ACCESO GRATIS a la Lectura en la Nube

Para visualizar el libro electrónico en la nube de lectura envíe junto a su nombre y apellidos una fotografía del código de barras situado en la contraportada del libro y otra del ticket de compra a la dirección:

ebooktirant@tirant.com

En un máximo de 72 horas laborales le enviaremos el código de acceso con sus instrucciones.

La visualización del libro en **NUBE DE LECTURA** excluye los usos bibliotecarios y públicos que puedan poner el archivo electrónico a disposición de una comunidad de lectores. Se permite tan solo un uso individual y privado

GESTIÓN INTELIGENTE DE LOS DESTINOS TURÍSTICOS

GESTIÓN INTELIGENTE DE LOS DESTINOS TURÍSTICOS

EDITORES:

RAFAEL LAPIEDRA ALCAMÍ

ROSA Mª RODRÍGUEZ ARTOLA

Universitat Jaume I

HANAE ABDELOUAHAB REDDAM
OUAFAE ABDELOUAHAB REDDAM
JOSEP MARIA AGUSTÍ ROCA
JUAN MIGUEL ALBEROLA OLTRA
MAR ALGUERÓ-BORONAT
LUISA ANDREU
RUBEN ARNANDIS I AGRAMUNT
ESTEFANIA BALLESTER
ZINA BARGHOUTI ABRINI
VANESSA MIGUEL BARRADO
ENRIQUE BIGNÉ
TAMIA BELEN BOADA CHICO
ELISABETTA BORDA
MONTSERRAT BORONAT-NAVARRO
DANIELA BUZOVA
CONRADO CARRASCOSA-LÓPEZ
DANIEL CATALÁ-PÉREZ
AMPARO CERVERA-TAULET
RICARDO CHIVA GÓMEZ
ALEJANDRO COLOMINA MARTÍNEZ
KIRSTEN COWAN
BLANCA DE-MIGUEL-MOLINA
MARÍA DE-MIGUEL-MOLINA
FRANCISCA RAMÓN FERNÁNDEZ
JOSÉ MARÍA FERNÁNDEZ-YÁÑEZ
PAULA FIERRO-RUBIO
RAMÓN FISAC-GARCÍA
ALEXANDRA GARCÍA-JOERGER
BEATRIZ FORÉS
EDUARD CRISTÓBAL FRANSI
JACOB GUINOT REINDERS
ALENA KOSTYK
EVA MARÍA LÓPEZ TUBÍA
JAUME MACIÀ AMORÓS
OBDULIA MONTESERÍN ABELLA
DANIEL PAÜL AGUSTÍ
JOSÉ M.PAVÍA
ALBA PUIG-DENIA
MARÍA CRISTINA RODRÍGUEZ RANGEL
ROSA ROIG
NATALIA RUBIO
CARLA RUIZ
MARCELINO SÁNCHEZ RIVERO
SILVIA SANZ-BLAS
WALESSKA SCHLESINGER
KARIM SMAHA
MARÍA-DOLORES TERUEL-SERRANO
PENÉLOPE TERUEL
ISABEL TORRES
BERTA TUBILLEJAS ANDRÉS
ELENA VICTORIA VALERO BOTELLA
DAHIANA VICENTE GONZÁLEZ
MARÍA JOSÉ VIÑALS
ANA MARÍA ZAMORA ORTIZ
MARINA ZANFARDINI

tirant lo blanch

Valencia, 2025

En caso de erratas y actualizaciones, la Editorial Tirant lo Blanch publicará la pertinente corrección en la página web www.tirant.com.

EDITA: TIRANT LO BLANCH
C/ Artes Gráficas, 14 - 46010 - Valencia
TELFS.: 96/361 00 48 - 50
FAX: 96/369 41 51
Email:tlb@tirant.com
www.tirant.com
Librería virtual: www.tirant.es
DEPÓSITO LEGAL: V-4800-2025
ISBN: 979-13-7021-503-3
MAQUETA: Innovatext

Si tiene alguna queja o sugerencia, envíenos un mail a: *atencioncliente@tirant.com*. En caso de no ser atendida su sugerencia, por favor, lea en *www.tirant.net/index.php/empresa/politicas-de-empresa* nuestro Procedimiento de quejas.

Responsabilidad Social Corporativa: *http://www.tirant.net/Docs/RSCTirant.pdf*

COMITÉ CIENTÍFICO DE LA OBRA

Índice

BLOQUE 1
SOSTENIBILIDAD Y TERRITORIO

LA HUERTA DE VALÈNCIA: UNA OPORTUNIDAD TURÍSTICA PARA LA SOSTENIBILIDAD DEL TERRITORIO Y EL ALCANCE DE LOS OBJETIVOS DE DESARROLLO SOSTENIBLE

Francisca Ramón Fernández

TERRITORIOS RURALES QUE LATEN: UNA MIRADA EXPLORATORIA A LA VALORIZACIÓN DEL PATRIMONIO CULTURAL INMATERIAL

Berta Tubillejas Andrés
Amparo Cervera-Taulet
Walesska Schlesinger

EL VALOR CULTURAL DE LA MÚSICA EN LA OFRENDA DE FLORES EN LAS FALLAS DE TORRENT

Blanca de-Miguel-Molina
María de-Miguel-Molina
Daniel Catalá-Pérez
Conrado Carrascosa-López

CASA CANSAT. CREACIÓN DE 7 ALOJAMIENTOS TURÍSTICOS ACCESIBLES EN LA VALL FOSCA (PIRINEO DE LLEIDA)

Josep Maria Agustí Roca
Jaume Macià Amorós
Eduard Cristóbal Fransi
Daniel Paül Agustí

EU-FUNDED TOURISM PROJECTS FOR A GREEN TRANSITION: THE CASE OF TOURISM SUSTAINABILITY PLANS AT DESTINATIONS (PSTD) IN SPAIN

Isabel Torres
María-Dolores Teruel-Serrano
María José Viñals

BLOQUE 2
TECNOLOGÍA, DIGITALIZACIÓN Y EXPERIENCIA DEL TURISTA

ONTOLOGÍAS DEL TURISMO COMO HERRAMIENTA PARA LA GESTIÓN INTELIGENTE Y SOSTENIBLE DE DESTINOS

Ouafae Abdelouahab Reddam
Hanae Abdelouahab Reddam
Obdulia Monteserín Abella

PERCEPCIÓN DE LOS TURISTAS SOBRE APLICACIONES INTELIGENTES PARA LA MEJORA DE LA EXPERIENCIA EN DESTINOS TURÍSTICOS INTELIGENTES (DTI)

Marcelino Sánchez Rivero
María Cristina Rodríguez Rangel
Vanessa Miguel Barrado

TURISMO DIGITAL EMERGENTE: PERCEPCIONES Y ACTITUDES HACIA EL METAVERSO

Silvia Sanz-Blas
Daniela Buzova
Paula Fierro-Rubio
Mar Algueró-Boronat

¿CÓMO INFLUYEN LOS INFLUENCERS VIRTUALES EN LA ENVIDIA BENIGNA, EL FOMO Y EL MATERIALISMO EN EL TURISMO ASPIRACIONAL?

Estefania Ballester
Enrique Bigné
Carla Ruiz
Natalia Rubio

TECNOLOGIAS DIGITALES PARA LA ESTIMACIÓN DE LA CAPACIDAD DE CARGA DE VISITANTES EN DIFERENTES TIPOS DE ESPACIOS PATRIMONIALES

Penélope Teruel
María José Viñals
Karim Smaha

DATOUR LAB 360: LABORATORIO DE INTELIGENCIA TURÍSTICA PARA LA TRANSFORMACIÓN DIGITAL, LA SOSTENIBILIDAD Y LA INNOVACIÓN EN DESTINOS

TAMIA BELEN BOADA CHICO
DAHIANA VICENTE GONZÁLEZ
ANA MARÍA ZAMORA ORTIZ

GESTIÓN SOSTENIBLE DE LA MOVILIDAD TURÍSTICA EN ESPACIOS NATURALES PROTEGIDOS: EL CASO DE L'ALBUFERA Y LA PLATAFORMA CONNECTA VALÈNCIA

ROSA ROIG
LUISA ANDREU
JOSÉ Mª PAVÍA

BLOQUE 3

GESTIÓN Y GOBERNANZA INTELIGENTE

MARCO JURÍDICO DE LA GESTIÓN DE RIESGOS Y CRISIS EN DESTINOS TURÍSTICOS INTELIGENTES: LA RESILIENCIA Y LA SOSTENIBILIDAD EN EL PAÍS VASCO. EL EJEMPLO DE SAN SEBASTIÁN DTI

EVA MARÍA LÓPEZ TUBÍA

LA PERCEPCIÓN DE LOS ACTORES PÚBLICOS SOBRE LA CORRESPONSABILIDAD EN LAS DECISIONES ESTRATÉGICAS EN TURISMO. LOS LÍMITES A LA PARTICIPACIÓN EN TIERRA BOBAL (VALÈNCIA, SPAIN)

Ruben Arnandis i Agramunt
Alejandro Colomina Martínez

TRANSPARENCIA EN LAS EMPRESAS TURÍSTICAS: UN ANÁLISIS SOBRE SUS EFECTOS EN EL COMPROMISO Y LOS COMPORTAMIENTOS DE AYUDA

JACOB GUINOT REINDERS
RICARDO CHIVA GÓMEZ
ZINA BARGHOUTI ABRINI

FROM TECHNOLOGY TO GOVERNANCE: THEMATIC EVOLUTION OF SMART TOURISM DESTINATION RESEARCH

BEATRIZ FORÉS
JOSÉ MARÍA FERNÁNDEZ-YÁÑEZ
ALBA PUIG-DENIA
MONTSERRAT BORONAT-NAVARRO
ALEXANDRA GARCÍA-JOERGER

PRÓLOGO

Esta publicación titulada “Gestión inteligente de los destinos turísticos” recopila las aportaciones realizadas en el XXVIII Congreso de Turismo Universidad-Empresa celebrado en Castellón durante los días 22 y 23 de octubre de 2025.

Una gestión inteligente de un destino puede ser considerada como una visión moderna y eficiente de la actividad turística, desarrollada en una industria más responsable, en la que se busca atraer a turistas conectados a las redes sociales, que disfrutan del ocio de una forma activa, y que mantienen una fluida interacción con el entorno de forma inmediata, donde lo importante es la calidad de la experiencia que se vive. Las tecnologías de la información y comunicación (TIC) están modificando el conocimiento y la forma de planificar, organizar y gestionar los viajes. Las TIC también están cambiando la forma en la que el turista interactúa con el destino, y comparte sus experiencias. El turista, cada vez más exigente, busca y encuentra la mejor relación calidad-precio, servicios y experiencias más personalizadas y adaptadas a sus gustos y necesidades, valora las opciones más respetuosas con el entorno y, particularmente, demanda estar conectado de manera permanente para poder hacer uso de las nuevas tecnologías a lo largo de todo el ciclo de vida del viaje.

No obstante, la consideración de un destino turístico inteligente (DTI) va más allá del uso de la tecnología. En este libro se trata el concepto de gestión inteligente desde los diferentes ámbitos que engloba: gobernanza, innovación, tecnología, accesibilidad universal y sostenibilidad en sus vertientes económica, sociocultural y medioambiental. Estos cinco ejes influyen unos en otros y están interrelacionados entre sí. Estos pilares permiten que los destinos turísticos evolucionen hacia un modelo más eficiente y resiliente, en el que una toma de decisiones más participativa se basa en datos y evidencias, la digitalización optimiza los servicios y la sostenibilidad se convierte en el eje central de la gestión. La implantación de este modelo ha demostrado su efectividad en la mejora de la planificación turística, la optimización de los recursos y la capacidad de adaptación de los destinos a los cambios en la demanda y las tendencias del mercado.

La decisión de un territorio de convertirse en un DTI supone establecer una estrategia que revaloriza el destino ya que promueve un aumento de su competitividad, un mejor aprovechamiento de sus atractivos naturales y culturales, la creación de otros recursos innovadores, la mejora en la eficiencia de los servicios, el impulso del desarrollo sostenible, la accesibilidad universal y el uso de las tecnologías de la información y comunicación. Todo ello contribuye a la mejora de la experiencia del turista, y también aporta beneficios adicionales como contribuir a incrementar la calidad de vida de los residentes y/o la creación de sinergias positivas entre los distintos agentes del destino. Los destinos turísticos integran múltiples interlocutores, tanto públicos como privados, que interactúan entre ellos y con el turista. Pero, además, el turismo es transversal en los destinos siendo, en ocasiones, difícilmente separable el turista y el ciudadano. Por todo ello, las acciones que mejoren el modelo turístico van a beneficiar necesariamente a la gestión de otros sectores y ámbitos del destino, y a distintos actores del mismo. Así, por ejemplo, las mejoras en la seguridad, las comunicaciones, la sanidad, el transporte, las telecomunicaciones, la accesibilidad, el sector alimentario, la hostelería, la restauración, equipamientos y actividades deportivas y culturales, y el ocio en general, van a tener una repercusión positiva sobre la actividad turística, pero también van a suponer una mejora en la calidad de la oferta de actividades que podrá disfrutar el ciudadano que reside habitualmente en un territorio.

En este libro se pretende recopilar los trabajos realizados sobre las últimas tendencias en el estudio de la gestión inteligente de los destinos turísticos, agrupando su contenido en tres grandes bloques. El primer apartado está orientado hacia el estudio de la sostenibilidad y el territorio. Los temas incluyen la regeneración de destinos, la conservación ambiental y la promoción del patrimonio cultural inmaterial. El segundo bloque titulado Tecnología, Digitalización y Experiencia del Turista agrupa las comunicaciones que exploran cómo la tecnología transforma la experiencia del turista y la gestión de los destinos. Los temas van desde el uso de la realidad virtual y el metaverso, hasta la percepción de los viajeros sobre aplicaciones digitales y la comunicación en línea. El tercer bloque se centra en la gestión de los destinos turísticos, con un énfasis en la toma de decisiones estratégicas, la resiliencia y la participación de los actores locales. También incluye el análisis de la gobernanza, las crisis y la comunicación institucional.

La lectura de cada una de las comunicaciones se puede realizar de forma individualizada; no obstante, se recomienda la lectura en conjunto de los artículos pertenecientes a cada uno de los bloques temáticos para dotar de mayor consistencia a los argumentos expuestos, facilitando la comprensión global de los objetivos planteados para cada uno de los apartados temáticos.

Finalmente, nos gustaría agradecer a la Diputación Provincial de Castellón por su esfuerzo y apoyo en la realización del XXVIII Congreso de Turismo. También, queremos agradecer a Turisme Comunitat Valenciana y a todas las entidades que de una u otra forma han contribuido para que se haya podido celebrar este evento. Por último, agradecer al Comité Organizador, Comité Científico y sobre todo a ponentes, comunicantes y participantes en los paneles de expertos porque todos ellos han aportado su sabiduría para generar un espacio de generación y compartición de conocimiento vinculado a las diferentes dimensiones de una gestión inteligente del turismo.

RAFAEL LAPIEDRA ALCAMÍ
ROSA Mª RODRÍGUEZ ARTOLA

BLOQUE 1

SOSTENIBILIDAD Y TERRITORIO

REGENERATIVE TOURISM IN THE CANARY ISLANDS: STRATEGIES TO CONSERVE THE ENVIRONMENT AND TO IMPROVE THE LOCAL COMMUNITY IN THE ISLANDS

Elisabetta Borda
Ramón Fisac-García
ESCP Business School

THEMATIC: Sustainable Tourism in the Canary Islands

ABSTRACT: Tourism has been the main driver of economic growth in the Canary Islands, but mass tourism has also generated environmental degradation, social pressure and economic leakage. This paper explores the concept of regenerative tourism as an innovative model that not only mitigates negative impacts but actively contributes to restoring ecosystems, enhancing community well-being and promoting sustainable economic development. A survey of 50 respondents (tourists and locals) and documental analysis of strategic plans reveal that although awareness of regenerative tourism is still limited, there is a clear recognition of its potential. A strategic plan is proposed to transition the Canary Islands toward a regenerative model with three main objectives: environmental regeneration, social well-being and sustainable economic growth. The findings are relevant for destinations facing challenges of overtourism and environmental vulnerability.

Keywords: Regenerative tourism, sustainable tourism, Canary Islands, community involvement, environmental conservation.

RESUMEN: El turismo ha sido el principal motor del crecimiento económico en las Islas Canarias, pero el turismo de masas también ha generado degradación ambiental, presión social y fugas económicas. Este trabajo explora el concepto de turismo regenerativo como un modelo innovador que no solo mitiga los impactos negativos, sino que contribuye activamente a restaurar los ecosistemas, mejorar el bienestar comunitario y promover un desarrollo económico sostenible. A partir de una encuesta a 50 participantes (turistas y residentes) y del análisis documental de planes estratégicos, se observa que, aunque el conocimiento sobre turismo regenerativo es aún limitado, existe un claro reconocimiento de su potencial. Se propone un plan estratégico para la transición hacia un modelo regenerativo con tres objetivos principales: regeneración ambiental, bienestar social y crecimiento económico sostenible. Los hallazgos resultan relevantes para destinos que enfrentan retos de sobrecarga turística y vulnerabilidad ambiental.

Palabras clave: Turismo regenerativo, turismo sostenible, Islas Canarias, participación comunitaria, conservación ambiental.

1. INTRODUCTION

Tourism has always been a driver of the economic development in many countries, creating growth, jobs and allowing a cultural exchange. An example of it is the Canary Islands, where tourism plays a crucial role due to the region's favourable climate, unique landscapes and rich biodiversity.

However, lately, it has been recognized that this approach led to serious challenges, such as the environmental degradation, the overcrowding and the depletion of natural resources. Over time, this pressure had serious repercussions on local ecosystems and communities, generating negative socio-economic and environmental impacts.

While this was a step forward, this concept of tourism was focusing only on the minimization of the negative impacts of tourism on the environment, society and economy, rather than fostering long-term positive changes. The need for more initiative-taking measures to not only preserve but actively contribute to the regeneration of the environment and society, led to the rise of the regenerative tourism model.

Regenerative tourism seeks to restore and enhance the ecosystem, the culture and the community in a destination, leaving the place better than it was before (Bishnu, 2023).

This event highlighted the fragility of tourism depending on the pure economy, exposing its weaknesses such as excessed resilience on international tourism and mass tourism.

It has become evident the need to embrace tourism strategies that contribute to the environmental conservation, which foster the community engagement and that created a more resilient and sustainable economy.

1.1. The gap

Sustainable tourism primarily aims to reduce the negative impacts on the environment and local communities but is not enough efficient to regenerate and improve these areas. It focuses on the minimization of the negative impact rather than adopting a proactive approach that could actually restore and enhance the ecosystem and the community impacted by tourism. This led to the realization that in the tourism industry there is a gap in its ability to truly safeguard and rejuvenate a destination, particularly those ones affected by overtourism, environmental degradation and socio-economic imbalances.

Regenerative tourism could really fill this gap in the sector since it would foster a shift in the tourism mindset, moving beyond sustainability to ensure that tourism actively contributes to the restoration of ecosystems, communities and local economies. Most of the literature review that will be analysed is conceptual, with limited studies that examine how it can be applied in a real-world scenario.

The Canary Islands, for instance, face specific challenges such as the dependence on mass tourism, overcrowding, and dependence on all-inclusive tourism packages. These issues are exacerbated by the fact that there is a lack of communication and unified work among the stakeholders and a limited local involvement in the decision-making process.

As many other destinations that depend on tourism, the Canary Islands face economic challenges that through regenerative tourism could be addressed by promoting local businesses, supporting sustainable agriculture and fostering circular economy.

1.2. Research questions

This research aims to be the starting point to develop a strategic plan to make the Canary Islands more sustainable and ready to embrace regenerative tourism at 360°. The primary research questions that guided this study are:

a. *How can regenerative tourism conserve the natural environment?* It will analyse how regenerative tourism is able to mitigate the negative impact of mass tourism on the environment and to protect the biodiversity of the archipelago. Sustainable practices in the tourism operations and initiatives will be illustrated.

b. *How can regenerative tourism improve the lives of the local community and include it in the tourism industry without damaging them?* This question focuses on understanding how the local community could be more engaged in the tourism sector establishing a meaningful relationship, where their voices are ensured to be heard and their needs are prioritized.

c. *What challenges and opportunities exist for the implementation of regenerative tourism in the Canary Islands?* In this question will be analysed the barriers that at the current day don't allow the archipelago to transition to regenerative tourism, such as the infrastructure limitations, the lack of awareness and the insufficient stakeholder collaboration.

d. *How can the strategic plan for regenerative tourism can be tailored to the unique characteristics of the Canary Islands?* To answer this question, the challenges and assets of the region will be analysed to figure out how a tailor-made strategy can be designed to satisfy both local and global sustainable need and achieve the regenerative goals.

Understanding regenerative tourism is very important in today's world, since the tourism industry is always evolving and it must be directed towards the right path where environmental pressure and social challenges must be addressed. The findings of this study are not only useful for the Canary Islands but for all those destinations that are struggling with sustainability challenges.

2. LITERATURE REVIEW

This literature review aims to explore the evolution of tourism practices, focusing on the transition from traditional to sustainable and regenerative approaches. Central to this research is understanding how regenerative tourism can protect the natural environment and enhance the life of the local community in the context of the Canary Islands.

2.1. The history and impact of traditional tourism

Traditional tourism has evolved over the years. Today, it increasingly considers the sustainability and regeneration of destinations. Tourism has changed significantly over the centuries, influenced by the changes in the society, in the economy and in the culture. Looking back at its beginning, the concept of tourism as we understand it today, began with the "Grand Tour", which emerged in the late 16th century and reached its peak in the 17th and 18th centuries.

The Grand Tour was intended to complete the education of aristocrats by visiting major cultural, historical and classical sites across Europe, specifically in France, Italy and Greece.

This concept comes from the industrial revolution era since the industrialization advanced, labour movements pushed for workers' rights, including shorter working hours and paid leave. With paid vacations, more people, including the emerging middle class, could afford to travel for leisure and this expanded tourism beyond the only elite. The democratization of tourism refers to the broadening of travel opportunities to wider segments of society.

- The mass transportation with the development of the railways in the 19th century, followed by the advancement of the commercial aviation.
- The economic growth following the World War II increased the disposal incomes, allowing more people to travel.
- The rise of the travel agencies and tour operators, such as Thomas Cook in the 19th century, offering organized travel packages that simplified the travel organization and experience.

In the '90, during the "globalization era", traditional tourist took a global dimension where each destination could become a potential tourist destination. According to Poon (1993) "mass tourism refers to the movement of a large number of organised tourists to popular holiday destinations for recreational purposes". This phenomenon was characterised by standardised package products and mass consumption, appealing to tourists due to its convenience, comfort and predictability. This approach resulted in a standardised product offering with minimal levels of services and facilities (Williams, 2010).

The mass tourism had a huge impact on the carrying capacity of a destination, as large numbers of tourists went to the same place at the same time of the year, leading to the exploitation of the local communities and ecosystems. Additionally, mass tourism often destroyed the culture and brought to economic leakage, where the profit from tourism failed to benefit the local economy and instead flowed out to external entities.

In conclusion, traditional tourism provided economic benefits for the destination but at the cost of the sustainable conservation of culture, environment and biodiversity of it, since it didn't prioritize sustainability (Hayward, 2024).

2.2. Sustainable tourism

Sustainable tourism emerged as a response to the challenges posed by mass tourism and it focuses on using efficiently the resources to minimize the negative impacts of tourism activities on the environment and communities, ensuring that future generations can enjoy the same possibilities society has now. This concept was introduced for the first time in the Brundtland report published in 1987 and it was defined by UNEP & UNWTO (2005) as "tourism that takes full account of its current and future economic, social and environmental impacts, addressing the needs of visitors, the industry, the environment and host communities".

The foundation of a sustainable tourism lies in the protection and preservation of the natural environment, yet tourism has historically contributed to its degradation.

According to UNWTO (2023), the CO2 emissions related to tourism are accounted for 5% of all emissions made by humans, with transportation for tourism responsible for 75% and accommodation 21%. To mitigate these impacts, industries and the destinations must put in practice effective resource and emission management strategies to save resources, decrease pollution and preserve the biodiversity. Where do the restaurants, hotel or tour operator source their product? are they local? How do they manage the food waste? In 2023 62% of hotels, 57% of restaurants and 48 % of tour operators sourced locally (GSTC, 2023) whereas 70% of hotels, 64% of restaurants and 53% tour operators manage food waste in a sustainable way (Food Waste Reduction Alliance, 2023).

Sustainable tourism includes the protection, preservation and enhancement of local places as well as the tradition and the culture of the people who live there, the so called "intangible heritage".

This partnership should integrate cultural habits and traditions into the traveller's experience so that the life of local people is not hindered by tourists. Accordingly to a study made by Booking.com (2019), tourists are more willingly to take part in a sustainable friendly tourism rather than the mass one, showing a preference for eco-friendly hotel over the standard one or making sustainable travel decisions choosing less CO2 gas emissions flights or travelling by car. Sustainable tourism, according to the World Tourism Organization (UNWTO) (2024), "*should make the best use of environmental resources while also contributing to the conservation of natural heritage and biodiversity, respect the socio-culture of local host communities and contribute to intercultural understanding. Economically, it should also assure long-term viability of operations that will benefit all stakeholders, whether that is permanent employment for locals, social services, or contributions to poverty alleviation*".

The definition of sustainable tourism provided by the World Tourism Organization (UNWTO) encompasses three primary dimensions: environmental, socio-cultural and economical. Despite the promising aspects of sustainable tourism, it has some limitation. One of the main drawbacks is the lack of motivation and incentives for people to engage in proactive measures that go beyond the mere impact reduction. As a result, opportunities to enhance biodiversity, support local development and foster community empowerment are often missed (Truyols, 2023).

2.3. Regenerative tourism and its application to destinations

Regenerative tourism emerges as an essential strategy to apply because the sector needs to go beyond the sustainable and responsible tourism, aiming to build this back better than it was before. Regenerative tourism is a new concept that accordingly to Sharma (2023) "creates opportunities for healing the tourist destinations, balancing the social-economic-environmental impacts of tourism transformation, address the issue of climate crisis and depleting resources from the planet, reducing and managing tourism's environmental impacts to make tourism more meaningful".

This approach considers all its elements and their interconnectedness, creating a synergy between them. Regenerative tourism goes beyond the simple help to preserve the destination by aiming to leave a positive impact on it.

It emphasizes the achievement of a net positive impact both on society and the environment, positioning these outcomes at the centre of tourism development and management strategies. This shift has been possible because regenerative tourism considers the expectations of different stakeholders involved in this sector like tourists, residents, communities, government, organizations and businesses.

Some of these positive initiatives that regenerative tourism helps to enhance are helping to clean the environment, assisting in building a better habitat for local wildlife and contributing to the revitalization of the ecosystem. The ESG framework requires all the stakeholders to be more involved and accountable in the tourism industry and to look toward to future-oriented strategies that can creates new values, especially for the local communities.

The main point of regenerative tourism is not the restoration or renewal of tourism, but rather it's about a change in mindset in terms of reinventing and discovering the industry. This transformative approach aims to achieve two goals at the same time: the preservation and improvement of the environment, eliminating the negative impacts and the degradation that tourism activity causes on destinations. The outcome that is expected is "leaving the place behind, better than before" and in this perspective, regenerative tourism is important because it creates chances to renew and heal the natural and human environment (Sharma, 2023).

In contrast to traditional tourism that focuses on exploring the world and discover new and exciting destinations, without taking into consideration its impacts, the regenerative one creates a deeper connection between many aspects such as economy, society, culture and nature, as explain before with the holistic approach. Therefore, starting from a comprehensive and evolutionary planning, the objective is to create a life-changing experience for the visitor. An experience that establishes a bond between him and the place. This will allow the traveller to dive deeper in the nature and cultural atmosphere, generating a meaningful change in the inner-self (Socatelli, 2020).

Teruel Avecilla (2018) emphasizes some key factors that drive this transformative experience.

- Firstly, the connection should come primarily from the history of the destination. This historical context forms the foundation for a meaningful bond between travellers and the place they visit.
- Secondly, the tourist should feel a sense of belonging to the local community. This connection goes beyond superficial interactions, fostering a deeper understanding and appreciation of the destination as a living system.
- Lastly, there is a triple relationship at play: between the human with himself, with the others and with the hearth. This holistic perspective fosters a deeper connection with the environment and people who live on it (Teruel Avecilla, 2018).

As previously highlighted, unlike sustainable tourism, regenerative tourism seeks to leave the place better than they found it. The difference between these two concepts is well explained in the article by Truyols (2023) who points out that in the common imagination of people, they think that these two terms can be interchanged but they actually represent two different concepts.

This article speaks about 9 key aspects of regenerative tourism that provide a comprehensive explanation that help to understand and foster this type of tourism. They focus on the broader goals of restoring and enhancing the natural, social and economic systems of tourism destinations. These 9 aspects are shown in figure 1.

Figure 1. Relevant aspects of regenerative tourism.

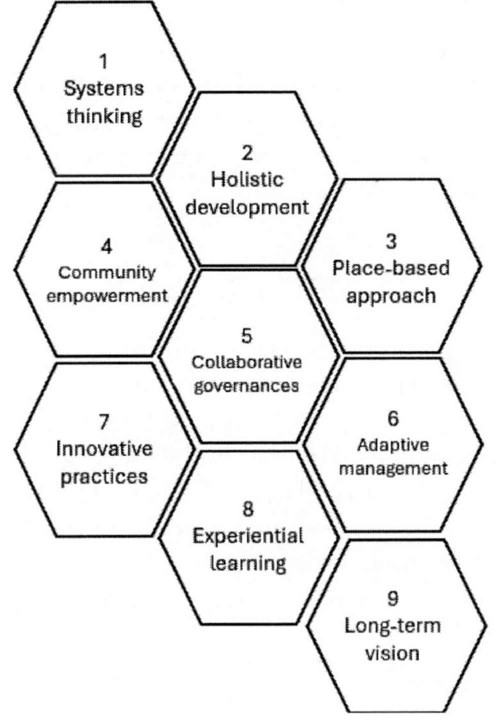

Source: own elaboration based on Truyols (2023)

Out of these 9 key aspects in which these two approaches differ, we can summarize them in three that are particularly compelling for an analysis: the paradigm, the purpose and the approach. The regenerative one aligns with nature and aims reaching a harmony in the economic, social, cultural, spiritual and ecological development.

According to what Teruel Avecilla (2018) says, the big leap that is required to move from sustainable to regenerative tourism is a change in the mindset of people: the change in the mindset of the zero negative impact of nature environment and community to the creations of a positive one.

Having said all this, the benefits that regenerative tourism could bring to a destination are many more respects to the merely sustainable one:

1. It enhances the ecosystem and local community resilience ensuring long-term enjoyment of destinations for tourists.
2. It benefits travel companies financially and creating stability in both natural and business environments.

3. It provides local support for tourism, improved quality of life for communities, and preservation of cultural heritage (Truyols, 2023).

A key starting point is to design project tailored specifically to each destination, avoiding reliance on standard formulas. Another crucial aspect highlighted in the article is the importance of educating travellers. This education aims to make them see the place as a living system and to get to know the true essence of the destination.

3. METHODOLOGY

This research adopts a quantitative method to provide a comprehensive understanding of regenerative tourism's situation and impact. The quantitative method, a survey, was used to gather a broader insight from a diverse range of respondents (tourists and locals), giving the possibility to analyse the trends and patterns related to regenerative tourism in the Canary Islands. In addition to them a documental analysis was done, which has been useful to better understand what the Canary Islands are really applying, nowadays, in terms of sustainable and regenerative strategies.

3.1. Documental analysis

In addition to the quantitative and qualitative methods, a documental analysis was conducted to assess the sustainability efforts and to explore the current implemented strategies in the tourism sector in the Canary Islands. This method was based on the analysis of existing documents about the topic, about the tourism action plans of the islands and sustainability reports to assess how regenerative tourism practices are integrated into the region's current tourism strategy.

The main document used in this research method is the 2022-2023 Action Plan of Tourism in the Canary Islands, which outlines the commitment of the archipelago to transitioning toward a regenerative tourism model. This plan focuses on fostering the resilience in the sector, aligning with the Sustainable Development Goals (SDGs) and achieving climate neutrality.

In addition to this document, to better understand the effort of each island towards sustainable and regenerative tourism, documents and reports about specific initiatives from individual island were analysed. For example, El Hierro is progressing with renewable energy projects like the Gorono Wind Hydro Power Plant, Fuerteventura focuses on ocean conservation through the Marine Garbage Observatory and Tenerife promotes biodiversity protection with its initiative Loro Parque Fundación. These initiatives highlight the unique contributions of each island toward the shared goal of sustainable and regenerative tourism.

3.2. Quantitative method: The survey

3.2.1. Rationale and structure of the survey

A survey was conducted to gather quantitative data from tourists and locals about how they perceive the level of regenerative tourism in the Canary Islands. Its aim was to obtain an exhaustive understanding of the level of regenerative tourism from a double point of view: the tourists and the residents. In addition to this, it allowed to highlight the strengths and weaknesses or areas for improvement to foster sustainable and regenerative development in the islands.

Table 1. Interviews' main characteristics

Duration	5 to 10 minutes
Anonymity	Anonymous responses and used solely for research purposes
Distribution	Social media and survey applications
Number of respondents	50

The survey was composed of 31 questions divided into 5 sections:

1. Demographic information: Basic demographic data were collected to classify responses and guarantee a diverse sample for a more comprehensive viewpoint.

2. Regenerative tourism perception: Here, the aim of the questions was to assess awareness and perceptions of regenerative tourism. Then the surveyed were asked several questions about their perceptions.

3. Regenerative practices evaluation: The third section deepened on "the regenerative practices evaluation" and it assesses the satisfaction of tourists and residents with the current regenerative practices on the islands.

4. Strengths and weaknesses: this section identified the perceived strengths and weaknesses of regenerative tourism practices in the Canary Islands: the main strengths and the main weaknesses of regenerative tourism in the Canary Islands, and ideas or suggestions to improve tourism practices

5. Specific aspects for residents and tourists: it asked targeted questions for tourists and residents to better understand better their specific experiences and perceptions.

Then 3 specific questions were asked depending on the type of survey (tourist and residents). They explored the experience, expectations and impacts of the tourism phenomenon.

3.2.2. Sampling and data collection

The sampling for this survey on regenerative tourism in the Canary Islands was designed to be inclusive and diverse. This strategy allowed for a comprehensive representation of different point of views. The survey was open to all individuals who have visited the Canary Islands, including both tourists and residents. This survey was not limited to only tourists but also aimed at reaching locals too. Having a double perspective is an added value in order to have a clear and 360 degrees view of the situation. As said before, this survey aimed to capture a wide range of demographics, which includes tourists from different countries and regions, residents of the archipelago and different age groups, genders and occupations.

Distribution through social media, particularly on WhatsApp and through survey applications was the recruitment strategy employed to help gather responses. Despite reaching 50 respondents, the survey's sample size was considered medium to low. The survey was conducted though Google Survey, which automatically analysed the responses creating for each one, interpretable graphs and providing percentages for each answer. Each section of questions was represented through these graphical summaries that gave a clear view of public opinion on key regenerative tourism topics in the Canary Islands.

4. THE CANARY ISLANDS: CURRENT SITUATION AND POTENTIAL FOR REGENERATIVE TOURISM

4.1. Tourism overview in the Canary Islands

Since 1960s tourism has experienced a rapid growth driven by foreign investments and tour operators. This growth has improved the local economic conditions, but it also created a disequilibrium among the economy, society and the environment. As a result, mass tourism, supported by international tour operators, has become the dominant form of tourism.

The main attraction of this destination is the landscape but especially the climate that due to a lack of a distinct seasonal pattern allows the arrival of tourist all year around.

Nowadays, among all the tourism destinations of "sol y playa", Canary Islands are a leader in the sector, positing at the top ranking in several main touristic indicators such as the overnight stay, the travel expense, the number of arrivals etc (Hernández-Martín, 2021).

Figure 2. Overnight stays of non-residents in the main European tourism regions, 2018 (millions)

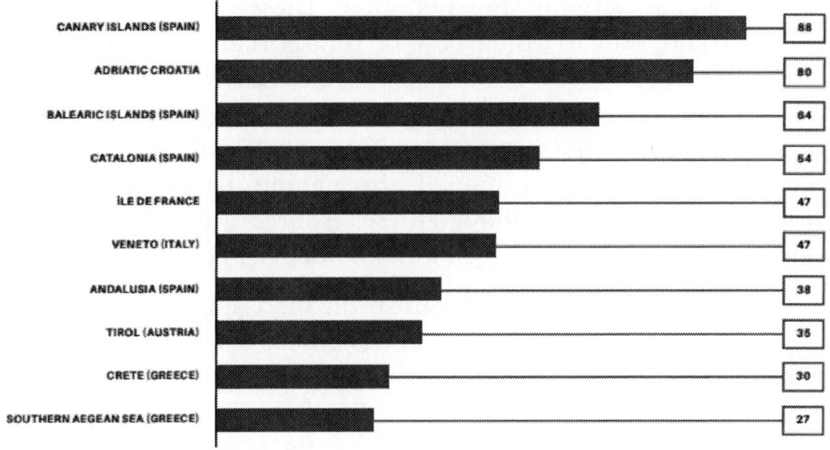

Source: EUROSTAT (2018)

Figure 3. Concentration of overnight stays in the main tourism municipalities of the Canary Islands.

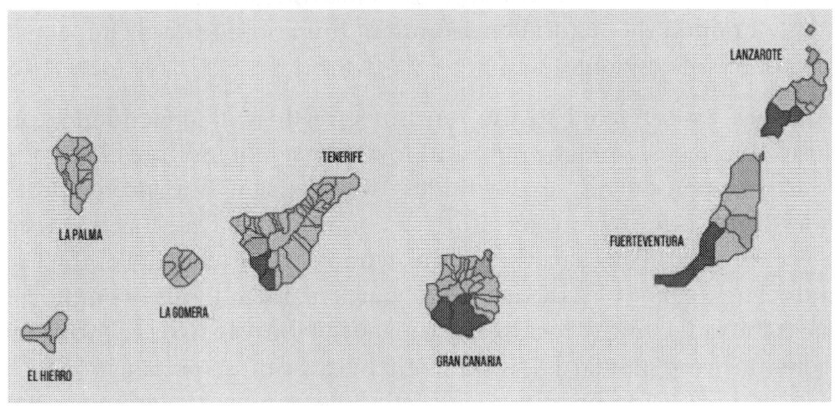

Source: Hernández-Martín et al. (2021)

The tourism model of Canary Islands relates heavily on natural resources but lack adequate support from intelligence and knowledge of people from the tourism sector and from the administration. Consequently, the destination attracts a high volume of tourists while depending on finite environmental resources, which are at risk of being exploited to the point of no return. As previously mentioned, the primary drivers of tourism in the islands are their unique climate conditions and the richness of landscape. However, relying solely on these resources constrains the development capacity of the region.

While climate and landscape are traditionally considered non-exhaustible for the Canary Islands' tourism, they are increasingly vulnerable to the impacts of global warming and pollution. These changes affect tourism flows and could lead to rising cost of transportation due to mitigation policies, increased of flights and fuel prices. Eventually, the tourism in these islands depends largely on the territory and the natural landscape, which are being constantly and intensively exploited. If this trend persists, the essential attractions may be drained, threatening the sustainability of the tourism industry. Thus, even though these resources are supposed to be non-exhaustible, they must be managed with knowledge to create an added value.

As said before, the growth of tourism in the Canary Islands, thanks to inversion from tour operators and international companies, led to mass tourism focusing on increase production and volumes' scale. This model proved to be strategically inappropriate for the industry, as any decline in tourist inflows often led to economic crisis in the region.

The underlying issue is closely related to real estate. To sustain the economic growth, the archipelago expanded real estate assets to attract more tourists, resulting in a situation where twice as many properties are dedicated to tourism as to the local community. This unrestricted construction has not only strained the natural environment but also negatively impacted the quality of life of residents.

Another issue related to the tourism growth is its dependence on all-inclusive packages, foreign trade and low tourist expenditure. The industry tries to compensate these downsides by increasing the production and standardizing offerings in an effort to continually set new arrival records. However, this strategy exacerbated the economic vulnerability of the Canary Islands. The weakness of the economy, particularly in terms of employment, impacts the well-being of locals. The capacity of tourism to drive the economy and elevate living standards is insufficient because most tourism income flows back to companies at the source with only 30% of tourist spending occurring within the islands. In 2018, 30% of tourists opted for all-inclusive packages and 59% chose package deals overall. This resilience on all-inclusive options reduces the local spending and hinders the creation of jobs. Moreover, the lack of entrepreneurship, of innovation system and the dominance of international firms don't encourage positive economic impacts, leaving the local economy dependent and constrained.

Furthermore, Canary Islands need better coordination among the institutions and the stakeholders involved in tourism. A critical issue is that the tourism departments of each region face competencies and economic capacity challenges. They don't have the capacity to really influence the management of the destination. Additionally, institutional decisions affecting tourism are often not driven by tourism needs. Another weakness is that citizens are excluded from the decision-making process. Involving them could make the difference enhancing the understanding of the destination and contributing to design a better tourism model that considers social aspect.

The Canary Islands benefit from several advantages that set them apart from other destinations: the lack of seasonality and the high levels of safety and security. As previously mentioned, the stable weather conditions attract a consistent flow of foreign tourists, particularly making winter the high season with higher prices. This stability is a significant asset, as evidenced by the hotel RevPAR in the Canary Islands, which during the winter of 2018–19 ranged between €79 and €86. In contrast, other "sol y playa" destination in the same year had most establishments closed during this period, with RevPAR ranging from €30 to €40 (Hernández-Martín, 2021).

4.2. Sustainability challenges in the Canary Islands

The key sustainable issues areas in the Canary Islands for the development of tourism can be divided into 4 subjects: environmental, human, economic and territorial.

a. Environmental factor

An urgent issue, that Canary Islands have to deal with, is the fragility of their environment, which is very vulnerable and influenced by the pressures of mass tourism and development like the one of the real estate constructions. Innovation in environmental practices is essential and Canary Islands lack in the implementation of effective and modern measures within the tourism sector. Effective environmental management remains inconsistent due limited authority and initiatives from the regional tourism administrations. Inadequate resource management and a lack of sustainable awareness exacerbate the situation in the coastal urban areas that are already particularly impacted by climate changes (Hernández-Martín, 2021).

b. Human factor

One of the social challenges facing Canary Islands is the integration of tourism in the local society.

The Canary Islands are struggling on different topics related to employment such as: high unemployment rates, deficits in training and unequal access to educational opportunities. Many workers in the tourism sector lack of essential language skills, problem that can only be addressed through collaborative efforts between institutions and businesses. Other critical weaknesses include the lack of a balanced perspective between demand and supply in the current model and inadequate awareness of the importance of sustainability.

c. Economic factor

The Canary Island face significant economic challenges as they strive to sustain and innovate in the tourism sector. Canary Islands don't support as much as they should the self-employed individuals and small businesses, particularly in rural areas. Despite these issues, the archipelago possesses a robust information system developed by ISTAC and a network of small business that promote local products.

To further stimulate economic growth, initiatives supporting SMEs and start-ups in tourism innovation project are crucial.

d. Territorial factor

The primary challenge related to the territorial is the need to rejuvenate the tourism infrastructure while ensuring sustainable use of the land. The objective should be the integration of public and private spaces such as urban areas, rural landscapes, and coastal zones. Despite these obstacles, there are some strengths that Canary Islands have that can support improvements in landscape and urban spaces. This includes urban planning legislation that favours renewal over expansion and tax

5. FINDINGS

5.1. Results of quantitative individual perceptions of "Regenerative tourism in Canary Islands"

The conducted survey was thought to assess the level of regeneration and sustainability in tourism within the Canary Islands with a specific focus on how the visitors and residents perceive it. It seeks to identify the strengths and weaknesses of possible existing practices and provide insights for enhancing sustainable development as well as ensuring positive impacts on the environment, local culture and community wellbeing.

Perception of regenerative tourism

One of the primary objectives of the survey was to understand how different stakeholders perceive the level of regeneration of tourism activities in the Canary Islands. The data collected reveals that 61,2 % of respondents were unfamiliar with the concept of regenerative tourism.

However, after being provided an explanation of the concept and examples, they were able to evaluate how the regenerative tourism level in Canary Islands was. From this question it can be assessed that regenerative practices are not so implemented in the islands, with a 37.5 % rating the regenerative practices level as 2 and a 43.8 % rating it as 3 on a scale of 1 to 5.

Figure 4. How do you think regenerative tourism is currently practiced in the Canary Islands?

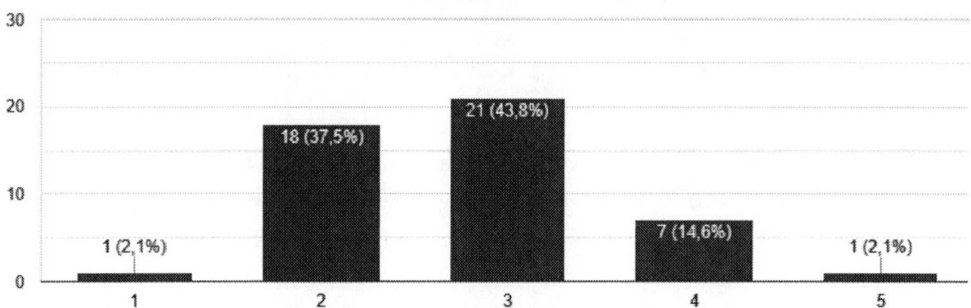

Despite this, the majority of respondents agree about the usefulness of regenerative tourism in the islands with a 83.4% who believe that applying regenerative tourism strategies could positively impact the current situation in the Canary Islands.

Figure 5. Do you believe that making changes to current tourism practices related to the overtourism can improve the situation of regenerative tourism in the Canary Islands?

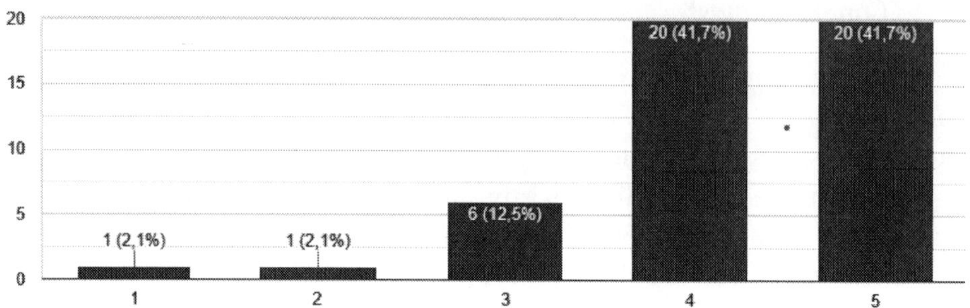

Regenerative practices evaluation

Another crucial aspect exanimated was the actual implementation of regenerative practices. The results show that the respondents perceive a lack of environmental conservation projects, with 48.9% of them rating a neutral 3 on a scale from 1 to 5.

Figure 6. How satisfied are you with the environmental conservation projects in the Canary Islands?

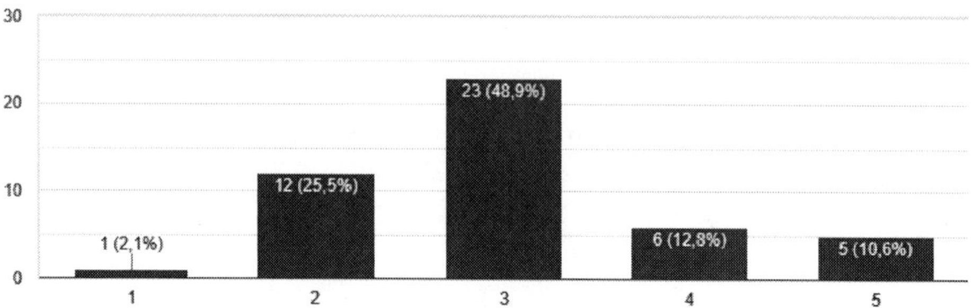

Furthermore, another factor that underline the scarce implementation of regenerative practices is that the integration with the local community is seen as insufficient, as evidenced by 36.2 % rating it as 2 and 31.9% rating it as 3. This highlights a need for more robust cultural exchange programs, local craft markets, community tours, and participating in local festivals and events were done on the islands.

Figure 7. Do tourist activities in the Canary Islands promote integration with the local community?

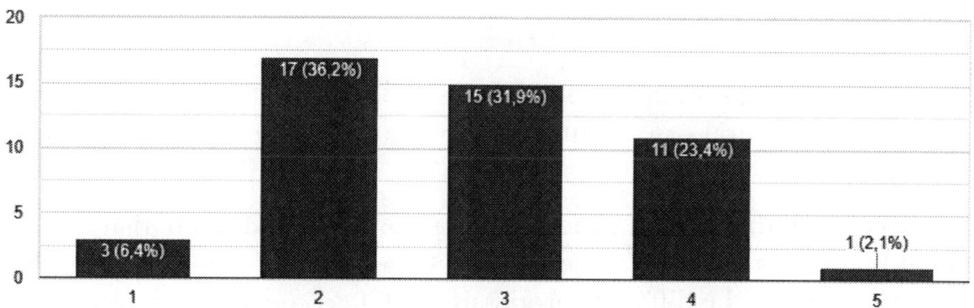

Additionally, when asked about respect for promotion of local culture, 47.8% of respondents remained neutral, while 28.3% rated it as 4, suggesting that there is potential for improvement in this area.

Figure 8. Does tourism in the Canary Islands respect and value local culture and traditions?

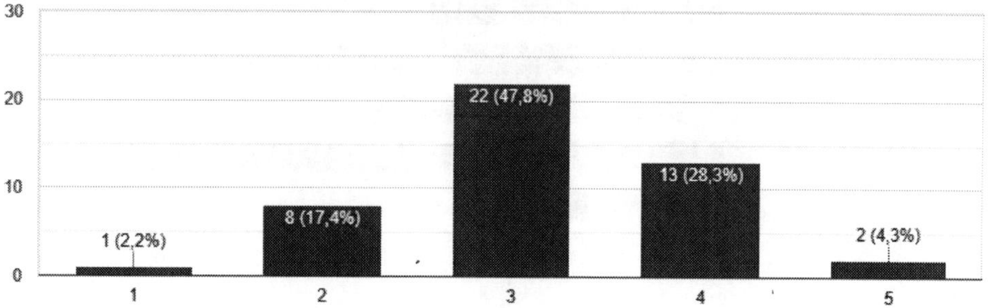

Strengths and weaknesses of regenerative tourism and the current tourism situation

The survey results underscore that regenerative tourism in Canary Islands is recognized for its strong preservation of natural landscapes, promotion of local culture and economic benefits to communities. However, significant challenges remain, including the overcrowding of popular areas, the environmental degradation and the insufficient infrastructure for sustainable tourism. Additionally, there is an urgent need to enhance the involvement of the local community and the improvement of the promotion of the local culture in the tourism industry.

To address these weaknesses and to advance towards a more sustainable and regenerative tourism model, respondents suggested three key areas for improvement

1. Increase of the investment in sustainable infrastructure
2. Encourage of eco-friendly and accessible transportation
3. Improve local markets and economies

All these 3 suggestions emphasize the importance of not only leveraging the islands' natural assets but also proving infrastructures and practices created by man.

Regarding the tourist experience, respondents indicated that Canary Islands already pay lots of attention to the natural and cultural aspects. For instance, among the different proposals, wildlife conservation projects were rated 42.9% and cultural heritage tours of not touristic areas scored a 31%. The most significant regenerative experience noted was dinning at local restaurants, providing an authentic cultural immersion.

Figure 9. Which regenerative tourist experiences have you found most significant in the Canary Islands

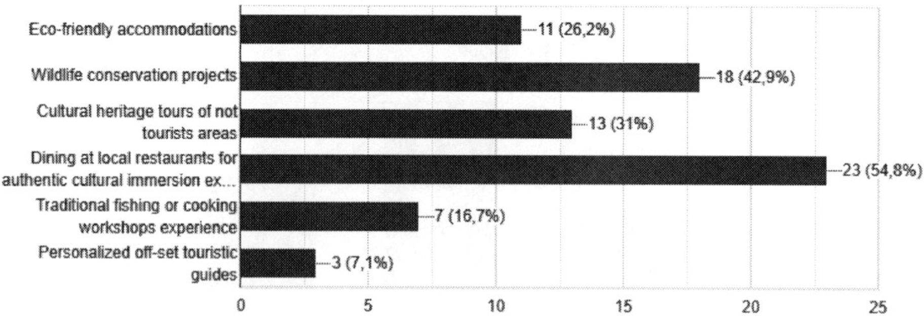

However, there is a clear desire for more personalized and meaningful tourist experiences, with an emphasis on deeper engagement with the local community and cultural heritage.

The current tourism situation in this survey was further assessed through questions directed at the local residents.

The survey revealed a clear division between those who perceive a negative impact and those who observe a positive impact. 45.8% of locals feel that tourism has increased the cost of living, while 20.8% recognize the positive aspects of it since it increased the job opportunities.

Figure 10. In what ways has tourism affected your community?

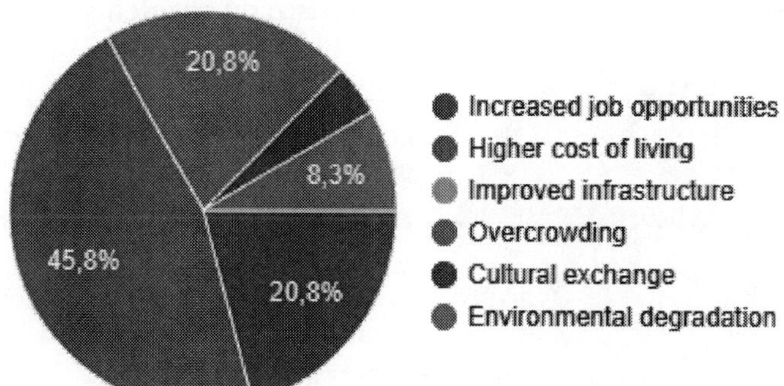

Furthermore, 53.8% of the respondents clearly identified that tourism has negative impact in their life regarding environmental impact especially the topic of hotel construction too closed to the beaches or in protected areas, cost of living and the real estate market and overcrowding.

Figure 11. How do you perceive the impact of tourism in your life and community in the Canary Islands?

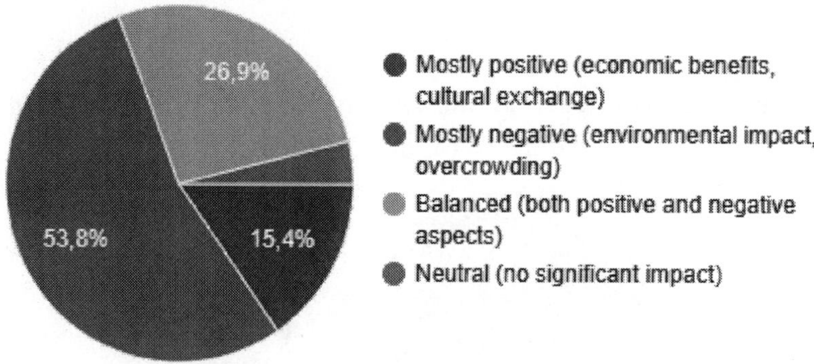

To mitigate the negative impacts of tourism on residents, the respondents suggested several measures, with nearly 20% support across all the following categories:

- Stricter environmental regulations
- Better infrastructure planning
- Increased community involvement in tourism planning
- Promotion of sustainable tourism practices
- Limits on tourist number

Figure 12. What measures do you think should be taken to mitigate the negative impacts of tourism on residents?

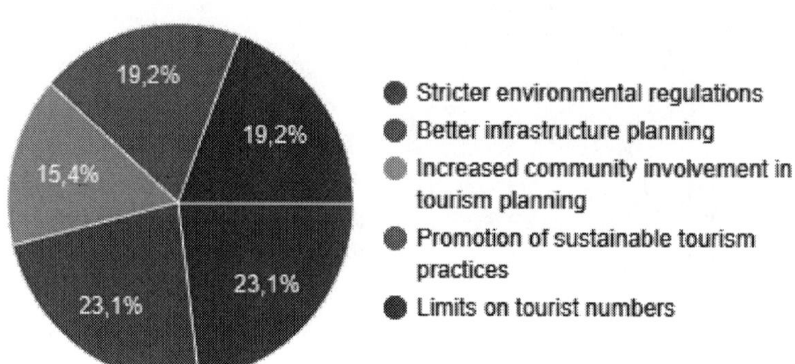

These responses highlight that urgent need for comprehensible strategies across multiple areas. Only the 19.2% feel that tourism takes into consideration the residents need when it comes to take decisions. This low percentage is not enough to counterpart the negative point of view that the majority has about this topic. The 38.5% says that sometimes the need of the local are heard in matter of tourism projects and the 30.8% confirms that they are rarely listened to.

Figure 13. Do you feel that tourism development projects consider the needs of local residents?

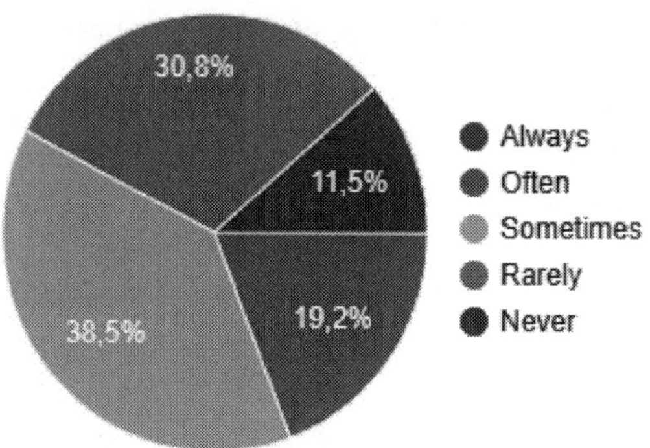

The survey concludes with the question on the potential contribution that regenerative tourism could have on the well-being of the community. While 38.5% of respondents remains neutral to this topic, 57.7% clearly stated that it could have a positive impact, suggesting that more work is needed to raise awareness and understanding of regenerative tourism's benefits.

Figure 14. How much do you think regenerative tourism could contribute to the well-being of your community?

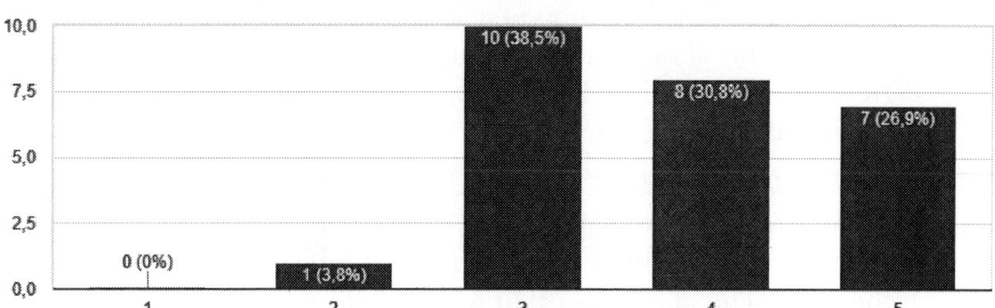

6. A PROPOSAL OF A REGENERATIVE STRATEGIC PLAN FOR THE CANARY ISLANDS

Having analysed the tourism situation and specifically the regenerative one in the Canary Islands, allowed to come to the conclusion that for true progress, it is essential that hotels along with the other stakeholders, work together to create a cohesive strategy.

Only through collaboration, sharing best practices and establishing common goals, the hospitality sector can leave truly positive impact on the territory.

These synergies would not only enhance the effectiveness of environmental initiatives but also contribute to creating a more sustainable and regenerative tourism model for the entire region.

This approach is crucial if the Canary Islands want to balance the demands of tourism with their need to preserve the natural and cultural heritage. Therefore, the purpose of this master thesis is to propose am action plan with a series of strategies that could implement regenerative practices to enhance the current tourism situation in the Canary Islands.

6.1. Objectives

This strategy aims to transitioning the Canary Islands towards a regenerative tourism model that envisions 3 objectives:

1. *Environmental regeneration:* this primary objective aims to enhance the health of the Canary Island's natural environment, making it more resilient, by reducing the negative impacts of tourism. The strategy

will address issues like overcrowding, environmental degradation and the need for improved and more sustainable infrastructure to support the development of regenerative tourism. An important aspect is the align of tourism practices with the UN's Sustainable Development Goals (SDGs) though the achievement of sustainable certifications.

2. *Social well-being and community involvement:* the focus of this objective is the involvement of the local community in the tourism sector, ensuring that tourism contributes in a positive and beneficial way to their life. The challenges that will be addressed in the strategy are: the insufficient integration of local communities, the negative impact of tourism and the need for more respect and promotion of local culture and traditions. This strategy wants to foster the connection between tourism and the local community, trying to raise awareness about it.
3. *Sustainable economic development:* the third objective aims to strengthening the economic benefits of tourism for the archipelago through sustainable and regenerative practices.

What this strategy wants to achieve is to add value to the islands' economy though sustainable and regenerative practices, to improve job conditions and to ensure that the economic growth will be beneficial and will include the community. It also stressed out the need of collaboration between public and private sectors to create a synergy in the tourism industry.

6.2. General approach

The Canary Islands represents one of the main and most popular destinations in Europe thanks to their extraordinary biodiversity, unique landscapes and to the weather which allows an all-yearlong tourism. Despite this, the archipelago suffers from great issues such as overtourism which has created pressures in other fields such as the environment, the society and the economy. These challenges in the long term can damage and put in danger the sustainability of the destination. To face these challenges, the destination must rethink about the type of tourism they apply and opt for a more regenerative one that doesn't limit only to the minimization of negative impacts. This strategic plan offers a real path to implement regenerative tourism in the Canary Islands. The 4 main sectors on which this strategic plan will focus are represented in figure 15.

Figure 15. The four sections of the strategic plan

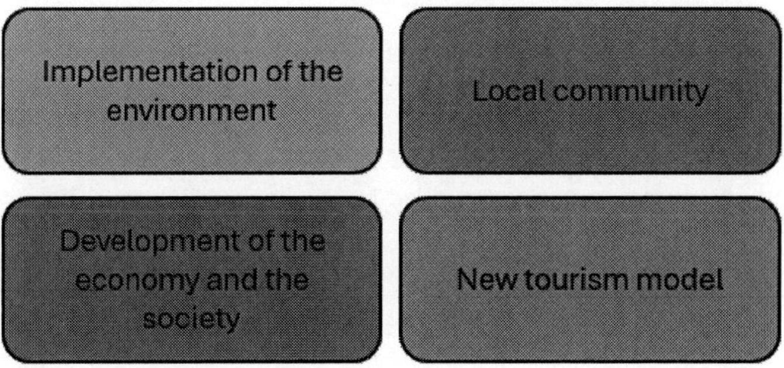

Some initiatives that can be taken in the environmental, social and economic dimensions are contained in table 2.

Table 2. Potential initiatives to the strategic plan

Environmental initiatives
• Raising the price of the stay tax: this strategy has already been applied in New Zealand and will help the islands to contrast the mass tourism. • Implementing the construction of sustainable hotels: stay in eco-friendly hotels reduce the tourism impact on the environment. • Energy efficiency: investing in technologies that reduce the energy consume, in sensors of movements, efficient heating and cooling systems can make the difference. • Water management: starting from technical aspects such as the installation of low-flow faucets, showers and dual-flush toilets. • Waste management: reduce plastic and single-use waste by fostering the use of renewable materials. • Implement the use of sustainable transportation: taking the public transportation reduce air pollution and the traffic. • Sustainable certification: obtaining a recognize sustainable certification for hotels and accommodations such as Green Key, EarthCeck or ISO 14001. • Carbon neutral tourist packages: offer carbon-neutral holiday packages that include sustainable accommodation, eco-friendly transportation options. • Restoration programs: promote restoration programs where tourists can participate in hands-on environmental restoration projects. • Eco-trails and biodiversity tours: develop eco-trails and off-set tourism route that showcase the unique biodiversity of each island.
Economic initiatives
• Government incentives for regenerative practices: defining monetary incentives that support local entrepreneurs. • Tourist incentives for green practices: retribution for tourists that participate in sustainable initiatives.

• Sustainable art and craft markets: promotion of local markets that sell recycled, up-cycled or locally sourced products. • Local food experiences: develop farm to table experiences that help local industries to grow and to expand their business.
Social initiatives
• Community tours: promoting tours led by local people where visitors can learn directly from residents. • Local tour operators: supporting local tours operator choosing them over the mass one. • Heritage preservation initiatives: host cultural exchange events such as traditional music, dance performances or cultural festivals. • Marketing campaigns: develop marketing campaigns that aims to attract young and conscious travellers. • Local language and cultural immersion programs: promote language and cultural immersion programs that encourage tourist to learn Spanish and Canarian dialects.

On the one hand, the strong points of this destination are: i) the integration of sustainable development goals (SDGs) in their strategic planning and investment, ii) the promotion of local culture and heritage, iii) the public awareness and marketing campaigns and iv) the sustainable certifications and targeted initiatives.

On the other hand, the potential weaknesses and gaps to work on are: i) the limited awareness and understanding of regenerative tourism, ii) the overcrowding and environmental degradation, iii) the insufficient sustainable infrastructures, iv) the challenges in community integration and negative impacts on residents and v) the inconsistent implementation across islands. This new approach should be implemented not only for its benefits on the environment and society, but also because the destination can count on the global trend towards sustainable tourism.

7. CONCLUSIONS

Beyond theoretical contributions, these results demonstrate that regenerative tourism is not just a theoretical framework but can also be implemented in real-world settings, like the Canary Islands, which are an overtourism destination. Some specific ways that regenerative practices could change the archipelago's current tourism model include enacting eco-taxes to restrict large-scale tourist inflows, creating eco-trails that highlight biodiversity while distributing visitor flows, and giving priority to farm-to-table projects to support regional food systems. The study is made more unique by the integration of theory and practical recommendations illustrated in the strategic plan, which also makes it immediately applicable to practitioners and policymakers looking for workable answers.

7.1. Recommendations To achieve a successful transition to regenerative tourism, the following recommendations are provided in table 3

Table 3. Potential initiatives to the strategic plan

For public organizations
• *Promote education and awareness:* the pioneers in raising awareness among the tourists and the local community should be the public organisations by educating residents, businesses and tourists about the benefits of regenerative tourism. • *Facilitate collaborative online platforms:* the creation of an online platform of the Tourism of Canary Island that facilitate the collaboration among various stakeholders. • *Support local initiatives:* choosing to support local initiatives that align with regenerative tourism practices such as local artisan markets, conservation projects and cultural heritage programs.
For governments
• *Enhance policy and regulatory framework:* Government should make stricter the environmental regulations, enact zoning laws that protect natural areas and establish policies that limit the environmental footprint of tourism developments. • *Investments in sustainable infrastructure:* they should prioritize the investments in sustainable infrastructures such as public transportation and energy-efficient buildings. • *Provide economic incentives:* economic incentives such as tax breaks or grants should be offered to businesses that adopt and adapt to regenerative practices.

7.2. Further research

This research tries to provide a solid foundation to understand and to implement regenerative tourism in the Canary Islands, but there are still some areas that could be investigated further. This will not only help to perfect the strategies proposed but also to contribute to expand the application of regenerative tourism principles across different context.

The following areas offer opportunities for further investigation:

- Longitudinal studies on the impact of regenerative tourism
- Broader stakeholders' involvement
- Comparative studies across destinations

To conclude, while this thesis sets the basis for implementing regenerative tourism in the Canary Islands, it also creates opportunities for further explorations and refinements. The proposed strategic plan should be considered as a starting point, from which one must always try to improve.

8. REFERENCES

Bishnu, S. A. T. (2023). Regenerative tourism: Opportunities and challenges. Journal of Responsible Tourism Management, 3(1). Australia.

Booking.com. (2019). Sustainable travel report. Retrieved from https://www.booking.com

EUROSTAT (2018). Tourism statistics – winter season occupancy. Statistical office of the European Union. Retireved from: https://ec.europa.eu/eurostat/statistics-explained/index.php?title=Tourism_statistics_-_winter_season_occupancy

Food Waste Reduction Alliance. (2023). Report: Food waste policy. Retrieved from https://www.foodwastealliance.org

Future of Tourism (2020),

GSTC. (2023). Annual report 2023. Global Sustainable Tourism Council. Retrieved from https://www.gstcouncil.org

Hernández-Martín, R., Antonova, N., Celis Sosa, D.F., Fernández Hernández, C. (2021).

Tourism Observatory of the Canary Islands. Preliminary Report. Consejería de Turismo, Industria y Empleo, Gobierno de Canarias. January 2021

Poon, A. (1993). Tourism, technology and competitive strategies. London: CABI.

Socatelli, M. A. (2020). Fundamentos del desarrollo regenerativo y turismo regenerativo. San José, Costa Rica: Universidad para la Cooperación Internacional. Retrieved from https://www.ucipfg.com

Teruel Avecilla, S. (2018). Análisis y aproximación a la definición del paradigma del

turismo regenerativo. San José, Costa Rica: Universidad para la Cooperación Internacional.

Truyols, M. (2023). Regenerative tourism 101: What it is, examples, implementation and more. Retrieved from https://www.mize.com

Turismo Islas Canarias (2022). Turismo de Canarias refuerza la descarbonización del sector con un plan para reducir al 50% sus emisiones en ocho años. Retrieved from https://www.turismodeislascanarias.com

UNEP & UNWTO (2005). Making tourism more sustainable – A guide for policy makers. United Nations Environment Programme and United Nations

World Tourism Organization Retrieved from https://www.unep.fr/shared/publications/pdf/DTIx0592xPA-TourismPolicyEN.pdf

UNWTO (2023). Transport-related CO_2 emissions of the tourism sector: From measurement to decarbonization. United Nations World Tourism Organization. Retrieved from https://www.unwto.org

UNWTO (2024). Sustainable development of tourism. United Nations World Tourism Organization. Retrieved from https://www.unwto.org/sustainable-development

LA HUERTA DE VALÈNCIA: UNA OPORTUNIDAD TURÍSTICA PARA LA SOSTENIBILIDAD DEL TERRITORIO Y EL ALCANCE DE LOS OBJETIVOS DE DESARROLLO SOSTENIBLE

FRANCISCA RAMÓN FERNÁNDEZ
Universitat Politècnica de València

TEMÁTICA: Turismo y comunidades locales: Oportunidades y desafíos para la sostenibilidad sociocultural

RESUMEN: La Huerta de València representa un espacio identificador del territorio. Su protección se contempla en la Ley 5/2018 y constituye una oportunidad turística al estar vinculada la Huerta con el milenario Tribunal de las Aguas de la Vega de Valencia. El mantenimiento del espacio de la Huerta resulta fundamental para la agricultura de proximidad y la sostenibilidad de los recursos. Además se establece su íntima relación con el alcance de los Objetivos de Desarrollo Sostenible. Nos proponemos reflexionar sobre dicho espacio y su potenciación en el ámbito turístico, su también relación con los huertos urbanos y el establecimiento de un tipo de turismo respetuoso con el medio ambiente y la sostenibilidad.

Palabras clave: Huerta, València, Turismo, Regional, Territorio, Objetivos de Desarrollo Sostenible

ABSTRACT: The Huerta de València represents a space that identifies the territory. Its protection is contemplated in Law 5/2018 and constitutes a tourism opportunity, as the Huerta is linked to the ancient Water Tribunal of the Vega de Valencia. Maintaining the Huerta space is essential for local agriculture and the sustainability of resources. Its close relationship with achieving the Sustainable Development Goals is also established. We propose to reflect on this space and its promotion in the tourism sector, its relationship with urban gardens, and the establishment of a type of tourism that respects the environment and sustainability.

Keywords: Huerta, València, Tourism, Regional, Territory, Sustainable Development Goals

1. INTRODUCCIÓN

El espacio de la Huerta de València forma parte de territorio valenciano y es identificatorio de su paisaje. Tiene un valor agrario muy relevante, ya que dispone de un suelo muy fértil y destaca por los cultivos de especies autóctonas dando lugar al comercio de productos de proximidad.

En el ámbito turístico la zona de la Huerta de València se caracteriza por su peculiaridad, su singularidad, y también por atraer a una tipología de turistas concienciados con el medio ambiente, la sostenibilidad y el patrimonio cultural.

En este trabajo nos proponemos aproximarnos a la Huerta de València como una oportunidad turística y revalorización de dicho espacio, cada vez más reducido, que tiene un valor caracterizado por su riqueza y por estar vinculado de una forma muy estrecha a una institución milenaria como es el Tribunal de las Aguas de la Vega de Valencia. Sin la Huerta de València el Tribunal no existiría, ya que que se ocupa de resolver los conflictos de agua de las acequias del margen derecho e izquierdo del río Turia, y su pervivencia depende de dicho territorio.

Veremos también los distintos recursos turísticos que ofrece el espacio de la Huerta de València, y su relación con los Objetivos de Desarrollo Sostenible, ya que dicho espacio debe respetarse y cuidarse para evitar su desaparición.

2. LA HUERTA DE VALÈNCIA: SOSTENIBILIDAD, TERRITORIO Y SU ATRACTIVO TURÍSTICO

La Huerta de València tiene una regulación específica y se le aplica la Ley 5/2018, de 6 de marzo, de la Huerta de València (BOE núm. 96, de 20 de abril de 2018), el Decreto 219/2018, de 30 de noviembre, del Consell, por el que se aprueba el Plan de acción territorial de ordenación y dinamización de la Huerta de València (DOGV núm. 8448, de 20 de diciembre de 2018), y el Decreto-ley 4/2025, de 4 de febrero, del Consell, de modificación de la Ley 5/2018, de 6 de marzo, de la Generalitat, de la Huerta de València, y del Decreto 219/2018, de 30 de noviembre, del Consell, por el que se aprueba el Plan de acción territorial de ordenación y dinamización de la Huerta de València (DOGV núm. 10040, de 5 de febrero de 2025).

Además, por Resolución 252/XI, del Pleno de Les Corts Valencianes, adoptada en la reunión del día 20 de febrero de 2025, se convalidó el Decreto ley 4/2025, de 4 de febrero, del Consell, de modificación de la Ley 5/2018, de 6 de marzo, de la Generalitat, de la Huerta de València, y del Decreto 219/2018, de 30 de noviembre, del Consell, por el que se aprueba el Plan de acción territorial de ordenación y dinamización de la Huerta de València (DOGV núm. 10058, de 3 de marzo de 2025).

La importancia de la Huerta de València también se manifiesta en la calidad del suelo con una alta capacidad agrológica, así como la vinculación con el Derecho civil valenciano a través de los arrendamientos rústicos históricos regulados actualmente por la Ley 3/2013, de 26 de julio, de los Contratos y otras Relaciones Jurídicas Agrarias (BOE núm. 222, de 16 de septiembre de 2013)., modificada por Ley 2/2019, de 6 de febrero (BOE núm. 51, de 28 de febrero de 2019)., en el que se reconoce el "derecho a la tierra flor" por parte del arrendatario en el caso de terminación del arriendo. Se trata de la parte más superficial de la tierra que ha sido enriquecida a lo largo de los sucesivos cultivos y generaciones de labradores. Esta capa es la que determina la productividad de la tierra, y que ha sido fruto del esfuerzo, abono y mantenimiento de prácticas agrícolas adecuadas (Figura 1)

Figura 1. Huerta de València

Fuente: https://valenciasecreta.com/huerta-de-valencia-patrimonio-mundial/ (Consultado el 11 de abril de 2025).

En el ámbito turístico, la Huerta de València tiene distintos aspectos que hacen del espacio que sea atractivo para el turista:

2.1. El Tribunal de las Aguas de la Vega de Valencia

La mayoría de las acequias que forman parte del ámbito del Tribunal de las Aguas de la Vega de València, que fue declarado patrimonio inmaterial de la humanidad por la UNESCO el 13 de septiembre de 2009, han visto reducida su superficie de riego de tal forma que en algunos casos es testimonial en el momento actual. En algunos tramos la zona que se puede considerar como regable ha desaparecido por completo o únicamente subsisten áreas inconexas de huerta residual, las cuales corren peligro de desaparecer definitivamente en una nueva pulsión expansiva del ciclo urbanístico (Figura 2).

La pervivencia de la Huerta de València es condición necesaria para la protección del patrimonio inmaterial reconocido al Tribunal de las Aguas de la Vega de València, que se encuentra indisolublemente vinculado a la propia existencia de este espacio en óptimas condiciones productivas y ambientales.

El reconocido Tribunal está declarado bien de interés cultural inmaterial por el Decreto 73/2006, de 26 de mayo (BOE núm. 224, de 19 de septiembre de 2006), y también interesa destacar el Decreto 148/2006, de 6 de octubre, por el que se declaran bienes de interés cultural, con la categoría de monumento, los Azudes de las Acequias del Tribunal de las Aguas de Valencia y de la Real Acequia de Moncada, situados en Valencia, Paterna, Quart de Poblet y Manises, así como se declara el Conjunto Histórico que forman los mismos (BOE núm. 309, de 27 de diciembre de 2006).

Figura 2. Tribunal de las Aguas de la Vega de València

Fuente: https://tribunaldelasaguas.org/es/el-tribunal/historia
(Consultado el 11 de abril de 2025).

2.2. El patrimonio cultural de la Huerta

Teniendo en cuenta la legislación del patrimonio cultural constituida por la Ley 4/1998, de 11 de junio, del Patrimonio Cultural Valenciano (BOE núm. 174, de 22 de julio de 1998), la Ley 7/2004, de 19 de octubre, de modificación de la Ley 4/1998, de 11 de junio, del Patrimonio Cultural Valenciano (BOE núm. 279, de 19 de noviembre de 2004), la Ley 5/2007, de 9 de febrero, de modificación de la Ley 4/1998, de 11 de junio, del Patrimonio Cultural Valenciano (BOE núm. 71, de 23 de marzo de 2007), y la Ley 9/2017, de 7 de abril, de modificación de la Ley 4/1998, del patrimonio cultural valenciano (BOE núm. 112, de 11 de mayo de 2017), en el espacio de la Huerta se encuentran distintos elementos de gran interés para el turismo.

También hay que tener en cuenta la Ley 10/2015, de 26 de mayo, para la salvaguardia del Patrimonio Cultural Inmaterial (BOE núm. 126, de 27 de mayo de 2015) en tanto que dentro de dicho espacio las manifestaciones culturales transmitidas de generación en generación también forman parte de la idiosincrasia de dicho espacio.

La Huerta de València y su área metropolitana, como espacio de acreditados valores productivos (Figura 3), ambientales, culturales, históricos y paisajísticos, es uno de los paisajes agrarios más relevantes y singulares del contexto europeo y mediterráneo. Así lo reconocía el Informe Dobris de la Agencia Europea del Medio Ambiente, que advertía que sólo restan cinco pequeños ámbitos de huerta semejantes en la Unión Europea y que estos deben preservarse mediante mecanismos necesarios para su conservación activa.

Este paisaje productivo y cultural de elevado valor simbólico, que contribuye a la excelencia y diferenciación del área metropolitana de València, dentro del contexto global de los espacios urbanos europeos, estuvo seriamente amenazado de desaparición en las últimas décadas por la crisis y el abandono de la actividad agraria, por el fraccionamiento producido por las infraestructuras de movilidad y por la propia presión de la actividad urbanística, que redujo su superficie sensiblemente. Así, la mayoría de las acequias que forman parte del ámbito del Tribunal de las Aguas de la Vega de València, declarado patrimonio inmaterial de la humanidad por la UNESCO el 13 de septiembre de 2009, vieron reducida su superficie de riego, siendo testimonial en algunos casos en el momento actual. Estamos, por tanto, ante un espacio merecedor de un adecuado régimen de protección y dinamización que garantice su recuperación y pervivencia para las generaciones futuras.

Figura 3. Productos típicos de la Huerta de València

Fuente: elaboración propia

El artículo 4 de la Ley 5/2018 se centra en la función social y pública de la Huerta de València estableciendo que la actividad agraria y el patrimonio natural, cultural y paisajístico de la Huerta de València desempeña una función social relevante al favorecer el desarrollo del sector agrario, la soberanía alimentaria, el bienestar de las personas, el uso sostenible del territorio y la prevención del cambio climático.

Las acciones encaminadas a la consecución de los fines de esta ley se declararán de utilidad pública e interés social a todos los efectos y en particular a los expropiatorios, respecto a los bienes o a los derechos que puedan estar afectados.

En la planificación y gestión de los valores del patrimonio natural, cultural y paisajístico y en la gestión de la actividad agraria de la Huerta de València, se fomentarán los acuerdos voluntarios con los titulares y usuarios de ésta, así como fórmulas de custodia del territorio u otras de naturaleza similar.

2.2.1. Patrimonio hidráulico y el agua

El artículo 10 de la Ley 5/2018 se refiere a que el patrimonio hidráulico de la Huerta de València es la red del riego por gravedad, la red de drenaje y los elementos que colaboran en el reparto de los recursos hídricos y su aprovechamiento, incluyendo los siguientes:

a) La red de acequias compuesta jerárquicamente de acequias madre, brazos, *rolls, files* y regadoras.

b) Otros elementos de reparto y distribución del agua como azudes, acueductos, *canos* y lenguas.

c) Los molinos que aprovechan los caudales de reparto que discurren por las acequias.

d) El agua es el elemento esencial que ha permitido la existencia de la huerta. Siendo mayoritarios los aportes provenientes del río Turia, no hay que olvidar los aportes realizados a través de multitud de pozos distribuidos en su ámbito y de otras fuentes, como las aguas regeneradas. La supervivencia de la huerta está supeditada a la existencia de recursos hídricos suficientes, tanto en cantidad como en calidad.

2.2.2. Patrimonio arquitectónico

El artículo 11 de la Ley 5/2018 indica que el patrimonio arquitectónico de la Huerta de València está integrado por los siguientes elementos:

a) Construcciones de habitación, resguardo y almacenamiento, entre otras y en particular las casas, alquerías y barracas de la huerta.

b) Construcciones de actividades agrarias y complementarias.

c) Construcciones religiosas como las cartujas, monasterios y ermitas.

2.2.3. Patrimonio etnológico

El artículo 12 de la Ley 5/2018 preceptúa que el patrimonio material etnológico está compuesto, con carácter general, por aquellos bienes materiales vinculados a tradiciones y costumbres de la huerta y en particular los calvarios, cruces, mojones de término y paneles cerámicos y chimeneas, así como los aperos y herramientas de labranza tradicionales.

El patrimonio inmaterial etnológico lo constituyen los jurados de riego, las costumbres generalmente transmitidas de manera oral y una gran variedad de manifestaciones folclóricas.

2.2.4. Patrimonio natural

Se regula en el artículo 13 de la Ley 5/2018, de tal forma que la Huerta de València presenta un patrimonio natural de flora y fauna en el que sobresalen las masas vegetales no agrícolas, así como las especies presentes en los márgenes de caminos y acequias. Su mantenimiento y regeneración será una acción prioritaria de esta ley y de los instrumentos que la desarrollen.

Los espacios naturales protegidos situados en el ámbito de la huerta se regirán por su legislación y sus instrumentos de ordenación y gestión específicos, los cuales prevalecerán sobre los de naturaleza urbanística o territorial.

2.3. Las vías pecuarias en relación con la Huerta

El artículo 14 de la Ley 5/2018 se refiere a la red de caminos y sendas históricas. La red de caminos de la Huerta de València está compuesta por las vías históricas de comunicación entre localidades, las vías pecuarias, los caminos rurales de acceso a la parcela y al hábitat disperso y las que facilitan la comunicación con puntos de interés turístico, cultural o patrimonial. En los instrumentos de desarrollo de esta ley se identificará esta red de caminos.

Se aplicará lo indicado en la Ley 3/1995, de 23 de marzo, de vías pecuarias (BOE núm. 71, de 24 de marzo de 1995), y la Ley 3/2014, de 11 de julio, de la Generalitat, de vías pecuarias de la Comunitat Valenciana (BOE núm. 186, de 1 de agosto de 2014).

2.4. El catálogo de protección de los bienes culturales

El artículo 17 de la Ley 5/2018 contempla el catálogo de protección de los bienes culturales. Indica que el instrumento de ordenación de la Huerta de València, regulado en el artículo siguiente, incluirá un catálogo de protección de los bienes culturales de relevancia supralocal e identificará y determinará su régimen de conservación y recuperación.

El planeamiento urbanístico municipal deberá completar este catálogo mediante la inclusión de los elementos del patrimonio cultural que posean rango local y podrá modificar las correspondientes fichas, de acuerdo con lo previsto en la legislación urbanística y de patrimonio cultural.

La conselleria competente, en colaboración con las administraciones locales, establecerá y promocionará mecanismos para hacer efectiva la participación ciudadana en la elaboración del catálogo de protección de los bienes culturales.

Decreto 219/2018 dispone que en el ámbito del espacio de la Huerta se contempla la implantación en estas edificaciones de usos complementarios a la agricultura que contribuyan a la dinamización, conocimiento y uso público sostenible del paisaje de la Huerta tales como espacios gastronómicos, viviendas de uso turístico y alojamiento turístico rural, artesanía, mercadillos y puntos de venta, entre otros.

En este sentido, el Plan de acción territorial identifica como elementos idóneos una red de huertos de ocio, las puertas de entrada a la Huerta, los itinerarios verdes, los puntos de encuentro y miradores, los museos vivos, las alquerías escuela, las viviendas de uso turístico y los alojamientos turísticos rurales y establecimientos de restauración. También se regulan las condiciones de señalización, la publicidad y la disposición del arbolado y las masas forestales en el ámbito de la Huerta.

2.5. Usos y actividades permitidas en la Huerta de València

Los usos y actividades permitidas en la Huerta se regulan en el artículo 37 del Decreto 219/2018. Los usos terciarios admitidos en la Huerta de València, con las particularidades que se especifican en el presente Plan son: restauración, alojamiento turístico, hípica, cría de animales para uso particular o comercial, huertos de ocio o sociales, usos de disfrute de la Huerta relacionados con sistemas de movilidad no motorizada, investigación agraria o ambiental.

El artículo 42 del Decreto 219/2018 contempla los alojamientos turísticos y establecimientos de restauración. Se permite la implantación de viviendas de uso turístico, alojamientos turísticos rurales y establecimientos de restauración.

En Huerta Grado 1 y 2 (H1 y H2) se situarán en edificios preexistentes de arquitectura tradicional y en Huerta Grado 3 (H3), y con carácter restringido, podrán situarse en todo tipo de construcciones, incluso de nueva planta. En todo caso, las actuaciones respetarán la trama viaria, la red de riego, las condiciones de la parcelación tradicional y la parcela libre de edificación deberá destinarse a uso agrario y mantenerse en buen estado de cultivo.

Cuando se implanten sobre edificación existentes y sea necesario un incremento del volumen edificado, no podrá superar el 20 % de la huella de la edificación existente a la entrada en vigor del Plan de acción territorial, cuando se trate de edificios catalogados, y al 10 % cuando se trate de edificios no catalogados. Dichos incrementos no superarán los 200 metros cuadrados.

Los parámetros urbanísticos de las nuevas edificaciones serán los establecidos en la legislación urbanística vigente en materia de suelo no urbanizable.

Figuras 4 y 5. Agromuseu de Vera.

Fuente: elaboración propia

La capacidad máxima de las actividades de alojamiento turístico permitidas se limitará: en Huerta Grado 1 (H1) a 12 plazas, y el aforo máximo de los restaurantes a 40 personas; en Huerta Grado 2 (H2) a 16 plazas, y el aforo máximo de los restaurantes a 60 personas y en Huerta Grado 3 (H3) a 20 plazas, y el aforo máximo de los restaurantes a 80 personas.

Las limitaciones de capacidad establecidas en el apartado anterior, no serán de aplicación a los alojamientos turísticos permitidos y establecimientos de restauración que se instalen en alquerías, masías u otras construcciones rurales que gocen de especial protección, que estén en suelo en situación de suelo urbanizado, que se localicen dentro de la trama urbana o contiguas a esta y sea posible el acceso no motorizado.

En este caso quedarán sometidas a lo dispuesto en la legislación vigente en materia de turismo y actividades.

Respecto de los puntos de encuentro y miradores, el artículo 72 del Decreto 218/2018 determina que los puntos de encuentro son lugares integrados en la red de itinerarios verdes, situados en espacios con elevado potencial para el uso turístico y recreativo. Deberán tener una incidencia mínima sobre la superficie y actividad agrarias.

Los puntos de encuentro, por su condición de área recreativa, contarán con arbolado de sombra, mobiliario urbano para el descanso y señalización informativa de los elementos de interés próximos. Con carácter general se localizarán en suelo público y no podrán tener una superficie superior a 40 m^2. El Plan de acción territorial propone con carácter orientativo diversos puntos de encuentro en los planos de ordenación.

En los puntos de dominancia visual y con vistas de valor perceptual se habilitarán miradores para la contemplación del paisaje, los cuales están señalados con carácter orientativo en los planos de ordenación.

Los Museos vivos se regulan en el artículo 73 del Decreto 219/2018, el Plan de acción territorial propone crear una red de cooperación entre los museos vinculados con la Huerta, su regulación será establecida por el Consejo de la Huerta de València. Como mínimo, formarán parte de esta red:

a) El Museu Valencià d'Etnologia (València).

b) El Museu de L'Horta (Almàssera).

c) El Museu de L'Horta Sud Josep Ferrís March (Torrent).

d) El Museo de la Horchata y de la Chufa (Alboraia).

e) El Museo del Arroz (València).

f) El Museo de Historia de València (València).

g) El Museo del Colegio del Arte Mayor de la Seda (València).

h) El Agromuseu de Vera (València) (Figuras 4 y 5)

2.6. Los huertos de ocio o sociales

El artículo 40 del Decreto 219/2018, regula los huertos de ocio o sociales. Se permiten huertos de ocio o sociales como espacios agrarios de reducidas dimensiones que cumplen funciones productivas de autoconsumo, ambientales, sociales, de salud o culturales. En ningún caso se considerará una actividad agraria profesional.

Se situarán de manera preferente en zonas próximas a los núcleos urbanos, o dentro del propio casco urbano.

Los huertos de ocio o sociales en Huerta Grado 1 y 2 (H1 y H2) serán de iniciativa pública, municipales o coordinadas por el Consejo de la Huerta de València. Para este fin, el Consejo de la Huerta de València aprobarán bases reguladoras de las condiciones de uso de estas instalaciones que incluirán criterios que promocionen la paridad de mujeres y hombres. En Huerta Grado 3 (H3) podrán ser de carácter privado.

La superficie vinculada de accesos y aparcamiento para huertos de ocio o sociales deberá cumplir lo dispuesto en el artículo 37.4, a excepción de la ocupación máxima que será del 50 %.

En ningún caso interferirán la actividad agraria habitual y la disposición de las unidades de cultivo responderá a composiciones ordenadas y respetuosas con los patrones del territorio.

El Decreto-ley 4/2025 introduce determinadas correcciones técnicas que han de servir para dar un impulso a la recuperación y dinamización de dicho espacio agrario, clarificando el régimen aplicable respecto al catálogo de protección de los bienes culturales, con la finalidad también de facilitar su urgente tramitación, cuyo inicio se remonta a enero de 2019 y, en conexión de sentido con alguna de las medidas previstas en el Decreto ley 20/2024, de 30 de diciembre, del Consell, de medidas urbanísticas urgentes para favorecer las tareas de reconstrucción tras los daños producidos por la DANA (DOGV núm. 10017, de 2 de enero de 2025), a la minoración de estándares de zonas verdes y parques públicos del planeamiento municipal. También permitiendo flexibilizar determinados parámetros urbanísticos para las construcciones e instalaciones agrarias, mediante informe de la conselleria competente en materia de agricultura y desarrollo rural, fundado en necesidades de la actividad agraria, lo que indudablemente facilitará las urgentes tareas de recuperación de las explotaciones agrarias afectadas.

De acuerdo con aportaciones recibidas, y por razones de conexión de sentido con la modificación introducida en el texto legal respecto al catálogo de protección de los bienes culturales, se introduce una modificación respecto a las ampliaciones sobre edificaciones catalogadas, exceptuando la regla general prevista y realizando una remisión a la correspondiente ficha de catálogo, habiéndose detectado ya esta necesidad con ocasión de la redacción del citado catálogo de protección. Por otra parte, y consecuentemente con lo anterior, se clarifica el concepto «huella de la edificación», sustituyendo el término construcción por el de edificación, que es más específico, de acuerdo con lo previsto en la legislación sobre ordenación de la edificación.

El uso global predominante en la Huerta de València, según el artículo 22 de la Ley 5/2018 es el agropecuario. Por ello, se podrán autorizar construcciones, instalaciones y obras que sean necesarias y compatibles con el mejor aprovechamiento, conservación, cuidado y restauración de los recursos propios de esta actividad, y mediante informe favorable de la conselleria competente en materia de agricultura, fundado en necesidades de la actividad agraria, podrá eximirse en casos determinados del cumplimiento de las limitaciones urbanísticas o territoriales reglamentarias establecidas con carácter general. Este uso global admite la compatibilidad de otros usos complementarios o dinamizadores de la actividad principal.

En la modificación operada por el artículo 43-2 de la normativa del Plan de acción territorial de ordenación y dinamización de la Huerta de València, que queda redactado como sigue: en huerta grado 3 (H3) se permiten las dotaciones deportivas, recreativas, educativas, culturales y científicas, sanitarias y asistenciales, residenciales dotacionales, administrativas e institucionales. En huerta grado 1 y 2 (H1 y H2) estas dotaciones únicamente se permiten en edificación existente a la entrada en vigor de este plan, que podrá justificadamente ampliarse como máximo en un 20% de su superficie construida cuando se trate de edificaciones catalogadas y del 10% para el resto.

Las ampliaciones sobre edificaciones catalogadas se ajustarán a lo previsto en su correspondiente catálogo, pudiendo superar el 20% señalado siempre que se justifique que la ampliación se adecúa a la ficha del bien y resto de determinaciones normativas del Catálogo.

3. LOS RECURSOS DE LA HUERTA EN RELACIÓN CON LOS OBJETIVOS DE DESARROLLO SOSTENIBLE

La Ley 15/2018, de 7 de junio, de turismo, ocio y hospitalidad de la Comunitat Valenciana (BOE núm. 157,de 29 de junio de 2018) indica que resulta, pues, ineludible tomar en consideración las disposiciones del Código ético mundial para el turismo que aprobó la Organización Mundial de Turismo (OMT) y que se ha adaptado a los rasgos propios e identitarios de la Comunitat Valenciana como destino europeo y mediterráneo a través de la implementación del Código ético del turismo valenciano. Si bien, *de facto,* ambos códigos no son jurídicamente vinculantes, en ellos se enuncian los principios que deben guiar el desarrollo del turismo, siendo un marco de referencia para las personas interesadas en el sector con el objetivo de reducir al mínimo los efectos negativos que puede generar sobre el medio ambiente y el patrimonio cultural al tiempo que se fijan las directrices para aprovechar los beneficios de la actividad turística en la promoción del desarrollo.

Además, el código propugna la comprensión y la promoción de los valores éticos comunes de la humanidad en un espíritu de tolerancia y respeto a la diversidad de las creencias religiosas, filosóficas y morales y a la libertad de conciencia que son, a la vez, fundamento y consecuencia de un turismo responsable, lo que conlleva una necesidad de formación específica de los agentes profesionales sobre la forma de vida, gustos y expectativas de las personas que nos visitan como turistas y su contribución al pleno desarrollo cultural y espiritual de las mismas, con el fin de garantizar un tratamiento hospitalario. En este sentido, el código insta al fomento de los desplazamientos por motivos históricos, patrimoniales, medioambientales, de religión, salud, educación e intercambio cultural o lingüístico. Unos principios que son básicos en el camino hacia una legislación moderna y que encuentran su trasunto en esta ley.

3.1. Obligaciones de las personas usuarias de servicios turísticos

El artículo 17 de la Ley 15/2018 regula las obligaciones de las personas usuarias de servicios turísticos. Éstas, sin perjuicio de lo que dispongan las normativas sectoriales que sean de aplicación, tendrán las siguientes obligaciones:

a) Respetar las tradiciones y prácticas sociales y culturales de los destinos turísticos así como su riqueza y valor.

b) Respetar el entorno medioambiental, el patrimonio histórico y cultural y los recursos turísticos.

3.2. La orientación turística del patrimonio natural y cultural

Según dispone el artículo 23 de la Ley 15/2018, los bienes declarados de interés cultural y los bienes declarados de relevancia local, recogidos como tales en los catálogos locales de bienes y espacios protegidos y en el Inventario general del patrimonio cultural valenciano, constituyen un activo turístico que será objeto de las actuaciones de fomento de los recursos turísticos de los departamentos de las administraciones públicas competentes en materia de turismo, especialmente mediante acciones dirigidas a mejorar su señalización, su descripción y su correcto uso, así como a mejorar la conservación de sus infraestructuras.

Los bienes declarados de interés cultural y los centros históricos que alberguen establecimientos y actividades turísticas serán objeto de una atención específica en las acciones de promoción turística de la Comunitat Valenciana. Se establecerán criterios que alerten sobre la posible saturación para evitarla y garantizar las excelentes relaciones entre visitantes y personas residentes.

Los espacios naturales protegidos de la Comunitat Valenciana, como parte esencial de su patrimonio natural, constituyen un elemento esencial del territorio como activo turístico que será objeto de actuaciones de las administraciones públicas competentes en materia de turismo, dirigidas tanto a su promoción como a su preservación y utilización racional, para no poner en riesgo su sostenibilidad, debiendo primar las actuaciones de conservación y preservación sobre las de promoción.

3.3. Los recursos turísticos

Como indica el artículo 24 de la Ley 15/2018, que fue modificado por la Ley 8/2022, de 29 de diciembre, de medidas fiscales, de gestión administrativa y financiera, y de organización de la Generalitat (BOE núm. 52, de 2 de marzo de 2023) constituye un recurso turístico cualquier bien, valor, elemento o manifestación, tanto material como inmaterial, expresivo de la realidad geográfica, natural, cultural, deportiva, histórica, social o económica de la Comunitat Valenciana que pueda generar o incrementar de manera directa o indirecta flujos turísticos, proporcionando repercusiones económicas favorables.

Tendrán la consideración de recursos turísticos de primer orden aquellos elementos que, aislada o conjuntamente, tengan capacidad por sí mismos de generar flujos y corrientes de turismo relevantes y contribuyan a reforzar la imagen de marca turística de la Comunitat Valenciana, así como su promoción como destino turístico.

A los efectos de esta ley, sin carácter exhaustivo, tienen la consideración de recursos turísticos de primer orden de la Comunitat Valenciana las manifestaciones festivas que cuenten con la correspondiente declaración de interés turístico, las playas, los recintos congresuales y feriales, los acontecimientos deportivos y los festivales de música con proyección nacional e internacional, las sociedades musicales de la Comunitat Valenciana en todas sus variantes, la gastronomía propia de la Comunitat Valenciana, la pirotecnia, el paisaje agrario e industrial y sus usos y valores etnológicos, las aguas termales y los balnearios, los bienes declarados patrimonio de la humanidad, los de interés cultural así como los espacios naturales y territoriales declarados protegidos.

Las administraciones públicas que, en razón de sus competencias sectoriales intervengan, gestionen o autoricen recursos turísticos de primer orden, valorarán dicha circunstancia en el ejercicio de sus atribuciones.

El departamento del Consell competente en materia de turismo elaborará un catálogo de los recursos turísticos de primer orden de la Comunitat Valenciana, con el fin de impulsar su difusión, promoción y protección.

El Consell velará, en alianza con las empresas y los profesionales del sector, por la conservación y adecuación, para su uso turístico sostenible, de los recursos turísticos al tiempo que fomentará su transformación en activos que contribuyan a la configuración de productos turísticos diferenciados, siempre que se garantice su cuidado

3.4. El impulso del turismo

Como establece el artículo 36 de la Ley 15/2018, se entiende por impulso del turismo la actividad encaminada a la potenciación de la oferta turística de la Comunitat Valenciana a través de medidas concretas tendentes a la mejora de la competitividad, el empleo y la internacionalización de las empresas y sus profesionales.

Las acciones de impulso del turismo que realicen las administraciones públicas en la Comunitat Valenciana serán acordes con los programas de impulso de la actividad turística que apruebe el Consell.

El departamento del Consell que tenga atribuidas las competencias en materia de turismo ofrecerá apoyo técnico al resto de administraciones en relación con las iniciativas de impulso del turismo que emprendan, con el objetivo de generar sinergias tendentes a mejorar conjuntamente la oferta turística valenciana, en el marco de la sostenibilidad del medio ambiente y la óptima relación entre visitantes y residentes.

La acción de impulso del turismo perseguirá los siguientes objetivos:

a) Diversificación, segmentación y desestacionalización de la oferta turística, así como impulso del desarrollo turístico sostenible.

b) Puesta en valor y conservación de los recursos turísticos vinculados esencialmente al patrimonio cultural y natural, en coordinación con el resto de administraciones con competencias en el mismo, así como revitalización y difusión de las costumbres, fiestas, tradiciones o gastronomía de la Comunitat Valenciana.

c) Modernización de la oferta turística mediante la actualización de instalaciones, infraestructuras y servicios y la mejora de la productividad y competitividad,

d) Potenciación de las enseñanzas turísticas y de la cualificación de los profesionales del sector mediante su reciclaje profesional, especialización y formación continuada y permanente.

3.5. Sostenibilidad e integración paisajística

El artículo 57 de la Ley 15/2018 indica que la actividad de los establecimientos turísticos se ajustará a las buenas prácticas medioambientales incorporando técnicas de sostenibilidad dirigidas a reducir el consumo energético y la producción de residuos, utilizar productos reciclables, minimizar la emisión de humos y olores al exterior, insonorizar áreas concurridas y ruidosas y trasladar a las personas usuarias dichas buenas prácticas.

Los establecimientos turísticos procurarán contribuir a la mejora del entorno y a la integración paisajística en el mismo, mejorando su valor estético y minimizando el impacto visual mediante una limpieza y apariencia exterior adecuada, especialmente en zonas naturales y centros históricos.

La aplicación de buenas prácticas medioambientales y de elementos de mejora del entorno e integración paisajística podrán ser considerados para asignar una determinada categoría a un establecimiento turístico en los términos que reglamentariamente se determine.

Las actividades turísticas respetarán y conservarán el patrimonio cultural y natural de la Comunitat Valenciana y procurarán la armonía con otros sectores productivos.

3.6. Las empresas de turismo activo y ecoturismo

Según dispone el artículo 71 de la Ley 15/2018, modificado por la Ley 7/2021, de 29 de diciembre, de medidas fiscales, de gestión administrativa y financiera y de organización de la Generalitat 2022 (BOE núm. 19, de 22 de enero de 2022) son empresas de turismo activo las dedicadas a proporcionar al público en general, de forma habitual y profesional, mediante precio, actividades turísticas de recreo, deportivas y de aventura que se practican sirviéndose, sin degradarlos, básicamente de los recursos que ofrece la propia naturaleza en el medio en que se desarrollan y a las que es inherente el factor riesgo o cierto grado de destreza para su práctica. Para la práctica de las actividades dispondrán de equipos y material homologados y, excepcionalmente, se podrán utilizar recursos distintos a los que ofrece la naturaleza.

Son empresas de ecoturismo aquellas que realizan actividades turísticas dirigidas al público en general, de forma habitual y profesional, mediante precio en espacios naturales de la Comunitat Valenciana, con la finalidad de conocer, interpretar y contribuir a la conservación del territorio, del patrimonio etnográfico rural y natural, a la educación ambiental, y a la observación de especies de flora y fauna, sin generar impactos sobre el medio y repercutiendo positivamente en la población local.

Las empresas de turismo activo y ecoturismo deberán tener suscritos contratos de seguro por accidentes y de responsabilidad civil que cubran de forma suficiente los posibles riesgos imputables a la empresa por la oferta y práctica de las actividades que oferten y presten, así como una póliza de seguros de rescate, traslado y asistencia derivados de accidente en la prestación de dichos servicios.

Reglamentariamente se determinarán los requisitos y el régimen administrativo aplicable a estas empresas.

No tendrán la consideración de empresas de turismo activo y ecoturismo los clubes y federaciones deportivas cuando organicen la realización de actividades en el medio natural, dirigidas única y exclusivamente a sus asociados o federados y no al público en general.

3.7. La relación con los Objetivos de Desarrollo Sostenible

Los 17 Objetivos de Desarrollo Sostenible (Figura 6) están relacionados con diversos ámbitos.

Figura 6. Objetivos de Desarrollo Sostenible

Fuente: Naciones Unidas.
https://www.un.org/sustainabledevelopment/es/2015/09/la-asamblea-general-adopta-la-agenda-2030-para-el-desarrollo-sostenible/ (Consultado el 10 de abril de 2025).

La importancia de la Huerta de València se relaciona con los Objetivos de Desarrollo Sostenible, no sólo con el objetivo 2 “Hambre Cero”, sino también con objetivo 12 “Producción y consumo responsable”, a través de las buenas prácticas en la agricultura, y el comercio de proximidad. En la actualidad, ese comercio de proximidad, y su gestión en el caso de los productos de la Huerta de València se realiza a través de la venta directa del agricultor al consumidor, a través de los mercados de venta directa.

Siendo aplicable la reciente Ley 1/2025, de 1 de abril, de prevención de las pérdidas y el desperdicio alimentario (BOE núm. 80, de 2 de abril de 2025).

La Ley 3/2011, de 23 de marzo, de comercio de la Comunitat Valenciana (BOE núm. 91, de 16 de abril de 2011) establece en su Preámbulo, la promoción por parte de la norma respecto del comercio de proximidad, para evitar desplazamientos y el uso de los modos de movilidad menos sostenibles. Se establece la necesidad de actuar en determinadas zonas, indicando razones de carácter histórico, en que tiene que realizarse una intervención por parte de la administración, los agentes económicos y las empresas. Se reconoce la figura de los centros comerciales urbanos como una figura concertada entre el sector público y privado para

proyectos de mejora y desarrollo comercial en los ámbitos donde se produce mayor concentración comercial.

El artículo 29 referente a los objetivos de la ordenación comercial, los relaciona con los objetivos de ordenación del territorio y protección del paisaje y del desarrollo urbanístico de la Comunitat Valenciana, y menciona la creación de un marco de implantaciones comerciales en los que prime la sostenibilidad territorial.

Esta política comercial estará dirigida a mejorar la calidad de vida de los ciudadanos y tendrá como base asegurar el mantenimiento de las condiciones de proximidad, accesibilidad, diversidad y servicio del comercio valenciano.

El artículo 32 que regula las normas para el tratamiento de la actividad comercial en el planeamiento urbanístico indica el fomento del desarrollo de dotaciones comerciales que satisfagan de forma equilibrada las necesidades de la población, potenciando la proximidad y la mezcla de usos.

Uno de los puntos de venta de productos agrícolas más importante es el conocido como "Tira de Contar", que está situado en MercaValencia, y que anteriormente se había realizado este sistema de venta en el Mercado Central, y posteriormente en el Mercado de Abastos, edificio para la venta de fruta y verdura por los comerciantes mayoritarios. Se distinguen a través del etiquetado ApHorta (Figura 7).

Figura 7. Etiquetado Aphorta

Fuente: https://uniodeconsumidors.org/es/en-la-union-de-consumidores-apostamos-por-el-comercio-de-proximidad/ (Consultado el 11 de abril de 2025)

Se relaciona la Huerta de València con el Objetivo 11 referente a "Ciudades y Comunidades Sostenibles", ya que apuesta por la sostenibilidad, ya que el espacio destinado a la Huerta se encuentra en el ámbito urbano, así como con el Objetivo 15 "Gestionar sosteniblemente los bosques, luchas contra la desertificación, detener e invertir la degradación de las tierras y detener la pérdida de biodiversidad". En el caso de la Huerta de València se contemplan en la legislación referida medidas para evitar la pérdida del espacio, a través de la declaración como suelo agrario infrautilizado (SAI) y la expropiación de la tierra. También se indica en la normativa el tipo de actividades que se pueden realizar dentro del espacio de la Huerta para evitar la pérdida de biodiversidad, y que no afecte a las especies.

4. CONCLUSIONES

La Huerta de València muestra una distinta perspectiva en la gestión y participación de los recursos de los que dispone, tanto en el ámbito patrimonial como agrícola y alimentario, lo que enlaza con los Objetivos de Desarrollo Sostenible (ODS) sirviendo de foco de atención para su alcance.

La Huerta de València hemos visto que se relaciona con distintos ODS, ya que se centra en el ámbito de la alimentación y de los recursos naturales, teniendo en cuenta que en la Huerta se cultivan los productos típicos y de proximidad.

De especial interés resulta el comercio de proximidad que se desarrolla con los productos de la Huerta y la actividad de la "Tira de Contar" como ejemplo de organización para la puesta a disposición de los productos por parte de los agricultores. Esta institución que pervive a lo largo del tiempo es un ejemplo de la importancia del comercio local, y de ser una figura que data de la época foral, siendo coetánea con el Tribunal de las Aguas de la Vega de Valencia, teniendo como denominador común la Huerta de València.

Estos productos disponen de un distintivo típico que forman parte también de las rutas de la Huerta, al encontrarse en los mercados de productos y que tienen un componente de respeto al medio ambiente.

Actualmente está regulada por un Reglamento interno que establece los requisitos tanto de comercio, como de acceso a la "Tira de Contar", así como las infracciones y sanciones que se contemplan en el caso de se incumplan las obligaciones que se recogen en el texto.

La necesidad de dotar a los productos agrarios de una puesta en valor se creó una etiqueta "Aphorta" para acreditar su calidad y origen, así como de respeto medioambiental.

La creación de un distintivo de estos productos en apoyo del comercio de proximidad y de los productos locales constituye una iniciativa altamente loable para conseguir la revitalización de un sector que está afectado por una crisis no sólo económica, sino también de explotación de la tierra. Es una realidad que muchos cultivos son abandonados, y que a raíz de la Ley que hemos visto que regula la Huerta se contempla la posibilidad de declarar como suelo agrario infrautilizado el espacio destinado al cultivo, y poder ser explotado por un tercero.

Hemos visto también cómo a través de la normativa de protección de la Huerta de València, el espacio cobra una importancia relevante, y que precisamente a través del Agromuseu de Vera se perpetua el conocimiento de los procesos agrarios propios de una cultura, para evitar su pérdida y desaparición.

AGRADECIMIENTOS

Trabajo realizado en el marco del Grupo de Investigación de Excelencia Generalitat Valenciana (Proyecto Prometeu 2021/009, 2021-2024), Proyecto de I+D+i 2023-2025 (PID2022-136439OB-I00) financiado por MCIN/AEI/10.13039/501100011033/ FEDER, UE, y

Proyecto "Promoting capacity building and knowledge for the extension of urban gardens in European cities" (PCI2022-132963) (02/06/22-01/06/25).

5. REFERENCIAS

De la Vega Zamorano, E. e Iranzo García, E. (2021): "El patrimonio y paisaje del agua de l´ Horta Sud como recursos para una propuesta didáctica", *Cuadernos geográficos de la Universidad de Granada*, 60(2): 192-213. https://dialnet.unirioja.es/descarga/articulo/8001823.pdf (Consultado el 4 de abril de 2025).

García Álvarez-Coque, J. M. y Bigné, G. (2020): "El regadío histórico de la Huerta de València (España) como Sistema Importante del Patrimonio Agrícola Mundial (SIPAM)", *Revista agroalimentaria*, 26(50): 281-301. http://erevistas.saber.ula.ve/index.php/agroalimentaria/article/view/16567 (Consultado el 10 de abril de 2025).

Iranzo García, E. y De la Vega Zamorano, E. (2019): "El paisaje de la Huerta de Valencia como herramienta pedagógica", *Crisis y espacios de oportunidad. Retos para la Geografía: Libro de Actas. XXVI Congreso de la Asociación Española de Geografía.* Universitat de València. Valencia: 1129-1145. https://www.age-geografia.es/site/wp-content/uploads/2020/01/Actas-Congreso-Conclusiones-AGE-VLC2019_compressed_reduce.pdf (Consultado el 10 de abril de 2025).

López Pérez, F. (2018): "Ley 5/2018, de 6 de marzo, de la Generalitat, de la Huerta de Valencia", *Actualidad Jurídica Ambiental*, 18: 82-85. https://www.actualidadjuridicaambiental.com/wp-content/uploads/2012/01/2018_04_Recopilatorio_78_AJA_Abril.pdf (Consultado el 10 de abril de 2025).

Marzal Raga, R. (2024): "La protección de tierras agrícolas desde el derecho administrativo urbanístico", *Revista Catalana de Dret Ambiental*, 15(1): 1-40. https://revistes.urv.cat/index.php/rcda/article/view/3810/4306 (Consultado el 9 de abril de 2025).

Mayordomo Maya, S. y Hermosilla Pla, J. (2019): "Evaluación del patrimonio cultural: la Huerta de Valencia como recurso territorial", *BAGE. Boletín de la Asociación Española de Geografía*, 82:1-57. https://dialnet.unirioja.es/descarga/articulo/7042646.pdf (Consultado el 10 de abril de 2025).

Naciones Unidas (2015): *Objetivos de Desarrollo Sostenible.* https://www.un.org/sustainabledevelopment/es/objetivos-de-desarrollo-sostenible/ (Consultado el 10 de abril de 2025).

Ramón Fernández, F. (2012): "La declaración de bienes de interés cultural inmaterial y su regulación en la legislación sobre patrimonio cultural valenciano", *América Latina, globalidad e integración*, III, Ediciones del Orto, Madrid: 1535-1546.

Ramón Fernández, F. (2013): "La huerta valenciana y su revitalización como opción turística a través del diseño de rutas guiadas", *Espacios de ocio y deporte como dinamizadores turísticos. XVI Congreso Internacional de Turismo Universidad-Empresa.* Tirant lo Blanch, Valencia: 345-356.

Ramón Fernández, F. (2015): "La delimitación del entorno de protección y su influencia en la conservación de los Bienes de Interés Cultural Inmaterial", *ANIAV Asociación Nacional de Investigación en Artes Visuales*, Universitat Politècnica de València, Valencia: 610-614. Disponible en: https://riunet.upv.es/handle/10251/97828 (Consultado el 9 de abril de 2025).

Ramón Fernández, F. (2016a): "Protección del patrimonio cultural inmaterial", *Revista General de Legislación y Jurisprudencia*, 4:639-670.

Ramón Fernández, F. (2016b): "La dinamización en el ámbito turístico mediante la puesta en valor de los Bienes de Interés Cultural Inmaterial», *Culturas. Revista de Gestión Cultural*, 3(1): 36-47. http://polipapers.upv.es/index.php/cs/article/view/4940/5835 (Consultado el 4 de abril de 2025).

Ramón Fernández, F. (2016c): "Las vías pecuarias: aspectos en relación con el patrimonio, el urbanismo y el paisaje. Especial referencia a la Comunitat Valenciana", *Revista de Derecho Urbanístico y Medio Ambiente*, 309: 159-194.

Ramón Fernández, F. (2018): "Del turismo sostenible al ecoturismo: una perspectiva legal", *Turismo y sostenibilidad.* Aranzadi Thomson Reuters. Cizur Menor: 171-197.

Ramón Fernández, F. (2020): "Objetivos de Desarrollo Sostenible (ODS) y gestión del patrimonio cultural de la Huerta de València: la importancia del comercio de proximidad y la puesta en valor de sus bienes y recursos. La tira de contar y la Agromuseu de Vera, Valencia",

Revista jurídica valenciana. Associació de Juristes Valencians (anteriormente Revista Internauta de Práctica Jurídica), 36: 1-20. https://www.revistajuridicavalenciana.org/wp-content/uploads/0036_0007_01.pdf (Consultado el 4 de abril de 2025).

Ramón Fernández, F. (2021): "La Huerta valenciana: propiedad, ordenación del territorio y protección", *Revista de Derecho Urbanístico y Medio Ambiente*, 344: 109-126.

Ramón Fernández, F. (2022): "Huerta y productos de proximidad. La Tira de Contar como forma de venta en el ámbito de la competencia", *Retos en el sector agroalimentario: regulación, competencia y propiedad industrial.* Tirant lo Blanch. Valencia: 479-491.

Ramón Fernández, F. (2024a): "El Tribunal de las Aguas de la Vega de Valencia y la Huerta Valenciana: aspectos referentes a la solución de conflictos", *Anales de la Facultad de Ciencias Jurídicas y Sociales de la Universidad Nacional de La Plata*, 54: 345-356. https://revistas.unlp.edu.ar/RevistaAnalesJursoc/article/view/16445/18690 (Consultado el 4 de abril de 2025).

Ramón Fernández, F. (2024b): "El ecoturismo: un modelo de turismo alienado con los Objetivos de Desarrollo Sostenible", *International Journal of Travel, Tourism and Hospitality Law*, 1: 221-265. https://files.tourismlaw.pt/IJTTHL-1-2024/14/ (Consultado el 10 de abril de 2025).

Ramón Fernández, F. y Payri, B. (2013): "The Court of Waters of the fertile valley of Valencia (Spain): beyond the tourist attraction", *Tourism & Creative Industry Sustanible tourism, cultural tourism, creative tourism, culinary tourism, heritage & tourism.* Universitat Politècnica de València. Valencia: 85-91.

Ramón Fernández, F., Lull Noguera, C., Soriano Soto, Mª. D. y García-España Soriano, L. (2020): "Role of soils in the context of the regulation of the Huerta de València", *XVI European Society for Agronomy Congress. Smart agricultura for great human challenges*, Sevilla: 146-147.

Segura Calero, S. (2021): "El plan de acción territorial de ordenación y dinamización de la huerta de Valencia. Aproximación transformativa al proceso de elaboración del plan", *Libro de resúmenes de los trabajos del XXVII Congreso de la Asociación Española de Geografía*, Universidad de La Laguna. La Laguna: 241-242. https://www.age-geografia.es/site/wp-content/uploads/2021/12/Libro-Resumenes-Aportaciones-al-XXVII-Congreso-de-Geografia.pdf (Consultado el 10 de abril de 2025).

Vercher Savall, N. (2025): "Territorios rurales en transformación: desafíos y oportunidades frente al reto de la despoblación", *BAGE. Boletín de la Asociación Es-*

pañola de Geografía, 103. https://bage.age-geografia.es/ojs/index.php/bage/article/view/3672 (Consultado el 10 de abril de 2025).

Referencias webs

Etiquetado Aphorta. Fuente: https://uniodeconsumidors.org/es/en-la-union-de-consumidores-apostamos-por-el-comercio-de-proximidad/ (Consultado el 11 de abril de 2025)

Huerta de València. Fuente: https://valenciasecreta.com/huerta-de-valencia-patrimonio-mundial/ (Consultado el 11 de abril de 2025).

Objetivos de Desarrollo Sostenible. Fuente: Naciones Unidas. https://www.un.org/sustainabledevelopment/es/2015/09/la-asamblea-general-adopta-la-agenda-2030-para-el-desarrollo-sostenible/ (Consultado el 10 de abril de 2025).

Tribunal de las Aguas de la Vega de València. Fuente: https://tribunaldelasaguas.org/es/el-tribunal/historia (Consultado el 11 de abril de 2025).

Referencias legislativas

Ley 3/1995, de 23 de marzo, de vías pecuarias (BOE núm. 71, de 24 de marzo de 1995).

Ley 4/1998, de 11 de junio, del Patrimonio Cultural Valenciano (BOE núm. 174, de 22 de julio de 1998).

Ley 7/2004, de 19 de octubre, de modificación de la Ley 4/1998, de 11 de junio, del Patrimonio Cultural Valenciano (BOE núm. 279, de 19 de noviembre de 2004).

Decreto 73/2006, de 26 de mayo, por el que se declara bien de interés cultural inmaterial el Tribunal de las Aguas de la Vega de Valencia (BOE núm. 224, de 19 de septiembre de 2006).

Decreto 148/2006, de 6 de octubre, por el que se declaran bienes de interés cultural, con la categoría de monumento, los Azudes de las Acequias del Tribunal de las Aguas de Valencia y de la Real Acequia de Moncada, situados en Valencia, Paterna, Quart de Poblet y Manises, así como se declara el Conjunto Histórico que forman los mismos (BOE núm. 309, de 27 de diciembre de 2006).

Ley 5/2007, de 9 de febrero, de modificación de la Ley 4/1998, de 11 de junio, del Patrimonio Cultural Valenciano (BOE núm. 71, de 23 de marzo de 2007).

Ley 3/2011, de 23 de marzo, de comercio de la Comunitat Valenciana (BOE núm. 91, de 16 de abril de 2011).

Ley 3/2013, de 26 de julio, de los Contratos y otras Relaciones Jurídicas Agrarias (BOE núm. 222, de 16 de septiembre de 2013).

Ley 3/2014, de 11 de julio, de la Generalitat, de vías pecuarias de la Comunitat Valenciana (BOE núm. 186, de 1 de agosto de 2014).

Ley 10/2015, de 26 de mayo, para la salvaguardia del Patrimonio Cultural Inmaterial (BOE núm. 126, de 27 de mayo de 2015).

Ley 9/2017, de 7 de abril, de modificación de la Ley 4/1998, del patrimonio cultural valenciano (BOE núm. 112, de 11 de mayo de 2017).

Ley 5/2018, de 6 de marzo, de la Huerta de València (BOE núm. 96, de 20 de abril de 2018).

Ley 15/2018, de 7 de junio, de turismo, ocio y hospitalidad de la Comunitat Valenciana (BOE núm. 157,de 29 de junio de 2018).

Decreto 219/2018, de 30 de noviembre, del Consell, por el que se aprueba el Plan de acción territorial de ordenación y dinamización de la Huerta de València (DOGV núm. 8448, de 20 de diciembre de 2018).

Ley 2/2019, de 6 de febrero, de reforma de la Ley 3/2013, de 26 de julio, de los contratos y otras relaciones jurídicas agrarias, para exigencia de la forma escrita y para la creación del Registro de Operadores, Contratos y Relaciones Jurídicas Agrarias (BOE núm. 51, de 28 de febrero de 2019).

Ley 7/2021, de 29 de diciembre, de medidas fiscales, de gestión administrativa y financiera y de organización de la Generalitat 2022 (BOE núm. 19, de 22 de enero de 2022).

Ley 8/2022, de 29 de diciembre, de medidas fiscales, de gestión administrativa y financiera, y de organización de la Generalitat (BOE núm. 52, de 2 de marzo de 2023).

Decreto-ley 20/2024, de 30 de diciembre, del Consell, de medidas urbanísticas urgentes para favorecer las tareas de reconstrucción tras los daños producidos por la DANA (DOGV núm. 10017, de 2 de enero de 2025).

Decreto-ley 4/2025, de 4 de febrero, del Consell, de modificación de la Ley 5/2018, de 6 de marzo, de la Generalitat, de la Huerta de València, y del Decreto 219/2018, de 30 de noviembre, del Consell, por el que se aprueba el Plan de acción territorial de ordenación y dinamización de la Huerta de València (DOGV núm. 10040, de 5 de febrero de 2025).

Resolución 252/XI, del Pleno de Les Corts Valencianes, adoptada en la reunión del día 20 de febrero de 2025, de convalidación del Decreto ley 4/2025, de 4 de febrero, del Consell, de modificación de la Ley 5/2018, de 6 de marzo, de la Generalitat, de la Huerta de València, y del Decreto 219/2018, de 30 de noviembre, del Consell, por el que se aprueba el Plan de acción territorial de ordenación y dinamización de la Huerta de València (DOGV núm. 10058, de 3 de marzo de 2025).

Ley 1/2025, de 1 de abril, de prevención de las pérdidas y el desperdicio alimentario (BOE núm. 80, de 2 de abril de 2025).

TERRITORIOS RURALES QUE LATEN: UNA MIRADA EXPLORATORIA A LA VALORIZACIÓN DEL PATRIMONIO CULTURAL INMATERIAL

Berta Tubillejas Andrés
Amparo Cervera-Taulet
Walesska Schlesinger
Universidad de Valencia

TEMÁTICA: Gobernanza, Sostenibilidad

RESUMEN: En un contexto europeo marcado por el despoblamiento rural y el éxodo juvenil, el patrimonio cultural inmaterial se presenta como un recurso estratégico para fortalecer la cohesión social, la identidad territorial y la retención de talento. Sin embargo, su gestión y valorización en entornos rurales sigue enfrentando importantes retos de legitimidad, participación y sostenibilidad. Este estudio, enmarcado en el proyecto europeo THRIVE, analiza de forma cualitativa las percepciones de actores clave que gestionan dicho patrimonio—sector público, sector privado y residentes—en la provincia de Bérgamo (Italia). Se realizaron dinámicas de grupo y se ejecutó un análisis de coocurrencias discursivas. Los resultados muestran una diversidad de visiones que, si bien comparten ejes comunes como la identidad, la innovación y la participación comunitaria, revelan tensiones generacionales, obstáculos estructurales y oportunidades para repensar el papel del patrimonio cultural inmaterial como motor de desarrollo. Nuestra investigación visibiliza el valor del patrimonio desde lo local y propone caminos para una gobernanza más inclusiva, creativa y sostenible en territorios rurales.

Palabras clave: Patrimonio cultural inmaterial, desarrollo rural, participación, talento, territorio

TEMÁTICA: Governance, sustainability

ABSTRACT: In a European context marked by rural depopulation and youth outmigration, intangible cultural heritage emerges as a strategic resource for strengthening social cohesion, territorial identity, and talent retention. However, its management and valorization in rural areas continue to face major challenges related to legitimacy, participation, and sustainability. This study, conducted within the framework of the European THRIVE project, qualitatively analyzes the perceptions of key actors involved in the management of this heritage—public sector, private sector, and local residents—in the province of Bergamo (Italy). Focus group discussions were carried out, complemented by a co-occurrence analysis of discourse. The results reveal a diversity of perspectives that, while aligned around shared themes such as identity, innovation, and community participation, also expose generational tensions, structural barriers, and opportunities to rethink the role of intangible cultural heritage as a driver of development. Our research highlights the locally rooted value of heritage and proposes pathways toward more inclusive, creative, and sustainable governance in rural territories.

Keywords: Intangible cultural heritage, rural development, participation, talent, territory

1. INTRODUCCIÓN

Actualmente, aproximadamente el 30% de las regiones europeas están afrontando una rápida caída de la fuerza laboral con una baja proporción de personas con educación superior y un marcado éxodo juvenil. Las zonas rurales son las más afectadas por la partida de jóvenes, el envejecimiento y el declive demográfico, situación que agrava la brecha urbano-rural y las disparidades territoriales en Europa, según informes recientes (European Comission, 2023b, 2023a). En este contexto, el patrimonio cultural inmaterial emerge como un recurso estratégico fundamental. La declaración de reconocimiento por parte de la UNESCO de un patrimonio mundial, en cualquiera de sus modalidades, sin pretenderlo lo conecta con el turismo al convertirlo en atractivo para visitar. generando un aumento significativo de visitantes e ingresos turísticos (Nguyen & Cheung, 2014). La relación entre turismo y patrimonio cultural inmaterial es muy estrecha, dado que el turismo cultural —que abarca experiencias tanto del patrimonio tangible como inmaterial— es un segmento en crecimiento que facilita un desarrollo sostenible y, por ende, un turismo cultural sostenible (UNESCO, 2007). Por ello, resulta urgente implementar estrategias innovadoras que combinen la protección del patrimonio inmaterial con su valorización social y económica, promoviendo la sostenibilidad y maximizando los beneficios para territorios y comunidades.

La Organización Mundial del Turismo enfatiza la necesidad de estudios académicos que analicen los efectos de este tipo de turismo y recopilen datos sobre productos asociados al patrimonio cultural inmaterial (UNWTO, 2012). Así pues, el objetivo general de este estudio es analizar las percepciones de actores clave respecto a la valorización del patrimonio cultural inmaterial en un contexto rural. Como objetivos específicos, se plantea en primer lugar explorar y comparar las perspectivas de estos actores sobre la gestión y valorización del patrimonio cultural inmaterial en entornos rurales; y en segundo lugar, comprender las estructuras discursivas que sustentan dichas percepciones.

El estudio ofrece un análisis comparado y cualitativo donde el uso de mapas de coocurrencias permite entender las dinámicas sociales implicadas en la valorización del patrimonio cultural inmaterial. En el marco del proyecto europeo THRIVE, se ha desarrollado esta investigación exploratoria de carácter cualitativo en la provincia de Bérgamo (Italia). Los resultados generados proporcionarán conocimiento útil para diseñar políticas culturales y estrategias de retención de talento basada en la valorización del patrimonio cultural inmaterial con impacto real en territorios rurales europeos.

2. EL PATRIMONIO CULTURAL INMATERIAL

Los orígenes de la protección del patrimonio cultural inmaterial datan de las negociaciones multilaterales de los años 50, cuando se buscó establecer derechos de autor para el folclore y tradiciones culturales. Desde entonces, la UNESCO ha impulsado diversos hitos normativos, culminando en la Convención para la Salvaguardia del Patrimonio Cultural Inmaterial en 2003 (UNESCO, 2003). Así pues, actualmente el patrimonio cultural inmaterial comprende las prácticas, representaciones, expresiones, conocimientos y habilidades —así como los instrumentos, objetos, artefactos y espacios culturales asociados— que las comunidades, grupos e individuos reconocen como parte esencial de su patrimonio cultural (UNWTO, 2012). Este patrimonio cultural inmaterial se manifiesta en diversas áreas, incluyendo la artesanía y las artes visuales tradicionales que demuestran técnicas ancestrales; la gastronomía y las prácticas culinarias; las prácticas sociales, rituales y eventos festivos; la música y las artes escénicas; las tradiciones orales y expresiones, incluyendo el lenguaje como vehículo del patrimonio inmaterial; los conocimientos y prácticas relacionados con la naturaleza y el universo; y la preparación y gestión de auditorías y recursos culturales.

Aunque la literatura científica ha puesto un fuerte énfasis en el patrimonio tangible y los sitios declarados patrimonio mundial, la investigación sobre la relación entre patrimonio cultural inmaterial y turismo es aún limitada (Lopez-Guzman & Gonzalez Santa-Cruz, 2016), especialmente desde la perspectiva de la oferta y los retos sectoriales. Las estrategias para convertir el patrimonio cultural inmaterial en productos culturales turísticos incluyen la creación de atractivos específicos, la combinación de múltiples atractivos, la generación de espacios culturales para manifestaciones vivas, el diseño o revitalización de rutas y la promoción de festivales y eventos (UNWTO, 2012). Si bien, la UNWTO (2012) advierte que los principales riesgos para el patrimonio cultural inmaterial en países desarrollados son la pérdida de autenticidad y la mercantilización.

El patrimonio cultural inmaterial no solo constituye un pilar de la identidad y cohesión social de las comunidades, sino que también puede actuar como motor de innovación económica y social (Shakya & Vagnarelli, 2024; Zain & Shandidy, 2023). La cultura y el patrimonio, incluidas las industrias culturales y creativas, son activos clave para la competitividad regional y el bienestar de los residentes, ya que fomentan su sentido de pertenencia y calidad de vida. Sin embargo, la transmisión y conservación del patrimonio cultural inmaterial están amenazadas por la globalización, la industrialización y los desafíos ambientales, especialmente en áreas rurales donde las tradiciones se transmiten de forma frágil de generación en generación (Wang, 2023). La participación activa y la inclusión social, así como el uso de nuevas tecnologías digitales (Wen & Xu, 2024), son esenciales para preservar este patrimonio vivo, según lo estipulado en el convenio de Faro (Council of Europe, 2005). El patrimonio también contribuye a la memoria colectiva, la identidad cultural y la cohesión social (Del Soldato & Massari, 2024), aspectos vinculados a la salud mental y el bienestar, al promover el apoyo social, la solidaridad y la resiliencia comunitaria. Frente a estos retos, es imprescindible cultivar y retener talento en las zonas rurales mediante la cultura y la creatividad, impulsando así el desarrollo sostenible, la cohesión social y la reducción de las brechas territoriales. En este sentido, Paulino et al. (2023) subrayan la importancia de una gobernanza participativa del patrimonio inmaterial, involucrando actores públicos, privados y comunitarios para construir un modelo sostenible desde lo local

Por todo ello, y de acuerdo con nuestros objetivos de investigación, se derivan dos preguntas de investigación; la primera de carácter exploratorio, enfocada en percepciones, y la segunda de carácter analítico, enfocada en discurso:

- RQ1: ¿Cuáles son las diferencias y similitudes en las percepciones de los sectores público, privado y residentes sobre la gestión y valorización del patrimonio cultural inmaterial en contextos rurales?
- RQ2: ¿Cómo se estructuran y relacionan las percepciones de los actores clave en torno al patrimonio cultural inmaterial en sus discursos?

3. METODOLOGÍA DE INVESTIGACIÓN

La provincia de Bérgamo, ubicada en la región de Lombardía en el norte de Italia, es un territorio caracterizado por su diversidad paisajística que abarca zonas alpinas, valles prealpinos, áreas urbanas y llanuras. Esta variedad geográfica se acompaña de una rica herencia cultural, fruto de su herencia histórico-artística, tanto material como inmaterial, que se ha mantenido viva gracias a la tradición, la artesanía y las prácticas comunitarias locales. Bérgamo lidera el proyecto europeo THRIVE, una iniciativa cofinanciada por la Unión Europea, cuyo objetivo es fortalecer la retención y atracción de talento en áreas rurales a través del desarrollo sostenible del patrimonio cultural inmaterial. Mediante un camino conjunto de sistematización y transferencia de experiencias entre diferentes organizaciones europeas, el proyecto facilitará, a través de varias acciones estructuradas y sinérgicas, la formación y retención de talentos mediante la preservación y valorización del patrimonio cultural inmaterial, fomentando el empoderamiento y la resiliencia de las comunidades rurales y reduciendo los desequilibrios territoriales (brecha urbano-rural). Las acciones se llevarán a cabo en la provincia de Bérgamo como territorio piloto, aprovechando y complementando diferentes habilidades y conocimientos europeos. El modelo será replicable para su implementación en otros países europeos, y acciones específicas de capitalización promoverán su adopción en territorios con características similares.

Dentro del marco de THRIVE, en su primera fase, se diseñó un estudio exploratorio cualitativo-descriptivo orientado a comprender las barreras, oportunidades, innovaciones, iniciativas y dinámicas de cooperación relacionadas con la valorización del patrimonio cultural inmaterial en las zonas rurales de Bérgamo. Este enfoque permite captar percepciones, valores simbólicos, relaciones comunitarias y la participación generacional, elementos esenciales para entender las complejas dinámicas sociales que sustentan la gestión del patrimonio y diseñar políticas culturales y turísticas inteligentes y sostenibles. La recolección de información se realizó en abril de 2025, mediante tres dinámicas de grupo con un total de 11 participantes vinculados a la gestión del patrimonio cultural en Bérgamo, organizados por sectores de actividad:

- Dinámica 1: representantes del sector público. Cinco participantes (2 hombres y 3 mujeres), vinculados a administraciones locales y organismos públicos dedicados a la gestión cultural y turística.

- Dinámica 2: representantes del sector privado. Tres participantes (2 hombres y 1 mujer), pertenecientes a empresas innovadoras y startups locales.
- Dinámica 3: residentes y miembros de la comunidad local. Tres mujeres con experiencia en iniciativas culturales y patrimonio inmaterial de diversas entidades y asociaciones culturales.

Dos de las sesiones se realizaron presencialmente y una de ellas (dinámica 1) en formato híbrido, con una duración aproximada de 45 minutos cada una. Las reuniones se grabaron mediante Zoom y se transcribieron con el software Happyscriber, complementado con revisión manual para garantizar la precisión. Para optimizar el tiempo de la dinámica, los participantes recibieron con anticipación un documento con preguntas guía orientadas a explorar las barreras percibidas para aprovechar el patrimonio cultural inmaterial en la retención y atracción de talento en entornos rurales, las oportunidades para preservar y promover dicho patrimonio, las innovaciones tecnológicas, digitales, sociales y otras necesarias para valorizar el mismo, las iniciativas concretas lanzadas para retener talento joven a través del patrimonio cultural inmaterial, las ideas para fomentar la cooperación público-privada para estos fines, la valoración y participación de las nuevas generaciones en las tradiciones culturales, y las características físicas, sociales e históricas de Bérgamo. El análisis de los datos cualitativos se realizó con el software KH Coder, aplicando mapas de coocurrencias para identificar patrones temáticos, relaciones entre conceptos y la frecuencia de términos clave, lo que permitió un análisis profundo y estructurado de los discursos. Este diseño metodológico facilitó la obtención de una visión holística y detallada sobre las percepciones y dinámicas que impactan la gestión y valorización del patrimonio cultural inmaterial en Bérgamo, sentando las bases para recomendaciones aplicables a otros contextos rurales europeos.

4. RESULTADOS

En primer lugar y atendiendo al guion temático de preguntas se clasificaron las diversas respuestas comparativamente por colectivo de acuerdo con la tabla 1 y que nos permitirán dar respuesta a la RQ1.

Tabla 1. Principales respuestas de los colectivos de estudio por temáticas.

	Sector Público	Sector Privado	Residentes
Barreras	– Transporte público deficiente, especialmente en zonas montañosas. – Escasa oferta de vivienda adecuada para jóvenes. – Falta de continuidad institucional en proyectos culturales. – Fragmentación territorial y digital. – Cultura no vista como oportunidad profesional.	– Desconexión emocional y funcional de jóvenes con el patrimonio. – Imagen anticuada de las tradiciones. – Falta de mediadores para coordinar iniciativas. – Dificultad para crear modelos aspiracionales territoriales. – Ausencia de redes para jóvenes talentos en tecnología e innovación. – Baja conciencia y valoración patrimonial entre residentes. – Estrategias comunicativas inadecuadas y obsoletas para jóvenes. – Mala organización de eventos o talleres atractivos.	– Pérdida de narrativas locales y débil vínculo territorial. – Tradición vista como atraso; uso político del patrimonio. – Folklore estigmatizado y vergüenza juvenil. – Bajo compromiso comunitario y falta de orgullo patrimonial. – Escasas oportunidades laborales en promoción cultural juvenil. – Patrimonio mal integrado en educación y comunicación. – Declive demográfico, desapego social y resistencia generacional.
Oportunidades	– Eventos destacados como "Bérgamo-Brescia Capital Cultural". – Red activa de bibliotecas, museos y festivales. – Experiencia colaborativa entre municipios. – Recursos naturales e históricos para turismo cultural.	– Tradiciones culinarias con fuerte identidad y valor comercial. – Narrativas locales aplicables al marketing territorial. – Potencial para reinterpretar el patrimonio con enfoque emprendedor. – Participación en redes internacionales (Slow Food, UNESCO). – Creación de experiencias que combinan tradición con formatos modernos como podcasts, escape rooms o VR/AR. – Incremento de la conciencia comunitaria mediante estrategias comunicativas juveniles en redes sociales.	– Cultura como empoderamiento: patrimonio, folklore y juegos tradicionales fomentan la cohesión e identidad comunitaria. – Espacios rurales vacíos y brechas culturales pueden reimaginarse para la juventud y la innovación social. – Educación y museos: escuelas y museos pueden reconectar a las comunidades con su patrimonio. – La diversidad como fortaleza: identidad local y culturas migrantes enriquecen la vida social. – Juventud y turismo: promover empleos en turismo cultural y eventos inclusivos para jóvenes.

	Sector Público	Sector Privado	Residentes
Innovaciones	- Unificación de plataformas digitales municipales. - Uso de tecnologías inmersivas (AR, IA, avatares). - Capacitación técnica para operadores culturales y turísticos. - Sostenibilidad tecnológica (actualizaciones y soporte).	- Comunicación digital creativa (gamificación, reels, storytelling). - Contenido verificado y atractivo para jóvenes. - Aplicación del patrimonio en experiencias participativas multisensoriales. - Uso de VR/AR, podcasts y formatos digitales interactivos. - Talleres presenciales y virtuales para artes y oficios tradicionales.	- Digitalización de archivos orales y prácticas locales. - Nuevos formatos museísticos: video, podcasts, interacción. - Actualización y adaptación móvil de webs de ecomuseos. - Tecnología respetuosa con la intimidad de las tradiciones. - Acceso libre a documentos históricos y científicos. - Innovación social: diálogo comunitario y proyectos juveniles. - Uso de dialecto y storytelling para fortalecer identidad. - Mejorar acceso a internet estable en zonas remotas.
Cooperación público-privada	- Fortalecer redes culturales. - Cofinanciar proyectos con impacto social. - Promover co-diseño y alianzas especiales. - Profesionalizar el trabajo cultural más allá del voluntariado.	- Modelos colaborativos (región-fundación–empresarios). - Asistencia técnica y créditos para proyectos rurales. - Crear clústeres culturales por microregión. - Organizar eventos colaborativos con gobiernos, escuelas y residentes. - Fomentar patrocinios empresariales en eventos tradicionales. - Facilitar alianzas entre municipios y startups para fusionar patrimonio e innovación. - Usar storytelling y eventos comunitarios para conectar sector privado y público.	- Alianzas entre escuelas, museos y asociaciones. - Museos como espacios de participación y mediación. - Apoyar redes comunitarias para activar patrimonio desde la base. - Crear mesas redondas para diálogo entre instituciones y ciudadanía. - Escuelas transfieren conocimiento; municipios apoyan estrategias intercomunales. - Fomentar participación juvenil con proyectos escolares y voluntariado.

	Sector Público	Sector Privado	Residentes
Nuevas generaciones	- Participación limitada sin continuidad ni sentido. - Trabajar desde edades tempranas. - Fomentar pertenencia vía escuelas y espacios públicos.	- Comunicar tradición como vida moderna y atractiva. - Vincular valores actuales con tradiciones. - Promover orgullo cultural y liderazgo juvenil con formatos renovados y multisensoriales.	- Educar en valor cultural desde la infancia. - Superar estigmas y prejuicios con mediación afectiva. - Crear espacios para que jóvenes reclamen su cultura.

El análisis comparado de las percepciones de los tres grupos clave —sector público, sector privado y residentes— evidencia que, si bien comparten la percepción de desafíos importantes para la valorización del patrimonio cultural inmaterial y la retención de talento, cada uno aporta perspectivas y prioridades complementarias que enriquecen el diagnóstico y orientan las soluciones.

En cuanto a las barreras, el sector público destaca problemas estructurales y organizativos, como el desconocimiento institucional sobre la importancia del patrimonio cultural inmaterial, la fragmentación territorial y digital, así como la falta de continuidad en proyectos culturales y deficiencias en servicios básicos como el transporte y la vivienda. Por su parte, el sector privado resalta la carencia de espacios para la innovación, la desconexión emocional y funcional de los jóvenes con el patrimonio, y la insuficiente comunicación adaptada a las nuevas generaciones, además de la ausencia de oportunidades laborales vinculadas al patrimonio. Los residentes, finalmente, evidencian una crisis demográfica acompañada de bajo orgullo cultural, pérdida de narrativas locales, estigmatización del folklore y bajo compromiso comunitario. Esta diversidad revela que la problemática del patrimonio cultural inmaterial es tanto institucional y técnica como profundamente social y cultural, requiriendo un abordaje integral para ser superada.

Respecto a las oportunidades, se observa una complementariedad clara: el sector público resalta eventos culturales consolidados, redes activas y recursos naturales e históricos que pueden potenciar el turismo cultural, además de valorar asociaciones estratégicas como las impulsadas por la UNESCO. El sector privado enfatiza la formación local, el potencial emprendedor vinculado al patrimonio y la innovación en comunicación digital para conectar con públicos jóvenes. Los residentes apuestan por la reactivación de espacios comunitarios, el papel del patrimonio como motor de empoderamiento y cohesión social, y la valorización de la diversidad cultural para fomentar la inclusión y el desarrollo social. La proximidad estratégica a infraestructuras como el aeropuerto también se considera una ventaja para fortalecer la economía local.

En cuanto a las innovaciones necesarias para potenciar el patrimonio cultural inmaterial, el sector público enfatiza la modernización tecnológica y la innovación sostenible, particularmente en sectores como el agroalimentario, junto con la capacitación técnica de los operadores culturales. El sector privado apuesta por el uso creativo de las redes sociales, el aprendizaje virtual y experiencias participativas e inmersivas (VR/AR, podcasts), buscando atraer y fidelizar a públicos jóvenes. Los residentes valoran la digitalización del patrimonio inmaterial, las acciones inclusivas, el acceso abierto a recursos culturales, y la protección de la intimidad cultural, además de la mejora del acceso a internet en zonas remotas.

En materia de cooperación público-privada, existe consenso sobre la necesidad de conectar eficazmente instituciones, educación y comunidades. El sector público insiste en fortalecer redes institucionales, universidades y municipios; el sector privado promueve convocatorias de innovación, apoyo técnico y financiero a proyectos rurales y la integración de startups innovadoras; mientras que los residentes destacan el papel del voluntariado, el patrocinio empresarial y el diálogo comunitario para activar el patrimonio desde la base.

Respecto a la participación juvenil, aunque hay cierto desinterés inicial, se reconoce un gran potencial. El sector público observa un creciente sentido de apropiación cultural por parte de los jóvenes; el sector privado señala la necesidad de modernizar las comunicaciones y los formatos para hacer la tradición más atractiva; y los residentes abogan por superar estigmas mediante mediación afectiva y crear espacios donde los jóvenes puedan apropiarse activamente de su cultura.

La identidad de Bérgamo se destaca por su diversidad de recursos, historia y gastronomía. El sector privado resalta referencias históricas y el potencial comercial; los residentes enfatizan la cultura agraria y la cohesión social; y el sector público subraya los vínculos entre zonas urbanas y rurales que favorecen la integración territorial. Finalmente, el turismo se reconoce como un motor clave para la valorización del patrimonio cultural inmaterial, promoviendo identidad y sostenibilidad. Mientras que los sectores privado y residentes combinan una visión global con un enfoque local, el sector público lo integra en estrategias amplias de calidad de vida, en línea con las directrices de la UNESCO.

Para responder a la RQ2 y analizar en profundidad los discursos generados en cada una de las dinámicas grupales, se realizó un análisis de coocurrencias que permite representar las redes de palabras que aparecen conjuntamente en las transcripciones. Estos mapas se elaboraron a partir de sustantivos, verbos y adjetivos extraídos de las oraciones, lo que permite captar micro-narrativas y relaciones directas más allá de los tópicos generales. La combinación de estas tres categorías gramaticales permite identificar (1) los conceptos clave que estructuran el discurso (nombres), (2) las acciones y relaciones entre ellos (verbos), y (3) los matices valorativos o emocionales que definen su interpretación (adjetivos). Este enfoque proporciona una comprensión más profunda y estructurada de los significados compartidos, las tensiones y las prioridades expresadas por los distintos actores.

Las figuras 1, 2 y 3 presentan los mapas correspondientes a las dinámicas 1, 2 y 3, con la participación de representantes del sector público, privado y residentes, respectivamente. En relación con la primera de las figuras, figura 1, el análisis del mapa de coocurrencias del discurso de representantes del sector público (ver tabla 2) revela una estructura temática claramente jerarquizada, en la que destaca de manera significativa el clúster centrado en los conceptos de "essere" (ser) y "potere" (poder). La magnitud y centralidad de este clúster evidencian que, para los actores institucionales, la construcción de identidad y el empoderamiento colectivo constituyen los pilares fundamentales sobre los cuales se articulan las demás dimensiones vinculadas a la valorización del patrimonio cultural y la retención de talento. Este predominio temático sugiere que el sentido de pertenencia y la capacidad de acción comunitaria son considerados precondiciones esenciales para el desarrollo y la implementación de políticas culturales efectivas. En este sentido, los clústeres de mayor tamaño que acompañan este núcleo central —relacionados con el voluntariado y la comunidad, la valorización patrimonial en relación con la empresa, la formación estratégica, la accesibilidad territorial y la incorporación tecnológica— configuran un entramado de áreas prioritarias que, aunque distintas, se complementan para sustentar una estrategia integral. Por otro lado, los clústeres de menor tamaño, como aquellos relacionados con el trabajo cultural, la tecnología aplicada al turismo, la gestión de proyectos y la colaboración en red, si bien son reconocidos en el discurso, parecen ocupar un lugar secundario, lo que refleja un enfoque institucional que prioriza primero el fortalecimiento identitario y la capacidad colectiva como base para cualquier otra iniciativa. Esta jerarquización temática permite concluir que, desde la perspectiva del sector público, el éxito en la valorización del patrimonio y en la retención de talento en territorios rurales depende en gran medida de la consolidación de una identidad sólida y de un empoderamiento comunitario efectivo. Sin esta base, las acciones sectoriales corren el riesgo de fragmentarse y perder impacto. Finalmente, esta configuración invita a una reflexión sobre la necesidad de transversalidad en las políticas culturales, integrando de manera equilibrada identidad, formación, accesibilidad, innovación y colaboración para lograr un desarrollo cultural sostenible y eficaz.

Figura 1. Mapa de coocurrencias con representantes del sector público

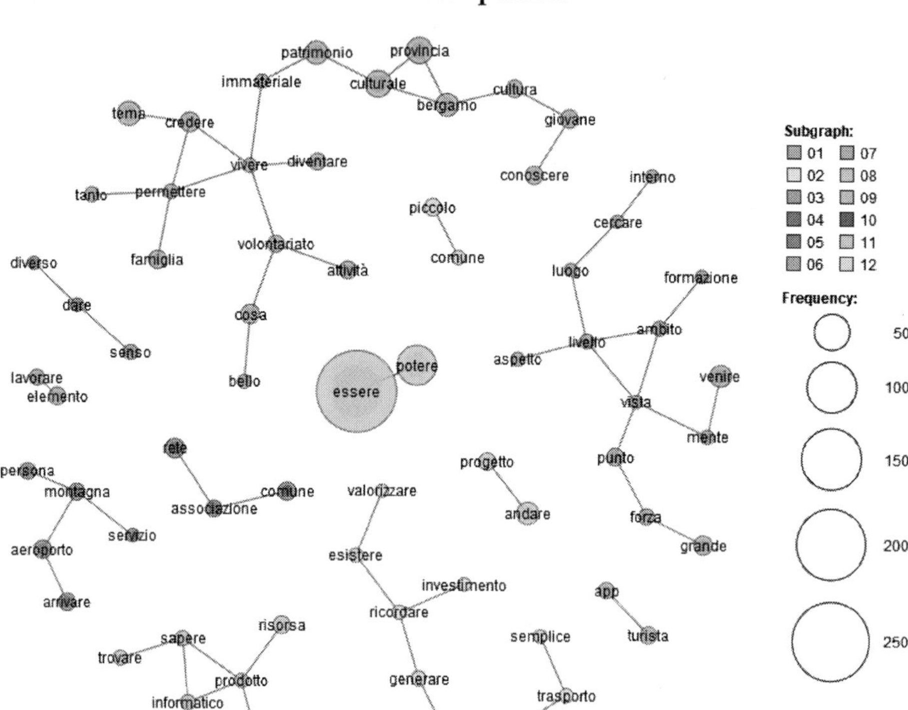

Tabla 2. Interpretación de los clústeres del mapa de coocurrencias con representantes del sector público

Clúster	Titulo	Interpretación
1	*Voluntariado y comunidad*	***El voluntariado es una forma de vida y transformación personal/comunitaria, valorado como algo "bello". Resalta el apoyo familiar y la creencia como facilitadores del compromiso. Jóvenes y conocimiento están presentes aunque menos centrales.***

Clúster	Titulo	Interpretación
2	*Valorización del patrimonio vinculada a empresa, tradición y accesibilidad*	***Recuperación y valorización de la tradición a través de iniciativas empresariales e inversión, con un enfoque que también incluye la accesibilidad y facilidad de acceso mediante transporte público sencillo, facilitando así la conexión entre patrimonio, comunidad y visitantes.***
3	***Formación, visión y potencial***	***Importancia de la formación y conocimiento, junto al reconocimiento del potencial y visión estratégica para impulsar cultura y turismo***
4	***Accesibilidad y territorio***	***Rretos de accesibilidad (aeropuerto, servicios) y vida en zonas montañosas, destacando el papel de personas en esos entornos.***
5	Pluralidad y significado	Reconocimiento de la pluralidad y riqueza diversa del patrimonio cultural y social, con énfasis en la necesidad de trabajar con sentido y propósito para fortalecer la identidad cultural y social.
6	Trabajo y elementos culturales	Importancia del trabajo y los elementos culturales en la transmisión y conservación del patrimonio.
7	Tecnología y turismo	Interñes en el uso de aplicaciones digitales para mejorar la experiencia turística, facilitando la interacción y el acceso de los visitantes al patrimonio y servicios culturales.
8	***Conocimiento y tecnología***	***El conocimiento y la tecnología informática son recursos para desarrollo o gestión del patrimonio, con interés en herramientas digitales para fortalecer la cultura.***
9	Proyecto y avance	Importancia de desarrollar proyectos culturales y avanzar en procesos vinculados a la gestión y promoción del patrimonio.
10	Redes y colaboración	Trabajo en red y colaboración entre asociaciones y municipios para potenciar patrimonio y cultura local, resaltando la organización comunitaria.
11	Identidad y poder	Se focaliza en la noción de "ser" y "poder hacer" dentro del contexto comunitario y cultural, reflejando empoderamiento existencial para los actores.
12	Municipios pequeños	Enfoque en gestión cultural y oportunidades en pequeñas comunidades.

Nota: en negrita y cursiva, clústeres con más de 3 nodos

En relación con la segunda de las figuras, figura 2, el análisis del mapa de coocurrencias del discurso de representantes del sector privado (ver tabla 3) muestra una estructura temática compleja, donde los clústeres con mayor número de nodos reflejan los conceptos clave en el discurso del sector privado. Estos núcleos temáticos no solo evidencian la diversidad de temas abordados, sino también cómo se interrelacionan en un ecosistema dinámico orientado a la innovación y la revitalización cultural. Destaca un clúster central vinculado a redes y comunicación, que subraya la importancia de la colaboración y el flujo constante de información para la gestión cultural y territorial. Esta red comunicativa actúa como plataforma fundamental para la generación de ideas, el desarrollo de proyectos y la consolidación del talento. La juventud y la innovación tecnológica conforman otro clúster relevante, mostrando que el sector privado identifica claramente a los jóvenes no solo como destinatarios, sino como actores activos indispensables para la renovación del patrimonio cultural. Las tecnologías digitales, el juego y nuevas formas de expresión artística se perciben como herramientas esenciales para conectar con este público y fomentar su participación. Los clústeres que abordan la innovación cultural y la comunicación de ideas reflejan un enfoque estratégico centrado en la generación continua de propuestas creativas, vitales para mantener la competitividad y la sostenibilidad en un entorno cultural en constante transformación. Esto revela una apuesta por modelos flexibles y adaptativos capaces de responder a los cambios sociales y tecnológicos. Asimismo, el clúster dedicado a la reflexión y la acción muestra un nivel de conciencia crítica dentro del sector privado, que reconoce la necesidad de procesos deliberados, evaluación constante y adaptación en la gestión cultural. La innovación, por tanto, se concibe no solo desde un punto de vista técnico, sino también conceptual y estratégico. Finalmente, aunque la modernidad y la innovación son prioritarias, se mantiene un respeto y reconocimiento por el valor temporal y cultural del patrimonio, evidenciado en clústeres relacionados con el producto, la edad y el estilo de vida local. Este equilibrio entre tradición y modernidad constituye un eje fundamental en la visión del sector privado. En resumen, el sector privado aborda la valorización del patrimonio cultural desde una perspectiva integradora que combina colaboración, innovación juvenil, creatividad permanente y reflexión estratégica, sin perder de vista la identidad local y la tradición. Este enfoque representa un modelo dinámico para promover el desarrollo cultural sostenible y competitivo.

Figura 2. Mapa de coocurrencias con representantes del sector privado

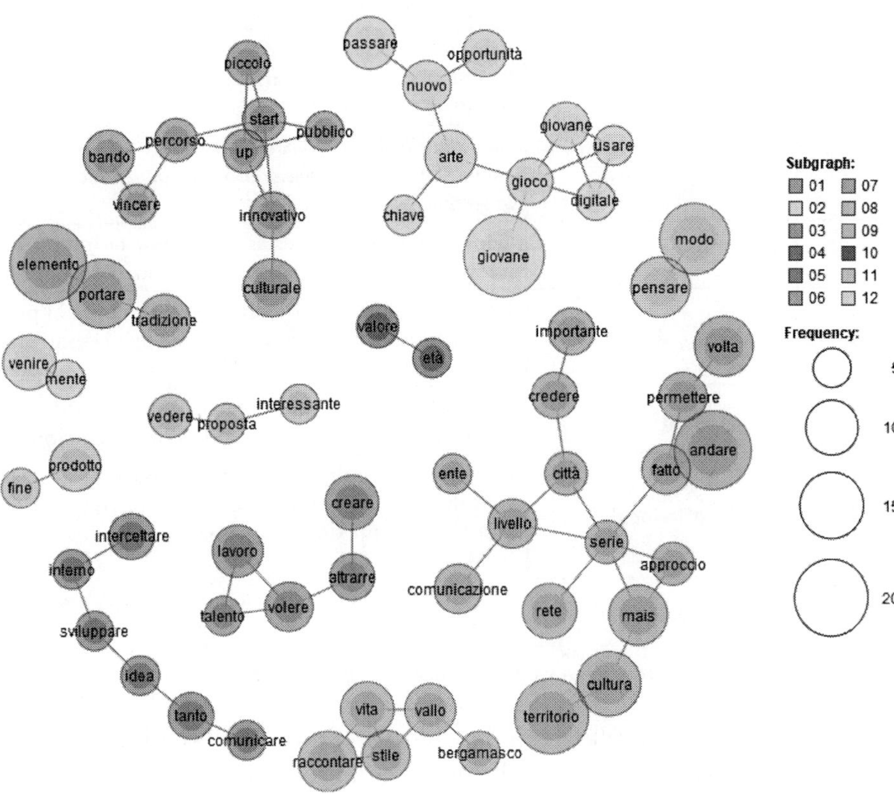

Tabla 3. Interpretación de los clústeres del mapa de coocurrencias con representantes del sector privado

Clúster	Titulo	Interpretación
1	*Redes y comunicación*	*Importancia de la comunicación y las redes colaborativas para gestionar cultura y territorio.*
2	*Juventud e innovación*	*Papel de la juventud y la innovación tecnológica para renovar y revitalizar patrimonio mediante nuevas herramientas y formatos.*
3	*Innovación cultural*	*Enfoque en el desarrollo de proyectos culturales innovadores y competitivos, con apoyo institucional y atención a pequeñas comunidades.*
4	*Comunicación e ideas*	*Importancia de captar y desarrollar ideas internas mediante una comunicación eficaz para impulsar la innovación cultural.*

Clúster	Titulo	Interpretación
5	***Talento y creación***	***Importancia de atraer y desarrollar talento a través de la creación y la motivación personal en el ámbito cultural.***
6	Tradición y elementos	Valoración de la tradición y los elementos culturales como base fundamental para la identidad y continuidad cultural.
7	***Reflexión y acción***	***Importancia de la reflexión estratégica y la consideración de diferentes enfoques o modos de actuación para la gestión cultural.***
8	Propuestas e interés	Generación de propuestas creativas y el interés en nuevas ideas como motor para el desarrollo cultural.
9	Producto y finalización	Relevancia dada a la finalización y calidad del producto cultural como resultado clave en el desarrollo de proyectos.
10	Valor y edad	Consideración del valor del patrimonio en relación con la dimensión temporal y el paso generacional.
11	Vida y estilo local	Cómo el patrimonio se vive y se relata a través de la vida diaria y los estilos propios del territorio, destacando la conexión emocional con la identidad local.
12	Finalización y resultado	Relevancia de la culminación exitosa y la reflexión en la gestión de proyectos culturales y patrimoniales.

Nota: en negrita y cursiva, clústeres con más de 3 nodos

En relación con la última de las figuras, figura 3, el análisis del mapa de coocurrencias del discurso de representantes residentes (ver tabla 4) revela una estructura temática centrada en la experiencia vivencial, la identidad social y la transmisión cultural. Los clústeres más relevantes destacan la importancia de comprender el patrimonio en todas sus dimensiones, integrando aspectos políticos, culturales y comunitarios. Se observa que el voluntariado y el emprendimiento familiar constituyen pilares esenciales para la vitalidad cultural, evidenciando el papel de las redes informales y la base social en la conservación y dinamización del patrimonio. Asimismo, emergen tensiones entre tradición y modernidad en la identidad juvenil, manifestadas a través de la expresión cultural y la apariencia, lo que plantea retos para la continuidad generacional. Además, la demanda social y el compromiso laboral aparecen como factores clave para fortalecer la cohesión comunitaria y promover oportunidades vinculadas al patrimonio. La música y los espacios escénicos se reconocen como escenarios privilegiados para la participación y la expresión artística. Finalmente, la comunidad identifica los espacios vacíos y las oportunidades emergentes como potenciales catalizadores de innovación social y cultural, siempre que se fomenten procesos participativos y colaborativos. En síntesis, la visión del sector residentes nos invita a concebir el patrimonio cultural inmaterial no solo como un legado para preservar, sino como un proceso dinámico que requiere de una participación activa, especialmente juvenil, y de un enfoque integrado que articule identidad, innovación y resiliencia comunitaria.

Figura 3. Mapa de coocurrencias con representantes residentes

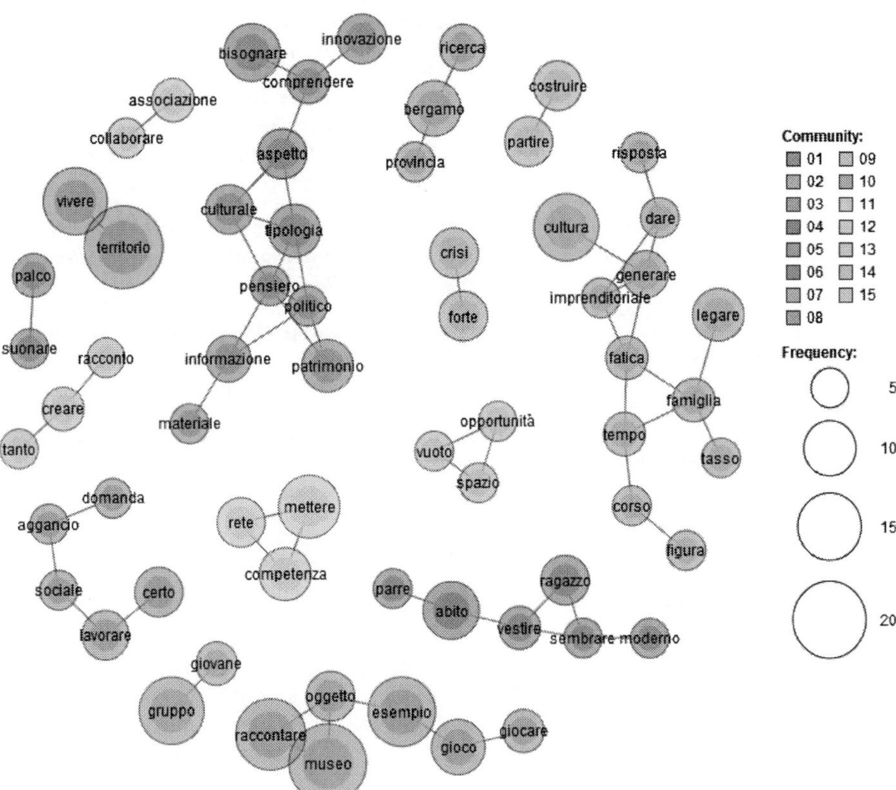

Tabla 4. Interpretación de los clústeres del mapa de coocurrencias con representantes residentes

Clúster	Titulo	Interpretación
1	*Comprensión y patrimonio*	***Necesidad de comprender y abordar diferentes tipologías y aspectos del patrimonio, integrando la innovación con la dimensión política y cultural. Se destaca la importancia de la información y la reflexión crítica para gestionar y valorar el patrimonio en su diversidad.***

Clúster	Titulo	Interpretación
2	*Emprendimiento y familia*	***Importancia del emprendimiento ligado a la familia como núcleo de apoyo, destacando el esfuerzo y la dedicación temporal necesarios para generar proyectos culturales y sociales. También se reconoce la necesidad de formación para consolidar estas iniciativas***
3	*Museo y narrativa*	***Función del museo como espacio narrativo y educativo, donde el juego y los objetos son utilizados para contar historias y ejemplificar el patrimonio, favoreciendo la participación activa y el aprendizaje experiencial.***
4	*Identidad y apariencia*	***Preocupaciones sobre la identidad juvenil y su expresión a través de la vestimenta y la apariencia, destacando la tensión entre tradición y modernidad en la percepción social.***
5	*Demanda y trabajo*	***Importancia de responder a la demanda social y la necesidad de compromiso laboral para fortalecer las dinámicas comunitarias y culturales.***
6	Escenario y música	Importancia del espacio escénico y la música como elementos centrales en las experiencias culturales y la expresión artística de la comunidad
7	Investigación y territorio	Importancia de la investigación y el conocimiento territorial para comprender y valorizar el patrimonio cultural en la provincia de Bérgamo.
8	Vida y territorio	Conexión entre la vida cotidiana y el territorio, subrayando la importancia del espacio local como contexto fundamental para la experiencia cultural y social.
9	Construcción y partida	Importancia de iniciar procesos y construir nuevas bases o estructuras dentro del patrimonio y la comunidad para promover su desarrollo y continuidad.
10	Juventud y comunidad	Importancia del trabajo en grupo y la participación juvenil como factores clave para la vitalidad cultural y social de la comunidad.
11	Colaboración y redes	Importancia de la colaboración y el trabajo en red entre asociaciones para fortalecer el patrimonio cultural y la comunidad.
12	Competencia y redes	Importancia de compartir competencias y fortalecer redes colaborativas para el desarrollo cultural y comunitario.
13	Creación y narrativa	Importancia de la creación cultural y la narrativa como herramientas para transmitir y fortalecer el patrimonio inmaterial.

Clúster	Titulo	Interpretación
14	Crisis y fortaleza	Percepción de que, pese a las crisis existentes, hay una fortaleza o resiliencia importante dentro de la comunidad o el patrimonio.
15	Espacios y oportunidades	Reflexión sobre la disponibilidad de espacios vacíos y su potencial para ser aprovechados como oportunidades para la comunidad y la innovación social.

Nota: en negrita y cursiva, clústeres con más de 3 nodos

Al comparar los mapas de coocurrencias de los tres grupos analizados, se observa que, pese a la diversidad de perspectivas, existe un núcleo común que enfatiza la importancia de la identidad cultural, la participación comunitaria y la innovación como pilares fundamentales para la valorización del patrimonio inmaterial y la retención de talento. Tanto el sector público como el privado y los residentes reconocen la necesidad de integrar tradición y modernidad, apoyándose en redes colaborativas y en la formación para impulsar proyectos culturales sostenibles y dinámicos.

Sin embargo, las diferencias entre grupos son igualmente reveladoras. El sector público tiende a focalizarse en aspectos estructurales y estratégicos, priorizando la construcción de identidad y el empoderamiento colectivo como base para políticas culturales efectivas. En cambio, el sector privado destaca la innovación tecnológica, la comunicación creativa y la juventud activa como motores de renovación y competitividad. Por último, los residentes aportan una mirada profundamente experiencial y social, centrada en la vivencia cotidiana, la cohesión comunitaria, la expresión cultural juvenil y la necesidad de fortalecer redes informales y espacios de participación.

5. CONCLUSIONES

Sobre la base de una filosofía de participación de los agentes sociales de un territorio para la toma de decisiones estratégicas, las complementariedades detectadas en el análisis evidencian que una estrategia eficaz para la valorización del patrimonio cultural inmaterial y la retención de talento debe integrar políticas institucionales sólidas, enfoques innovadores y una implicación genuina de las comunidades locales, especialmente de la juventud. Solo así será posible promover un desarrollo cultural sostenible, inclusivo y arraigado en las identidades territoriales. En este sentido, este estudio ofrece una contribución original al análisis del patrimonio cultural inmaterial desde el punto de vista de los agentes clave que gestionan el patrimonio en contextos rurales europeos. Su principal aportación consiste en visibilizar esta diversidad de percepciones entre actores públicos, privados y comunitarios sobre la gestión y valorización del patrimonio cultural inmaterial, así como en mostrar cómo estas percepciones se articulan discursivamente en torno a tres ejes clave: identidad territorial, participación comunitaria e innovación. Desde una perspectiva conceptual, el estudio propone superar la visión patrimonial centrada en la preservación pasiva, avanzando hacia una comprensión dinámica y relacional de dicho patrimonio, donde la juventud desempeñe un papel activo como reinterpretadora del legado cultural. Asimismo, subraya la necesidad de incorporar enfoques de innovación organizativa y narrativa —más allá de la tecnológica— que respeten la naturaleza compleja, simbólica y colectiva del patrimonio vivo.

Desde una perspectiva aplicada, los resultados de esta investigación ofrecen recomendaciones estratégicas relevantes para responsables de políticas culturales, gestores del patrimonio y entidades locales. En primer lugar, se señala la urgencia de diseñar estrategias de educación patrimonial intergeneracional, que combinen la transmisión formal en la escuela con metodologías creativas e inmersivas como el *storytelling* digital, la gamificación o las tecnologías inmersivas (VR/AR). Hacer el patrimonio cultural inmaterial relevante para la juventud es clave para su continuidad: los jóvenes no deben ser vistos como meros receptores, sino como narradores activos y reinterpretadores culturales. En segundo lugar, se evidencia el potencial económico del patrimonio cuando se vincula a herramientas digitales, el turismo sostenible y el emprendimiento local, especialmente si se desarrolla dentro de ecosistemas de apoyo estructurados, que incluyan formación, acompañamiento técnico y espacios de mediación público-privada. En tercer lugar, se destaca la necesidad de crear redes locales de mediadores culturales o “orquestadores” —universidades, museos, asociaciones, líderes comunitarios— que actúen como puentes entre instituciones, ciudadanía y sector privado, articulando esfuerzos dispersos y legitimando socialmente las prácticas patrimoniales. Para que el patrimonio cultural inmaterial contribuya a frenar la fuga de talento y atraer a jóvenes retornados, es necesario construir un relato compartido que revalorice la identidad local, combata el estigma asociado a lo tradicional y refuerce el sentido de pertenencia. Por último, se recomienda aplicar estrategias de innovación contextualmente sensibles, capaces de adaptarse a la singularidad de cada expresión patrimonial, respetando sus tiempos, lenguajes y significados.

Este estudio, de carácter exploratorio y limitado al territorio de Bérgamo, requiere ser ampliado en futuras investigaciones comparativas en otros contextos rurales europeos para validar y enriquecer los hallazgos. Además, la naturaleza cualitativa del análisis restringe la generalización estadística de los resultados, aunque permite una comprensión profunda y situada. Futuros estudios deben integrar metodologías mixtas que combinen análisis discursivos con encuestas o análisis de redes sociales para mapear percepciones y dinámicas a mayor escala. También se recomienda investigar más a fondo la legitimación social del patrimonio entre jóvenes, explorando las condiciones bajo las cuales se transforma de "tradición vergonzante" en fuente de orgullo e innovación. Otra línea prometedora es el análisis longitudinal de cómo evolucionan los discursos y las prácticas patrimoniales en comunidades que implementan políticas de gobernanza participativa o que experimentan procesos de digitalización patrimonial. Finalmente, será interesante considerar la voz del turista, actual o potencial, respecto a la valorización del patrimonio cultural inmaterial y su experiencia como visitante a un territorio.

FINANCIACIÓN
Las autoras declaran que esta investigación ha sido financiada en el marco del proyecto Project 101173661-THRIVE (UE).

6. REFERENCIAS

Council of Europe. (2005). *Council of Europe Framework Convention on the Value of Cultural Heritage for Society* (p. 9). https://rm.coe.int/1680083746

Del Soldato, E., & Massari, S. (2024). Creativity and digital strategies to support food cultural heritage in Mediterranean rural areas. *EuroMed Journal of Business, 19*(1), 113–137. https://doi.org/10.1108/EMJB-05-2023-0152/FULL/PDF

European Comission. (2023a). *Harnessing talent in Europe's regions.* https://ec.europa.eu/regional_policy/sources/communication/harnessing-talents/harnessing-talents-regions_en.pdf

European Comission. (2023b). *The impact of demographic change-in a changing environment.* https://commission.europa.eu/system/files/2023-01/the_impact_of_demographic_change_in_a_changing_environment_2023.PDF

Lopez-Guzman, T., & Gonzalez Santa-Cruz, F. (2016). International tourism and the UNESCO category of intangible cultural heritage. *International Journal of Culture, Tourism, and Hospitality Research, 10*(3), 310–322. https://doi.org/10.1108/IJCTHR-03-2015-0025/FULL/PDF

Nguyen, T. H. H., & Cheung, C. (2014). The classification of heritage tourists: a case of Hue City, Vietnam. *Journal of Heritage Tourism*, *9*(1), 35–50. https://doi.org/10.1080/1743873X.2013.818677

Paulino, I., Burgos-Tartera, C., & Aulet, S. (2023). Participatory governance of intangible heritage to develop sustainable rural tourism: the timber-raftsmen of La Pobla de Segur, Spain. *Journal of Heritage Tourism*, *18*(5), 710–729. https://doi.org/10.1080/1743873X.2023.2235440

Shakya, M., & Vagnarelli, G. (2024). Creating value from intangible cultural heritage—the role of innovation for sustainable tourism and regional rural development. *European Journal of Cultural Management and Policy*, *14*, 12057. https://doi.org/10.3389/EJCMP.2024.12057

UNESCO. (2003). *Textos fundamentales de la Convención para la Salvaguardia del Patrimonio Cultural Inmaterial.*

UNESCO. (2007). *Safeguarding Intangible Heritage and Sustainable Cultural Tourism: Opportunities and Challenges.* UNESCO. https://unesdoc.unesco.org/ark:/48223/pf0000178732

UNWTO. (2012). *Tourism and Intangible Cultural Heritage.* https://www.unwto.org/archive/global/publication/study-tourism-and-intangible-cultural-heritage

Wang, J. (2023). Intangible Cultural Heritage Boosts Rural Revitalization: Dilemma and Way out: Take Guier Opera in Qiaotou Town, Huaiji County as an Example. *Journal of Innovation and Development*, *5*(1), 71–75. https://doi.org/10.54097/JID.V5I1.16

Wen, Y., & Xu, K. (2024). Dissemination of Intangible Cultural Heritage Based on Digital Twin Technology. *Proceedings-2024 International Conference on Culture-Oriented Science and Technology, CoST 2024*, 94–98. https://doi.org/10.1109/COST64302.2024.00027

Zain, M., & Shandidy, E. (2023). The power of intangible heritage in sustainable development. *International Journal of Advanced Studies in World Archaeology*, *6*(2), 92–97. https://doi.org/10.21608/IJASWA.2024.275163.1043

EL VALOR CULTURAL DE LA MÚSICA EN LA OFRENDA DE FLORES EN LAS FALLAS DE TORRENT

Blanca de-Miguel-Molina
María de-Miguel-Molina
Daniel Catalá-Pérez
Conrado Carrascosa-López
Universitat Politècnica de València

TEMÁTICA: Turismo y comunidades locales: Oportunidades y desafíos para la sostenibilidad sociocultural

RESUMEN: Este trabajo analiza el valor de la música en un evento, la Ofrenda de Flores en las Fallas de Torrent (Valencia). A través de datos obtenidos de una encuesta distribuida entre personas que participan en el evento, se evalúa si su valor cultural y el de la música que acompaña son condiciones necesarias y suficientes para que los asistentes consideren el evento como auténtico y memorable. Para realizar el estudio se utilizan el análisis cualitativo comparado (QCA) y el análisis de condiciones necesarias (NCA). Los resultados muestran que la música es condición suficiente tanto para la autenticidad como para que el evento sea memorable, mientras que la cultura está ausente cuando la música está presente. El análisis NCA muestra que la música se convierte en necesaria a partir de un nivel concreto de los dos outcomes, aunque el tamaño del efecto es muy pequeño.

Palabras clave: valor cultural, evento, música, Fallas, Torrent, QCA, NCA

Keywords: cultural value, event, music, Fallas, Torrent, QCA, NCA

1. INTRODUCCIÓN

La Ofrenda de Flores es un evento importante que se celebra durante la fiesta de las Fallas de la ciudad de Valencia, así como en otros municipios, principal pero no únicamente, de la propia provincia. La fiesta de las Fallas de Valencia fue declarada Patrimonio Cultural Inmaterial de la Humanidad en 2016 y se caracteriza por la participación de los habitantes, agrupados en comisiones falleras. Aunque la fiesta es conocida por los monumentos falleros y su quema el día 19 de marzo, los artesanos falleros, los artesanos encargados de la vestimenta y accesorios, los pirotécnicos y las bandas de música, ayudan a preservar el patrimonio cultural de la zona (UNESCO, 2016).

Los estudios sobre eventos culturales locales basados en tradiciones y patrimonio cultural muestran que estas tradiciones ofrecen un valor de autenticidad y generan una experiencia única y memorable (Folgado-Fernández et al. 2021). Como en estos eventos la población local se involucra activamente, se potencia el sentido de pertenencia a la comunidad (Rodríguez-Campo et al., 2022), lo que ayuda a su sostenibilidad socioeconómica (De Miguel et al., 2021). Turel et al. (2010) incluyeron la música como un valor cultural asociado a la calidad, pero el valor cultural de la música en los eventos locales está asociado con la preservación de las tradiciones musicales y con el valor percibido por los participantes en los eventos. El valor ético de la música ha sido menos estudiado en la literatura de este tipo de eventos, aunque puede ayudar a preservar la música tradicional local y a los músicos locales (Green et al., 2016).

Este trabajo trata de responder a dos preguntas de investigación:

- RQ1. ¿El valor cultural del evento es condición necesaria y/o suficiente en la percepción de autenticidad y de evento memorable?
- RQ2. ¿El valor cultural y ético de la música es condición necesaria y/o suficiente en la percepción de autenticidad y de evento memorable?

El trabajo se estructura en cinco apartados principales; después de esta introducción, se explican las principales líneas en la literatura relacionadas con valores percibidos por los asistentes a un evento y su impacto en la autenticidad y que se considere memorable. En el apartado de metodología se especifican los datos utilizados y los métodos seleccionados para su análisis. En el apartado de resultados se presentan las respuestas a las preguntas de investigación a partir de los análisis realizados. Por último, se ofrecen las principales conclusiones a este trabajo.

2. LITERATURA SOBRE EL VALOR CULTURAL Y ÉTICO DE LA MÚSICA Y SU IMPACTO EN UN EVENTO

La literatura sobre eventos ha analizado con detalle los valores que explican la asistencia a dichos eventos, utilizando como una referencia importante la teoría de los valores en el consumo desarrollada por Sheth et al. (1991) y posteriormente revisada por otros autores como Sweeney & Soutar (2001).

Sheth et al. (1991) consideraron cinco valores que influyen en la elección del consumidor: valor funcional, condicional, social, emocional y epistémico. El valor funcional lo asocian a los atributos utilitarios y físicos del producto o servicio, el valor condicional con situaciones y circunstancias concretas, el valor social con la pertenencia a grupos, el valor emocional con sentimientos y el valor epistémico con la curiosidad, novedad y satisfacer un deseo de conocimiento. Sweeney & Soutar (2001) utilizan también los valores emocional y social, pero el funcional los dividen en dos, un valor para la calidad percibida y otro para el precio. Además, definen constructos multidimensionales para los cuatro valores, siendo su trabajo altamente citado en estudios que analizan el valor de la música en eventos. Turel et al. (2010) utilizan el valor social y el del precio de Sweeney & Soutar (2001) y añaden el valor visual/música y el de la alegría. El primero lo relacionan con los elementos estéticos y el segundo con la participación y, a su vez, lo asocian a dos tipos de valores adicionales, escapismo (de las actividades diarias) y disfrute (ganancia emocional).

El valor cultural es utilizado por algunos autores para indicar las cualidades artísticas de la música en los eventos, las actuaciones de los artistas, la diversidad de géneros y la experimentación artística (Behr et al., 2016; Van der Hoeven and Hitters, 2019). El valor cultural es equivalente a los valores funcional y epistémico de Sheth et al. (1991), el de la calidad/actuación de Sweeney & Soutar (2001) y el de visual/música de Turel et al. (2010). Toldos et al. (2019) consideran el idioma entre los elementos del valor cultural, aunque se centran en la música en tiendas.

Entre los trabajos más recientes relacionados con la música y que incluyen algunos de estos valores se encuentran los de Mulder and Hitters (2021), Gallarza et al. (2023) y Saha et al. (2023). Los tres trabajos analizan los valores cultural, social y emocional, pero Gallarza et al. (2023) añade el valor económico y Saha et al. (2023) el funcional. Los resultados a los que llegan son diferentes, ya que Mulder and Hitters (2021) encuentran que el valor cultural es el más importante en los conciertos, mientras que Saha et al. (2023) obtienen que los importantes son el social y el emocional. Sin embargo, los resultados de Gallarza et al. (2023) no hallan impacto del valor social, pero sí del contenido de la música y del valor emocional.

El valor ético de la música ha sido menos utilizado en la literatura, pero cuando es utilizado se observa que hacen referencia al comportamiento de los artistas, el contenido de las letras, la aceptación del pago de derechos a los autores por la audiencia. Los tipos de valores éticos se pueden agrupar en seis temas: ética, soporte social, legalidad, comportamiento positivo, trascendencia y valores morales. El valor ético lo utilizan Weijters et al. (2014) para referirse al pago por la música y a que los artistas reciban un porcentaje de los ingresos, mientras que el soporte social aparece en el trabajo de Green et al. (2016) y abogan por el soporte a la música y músicos locales. Los dos trabajos utilizan el valor de la legalidad para referirse al pago por la música, pero a través de canales legales. Green et al. (2016), además, exponen la importancia del comportamiento positivo de los artistas por su influencia en los niños. Recientemente, encontramos los trabajos de Preniqi et al. (2023) y de Higgins (2023), el primero centrado en los valores morales y la letra de las canciones y el segundo en la trascendencia moral, ya que consideran que la evaluación moral de una canción dependerá del contexto en el que se utiliza.

Volviendo al valor cultural de un evento, dicho valor incluye otros elementos diferentes a la música y más relacionados con el patrimonio cultural del lugar y las tradiciones. Los estudios sobre eventos culturales basados en tradiciones locales muestran que estas tradiciones ofrecen un valor de autenticidad y generan una experiencia única y memorable (Folgado-Fernández et al. (2021). El análisis de la autenticidad ha sido un tema de interés en los últimos años y entre las aportaciones de la literatura destaca el desarrollo de una escala de dimensiones por He et al. (2023) y los tres tipos de autenticidad apuntados por Liu et al. (2022): objetiva, construida y existencial. Sobre la influencia de otros valores en la autenticidad, los estudios tienen planteamientos contrarios, tal como apuntan Liu et al. (2022). Para ellos, es la autenticidad la que influye en el valor percibido, mientras otros estudios apuntan a que son los valores los que influyen en la autenticidad.

Por otra parte, para que un evento se considere único, debe reunir características difíciles de imitar por otros eventos, como las experiencias, atmósfera y el entorno (He et al., 2023). También son recientes los estudios que analizan los factores que hacen que un evento se considere una experiencia memorable (Chen, 2022) que implica que el evento produce recuerdos positivos en quienes participan en ellos (Ding and Hung, 2021).

La Figura 1 muestra las relaciones que se exploran en este trabajo a partir de la revisión de literatura: la influencia del valor cultural del evento y de la música en que el evento sea percibido como auténtico y único.

Figura 1. Modelo conceptual

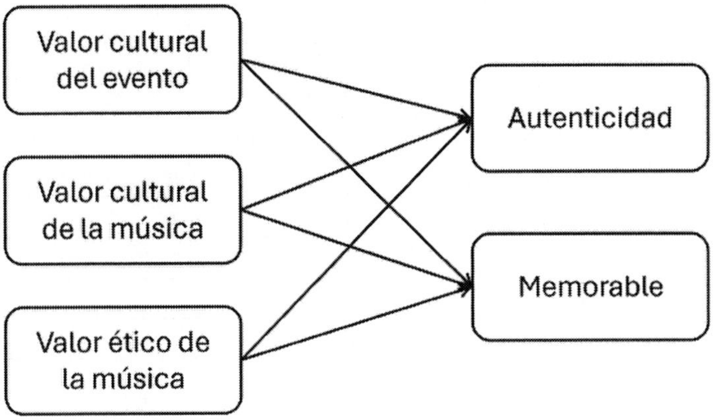

Fuente: elaboración propia

3. METODOLOGÍA

3.1. Datos y muestra

Los datos utilizados para el análisis proceden de la encuesta, llevada a cabo en julio de 2024, a participantes en la Ofrenda de Torrent (Valencia). La encuesta incluía 34 preguntas organizadas en nueve grupos, el primero centrado en el perfil de los participantes y los otros ocho grupos en las ocho variables latentes y sus ítems. La encuesta fue respondida por 82 personas, pero 18 respuestas eran muy incompletas, por lo que no se consideran. Otras cuatro respuestas no ofrecen respuestas para todos los ítems de variables latentes y también se excluyen. Por tanto, el número de respuestas completas es de 60. Dado que el número de respuestas no es elevado, el análisis que se realizará será cualitativo y exploratorio.

El perfil demográfico de las personas encuestadas se muestra en la Tabla 1. El género es mayoritariamente femenino, ya que supone el 73,33% de las personas de la muestra. Respecto a generaciones, destaca la generación X con más de la mitad de los casos. En la motivación para participar en la Ofrenda, la principal es la cultural, seguida de la religiosa, mientras que la motivación social es menos importante.

Tabla 1. Perfil de los participantes en la encuesta

Género	Total	%	Motivación para asistir	Total	%
Femenino	44	73,33%	Cultural	35	58,33%
Masculino	16	26,67%	Religiosa	20	33,33%
			Social	5	8,33%
Generación	**Total**	%			
Generación Z	16	26,67%			
Generación Y	12	20%			
Generación X	31	51,67%			
Boomers	1	1,66%			

3.2. Variables

De las 34 preguntas de la encuesta, las variables utilizadas en el análisis corresponden a 17 preguntas que se centran en los ítems de cinco variables latentes: valor cultural del evento, valor de la música, ética de la música, autenticidad y evento memorable. La Tabla 2 muestra los ítems de las cinco variables.

Tabla 2. Variables e ítems

Variables and items	Description	Mean	Referencia
CULTURA			Rivetti & Lucadamo (2023)
cultura 1	Participo en la Ofrenda Fallera de Torrent para aumentar mi bagaje cultural	6.9	
cultura 2	Participo en la Ofrenda Fallera de Torrent para aprender y entender la cultura y tradiciones de las Fallas	7.47	
cultura 3	Participo en la Ofrenda Fallera de Torrent para aprender y entender la cultura y tradiciones de esta ciudad	7.08	
MUSICA			Nguyen et al. (2020)
musica 1	En la Ofrenda Fallera de Torrent, la calidad de la música es muy alta	8.05	
musica 2	En la Ofrenda Fallera de Torrent, la lista de obras/piezas interpretadas es extraordinaria	7.52	

Variables and items	Description	Mean	Referencia
musica 3	En la Ofrenda Fallera de Torrent, la lista de obras/piezas interpretadas es creativa	6.13	
musica 4	En la Ofrenda Fallera de Torrent, el orden de las obras/piezas interpretadas está bien planificado	7.52	
ETICA			Green et al. (2016)
etica 1	Es importante que la selección de la música en la Ofrenda represente un buen ejemplo para niños/as y jóvenes	8.43	
etica 2	Es importante que la selección de la música en la Ofrenda apoye la música de artistas locales y de la provincia	8.72	
etica 3	Es importante que se asegure el pago de derechos a los/las artistas por el uso de su música en la Ofrenda	8.27	
AUTENTICIDAD			Liu et al. (2022)
autenticidad 1	En la Ofrenda Fallera de Torrent, el patrimonio cultural de las Fallas está bien conservado	8.35	
autenticidad 2	En la Ofrenda Fallera de Torrent, se mantiene la tradición histórica y cultural	8.32	
autenticidad 3	En la Ofrenda Fallera de Torrent, la atmósfera de cultura tradicional es real y firme	8.22	
MEMORABLE			He et al. (2023)
memorable 1	La Ofrenda Fallera de Torrent ofrece experiencias que otros eventos no pueden imitar	8.07	
memorable 2	La atmósfera de la Ofrenda Fallera de Torrent es difícil de encontrar en otros eventos	7.38	
memorable 3	La Ofrenda Fallera de Torrent se celebra en un entorno que otros eventos no pueden ofrecer	7.13	
memorable 4	Las actividades que incluye la Ofrenda Fallera de Torrent son difíciles de repetir por otros eventos	7.23	

3.3. Análisis

El análisis se estructura en cuatro pasos en base a los análisis realizados. El primero de ellos es una descripción más profunda de los perfiles de los participantes, diferenciando los datos de las medias de la Tabla 2 en base a generación, género y motivo para participar en la Ofrenda. Se utiliza el software JASP (JASP Team, 2024).

El segundo análisis es un análisis factorial exploratorio (EFA) para seleccionar los ítems que se incluyen en el tercer análisis, que consiste en el análisis cualitativo comparado (QCA) y que identifica las condiciones necesarias y suficientes para los outcomes. El cuarto análisis, de condiciones necesarias (NCA), sirve para reforzar los resultados del QCA. Estos tres análisis se realizan con librerías de R.

El **análisis factorial** se realiza para cada una de las dos variables a explicar, autenticidad y evento memorable. Antes de llevar a cabo el análisis factorial se calcula la matriz de correlación entre los ítems para determinar si es necesario elegir entre ítems de una variable latente. La matriz de correlación de Spearman muestra alta correlación (>0.8) entre los tres ítems de autenticidad, por lo que el análisis factorial trata de explorar que los ítems de las variables latentes CULTURA, MÚSICA y ÉTICA correlacionan sólo con la variable latente que representa su concepto. En cuanto a las variables latentes que representan los conceptos de autenticidad y evento memorable, sus ítems se van probando individualmente como outcome en los análisis de QCA para comprobar cuál ofrece mejores resultados.

Después de revisar las correlaciones, se calculan el KMO y el test de Bartlett y se comprueba que KMO es mayor que 0.7 y que el análisis factorial es adecuado (test de Bartlett significativo). Para el EFA se utiliza la librería *psych* de R (Revelle, 2025), que incluye la función *fa*, en la que se selecciona el método "*pa*" (principal axis) y la rotación oblicua oblimin. Se prueban varios números de factores hasta que se alcanza la mejor solución. La función *fa* ofrece datos de ajuste del modelo como Chi2, p-valor, grados de libertad, TLI (Tucker Lewis fit index), RMSEA (Root mean square error of approximation), RMSR (root mean square of the residuals) y CFI (comparative fix index). Después se obtiene el alfa de Cronbach para las variables latentes, con el objeto de comprobar su consistencia interna y que cada una de ellas puede ser tratada como un único concepto.

El **análisis cualitativo comparado** se realiza con la librería QCA de R (Dusa, 2019) para obtener las condiciones necesarias y/o suficientes finales. Previamente, se utiliza el software fsQCA (Ragin & Davey, 2022) para escoger qué ítems de las variables autenticidad y memorable utilizar como outcomes, en base a los niveles de consistencia y cobertura. El análisis que se lleva a cabo es QCA fuzzy set y las condiciones de cultura y música se han obtenido con el promedio de los ítems de cada una. Después, se realizan calibraciones de las condiciones y los outcomes utilizando la calibración directa con tres medidas de referencia, los percentiles 10%, 50% y 90%. Las soluciones finales que se presentan incluyen las parsimoniosas e intermedias conjuntamente.

El **análisis de condiciones necesarias** con la librería NCA de R (Dul, 2024) complementa los análisis realizados con QCA, ya que puede detectar condiciones necesarias no identificadas por el análisis previo. Además, NCA permite comprobar en qué grado debe darse una condición para ser considerada como necesaria para un grado específico del outcome (Vis & Dul, 2018). En el análisis del tamaño del efecto se utilizan 10,000 muestras (Dul, 2024). Para la obtención de la tabla de cuello de botella se CR_FDH. Las figuras se obtienen con la opción plotly en la función nca_output de la misma librería.

4. RESULTADOS

4.1. Resultados según perfil

La Tabla 3 muestra la media de cada uno de los ítems en base a su generación, género y motivo por el que participan en la Ofrenda. Se observan diferencias entre las tres generaciones para los ítems de cultura, autenticidad y evento memorable, con la generación más joven puntuando más alto en cultura y la generación Y menos en autenticidad y evento memorable. En cuanto a género, las diferencias más importantes se dan en la valoración de autenticidad y evento memorable, con puntuaciones menores por parte del género masculino. Por último, la motivación para asistir también influye en las puntuaciones, ya que las valoraciones a los ítems de cultura son más altas cuando la motivación para asistir es cultural, pero menores cuando es religiosa. Cuando la motivación para asistir es religiosa, las puntuaciones son más bajas en autenticidad y evento memorable. En el caso de la motivación social para asistir, aunque hay pocas respuestas, se comprueba que la puntuación a los ítems de música es más alta, así como a los ítems de ética.

Tabla 3. Análisis del perfil de los participantes (medias de las respuestas)

Variables e items	Gen. X	Gen. Y	Gen. Z	Género F	Género M	Cultura	Religión	Social
CULTURA								
cultura 1	6.9	6.3	7.3	6.9	6.9	7.3	5.9	8.0
cultura 2	7.4	7.0	8.1	7.7	6.9	8.1	6.7	6.6
cultura 3	6.9	6.8	7.7	7.2	6.8	7.5	6.5	6.4
MUSICA								
musica 1	8.3	8.0	7.4	8.3	7.5	8.0	8.0	9.0
musica 2	7.7	7.2	7.3	7.7	7.0	7.6	7.1	8.4
musica 3	6.6	4.7	6.1	6.1	6.1	6.0	5.7	8.6
musica 4	7.8	7.0	7.3	7.6	7.2	7.5	7.4	8.6
ETICA								
etica 1	8.6	8.3	8.1	8.4	8.6	8.3	8.4	9.6
etica 2	8.8	8.6	8.6	8.8	8.4	8.7	8.6	9.0
etica 3	8.2	8.6	8.1	8.3	8.3	8.1	8.2	10.0
AUTENTICIDAD								
autenticidad 1	8.6	7.6	8.4	8.8	7.3	8.7	7.6	8.8
autenticidad 2	8.7	7.3	8.3	8.7	7.4	8.8	7.4	8.8
autenticidad 3	8.5	7.3	8.1	8.6	7.1	8.5	7.4	9.2
MEMORABLE								
memorable 1	7.8	7.8	8.6	8.5	7.0	8.1	7.6	8.8
memorable 2	7.7	6.3	7.4	7.8	6.1	7.5	6.8	8.6
memorable 3	7.6	5.6	7.3	7.6	5.9	7.4	6.5	8.2
memorable 4	7.7	6.3	6.9	7.5	6.6	7.4	6.8	8.2

Fuente: elaboración a partir de las respuestas de la encuesta

4.2. Resultados del análisis factorial exploratorio

La Tabla 4 presenta los resultados finales del análisis factorial. Como se observa en la tabla, sólo dos de las tres variables han aparecido entre los factores encontrados, cultura y música. Sin embargo, la variable de ética no ha generado un tercer factor. Sólo el ítem ética1 aparecía con los ítems de música en el mismo factor, pero no representa el concepto que define a los tres ítems de música, por lo que no se ha incorporado a la selección final. La varianza acumulada explicada por los dos factores es del 67%, la prueba KMO para los tres factores en conjunto es de 0.84 y el test de Bartlett es significativo. Las medidas de ajuste del modelo obtenidas son Chi2=3.15 (p-valor > 0.05), RMSEA=0 (CI 90% [0, 0.049], RMSR=0.02.

Tabla 4. Factores e ítems

Ítems	Factor 1_C	Factor 2_M	MSA	Alpha Cronbach
CULTURAL				0.863
cultural 1	0.59		0.90	0.88
cultural 2	0.84		0.78	0.78
cultural 3	0.95		0.75	0.74
MUSICA				0.892
musica 1		0.84	0.87	0.87
musica 2		0.92	0.82	0.83
musica 3		0.56	0.93	0.90
musica 4		0.84	0.87	0.85

4.3. Análisis cualitativo comparado

El primer paso en este análisis ha sido la selección del outcome a utilizar para autenticidad y memorable a partir del software fsQCA (Ragin & Davey, 2022). Los resultados de consistencia y convergencia con las dos condiciones de música y cultura se muestran en la Tabla 5. Como se puede comprobar, en el caso de autenticidad los tres resultados muestran valores elevados de consistencia y cobertura, con la misma condición en sus soluciones. Sin embargo, el segundo ítem muestra un valor más alto en consistencia con una cobertura parecida a la del ítem 3. Por tanto, se selecciona el ítem autenticidad2 como outcome. En el caso de memorable, los cuatro ítems muestran alta consistencia, aunque baja cobertura. Sin embargo, el ítem memorable4 muestra un nivel más alto en las dos medidas, por lo que se selecciona como outcome.

Tabla 5. Selección de outcomes para QCA

Outcome	Consistencia	Cobertura
autenticidad 1	0.833	0.789
autenticidad 2	**0.816**	**0.812**
autenticidad 3	0.805	0.817
memorable 1	0.837	0.390

Outcome	Consistencia	Cobertura
memorable 2	0.901	0.408
memorable 3	0.886	0.396
memorable 4	**0.925**	**0.419**

Una vez determinados los outcomes y las condiciones a incluir en el análisis, el siguiente paso es utilizar la librería QCA para explorar si el valor cultural del evento y de la música son condiciones necesarias y/o suficientes para la autenticidad del evento y que sea memorable. Una condición es necesaria si está siempre presente cuando el outcome lo está. La Tabla 6 muestra los resultados del análisis de necesidad para el outcome de autenticidad, considerando todas las posibles situaciones de presencia y ausencia de condiciones y outcomes. La Tabla 7 muestra el análisis para el outcome memorable, incluyendo todas las opciones posibles. La librería QCA ofrece tres datos: consistencia, cobertura y RoN (relevancia de la necesidad). Siguiendo el criterio de Mello (2021), para que una condición sea necesaria, debe darse a la vez que la consistencia sea ≥0.9 y la cobertura y la relevancia de necesidad ≥0.5. Como ninguna de las dos tablas muestra estos valores conjuntamente, desde el análisis QCA se obtiene que ninguna de las condiciones es necesaria para alguno de los outcomes.

Tabla 6. Análisis de condiciones necesarias con QCA

autenticidad 2				~autenticidad 2			
Condiciones	**Consist.**	**Cob.**	**RoN**	**Condiciones**	**Consist.**	**Cob.**	**RoN**
Cultura_c	0.691	0.693	0.744	Cultura_c	0.592	0.527	0.653
Música_c	0.812	0.816	0.830	Música_c	0.460	0.411	0.604
~Cultura_c	0.528	0.593	0.734	~Cultura_c	0.655	0.653	0.764
~Música_c	0.414	0.463	0.675	~Música_c	0.794	0.789	0.841

Tabla 7. Análisis de condiciones necesarias con QCA

memorable 4				~memorable 4			
Condiciones	**Consist.**	**Cob.**	**RoN**	**Condiciones**	**Consist.**	**Cob.**	**RoN**
Cultura_c	0.668	0.628	0.706	Cultura_c	0.622	0.592	0.686
Música_c	0.786	0.742	0.776	Música_c	0.505	0.482	0.634
~Cultura_c	0.566	0.596	0.735	~Cultura_c	0.609	0.650	0.762
~Música_c	0.451	0.473	0.679	~Música_c	0.729	0.775	0.832

El siguiente paso es el análisis de condiciones suficientes, es decir, encontrar condiciones que siempre que están presentes entonces el outcome estará presente. Para ello, se obtiene primero la tabla de verdad y, a partir de ella, las soluciones compleja, parsimoniosa e intermedia. La Tabla 8 muestra los resultados obtenidos de las dos últimas soluciones conjuntamente, que en este caso arrojan el mismo resultado. Cada columna hace referencia a las condiciones suficientes encontradas a partir de las cuatro tablas de verdad obtenidas, en función de si el outcome está presente o ausente. En todas las soluciones, la medida de ajuste de consistencia es >0.80. La primera columna muestra que, para la autenticidad presente, sólo la música es condición suficiente. Esta solución es la que incluye más respuestas (30), por lo que tiene mayor nivel de cobertura, lo que implica una mayor relevancia en la relación entre la condición y el outcome (Mello, 2021). La tercera columna muestra el resultado para evento memorable, con la diferencia de que la solución suficiente requiere que se den a la vez la presencia de la música y la ausencia de la cultura, por lo que está reflejando valores menores en las respuestas de esta condición. La segunda y cuarta columna muestra resultados similares, de manera que cuando la música no está presente, los dos outcomes tampoco lo están.

Tabla 8. Análisis de condiciones suficientes con QCA

	autenticidad 2	~autenticidad 2	memorable 4	~memorable 4
Condiciones				
Cultura_c		•	o	•
Música_c	•	o	•	o
Inclusión solución	0.816	0.877	0.925	0.852
Cobertura solución	0.812	0.423	0.419	0.384
Inclusión modelo	0.816	0.877	0.925	0.852
Cobertura modelo	0.812	0.423	0.419	0.384
Casos (nº)	30	8	8	8
Deviant cases consistency (nº casos)	3	0	0	3
•	Condición presente en soluciones parsimoniosa e intermedia			
o	Condición ausente en soluciones parsimoniosa e intermedia			

4.4. Análisis de condiciones necesarias

En el análisis de condiciones necesarias propuesto por Dul (2020) hay que comprobar que el tamaño del efecto es > 0 y el p-valor es significativo.

La Tabla 9 muestra que sólo la música es estadísticamente significativa (p-valor < 0.05) en la autenticidad del evento y en que sea memorable. Sin embargo, el tamaño del efecto (d = 0.025 para autenticidad y d = 0.04 para memorable) está entre 0 y 0.1, por lo tanto, el tamaño del efecto es pequeño (Vis & Dul, 2018). La Tabla 10 representa la conocida como tabla de cuello de botella e indica el nivel necesario en cada condición para alcanzar un nivel determinado del outcome. Por ejemplo, para alcanzar un nivel del 50% en autenticidad, la música debe alcanzar un nivel mínimo del 2.4%. En el caso de memorable, para alcanzar el 50% en el nivel de este outcome, la música debe alcanzar un nivel mínimo del 2.9%. En cada uno de los outcomes, la música empieza a mostrarse como condición necesaria a partir de un nivel determinado del outcome: de un nivel del 0.5% de la música para un nivel del 20% de autenticidad, de un 1.2% de la música para un nivel de memorable del 40%. Para alcanzar un 90% de memorable, son necesarias las condiciones de música a un nivel mínimo del 9.5%.

Tabla 9. NCA tamaños de efecto

Condiciones	autenticidad 2				memorable 4			
	CE_ FDH	p-valor	CR_ FDH	p-valor	CE_ FDH	p-valor	CR_ FDH	p-valor
Cultura_c	0.00	1.000	0.000	1.000	0.01	0.323	0.00	0.323
Música_c	0.04	0.007	0.025	0.009	0.04	0.015	0.04	0.015

Tabla 10. Tabla de cuello de Botella (Bottleneck table) (CR_FDH)

autenticidad 2	Música_c	memorable 4	Música_c
0	NN	0	NN
10	NN	10	NN
20	0.5	20	NN
30	1.2	30	NN
40	1.8	40	1.2
50	2.4	50	2.9
60	3.1	60	4.6

autenticidad 2	Música_c	memorable 4	Música_c
70	3.7	70	6.2
80	4.3	80	7.9
90	4.9	90	9.5
100	5.6	100	11.2

Las Figuras 2 y 3 muestran los diagramas de dispersión entre la condición música y cada uno de los dos outcomes. Se puede observar, como se ha comprobado en la Tabla 10, que los espacios vacíos de la zona superior izquierda de la figura son pequeños (tamaño del efecto <0.1), pero que a niveles más altos de autenticidad y memorable, la música se vuelve algo más necesaria. También se observa que el efecto es mayor en memorable que en autenticidad, aunque se mantiene pequeño.

Figura 2. Diagrama de dispersión para música condición necesaria de autenticidad

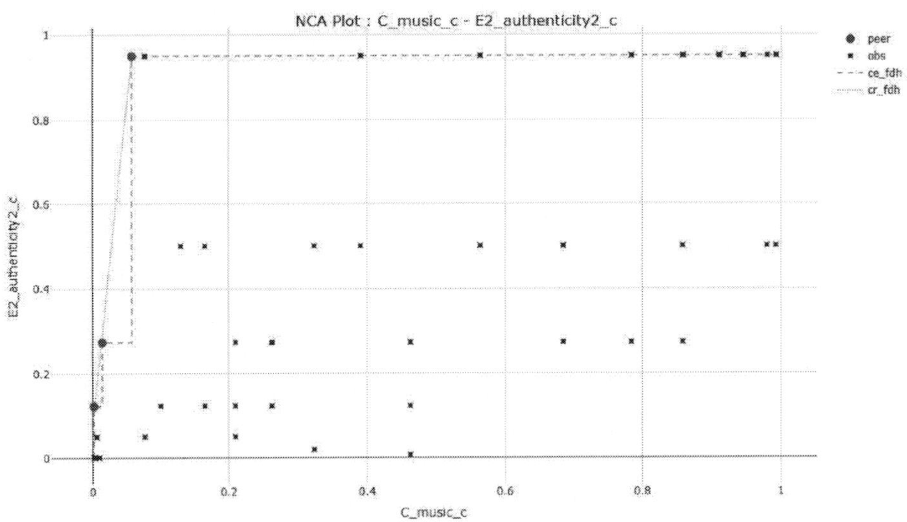

Fuente: elaboración con la librería NCA de R (opción plotly)

Figura 3. Diagrama de dispersión para música condición necesaria de memorable

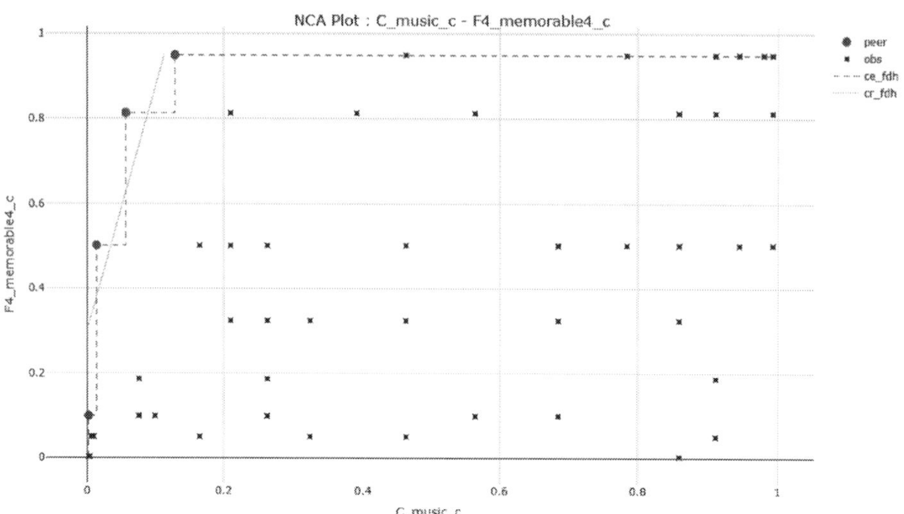

Fuente: elaboración con la librería NCA de R (opción plotly)

5. CONCLUSIONES

En este trabajo se ha presentado el análisis de la influencia de la cultura y la música en un evento concreto, la Ofrenda de Flores que se celebra durante la fiesta de Fallas en Torrent (Valencia). Este evento, al igual que las Fallas, se celebra en la ciudad de Valencia y en otros municipios de la provincia durante el mes de marzo. A partir de los datos de una encuesta recogida en 2024, se utilizan las metodologías QCA y NCA para evaluar si la cultura del evento analizado y la música tradicional que acompaña a la Ofrenda pueden considerarse condiciones necesarias y/o suficientes para que el evento se considere auténtico y memorable.

Del análisis de los resultados se pueden concluir tres ideas principales. La primera se refiere a las diferencias detectadas en el perfil de los participantes en la encuesta, que muestra diferencias basadas en el motivo de su participación. Destaca que las valoraciones a los ítems de cultura son más altas cuando la motivación para asistir es cultural, pero menores cuando es religiosa. Cuando la motivación es social, la puntuación a los ítems de música es más alta, así como a los ítems de ética.

La segunda conclusión se basa en las condiciones suficientes encontradas al analizar la presencia y ausencia de los dos outcomes. El resultado con mayor consistencia y cobertura muestra que sólo la presencia de la música es condición suficiente para que la autenticidad esté presente. Sin embargo, cuando la música está ausente, aunque la cultura esté presente, la autenticidad está ausente. Las soluciones para memorable tienen una baja cobertura, aunque son congruentes con los resultados para autenticidad, de manera que cuando la música está presente, aunque la cultura esté ausente, el evento es percibido como memorable. Por el contrario, cuando la música está ausente, aunque la cultura esté presente, el outcome memorable está ausente.

La tercera conclusión se centra en el estudio de las condiciones necesarias para cada outcome. Aunque el análisis QCA no muestra que las condiciones sean necesarias, el análisis NCA muestra un efecto, aunque muy pequeño, de la música como condición necesaria para la presencia de autenticidad y evento memorable. Por el contrario, la cultura del evento no es significativa para generar el efecto de condición necesaria.

La principal limitación de este trabajo está en el número de respuestas a la encuesta, que sólo ha permitido llevar a cabo un análisis exploratorio. Estudios futuros con un mayor número de respuestas permitirán no sólo comparar los resultados alcanzados en este estudio sino ampliar el número de variables latentes a incluir y el uso de otros métodos que mejoren los resultados alcanzados.

AGRADECIMIENTOS

La investigación de este trabajo ha sido realizada dentro del proyecto Music360 (https://music-360.eu/), que ha recibido financiación del programa de investigación e innovación Horizon Europe de la Unión Europea bajo el acuerdo de subvención n.º 101094872 (https://cordis.europa.eu/project/id/101094872).

6. REFERENCIAS

Behr et al (2016): "Live concert performance: an ecological approach". Rock Music Studies. 3.5–23

Chen, LH. (2022): "Unobserved heterogeneity in music festivalgoers' experience processing". Tourism Management Perspectives, 44. 101026.

De-Miguel-Molina et al (2021): "Music as intangible cultural heritage: economic, cultural and social identity". Springer Nature. Switzerland.

Ding, HM & Hung, KP (2021): "The antecedents of visitors' flow experience and its influence on memory and behavioral intentions in the music festival context". Journal of Destination Marketing & Management. 19. 100551.

Dul, J. (2020): "Conducting Necessary Condition Analysis for Business and Management Students". SAGE. UK.

Dul, J. (2024): "Necessary Condition Analysis. R Package Version 4.0.1". https://cran.r-project.org/web/packages/NCA/

Dusa, A. (2019): "QCA with R. A Comprehensive Resource". Springer International Publishing. Switzerland.

Folgado-Fernández et al (2021): "Tourist's rational and emotional engagement across events: A multi-event integration view". International Journal of Contemporary Hospitality Management. 33. 2371-2390

Gallarza, MG et al (2023): "Consumer value of virtual music festivals". International Journal of Consumer Studies. 47. 2012-2030

Green, T. et al (2016): "Do they Know it's CSR at all? An Exploration of Socially Responsible Music Consumption". Journal of Business Ethics. 138. 231-246

He, Y. et al (2023): "Perceived authenticity of hallmark event brands: Conceptualization, measurement, and an integrative framework". Journal of Destination Marketing & Management. 27. 100766

Higgins, K. (2023): "Ethics and music". The Oxford Handbook of Ethics and Art. Oxford University Press, New York.

JASP Team (2024): "JASP (Version 0.18.3) Computer software". Retrieved from https://jasp-stats.org/

Liu, H. et al (2022): "An extended stimulus-organism-response model of Hanfu experience in cultural heritage tourism". Journal of Vacation Marketing. 30. 288–310

Mello, P. (2021): "Qualitative Comparative Analysis. An Introduction to Research Design and Application". Georgetown University Press, Washington, DC.

Mulder, M., & Hitters, E. (2021): "Visiting pop concerts and festivals: measuring the value of an integrated live music motivation scale". Cultural Trends. 30. 355–375

Nguyen, T. et al (2020): "The way of generation Y enjoying Jazz festival: a case of the Korea (Jarasum) music festival". Asia Pacific Journal of Tourism Research. 25. 52-63

Preniqi V, et al (2023): "Soundscapes of morality: Linking music preferences and moral values through lyrics and audio". PLoS ONE. 18. e0294402

Ragin, C.C. & Davey, S. (2022): "Fuzzy-Set/Qualitative Comparative Analysis 4.0". Irvine, California: Department of Sociology, University of California. (https://sites.socsci.uci.edu/~cragin/fsQCA/software.shtml)

Revelle, W. (2025): "psych: Procedures for Psychological, Psychometric, and Personality Research". Northwestern University, Evanston, Illinois. R package version 2.5.3, https://CRAN.R-project.org/package=psych

Rivetti, F. & Lucadamo, A. (2023): "Cultural festival attendees: a path from motivation to loyalty". Current Issues in Tourism. 26. 3499-3515

Rodríguez-Campo, L. et al (2022): "A holistic understanding of the emotional experience of festival attendees". Leisure Sciences. 44. 421-439

Saha, P. et al (2023): "Re-examining the roles of experience quality at festivals: a comparative analysis using SEM and fsQCA". International Journal of Contemporary Hospitality Management. 35. 1802-1823

Sheth, J. N. et al (1991): "Why we buy what we buy: A theory of consumption values". Journal of Business Research. 22. 159-170

Sweeney, J. C., & Soutar, G. N. (2001): "Consumer perceived value: The development of a multiple item scale". Journal of Retailing. 77. 203-220

Toldos, M.P. et al (2019). "Exploring international atmospherics: The impact on shopping behaviors based on the language of the lyrics of music played in global apparel retailers' stores". International Journal of Retail and Distribution Management. 47. 368-383

Turel, O. et al (2010): "User acceptance of hedonic digital artifacts: A theory of consumption values perspective". Information & Management. 47. 53-59

UNESCO (2016): "La fiesta de las Fallas de Valencia". Disponible en https://ich.unesco.org/es/RL/la-fiesta-de-las-fallas-de-valencia-00859

Van der Hoeven, A., & Hitters, E. (2019): "The social and cultural values of live music: Sustaining urban live music ecologies". Cities. 90. 263–271.

Vis, B. & Dul, J. (2018): "Analyzing Relationships of Necessity Not Just in Kind But Also in Degree: Complementing fsQCA With NCA". Sociological Methods & Research. 47. 872-899

Weijters, B. et al (2014): "Online Music Consumption in Today's Technological Context: Putting the Influence of Ethics in Perspective". Journal of Business Ethics. 124. 537–550.

CASA CANSAT. CREACIÓN DE 7 ALOJAMIENTOS TURÍSTICOS ACCESIBLES EN LA VALL FOSCA (PIRINEO DE LLEIDA)

Josep Maria Agustí Roca
Jaume Macià Amorós
Eduard Cristóbal Fransi
Daniel Paül Agustí
Universidad de Lleida

TEMÁTICA: Accesibilidad Universal – Accesibilidad y diseño inclusivo en infraestructuras turísticas

RESUMEN: El presente trabajo presenta el desarrollo de un proyecto turístico de alto valor social y económico: la creación de siete alojamientos turísticos totalmente accesibles en la Vall Fosca, en el Pirineo de Lleida. La iniciativa nace de la colaboración con la Fundació Aremi y busca rehabilitar un edificio cedido a tal efecto para ofrecer estancias dignas, adaptadas y confortables a personas con parálisis cerebral y otras discapacidades graves. La propuesta plantea un modelo de negocio sostenible, con un enfoque en el turismo inclusivo y accesible, alineado con las tendencias del sector y las necesidades sociales actuales.

Palabras clave: turismo accesible, Vall Fosca, parálisis cerebral, inclusión, accesibilidad

ABSTRACT: This paper presents the development of a tourism project with high social and economic value: the creation of seven fully accessible tourist accommodations in Vall Fosca, in the Pyrenees of Lleida. The initiative is promoted by Fundació Aremi and aims to rehabilitate a donated building to offer adapted, dignified and comfortable stays for people with cerebral palsy and other severe disabilities. The proposal outlines a sustainable business model focused on inclusive and accessible tourism, aligned with current sector trends and social needs.

Keywords: accessible tourism, Vall Fosca, cerebral palsy, inclusion, accessibility

1. INTRODUCCIÓN

El presente proyecto tiene como objetivo la creación de siete alojamientos turísticos completamente accesibles en la Vall Fosca, en el Pirineo de Lleida. La propuesta nace de una necesidad social real identificada por la

Fundació Privada AREMI, entidad sin ánimo de lucro dedicada a la atención de personas con parálisis cerebral y discapacidades similares. Este trabajo busca proporcionar una solución de alojamiento inclusiva, digna y adaptada, con alto impacto social y valor añadido turístico.

La idea surge a partir de la cesión de un edificio situado en La Pobleta de Bellveí, un núcleo rural en pleno entorno natural de alta montaña. Este inmueble, actualmente en desuso, ofrece una ubicación estratégica para desarrollar un proyecto de turismo accesible que combine la tranquilidad del medio rural con todas las condiciones necesarias para garantizar la autonomía y el bienestar de personas con movilidad reducida. Lejos de tratarse de una simple mejora arquitectónica, el proyecto aborda el concepto de accesibilidad desde una perspectiva integral: física, sensorial, cognitiva y emocional.

CASA CANSAT no solo aspira a convertirse en un modelo de referencia en turismo inclusivo, sino que también busca contribuir al desarrollo económico local, creando oportunidades de empleo, fortaleciendo el tejido comunitario y favoreciendo la repoblación rural. Asimismo, el proyecto se alinea con los Objetivos de Desarrollo Sostenible (ODS), especialmente en lo relativo a la reducción de desigualdades (ODS 10) y la promoción de comunidades sostenibles (ODS 11), lo que refuerza su valor estratégico y social.

Figuras 1 y 2. Fachada del edificio que debe albergar la futura CASA CANSAT

Fuente: Josep Maria Agustí Roca

2. METODOLOGÍA

El diseño metodológico del proyecto CASA CANSAT se ha basado en el modelo de Aprendizaje y Servicio (ApS), una propuesta pedagógica que combina procesos de formación con la realización de un servicio a la comunidad. Esta metodología se ha mostrado especialmente adecuada para un trabajo final de máster con vocación transformadora, ya que permite al estudiante aplicar los conocimientos adquiridos a lo largo del programa académico a una situación real, colaborando con una entidad del tercer sector —en este caso, la Fundació AREMI— que plantea una necesidad concreta.

La elaboración del plan ha partido de un diagnóstico preliminar de la situación: la carencia de alojamientos turísticos accesibles en el entorno rural de montaña. A partir de esta identificación, se ha planteado una hoja de ruta estructurada en varias fases de análisis y desarrollo.

En primer lugar, se ha realizado un análisis del entorno desde una perspectiva macroeconómica, social y legal, recopilando información de fuentes oficiales como el INE, el Idescat o el Observatorio del Turismo Rural. Posteriormente, se ha llevado a cabo un benchmarking de proyectos similares en el ámbito estatal, con el fin de identificar buenas prácticas y modelos de gestión replicables.

La siguiente fase ha consistido en el diseño del modelo de negocio utilizando herramientas como el Business Model Canvas, lo que ha permitido estructurar la propuesta en torno a segmentos de clientes, canales de distribución, fuentes de ingresos y estructura de costes. A continuación, se ha desarrollado el plan estratégico y el plan de marketing, con una fuerte orientación digital, definiendo estrategias de posicionamiento SEO, presencia en redes sociales y alianzas con plataformas turísticas y entidades sociales.

Finalmente, se ha construido un plan económico-financiero que incluye previsión de ingresos, cálculo del punto de equilibrio, análisis de viabilidad (VAN y TIR) y propuesta de estructura financiera basada en capital propio, préstamos y subvenciones. Todo ello ha sido validado a través de entrevistas informales con agentes del territorio: representantes municipales, técnicos del parque natural, operadores turísticos y potenciales usuarios.

La metodología empleada, por tanto, no solo garantiza la solidez académica del proyecto, sino también su aplicabilidad y conexión con el contexto real, asegurando que CASA CANSAT no sea una propuesta teórica, sino una iniciativa viable y transformadora.

3. ANÁLISIS DEL ENTORNO

3.1. Entorno económico y social

El contexto económico y social en el que se enmarca el proyecto CASA CANSAT es particularmente relevante para comprender tanto su necesidad como su viabilidad. En los últimos años, el turismo de interior y de naturaleza ha experimentado un repunte significativo, impulsado por la pandemia de la COVID-19 y por cambios en los hábitos de consumo vacacional. Cada vez más personas optan por destinos rurales que ofrezcan tranquilidad, contacto con el medio ambiente y una experiencia personalizada.

En este escenario, el Pirineo de Lleida ha visto un aumento progresivo del número de visitantes, especialmente catalanes, que representan más del 80% de los turistas en la zona. Sin embargo, la oferta turística todavía presenta grandes limitaciones en materia de accesibilidad universal, lo que excluye a un amplio colectivo de potenciales usuarios: personas con discapacidad, personas mayores, familias con necesidades especiales, etc.

Según datos del Departament de Drets Socials de la Generalitat de Catalunya, existen 677.540 personas con algún tipo de discapacidad en Cataluña, de las cuales una parte significativa presenta limitaciones motoras severas. Esta cifra, sumada al proceso de envejecimiento poblacional, hace prever un aumento en la demanda de servicios turísticos adaptados en los próximos años.

Por otro lado, el entorno social del Pallars Jussà —comarca donde se ubica el proyecto— presenta un tejido comunitario cohesionado, con entidades locales activas y una fuerte implicación ciudadana. La posibilidad de crear un recurso como CASA CANSAT contribuye no solo a mejorar la calidad de vida de las personas con discapacidad, sino también a dinamizar la economía local y fijar población en zonas rurales, objetivos alineados con las políticas de desarrollo rural y cohesión territorial.

Desde una perspectiva institucional, el apoyo de la Fundació AREMI y la colaboración con entidades como Lleida Solidària o el Ayuntamiento de La Torre de Cabdella refuerzan el carácter inclusivo y estratégico del proyecto, dotándolo de una legitimidad social que facilitará su implementación.

3.2. Análisis de mercado

El mercado turístico en la comarca del Pallars Jussà muestra una tendencia positiva de crecimiento, aunque todavía por debajo de otras zonas del Pirineo catalán. Según el Observatorio de Turismo del Interior, el número de pernoctaciones en alojamientos rurales ha aumentado un 10% entre 2020 y 2023. Aun así, la ocupación media anual sigue siendo baja

(15-17%), lo que revela un margen importante de mejora a través de propuestas diferenciadas como CASA CANSAT.

Figura 3. Evolución del grado de ocupación por plazas (%) en establecimientos de turismo rural en la demarcación de Lleida (2003-2022)*

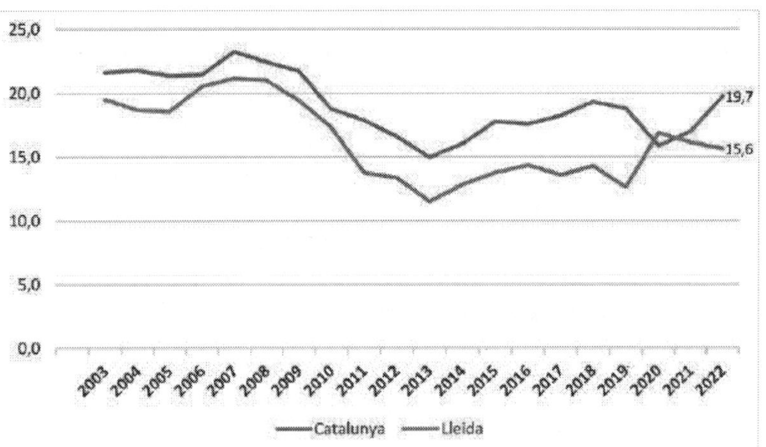

Fuente: Càtedra de Turisme d'Interior i de Muntanya de la Universitat de Lleida i la Diputació de Lleida. Informe sobre el turisme rural a la demarcació de Lleida 2002-2022 [Internet]. 2023. Disponible en: https://observatorituristic.aralleida.cat/ftp/documents/Estudis_i_Analisis/Flash informatiu 026 Informe de turisme rural sobre la demarcació de Lleida 2002-2022.pdf

Uno de los elementos más destacados del análisis de mercado es la escasez de alojamientos adaptados a personas con movilidad reducida. A pesar de que algunas casas rurales declaran ser "accesibles", muy pocas cumplen con los requisitos técnicos del Codi d'Accessibilitat de Catalunya. Esta carencia convierte a CASA CANSAT en una propuesta pionera, no solo en su comarca, sino en todo el ámbito del turismo de montaña.

El perfil del cliente objetivo ha sido estudiado mediante la técnica de Buyer Persona, identificando dos segmentos principales:

1. Familias con al menos un hijo/a con discapacidad física severa, que buscan lugares tranquilos, accesibles y con servicios complementarios como restauración adaptada o transporte asistido.
2. Personas mayores o con movilidad reducida temporal, interesadas en disfrutar de la naturaleza con condiciones de confort y seguridad.

A nivel competitivo, la presencia de plataformas como Airbnb o Booking permite tener una idea clara de los precios de mercado, que oscilan entre 85 y 140 €/noche, con estancias mínimas de 2-3 días. CASA CANSAT se posicionará en la franja media-alta del segmento, pero con una propuesta de valor claramente diferenciada basada en accesibilidad, atención personalizada y colaboración con entidades sociales.

Además, el análisis muestra una cierta estacionalidad con gran afluencia especialmente en puentes, fines de semana y periodos vacacionales estivales. Esta característica permite estabilizar ingresos y optimizar recursos operativos.

El análisis de mercado justifica la oportunidad que representa CASA CANSAT, tanto desde una perspectiva social como desde una lógica empresarial de nicho bien definido.

Figura 4. Grado de ocupación mensual (%) de los establecimientos de turismo rural en la demarcación de Lleida (2022).

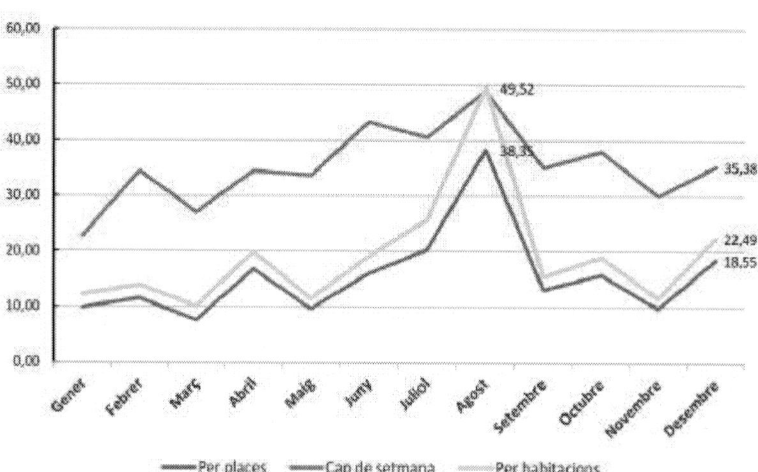

Fuente: Càtedra de Turisme d'Interior i de Muntanya de la Universitat de Lleida i la Diputació de Lleida. Informe sobre el turisme rural a la demarcació de Lleida 2002 - 2022 [Internet]. 2023. Disponible en: https://observatorituristic.aralleida.cat/ftp/documents/Estudis_i_Analisis/Flash informatiu 026 Informe de turisme rural sobre la demarcació de Lleida 2002-2022.pdf

4. PLAN ESTRATÉGICO

El plan estratégico de CASA CANSAT se construye a partir de una propuesta de valor claramente diferenciada: ofrecer alojamientos rurales totalmente accesibles en una zona de alta montaña, con una orientación social y comunitaria. A diferencia de otros proyectos turísticos, este plan no se limita a la generación de beneficios económicos, sino que persigue un impacto transformador tanto en el territorio como en las personas usuarias.

La **misión** del proyecto es facilitar el derecho al ocio y al descanso a personas con movilidad reducida o discapacidades severas, en condiciones de igualdad y dignidad. Para ello, se integran criterios de accesibilidad universal, diseño para todos y atención centrada en la persona. La **visión** a medio plazo es posicionar CASA CANSAT como un referente de turismo inclusivo en los Pirineos y como ejemplo replicable para otras zonas rurales.

En cuanto a los objetivos estratégicos, se definen tres líneas prioritarias:

1. Sostenibilidad económica y operativa: garantizar la viabilidad financiera del proyecto a través de una combinación de ingresos por reservas, subvenciones y alianzas con entidades públicas y privadas.
2. Impacto social: medir y maximizar la mejora en la calidad de vida de las personas usuarias, promoviendo su autonomía, integración y bienestar.
3. Articulación territorial: colaborar con proveedores, empresas y administraciones del entorno para fortalecer el tejido socioeconómico de la Vall Fosca.

Este enfoque se concreta en acciones como la contratación local, la dinamización de actividades culturales accesibles, la participación en redes de turismo social y la generación de sinergias con centros educativos, sanitarios y sociales. El plan estratégico también contempla un modelo de gobernanza participativo, donde las personas con discapacidad y sus familias puedan formar parte de los órganos de decisión del proyecto, reforzando así su carácter inclusivo y democrático.

5. PLAN DE MARKETING

5.1. Público objetivo

El público objetivo de CASA CANSAT ha sido identificado tras un proceso de segmentación basado en necesidades específicas, más allá de criterios sociodemográficos tradicionales. El foco está en colectivos que enfrentan barreras de acceso al turismo convencional, principalmente:

- Personas con parálisis cerebral, daño cerebral adquirido, enfermedades neuromusculares o neurodegenerativas.

- Personas mayores con movilidad reducida o dependencia moderada.
- Familias que viajan con algún miembro con discapacidad.
- Cuidadores/as profesionales o acompañantes que buscan alojamientos adaptados.
- Colectivos vinculados al ámbito de la diversidad funcional (entidades, asociaciones, centros ocupacionales, etc.).

Este público comparte demandas comunes: espacios sin barreras, habitaciones amplias, baños adaptados, accesos seguros, mobiliario ergonómico, señalización clara, y, sobre todo, personal formado en atención inclusiva. CASA CANSAT responde a estas demandas con una propuesta orientada al detalle, capaz de ofrecer experiencias personalizadas en un entorno natural único.

El análisis de Buyer Persona ha permitido detectar motivaciones concretas como el deseo de normalización, la necesidad de descanso para las familias cuidadoras, el valor emocional del contacto con la naturaleza o la posibilidad de compartir vacaciones con otras personas en situación similar. Todo ello convierte a CASA CANSAT en mucho más que un alojamiento: es un espacio de encuentro, descanso y dignificación personal.

5.2. Estrategia de comunicación

La estrategia de comunicación se centrará en posicionar la marca CASA CANSAT como sinónimo de turismo accesible, digno y transformador. Para ello, se han definido diversas acciones:

1. Presencia digital sólida: desarrollo de una página web con criterios de accesibilidad (cumplimiento de las WCAG 2.1), navegación intuitiva, lectura fácil y opción de audiodescripción. La web incluirá galería fotográfica, calendario de disponibilidad, precios dinámicos y formularios accesibles.
2. Marketing de contenidos: generación de contenidos informativos y emocionales en blog, redes sociales y newsletters. Se priorizarán testimonios reales, vídeos subtitulados, experiencias compartidas y consejos de viaje accesible.
3. Redes sociales: uso activo de Instagram, Facebook y TikTok, con una línea gráfica coherente y un tono empático. Las redes servirán para

visibilizar el día a día del proyecto, generar comunidad y fomentar la interacción con los usuarios.

4. Colaboraciones estratégicas: alianzas con asociaciones como ASPACE, ECOM o PREDIF; acuerdos con centros de atención precoz, hospitales de rehabilitación y ayuntamientos; participación en ferias de turismo accesible y jornadas de turismo social.

5. Plataformas de reserva: presencia en Booking, EscapadaRural y Airbnb, asegurando una ficha clara y adaptada, con indicaciones precisas sobre accesibilidad (anchura de puertas, tipo de camas, altura de interruptores, etc.).

La estrategia de marketing tiene un doble objetivo: dar visibilidad al proyecto entre sus públicos prioritarios y normalizar el turismo accesible como una práctica de justicia social. La comunicación no solo debe informar, sino también emocionar, conectar y transformar percepciones.

6. PLAN ECONÓMICO-FINANCIERO

La viabilidad económica de CASA CANSAT se ha estudiado desde una perspectiva realista, equilibrando el compromiso social con la necesidad de sostenibilidad financiera. El presupuesto inicial estimado para la rehabilitación integral del edificio y su adaptación completa a criterios de accesibilidad universal asciende a 640.000 €. Esta cifra incluye obra civil, equipamiento, mobiliario adaptado, señalética accesible, diseño web, y puesta en marcha operativa.

La estructura financiera se plantea en tres pilares:

1. Capital propio: 200.000 € aportados por la Fundació AREMI, procedentes de fondos propios y excedentes de ejercicios anteriores.

2. Financiación externa: 200.000 € a través de un préstamo bancario a interés reducido, con carencia de un año y amortización en ocho ejercicios.

3. Subvenciones y donaciones: 240.000 € solicitados a entidades como la Generalitat de Catalunya, Fundación ONCE, Next Generation EU y micromecenazgo social.

Las proyecciones de ingresos se han calculado con base en un precio medio de 125 €/noche y una estancia mínima de dos noches. Con una capacidad estimada para 34 personas, se prevé alcanzar el punto de equilibrio con solo 33 estancias anuales, cifra conservadora que refuerza la viabilidad del modelo. A partir del segundo año, se espera un rendimiento positivo que permita cubrir costes fijos y generar beneficios modestos.

Los indicadores financieros clásicos como el Valor Actual Neto (VAN) y la Tasa Interna de Retorno (TIR) resultan negativos debido a la elevada inversión inicial y al modelo basado en impacto social, no en rentabilidad económica inmediata. Sin embargo, el análisis cualitativo indica que el proyecto es perfectamente viable operativamente, ya que los gastos recurrentes son bajos y existe una fuerte demanda potencial no cubierta.

Además, se prevé un retorno social de la inversión (SROI) elevado, especialmente en términos de inclusión, mejora del bienestar, autonomía, visibilidad y desarrollo territorial. En este sentido, el proyecto se alinea con modelos híbridos de economía social, combinando eficacia económica y vocación transformadora.

7. RESULTADOS ESPERADOS

El proyecto CASA CANSAT tiene como principal expectativa generar impacto social positivo en múltiples niveles. A corto plazo, se espera completar la rehabilitación del inmueble y poner en marcha el servicio en condiciones óptimas, permitiendo acoger a los primeros usuarios en el segundo semestre posterior a la inversión.

En cuanto a indicadores cuantificables, se han definido los siguientes resultados esperados:

- Ocupación progresiva hasta alcanzar el 20% en el segundo año, con una media de 180 noches vendidas anualmente.
- Al menos 120 beneficiarios directos por año, incluyendo personas con discapacidad y sus acompañantes.
- Creación de 2 puestos de trabajo directos (coordinación y mantenimiento) y al menos 2 indirectos (limpieza, logística).
- Participación en redes de turismo social y accesible, como la Xarxa de Turisme Inclusiu de Catalunya.
- Captación de al menos 4 subvenciones anuales que permitan reinvertir en mejoras, formación del personal o dinamización territorial.

En términos cualitativos, los beneficios serán aún más significativos. CASA CANSAT permitirá a personas tradicionalmente excluidas del ocio turístico acceder a experiencias vitales en igualdad de condiciones. El entorno natural, la autonomía promovida por el diseño del espacio y la atención personalizada contribuirán a mejorar el bienestar emocional de los usuarios.

Además, el proyecto tiene vocación de modelo replicable, tanto en otras comarcas rurales como en contextos urbanos, adaptando el enfoque a las particularidades de cada territorio. Las alianzas generadas con asociaciones, ayuntamientos y entidades del tercer sector facilitarán esta expansión.

También se prevé una mejora en la sensibilización social, ya que el proyecto servirá como ejemplo visible de cómo la accesibilidad no es un coste, sino una inversión ética, social y estratégica. En definitiva, los resultados esperados trascienden lo económico para inscribirse en el ámbito de los derechos, la equidad y la justicia social.

8. CONCLUSIONES

CASA CANSAT representa una propuesta pionera e innovadora en el panorama del turismo inclusivo en España. Su origen en el seno de una fundación con amplia trayectoria en el ámbito de la discapacidad garantiza la sensibilidad, el conocimiento del colectivo y el compromiso con la calidad de vida de las personas usuarias.

El proyecto ha demostrado ser viable operativamente, incluso en un contexto de baja densidad poblacional y en un entorno rural de difícil acceso. Gracias a su diseño integral, a la colaboración intersectorial y a la identificación precisa de un nicho desatendido, se ha logrado configurar un plan sólido, con capacidad de ejecución y con impacto a corto, medio y largo plazo.

Las conclusiones principales que se desprenden del trabajo son las siguientes:

1. El turismo inclusivo no es una tendencia pasajera, sino una necesidad estructural en una sociedad cada vez más diversa.
2. Es posible diseñar modelos híbridos que combinen sostenibilidad económica con impacto social sin comprometer la calidad.
3. Las zonas rurales tienen un enorme potencial para ofrecer experiencias accesibles, siempre que se apueste por la rehabilitación, la innovación social y la colaboración entre actores.

4. El enfoque de accesibilidad universal no debe limitarse al diseño arquitectónico, sino abarcar también la comunicación, la atención, la tecnología y la participación de los usuarios.

El proyecto CASA CANSAT no solo persigue llenar un vacío en la oferta turística, sino que aspira a redefinir el concepto mismo de hospitalidad: un turismo que pone a las personas en el centro, que respeta el territorio y que actúa como palanca de transformación social. Su implementación abre una puerta hacia un turismo más justo, más humano y verdaderamente para todos y todas.

9. REFERENCIAS

Any 2023. (2023). Departament de Drets Socials i Inclusió. Recuperat el 4 de setembre de 2024, de https://dretssocials.gencat.cat/ca/ambits_tematics/persones_amb_discapacitat/estadistiquesdiscapacitat/2023/

ApS. (n.d.). Universitat de Lleida. Recuperat el 4 de setembre de 2024, de https://udl.cat/ca/serveis/ODEC/aps/

Askalidis, G., & Malthouse, E. C. (2016). The value of online customer reviews. En *Proceedings of the 10th ACM Conference on Recommender Systems.* ACM. https://doi.org/10.1145/2959100.2959181

Càtedra de Turisme d'Interior i de Muntanya de la Universitat de Lleida i la Diputació de Lleida. (2023). *Informe sobre el turisme rural a la demarcació de Lleida 2002–2022.* Recuperado de https://observatorituristic.aralleida.cat/ftp/documents/Estudis_i_Analisis/Flash%20informatiu%20026%20Informe%20de%20turisme%20rural%20sobre%20la%20demarcaci%C3%B3%20de%20Lleida%202002-2022.pdf

Càtedra de Turisme d'Interior i de Muntanya de la Universitat de Lleida i la Diputació de Lleida. (2023). *Informe sobre la superació de la COVID-19 pel sector turístic de la demarcació de Lleida.* Recuperado de https://observatorituristic.aralleida.cat/ftp/documents/Estudis_i_Analisis/Informe%20sobre%20la%20superaci%C3%B3%20de%20la%20COVID-19%20pel%20sector%20tur%C3%ADstic%20de%20la%20demarcaci%C3%B3%20de%20Lleida%20(maig%202023).pdf

Càtedra de Turisme Interior i de Muntanya de la Universitat de Lleida i la Diputació de Lleida. (2024). *Canvi climàtic, paisatge i turisme: impactes i reptes a la demarcació de Lleida.* Recuperado de https://observatorituristic.aralleida.cat/ftp/documents/Estudis_i_Analisis/Informe%20Canvi%20Clim%C3%A0tic,%20Paisatge%20i%20Turisme.pdf

Caldwell, B., Cooper, M., Reid, L. G., & Vanderheiden, G. (2008). *Web Content Accessibility Guidelines (WCAG) 2.0.* Recuperado el 4 de septiembre de 2024, de https://www.w3.org/TR/WCAG21/

Castro, R. M. (2021). SEO on page: Qué es y cómo hacerlo. *Semrush Blog.* Recuperado el 4 de septiembre de 2024, de https://es.semrush.com/blog/guia-de-seo-on-page/

COCEMFE. (2024). *Programa de vacaciones febrero-noviembre 2024.* Recuperado de https://www.cocemfe.es/wp-content/uploads/2023/12/vacaciones-cocemfe-2024-folleto.pdf

DECRET 159/2012, de 20 de novembre, d'establiments d'allotjament turístic i d'habitatges d'ús turístic. (2012). *Portal Jurídic de Catalunya.* Recuperado de https://portaljuridic.gencat.cat/eli/es-ct/d/2012/11/20/159#1398552

DECRET 75/2020, de 4 d'agost, de turisme de Catalunya. (2020). *Portal Jurídic de Catalunya.* Recuperado de https://portaljuridic.gencat.cat/ca/document-del-pjur/?documentId=879876

DECRET LLEI 3/2023, de 7 de novembre, de mesures urgents sobre el règim urbanístic dels habitatges d'ús turístic. (2023). *Portal Jurídic de Catalunya.* Recuperado de https://portaljuridic.gencat.cat/eli/es-ct/dl/2023/11/07/3

de la Serna, J. B. (2018). SEO para imágenes o contenido multimedia. *Semrush Blog.* Recuperado el 4 de septiembre de 2024, de https://es.semrush.com/blog/seo-para-imagenes-contenido-multimedia/

FEM. (2024). Llancen un programa de vacances per a persones amb discapacitat física. *Fundación Esclerosis Múltiple.* Recuperado el 4 de septiembre de 2024, de https://www.fem.es/llancen-un-programa-de-vacances-per-a-persones-amb-discapacitat-fisica/

Gencat.cat. (n.d.). Som 8 milions. Recuperat el 4 de setembre de 2024, de https://web.gencat.cat/ca/actualitat/detall/Som-8-milions

GLOBALLEIDA. (2020). *Cuaderno del emprendedor: Guía para la elaboración del plan de empresa.* Recuperado de https://ceeilleida.com/wp-content/uploads/Quadern_Emprenedor_18_tahoma10CASTELLANO_compressed.pdf

Gobierno de España. Ministerio de Sanidad. (n.d.). *Indicadores clave: Sistema Nacional de Salud.* Recuperado el 4 de septiembre de 2024, de https://inclasns.sanidad.gob.es/report/population/

INE-Instituto Nacional de Estadística. (2024). *Contabilidad Nacional Trimestral de España.* Recuperado el 4 de septiembre de 2024, de https://www.ine.es/dyngs/Prensa/avCNTR4T23.htm

INE-Instituto Nacional de Estadística. (2024). *Encuesta de ocupación en alojamientos turísticos extrahoteleros.* Recuperado el 4 de septiembre de 2024, de https://www.ine.es/dyngs/Prensa/EOAT1223.htm

Institut Obert de Catalunya. (n.d.). *Disseny d'interfícies web.* Recuperat el 4 de setembre de 2024, de https://ioc.xtec.cat/materials/FP/Recursos/fp_daw_m09_/web/fp_daw_m09_htmlindex/WebContent/u5/a1/continguts.html

Introducción a los archivos robots.txt. (n.d.). *Google for Developers.* Recuperado el 4 de septiembre, de https://developers.google.com/search/docs/crawling-indexing/robots/intro?hl=es

Larreina, I. A. (2005). Posicionamiento en buscadores: una metodología práctica de optimización de sitios web. *El Profesional de la Información, 14*(2), 108–124. https://doi.org/10.3145/epi.2005.mar.03

LLEI 13/2002, de 21 de juny, de turisme de Catalunya. (2002). *Portal Jurídic de Catalunya.* Recuperado de https://portaljuridic.gencat.cat/ca/document-del-pjur/?documentId=288384#1068236

Lodgify.com. (n.d.). *Las 16 mejores plataformas para anunciar tu alquiler vacacional.* Recuperado el 4 de septiembre de 2024, de https://www.lodgify.com/blog/es/anunciar-alquiler-vacacional/

Monclús, J. R. A. (n.d.). Presentación de datos del turismo rural en Cataluña 2022. *Web Grup CETT.* Recuperado el 4 de septiembre, de https://www.cett.es/es/turismo-rural-cataluna-2022

Monmany, J. (2024). Observatorio del Turismo Rural: situación, tendencias y oportunidades. *EscapadaRural Magazine.* Recuperado el 4 de septiembre de 2024, de https://www.escapadarural.com/blog/observatorio-del-turismo-rural-2023-2024/

Monmany, J. (2024). Tendencias y oportunidades para el turismo rural en Cataluña en 2024. *EscapadaRural Magazine.* Recuperado el 4 de septiembre de 2024, de https://www.escapadarural.com/blog/datos-del-turismo-rural-catalunya-2024/

Moreno, M. (2011). *Plan de empresa: guía para emprender.* Ediciones Pirámide.

OCDE. (2021). *Perspectivas del turismo 2021.* Organización para la Cooperación y el Desarrollo Económicos. https://www.oecd.org/cfe/tourism/oecd-tourism-trends-and-policies-20767773.htm

Organización Mundial de la Salud (OMS). (2001). *Clasificación Internacional del Funcionamiento, de la Discapacidad y de la Salud (CIF).* https://iris.who.int/handle/10665/42407

PARES-Portal de Archivos Españoles. (s. f.). *Ley de Integración Social de los Minusválidos (LISMI), 1982.* Recuperado el 4 de septiembre de 2024, de http://pares.mcu.es/ParesBusquedas20/catalogo/description/16034

Pine, B. J., & Gilmore, J. H. (1999). *The experience economy: Work is theatre & every business a stage.* Harvard Business Press.

Pujol, T. (2020). *Diseño gráfico y comunicación visual: fundamentos, aplicaciones y desarrollos.* Ediciones UOC.

Statista Research Department. (2023). *Ingresos por turismo accesible en Europa 2018-2023.* Recuperado el 4 de septiembre de 2024, de https://es.statista.com/estadisticas/1017159/ingresos-por-turismo-accesible-en-europa/

Turisme de Catalunya. (2023). *Informe de tendències turístiques 2023.* Agència Catalana de Turisme. https://act.gencat.cat/informes-i-estudis/

UNWTO-Organización Mundial del Turismo. (2023). *Tourism for Inclusive Growth.* https://www.unwto.org/tourism-for-inclusive-growth

Yotpo. (n.d.). *Qué es una reseña de cliente.* Recuperado el 4 de septiembre de 2024, de https://www.yotpo.com/resources/customer-review-definition/

EU-FUNDED TOURISM PROJECTS FOR A GREEN TRANSITION: THE CASE OF TOURISM SUSTAINABILITY PLANS AT DESTINATIONS (PSTD) IN SPAIN

Isabel Torres
Universitat Politècnica de València
Universidad Europea de València

María-Dolores Teruel-Serrano
María José Viñals
Universitat Politècnica de València

THEME: Sustainability

ABSTRACT: Tourism is a key sector in the European economy, yet EU tourism policy remains weakly integrated into broader sustainability and cohesion frameworks. This paper analyses Spain's Tourism Sustainability Plans in Destinations (PSTD), funded under the Recovery and Resilience Facility (RRF) of Next Generation EU. Of the €140 billion in EU-backed investment allocated to Spain, €1.86 billion has supported PSTD implementation in over 400 destinations. Using a combination of policy and literature review and a systematic analysis of 540 funded interventions between 2021 and 2023, the study assesses whether the PSTD contribute to a green and sustainable tourism transition. Results show a strong focus on infrastructure and energy efficiency, but limited incorporation of climate action, circular economy, or governance innovation. The paper concludes that while PSTDs represent a major financial commitment, their transformative potential remains constrained. Greater policy coherence and stronger evaluation frameworks are needed to align these initiatives with the European Agenda for Tourism 2030 and long-term sustainability goals.

Keywords: EU tourism policy, sustainable tourism, green transition, Spain, Plan Sostenibilidad Turística en Destino (PSTD)

RESUMEN: El turismo es un sector clave en la economía europea, pero la política turística de la Unión Europea sigue estando débilmente integrada en los marcos más amplios de sostenibilidad y cohesión. Este artículo analiza los Planes de Sostenibilidad Turística en Destinos (PSTD) de España, financiados a través del Mecanismo de Recuperación y Resiliencia (MRR) del programa Next Generation EU. De los 140.000 millones de euros en inversión pública respaldada por la UE asignados a España, 1.860 millones se han destinado a la implementación de PSTD en más de 400 destinos. Mediante una revisión de políticas y literatura especializada, junto con un análisis sistemático de 540 intervenciones financiadas entre 2021 y 2023, el estudio evalúa si los PSTD contribuyen a una transición turística verde y sostenible. Los resultados muestran un fuerte enfoque en infraestructura y eficiencia energética, pero una integración limitada de la acción climática, la economía circular o la innovación en gobernanza. El artículo concluye que, si bien los PSTD representan un importante compromiso financiero, su potencial transformador sigue siendo limitado. Para alinear estas iniciativas con la Agenda Europea de Turismo 2030 y los objetivos de sostenibilidad a largo plazo, se requiere una mayor coherencia política y marcos de evaluación más sólidos.

Palabras clave: Política turística europea, turismo sostenible, transición verde, España, Plan de Sostenibilidad Turística en Destino (PSTD)

1. INTRODUCTION

Europe remains the world's leading tourist destination, welcoming over 747 million international arrivals in 2024 – 1% above pre-pandemic levels (UN Tourism, 2025). Prior to the COVID-19 pandemic, tourism contributed approximately 10% to the EU's GDP and supported over 23 million jobs (WTTC, 2023). As such, the European Union (EU) has increasingly sought to maintain its global leadership while transforming the sector into a more sustainable, resilient, and inclusive one (European Commission, 2010, 2022).

However, despite the sector's importance, tourism policy at the EU level has historically evolved very slowly, lacking institutional power (Estol & Font, 2016; Torres et al., 2025). The COVID-19 pandemic catalysed unprecedented public investment, notably through the Recovery and Resilience Facility (RRF), which offered a window of opportunity to accelerate the transition towards more sustainable tourism models. Spain, one of the top recipients of RRF funding, launched the Tourism Sustainability Plans at Destinations (PSTD) as a flagship initiative to support modernisation, smart destination development, and green transition.

This paper investigates to what extent these plans reflect the EU's stated ambitions for a green transition in tourism. It introduces the theoretical evolution of EU tourism policy, analyses the nature and distribution of PSTD funding, and assesses the degree to which supported interventions align with sustainability objectives. In doing so, it contributes to current debates on the role of EU funding in delivering place-based and environmentally responsible tourism futures.

2. THEORETICAL FRAMEWORK

The trajectory of EU tourism policy has been marked by incremental recognition rather than structural consolidation. Initial communications from the 1980s were followed by the Treaty of Lisbon (2007) which for the first time formally acknowledged the EU's role in promoting tourism. Yet, as scholars argue, this formalisation has not translated into substantial influence or budgetary power (Anastasiadou, 2011). Tourism remains an area of shared competence, with limited authority delegated to EU institutions.

The policy framework has evolved through strategic documents emphasising competitiveness, sustainability, and digitalisation. Estol & Font (2016) note that the sector's positioning within the EU has been increasingly shaped by broader goals of market integration and sustainable development. The European Commission has sought to address this gap through strategic guidance documents and by embedding tourism within broader agendas of cohesion, sustainability, and resilience. A significant turning point came with the publication of the Transition Pathway for Tourism (European Commission, 2022), which outlined a collaborative roadmap for the green and digital transformation of the sector. The pathway encourages voluntary commitments and action from Member States and stakeholders, supported by initiatives such as the European Agenda for Tourism 2030, which further outlines priorities around resilience, innovation, and cohesion. While a new EU Sustainable Tourism Strategy is currently being developed, stronger efforts and more coherent and holistic approaches are needed to achieve enhanced policy enforcement (Torres et al., 2025).

The green transition in tourism is increasingly understood as part of a broader "twin transition" that also includes digital innovation. Jones (2023) emphasises that the EU's Transition Pathway for Tourism promotes a systemic shift toward climate neutrality, circularity, and sustainable mobility, underpinned by stakeholder pledges and public funding. However, evidence suggests that digitalisation alone may increase emissions unless paired with strong environmental technologies. Bianchini et al. (2023) find that while green research and development reduces emissions, digital technologies can raise them, unless integrated with robust environmental strategies. This highlights the need for coordinated green and digital investments in tourism. At the same time, the EU has activated a series of financial instruments to support this transition, including extensions to traditional structural funds, such as *Recovery assistance for cohesion and the territories of Europe* (REACT-EU), and temporary mechanisms such as the *Recovery and Resilience Facility* (RRF) and *Support to mitigate Unemployment Risks in an Emergency* (SURE) (Kiss-Gálfalvi et al., 2024).

Among EU member states, Spain has adopted these narratives while designing its post-pandemic tourism recovery. The PSTD, financed via the Next Generation EU (NGEU) mechanism, represents an attempt to operationalise sustainability in tourism through decentralised action. However, Spain's recovery approach has privileged economic reactivation over environmental and social transformation, echoing pre-existing growth paradigms (Capdepón Frías, 2023). Similarly, evaluations of previous EU-funded tourism programmes have flagged significant shortcomings in planning, needs assessment, and impact tracking (European Court of Auditors, 2021).

Spain, one of the main beneficiaries of EU recovery funds, has long faced the challenges of mass tourism and seasonal overconcentration. The Spanish tourism model, rooted in rapid coastal development in the second half of the nineteenth century, has led to environmental degradation, infrastructural pressure, and socio-economic imbalances. Planning efforts since the 1990s have attempted to diversify tourism offerings and introduce sustainability principles through national strategies such as Plan Horizonte 2020 and the Plan Nacional e Integral de Turismo (2012-2015), yet implementation has often been fragmented or short-lived (Ivars Baidal, 2014; López Palomeque et al., 2022).

With the adoption of the Plan de Recuperación, Transformación y Resiliencia ("España Puede"), Spain committed to accelerating its tourism transition through the Plan de Modernización y Competitividad del sector turístico. This includes the expansion of the Planes de Sostenibilidad Turística en Destinos (PSTD), co-financed by the RRF. These plans aim to empower regional and local authorities to implement projects across four strategic axes: green transition, energy efficiency, digitalisation, and competitiveness (Gobierno de España, 2021).

Initial results have been mixed. While the PSTD initiative has succeeded in mobilising significant resources —over €1.8 billion between 2021 and 2023— and activating over 500 projects nationwide, it is unclear the impact and alignment with tourism sustainability policies. Recent research highlights several structural limitations in the implementation of the Planes de Sostenibilidad Turística en Destino (PSTD), particularly regarding territorial coherence and planning integration (Capdepón Frías et al., 2024). For instance, the implementation of PSTDs within natural protected areas has been marked by fragmentation and territorial imbalance, fostering the continuation of growth-oriented logics within sensitive ecosystems, instead of integrated management approaches that reconcile conservation objectives with tourism development limitations (Capdepón Frías, 2023). While these plans have enabled significant funding mobilisation, their application in some regions has led to overlaps, fragmented strategies, or support for locations with questionable suitability as tourism destinations. Garzón García & Ramírez López (2025) observe that in Andalusia, multiple PSTD were approved for small municipalities with limited tourism capacity or for areas already covered by other plans, contributing to incoherence and administrative inefficiency. Furthermore, the content of many PSTD remains publicly inaccessible, limiting transparency and hindering critical evaluation of their strategic orientation.

The literature consistently points to a gap between strategic discourse and implementation. Scholars have warned of the risk of path dependency, where investments reproduce established patterns rather than catalysing change (Ivars Baidal, 2014; López Palomeque et al., 2022). Despite the narrative of sustainability, tourism planning in Spain remains deeply conditioned by economic recovery imperatives and local absorptive capacity, echoing broader concerns identified at the EU level regarding the dilution of cohesion policy's long-term objectives in the face of successive crises (Kiss-Gálfalvi et al., 2024). This paper builds on these insights to interrogate whether the PSTD signify a substantive shift towards sustainability, or whether they reflect a continuation of infrastructuralist, growth-driven approaches covered in green rhetoric.

3. METHODOLOGY

This study employed a mixed-methods approach combining a literature review with a systematic analysis of publicly available data on the implementation of the Tourism Sustainability Plans in Destinations (Planes de Sostenibilidad Turística en Destinos, PSTD) in Spain from 2021 to 2023.

Three main sources were used: i) Official calls and results from the Spanish Ministry of Industry, Trade and Tourism for the PSTD (2021, 2022, 2023), identifying 540 interventions with €1.808 billion allocated; ii) The complete funding and intervention dataset for the Comunitat Valenciana (CV), obtained from Turisme Comunitat Valenciana, including 122 individual actions within 21 interventions; and iii) The territorial PSTD strategy for CV (2022), which provided a regional case to analyse priorities, implementation choices, and typologies of funded actions.

All interventions were categorised according to the four strategic axes defined by the national PSTD framework: 1) Green and sustainable transition, 2) Energy efficiency, 3) Digital transition and 4) Competitiveness. Special emphasis was placed on analysing axis 1 and 2 (green transition and energy efficiency), to assess whether systemic sustainability principles, such as circular economy, climate change adaptation, or low-carbon mobility; were integrated into project design. A categorisation system was developed to group actions by type of investment (e.g., infrastructure, services, planning tools) and by thematic area (e.g., solid waste, renewable energy, mobility). Descriptive statistics and comparative analysis were used to assess funding distribution over time, by region, and by intervention type. The results were interpreted in relation to national tourism priorities, and the EU's green transition objectives.

4. RESULTS

4.1 National funding allocation

Between 2021 and 2023, the Spanish government allocated a total of €1.808 billion to 540 PSTD interventions across the country (Figure 1). The annual distribution of funds was relatively balanced, with slight increases year-on-year and a decrease in the last call in 2023. Interventions were implemented across a diversity of destination types, including rural areas, coastal towns, natural areas, and urban tourism zones.

Figure 1. EU Funding for Tourism Sustainability Plans at Destinations in Spain and Number of funded interventions (2021-2023)

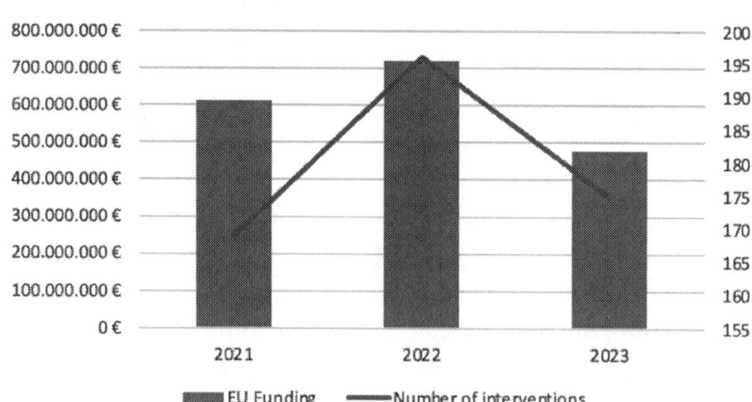

Source: own elaboration with data from the Ministry of Industry, Trade and Tourism (2023)

The five regions with the highest tourism arrivals in 2023 —Cataluña, Illes Balears, Islas Canarias, Andalucía, and Comunitat Valenciana— also received the largest shares of funding. For example, Cataluña, with 18.2 million tourist arrivals in 2023 (INE, 2024), received over €200 million during the three-year period, while Andalucía with 12.2 million tourist arrivals also received a similar amount (Figure 2).

Figure 2. Total funding for PSTD by region and year

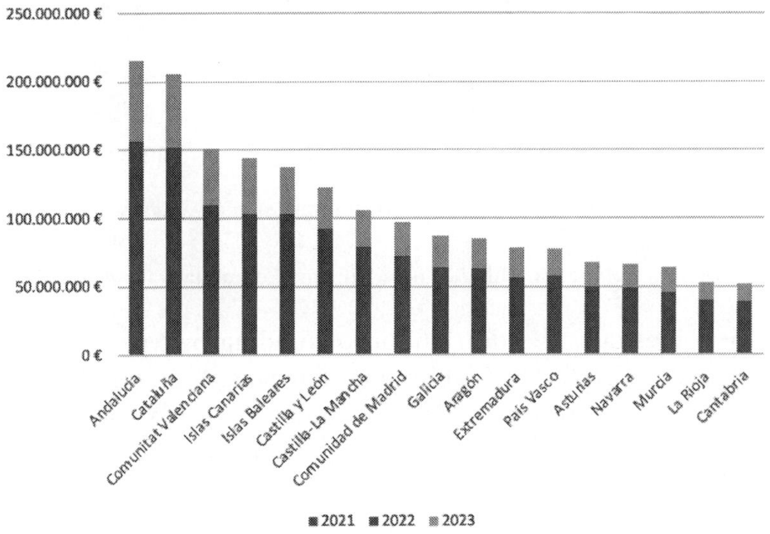

Source: own elaboration with data from the Ministry of Industry, Trade and Tourism (2023)

4.2. Focus on Comunitat Valenciana

A more detailed analysis was conducted for the Comunitat Valenciana, which received over €151 million through 55 interventions between 2021 and 2023. Within the 2022 programme alone, €31.3 million —equivalent to 52% of the total budget— was allocated to actions under axes 1 and 2 (Figure 3).

Figure 3. EU Funding for PSTD in Comunitat Valenciana and Number of funded interventions (2021-2023)

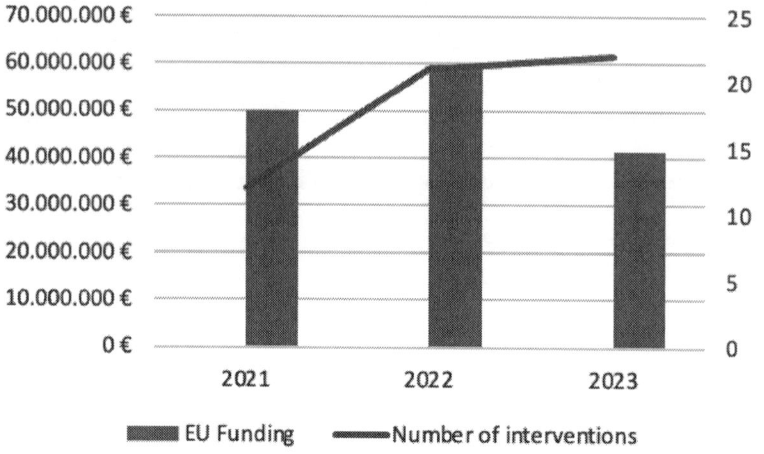

Source: own elaboration with data from Turisme Comunitat Valenciana (2023)

Figure 4 illustrates the distribution of funding by type of intervention within the 2022 PSTD for the Comunitat Valenciana. A total of €31.3 million—representing 52% of the overall PSTD budget for that year—was allocated to 122 individual actions implemented across 21 different plans. The funding was heavily concentrated in infrastructure and environmental improvement projects. The largest share was directed toward energy efficiency upgrades, particularly in lighting and equipment, which accounted for approximately 16% of the total allocation. This was matched by investments in public use infrastructure and tourism service facilities, also at 16%. Environmental restoration initiatives, such as landscape rehabilitation, received 14% of the funds, while cycling infrastructure projects made up a further 12%. By contrast, less emphasis was placed on systemic sustainability tools, such as solid waste management, circular economy practices, and fire prevention, which received minimal investment. Notably, only three destinations incorporated climate action or circular economy frameworks into their plans. This distribution reflects a continued prioritisation of visible, short-term infrastructure over long-term transformational strategies.

Figure 4. Funding by type of intervention (PTSD CV 2022)

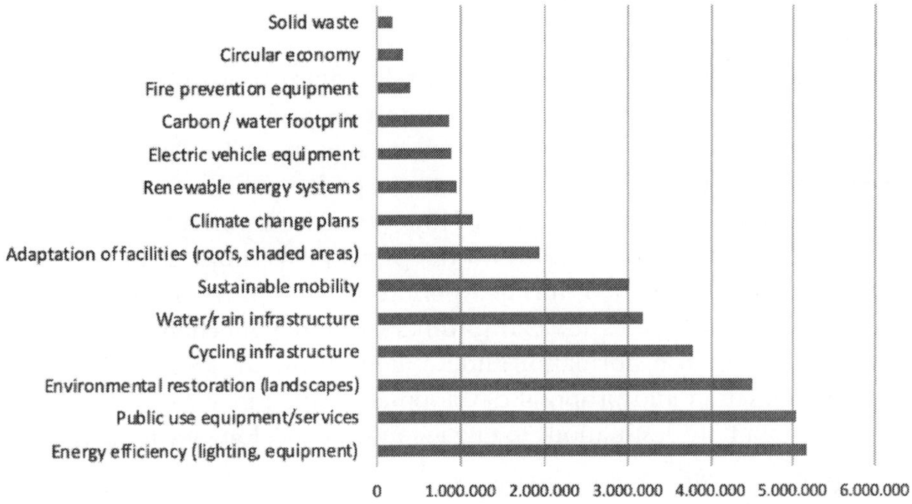

Source: own elaboration with data from Turisme Comunitat Valenciana (2023)

5. DISCUSSION

The analysis of the 2022 Tourism Sustainability Plans in Destinations in the Comunitat Valenciana reveals a series of important patterns and limitations in both the design and the execution of the programme. The 122 actions funded that year were, according to the original plans, predominantly oriented toward infrastructure-based investments that could be implemented within short timeframes and produce visible, quantifiable outputs. These included energy efficiency upgrades (such as lighting and equipment), construction of cycling paths, improvements to public use facilities, and environmental restoration efforts. Such measures are politically attractive, relatively low-risk, and facilitate straightforward compliance with funding and reporting requirements.

By contrast, more complex interventions, such as climate vulnerability assessments, stakeholder engagement processes, circular economy strategies, or governance innovation; were largely absent from the submitted plans. Their limited inclusion suggests a structural bias in the programme towards short-term, deliverable actions, possibly shaped by limitations in local planning capacity or by the technical structure of the call itself. This observation resonates with critiques in the literature that point to a gap between sustainability narratives and their actual implementation on the ground (Capdepón Frías, 2023).

The diversity of interventions across municipalities also points to considerable variation in how different localities approached the PSTD framework. Some opted for a broader interpretation of sustainability, while others focused narrowly on physical infrastructure upgrades. This unevenness likely reflects differences in administrative capacity, political leadership, and existing institutional arrangements. However, it is important to emphasise that these observations are based on the initial plans submitted in response to a national call launched during a period of acute pressure caused by the COVID-19 pandemic. As an extraordinary funding mechanism linked to Spain's Recovery, Transformation and Resilience Plan, the PSTD call required rapid mobilisation and proposal development, which may have constrained the ability of many destinations to engage in strategic, long-term planning.

Given this context, further research is necessary to assess the actual implementation and impact of the PSTD interventions. It remains unclear to what extent the original measures were executed as planned, or whether they were modified during the course of delivery in response to evolving local priorities, technical challenges, or administrative requirements. In addition, the specific content of the plans is not always publicly available, hindering its analysis (Garzón García & Ramírez López, 2025). A systematic evaluation of the final projects, beyond their initial design, will be essential to understand whether these plans have contributed meaningfully to the goals of sustainability, resilience, and territorial equity. Such an evaluation would also shed light on whether the PSTD initiative has fulfilled its potential as a transformative policy instrument, or whether it has largely reproduced pre-existing development patterns under the banner of sustainability.

Moreover, these findings echo concerns raised by the European Court of Auditors (2021, 2022), Kiss-Gálfalvi et al. (2024) and Valente & Uršič (2025) regarding the limitations of performance tracking and monitoring systems within EU crisis-response funding instruments. The voluntary nature of performance indicators, the lack of harmonised frameworks, and the urgency of fund disbursement have often undermined transparency and accountability. In the case of the PSTD, the absence of robust evaluation mechanisms means that assessing long-term sustainability outcomes remains an open challenge.

In summary, while the PSTD programme has enabled the mobilisation of substantial resources and has offered municipalities a platform for recovery-focused tourism investment, its potential as a tool for systemic transition appears limited. To bridge the gap between discourse and delivery, future calls must prioritise governance capacity, systemic planning, and evaluation practices capable of aligning short-term recovery with long-term transformation.

6. CONCLUSIONS

This paper has examined the contribution of EU-funded tourism programmes to advancing a green and sustainable transition, with a particular focus on Spain's Tourism Sustainability Plans in Destinations (PSTD) under the Recovery and Resilience Facility (RRF). Based on a mixed-methods analysis of policy frameworks and intervention data, the study shows that while the PSTD represent a significant mobilisation of resources—totalling €1.808 billion between 2021 and 2023—the nature of funded actions remains largely conventional. The emphasis continues to fall on infrastructure investments, particularly energy efficiency and public amenities, with limited integration of more transformative approaches such as circular economy strategies, climate adaptation planning, or mechanisms for community empowerment.

These findings highlight a persistent gap between the EU's evolving policy discourse, notably the European Agenda for Tourism 2030 and the Transition Pathway for Tourism, and the way these ambitions are operationalised at national and regional levels. Despite growing recognition of the need for a sustainability-driven tourism transition, implementation remains uneven, and governance systems often lack the capacity or incentives to move beyond traditional project formats.

Addressing these challenges will require the reinforcement of sustainability governance across multiple dimensions. In particular, improved monitoring frameworks, more inclusive and participatory planning processes, and stronger policy coherence between levels of government are essential. Unlocking the transformative potential of EU-funded tourism interventions demands not only financial investment but also institutional alignment, robust evaluative tools, and support for place-based innovation tailored to local needs and ecological contexts.

The analysis presented in this paper offers several policy-relevant recommendations:

- Strengthen alignment between EU-level policy objectives and national implementation mechanisms to ensure consistency and ambition.
- Establish standardised, outcome-oriented evaluation criteria to measure the sustainability impact of tourism investments.

- Promote planning frameworks that support localised, participatory, and adaptive approaches to tourism development.
- Ensure equitable access to funding and technical support, particularly for territories with weaker institutional capacity or emerging tourism potential.

Future research should prioritise the longitudinal tracking of PSTD implementation outcomes, including changes introduced during project delivery, and the extent to which these initiatives generate measurable progress toward decarbonisation, territorial cohesion, and social equity. More broadly, there is a pressing need to critically assess the institutional and political conditions that enable, or constrain, the systemic transformation of tourism through EU recovery instruments.

7. REFERENCES

Anastasiadou, C. (2011). Promoting sustainability from above: reflections on the influence of the European Union on tourism governance. *Policy Quarterly*, 7(4), 27–33. https://doi.org/10.26686/pq.v7i4.4403

Bianchini, S., Damioli, G., & Ghisetti, C. (2023). The environmental effects of the "twin" green and digital transition in European regions. *Environmental and Resource Economics, 84*(4), 877–918. https://doi.org/10.1007/s10640-022-00741-7

Capdepón Frías, M. (2023). El turismo de naturaleza en España: de las políticas de recuperación post-pandemia a la propuesta de alternativas. *Boletín de La Asociación de Geógrafos Españoles, 99*. https://doi.org/10.21138/bage.3444

Capdepón Frías, M., Durá Alemañ, C. J., & Vera Rebollo, J. F. (2024). Análisis de relaciones entre planes de sostenibilidad turística en destinos y áreas naturales protegidas en España. In A. Ferrandis Martínez, C. Zornoza Gallego, & J. V. Sánchez Cabrera (Eds.), *Repensando los destinos turísticos en tiempos de cambio global* (pp. 139–156).

Estol, J., & Font, X. (2016). European tourism policy: Its evolution and structure. *Tourism Management, 52*, 230–241. https://doi.org/10.1016/j.tourman.2015.06.007

European Commission. (2010). *COM(2010) 352 final – Europe, the world's No 1 tourist destination – a new political framework for tourism in Europe.*

European Commission. (2022). *Transition Pathway for Tourism.* https://data.europa.eu/doi/10.2873/344425

European Court of Auditors. (2021). *EU Support to tourism. Need for a fresh strategic orientation and a better funding approach. Special Report.* https://www.eca.europa.eu/Lists/ECADocuments/SR21_27/SR_EU-invest-tourism_EN.pdf

European Court of Auditors. (2022). *The Commission's assessment of national recovery and resilience plans. Special report.* https://www.eca.europa.eu/Lists/ECADocuments/SR22_21/SR_NRRPs_EN.pdf

Garzón García, R., & Ramírez López, M. L. (2025). Tourism Management and Planning: evolution and challenges based on the case of Andalusia (Spain). *Cuadernos Geograficos, 64*(1), 173–197. https://doi.org/10.30827/cuadgeo.v64i1.30633

Gobierno de España. (2021). *Plan de Recuperación, Transformación y Resiliencia.* https://www.lamoncloa.gob.es/temas/fondos-recuperacion/Documents/160621-Plan_Recuperacion_Transformacion_Resiliencia.pdf

INE. (2024). *Estadística de Movimientos Turísticos en Fronteras (FRONTUR).* https://Www.Ine.Es/Dyngs/INEbase/Es/Operacion.Htm?C=Estadistica_C&cid=1254736176996&menu=ultiDatos&idp=1254735576863.

Ivars Baidal, J. A. (2014). Spain: From the Mass Model to a New Tourism Economy. In D. Buhalis, C. Costa, & E. Panyik (Eds.), *European Tourism Planning and Organisation Systems: The EU Member States* (pp. 384–398). Channel View Publications. https://doi.org/10.21832/9781845414344

Jones, P. (2023). Towards a Green and Digital Transition for European Tourism. *Athens Journal of Tourism, 10*(4), 281–294. https://doi.org/10.30958/ajt.10-4-3

Kiss-Gálfalvi, T., Alcidi, C., Ounnas, A., Rubio, E., Crichton-Miller, H., & Gogsic, D. (2024). *Lessons learned from the implementation of crisis response tools at EU level – Part 1: Assessing implementation and implications.* https://www.europarl.europa.eu/RegData/etudes/STUD/2024/760343/IPOL_STU(2024)760343_EN.pdf

López Palomeque, F., Vera Rebollo, J. F., Torres Delgado, A., & Ivars Baidal, J. A. (2022). *El turismo, ¿fin de época? Desafíos de España como destino turístico en un nuevo escenario.* Publicacions de la Universitat de València. https://doi.org/http://dx.doi.org/10.7203/PUV-OA-863-4

Torres, I., Teruel-Serrano, M. D., & Viñals, M. J. (2025). Tourism policy in the European Union: progress, challenges and prospects. *Journal of Policy Research in Tourism, Leisure and Events.* https://doi.org/10.1080/19407963.2025.2527652

Treaty of Lisbon Amending the Treaty on European Union and the Treaty Establishing the European Community Signed on 13 December 2007, Office for Official Publications of the European Communities (2007).

UN Tourism. (2025, January 25). *International tourism recovers pre-pandemic levels in 2024.* https://www.unwto.org/news/international-tourism-recovers-pre-pandemic-levels-in-2024

Valente, B., & Uršič, E. D. (2025). An Ex Ante Approach to the Resilience and Recovery Plan's Impacts on Sustainable Tourism in Algarve and Alentejo. *Tourism and Hospitality, 6*(1). https://doi.org/10.3390/tourhosp6010038

BLOQUE 2

TECNOLOGÍA, DIGITALIZACIÓN Y EXPERIENCIA DEL TURISTA

ONTOLOGÍAS DEL TURISMO COMO HERRAMIENTA PARA LA GESTIÓN INTELIGENTE Y SOSTENIBLE DE DESTINOS

Ouafae Abdelouahab Reddam
Hanae Abdelouahab Reddam
Universidad Abdelmalek Essaadi

Obdulia Monteserín Abella
Universitat Jaume I

TEMÁTICA: Innovación / Tecnologías emergentes (IoT, big data, inteligencia artificial) para la gestión de los destinos turísticos

RESUMEN: la comunicación analiza de forma descriptiva cómo las ontologías y tecnologías emergentes (IA, *big data*, Web semántica) pueden contribuyen a la gestión eficiente y ágil del destino. Las ontologías organizan datos dinámicos de distinta naturaleza (oferta, accesibilidad, clima, etc.) en un marco estructurado, facilitando la interoperabilidad entre sistemas y permitiendo una gestión más inteligente y sostenible de destinos. España destaca con proyectos como ontologías para rutas naturales y modelos de Destinos Turísticos Inteligentes (DTI). A nivel global, ejemplos como EGYTOUR en Egipto y OTMV2 en Marruecos muestran aplicaciones prácticas. Los inventarios dinámicos actualizan información en tiempo real para optimizar la experiencia del turista y la planificación estratégica. Aunque persisten retos como la brecha digital y la estandarización de datos, el futuro apunta a una mayor integración con IA para personalizar servicios y mejorar la adaptación del sector.

Palabras clave: web semántica; inventario turístico; ontología turística; destinos inteligentes.

ABSTRACT: communication analyses descriptively how ontologies and emerging technologies (AI, big data, semantic web) can contribute to efficient and agile destination management. Ontologies organise dynamic data of different nature (supply, accessibility, climate, etc.) in a structured framework, facilitating interoperability between systems and enabling smarter and more sustainable destination management. Spain stands out with projects such as ontologies for nature routes and Smart Tourism Destination (ITD) models. Globally, examples such as EGYTOUR in Egypt and OTMV2 in Morocco show practical applications. Dynamic inventories update information in real time to optimise tourist experience and strategic planning. While challenges such as digital divide and data standardisation remain, the future points to further integration with AI to personalise services and improve industry customization.

Keywords: semantic web; tourism inventory; tourism ontology; smart destinations.

1. INTRODUCCIÓN

En los últimos años, las tecnologías semánticas han experimentado un desarrollo acelerado, impulsado por avances en inteligencia artificial, procesamiento del lenguaje natural y web semántica. Estas tecnologías han mejorado significativamente la capacidad de estructurar, organizar y recuperar información de manera más eficiente y contextualizada. Gracias a enfoques como la ontología, el *machine learning* y los gráficos de conocimiento, los sistemas digitales pueden interpretar y relacionar datos con mayor precisión, facilitando aplicaciones en sectores como el turismo, la sostenibilidad y la digitalización (Butowski & Butowski, 2023; Zhang et al., 2023). Este progreso ha permitido la creación de plataformas más inteligentes y adaptativas, capaces de ofrecer respuestas más relevantes y mejorar la toma de decisiones en distintos ámbitos.

La web semántica es una tecnología clave en la evolución digital, diseñada para convertir la web en un entorno accesible tanto para humanos como para máquinas. Su objetivo es optimizar la interpretación automática del contenido, permitiendo que los sistemas digitales comprendan y procesen la información de manera más eficiente (Tatane et al., 2024).

En este contexto, los modelos de datos semánticos, como las ontologías y los grafos de conocimiento, han ganado popularidad en los últimos años. Las ontologías, consideradas la columna vertebral de la web semántica, proporcionan una estructura formal para representar el conocimiento, facilitando la interoperabilidad entre sistemas (SEGITTUR, 2023; Haridy et al., 2023). Según una definición ampliamente aceptada, una ontología es una “especificación explícita de una conceptualización” (Gruber, 1993).

Dado que las ontologías proporcionan contexto y significado a los datos, son esenciales para la extracción y reutilización eficiente del conocimiento (Zhang et al., 2023). Además, ofrecen una solución para los problemas de interoperabilidad sintáctica y semántica, que obstaculizan el intercambio de información eficiente y la colaboración entre sistemas heterogéneos (Haridy et al., 2023).

En el ámbito turístico, la ontología no solo ayuda a sistematizar la enorme cantidad de información tradicional y estática dispersa en Internet (como catálogos de destinos, alojamientos o patrimonios culturales), sino que también es fundamental para representar y gestionar recursos turísticos, facilitando la interoperabilidad entre sistemas y la comprensión por parte de agentes tanto humanos como automatizados (Gutiérrez Losada et al., 2008).

Esta formalización se vuelve esencial ante la multiplicidad de actores, fuentes de datos y servicios, ofreciendo un lenguaje común que favorece desde la búsqueda de información hasta la toma de decisiones estratégicas en destinos turísticos (SEGITTUR, 2023).

Estos recursos incluyen datos en tiempo real sobre condiciones meteorológicas, eventos temporales, variaciones en la oferta de servicios y respuestas de los visitantes, entre otros aspectos que evolucionan constantemente. El reto consiste en integrar información de alto volumen y heterogénea, facilitando la interoperabilidad y la toma de decisiones tanto en el ámbito comercial como en el de planificación estratégica.

2. SOSTENIBILIDAD E IMPACTO DE LA DIGITALIZACIÓN EN LA EFICIENCIA DE LOS SISTEMAS TURÍSTICOS

La transformación digital se ha consolidado como uno de los pilares estratégicos para reconfigurar el modelo turístico español en un contexto de creciente demanda y desafíos ambientales. La integración de tecnologías de la información y la comunicación (TIC) —como análisis de Big data, inteligencia artificial, Internet de las Cosas (IoT) y plataformas de geolocalización— permite optimizar la gestión de los flujos de visitantes, reducir la sobrecarga en infraestructuras y mitigar el impacto ambiental derivado de la masificación turística (Gallego Gómez & Vaquero Frías, 2022). Esta sinergia entre digitalización y sostenibilidad se fundamenta en la triple dimensión del desarrollo sostenible: ambiental, económico y social, e impulsa modelos de gestión que equilibran la eficiencia operativa con la protección del patrimonio natural y cultural (Céspedes Morai, 2024).

El despliegue de soluciones digitales ha dado origen a la figura de los Destinos Turísticos Inteligentes (DTI), en los cuales la recopilación y el análisis en tiempo real de datos permiten anticipar comportamientos y ajustar estrategias de gestión. Este enfoque, que ha adquirido relevancia tras la crisis provocada por la pandemia de COVID-19, fomenta la descentralización de la oferta turística y facilita la implementación de medidas de control ambiental, como la monitorización de la congestión y la optimización en el uso de los recursos (Boulaalama et al., 2018). La digitalización, por tanto, se erige como un catalizador para transformar la experiencia turística, generando beneficios tanto en la reducción de la huella de carbono como en la mejora de la calidad del servicio ofrecido.

Desde la perspectiva de la política pública, la estrategia de modernización del sector turístico en España ha impulsado proyectos y planes de competitividad que integran la digitalización como herramienta para alcanzar la sostenibilidad. Documentos institucionales como el Plan de Modernización y Competitividad del Sector Turístico delinean objetivos que incluyen la transformación digital de destinos y empresas turísticas, orientados a mejorar indicadores económicos y ambientales, y a potenciar la resiliencia del sector ante crisis (Céspedes Morai, 2024). Estas intervenciones demuestran cómo las inversiones en infraestructura digital y en tecnologías habilitadoras pueden contribuir a redistribuir los flujos turísticos en destinos menos saturados, generar empleo local y, en última instancia, fortalecer el tejido socioeconómico de las comunidades receptoras.

No obstante, la incorporación de tecnologías digitales también presenta desafíos que deben ser abordados para lograr una integración equitativa y eficaz. La brecha digital, especialmente en regiones rurales o en destinos con infraestructuras tecnológicas limitadas, puede obstaculizar la adopción plena de soluciones inteligentes. Además, resulta esencial desarrollar métricas e indicadores que permitan evaluar en forma integral el impacto de la digitalización en términos de sostenibilidad, considerando variables ambientales, sociales y económicas (Cholat et al., 2019). La generación de indicadores compuestos y el diseño de metodologías de seguimiento robustas emergen como líneas prioritarias para la investigación futura, que contribuirán a perfeccionar las estrategias de digitalización turística y a maximizar sus retornos en términos de eficiencia y sostenibilidad a largo plazo.

En conclusión, la convergencia de la sostenibilidad con la digitalización (Figura 1) se presenta como una estrategia innovadora y necesaria para afrontar los retos contemporáneos del sector turístico español. La integración de herramientas digitales no solo optimiza la gestión operativa y la experiencia del visitante, sino que también habilita un modelo de turismo resiliente, capaz de responder de manera dinámica a las fluctuaciones de la demanda y a la presión ambiental. Este paradigma invita a repensar el desarrollo turístico desde una perspectiva holística, en la que cada avance tecnológico se traduzca en beneficios medibles para la sociedad y el medio ambiente, sentando las bases de un crecimiento equilibrado y sustentable (Gallego Gómez & Vaquero Frías, 2022).

Figura 1. Gestión inteligente de datos

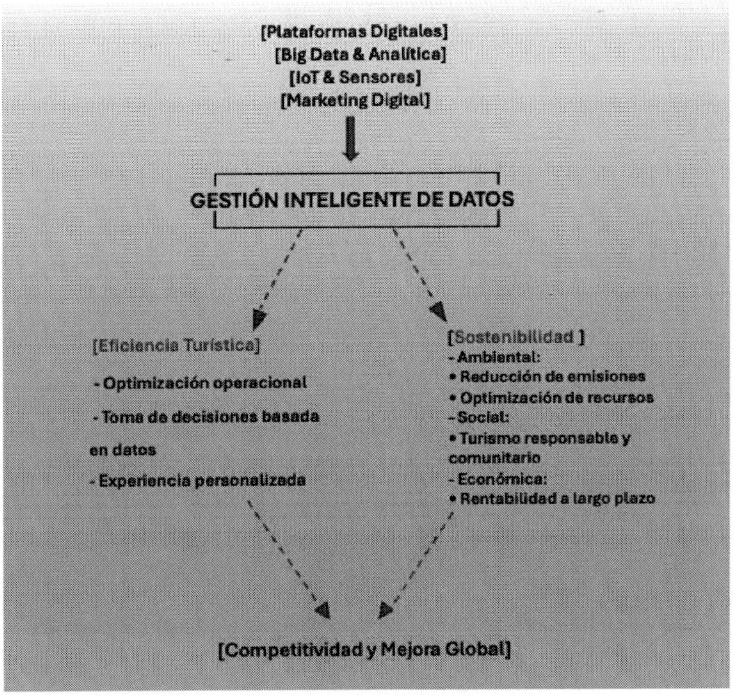

Fuente: elaboración propia.

3. FUNDAMENTOS DE LA ONTOLOGÍA DEL TURISMO

3.1. Definición y Objetivos

Las ontologías permiten que los datos dinámicos se integren y entiendan entre plataformas distintas. Una ontología turística formaliza conceptos tan variados como destinos, rutas turísticas, alojamientos, actividades culturales y gastronómicas, transporte o eventos, entre otros (Zhang et al., 2023). El objetivo principal es establecer un marco semántico que permita:

- La integración de datos heterogéneos: Conectar información proveniente de diversas fuentes, desde bases de datos institucionales hasta redes sociales y sensores IoT (Boulaalama et al., 2018).

- La interoperabilidad entre sistemas: Facilitar el intercambio de información entre gestores públicos, empresas privadas y plataformas digitales (SEGITTUR, 2023).
- La personalización y dinamización de la oferta: Permitir la actualización en tiempo real de la información, facilitando recomendaciones y servicios adaptados a las condiciones cambiantes del entorno turístico (Baizal et al., 2021).

Esta estructura semántica se vuelve especialmente adecuada para abordar la naturaleza dinámica del turismo, donde cada recurso, por ejemplo, la disponibilidad de transporte, eventos culturales o variaciones en la demanda, varían constantemente (Gutiérrez Losada et al., 2008).

Con estas bases, se puede construir un marco semántico en el que los elementos del turismo se relacionen de forma coherente y estructurada, permitiendo así el desarrollo de aplicaciones inteligentes, portales de información y soluciones de análisis de mercado (Figura 2).

Figura 2. Ontología de recursos turísticos

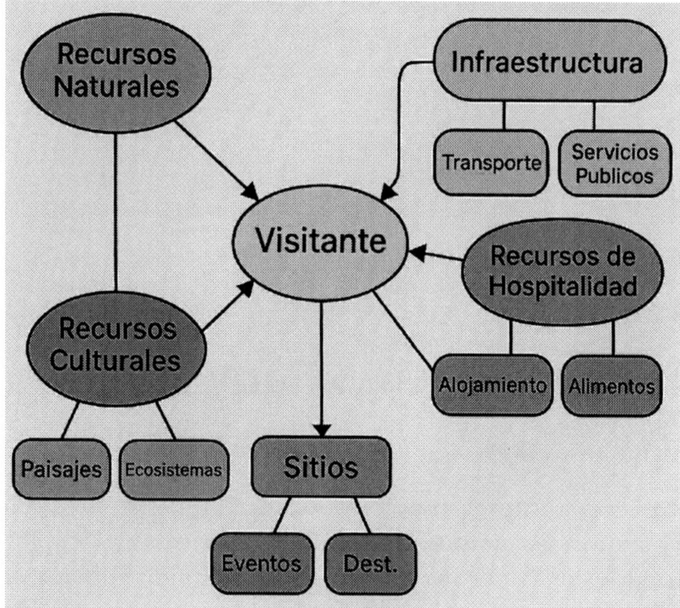

Fuente: elaboración propia. *Dest.: Destinos

3.2. El Rol de las Tecnologías Semánticas

La era digital ha favorecido la integración de tecnologías centradas en la semántica y la Web, permitiendo que las máquinas puedan interpretar el contenido de la información turística. La Web Semántica y las tecnologías afines han sido clave en este avance (como RDF, OWL y SPARQL) permiten que las ontologías no sean solo descripciones estáticas, sino herramientas dinámicas para la integración y consulta de datos (Haridy et al., 2023). Países como Marruecos, España y Egipto han liderado investigaciones en este ámbito (Tatane et al., 2024; Haridy et al., 2023).

4. EJEMPLOS Y APLICACIONES EN ESPAÑA

España es un destino pionero en el desarrollo y aplicación de la ontología en el turismo, y ya considera referente internacional en este ámbito (SEGITTUR, 2023). Entre sus aplicaciones destacan las ontologías geográficas para rutas naturales, creadas por la Universitat Oberta de Catalunya, que integran datos ambientales y de afluencia de usuarios para optimizar recomendaciones; y los modelos de destinos turísticos inteligentes (DTI), donde se usan datos en tiempo real para mejorar la gestión y sostenibilidad de los destinos.

4.1. Ontologías Turísticas Geográficas para Rutas Naturales

Investigadores de la Universitat Oberta de Catalunya desarrollaron una ontología para rutas naturales, incorporando datos dinámicos como afluencia de usuarios y condiciones ambientales (Gutiérrez Losada et al., 2008). Este enfoque mejora la precisión de las recomendaciones turísticas.

Este proyecto, desarrollado por investigadores de la Universitat Oberta de Catalunya, utiliza la semántica para catalogar información dispersa disponible en la web, facilitando al usuario la búsqueda de rutas adecuadas según sus intereses y condiciones del entorno natural.

4.2. Modelo Conceptual Ontológico del Dominio del Turismo

Por otro lado, el documento elaborado por SEGITTUR (2023) propone un marco conceptual robusto con el objetivo de integrar sistemas digitales y mejorar la coordinación entre entidades públicas y privadas. Este modelo no solo aboga por la estandarización en el sector, sino que también impulsa la evolución competitiva del turismo español mediante la interoperabilidad y el aprovechamiento de la economía del dato. La iniciativa se enmarca en proyectos de transformación digital que, en el contexto de los recientes desafíos sociales y económicos, buscan optimizar la gestión de la información turística.

Este modelo busca facilitar la toma de decisiones mediante la interoperabilidad de sistemas digitales y la incorporación de datos en tiempo real, lo que permite a los gestores turísticos optimizar la oferta y responder a eventos imprevistos de manera inmediata.

España ha vinculado las ontologías con su estrategia de transformación digital del turismo, como parte de planes nacionales para la sostenibilidad, competitividad y resiliencia del sector (por ejemplo, en el Plan de Modernización y Competitividad del Sector Turístico (2022) dentro de la Estrategia de Turismo Sostenible de España 2030, e impulsado por el Plan de Recuperación, Transformación y Resiliencia.

5. EJEMPLOS INTERNACIONALES Y PERSPECTIVAS GLOBALES

Aunque España ha logrado avances significativos en la aplicación de ontologías en el ámbito turístico, su liderazgo en ciertos aspectos no excluye el desarrollo de numerosas iniciativas internacionales que refuerzan la importancia de este enfoque. En diversas regiones del mundo, investigadores y profesionales del sector han impulsado proyectos que integran modelos semánticos para mejorar la estructuración del conocimiento turístico, la interoperabilidad de datos y la eficiencia de los sistemas digitales.

a) Egipto

El estudio de Haridy et al. (2023) aplica la metodología ON-ODM al turismo egipcio, centrándose en satisfacción del visitante y desarrollo económico. La ontología EGYTOUR ejemplifica este esfuerzo.

que ofrece pautas detalladas para todas las actividades cruciales, desde la especificación de requisitos hasta la evaluación de ontologías. En este documento, ON-ODM se aplica al contexto del turismo, debido a su importancia e impacto en la promoción de la economía de cualquier nación. Se sugiere el turismo egipcio como un estudio de caso debido al alto valor de su patrimonio histórico y cultural a dada la riqueza de las ciudades en monumentos de gran valor e importancia, lo que lleva a una abundancia de datos que se pueden utilizar en la aplicación.

Esta investigación se centra en una metodología determinada para el caso del turismo egipcio, especificando cuatro objetivos que son la satisfacción del visitante, el desarrollo comunitario, la protección de recursos y el desarrollo económico.

La investigación presenta como ejemplo EGYTOUR como ontología turística, es cierto que el estudio, puesto que está desarrollado por ingenieros informáticos, detalla toda la información en lenguaje informático y explica paso a paso como se elaboran las ontologías y como se desarrollan para llegar a los resultados requeridos. El ejemplo EGYTOUR se representa mediante ejemplos de procesamiento de datos, llegando a mostrar Ejemplos de los resultados de preprocesamiento de la ontología EGYTOUR.

La version diponible (en el momento de la publicaión del estudio) de la ontología de EGYTOUR está en inglés, pero estaba previsto, para el lanzamiento final crear un archivo de traducción al árabe. El trabajo fue minucioso y también complicado, ya que la cantidad de información y por consecuente la gran carga que supone para el ingeniero, pero en definitiva, se muestra la transversalidad del turismo y la necesidad de nuevas herramientas para mejorar y facilitat la experiencia del visitante.

b) Otros proyectos en Europa y América Latina

En Europa, especialmente en países nórdicos, las ontologías se han aplicado exitosamente a la gestión de destinos inteligentes, integrando datos meteorológicos, de movilidad, servicios culturales y fenómenos naturales para crear sistemas de recomendación predictivos y promover el turismo sostenible (Butowski & Butowski, 2023). Estos modelos no solo mejoran la experiencia del visitante, sino que también contribuyen a la planificación estratégica de rutas y eventos culturales. Por otro lado, en América, diversas universidades han explorado el uso de ontologías para la gestión de eventos locales y la optimización de servicios turísticos (Céspedes Morai, 2024), demostrando la versatilidad de este enfoque en contextos geográficos y culturales diversos.

En América, no ha alcanzado aún la misma sistematización que en Europa, pero diversas universidades y centros de investigación han explorado la creación de ontologías que permiten integrar datos de eventos locales, reservas y opiniones de los visitantes. Estas iniciativas, que se han desarrollado en México, Brasil, Colombia y Argentina, destacan la importancia de incorporar la variable tiempo para mejorar la eficiencia en la promoción y gestión del turismo, evidenciando la aplicabilidad de este enfoque en contextos tan heterogéneos como el urbano y el rural. En Brasil, por ejemplo, se ha impletando la ontología que permite integrar datos meteorológicos y de transporte mediante modelos semánticos en ciudades como Florianópolis y Recife; en Colombia, la Universidad Nacional de Colombia y la Universidad de los Andes, lo hacen con ontologías de eventos culturales y festivales o con el uso de tecnologías semánticas para destinos emergentes; en México, por ejemplo, se ha aplicado con el análisis de opiniones turísticas en redes sociales y portales digitales; o en Argentina, desde universidades públicas y el CONICET, han explorado el uso de ontologías para la integración de datos de reservas, alojamientos y circuitos turísticos, o para la planificación en parques nacionales y zonas de ecoturismo.

La capacidad para combinar datos dinámicos de distintas fuentes permite no solo la adaptación a cambios en tiempo real, sino también el fortalecimiento de la competitividad del destino.

c) Marruecos

Otro estudio realizado por la Escuela Nacional de Ciencias Aplicadas repersentada en su equipo de Investigación ESTIDMA de la Universidad Ibn Zohr, Agadir, Marruecos y por el Laboratorio de Reconocimiento de Imágenes y Patrones – Sistemas Inteligentes y Comunicantes (IRF-SIC) de la misma Universidad, publicado en un articulo "Mejoramiento del Análisis Semántico Basado en la Reingeniería de Ontología: Un Estudio de Caso sobre el Dominio del Turismo en Marruecos" Tatane et al. (2024), el cual tenía como objetivo establecer un nuevo enfoque metodológico para actualizar una ontología central que cubra el turismo marroquí y sus especificidades. El trabajo propuesto en este contexto se basaba en dos fases de estudio. La primera fase implicaba analizar y extraer nuevas entidades conceptuales y semánticas de un corpus textual representativo del dominio, siguiendo una explotación bien estudiada de un conjunto de herramientas de procesamiento de lenguaje natural. La segunda fase tenía como objetivo alinear la ontología base con otras sub-ontologías empresariales identificadas, tras un análisis exhaustivo de la estructura conceptual de OTMV1. Todo lo precedente llevó, al equipo de investigación a diseñar y desarrollar una serie de algoritmos específicos para proponer mapeos probables (terminológicos y estructurales) a expertos empresariales del dominio.

La experimentación con este enfoque facilitó la ampliación del modelo ontológico inicial a través de la creación de una nueva versión que es más representativa del dominio y semánticamente más rica. Sin embargo, el desarrollo de la plataforma WebApp OTMV2 asegura la participación remota de expertos en el dominio y así propone un conjunto de herramientas técnicas para facilitar la comprensión, el análisis y la interrogación del modelo ontológico en estudio, además de indicadores técnicos para asistir a los científicos cognitivos durante la fase de validación del mapeo.

6. LOS INVENTARIOS DINÁMICOS DE RECURSOS TURÍSTICOS

Los recursos turísticos son objeto de ordenación desde el ámbito jurídico español. A nivel estatal, la Ley 42/2007, de Patrimonio Natural y de la Biodiversidad, Ley 16/1985, del Patrimonio Histórico Español, e incluso la Ley 21/2013, de Evaluación Ambiental regulan recursos territoriales con funcionalidad turística, ya sean espacios protegidos, bienes culturales o proyectos turísticos. Aunque es a nivel autonómico desde donde que se define y clasifican los recursos turísticos. Así, la Ley 15/2018, 7 de junio, de la Generalitat, de turismo, ocio y hospitalidad de la Comunitat Valenciana introduce el concepto de inteligencia turística territorial y desarrolla la cuestión de los recursos patrimoniales del territorio como base para el desarrollo del producto turístico.

La Ley reconoce el papel central del territorio como soporte físico y cultural de la actividad turística y establece un marco normativo donde el desarrollo turístico debe estar vinculado al aprovechamiento sostenible del patrimonio natural, cultural y paisajístico del territorio. Y señala que el desarrollo turístico deberá ser coherente con la sostenibilidad territorial, incluyendo criterios de protección ambiental, social y económica. De acuerdo con los artículos 23 a 27, el inventario de recursos turísticos se presenta como una herramienta elemental para la gestión sostenible del destino, considerando que, además de la función turística, el territorio también desarrolla otras funciones como la ambiental o residencial.

Según lo señalado, las ontologías y tecnologías semánticas pueden ordenar y actualizar en tiempo real información sobre los recursos y otros factores geográficos (clima, accesibilidad, eventos, etc.), además de proporcionar datos clave para la gestión del destino.

De acuerdo con SEGITTUR (2023) en relación con el modelo de interacción oferta-turista-destinos en el contexto de la ontología del dominio turismo, existen 2 dominios que se retroalimentarían del inventario dinámico: el subdominio Destino, que <<se refiere a los espacios y servicios públicos que

intervienen en la actividad turística y son proporcionados, generalmente, por la administración local bajo el precepto de que le objetivo de los destinos es atraer visitantes, ofrecerles una experiencia satisfactoria y fidelizarlos. Entre sus entidades relevantes se encuentran los servicios públicos vinculables al turismo, los recursos turísticos (…), infraestructuras de transporte, servicios sanitarios y de emergencias, y la propia identidad digital que el destino mantiene en diferentes canales>> (SEGITTUR, 2023, p.15). Aunque de acuerdo con nuestro análisis, el objetivo de atraer visitantes podría relacionarse con el objetivo de considerar el destino como un ecosistema vivo y, por consiguiente, con visitantes que aporten valor al destino y se integren en modelos más integrales y respetuosos. Y al subdominio de la Oferta. Según el modelo, la oferta y el destino constituyen el escenario donde el turista entra en interacción con las entidades del sistema turístico. SEGITTUR concluye que estas entidades, que modelan de forma digital el entorno donde se desarrolla la interacción turística, contienen características importantes que ayudan a las máquinas a ofrecer al turista la información que necesita para su experiencia. Además, mantienen vínculos con distintas entidades de ambos subdominios, mostrando cómo se relacionan y funcionan entre sí (p.22) (Figura 3).

Figura 3. Interacción turística a través del subdominio de la oferta y el subdominio del destino

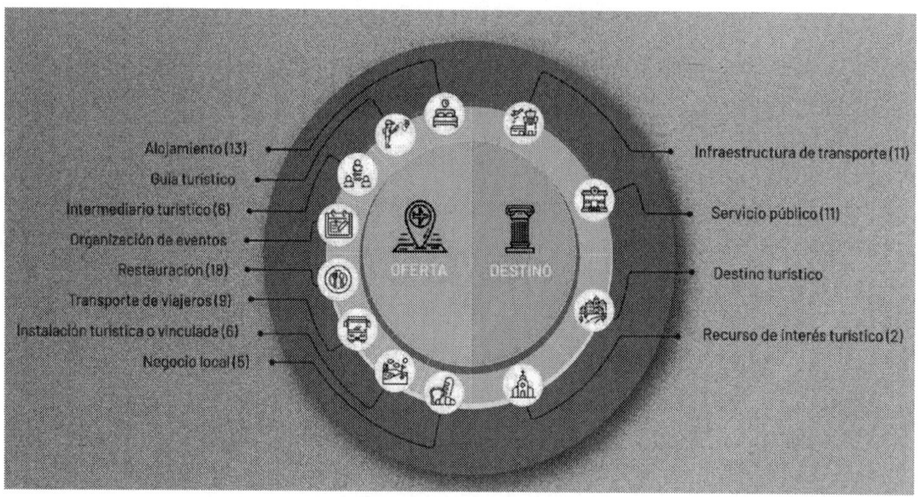

Fuente: SEGITUR, 2023, p. 22.

El inventario dinámico basado en ontologías del turismo puede constituir una herramienta ágil para garantizar una mejor experiencia del visitante, para generar datos e información para la gestión turística del destino y la gestión sostenible de recursos. Pero, sobre todo, se presenta como una herramienta accesible y eficiente para los destinos emergentes y/o que carezcan de procesos de digitalización avanzados. Además, el inventario dinámico puede favorecer la gobernanza turística y la participación colaborativa de los visitantes en algunos atributos, que, a su vez, pueden contribuir a mejorar su experiencia.

7. IMPLICACIONES PARA LA PLANIFICACIÓN Y SOSTENIBILIDAD

La gestión ontológica permite prever picos de demanda y responder a emergencias climáticas (Cholat et al., 2019). Revistas especializadas de alto impacto, como *Journal of Sustainable Tourism o Tourism Management,* han destacado el papel de las ontologías y la inteligencia semántica en la planificación turística basada en datos.

La gestión de recursos turísticos a través de ontologías no solo tiene implicaciones en la eficiencia operativa, sino que también resulta clave para la planificación estratégica y la sostenibilidad de un destino. La capacidad de prever picos de afluencia, gestionar la demanda y responder a imprevistos (como cambios climáticos o emergencias) contribuye a un desarrollo turístico más equilibrado y resiliente. En este contexto, publicaciones internacionales como *Journal of Sustainable Tourism* (Zhang et al., 2023) y *Tourism Management* (Butowski & Butowski, 2023) han resaltado la relevancia del enfoque semántico en la integración de información dinámica, lo cual permite promover una gestión territorial más inteligente, adaptable y sostenible. En este sentido, de acuerdo con los objetivos de SEGITTUR (2023), los desafíos cctuales consisten principalmente en:

- Estandarización y heterogeneidad de datos: La integración de datos provenientes de fuentes diversas (institucionales, sociales, sensores IoT) requiere estándares que faciliten la normalización y procesamiento (Adad et al., 2019).
- Actualización constante: Los recursos dinámicos exigen mecanismos que permitan la actualización en tiempo real sin comprometer la integridad de la ontología. (Tatane et al., 2015).
- Interoperabilidad sistémica: La implementación de ontologías en el turismo requiere la colaboración estrecha entre organismos públicos y privados, así como la inversión en infraestructura tecnológica.

En cuanto a las perspectivas de futuro, nos encontramos que la evolución de las tecnologías semánticas, la inteligencia artificial y el *big data* augura un futuro en el que las ontologías podrán gestionar de manera aún más eficiente los recursos turísticos dinámicos. Se vislumbra la creación de plataformas integradas que no solo permitan la monitorización en tiempo real, sino también la predicción de tendencias y la adaptación automática de la oferta turística. La ampliación de estas prácticas tanto en España como a nivel internacional contribuirá a la transformación digital del sector, fomentando una gestión más inteligente, sostenible y competitiva.

8. CONCLUSIONES Y PERSPECTIVAS FUTURAS

El desarrollo de ontologías en el turismo representa una herramienta poderosa que puede transformar la manera en que se gestiona, consulta y utiliza la información en este sector. En el caso de España, que se sitúa en pionero en el desarrollo y aplicación del aontología del turismo, busca una gestión más equilibrada del turismo, lo cual permitiría reducir la masificación, optimizar recursos y una mejor redistribución de flujos turísticos hacia zonas menos saturadas. En un futuro próximo se espera que el uso de tecnologías semánticas se profundice, integrándose con inteligencia artificial y *big data* para afrontar nuevos desafíos como la sostenibilidad, la personalización extrema y la adaptabilidad a escenarios cambiantes.

La consolidación de marcos ontológicos sólidos no solo contribuirá al avance científico, sino que también impulsará decisiones más informadas y colaborativas entre los diversos actores del turismo, promoviendo un desarrollo sectorial que compagine la innovación tecnológica con la preservación cultural y medioambiental.

En definitiva, la ontología del turismo no es solo una herramienta técnica, sino un puente que conecta el conocimiento, la cultura y la tecnología para transformar la experiencia turística en un mundo cada vez más digital y conectado. Y no solo incide en la experiencia turística del visitante, sino que aúna inteligencia territorial y competitividad turística, prácticamente, en todos los niveles, ya que puede favorecer la gestión pública del destino, como favorecer la toma de decisiones estratégicas para empresas, destinos y administraciones.

Agradecimientos:

La aportación de la autora a esta comunicación forma parte de los resultados del Proyecto MODELTUR desarrollado en el marco de los Proyectos IMPULSO a la investigación de la URJC (Convocatoria 2024).

9. REFERENCIAS

Adad, M. A., Semlali, E. H., El-Ayachi, M., & Ibannain, F. (2019). Ontology model and thesaurus for Moroccan land domain governance. African Journal of Land Policy and Geospatial Sciences, 2(2), 112-134.

Baizal, Z. K. A., Tarwidi, D., Adiwijaya, & Wijaya, B. (2021). Tourism Destination Recommendation Using Ontology-based Conversational Recommender System. International Journal of Computing and Digital Systems, 10(1), 176.

Boulaalama, O., Aghoutaneb, B., El Ouadghiria, D., Moumenc, A., & Cheikh Malinine, M. L. (2018). Proposal of a Big Data System Based on the Recommendation and Profiling Techniques for an Intelligent Management of Moroccan Tourism. Procedia Computer Science, 134, 346–351.

Butowski, L., & Butowski, S. (2023). Exploring Ontology of Tourism: A New-Realist Approach. Journal of Travel Research, 62(4), 719-733.

Céspedes Morai, J. M. (2024). Evolución de la Industria del Turismo Sostenible en España. Revista Ciencia y Reflexión, 3(2), 126-144.

Cholat, F., Gwiazdzinski, L., Tritz, C., & Tuppen, J. (2019). Tourismes et adaptations. Elya Ediciones.

Gallego Gómez, C., & Vaquero Frías, L. (2022). Artificial Intelligence and Sustainable Tourism Development: The Value of Partnerships. ESIC Market, 53(3), e281.

Gutiérrez Losada, I., Conesa Caralt, J., & Geva Urbano, F. (2008). Ontologías Turísticas Geográficas: Creación de una Ontología sobre Rutas Turísticas (a Pie o en Bicicleta) por Espacios Naturales. Universitat Oberta de Catalunya.

Gruber, T. R. (1993). A translation approach to portable ontology specifications. *Knowledge Acquisition*, 5(2), 199–220. https://doi.org/10.1006/knac.1993.1008bibsonomy.org+9

Haridy, S., Ismail, R. M., Badr, N., & Hashem, M. (2023). An ontology development methodology based on ontology-driven conceptual modeling and natural language processing: Tourism case study. Big Data Cogn. Comput., 7(2), 101.

SEGITTUR. (2023). Ontología del turismo: Un lenguaje común para la industria y la interacción turista-máquina. https://www.segittur.es/wp-content/uploads/2023/09/1.-Ontologia-de-Turismo-Documento-de-divulgacion.pdf

Tatane, K., Er-Raha, B., Cherkaoui, C., & Mouhim, S. (2015). *Alignment Methodological Approach of Evolving Domain Sub-Ontologies using Terminological and Structural Matchers Applied to Tourism Domain.* International Journal of Computer Applications, 123(15).

Tatane, K., Amalki, A., & Bouzit, A. (2023). The Impact of the Support of Semantic Layers on the Search for Tourist Information: Case of Digitalized Tourist Establishments and Services in Morocco. Revista Multidisciplinar, 5(3).

Tatane, K., Amalki, A., & Bouzit, A. (2024). Enhancement of Semantic Analysis Based on the Ontology Reengineering: A Case Study on Moroccan Tourism Domain. Journal of Computer Science, 20(8), 872-884.

Zhang, P., Wang, J., & Li, R. (2023). Tourism-type ontology framework for tourism-type classification, naming, and knowledge organization. Heliyon, 9(4), e15192

Ley 15/2018, de 7 de junio, de turismo, ocio y hospitalidad de la Comunitat Valenciana. [DOGV núm. 8317, de 11.06.2018].

PERCEPCIÓN DE LOS TURISTAS SOBRE APLICACIONES INTELIGENTES PARA LA MEJORA DE LA EXPERIENCIA EN DESTINOS TURÍSTICOS INTELIGENTES (DTI)

Marcelino Sánchez Rivero
María Cristina Rodríguez Rangel
Vanessa Miguel Barrado
Universidad de Extremadura

TEMÁTICA: Tecnología

RESUMEN: Uno de los objetivos últimos de los destinos turísticos inteligentes es adaptarse a las demandas de los turistas 4.0 y mejorar la experiencia turística. Para ello, los destinos turísticos inteligentes tienen a su disposición una amplia gama de aplicaciones y de servicios tecnológicos que pueden contribuir a este objetivo. Con independencia del grado de implantación de estas aplicaciones y servicios tecnológicos en los destinos, son muy escasos hasta la fecha los estudios que han analizado el interés que muestran los turistas por estas aplicaciones tecnológicas, así como aquellos que identifican los factores que pueden condicionar dicho interés. El objetivo de este trabajo es cubrir esta brecha de investigación. En concreto, se ha analizado el grado de interés, en una escala Likert de 11 puntos, que los turistas que visitan los destinos turísticos inteligentes de la provincia de Cáceres tienen en 10 aplicaciones inteligentes, utilizando para ello una muestra integrada por más de 1.000 turistas. Este grado de interés se ha utilizado como variable endógena en un modelo de regresión en el que las variables exógenas han sido el grado de conocimiento del concepto "Destino Turístico Inteligente", la importancia que los turistas conceden al hecho de que el destino visitado sea inteligente y la valoración que los mismos hacen de las cinco dimensiones del modelo DTI español (gobernanza, innovación, tecnología, sostenibilidad y accesibilidad). Los resultados obtenidos de la estimación de estos modelos de regresión servirán a los gestores de destino a elegir los módulos que incorporan a la Plataforma Inteligente de Destinos que en el futuro implantarán los destinos turísticos inteligentes españoles.

Palabras clave: aplicaciones inteligentes, destino turístico inteligente, percepción del turista, regresión.

ABSTRACT: One of the ultimate goals of smart destinations is to adapt to the demands of tourists 4.0 and improve the tourist experience. To do this, smart destinations have at their disposal a wide range of applications and technological services that can contribute to this goal. Regardless of the degree of implementation of these technological applications and services in destinations, very few studies to date have analyzed the interest shown by tourists in these technological applications, as well as those that identify the factors that may condition this interest. The aim of this study is to fill this research gap. Specifically, we have analyzed the degree of interest, on an 11-point Likert scale, that tourists visiting smart destinations in the province of Cáceres have in 10 smart applications, using a sample of more than 1,000 tourists. This level of interest was used as an endogenous variable in a regression model in which the exogenous variables were the level of knowledge of the 'Smart Tourism Destination' concept, the importance that tourists attach to the fact that the destination visited is smart and their assessment of the five dimensions of the Spanish STD model (governance, innovation, technology, sustainability and accessibility). The results obtained from the estimation of these regression models will help destination managers to choose the modules to incorporate into the Smart Destination Platform that will be implemented in the future by Spanish smart destinations.

Keywords: Smart apps, smart destination, tourist perception, regression.

1. INTRODUCCIÓN

El concepto de turismo inteligente hace alusión al actual contexto de la actividad turística caracterizada por su evolución desde el turismo tradicional mediante una paulatina inclusión de herramientas de Tecnologías de la Información y la Comunicación (TICs) en la infraestructura física, que implica realizar un uso activo de estas herramientas para el desarrollo de la actividad turística en un determinado destino (Xiang et al., 2015).

Los destinos turísticos inteligentes (DTI) surgen como una extensión de las ciudades inteligentes, ya que aplican los principios de estos espacios a áreas rurales o urbanas teniendo en consideración no solo a los residentes, como ocurre en las ciudades inteligentes, sino también a los diferentes stakeholders de la actividad turística, resaltando entre sus principales objetivos la mejora de la experiencia de los turistas (Gretzel et al., 2015).

Así, López Ávila y García (2013) definen los destinos turísticos inteligentes como espacios innovadores, construidos sobre una infraestructura de vanguardia que garantizan el desarrollo sostenible de las zonas turísticas, haciéndolas accesible para todos, facilitando la interacción del visitante con su entorno y su integración en él, aumentan la calidad de la experiencia en el destino y mejoran la calidad de vida de los residentes.

En el ámbito de los DTI España sobresale entre las naciones que han implementado con éxito iniciativas de "smart cities" (Palomo y Parra, 2024).

Además, destaca por ser país pionero en el desarrollo de un modelo de destinos turísticos inteligentes que goza de un reconocido prestigio internacional. Un ejemplo destacado de su influencia a nivel europeo es la creación del premio European Capital of Smart Tourism, cuyo objetivo es reconocer el desarrollo del turismo inteligente en ciudades europeas basándose en el modelo DTI español.

El modelo DTI español es una iniciativa gestionada por la Sociedad Mercantil Estatal para la Gestión de la Innovación y las Tecnologías Turísticas (Segittur). Su propósito es ofrecer un enfoque de gestión que asista a los responsables de los destinos en su camino para convertirse en DTI. El objetivo de este modelo de gestión es diferenciar a aquel destino que, según afirman destaca por ser "un destino turístico innovador, consolidado sobre una infraestructura tecnológica de vanguardia, que garantiza el desarrollo sostenible del territorio turístico, accesible para todos, que facilita la interacción e integración del visitante con el entorno e incrementa la calidad de su experiencia en el destino y mejora la calidad de vida del residente".

Como puede observarse en las diferentes definiciones planteadas a lo largo de esta introducción el turista ocupa un lugar central y su inclusión en el ecosistema inteligente resulta incuestionable. Sin embargo, a pesar de ello, los estudios sobre DTI suelen centrarse en abordar aspectos como la innovación tecnológica, la gobernanza o la prestación de servicios, pasando por alto la percepción de los viajeros (Hott & Sevihlha, 2020). Se detecta una falta de trabajos que aborden las preferencias de los consumidores en relación al uso de la tecnología (Femenia-Serra et al., 2019) que es especialmente notable cuando se centra la atención en la relación entre la experiencia de uso de las herramientas tecnológicas y cómo afectan a la percepción de la imagen de destino (Xia et al., 2018)

Por ello, la presente investigación pretende cubrir este gap de investigación mediante la propuesta de un estudio empírico que contribuya a avanzar en la teoría sobre cómo el grado de percepción de inteligencia del destino influye en la valoración de los servicios turísticos ofrecidos a través de herramientas turísticas inteligentes. Para ello, se han seleccionado como soluciones tecnológicas a evaluar los módulos dirigidos a turistas en la PID del modelo DTI español.

La Plataforma Inteligente de Destinos (PID) surge como una iniciativa pionera en el contexto de los DTI promovido por Segittur. Se trata de una infraestructura tecnológica, abierta y modular que tiene como objetivo conectar a todos los agentes del ecosistema turístico, es decir, destinos, empresas, turistas y residentes. Dentro de los diferentes módulos que propone, este trabajo ha centrado su atención en un conjunto de soluciones dirigidas a turistas para mejorar su experiencia en destino en las diferentes fases de planificación del viaje. Estos módulos han sido utilizados en para analizar la valoración que los turistas hacen de este servicio en función de la percepción de inteligencia que tengan sobre el destino.

Por su parte, la percepción del grado de inteligencia del destino se podrá definir como un constructo complejo basado en el grado de conocimiento e importancia relativa que el turista tiene respecto de la inclusión en la red DTI del destino que está visitando, junto con la valoración de las diferentes dimensiones que conforman la inteligencia turística, según el modelo español, es decir, según su percepción del grado de sostenibilidad, gobernanza, tecnología, innovación y accesibilidad del destino. Sería de esperar que, a un mayor grado de inteligencia turística percibida por el turista, éste otorgara una mayor valoración a los diferentes módulos de servicios turísticos inteligentes.

Para verificar esta teoría en la presente investigación se han planteado un conjunto de modelos de regresión que consideran como variable endógena la valoración que los turistas otorgan a cada uno de los módulos seleccionados, tomándola como un indicador del interés que estos servicios despiertan en los turistas, y como variables exógenas la percepción de inteligencia del destino turístico.

Para desarrollar este trabajo se ha realizado una encuesta a un total de 1046 turistas entre los meses de julio y septiembre de 2024 que estaban visitando diferentes territorios de la región de Extremadura (España) que están incluidos, todos ellos, en la red DTI española.

La región de Extremadura se presenta como un interesante caso de estudio por diferentes motivos. En primer lugar, se trata de una región ubicada en España, país pionero en el desarrollo de DTI En segundo lugar, el sector turístico de esta región ha estado tradicionalmente caracterizado por una baja competitividad, ocupando las últimas posiciones del ranking nacional elaborado por Monitur (2023). En tercer lugar, el sector turístico de esta región posee un escaso nivel de digitalización (Sánchez-Rivero et al., 2022). La Administración Regional, siendo consciente de esta realidad, ve en la conversión del destino en inteligente una oportunidad para revertir esta situación y está realizando un gran esfuerzo para alcanzar esta meta. Este esfuerzo se ve reflejado en el hecho de que se trata de la región con un mayor número de microterritorios trabajando en la actualidad bajo la metodología DTI para mejorar su grado de inteligencia turística, siendo especialmente relevante en la provincia de Cáceres, que se ha seleccionado como territorio objetivo para la realización de este estudio.

Por todo ello, se considera que los resultados de esta investigación presentan importantes implicaciones tanto a nivel teórico como práctico. A nivel teórico, contribuyen a la literatura sobre turismo inteligente en un tema poco explorado como la percepción del turista. A nivel práctico, permiten a los gestores de destinos obtener información sobre el turista que visita su destino, tanto sobre cómo percibe el destino como sobre su predisposición y valoración de las herramientas que el destino podría poner a su disposición.

Para alcanzar estos objetivos, la investigación se organiza como sigue: tras esta introducción, se presenta una revisión de la literatura centrada en la percepción del turista de destinos inteligentes y su valoración de las herramientas tecnológicas. A continuación, se describe la metodología, se presentan los principales resultados y se exponen las conclusiones.

2. PERCEPCIÓN DEL TURISTA SOBRE LA MEJORA DE LA EXPERIENCIA TURÍSTICA A TRAVÉS DE LA TECNOLOGÍA

Los Destinos Turísticos Inteligentes (DTI) pueden ser definidos como espacios turísticos que ofrecen servicios, instalaciones y formas de intervenir inteligentemente en la actividad turística (Ivars-Baidal et al., 2016; Buhalis & Amaranggana, 2014).

Tienen su origen en la estrecha relación entre el turismo y el uso en él cada vez más intensivo de las TICs en todo el ecosistema turístico, implicando a los diferentes agentes de esta actividad. Si se centra la atención en el turista, por ser el agente dentro del ecosistema turístico que ocupa el interés de este trabajo, los DTI son entendidos como un ecosistema establecido por una red de negocios inteligentes, destinos inteligentes e infraestructuras tecnológicas inteligentes para maximizar el valor de los servicios y la experiencia para los turistas (Femenia-Serra et al., 2015; Um & Chung, 2019), interceder en la experiencia turística (Tussyadiah et al, 2018; Wang et al., 2012) y proporcionar infraestructuras para la cocreación de valor (Buhalis, 2019).

Entre otras razones, dada la alta complejidad de las relaciones y cantidad de datos generados por la hiperconexión de los turistas en el destino, resulta necesario disponer de herramientas que cumplan una doble función, captar y gestionar datos procedentes de las actividades realizadas por el turista y mejorar la experiencia de éste en el destino.

Desde la perspectiva de los gestores de destinos, la provisión de herramientas tecnológicas les va a permitir recabar datos para, posteriormente, poder utilizarlos para mejorar la gestión del destino (López de Ávila &

García-Sánchez, 2013; Buhalis & Amaranggana 2014; Blanco, 2015; Cornejo Ortega & Malcom, 2020). Tal y como sugieren Huang et al. (2017) dentro de estas herramientas tecnológicas deben incluirse todas las formas posibles de aplicaciones turísticas online y fuentes de información como agencias online, blogs, websites, social media, etc. Todas ellas deben ser diseñadas con el objetivo de aumentar la conexión digital entre el viajero y el destino con el fin de recabar datos que serán utilizados para mejora la gestión consiguiendo el objetivo de mejorar la experiencia del turista.

Desde la perspectiva del turista, el uso de soluciones tecnológicas inteligentes afecta a su experiencia en destino. Como ya se ha señalado con anterioridad, pese a ser uno de los objetivos principal que se persiguen en la gestión inteligente de los destinos, hasta la fecha se ha prestado escasa atención a analizar cuál es la percepción del turista sobre las herramientas de turismo inteligente que los destinos ponen a su disposición para mejorar su experiencia. Sin embargo, se trata de un tema de creciente interés en la literatura (Mior Shariffuddin et al., 2023) que cuenta con diferentes casos de estudio que están permitiendo confirmar que disponer de tecnologías innovadoras mejora la calidad de los servicios turísticos e imagen de destino (Kock et al., 2016; Papadimitriou et al., 2014)

Hott y Sevilha (2020) realizar un estudio para ahondar en la importancia de la experiencia turística en los destinos inteligentes. El estudio destaca la importancia de entender cómo los viajeros perciben las experiencias de turismo inteligente (STEs), lo que puede ayudar a crear experiencias más satisfactorias y a promover el desarrollo sostenible de los destinos turísticos inteligentes. Azis et al. (2020) realizan un estudio en cuatro ciudades inteligentes en Indonesia para indagar sobre cómo las tecnologías de turismo inteligente (STT) y las experiencias turísticas memorables (MTE) afectan la satisfacción del turista y la lealtad hacia el destino turístico. Mediante una muestra de 360 encuestas consiguieron demostrar que tanto las tecnologías de turismo inteligente como la experiencia turística tienen un impacto positivo en la satisfacción del turista. Tavitiyama et al. (2021) realizan un estudio sobre turistas internaciones planteándolo como un estudio de casos sobre el destino inteligente de Hong Kong. Sus resultados demuestran que la percepción de los turistas de los atributos de las aplicaciones de turismo inteligente influye en la imagen que tienen del destino y en su comportamiento.

Uno de los trabajos más recientes es el elaborado por Aqilah et al. (2023) que se centran en analizar la disponibilidad de los turistas a utilizar códigos QR en sitios turísticos relacionándolo con los conceptos de tecnología y sostenibilidad. Los resultados resaltan la importancia de considerar los hábitos establecidos de los turistas y sus compromisos con la sostenibilidad para la implementación efectiva de iniciativas de turismo inteligente.

Todos estos estudios han contribuido, desde el estudio de casos y a través de diferentes metodologías, a avanzar en el conocimiento de la percepción del turista en el contexto de los destinos turísticos inteligentes. La presente investigación se plantea desde la misma óptica para ahondar en el conocimiento sobre cómo el grado de percepción de inteligencia del destino influye en la valoración de los servicios turísticos ofrecidos a través de herramientas turísticas inteligentes.

La imagen de un destino, con carácter general, se ha definido como una visión global que se conforma a través de la suma de cualquier creencia, opinión o expresión (Crompt, 1979). Es por ello, que este trabajo asume que la percepción de inteligentes del destino puede ser medida a través del conocimiento sobre la inclusión del destino que visita en la red DTI, que actúa como una etiqueta de esta cualidad del destino (Cornejo Ortega & Malcolm, 2020), la importancia que él mismo concede a este hecho y la identificación del destino con cada una de las dimensiones que conformen la inteligencia turística.

3. DATOS Y METODOLOGÍA

3.1. Datos

Los datos analizados en este trabajo proceden de una encuesta realizada a turistas que han visitado los destinos de la provincia de Cáceres incluidos en la Red DTI de Segittur (ciudades de Cáceres y de Plasencia, y comarcas de Las Hurdes, Sierra de Gata, La Vera, Valle del Jerte, Parque Nacional de Monfragüe y Valle del Ambroz-Cáparra). Las encuestas se realizaron a través de entrevista personal entre el 26 de julio y el 13 de septiembre de 2024. El tamaño muestral ascendió a 1.046 turistas. El error muestral máximo de la encuesta, para un nivel de confianza del 95% y en el caso más desfavorable (p=q=0,50), ascendió a un ±2,99%.

Uno de los objetivos de esta encuesta fue conocer el grado de interés (en una escala Likert de 11 puntos, donde 0=nada interesante y 10=absolutamente interesante) que el turista tenía sobre 10 soluciones tecnológicas a implantar por los destinos DTI anteriormente enumerados para que el turista considere que dicho destino debe ser considerado realmente como inteligente. Estas 10 soluciones tecnológicas fueron las siguientes: recomendaciones en destino (RECO), tourist card (CARD), app turista (APPT), asesor virtual cognitivo (ASES), realidad aumentada-realidad virtual (REAL), planificador de rutas (PLAN), pulsera inteligente (PULS), cuaderno de viaje (CUAD), gamificación (GAMI) y gestor de reclamaciones y quejas (GEST).

Por otro lado, se preguntó también a los turistas si conocían qué es un Destino Turístico Inteligente (CONO; 1=sí; 0=no), que valorasen la importancia que otorgaban al hecho de que el destino que estaban visitado sea reconocido oficialmente como DTI (IMPO; escala Likert de 11 puntos;0=ninguna importancia; 10=importancia absoluta) y que indicasen en una escala Likert de 0 a 10 puntos la percepción que tenían de las siguientes características del destino que estaban visitando: bien gobernado (GOBE), innovador (INNO), tecnológico (TECN), sostenible (SOST) y accesible (ACCE).

3.2. Metodología

El objetivo de este trabajo consiste en determinar si el grado de conocimiento del concepto DTI, la importancia que los turistas otorgan al mismo y las dimensiones del modelo DTI de Segittur que perciben los turistas al visitar el destino ejercen una influencia significativa sobre el interés que el turista tiene en la implantación de diferentes soluciones tecnológicas en el destino visitado. Esto es, si la valoración de las diferentes aplicaciones inteligentes está condicionada por la percepción de inteligencia del turista sobre el destino. Para ello, se han estimado modelos de regresión, en los que la variable endógena ha sido el interés demostrado por estas soluciones, mientras que las variables exógenas han sido las relacionadas con el conocimiento, con la importancia y con las dimensiones DTI percibidas en el destino, es decir:

donde =RECO, CARD, APPT, ..., GEST. Todos estos modelos de regresión han sido estimados por el método de los mínimos cuadrados ordinarios (MCO) con errores estándar robustos (HC1) para evitar posibles sesgos en las estimaciones de los parámetros por la presencia de heterocedasticidad. Además de los estimadores ELIO de los parámetros del modelo, sus valores *t* y sus *p*-valores asociados, en los resultados se presentarán también la bondad de ajuste de cada modelo, cuantificada a través de la prueba *F* y del coeficiente de determinación (R cuadrado) así como el Factor de Inflación de la Varianza (FIV) para detectar posibles problemas de multicolinealidad entre las variables explicativas. Los cálculos han sido realizados con el paquete estadístico Gretl.

4. RESULTADOS

A continuación, se presentan y se interpretan las estimaciones MCO-HC1 del modelo presentado en el apartado anterior de metodología para cada una de las 10 aplicaciones inteligentes analizadas en este trabajo.

4.1. Recomendaciones en destino

Como se puede observar en la Tabla 1, el interés de los turistas por las recomendaciones en destino depende únicamente del grado de importancia que el turista concede al concepto DTI y de su percepción de que el destino que está visitando es sostenible. Así, por cada punto adicional en la importancia concedida al concepto DTI el interés por las recomendaciones en destino se incrementaría en 0,1167 puntos (ceteris paribus: c.p.), mientras que por cada punto en que se incremente la valoración del turista sobre la sostenibilidad del destino, el interés por las recomendaciones en destino se incrementaría también en 0,1635 puntos (c.p.).

Por otro lado, no se han detectado (ni en este modelo ni en los restantes modelos estimados que se presentarán en este trabajo) problemas de multicolinealidad entre las variables exógenas, toda vez que los factores de inflación de varianza (FIV) alcanzan, en todos los casos, valores muy cercanos a 1.

Tabla 1. Estimación del modelo: variable endógena: RECO

RECO: generación de recomendaciones en tiempo real al usuario en base a sus preferencias y perfil de consumo y a los lugares que visita.

Variable	Estimación MCO	Valor t	p-valor	FIV
Intercepto	5,5659	13,830	0,0000 **	
CONO	-0,1388	-0,850	0,3954	1,010
IMP	0,1167	3,710	0,0002 **	1,095
GOBE	0,0872	1,771	0,0769	1,818
INNO	-0,0064	-0,120	0,9045	2,348
TECN	0,0185	0,548	0,5836	1,816
SOST	0,1635	3,133	0,0018 **	1,773
ACCE	0,0146	0,399	0,6902	1,451

Prueba F (7, 1038): 11,5310 (p-valor: 0,0000)
R cuadrado: 0,0870
* Parámetro significativo al 5%; ** Parámetro significativo al 1%.

Fuente: elaboración propia a partir de cálculos realizados con Gretl ©.

4.2. Tourist card

El interés de los turistas consultados por la tarjeta turística depende únicamente de la percepción del desarrollo tecnológico que tenga el destino (véase la Tabla 2). Así, el interés por solicitar y utilizar este tipo de tarjeta se incrementa a medida que aumenta también la implantación de tecnología en el destino percibida por el turista. En concreto, por cada punto adicional en la valoración de esta tecnología se estima que el interés de los turistas por la tarjeta turística se incrementaría en 0,1042 puntos.

Tabla 2. Estimación del modelo: variable endógena: CARD

CARD: tarjeta que ofrece una mejor experiencia al visitante, unificando servicios, haciendo upselling y venta cruzada, mejorando precios con descuentos, etc.

Variable	Estimación MCO	Valor t	p-valor	FIV
Intercepto	4,8410	9,176	0,0000 **	
CONO	0,0681	0,288	0,7735	1,010
IMP	-0,0024	-0,0580	0,9538	1,095
GOBE	0,1098	1,670	0,0953	1,818
INNO	0,0334	0,469	0,6392	2,348
TECN	0,1042	2,088	0,0371 *	1,816
SOST	0,1046	1,588	0,1126	1,773
ACCE	0,0661	1,176	0,2400	1,451

Prueba F (7, 1038): 7,0002 (p-valor: 0,0000)
R cuadrado: 0,0633
* Parámetro significativo al 5%; ** Parámetro significativo al 1%.

4.3. App turista

El interés de los viajeros que visitan los destinos turísticos inteligentes de la provincia de Cáceres por una app turística de dichos destinos o del conjunto de la provincia está condicionado tanto por la importancia que concedan al hecho de que el destino sea inteligente, como por su carácter innovador y sostenible (Tabla 3). Así, por cada punto adicional con que el turista consultado valore la sostenibilidad del destino, su interés en una app turística se incrementaría en 0,1795 puntos (c.p.). En algo menos se incrementaría este interés por cada punto que el turista incremente su valoración por la innovación que ha percibido durante su visita (0,1096, c.p.). Finalmente, el aumento estimado en el interés por disponer y utilizar una app turística por cada punto adicional en la valoración de la importancia que para el turista tiene conocer el concepto de DTI es de 0,1430 puntos.

Tabla 3. Estimación del modelo: variable endógena: APPT

APPT: aplicación para dispositivos móviles con información detallada y personalizada sobre el destino, como lugares de interés, eventos, restaurantes, alojamiento, transporte, mapas interactivos, guías turísticas, etc.

Variable	Estimación MCO	Valor t	p-valor	FIV
Intercepto	5,5154	12,410	0,0000 **	
CONO	-0,1067	-0,541	0,5886	1,010
IMP	0,1430	3,531	0,0004 **	1,095
GOBE	-0,0789	-1,604	0,1090	1,818
INNO	0,1096	-0,869	0,0137 *	2,348
TECN	-0,0325	3,208	0,3850	1,816
SOST	0,1795	1,813	0,0014 **	1,773
ACCE	0,0732		0,0702	1,451

Prueba F (7, 1038): 9,9621 (p-valor: 0,0000)
R cuadrado: 0,0988
* Parámetro significativo al 5%; ** Parámetro significativo al 1%.

4.4. Asesor virtual cognitivo

El interés de los turistas consultados por un asesor virtual cognitivo está directamente relacionado con la percepción de que el destino es innovador, es tecnológicamente avanzado y es accesible, e indirectamente relacionado con la percepción de que está bien gobernado (véase la Tabla 4). Así, el factor que más ayuda a incrementar el interés por esta aplicación inteligente es la tecnología (0,1938, c.p.), seguido de los procesos innovadores (0,1387, c.p.) y de la accesibilidad física y virtual del destino (0,1773, c.p.). Sin embargo, la percepción de que el destino está bien gobernado desincentiva el interés por esta aplicación inteligente, de forma que dicho interés se reduce en 0,1907 puntos (c.p.) por cada punto adicional con el que los turistas valoren la gobernanza del destino que visitan.

Tabla 4. Estimación del modelo: variable endógena: ASES

ASES: asistente de voz y texto. Este asesor ayuda y guía a los turistas durante todo el ciclo del viaje mediante una interacción dialogada en lenguaje natural, ofreciéndoles la información más relevante del destino, en relación a su perfil.

Variable	Estimación MCO	Valor t	p-valor	FIV
Intercepto	3,6255	6,732	0,0000 **	
CONO	0,0933	0,371	0,7111	1,010
IMP	0,0742	1,773	0,0764	1,095
GOBE	-0,1907	-3,194	0,0014 **	1,818
INNO	0,1387	2,472	0,0136 *	2,348
TECN	0,1938	4,324	0,0001 **	1,816
SOST	0,1215	1,760	0,0787	1,773
ACCE	0,1373	2,559	0,0106 *	1,451
Prueba F (7, 1038): 14,3721 (p-valor: 0,0000) R cuadrado: 0,1004 * Parámetro significativo al 5%; ** Parámetro significativo al 1%.				

4.5. Realidad aumentada-realidad virtual

El factor que, en mayor medida, condiciona el interés del turista por la realidad aumentada y la realidad virtual es la tecnología, de manera que por cada punto adicional que el turista otorgue al desarrollo tecnológico del destino, su interés por este tipo de aplicaciones inteligentes se incrementa en 0,2619 puntos (c.p.). Además de la tecnología, hay otros dos factores que favorecen el interés por la implantación en los destinos de la realidad aumentada y de la realidad virtual. Se trata de la accesibilidad (cuanto más accesible es el destino, mayor es también el interés por estas aplicaciones) y la importancia que el turista concede al hecho de que el destino sea oficialmente considerado como inteligente (cada vez que esta importancia se incremente en un punto, el interés de los turistas se incrementará en 0,1539 puntos, c.p.)

Tabla 5. Estimación del modelo: variable endógena: REAL

REAL: permite crear un destino turístico virtual e inmersivo, combinando el mundo físico con el virtual para identificar atractivos e información relevante alrededor del turista.				
Variable	**Estimación MCO**	**Valor t**	**p-valor**	**FIV**
Intercepto	2,2552	3,984	0,0000 **	
CONO	-0,5283	-1,661	0,0971	1,010
IMP	0,1539	3,355	0,0008 **	1,095
GOBE	-0,1136	-1,704	0,0887	1,818
INNO	0,0442	0,580	0,5622	2,348
TECN	0,2619	4,552	0,0000 **	1,816

Variable	Estimación MCO	Valor t	p-valor	FIV
SOST	0,0600	0,800	0,4238	1,773
ACCE	0,1551	2,625	0,0088 **	1,451
Prueba F (7, 1038): 13,8411 (p-valor: 0,0000) R cuadrado: 0,1004 * Parámetro significativo al 5%; ** Parámetro significativo al 1%.				

4.6. Planificador de rutas

El interés de los turistas por los planificadores de rutas está directamente relacionado con la percepción de los mismos sobre el carácter innovador y accesible de los destinos (Tabla 6). Así, por cada punto en que se incremente la percepción del turista de que está visitando un destino innovador, se estima que el interés por un planificador de rutas se incrementará en 0,1658 puntos (c.p.), mientras que lo hará en 0,1460 puntos por cada incremento unitario en la percepción de que el destino es accesible. El modelo estimado también ha identificado una relación directa entre el interés por esta aplicación inteligente y la importancia que el turista concede al hecho de que el destino sea inteligente (0,1360; c.p.) y una relación inversa entre dicho interés y la percepción de que el destino cuenta con una buena gobernanza (-0,1084; c.p.).

Tabla 6. Estimación del modelo: variable endógena: PLAN

PLAN: permite recomendar y agregar las diferentes rutas del destino y ofrecer un plan detallado en base a los días de estancia y preferencias del turista.				
Variable	**Estimación MCO**	**Valor t**	**p-valor**	**FIV**
Intercepto	5,3019	11,550	0,0000 **	
CONO	-0,0775	-0,442	0,6585	1,010
IMP	0,1360	3,655	0,0003 **	1,095
GOBE	-0,1084	-2,234	0,0257 *	1,818
INNO	0,1658	3,391	0,0007 **	2,348
TECN	-0,0275	-0,784	0,4331	1,816
SOST	0,0979	1,702	0,0890	1,773
ACCE	0,1460	3,372	0,0008 **	1,451
Prueba F (7, 1038): 9,7003 (p-valor: 0,0000) R cuadrado: 0,1072 * Parámetro significativo al 5%; ** Parámetro significativo al 1%.				

4.7. Pulsera inteligente

En el interés de los turistas por el uso de pulseras inteligentes confluyen factores que contribuyen a que el mismo se incremente, y factores que contribuyen a que se reduzca. Así, y según se desprende de la Tabla 7, cuanto más innovador (0,2411) y más accesible (0,1998) sea el destino, mayor será el interés de los turistas por las pulseras inteligentes. También se incrementa el interés por esta aplicación inteligente a medida que aumenta la importancia que el turista concede al hecho de estar visitando un destino inteligente (0,2526, c.p.). Sin embargo, el conocimiento del concepto DTI tiende a frenar el interés por estas pulseras inteligentes, ya que son los turistas que menor conocimiento tienen los que se más interesan por ellos y, por el contrario, los que mejor conocen el concepto DTI son los que muestren menor interés. Algo similar, aunque con un efecto más suavizado, sucede con la percepción del desarrollo tecnológico del destino (-0,1575).

Tabla 7. Estimación del modelo: variable endógena: PULS

PULS: wearable equipada con chip de radiofrecuencia que permite localizar a los portadores de la pulsera.

Variable	Estimación MCO	Valor t	p-valor	FIV
Intercepto	4,6933	8,974	0,0000 **	
CONO	-0,7229	-2,313	0,0209 *	1,010
IMP	0,2516	5,465	0,0000 **	1,095
GOBE	-0,0392	-0,641	0,5218	1,818
INNO	0,2411	3,240	0,0012 **	2,348
TECN	-0,1575	-3,142	0,0017 **	1,816
SOST	-0,1076	-1,614	0,1069	1,773
ACCE	0,1998	3,552	0,0004 **	1,451

Prueba F (7, 1038): 12,0740 (p-valor: 0,0000)
R cuadrado: 0,0877
* Parámetro significativo al 5%; ** Parámetro significativo al 1%.

4.8. Cuaderno de viaje

El interés por los cuadernos de viaje es la aplicación inteligente, de entre todas las analizadas en este trabajo, que en mayor medida depende de las variables exógenas del modelo (véase la Tabla 8). En concreto, la única variable que parece no condicionar este interés es la percepción de la sostenibilidad del destino. Sin embargo, no todas las variables exógenas con parámetros estadísticamente significativos contribuyen a incrementar el interés por los cuadernos de viaje. Así, este interés se incrementa cuando lo hace la importancia que el turista concede al hecho de que el destino sea inteligente (0,1027, c.p.), cuando aumenta la percepción de que el destino es innovador (0,2585; c.p.) y cuando lo hace la percepción de que el destino está desarrollado tecnológicamente (0,1550, c.p.). Sin embargo, el interés se reduce a medida que se incrementa el grado de conocimiento que el turista tiene del concepto DTI (-0,7601, c.p.) y a medida que lo hace la percepción de que el destino está bien gobernado (-0,1420; c.p.).

Tabla 8. Estimación del modelo: variable endógena: CUAD

CUAD: solución para la gestión del viaje en su globalidad, incluyendo todas las actividades y lugares contratados que lo conforman a modo de cuaderno.

Variable	Estimación MCO	Valor t	p-valor	FIV
Intercepto	3,8185	9,166	0,0000 **	
CONO	-0,7601	-3,036	0,0025 **	1,010
IMP	0,1027	2,728	0,0065 **	1,095
GOBE	-0,1420	-2,647	0,0083 **	1,818
INNO	0,2585	4,498	0,0000 **	2,348
TECN	0,1550	3,372	0,0008 **	1,816
SOST	-0,0337	-0,596	0,5515	1,773
ACCE	0,1537	3,394	0,0007 **	1,451

Prueba F (7, 1038): 24,5462 (p-valor: 0,0000)
R cuadrado: 0,1454
* Parámetro significativo al 5%; ** Parámetro significativo al 1%.

4.9. Gamificación

El interés de los turistas por la gamificación se incrementa cuando lo hace la importancia que el turista otorga a la inteligencia turística y cuando percibe que el destino es innovador (véase la Tabla 9). Así, por cada punto en que se incremente la importancia que el turista da al hecho de que el destino que está visitando sea inteligente, el interés por la gamificación se incrementa en 0,1958 puntos (c.p.). En mucha mayor medida se incrementa este interés (0,3286, c.p.) por cada punto adicional que el turista otorga al carácter innovador del destino. Sin embargo, la percepción de una buena gobernanza desincentiva el interés por la gamificación (-0,1352, c.p.), aunque el factor que, con diferencia, más frena este interés es el grado de conocimiento del concepto DTI, ya que por cada punto adicional en dicho grado de conocimiento que manifieste el turista, su interés promedio en la gamificación se reduce en 0,6105 puntos.

Tabla 9. Estimación del modelo: variable endógena: GAMI

GAMI: herramienta para el uso de la gamificación como sistema de interacción, estímulo del consumo y entretenimiento para los turistas durante su estancia.

Variable	Estimación MCO	Valor t	p-valor	FIV
Intercepto	3,9348	9,139	0,0000 **	
CONO	-0,6105	-2,258	0,0242 *	1,010
IMP	0,1958	4,648	0,0000 **	1,095
GOBE	-0,1352	-2,251	0,0246 *	1,818
INNO	0,3286	5,105	0,0000 **	2,348
TECN	-0,0794	-1,768	0,0773	1,816
SOST	0,0686	1,132	0,2578	1,773
ACCE	0,0709	1,503	0,1332	1,451

Prueba F (7, 1038): 16,9844 (p-valor: 0,0000)
R cuadrado: 0,1100
* Parámetro significativo al 5%; ** Parámetro significativo al 1%.

4.10. Gestor de reclamaciones y quejas

Finalmente, el interés de los turistas consultados por los gestores de reclamaciones y quejas se incrementa a medida que crece la importancia que el turista concede a estar en un destino inteligente y la percepción de que el destino es sostenible. Así, por cada punto adicional en la importancia que el turista otorga a la inteligencia de los destinos, el interés por estos gestores se incrementa en 0,1162 puntos (c.p.), mientras que por cada punto en que se incrementa la percepción de la sostenibilidad del destino, dicho interés experimenta un crecimiento estimado de 0,0972 puntos. Por el contrario, el grado de conocimiento que el turista tenga del concepto DTI contribuye a frenar el interés por este tipo de aplicación inteligente, de forma que cuando el grado de conocimiento se incrementa en un punto, el interés por los gestores de reclamaciones y quejas experimenta una reducción estimada de 0,6013 puntos.

Tabla 10. Estimación del modelo: variable endógena: GEST

GEST: generación y gestión de incidencias, quejas y reclamaciones por parte del turista hacia el destino y sus empresas.

Variable	Estimación MCO	Valor t	p-valor	FIV
Intercepto	5,8099	13,780	0,0000 **	
CONO	-0,6013	-2,721	0,0066 **	1,010
IMP	0,1162	3,649	0,0003 **	1,095
GOBE	0,0189	0,416	0,6775	1,818
INNO	0,0842	1,849	0,0647	2,348
TECN	0,0014	0,046	0,9637	1,816
SOST	0,0972	2,046	0,0410 *	1,773
ACCE	0,0639	1,710	0,0876	1,451
Prueba F (7, 1038): 10,6205 (p-valor: 0,0000) R cuadrado: 0,0978 * Parámetro significativo al 5%; ** Parámetro significativo al 1%.				

5. CONCLUSIONES

En este estudio se ha analizado la percepción de los turistas sobre la implantación de soluciones tecnológicas en destinos turísticos inteligentes a partir de una encuesta realizada a visitantes de los municipios de la provincia de Cáceres integrados en la Red DTI de Segittur. El objetivo ha sido comprobar si el conocimiento del concepto DTI, la importancia que se le atribuye y las dimensiones del modelo Segittur percibidas influyen en el interés por dichas soluciones.

Los factores considerados para explicar el interés que los turistas tienen por la implantación de aplicaciones tecnológicas en los destinos turísticos inteligentes tienen una influencia dispar, según se ha podido demostrar a partir de los modelos de regresión estimados en este trabajo. Así, el factor que contribuye en mayor medida a generar interés entre los turistas es la importancia que estos conceden a que el destino visitado forme parte oficialmente de la red DTI (para el 80% de las aplicaciones estudiadas, esta importancia tiene una influencia positiva y estadísticamente significativa). Esto se ve respaldado por estudios que evidencian cómo el reconocimiento oficial como DTI ha sido utilizado como herramienta estratégica para mejorar la infraestructura tecnológica y los servicios digitales, favoreciendo la atracción de nuevos modelos de negocio y reforzando el posicionamiento competitivo del destino (Cornejo-Ortega & Malcolm, 2020).

La innovación parece ser también un factor determinante en el interés mostrado por los turistas consultados, dado que la percepción de que el destino es innovador contribuye a incrementar el interés por las aplicaciones consideradas en el 60% de los casos. En esta línea, Femenia-Serra & Neuhofer (2018) subrayan que las experiencias turísticas inteligentes se desarrollan en entornos caracterizados por una interacción dinámica y con un claro espíritu innovador, lo que refuerza el papel central de la innovación en la percepción del destino. En consonancia con esta idea, varios estudios coinciden en que la incorporación de tecnologías innovadoras no solo moderniza la oferta digital del destino, sino que también incrementa la satisfacción del visitante y refuerza su imagen como destino competitivo e innovador (Ferràs et al., 2020; Ramanauskas et al., 2024).

Por el contrario, hay dos factores que, lejos de hacer que el turista muestre más interés por estas aplicaciones, influyen negativamente sobre dicho interés. El primero de estos factores es la gobernanza del destino, dado que en los cuatro casos en los que este factor ha sido estadísticamente significativo, el signo del parámetro estimado ha sido negativo, es decir, cuanto mayor es la percepción de que el destino está bien gobernado, menor es el interés por estas cuatro aplicaciones inteligentes. Esta aparente contradicción, como señalan Corrêa & Gosling (2020), puede deberse a que la gobernanza opera de forma estructural y poco visible, por lo que los turistas no la perciben directamente. Así, cuando consideran que todo funciona correctamente, tienden a confiar en los servicios presenciales, reduciendo su necesidad de recurrir a herramientas digitales. El segundo de estos factores es el grado de conocimiento del concepto DTI, ya que en otras cuatro aplicaciones inteligentes han sido los turistas que menos conocen el concepto lo que han demostrado más interés por los mismos. En esta línea, Jeong & Shin (2020) encontraron que los turistas con menor familiaridad con las tecnologías turísticas inteligentes valoraban especialmente la capacidad informativa de estas herramientas, lo que sugiere que, ante un conocimiento limitado del entorno inteligente, los usuarios tienden a apoyarse más en las aplicaciones para obtener información útil y en tiempo real que les ayude a enriquecer su experiencia.

Como demuestran varios estudios (Azis et al., 2020; Azmadi et al., 2023; Tavitiyaman et al., 2021), las percepciones de los visitantes sobre las soluciones tecnológicas son determinantes para su satisfacción, la imagen del destino y su intención de regresar o recomendarlo, lo que subraya la necesidad de diseñar tecnologías turísticas centradas en la experiencia del usuario. En este contexto, resulta imprescindible poner en valor el papel que desempeñan las tecnologías de la información y la comunicación en la consolidación de los destinos turísticos inteligentes, pues estas tecnologías permiten una interacción más fluida entre los distintos actores turísticos y facilitan la toma de decisiones. No obstante, como señalan Gomes et al.

(2017), la transición hacia un modelo de destino turístico inteligente requiere no solo de infraestructura tecnológica, sino también de planificación estratégica, cooperación público-privada y una gobernanza orientada a la innovación. En este sentido, se recomienda a los actores implicados avanzar hacia modelos de gestión basados en datos, promoviendo la interoperabilidad de sistemas, la integración de plataformas digitales y el uso de tecnologías emergentes, como la inteligencia artificial, el big data o el Internet de las Cosas (Palomo-Santiago & Parra-López, 2024).

Pese a estos hallazgos, este estudio presenta algunas limitaciones que deben ser consideradas en futuros estudios. En primer lugar, el trabajo se ha centrado en los destinos turísticos inteligentes de la provincia de Cáceres, lo que puede limitar la generalización de los resultados a otros contextos geográficos. Por tanto, sería oportuno replicar este estudio en otros destinos turísticos inteligentes con el fin de contrastar los resultados obtenidos. En segundo lugar, el estudio se ha apoyado en una metodología cuantitativa que ha permitido identificar tendencias generales en las percepciones de los turistas. No obstante, este enfoque limita la posibilidad de profundizar en aspectos más subjetivos y contextuales de la experiencia turística, que podrían explorarse mejor mediante técnicas cualitativas. Por último, es fundamental incorporar la perspectiva de otros actores turísticos, como residentes, gestores públicos o empresas tecnológicas, con el fin de avanzar hacia modelos de gobernanza colaborativa que garanticen un desarrollo turístico óptimo.

6. REFERENCIAS

Azis, N., Amin, M., Chan, S. and Aprilia, C. (2020), How smart tourism technologies affect tourist destination loyalty, Journal of Hospitality and Tourism Technology, Vol. 11 No. 4, pp. 603-625. https://doi.org/10.1108/JHTT-01-2020-0005

Azis, N., Amin, M., Chan, S., & Aprilia, C. (2020). How smart tourism technologies affect tourist destination loyalty. Journal of Hospitality and Tourism Technology, 11(4), 603–625. https://doi.org/10.1108/JHTT-01-2020-0005/FULL/PDF

Azmadi, A. S. A., Abdul Hamid, M., Hanafiah, M. H., Hariani, D., & Mior Shariffuddin, N. S. (2023). Measuring Tourist Preferences and Behavior Toward Smart Tourism Destination Planning. Planning Malaysia, 21(6), 342–356. https://doi.org/10.21837/PM.V21I30.1405

Blanco, J. (2015) Libro blanco de los destinos turísticos inteligentes: estrategias y soluciones para fomentar la innovación en el turismo digital. LID Editorial, Biblioteca ALTRAN.

Buhalis, D. & Amaranggana, A. (2014) Smart Tourism Destinations Enhancing Tourism Experience Through Personalisation of Services. Information and Communication Technologies in Tourism 2015, 377-389.

Buhalis, D. (2019), Technology in tourism-from information communication technologies to eTourism and smart tourism towards ambient intelligence tourism: a perspective article, Tourism Review, Vol. 75 No. 1, pp. 267-272.

Cornejo Ortega, J.L. and Malcolm, C.D. (2020) Touristic stakeholders' perceptions about the smart tourism destination concept in Puerto Vallarta, Jalisco, Mexico, Sustainability, 12(5), p. 1741. https://doi.org/10.3390/su12051741.

Cornejo-Ortega, J. L., & Malcolm, C. D. (2020). Touristic Stakeholders' Perceptions about the Smart Tourism Destination Concept in Puerto Vallarta, Jalisco, Mexico. Sustainability 2020, Vol. 12, Page 1741, 12(5), 1741. https://doi.org/10.3390/SU12051741

Corrêa, S. C. H., & Gosling, M. de S. (2020). Travelers' Perception of Smart Tourism Experiences in Smart Tourism Destinations. Tourism Planning and Development, 18(4), 415–434. https://doi.org/10.1080/21568316.2020.1798689

Crompton, J. L. (1979). An assessment of the image of Mexico as a vacation and the influence of geographical location upon that image. Journal of Travel Research, 17(4), 18–23. https://doi.org/10.1177/004728757901700404

Development, DOI: 10.1080/21568316.2020.1798689

Economia Industrial/RevistaEconomiaIndustrial/395/LOPEZ DE AVILA y GARCÍA.pdf

Femenia-Serra, F., & Neuhofer, B. (2018). Smart tourism experiences: conceptualisation, key dimensions and research agenda. Investigaciones Regionales – Journal of Regional Research, 2019(42). https://investigacionesregionales.org/en/article/smart-tourism-experiences-conceptualisation-key-dimensions-and-research-agenda/

Femenia-Serra, F., Neuhofer, B. and Ivars-Baidal, J.A. (2019), Towards a conceptualisation of smart tourists and their role within the smart destination scenario, The Service Industries Journal, Vol. 39 No. 2, pp. 109-133.

Femenia-Serra, F., Perless-Ribes, J. F., & Ivars-Baidal, J. A. (2019b). Smart destinations and tech-savvy millennial tourists: Hype versus reality. Tourism Review, 74(1), 63–81. https://doi.org/10.1108/TR-02-2018-0018.

Ferràs, X., Hitchen, E. L., Tarrats-Pons, E., & Arimany-Serrat, N. (2020). Smart Tourism Empowered by Artificial Intelligence: The Case of Lanzarote. Journal of Cases on Information Technology, 22(1), 1–13. https://doi.org/10.4018/JCIT.2020010101

Gomes, E. L., Gândara, J. M., & Ivars-Baidal, J. (2017). É importante ser um destino turístico inteligente? A compreensão dos gestores públicos dos destinos do

Estado do Paraná. Revista Brasileira de Pesquisa Em Turismo, 11(3), 503–536. https://doi.org/10.7784/RBTUR.V11I3.1318

Gretzel, U., Reino, S., Kopera, S. and Koo, C. (2015), Smart tourism challenges, Journal of Tourism, Vol. 16 No. 1, pp. 41-47.

Gretzel, U., Sigala, M., Xiang, Z. et al. (2015) Smart tourism: foundations and developments. Electron Markets 25, 179–188. https://doi.org/10.1007/s12525-015-0196-8

Huang, C.D.; Goo, J.; Nam, K.; Yoo, C.W. Smart tourism technologies in travel planning: The role of exploration and exploitation. Inf. Manag. 2017, 54, pp. 757–770. https://doi.org/10.1016/j.im.2016.11.010

Ivars-Baidal, J., Solsona Monzonís, F. J., & Giner Sánchez, D. (2016). Gestión turística y tecnologías de la información y la comunicación (TIC): El nuevo enfoque de los destinos inteligentes. https://doi.org/10.5565/rev/dag.285

Jeong, M., & Shin, H. H. (2020). Tourists' Experiences with Smart Tourism Technology at Smart Destinations and Their Behavior Intentions. Journal of Travel Research, 59(8), 1464–1477. https://doi.org/10.1177/0047287519883034

Kock, F., Josiassen, A., & Assaf, A. G. (2016). Advancing destination image: The destination content model. Annals of Tourism Research, 61, 28–44. https://doi.org/10.1016/j.annals.2016.07.003.

López de Ávila, A., & García, S. (2013). Destinos turísticos inteligentes. Economía Industrial, (395), 61–69. Retrieved from http://www.minetad.gob.es/Publicaciones/Publicacionesperiodicas/

Mior Shariffuddin, N. S., Azinuddin, M., Yahya, N. E., & Hanafiah, M. H. (2023). Navigating the tourism digital landscape: The interrelationship of online travel sites' affordances, technology readiness, online purchase intentions, trust, and Eloyalty. Heliyon, 9(8), 1-14. https://doi.org/10.1016/j.heliyon.2023.e19135

Monitur (2023) Disponible: https://www.exceltur.org/wp-content/uploads/2024/07/Exceltur-MONITUR-2023-junio-2024.pdf

Palomo-Santiago, M., & Parra-López, E. (2024). Intellectual influence of smart tourism destinations 2000-2023. Tourism and Hospitality Management, 30(3), 301–316. https://doi.org/10.20867/THM.30.3.1

Papadimitriou, D., Apostolopoulou, A., & Kaplanidou, K. K. (2014). Destination personality, affective image, and behavioral intentions in domestic urban tourism. Journal of Travel Research, 54(3), 302–315. https://doi.org/10.1177/0047287513516389.

Perception of Smart Tourism Experiences in Smart Tourism Destinations, Tourism Planning &

Ramanauskas, J., Banevičius, Š., & Bielskis, P. (2024). Evaluation of smartness of the tourism destination websites of the Klaipeda region. Baltic Journal of Economic Studies, 10(5), 31–39. https://doi.org/10.30525/2256-0742/2024-10-5-31-39

Sánchez-Rivero, M., Rodríguez-Rangel, M. C., & Ricci-Risquete, A. (2022). K-Means segmentation of tourism accommodation based on the active use of websites: Its application to an emerging destination (Extremadura, Spain). Journal of Vacation Marketing, 29(4), 654-669. https://doi.org/10.1177/13567667221117303

Stela Cristina Hott Corrêa & Marlusa de Sevilha Gosling (2020) Travelers' Perception of Smart Tourism Experiences in Smart Tourism Destinations, Tourism Planning & Development, DOI: 10.1080/21568316.2020.1798689

Tavitiyaman, P., Qu, H., Tsang, W. S. L., & Lam, C. W. R. (2021). The influence of smart tourism applications on perceived destination image and behavioral intention: The moderating role of information search behavior.Journal of Hospitality and Tourism Management,46, 476-487. https://doi.org/10.1016/j.jhtm.2021.02.003.

Tavitiyaman, P., Qu, H., Tsang, W. sze L., & Lam, C. wah R. (2021). The influence of smart tourism applications on perceived destination image and behavioral intention: The moderating role of information search behavior. Journal of Hospitality and Tourism Management, 46, 476–487. https://doi.org/10.1016/J.JHTM.2021.02.003

Tussyadiah, I.P., Jung, T.H. and Tom Dieck, M.C. (2018), Embodiment of wearable augmented reality technology in tourismexperiences, Journal of Travel Research, Vol. 57 No. 5, pp. 597-611.

Um, T. and Chung, N. (2019), Does smart tourism technology matter? Lessons from three smart tourism cities in South Korea, Asia Pacific Journal of TourismResearch:, pp. 1-19.

Wang, D., Park, S. and Fesenmaier, D.R. (2012), The role of smartphones in mediating the touristic experience, Journal of Travel Research, Vol. 51 No. 4, pp. 371-387.

Xia, M., Zhang, Y., & Zhang, C. (2018). A TAM-based approach to explore the effect of online experience on destination image: A smartphone user's perspective. Journal of Destination Marketing & Management, 8, 259–270. https://doi.org/10.1016/j.jdmm.2017.05.002.

Xiang, Z., Tussyadiah, I., & Buhalis, D. (2015). Smart destinations: Foundations, analytics, and applications. Journal of Destination Marketing and Management, 4(3), pp. 143-144. https://doi.org/10.1016/j.jdmm.2015.07.001

LA REALIDAD VIRTUAL COMO ESTRATEGIA DE RECUPERACIÓN EMOCIONAL Y GESTIÓN INTELIGENTE EN DESTINOS TURÍSTICOS

AMPARO CERVERA-TAULET
Universitat de València, España.

ALENA KOSTYK
EDHEC Business School, Francia

KIRSTEN COWAN
University of Edinburgh, UK

TEMÁTICA: Innovación – Innovación en la experiencia turística

RESUMEN: Este estudio presenta evidencia empírica sobre el uso de la realidad virtual (RV) como herramienta de recuperación emocional ante experiencias negativas en destinos turísticos. A través de dos experimentos de laboratorio, se demuestra que una experiencia inmersiva positiva en RV mejora significativamente las emociones negativas evocadas por experiencias turísticas desfavorables, aumentando la memorabilidad y fomentando el storytelling personal. Los resultados sugieren que la RV puede integrarse estratégicamente en la gestión inteligente de destinos para fortalecer la relación emocional con el turista, contribuir a la sostenibilidad emocional y apoyar políticas de innovación turística orientadas al bienestar del visitante.

Palabras clave: realidad virtual, turismo emocional, recuperación de servicios, memorabilidad, storytelling, innovación en destinos.

ABSTRACT: This study presents empirical evidence on the use of virtual reality (VR) as an emotional recovery tool for negative tourism experiences. Through two laboratory experiments, it demonstrates that a positive immersive VR experience significantly improves emotional responses associated with unfavorable tourism scenarios, enhancing memorability and fostering personal storytelling. The findings suggest that VR can be strategically integrated into smart destination management to reinforce the tourist's emotional connection, contribute to emotional sustainability, and support tourism innovation policies aimed at visitor wellbeing.

Keywords: virtual reality, emotional tourism, service recovery, memorability, storytelling, destination innovation.

1. INTRODUCCIÓN

Las emociones del consumidor desempeñan un papel fundamental en el consumo, especialmente en ofertas hedónicas y experienciales como el turismo (Knobloch et al., 2017). Si los turistas experimentan emociones negativas al interactuar con un destino turístico, estas reacciones negativas pueden tener un efecto negativo en sus futuras intenciones de comportamiento (Prayag et al., 2017).

La realidad virtual se utiliza cada vez más en el mercado para potenciar los beneficios del consumo gracias a sus características experienciales (Cowan et al., 2023). El contenido de realidad virtual relacionado con la marca está diseñado por profesionales del marketing y, por lo tanto, la representa con una imagen perfecta; sin embargo, a menudo se percibe como una experiencia en primera persona (Kostyk & Sheng, 2023). Esto sugiere que la realidad virtual podría remediar experiencias negativas de la vida real, ya que el contenido de realidad virtual puede inducir fuertes emociones positivas (Pavic et al., 2022) y evocar reacciones emocionales más positivas que otros formatos de marketing (Flavián et al., 2021). En consonancia con esto, la literatura previa sobre la recuperación del servicio subraya el papel de las emociones en la "remediación" de experiencias negativas de marca (Harrison-Walker, 2019).

Las emociones de los turistas son cruciales para que las experiencias sean memorables, influyendo en la planificación y el comportamiento (Pizam, 2010; Tung & Ritchie, 2011; Wood, 2020). Estudios preliminares sugieren que los recuerdos de la RV se transfieren al mundo real (Smith, 2019), lo que sugiere el potencial de la RV para crear nuevas experiencias memorables. Es importante destacar que las experiencias personales no se almacenan en la memoria como una unidad, más bien, el cerebro humano genera "marcadores de memoria" registrando los cambios ocurridos durante la experiencia (Ahn et al., 2009; Ezzyat & Davachi, 2011; Tulving, 1972). Es lógico que un mayor cambio resulte en más marcadores de memoria, haciendo que las experiencias sean más memorables.

Además, los recuerdos de los turistas se representan, reproducen y recrean posteriormente a través de narrativas personales y relatos (Cater et al., 2021). Los recuerdos más intensos se convierten en el punto focal de las historias que los turistas comparten con otros, lo que asegura que la experiencia permanezca vívida y 'viva' en su mente (Zhong et al., 2017). La narración de historias fomenta el interés y conduce a la persuasión narrativa (Ma et al., 2023). Este proceso construye una narrativa de la memoria que evoluciona con el tiempo y finalmente impacta en resultados de marketing, como la intención de comportamiento futuro (Alrawadieh et al., 2023; Zatori et al., 2018). La investigación previa ha explorado de forma limitada el papel de la tecnología inmersiva en la promoción de la memorabilidad y la construcción de relatos (Olya et al., 2020; Shin, 2018). En resumen, se plantea que la memorabilidad generada por una experiencia positiva de realidad virtual potencia la narrativa de los consumidores y, a su vez, influye en sus intenciones de comportamiento.

Por lo tanto, las emociones negativas de los turistas, aunque poco frecuentes, pueden tener efectos duraderos en la reputación del destino y en la intención de volver a visitarlo. La mayoría de las estrategias de recuperación se centran en los aspectos operativos, descuidando los componentes emocionales. La realidad virtual ofrece una vía inmersiva para reconfigurar dichas emociones, abriendo nuevas oportunidades para una gestión de destinos emocionalmente inteligentes. Este estudio se centra específicamente en el uso de la RV como herramienta de recuperación emocional tras una experiencia, más que como herramienta para la toma de decisiones previas al viaje. El objetivo es explorar cómo se puede implementar la RV tras una experiencia turística negativa para restaurar el afecto positivo y apoyar los procesos de recuperación del servicio.

A pesar de su escaso análisis, las reacciones emocionales negativas en el turismo pueden afectar significativamente la imagen del destino y la intención de volver a visitarlo. Sin embargo, la mayoría de las estrategias de recuperación se centran en aspectos operativos, a menudo ignorando la dimensión emocional. La RV ofrece una alternativa prometedora para la recuperación emocional posterior a la experiencia, fomentando una gestión del destino emocionalmente inteligente. Este estudio examina específicamente el papel de la RV no como una herramienta para la toma de decisiones previas al viaje, sino como una intervención de recuperación posterior al mismo. Dada la escasa investigación sobre la memorabilidad en el turismo de RV, este estudio examina específicamente cómo una experiencia inmersiva positiva en RV puede contrarrestar emociones negativas previas y cómo este cambio emocional se relaciona con la memorabilidad y el storytelling del turista, impactando finalmente en su intención de visita o recomendación. Para ello, se plantean cuatro preguntas de investigación:

- **RQ1:** ¿Qué procesos psicológicos explican la memorabilidad de una experiencia positiva de RV tras una experiencia turística negativa o positiva?
- **RQ2:** ¿En qué medida la RV mejora las emociones negativas evocadas por experiencias previas?

- **RQ3:** ¿Cómo la memorabilidad y el storytelling median este cambio emocional?
- **RQ4:** ¿Cuál es el impacto final en la intención de visita o recomendación?

Esta propuesta se alinea con el eje de innovación del congreso, mostrando cómo las tecnologías inmersivas pueden apoyar el diseño de estrategias de recuperación emocional basadas en la evidencia. Aboga por un enfoque centrado en el ser humano, tecnológico y sostenible para mejorar las experiencias turísticas.

2. MARCO TEÓRICO

2.1. Emociones y turismo

Las emociones son fundamentales en el turismo y la hostelería, ya que influyen significativamente en el comportamiento del consumidor, la toma de decisiones y los resultados de la experiencia. A menudo, las emociones se conceptualizan como (Hosany et al., 2021; Le et al., 2020) constructos multifacéticos que incluyen estados afectivos subjetivos, comportamientos expresivos y respuestas fisiológicas (Le et al., 2020).

Las investigaciones demuestran que los estímulos emocionalmente intensos, tanto positivos como negativos, mejoran la memorabilidad de los eventos (Kensinger & Corkin, 2003; Kim, 2014; Wirtz et al., 2003). Algunos estudios argumentan que los eventos negativos podrían estar más fuertemente codificados que los positivos (Kensinger & Schacter, 2006; Sthapit, Björk, et al., 2020). Sin embargo, los hallazgos empíricos sugieren que, en el contexto turístico, las emociones positivas predominan en la memoria en todas las etapas del servicio (Torres et al., 2017).

La implicación emocional es un factor clave para lograr experiencias turísticas memorables; sin embargo, muchos estudios descuidan los factores personales y emocionales en la formación de la memoria. La Teoría de la Evaluación Cognitiva (CAT) ofrece un marco sólido para comprender cómo las personas desarrollan respuestas emocionales (Skavronskaya et al., 2017). En concreto, la "regla del punto álgido" destaca que los momentos emotivos álgidos, ya sean positivos o negativos, y el estado emocional final influyen significativamente en la evaluación global y el recuerdo de la experiencia (Bastiaansen et al., 2019).

2.2. Realidad virtual y experiencias inmersivas

Se ha demostrado que las interfaces tecnológicas generan experiencias memorables, y características de los medios como la interactividad y la inmersión pueden mejorar la evocación de las escenas en entornos de realidad virtual (RV) (Golja & Paulišić, 2021; Marchiori et al., 2017). Las aplicaciones de RV tienen el potencial de enriquecer el turismo al amplificar la percepción del entorno físico, lo que genera experiencias más impactantes y memorables (Jung et al., 2016, 2017; Passebois Ducros & Euzéby, 2021).

La RV también puede servir como medio para almacenar y compartir recuerdos de viajes (Beck et al., 2019), y se ha demostrado que la realidad aumentada (RA) mejora todos los componentes de las experiencias turísticas memorables (S. Jiang et al., 2022). La inmersión sensorial y la presencia espacial son cruciales para la experiencia del usuario, ya que la RV/RA ofrece contenido detallado, entretenido e interactivo, que contribuye al disfrute, la autonomía y la formación (Flavián et al., 2019; Maubisson et al., 2022; Yung & Khoo-Lattimore, 2019; Zhu et al., 2023).

Además, se ha demostrado que la intensidad y la inmersión promueven una fuerte sensación de presencia, lo que a su vez potencia los componentes cognitivos, afectivos y conductuales de la experiencia turística (X. Jiang et al., 2023). Dado que las emociones son fundamentales para la evaluación y la recordación de las experiencias (Bastiaansen et al., 2019), la RV se perfila como una herramienta poderosa no para la promoción, sino para la recuperación y la reconfiguración emocional tras la experiencia.

2.3. Memorabilidad y Storytelling

La memorabilidad se refiere a la capacidad de codificar, almacenar y recuperar experiencias personales (Brown et al., 1977; Kim, 2014; Malone et al., 2018; Saket et al., 2016). En turismo, representa la evaluación que los turistas hacen de una experiencia y su grado de recordación (Campos et al., 2017; Oh et al., 2007; Sthapit, Del Chiappa, Coudounaris, & Bjork, 2020).

El Storytelling se reconoce cada vez más como un proceso cognitivo-afectivo en el que las personas reconstruyen y comunican sus experiencias mediante historias. Estas narrativas suelen surgir de momentos extraordinarios o de gran carga emocional (Cater et al., 2021). Si bien algunas investigaciones se han centrado en la narración positiva, las experiencias memorables negativas también merecen atención (Zhong et al., 2017).

En este estudio, conceptualizamos el storytelling no solo como una estrategia de comunicación, sino también como un mecanismo mediante el cual las emociones y la memorabilidad moldean el comportamiento del consumidor. Los recuerdos emocionalmente intensos tienen mayor probabilidad de ser compartidos y desarrollados a través del storytelling, lo que a su vez mejora la persuasión y la durabilidad del mensaje (Jensen et al., 2023; Zhong et al., 2017). Por lo tanto, postulamos que la memorabilidad actúa como precursor del storytelling, especialmente en contextos inmersivos como la realidad virtual (RV).

Las tecnologías inmersivas como la realidad virtual (RV) fomentan la interacción emocional y mejoran la memorabilidad de las experiencias (Olya et al., 2020; Shin, 2018). La RV destaca por su capacidad para facilitar un storytelling rico y significativo que fortalece el posicionamiento de marca (Kostyk & Sheng, 2023)y apoya objetivos educativos y culturales mediante storytelling con gran resonancia emocional (Marasco, 2020).

3. METODOLOGÍA

3.1. Diseño experimental

Se realizaron dos experimentos de laboratorio para abordar las preguntas de investigación. Cada uno empleó un diseño intersujetos para la variable manipulada (valencia del escenario: positiva vs. negativa) y un diseño intrasujetos para la variable medida (emociones antes y después de la exposición a la RV). Si bien todos los participantes experimentaron el mismo contenido positivo de RV, se evaluaron las respuestas emocionales en ambas condiciones y momentos para evaluar la variación en los resultados afectivos.

3.2. Procedimiento

Los participantes (Estudio 1: N=23; Estudio 2: N=39) fueron asignados aleatoriamente a leer escenarios turísticos validados, positivos o negativos. Tras leer el escenario, todos los participantes experimentaron la misma experiencia positiva de realidad virtual en la ciudad de Edimburgo.

Se midieron las emociones antes y después de la exposición a la RV. Otros constructos (memorabilidad, storytelling e intención de visita) también se evaluaron después de la exposición mediante escalas validadas.

Si bien el tamaño de la muestra en el Estudio 1 fue limitado (N = 23), esto coincide con el precedente de estudios exploratorios de laboratorio en turismo y psicología del consumidor (Cobos & Shapoval, 2024; Kingshott et al., 2020). El objetivo del primer estudio fue generar evidencia inicial y guiar el diseño de investigaciones posteriores con muestras más amplias.

3.3. Medidas

Las emociones se midieron mediante una escala Likert de 5 puntos de PANAS (Watson et al., 1988). La memorabilidad se midió mediante la escala adaptada de (Oh et al., 2007; Sthapit, Del Chiappa, Coudounaris, & Björk, 2020; Wang et al., 2020; Zatori et al., 2018); Storytelling mediante (Cater et al., 2021); y la intención de visita mediante (Assiouras et al., 2024).

El cambio en la emoción se calculó como una puntuación diferencial, que representa la diferencia entre las respuestas emocionales tras leer el escenario y tras experimentar la realidad virtual. Este enfoque nos permitió evaluar los estados emocionales presentes sin depender de la memoria retrospectiva, lo que aumentó la validez interna de los hallazgos.

En este estudio, el término «emociones» se refiere a la respuesta afectiva general de los participantes, medida inmediatamente después de la exposición a cada condición (escenario y RV). Si bien ciertos tipos de emociones (p. ej., básicas, complejas y autoconscientes) son relevantes en la investigación de las emociones, nuestro estudio se centró en la variación emocional general para evaluar el efecto neto de la intervención de RV. Este enfoque sigue las metodologías existentes en la investigación sobre turismo y recuperación de servicios.

3.4. Análisis

Para examinar el cambio emocional, realizamos un ANOVA de medidas repetidas y pruebas t para muestras pareadas para comparar las diferencias intragrupales. Se probó un modelo de mediación serial utilizando la macro PROCESS para SPSS (Hayes, 2013, Modelo 6), con 10 000 remuestreos bootstrap para estimar los efectos indirectos y los intervalos de confianza.

Antes de realizar el ANOVA y las pruebas t, se evaluó la normalidad de las variables emocionales mediante la prueba de Shapiro-Wilk. Los resultados no mostraron desviaciones significativas de la normalidad, lo que respalda el uso de pruebas paramétricas. Sin embargo, considerando el tamaño muestral relativamente pequeño del Estudio 1, reconocemos que esta suposición constituye una limitación metodológica que debería abordarse en futuros estudios mediante muestras más amplias y representativas.

4. RESULTADOS

Realizamos dos estudios experimentales y un análisis de mediación para abordar las preguntas de investigación planteadas.

En el primer estudio piloto, 23 participantes en un laboratorio de realidad virtual leyeron un escenario que describía una experiencia turística positiva o negativa, asignada aleatoriamente. Se evaluaron sus emociones resultantes, seguido de una tarea distractora y luego una experiencia de realidad virtual positiva del mismo destino turístico (Edimburgo, Escocia). Las emociones se reevaluaron después de la RV. Tras comprobar la manipulación y controlar posibles efectos de mareo cibernético, un ANOVA de diseño mixto mostró una interacción significativa entre el tipo de experiencia y el tiempo ($F(1,16) = 3.165$, $p = 0.09$, $\eta p^2 = 0.17$). Las comparaciones planificadas mediante pruebas t pareadas revelaron que las emociones derivadas de una experiencia turística negativa mejoraron después de la experiencia de realidad virtual positiva (Mneg1 = 3.44, DE = 0.46 vs. Mneg2 = 4.21, DE = 0.57, $p = 0.006$, d de Cohen = 0.56), en mayor medida que las emociones derivadas de una experiencia turística positiva, que también mejoraron levemente (Mpos1 = 4.08, DE = 0.27 vs. Mpos2 = 4.48, DE = 0.43, $p = 0.004$, d de Cohen = 0.33). También se observó un efecto principal del tiempo, mostrando emociones más positivas después de la RV (Mt1 = 3.79, DE = 0.49 vs. Mt2 = 4.36, DE = 0.50; $F(1,16) = 31.2$, $p < 0.001$, $\eta p^2 = 0.66$).

El segundo estudio replicó este efecto siguiendo el mismo procedimiento con 39 participantes adicionales. Después de las mismas comprobaciones, un ANOVA de diseño mixto reveló nuevamente una interacción significativa entre el tipo de experiencia y el tiempo ($F(1,32) = 12.87$, $p = 0.001$, ⊠$p^2 = 0.29$). Las comparaciones indicaron que las emociones negativas mejoraron después de la experiencia de realidad virtual positiva (Mneg1 = 3.24, DE = 0.61 vs. Mneg2 = 4.12, DE = 0.59, $p < 0.001$, d de Cohen = 0.57), mientras que las emociones de una experiencia positiva permanecieron estables ($p = 0.38$; ver Figura 1). Se encontró también un efecto principal del tiempo: las emociones fueron más positivas después de la RV (Mt1 = 3.64, DE = 0.72 vs. Mt2 = 4.15, DE = 0.63; $F(1,32) = 24.27$, $p < 0.001$, $\eta p^2 = 0.43$).

Para analizar la relación entre la recuperación emocional, la memorabilidad, el storytelling y la intención de visita, se calculó el cambio emocional inducido por la RV (emoción post-RV menos emoción pre-RV) y se ingresó en un análisis de mediación secuencial (Modelo PROCESS 6; Hayes, 2017) con 10,000 remuestreos bootstrap. Los resultados mostraron que un mayor cambio emocional predijo significativamente la memorabilidad ($b = 0.32$, $p < 0.05$); la memorabilidad predijo el storytelling ($b = 0.29$, $p < 0.05$); y el storytelling predijo la intención de visita ($b = 0.38$, $p < 0.01$). El efecto indirecto total fue significativo: $b = 0.49$, IC 95% [0.06, 1.12].

Estos hallazgos aportan evidencia empírica para responder a las preguntas de investigación: la realidad virtual facilita la recuperación emocional (RQ2), este cambio se asocia a una mayor memorabilidad y storytelling (RQ1 y RQ3) y, en conjunto, influyen positivamente en la intención de volver a visitar o recomendar el destino (RQ4).

4.1. Recuperación emocional significativa después de la RV

Ambos estudios demostraron que las emociones negativas experimentadas durante un escenario turístico mejoraron significativamente después de la exposición a una experiencia de realidad virtual positiva.

- **Estudio 1:** La valencia emocional media aumentó de $M = 3.44$ ($DE = 0.46$) a $M = 4.21$ ($DE = 0.57$), $p = 0.006$, $d = 0.56$.
- **Estudio 2:** La valencia emocional media aumentó de $M = 3.24$ ($DE = 0.61$) a $M = 4.12$ ($DE = 0.59$), $p < 0.001$, $d = 0.57$.

Estos resultados respaldan la efectividad de la RV para facilitar la recuperación emocional, en línea con la **RQ2**.

4.2. Las emociones positivas se mantuvieron estables

Por el contrario, las emociones positivas previas a la intervención se mantuvieron relativamente estables después de la exposición a RV:

- **Estudio 2:** $M = 4.08$ ($DE = 0.27$) a $M = 4.48$ ($DE = 0.43$), $p = 0.38$.

Esto refuerza la especificidad del efecto de la RV para resignificar emociones negativas.

4.3. Modelo de mediación serial compatible

El análisis de mediación mostró que la mejora emocional facilitada por la RV se relaciona con una mayor memorabilidad, lo que a su vez favorece el storytelling y finalmente impacta en la intención de visita. Específicamente:

- El cambio emocional predijo significativamente la memorabilidad (**$b = 0.32$, $p < 0.05$**).
- La memorabilidad predijo significativamente el storytelling (**$b = 0.29$, $p < 0.05$**).

- El storytelling predijo significativamente la intención de visita (**b = 0.38, p < 0.01**).
- Efecto indirecto total: **b = 0.49**, IC 95% [0.06, 1.12].

Esto aporta evidencia coherente para las **RQ1, RQ3 y RQ4** vía de mediación secuencial donde una mayor mejora emocional a través de la realidad virtual conduce a una codificación de la memoria más fuerte, lo que facilita el storytelling y, en última instancia, mejora la intención de los turistas de volver a visitar el destino.

4.4. Resumen gráfico

Figura 1. Mejora emocional post-RV en la condición negativa

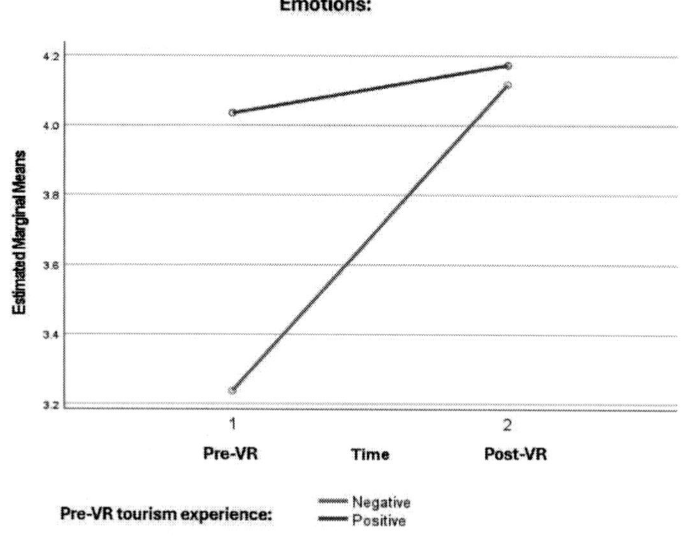

Figura 2. Modelo propuesto adaptado de (Hayes, 2013)

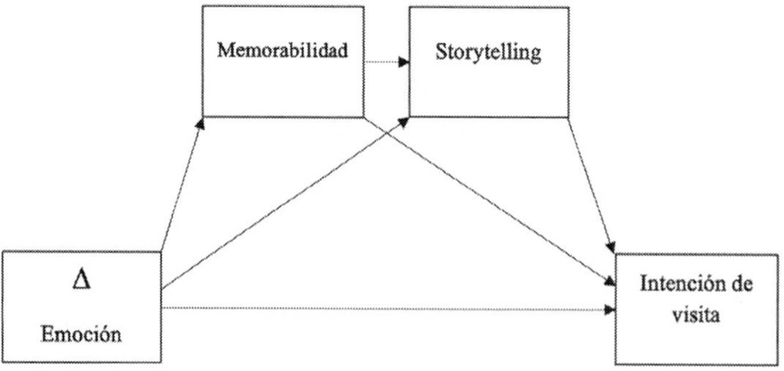

5. DISCUSIÓN

5.1. Interpretación de los hallazgos

Esta investigación demuestra que la realidad virtual permite la transformación emocional de experiencias turísticas negativas en estados afectivos redefinidos positivamente, con efectos posteriores en la memorabilidad, el storytelling y la intención de visita. Es importante destacar que la variación emocional se basó en afecto presente, capturado antes y después de la experiencia de RV, en lugar de emociones recordadas, lo que refuerza la validez interna de los resultados al aislar el impacto real de la intervención tecnológica.

La relación secuencial observada (cambio emocional → memorabilidad → storytelling → intención de visita) respalda la premisa teórica vinculada a las preguntas de investigación RQ1, RQ3 y RQ4, según la cual experiencias emocionalmente intensas y vívidas proporcionan la base para construir relatos personales significativos. Aunque podría existir influencia bidireccional entre memorabilidad y storytelling, los datos sugieren que el recuerdo fortalecido actúa como detonante para la construcción de relatos. Las características inmersivas de la RV parecen facilitar esta secuencia al ofrecer contenido emocionalmente atractivo y fácil de relatar.

Si bien no se modeló estadísticamente como interacción, el patrón observado refleja un proceso de mediación secuencial: cada variable intermedia transmite parte del efecto emocional hacia la intención de visita de manera acumulativa y estructurada.

5.2. Implicaciones académicas

El estudio contribuye a la literatura sobre marketing experiencial y psicología del turismo al proponer y validar empíricamente un proceso secuencial que conecta la recuperación emocional facilitada por RV con la generación de memorias memorables y relatos, aportando evidencia para responder a las preguntas de investigación planteadas. Este aporte refuerza la importancia de integrar tecnologías inmersivas en modelos de gestión emocional post-experiencia.

5.3. Aplicaciones prácticas para destinos

Los gestores de destinos pueden considerar la integración de experiencias RV en puntos estratégicos como aeropuertos, centros de visitantes o plataformas digitales, ofreciendo intervenciones diseñadas para mitigar emociones negativas tras incidentes o insatisfacciones. No obstante, la aplicación práctica de esta estrategia plantea desafíos operativos y motivacionales: será clave explorar la disposición real de los turistas a participar en actividades de RV tras un suceso desfavorable, el momento óptimo para ofrecer la experiencia y los canales de contacto más adecuados.

Diseñar intervenciones de RV eficaces requiere comprender la intensidad emocional y el umbral de recuperación de cada visitante. Una implementación personalizada, adaptada al contexto y combinada con otras tácticas de recuperación, puede maximizar el impacto positivo sobre la satisfacción y la fidelización.

5.4. Limitaciones

Una limitación importante de esta investigación es el uso de escenarios hipotéticos en lugar de experiencias turísticas reales. Aunque este enfoque es válido para la experimentación controlada, reduce la validez ecológica de los resultados. Por ello, se propone una fase de seguimiento con turistas reales en entornos auténticos (por ejemplo, museos), donde se registre en tiempo real el cambio afectivo tras la intervención de RV, fortaleciendo así la aplicabilidad de los hallazgos.

Además, no se contempló una condición comparativa con formatos no inmersivos o interacciones repetidas con la marca. A pesar de que la RV mostró resultados alentadores, futuros estudios deberían comparar su eficacia con otros medios para clarificar si el efecto de recuperación emocional es exclusivo de la inmersión o si puede lograrse mediante técnicas alternativas.

El tamaño limitado de las muestras en ambos estudios piloto reduce la generalización de los resultados y la potencia estadística de algunos análisis. Sin embargo, como etapa exploratoria, estos estudios cumplen su función al validar los supuestos teóricos bajo condiciones controladas. La finalidad no fue obtener conclusiones definitivas, sino sentar las bases para investigaciones futuras con muestras más amplias, aplicadas en escenarios reales de destino.

6. CONCLUSIONES

Esta investigación aporta evidencia empírica de que la realidad virtual (RV) puede funcionar como una herramienta eficaz para la recuperación emocional en contextos turísticos. Concretamente, una experiencia positiva de RV posterior a una vivencia turística negativa contribuye a mejorar significativamente el estado emocional, aumenta la memorabilidad y estimula la generación de storytelling personales, factores que, combinados, influyen en la intención de visita futura.

A través de dos estudios experimentales, se examinó y respaldó un proceso secuencial en el que la transformación emocional inducida por la RV se relaciona con la memoria y el storytelling del turista, cumpliendo con las preguntas de investigación planteadas. Estos hallazgos destacan la relevancia de diseñar intervenciones de marketing y estrategias de recuperación de servicios que contemplen la dimensión emocional de forma inteligente y basada en tecnología inmersiva.

Desde el ámbito teórico, este trabajo amplía el marco del marketing experiencial al proponer una nueva secuencia emocional-conductual apoyada en tecnología inmersiva. Asimismo, enriquece la literatura emergente sobre turismo digital y RV, demostrando cómo intervenciones aplicadas después de la experiencia —y no solo como herramientas de promoción previa— pueden influir de forma significativa en la percepción y la conducta del consumidor.

En la práctica, los resultados sugieren que la RV puede ser adoptada como solución innovadora dentro de la cadena de valor del turismo, especialmente en situaciones donde las respuestas tradicionales de recuperación de servicio resultan limitadas. Integrar contenido inmersivo y emocionalmente restaurador, a través de centros de visitantes, plataformas móviles o experiencias personalizadas con IA, abre nuevas oportunidades para gestionar la insatisfacción y fortalecer la lealtad del turista.

De cara al futuro, se proyecta ampliar esta línea de trabajo con estudios basados en experiencias reales y comparativas con otros formatos, con el fin de validar la aplicabilidad y eficacia de la RV en entornos auténticos y establecer su rol estratégico dentro de sistemas de gestión de destinos resilientes.

En resumen, este trabajo se alinea con la línea de innovación del Congreso Internacional de Turismo, al ofrecer un enfoque basado en evidencia y centrado en las personas para la recuperación emocional en turismo, integrando tecnología, narrativa y ciencia emocional para redefinir cómo los destinos enfrentan desafíos y fortalecen la conexión con sus visitantes.

7. DECLARACIÓN DE CONTRIBUCIÓN

Este artículo contribuye al campo de la innovación turística al conceptualizar y validar de forma empírica el papel de la realidad virtual (RV) como herramienta de recuperación emocional posterior a la experiencia turística. Presenta un proceso secuencial que vincula la mejora emocional con la intención de visita, mediado por la memorabilidad y el storytelling, respaldado por dos estudios experimentales que responden a preguntas de investigación clave para la gestión emocional del destino.

Al abordar una fase poco explorada del recorrido del turista —la recuperación emocional post-consumo— esta investigación abre nuevas perspectivas teóricas y prácticas para la gestión inteligente de destinos. Además, conecta la academia y la práctica profesional, al proponer vías claras para implementar la RV como intervención de recuperación, mejorando la satisfacción del visitante y fortaleciendo la resiliencia de la marca destino.

8. REFERENCIAS

Ahn, H. K., Liu, M. W., & Soman, D. (2009). Memory markers: How consumers recall the duration of experiences. *Journal of Consumer Psychology, 19*(3), 508–516. https://doi.org/10.1016/J.JCPS.2009.05.002

Alrawadieh, Z., Prayag, G., & Alrawadieh, Z. (2023). A cognitive appraisal perspective of emotional accessibility at heritage sites: empirical evidence from the UNESCO World Heritage Site of Petra. *Journal of Heritage Tourism, 18*(2), 145–163. https://doi.org/10.1080/1743873X.2023.2169152

Assiouras, I., Giannopoulos, A., Mavragani, E., & Buhalis, D. (2024). Virtual reality and mental imagery towards travel inspiration and visit intention. *International Journal of Tourism Research, 26*(2). https://doi.org/10.1002/jtr.2646

Bastiaansen, M., Lub, X. D., Mitas, O., Jung, T. H., Ascenção, M. P., Han, D. I., Moilanen, T., Smit, B., & Strijbosch, W. (2019). Emotions as core building blocks of an experience. *International Journal of Contemporary Hospitality Management, 31*(2), 651–668. https://doi.org/10.1108/IJCHM-11-2017-0761

Beck, J., Rainoldi, M., & Egger, R. (2019). Virtual reality in tourism: a state-of-the-art review. In *Tourism Review* (Vol. 74, Issue 3, pp. 586–612). Emerald Group Holdings Ltd. https://doi.org/10.1108/TR-03-2017-0049

Brown, J., Lewis, V. J., & Monk, A. F. (1977). Memorability, Word Frequency and Negative Recognition. *Quarterly Journal of Experimental Psychology, 29*(3), 461–473. https://doi.org/10.1080/14640747708400622

Campos, A. C., Mendes, J., Valle, P. O. do, & Scott, N. (2017). Co-creating animal-based tourist experiences: Attention, involvement and memorability. *Tourism Management, 63,* 100–114. https://doi.org/10.1016/j.tourman.2017.06.001

Cater, C., Albayrak, T., Caber, M., & Taylor, S. (2021). Flow, satisfaction and storytelling: a causal relationship? Evidence from scuba diving in Turkey. *Current Issues in Tourism, 24*(12), 1749–1767. https://doi.org/10.1080/13683500.2020.1803221

Cobos, L. M., & Shapoval, V. (2024). Leveraging Psychological Characteristics to Influence Mobile Hotel Bookings During a Global Health Crisis. *International Journal of Hospitality and Tourism Administration, 25*(2), 306–329. https://doi.org/10.1080/15256480.2022.2103485

Cowan, K., Ketron, S., Kostyk, A., & Kristofferson, K. (2023). Can you smell the (virtual) roses? The influence of olfactory cues in virtual reality on immersion and positive brand responses. *Journal of Retailing, 99*(3), 385–399. https://doi.org/10.1016/j.jretai.2023.07.004

Ezzyat, Y., & Davachi, L. (2011). What constitutes an episode in episodic memory? *Psychological Science, 22*(2), 243–252. https://doi.org/10.1177/0956797610393742

Flavián, C., Ibáñez-Sánchez, S., & Orús, C. (2019). The impact of virtual, augmented and mixed reality technologies on the customer experience. *Journal of Business Research, 100,* 547–560. https://doi.org/10.1016/j.jbusres.2018.10.050

Flavián, C., Ibáñez-Sánchez, S., & Orús, C. (2021). Impacts of technological embodiment through virtual reality on potential guests' emotions and engagement. *Journal of Hospitality Marketing & Management, 30*(1), 1–20. https://doi.org/10.1080/19368623.2020.1770146

Golja, T., & Paulišić, M. (2021). Managing-technology enhanced tourist experience: The case of scattered hotels in istria. *Management (Croatia), 26*(1), 63–95. https://doi.org/10.30924/MJCMI.26.1.5

Harrison-Walker, L. J. (2019). The effect of consumer emotions on outcome behaviors following service failure. *Journal of Services Marketing, 33*(3), 285–302. https://doi.org/10.1108/JSM-04-2018-0124

Hayes, A. F. (2013). *Model templates for PROCESS for SPSS and SAS.* New York: The Guilford Press.

Hosany, S., Martin, D., & Woodside, A. G. (2021). Emotions in Tourism: Theoretical Designs, Measurements, Analytics, and Interpretations. *Journal of Travel Research, 60*(7), 1391–1407. https://doi.org/10.1177/0047287520937079

Jensen, J. D., Krakow, M. M., Christy, K. R., Ratcliff, C. L., Pokharel, M., & Lillie, H. (2023). Validating cross-modal measures for comparative research: Message veracity, novelty, and memorability. *Psychology and Marketing, 40*(12), 2686–2710. https://doi.org/10.1002/mar.21910

Jiang, S., Moyle, B., Yung, R., Tao, L., & Scott, N. (2022). Augmented reality and the enhancement of memorable tourism experiences at heritage sites. *Current Issues in Tourism.* https://doi.org/10.1080/13683500.2022.2026303

Jiang, X., Deng, N., & Zheng, S. (2023). Understanding the core technological features of virtual and augmented reality in tourism: a qualitative and quantitative review. *Current Issues in Tourism*, 1–21. https://doi.org/10.1080/13683500.2023.2214847

Jung, T., Tom Dieck, C., Moorhouse, N., & Tom Dieck, D. (2017). Tourists' Experience of Virtual Reality Applications. *IEEE International Conference on Consumer Electronics.*

Jung, T., Tom Dieck, M. C., Lee, H., & Chung, N. (2016). Effects of Virtual Reality and Augmented Reality on Visitor Experiences in Museum. *Information and Communication Technologies in Tourism*, 621–635. https://doi.org/10.1007/978-3-319-28231-2-45

Kensinger, E., & Corkin, S. (2003). Memory enhancement for emotional words:Are emotional words more vividly rememberedthan neutral words? *Memory & Cognition, 31*(8), 1169–1180.

Kensinger, E., & Schacter, D. (2006). When the Red Sox shocked the Yankees: Comparing negative and positive memories. *Psychonomic Bulletin & Review*, 757–763.

Kim, J. H. (2014). The antecedents of memorable tourism experiences: The development of a scale to measure the destination attributes associated with memorable experiences. *Tourism Management, 44*, 34–45. https://doi.org/10.1016/j.tourman.2014.02.007

Kingshott, R. P. J., Gaur, S. S., Sharma, P., Yap, S. F., & Kucherenko, Y. (2020). Made for each other? Psychological contracts and service brands evaluations. *Journal of Services Marketing, 35*(3), 271–286. https://doi.org/10.1108/JSM-01-2020-0002

Knobloch, U., Robertson, K., & Aitken, R. (2017). Experience, Emotion, and Eudaimonia: A Consideration of Tourist Experiences and Well-being. *Journal of Travel Research, 56*(5), 651–662. https://doi.org/10.1177/0047287516650937

Kostyk, A., & Sheng, J. (2023). VR in customer-centered marketing: Purpose-driven design. *Business Horizons, 66*(2), 225–236. https://doi.org/10.1016/j.bushor.2022.06.005

Le, D., Pratt, M., Wang, Y., Scott, N., & Lohmann, G. (2020). How to win the consumer's heart? Exploring appraisal determinants of consumer pre-consumption emotions. *International Journal of Hospitality Management, 88.* https://doi.org/10.1016/j.ijhm.2020.102542

Malone, S., McKechnie, S., & Tynan, C. (2018). Tourists' Emotions as a Resource for Customer Value Creation, Co-Creation and Destruction: A Customer-Grounded Understanding. *Journal of Travel Research, 57*(7), 843–855. http://mc.manuscriptcentral.com/jotrhttp://mc.manuscriptcentral.com/jotr

Marasco, A. (2020). Beyond virtual cultural tourism: history-living experiences with cinematic virtual reality. *Tourism and Heritage Journal, 2*, 1–16. https://doi.org/10.1344/thj.2020.2.1

Marchiori, E., Niforatos, E., & Preto, L. (2017). Measuring the Media Effects of a Tourism-Related Virtual Reality Experience Using Biophysical Data. In *Information and Communication Technologies in Tourism 2017* (pp. 203–215). Springer International Publishing. https://doi.org/10.1007/978-3-319-51168-9_15

Maubisson, L., Rivière, A., & Coutelle, P. (2022). An Analytical and Comparative Approach to Cultural Heritage Experiences Enhanced With Augmented Reality. *International Journal of Arts Management, 25*(1), 68–91.

Oh, H., Fiore, A. M., & Jeoung, M. (2007). Measuring experience economy concepts: Tourism applications. *Journal of Travel Research, 46*(2), 119–132. https://doi.org/10.1177/0047287507304039

Olya, H., Jung, T. H., Tom Dieck, M. C., & Ryu, K. (2020). Engaging visitors of science festivals using augmented reality: asymmetrical modelling. *International Journal of Contemporary Hospitality Management, 32*(2), 769–796. https://doi.org/10.1108/IJCHM-10-2018-0820

Passebois Ducros, J., & Euzéby, F. (2021). Investigating consumer experience in hybrid museums: a netnographic study. *Qualitative Market Research, 24*(2), 180–199. https://doi.org/10.1108/QMR-07-2018-0077

Pavic, K., Vergilino-Perez, D., Gricourt, T., & Chaby, L. (2022). Because I'm Happy—An Overview on Fostering Positive Emotions Through Virtual Reality. In *Frontiers in Virtual Reality* (Vol. 3). Frontiers Media S.A. https://doi.org/10.3389/frvir.2022.788820

Pizam, A. (2010). Creating memorable experiences. In *International Journal of Hospitality Management* (Vol. 29, Issue 3, p. 343). https://doi.org/10.1016/j.ijhm.2010.04.003

Prayag, G., Hosany, S., Muskat, B., & Del Chiappa, G. (2017). Understanding the Relationships between Tourists' Emotional Experiences, Perceived Overall Image, Satisfaction, and Intention to Recommend. *Journal of Travel Research, 56*(1), 41–54. https://doi.org/10.1177/0047287515620567

Saket, B., Endert, A., & Stasko, J. (2016). Beyond usability and performance: A review of user experience-focused evaluations in Visualization. *ACM International Conference Proceeding Series, 24-October-2016*, 133–142. https://doi.org/10.1145/2993901.2993903

Shin, D. (2018). Empathy and embodied experience in virtual environment: To what extent can virtual reality stimulate empathy and embodied experience? *Computers in Human Behavior, 78*, 64–73. https://doi.org/10.1016/j.chb.2017.09.012

Skavronskaya, L., Scott, N., Moyle, B., Le, D., Hadinejad, A., Zhang, R., Gardiner, S., Coghlan, A., & Shakeela, A. (2017). Cognitive psychology and tourism research: state of the art. In *Tourism Review* (Vol. 72, Issue 2, pp. 221–237). Emerald Group Publishing Ltd. https://doi.org/10.1108/TR-03-2017-0041

Smith, S. A. (2019). Virtual reality in episodic memory research: A review. In *Psychonomic Bulletin and Review* (Vol. 26, Issue 4, pp. 1213–1237). Springer Science and Business Media, LLC. https://doi.org/10.3758/s13423-019-01605-w

Sthapit, E., Björk, P., & Jiménez Barreto, J. (2020). Negative memorable experience: North American and British Airbnb guests' perspectives. *Tourism Review, 76*(3), 639–653. https://doi.org/10.1108/TR-10-2019-0404

Sthapit, E., Del Chiappa, G., Coudounaris, D. N., & Bjork, P. (2020). Determinants of the continuance intention of Airbnb users: consumption values, co-creation, information overload and satisfaction. *Tourism Review, 75*(3), 511–531. https://doi.org/10.1108/TR-03-2019-0111

Sthapit, E., Del Chiappa, G., Coudounaris, D. N., & Björk, P. (2020). Tourism experiences, memorability and behavioural intentions: a study of tourists in Sardinia, Italy. *Tourism Review, 75*(3), 533–558. https://doi.org/10.1108/TR-03-2019-0102

Torres, E. N., Wei, W., & Hua, N. (2017). Towards understanding the effects of time and emotions on the vacation experience. *Tourism Review, 72*(4), 357–374. https://doi.org/10.1108/TR-05-2017-0088

Tulving, E. (1972). Episodic and semantic memory. In *Organization of Memory* (pp. 381–403).

Tung, V. W. S., & Ritchie, J. R. B. (2011). Exploring the essence of memorable tourism experiences. *Annals of Tourism Research, 38*(4), 1367–1386. https://doi.org/10.1016/j.annals.2011.03.009

Wang, C., Liu, J., Wei, L., & Zhang, T. (2020). Impact of tourist experience on memorability and authenticity: a study of creative tourism. *Journal of Travel and Tourism Marketing, 37*(1), 48–63. https://doi.org/10.1080/10548408.2020.1711846

Watson, D., Clark, L. A., & Tellegen, A. (1988). Development and Validation of Brief Measures of Positive and Negative Affect: The PANAS Scales. In *Journal of Personality and Social Psychology* (Vol. 54, Issue 6).

Wirtz, D., Kruger, J., Scollon, C. N., & Diener, E. (2003). What to do on spring break?The Role of Predicted, On-Line, and Remembered Experience in Future Choice. *Psychological Science, 14*(5), 520–524.

Wood, E. H. (2020). I Remember How We All Felt: Perceived Emotional Synchrony through Tourist Memory Sharing. *Journal of Travel Research, 59*(8), 1339–1352. https://doi.org/10.1177/0047287519888290/ASSET/IMAGES/LARGE/10.1177_0047287519888290-FIG1.JPEG

Yung, R., & Khoo-Lattimore, C. (2019). New realities: a systematic literature review on virtual reality and augmented reality in tourism research. In *Current Issues in Tourism* (Vol. 22, Issue 17, pp. 2056–2081). Routledge. https://doi.org/10.1080/13683500.2017.1417359

Zatori, A., Smith, M. K., & Puczko, L. (2018). Experience-involvement, memorability and authenticity: The service provider's effect on tourist experience. *Tourism Management, 67,* 111–126. https://doi.org/10.1016/j.tourman.2017.12.013

Zhong, Y. Y. (Susan), Busser, J., & Baloglu, S. (2017). A model of memorable tourism experience: The effects on satisfaction, affective commitment, and storytelling. *Tourism Analysis, 22*(2), 201–217. https://doi.org/10.3727/108354217X14888192562366

Zhu, C., Fong, L. H. N., & Gan, M. (2023). Rethinking the consequences of postmodern authenticity: the case of a World Cultural Heritage in Augmented Reality. *Current Issues in Tourism, 26*(4), 617–631. https://doi.org/10.1080/13683500.2022.2033181

9. ANEXOS

Tabla 1. Resultados del ANOVA de diseño mixto Estudio 1. Adaptado de SPSS

Source		df	Mean Square	F	Sig.	Partial Eta Squared
Time	Sphericity Assumed	1	3,068	31,069	0	0,66
	Greenhouse-Geisser	1	3,068	31,069	0	0,66
	Huynh-Feldt	1	3,068	31,069	0	0,66
	Lower-bound	1	3,068	31,069	0	0,66
Time * RGroup	Sphericity Assumed	1	0,313	3,165	0,094	0,165
	Greenhouse-Geisser	1	0,313	3,165	0,094	0,165
	Huynh-Feldt	1	0,313	3,165	0,094	0,165
	Lower-bound	1	0,313	3,165	0,094	0,165
Error(Time)	Sphericity Assumed	16	0,099			
	Greenhouse-Geisser	16	0,099			
	Huynh-Feldt	16	0,099			
	Lower-bound	16	0,099			

Tabla 2. Resultados de la prueba t del estudio 1. Adaptado de SPSS

Scenario +/-			Mean	N	Std. Deviation	Std. Error Mean
Negative	Pair 1	PANAS T1 Overall	3,44	8	0,463	0,164
		PANAS T2 Overall	4,21	8	0,568	0,201
Positive	Pair 1	PANAS T1 Overall	4,08	10	0,271	0,086
		PANAS T2 Overall	4,48	10	0,43	0,136

Tabla 3. Resultados de la prueba de muestras pareadas y tamaños del efecto de muestras pareadas Estudio 1. Adaptado de SPSS

			Significance Two-Sided p		Standardizer[a]
Negative	Pair 1	PANAS T1 Overall – PANAS T2 Overall	0,006	Cohen's d	0,555
				Hedges' correction	0,588
Positive	Pair 1	PANAS T1 Overall – PANAS T2 Overall	0,004	Cohen's d	0,333
				Hedges' correction	0,348
[a]The denominator used in estimating the effect sizes.					

Tabla 4. Resultados de la estadística descriptiva del modelo lineal general Estudio 1. Adaptado de SPSS

Scenario +/-		Mean	Std. Deviation	N
PANAS T1 Overall	Negative	3,44	0,463	8
	Positive	4,08	0,271	10
	Total	3,79	0,485	18
PANAS T2 Overall	Negative	4,21	0,568	8
	Positive	4,48	0,43	10
	Total	4,36	0,5	18

Tabla 5. Resultados del ANOVA de diseño mixto Estudio 2. Adaptado de SPSS

Source		df	Mean Square	F	Sig.	Partial Eta Squared
Time	Sphericity Assumed	1	4,401	24,267	0	0,431
	Greenhouse-Geisser	1	4,401	24,267	0	0,431
	Huynh-Feldt	1	4,401	24,267	0	0,431
	Lower-bound	1	4,401	24,267	0	0,431
Time * RGroup	Sphericity Assumed	1	2,335	12,872	0,001	0,287
	Greenhouse-Geisser	1	2,335	12,872	0,001	0,287
	Huynh-Feldt	1	2,335	12,872	0,001	0,287
	Lower-bound	1	2,335	12,872	0,001	0,287
Error (Time)	Sphericity Assumed	32	0,181			
	Greenhouse-Geisser	32	0,181			
	Huynh-Feldt	32	0,181			
	Lower-bound	32	0,181			

Tabla 6. Resultados de la prueba t del estudio 2. Adaptado de SPSS

Scenario +/-			Mean	N	Std. Deviation	Std. Error Mean
Negative	Pair 1	PANAS T1 Overall	3,24	17	0,613	0,149
		PANAS T2 Overall	4,12	17	0,491	0,119
Positive	Pair 1	PANAS T1 Overall	4,04	17	0,592	0,143
		PANAS T2 Overall	4,17	17	0,766	0,186

Tabla 7. Resultados de la prueba de muestras pareadas y tamaños del efecto de muestras pareadas, estudio 2. Adaptado de SPSS

			Significance Two-Sided p		Standardizer[a]
Negative	Pair 1	PANAS T1 Overall – PANAS T2 Overall	0	Cohen's d	0,572
				Hedges' correction	0,586
Positive	Pair 1	PANAS T1 Overall – PANAS T2 Overall	0,38	Cohen's d	0,631
				Hedges' correction	0,646
[a]The denominator used in estimating the effect sizes.					

Tabla 8. Resultados de la estadística descriptiva del modelo lineal general, estudio 2. Adaptado de SPSS

Scenario +/-		Mean	Std. Deviation	N
PANAS T1 Overall	Negative	3,24	0,613	17
	Positive	4,04	0,592	17
	Total	3,64	0,718	34
PANAS T2 Overall	Negative	4,12	0,491	17
	Positive	4,17	0,766	17
	Total	4,15	0,634	34

Tabla 9. Efectos indirectos de X sobre los resultados de Y Estudio 2. Adaptado de SPSS

Effect	BootSE	BootLLCI	BootULCI	
TOTAL	0,0568	0,4434	-0,9263	0,8355
Ind1	-0,1646	0,2741	-0,7848	0,3194
Ind2	-0,2640	0,3188	-1,0874	0,1989
Ind3	0,4854	0,2771	0,0527	1,1203
Indirect effect key:				
Ind1	EMTD_OV –> MB –> VI			
Ind2	EMTD_OV –> ST –> VI			
Ind3	EMTD_OV –> MB –> ST –> VI			

Figura 3. Ejemplos de estímulos de investigación en RV

TURISMO DIGITAL EMERGENTE: PERCEPCIONES Y ACTITUDES HACIA EL METAVERSO

Silvia Sanz-Blas
Daniela Buzova
Paula Fierro-Rubio
Mar Algueró-Boronat
Universidad de Valencia

TEMÁTICA: Innovación (Turismo digital y la creación de nuevas experiencias virtuales)

RESUMEN; Este trabajo analiza cómo potenciales usuarios perciben y valoran el turismo en el metaverso desde una aproximación cualitativa basada en grupos de discusión. Se realizaron un total de cinco focus groups (N=45; 21–40 años; 11 nacionalidades). Previamente, los participantes exploraron un espacio virtual turístico para contar con una referencia común. El corpus se codificó con NVivo mediante categorías a priori y emergentes, prestando especial atención a dimensiones emocionales (presencia, conexión) y a variables como autenticidad percibida, accesibilidad y sostenibilidad.

Los resultados muestran que el metaverso se concibe mayoritariamente como complemento del turismo físico, aporta utilidad en fases previas a la experiencia (planificación, inspiración) y en contextos con restricciones de tiempo, salud o presupuesto, y para accesos alternativos a recursos culturales. Sin embargo, persisten barreras: déficit sensorial (olfato, tacto), menor conexión humana, percepciones de autenticidad frágil, brechas tecnológicas y desigualdad de acceso. La reflexión comparativa genera una revalorización del viaje presencial por su densidad sensorial y sociocultural.

El estudio contribuye a cubrir el vacío de evidencia cualitativa sobre experiencias turísticas en entornos inmersivos, aportando una profunda comprensión de emociones y significados. Se derivan implicaciones para el diseño de experiencias virtuales centradas en el usuario (narrativas coherentes, interacción social significativa, personalización y criterios de accesibilidad), así como para la gobernanza ética de datos y la evaluación de impactos.

Palabras clave: autenticidad percibida, experiencia del usuario, focus groups, metaverso, turismo virtual.

ABSTRACT: This study examines how potential users perceive and evaluate tourism in the metaverse through a qualitative, focus groups–based approach. Five focus groups were conducted (N = 45; ages 21–40; 11 nationalities). Prior to the sessions, participants explored a virtual tourism space to establish a common frame of reference. The corpus was coded in NVivo using a priori and emergent categories, with particular attention to emotional dimensions (presence, connection) and to variables such as perceived authenticity, accessibility, and sustainability.

Findings indicate that the metaverse is predominantly conceived as a complement to physical tourism. It proves useful in pre-experience phases (planning, inspiration), in contexts with time, health, or budget constraints, and for alternative access to cultural resources. However, barriers persist: sensory deficits (smell, touch), weaker human connection, fragile perceptions of authenticity, technological hurdles, and unequal access. Comparative reflection leads to a reappraisal of in-person travel for its sensory and sociocultural richness.

The study helps address the scarcity of qualitative evidence on tourist experiences in immersive environments, providing a deeper understanding of emotions and meanings. It yields implications for the design of user-centered virtual experiences (coherent narratives, meaningful social interaction, personalization, and accessibility criteria), as well as for the ethical governance of data and impact assessment.

Keywords: focus groups, metaverse, perceived authenticity, user experience, virtual tourism.

1. INTRODUCCIÓN

La digitalización y el continuo desarrollo tecnológico está reconfigurando el sistema turístico hacia nuevos modelos donde tecnologías inmersivas y plataformas inteligentes median la planificación, la vivencia y el recuerdo del viaje. Este giro, vinculado al smart tourism y a las smart cities, abre oportunidades en accesibilidad y sostenibilidad, pero también pone en duda la autenticidad percibida (Hao et al., 2025; Monaco & Sacchi, 2023; Su et al., 2023; Zaman et al., 2022).

En este contexto, el metaverso emerge como escenario de interacción turística aún en consolidación, pero con implicaciones para la accesibilidad, la sostenibilidad y la autenticidad percibida y con usos que van del marketing inmersivo y la educación patrimonial a la gobernanza urbana y la inclusión social (Florido-Benítez, 2024).

La literatura reciente perfila beneficios potenciales (como presencia, inmersión y disfrute) cuando el diseño es de alta calidad, junto a límites persistentes por brechas de acceso, alfabetización digital y dudas sobre la autenticidad y la conexión emocional (Flavián et al., 2024; Nazli et al.,

2024; Özdemir Uçgun & Zeki Şahin, 2024). A su vez, la pandemia aceleró soluciones digitales (visitas 3D, recreaciones inmersivas), consolidando el potencial estructural del entorno virtual en la oferta turística (Zaman et al., 2022; Monaco & Sacchi, 2023).

No obstante, persiste un vacío claro de evidencia cualitativa centrada en vivencias subjetivas: predominan enfoques tecnológicos o de mercado y diseños cuantitativos o revisiones, mientras apenas se encuentran estudios que exploren en profundidad emociones, significados y tensiones que los usuarios atribuyen a la experiencia virtual y su comparación con el turismo físico (p. ej., autenticidad y conexión afectiva). Este vacío es especialmente relevante porque los métodos cualitativos captan matices afectivos y relacionales que difícilmente afloran en encuestas estandarizadas.

Este trabajo aborda ese gap mediante un diseño cualitativo de focus groups con 45 participantes de 11 nacionalidades, orientado a comprender cómo perciben, sienten y valoran el turismo en el metaverso frente al turismo físico. La estrategia combina codificación temática asistida por el software NVivo, análisis de emociones y segmentación por perfiles sociodemográficos y familiaridad tecnológica, para identificar patrones y discrepancias significativas en torno a autenticidad, conexión emocional, accesibilidad e impacto.

El objetivo principal es aportar evidencia empírica cualitativa que permita aflorar las motivaciones, barreras y dilemas éticos de la experiencia turística virtual, y que oriente el diseño de experiencias más inclusivas y transformadoras, consistentes con las expectativas reales de los usuarios y con criterios de sostenibilidad.

2. REVISIÓN DE LA LITERATURA

En este contexto, el metaverso ha irrumpido en el ámbito del turismo como un entorno digital inmersivo que desafía las formas tradicionales de interacción entre turistas, destinos y proveedores de servicios. Aunque aún se encuentra en una fase incipiente de desarrollo, el metaverso ha sido conceptualizado de múltiples formas en la literatura académica. Una revisión sistemática realizada por Florido-Benítez (2024) recoge definiciones de más de 30 autores y organismos, destacando que este espacio ha sido interpretado desde perspectivas funcionales muy diversas: como herramienta de colaboración, canal de ventas, espacio social, instrumento educativo o recurso para la gobernanza urbana y la inclusión social. Esta pluralidad conceptual refleja tanto el potencial transformador del metaverso como la falta de consenso sobre sus límites y usos en el contexto turístico.

Desde una perspectiva turística, el metaverso se presenta como una extensión digital del destino que puede facilitar la promoción, la planificación del viaje, la educación cultural o incluso la sustitución parcial de la experiencia física cuando el desplazamiento no es viable (Buhalis, Leung, et al., 2023; Hennig-Thurau et al., 2022; Zaman et al., 2022).

No obstante, su valor como herramienta de consumo turístico no está exento de desafíos. La autenticidad percibida constituye uno de los principales factores diferenciadores entre la experiencia física y la digital. En entornos virtuales, esta se construye de manera simbólica a través del diseño de los escenarios, la interacción con avatares y la narrativa inmersiva. Sin embargo, varios autores advierten que esta autenticidad es, en muchos casos, frágil y dependiente del grado de realismo y personalización de la experiencia (Flavián et al., 2024; Florido-Benítez, 2024; Hao et al., 2025). Por ejemplo, Nazli et al. (2024) evidencian que muchos usuarios, especialmente jóvenes, valoran positivamente la posibilidad de interactuar con entornos virtuales, pero reconocen que la falta de estimulación sensorial completa y de interacción humana limita el impacto emocional de la experiencia.

A pesar de estas limitaciones, algunos estudios sugieren que las experiencias turísticas virtuales pueden ser emocionalmente significativas si se diseñan con enfoques centrados en el usuario y se integran elementos gamificados o participativos (Hennig-Thurau et al., 2022; Triviño-Tarradas et al., 2024; Zaman et al., 2022). La calidad gráfica, la fluidez de la interacción, la posibilidad de personalización y la coherencia narrativa se consolidan así como variables clave para fomentar el compromiso y la satisfacción del visitante digital (Su et al., 2023).

El crecimiento del turismo en el metaverso está vinculado no solo al desarrollo tecnológico, sino también a la evolución de las motivaciones, expectativas y actitudes de los usuarios frente a nuevas formas de experimentar los destinos. Entre las motivaciones más frecuentes destacan la curiosidad tecnológica, la búsqueda de experiencias nuevas, la posibilidad de ahorrar costes económicos y la conveniencia de poder "viajar" sin limitaciones físicas o logísticas (Su et al., 2023).

Sin embargo, la literatura también identifica barreras relevantes para la adopción del turismo virtual. Una de las más señaladas es la percepción de falta de autenticidad, asociada a la escasa estimulación sensorial y a la ausencia de interacción directa con personas, lugares y culturas (Özdemir

Uçgun & Zeki Şahin, 2024). Esta limitación afecta especialmente a usuarios que valoran el componente emocional, espontáneo y relacional del turismo físico, y que consideran que la experiencia virtual no puede replicar la riqueza simbólica del contacto real (Florido-Benítez, 2024).

Otras barreras detectadas incluyen la dificultad tecnológica (falta de familiaridad con las plataformas), la escasez de infraestructuras adecuadas, o la desigualdad en el acceso a dispositivos y conectividad, lo que genera formas de exclusión digital. Además, algunos estudios destacan el riesgo de sobrecarga sensorial, fatiga visual o desconexión emocional, cuando las experiencias no están bien diseñadas o no se adaptan a las expectativas del usuario (Flavián et al., 2024; Triviño-Tarradas et al., 2024). Desde una perspectiva crítica, autores como Florido-Benítez (2024) advierten que una adopción acrítica del metaverso puede reforzar lógicas de consumo extractivistas, invisibilizar a las comunidades locales y trivializar la sostenibilidad, si no se acompaña de mecanismos participativos, transparentes y orientados al bien común.

En este escenario, el presente estudio aporta una visión profunda de las motivaciones y barreras percibidas por los usuarios, así como de sus preocupaciones éticas en relación con la autenticidad, la accesibilidad, la privacidad y la representación cultural. Estas percepciones constituyen una base empírica fundamental para orientar el diseño de experiencias turísticas en el metaverso que sean más inclusivas, respetuosas y emocionalmente significativas.

3. METODOLOGÍA

El enfoque cualitativo de esta investigación se estructuró en torno a la técnica de focus groups. Recientes estudios han destacado la eficacia de los focus groups para investigar experiencias en entornos virtuales (Amestoy Alonso et al., 2024; Flavián et al., 2024).

Se realizaron un total de 5 focus groups, cada uno de ellos compuesto de entre ocho y diez participantes. La muestra total estuvo compuesta de 45 turistas, con edades comprendidas entre los 21 y 40 años. La diversidad nacional (11 nacionalidades representadas) y el nivel educativo elevado de los integrantes de las dinámicas (60 % con estudios universitarios finalizados y 40 % con formación de posgrado) aportaron una riqueza de perspectivas que enriqueció el análisis cualitativo.

Cabe destacar que el 100% de los participantes habían estado expuestos previamente a entornos digitales con elementos inmersivos o de simulación, como videojuegos de mundo abierto (por ejemplo, Second Life, The Sims, VRChat), entornos educativos en realidad virtual, o experiencias con dispositivos como Oculus o PlayStation VR, lo que proporcionó una base conceptual compartida desde la cual reflexionar sobre las posibilidades y limitaciones del turismo en el metaverso. Adicionalmente, la experiencia acumulada en este tipo de plataformas permitió enriquecer los debates grupales con valoraciones sobre la autenticidad, la sostenibilidad y el grado de inmersión emocional que puede llegar a ofrecer el turismo virtual.

Sin embargo, no todos los participantes habían tenido experiencias directas previas con el turismo virtual, ya que solo el 60% de los participantes lo había probado, bien a través de visitas guiadas online, museos virtuales o plataformas interactivas promocionales de destinos. Por tanto, se pidió a los participantes que, previamente a la participación en los grupos de debate, accedieran a un espacio virtual concreto que les fue facilitado para familiarizarse con la navegación y tener contacto con el turismo en el metaverso. Esta exposición previa, junto a la experiencia en entornos digitales, sirvió como punto de referencia para evaluar el potencial del turismo en el metaverso.

Para el análisis de los datos cualitativos se utilizó el software NVivo, que permitió realizar una codificación sistemática y detallada de los discursos, basada en un análisis temático apoyado en categorías a priori derivadas del guion de investigación, y enriquecido con categorías emergentes identificadas mediante codificación abierta. Esta codificación se realizó tanto a nivel de contenido como de emociones expresadas, actitudes y valoraciones, y se aplicó de forma transversal a todas las sesiones. Esto permitió identificar patrones discursivos, divergencias y matices dentro de cada eje temático y obtener también datos complementarios como la frecuencia de aparición de términos clave, el número de participantes que compartían posturas similares o la intensidad emocional asociada a determinadas opiniones. Además, se segmentaron los discursos según variables sociodemográficas como edad, nacionalidad o grado de familiaridad con tecnologías digitales, lo que permitió establecer comparaciones cruzadas entre diferentes perfiles de participantes.

4. RESULTADOS

La Tabla 1 recoge, a modo de resumen, los códigos, las categorías y temáticas identificadas tras la transcripción de las dinámicas.

A continuación, se presentan los principales hallazgos obtenidos a partir del análisis de las cinco dinámicas de grupo, organizados según los bloques temáticos y categorías identificadas en la transcripción. Cada sección recoge las percepciones, argumentos y experiencias compartidas por los participantes, ilustradas mediante fragmentos textuales significativos que permiten profundizar en la comprensión del fenómeno estudiado.

Tabla 1. Tabla de códigos, categorías y temáticas

Códigos asociados	Categoría	Temática
más real, menos conexión, igual de interesante, diferente pero útil	Comparación entre experiencias físicas y virtuales	Experiencia en turismo
comodidad, ahorro, flexibilidad, seguridad, accesibilidad	Razones para elegir el turismo en el metaverso	Motivaciones y barreras en el turismo en el metaverso
tecnología compleja, falta de realismo, no es lo mismo, dificultades técnicas	Barreras percibidas en el turismo en el metaverso	
menos necesario, experiencia complementaria, más sostenible	Cambios en la percepción del turismo físico	Cambios de percepciones y de preferencias turísticas
enfermedad, restricciones, clima adverso, movilidad reducida	Situaciones donde se prefiere el turismo en el metaverso	
sustitución, equivalente, preferencia digital, alternativa viable	Posibilidad de sustituir viajes físicos por virtuales	

Fuente: Elaboración propia.

4.1. *Comparación entre experiencias reales y digitales*

En primer lugar, cabe destacar que el metaverso es percibido generalmente como una posibilidad de acceso universal, económico y funcional, especialmente para personas con limitaciones de recursos o movilidad. Otros se mostraron más escépticos, subrayando la dificultad de reemplazar un viaje real por una experiencia digital. En lo que se refiere a las diferencias percibidas entre el metaverso y el turismo físico, uno de los puntos más comentados fue la experiencia sensorial y emocional. La mayoría de los participantes destacaron que el turismo tradicional ofrece una vivencia más completa, donde los cinco sentidos están involucrados y donde se generan recuerdos emocionales más intensos. Una de las ideas más repetidas fue la imposibilidad del metaverso de replicar la sensación real de "estar allí", así como las diferencias en el alcance sensorial. Algunos participantes afirmaban:

> *"Creo que no podemos hablar de similitudes en el turismo físico y en el metaverso. Yo creo que en el metaverso hay cosas que no llegas a sentir"*

> *"El viaje físico te deja una mayor satisfacción [...] viajando en el metaverso no tienes la sensación de estar al 100% en el lugar."*

Algunos participantes reconocieron similitudes parciales, especialmente en cuanto al entretenimiento o la motivación por explorar nuevos lugares. Sin embargo, incluso en esos casos, se señalaba que la calidad de la experiencia es diferente: *"la experiencia en todos los sentidos, quitando la visual, es totalmente diferente"*.

Se plantearon también limitaciones físicas del metaverso, como el hecho de que la interacción está sujeta a un espacio cerrado y a restricciones tecnológicas: *"en el metaverso estás muy inmerso visualmente, entonces es como si estuvieras ahí, pero la verdad que las diferencias se encuentran en generar barreras físicas porque tienes que seguir dentro de un espacio porque si te sales, te chocas contra la pared"*.

Otras diferencias se situaron en el nivel de satisfacción y autenticidad: *"nunca vas a quedar más satisfecho que visitarlo en persona, siempre y cuando hayas tenido una buena experiencia durante el viaje, ya que el estar in situ en un destino te hace desarrollar y vivir experiencias únicas que con el metaverso no puedes experimentar"*.

La Tabla 2 identifica las principales diferencias identificadas por los participantes entre el turismo físico y virtual.

Tabla 2. Comparativa entre turismo físico vs. Metaverso

Aspecto	Turismo físico	Metaverso
Estimulación sensorial	Elevada: involucra los cinco sentidos	Reducida: centrada en lo visual y lo auditivo
Impacto emocional y memorias	Intenso: genera vivencias con gran carga afectiva	Menor: la conexión emocional se atenúa
Accesibilidad y gasto	Mayor coste y, en ocasiones, acceso limitado	Menor coste y mayor accesibilidad económica

Aspecto	Turismo físico	Metaverso
Interacción social y cultural	Relación directa con personas y cultura del lugar	Interacción simulada en entornos virtuales
Grado de autenticidad y satisfacción	Alta fidelidad y experiencia plena	Autenticidad reducida, vivencia parcial
Restricciones técnicas o físicas	Sin limitaciones de tipo tecnológico	Condicionada por la infraestructura y soporte tecnológico

Fuente: Elaboración propia.

4.2. Motivaciones para elegir el metaverso como opción turística

Los participantes señalaron una variedad de motivaciones personales y prácticas que los llevarían a considerar el turismo en el metaverso como una opción válida, aunque en la mayoría de los casos lo veían más como un complemento al turismo físico que como un sustituto total.

Entre las razones de carácter práctico, destacaron la comodidad de poder viajar desde casa sin necesidad de desplazamientos ni preparativos, así como el ahorro de tiempo que esto supondría, especialmente para quienes cuentan con agendas limitadas por motivos laborales, familiares o académicos. Algunos también subrayaron la utilidad de esta modalidad para evitar viajes largos o incómodos, así como la posibilidad de acceder de forma inmediata a cualquier destino. Tal y como expresaba una participante: *"Yo también preferiría el turismo en el metaverso en algunas ocasiones, especialmente por la comodidad que ofrece frente a las largas distancias y el tiempo que implican los viajes físicos."*

En el plano económico, varios participantes coincidieron en que el turismo en el metaverso podría representar un importante ahorro al evitar gastos de transporte, alojamiento o manutención. Además, se mencionó la posibilidad de visitar destinos normalmente inaccesibles por su elevado coste, como viajes espaciales o actividades exclusivas como el buceo en localizaciones remotas. Para algunos, también sería una alternativa en casos donde un viaje físico requiere preparación física o médica previa. Una participante lo resumía así: *"Mis principales motivaciones serían el ahorro económico y la comodidad ya que puedes viajar de inmediato y visitar cualquier destino como ha dicho mi compañera, a un click."* Otro participante añadía: *"Me gustaría probarlo para viajes que son bastante difíciles de conseguir por la escasa oferta y el precio muy alto o también muy difíciles para cumplir físicamente (previa preparación física antes del viaje)."*

Los motivos de naturaleza medioambiental también tuvieron peso en las opiniones recogidas. Algunos valoraron el potencial del turismo en el metaverso para reducir el impacto ambiental asociado al transporte, especialmente en trayectos en avión o en coche, así como para disminuir la presión turística sobre destinos físicos ya saturados. La descongestión de estos lugares se veía como una oportunidad para equilibrar la carga de visitantes, favoreciendo una distribución más sostenible.

En cuanto a las razones vinculadas con la accesibilidad, el metaverso se percibió como una herramienta valiosa para personas con dificultades físicas o de movilidad, así como en contextos donde el desplazamiento está limitado por conflictos, pandemias o restricciones de seguridad. Un participante mencionó: *"Personalmente, usaría el metaverso para ver alguna exposición interesante en un lugar al que, en ese momento, no pueda viajar, ya sea por cuestiones laborales o de tiempo."*

Finalmente, se identificaron también motivaciones de carácter cultural y educativo. El acceso a exposiciones o eventos temporales que, por razones de tiempo o disponibilidad, no podrían visitarse de forma presencial, fue una de las más señaladas. Igualmente, se destacó el valor del metaverso como medio para descubrir anticipadamente un destino, explorarlo virtualmente antes de una visita física y así optimizar la experiencia real.

4.3. Limitaciones y barreras percibidas para la adopción del turismo en el metaverso

A pesar de los motivos variados de uso del metaverso, se perciben ciertas limitaciones y barreras a la hora de adoptar esa nueva tecnología en el ámbito turístico. Las más mencionadas han sido de tipo tecnológico, la falta de autenticidad y conexión emocional, así como barreras económicas, culturales y sociales.

En cuanto a las barreras de tipo tecnológico, una de las limitaciones más frecuentes señaladas por los participantes fue la necesidad de disponer de equipamiento avanzado para acceder al metaverso (como gafas de realidad virtual, dispositivos con alta capacidad gráfica, buena conexión a internet). Además, surgieron preocupaciones por la desigualdad de acceso tecnológico entre países desarrollados y aquellos con menores recursos. Un participante afirmaba: *"Otra barrera que veo es que por ejemplo los adultos no están muy abiertos a la tecnología no sé lo abiertos que podrían estar a realizar una experiencia virtual."*

Otra barrera ampliamente señalada fue la falta de conexión emocional y la dificultad para vivir una experiencia auténtica y significativa a través del entorno digital. Muchos participantes indicaron que el proceso mismo del viaje, las sensaciones físicas y el entorno real no pueden ser replicados de forma satisfactoria. Una de las opiniones expresadas fue la siguiente: *"Para mí no sería lo mismo estar en un lugar y a la vez no estar. El trayecto, el proceso y todas esas sensaciones no las obtienes en el metaverso desde la comodidad de tu casa". Otro participante añadía: "Me preocupa la barrera de autenticidad y conexión emocional con el lugar de destino y con las personas con quien viajes o conozcas en el viaje."*

Como barreras culturales y sociales, varios participantes señalaron como problema la imposibilidad de interactuar directamente con las personas del destino, algo que consideran esencial para una experiencia turística real. También se menciona la imposibilidad de experimentar la cultura local, su gastronomía, sus costumbres o sus recomendaciones espontáneas.

Aunque el turismo en el metaverso puede ser más barato a largo plazo, algunos participantes advirtieron que su adopción inicial implica costes elevados, especialmente en tecnología de acceso y software. Un participante afirmaba: *"Necesitas un equipamiento considerablemente bueno y necesitas hacer un gran desembolso inicial y en comparación con el turismo convencional, una escapada económica es más inaccesible."*

El Gráfico 2 representa la distribución de las principales barreras percibidas por los participantes para adoptar el turismo en el metaverso. Esta representación visual permite apreciar que, aunque el turismo virtual ofrece oportunidades, todavía enfrenta importantes retos que condicionan su aceptación generalizada.

Gráfico 2. Barreras para adoptar el turismo virtual

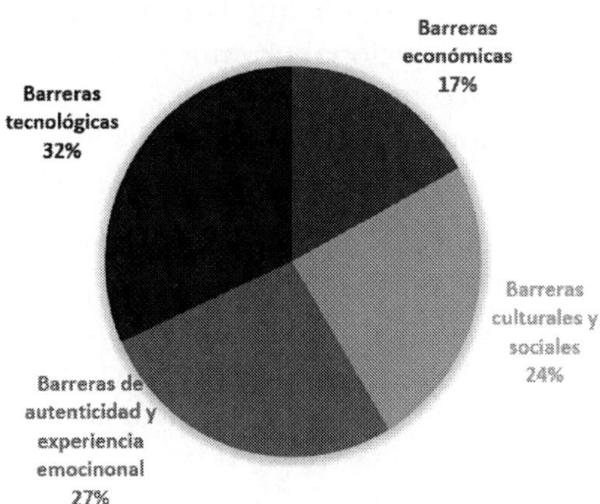

Fuente: Elaboración propia.

4.4. Cambios en la percepción del turismo físico

Tras reflexionar sobre el turismo en el metaverso, muchos participantes manifestaron un mayor aprecio por las experiencias del turismo físico, resaltando aspectos como la conexión cultural, la autenticidad, los sentidos involucrados y el valor emocional del viaje. La Tabla 3 realiza una comparación entre la percepción del turismo físico antes y después de reflexionar sobre el turismo en el metaverso. Esta reflexión ha despertado en muchos sentimientos de aprecio, nostalgia y conciencia sobre la importancia del contacto humano, la autenticidad y la vivencia real de los entornos, aspectos que consideran imposibles de replicar de manera virtual.

Tabla 3. Turismo físico antes vs. después de reflexionar sobre el metaverso

Antes de reflexionar sobre el metaverso	**Después de reflexionar sobre el metaverso**
Viajar es ocio	El turismo es una experiencia sensorial completa
Interés centrado en el destino	Valoración del trayecto y del contacto humano
Viajar como hábito o costumbre	Mayor conciencia sobre el valor del turismo y del entorno
Enfoque en el descanso	Enfoque en el aprendizaje y la vivencia
Desconexión del entorno local	Revalorización de la cultura y naturaleza locales

Fuente: Elaboración propia.

El análisis de las respuestas revela que la reflexión sobre estas diferencias ha tenido un impacto emocional profundo en los participantes, quienes valoran el turismo físico no solo como una actividad, sino como una fuente de experiencias significativas, recuerdos y sentimientos únicos que consideran irremplazables en entornos virtuales.

La Figura 1 muestra un diagrama de Venn que compara los elementos que solo ofrece el turismo físico, aquellos que son propios del metaverso y los aspectos que ambos comparten, según las opiniones expresadas por los participantes. Este enfoque ayuda a visualizar claramente el valor diferencial del turismo físico, donde la autenticidad, la riqueza sensorial y el contacto humano ocupan un lugar central.

Figura 1. Comparativa metaverso y turismo físico

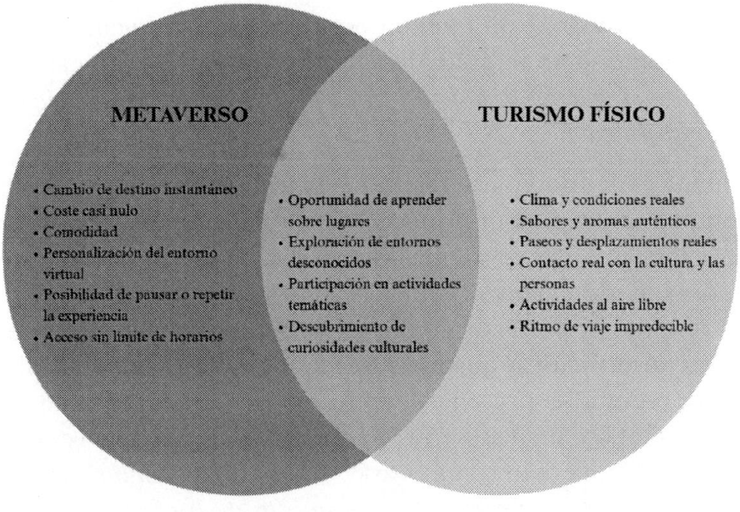

Fuente: Elaboración propia.

4.5. Situaciones donde se prefiere el turismo en el metaverso

Aunque los participantes no conciben el metaverso como un sustituto del turismo físico, sí identificaron situaciones concretas en las que podrían optar por él como alternativa temporal, complementaria o accesoria. Una de las más recurrentes fue la relacionada con limitaciones económicas. Muchos afirmaron que, en contextos de dificultad financiera, el metaverso podría ser una solución para seguir viajando sin incurrir en los gastos asociados a un desplazamiento físico.

Otra circunstancia señalada con frecuencia fue la falta de tiempo. En estos casos, la posibilidad de realizar una experiencia turística virtual permitiría a quienes cuentan con agendas limitadas por el trabajo, los estudios o la familia, conocer lugares sin la necesidad de largos desplazamientos ni preparativos.

Las condiciones de salud o la movilidad reducida también fueron identificadas como un contexto en el que el metaverso podría resultar especialmente útil. Algunos lo imaginaron como una herramienta para personas enfermas, hospitalizadas o con discapacidades que les impidan desplazarse físicamente. Un participante lo expresaba así: *"En los hospitales, para gente enferma que no puede moverse sería una buena forma de reemplazar esos viajes."*

Asimismo, se mencionaron situaciones de crisis, como la pandemia de la COVID-19, en las que el turismo virtual podría ofrecer una solución real y valiosa. Varios recordaron que, en ese periodo, esta tecnología hubiera sido una opción que no habrían descartado. Un participante afirmaba: *"Si hay otra pandemia, guerras o cualquier razón por la que yo no pueda viajar, tendría en cuenta esa posibilidad"*.

Finalmente, algunos participantes propusieron el uso del metaverso como complemento para enriquecer o completar una visita física incompleta. En estos casos, la experiencia virtual podría servir para acceder a museos, exposiciones o eventos cuando las entradas estén agotadas, explorar áreas restringidas al público (como excavaciones arqueológicas en curso o zonas de conservación), asistir de forma inmersiva a espectáculos culturales sin disponibilidad presencial, recorrer partes del destino no visitadas por falta de tiempo o incluso revivir momentos del viaje una vez de regreso a casa. Una participante lo resumía así: *"Si has visitado un lugar recientemente, pero no tuviste tiempo de conocer todo lo que querías, podría ayudar a completar la experiencia"*. Otros añadían ejemplos concretos: *"El metaverso podría ser útil, por ejemplo, si en el Louvre no quedan entradas o si no puedes acceder a una zona por restauración"* o *"Serviría para ir más allá de lo que se ha podido ver físicamente. A veces los horarios o las colas no permiten visitar todo, y en esos casos sería una ayuda"*.

4.6. Posibilidad de sustituir viajes físicos por virtuales

La percepción mayoritaria entre los participantes fue que el turismo en el metaverso no puede reemplazar completamente al turismo físico. Una de las principales razones que sostienen esta opinión es la incompletitud emocional y sensorial del viaje virtual. Además, se considera que el contacto humano, la autenticidad, los sentidos (como el olfato, el tacto o la temperatura del entorno) no son replicables en el entorno virtual. De este modo, se vislumbra un futuro donde el metaverso sea útil para fines específicos dentro de la experiencia turística, pero no como alternativa integral que sustituya al turismo físico. La posibilidad de combinar ambos formatos abre nuevas oportunidades para enriquecer las experiencias de viaje, permitiendo ampliar, profundizar o mantener el contacto con los destinos de forma más flexible e inclusiva.

La Tabla 4 recoge los principales argumentos a favor y en contra de la sustitución del turismo físico por el turismo virtual, tal y como han sido expresados por los participantes.

Tabla 4. Argumentos a favor y en contra de la sustitución del turismo físico

A favor de la sustitución	En contra de la sustitución
– Permite viajar en situaciones donde el turismo físico no es viable (enfermedad o movilidad reducida) – Facilita el acceso durante pandemias o conflictos – Accesibilidad a destinos lejanos o costosos – Puede ofrecer experiencias complementarias en destino – Puede ser más accesible económicamente	– No se replican las sensaciones físicas (olfato, tacto, clima) ni emociones – Falta de contacto humano y conexión cultural auténtica e interacción real – Impacto negativo en la economía local e industrias turísticas físicas (hoteles, restaurantes, guías…) – Pérdida de autenticidad y riqueza sensorial y cultural de la experiencia

Fuente: Elaboración propia.

5. CONCLUSIONES

Los resultados obtenidos a través de las dinámicas de grupo confirman que el metaverso se percibe como un complemento del turismo presencial más que como su reemplazo. Los participantes reconocen su utilidad para ampliar el acceso y para apoyar momentos concretos del itinerario de viaje (preparación, inspiración y recuerdo) especialmente cuando existen límites físicos, económicos o temporales. Sin embargo, la comparación directa con el viaje físico refuerza la primacía del viaje real por su densidad sensorial y sociocultural, asociada al contacto humano, a la interacción espontánea y a la imprevisibilidad del contexto, dimensiones que los entornos virtuales actuales no reproducen de manera equivalente.

A lo largo del estudio, se ha observado que la reflexión sobre el metaverso ha impulsado una revalorización emocional del turismo tradicional. Los participantes mostraron un fuerte apego a las vivencias físicas, destacando el contacto humano, la autenticidad cultural, la experiencia sensorial completa y la generación de recuerdos imborrables como elementos insustituibles. Esta dimensión emocional ha sido especialmente relevante en las respuestas, revelando que el turismo físico es percibido no solo como un acto de desplazamiento, sino como una fuente de identidad, aprendizaje y conexión interpersonal.

El componente emocional aparece de manera transversal: junto al reconocimiento del potencial tecnológico persisten reticencias motivadas por la reducción de estímulos no visuales y por la interacción social mediada. En este sentido, la experiencia virtual resulta más significativa cuando concibe el metaverso como etapa previa que facilita comprensión, accesibilidad y aprendizaje, y no como sustituto pleno del encuentro con el destino. Este patrón dialoga con la literatura sobre autenticidad percibida y experiencia turística, donde la atribución de valor depende de la capacidad del entorno para evocar emociones, transmitir identidad cultural y generar sentido, más allá del realismo gráfico (Florido-Benítez, 2024). Asimismo, los resultados son coherentes con trabajos que señalan el atractivo del metaverso entre públicos familiarizados con tecnologías inmersivas, pero también sus límites cuando faltan sensaciones corporales y vínculo emocional (Flavián et al., 2024; Nazli et al., 2024).

En conjunto, el metaverso aparece como un dispositivo con potencial para la accesibilidad y la educación patrimonial, siempre que su diseño incorpore criterios de calidad de experiencia, inclusión y ética de datos (Kılıçarslan et al., 2024; Özdemir Uçgun & Zeki Şahin, 2024; Su et al., 2023). A este respecto, este trabajo aporta evidencia cualitativa original sobre cómo se configuran emociones y autenticidad en experiencias turísticas inmersivas; delimita las condiciones bajo las que el metaverso opera como complemento del viaje y no como sustituto y propone un marco de diseño centrado en el usuario transferible a destinos, museos y agencias. Esta síntesis ofrece bases empíricas y operativas para orientar decisiones de diseño, segmentación y gobernanza del turismo virtual en contextos reales.

5.1. Implicaciones prácticas

Para destinos, museos y agencias de viajes, los hallazgos sugieren orientar las inversiones hacia usos complementarios: recorridos previos para planificación informada, accesos alternativos cuando la visita presencial no es viable, y extensiones post-visita que consoliden aprendizaje y memoria. Estas aplicaciones exigen coherencia narrativa, interacción social mediada con sentido, opciones de personalización y estándares de accesibilidad que reduzcan brechas tecnológicas. La gobernanza debe contemplar transparencia en datos, criterios de representación cultural y métricas que conecten el desempeño virtual con objetivos del destino (satisfacción, tiempo de interacción, conversión a visita presencial, etc). Además, una estrategia de segmentación por familiaridad digital y motivaciones permitirá alinear expectativas y evitar promesas de sustitución que los propios usuarios no demandan.

5.2. Limitaciones y futuras líneas de investigación

Al tratarse de un estudio cualitativo, esta investigación presenta una serie de limitaciones metodológicas que deben considerarse al interpretar los resultados. En primer lugar, la muestra utilizada (aunque diversa en términos de edad, nacionalidad y género) está compuesta exclusivamente por personas jóvenes con cierta familiaridad con las tecnologías digitales. Este perfil puede sesgar tanto la receptividad hacia el turismo virtual como la capacidad de imaginar sus usos y límites, reduciendo la transferibilidad de los hallazgos a otros colectivos.

En segundo lugar, el diseño basado en dinámicas de grupo implica que la interacción entre participantes pudo influir en la configuración de discursos compartidos, atenuando, reforzando o desplazando opiniones individuales. No obstante, esta misma configuración facilitó el acceso a un registro emocional y relacional especialmente útil, aportando una profundidad analítica poco habitual en trabajos previos sobre el tema.

Asimismo, gran parte de la discusión se centró en escenarios hipotéticos, dado que la mayoría de los participantes carecía de experiencias directas de turismo en el metaverso. En consecuencia, muchas percepciones reflejan expectativas, preocupaciones y proyecciones más que vivencias concretas. A medida que estas tecnologías se integren en la vida cotidiana, será necesario examinar cómo evolucionan dichas percepciones a partir de experiencias reales.

De cara al futuro, sería relevante ampliar el estudio a otros segmentos poblacionales (personas más mayores, colectivos con baja accesibilidad digital y perfiles profesionales del sector). También resultaría pertinente explorar, mediante métodos mixtos, cómo varía la percepción del turismo virtual antes y después de experimentar una simulación real, lo que permitiría comparar las expectativas iniciales con las vivencias efectivas.

Por último, otra interesante línea de investigación futura consistiría en analizar el papel del turismo virtual en procesos de inclusión social y educativa, así como en contextos de emergencia climática o conflictos geopolíticos, donde las restricciones al turismo físico podrían abrir nuevas oportunidades para su desarrollo responsable.

6. REFERENCIAS

Amestoy Alonso, B., Donegan, T., Calvis, I., Swidrak, J., Rodriguez, E., Vargas-Reverón, C. L., Combalia, A., Oliva Martinez, R., & Sanchez-Vives, M. V. (2024). Focus groups in the metaverse: shared virtual spaces for patients, clinicians, and researchers. *Frontiers in Virtual Reality, 5*, 1432282. https://doi.org/10.3389/FRVIR.2024.1432282

Buhalis, D., Leung, D., & Lin, M. (2023). Metaverse as a disruptive technology revolutionising tourism management and marketing. *Tourism Management, 97*, 104724. https://doi.org/10.1016/J.TOURMAN.2023.104724

Buhalis, D., Lin, M. S., & Leung, D. (2023). Metaverse as a driver for customer experience and value co-creation: implications for hospitality and tourism management and marketing. *International Journal of Contemporary Hospitality Management, 35*(2), 701–716. https://doi.org/10.1108/IJCHM-05-2022-0631

Flavián, C., Ibáñez-Sánchez, S., Orús, C., & Barta, S. (2024). The dark side of the metaverse: The role of gamification in event virtualization. *International Journal of Information Management, 75*(November 2023). https://doi.org/10.1016/j.ijinfomgt.2023.102726

Florido-Benítez, L. (2024). Metaverse cannot be an extra marketing immersive tool to increase sales in tourism cities. *International Journal of Tourism Cities, 10*(3), 974–994. https://doi.org/10.1108/IJTC-01-2024-0001

Go, H., & Kang, M. (2023). Metaverse tourism for sustainable tourism development: Tourism Agenda 2030. *Tourism Review, 78*(2), 381–394. https://doi.org/10.1108/TR-02-2022-0102

Hao, F., Liu, S., Zhang, C., & Chon, K. K. S. (2025). Metaverse in tourism: from virtual worlds to sustainable worlds. *Tourism Review*. https://doi.org/10.1108/TR-03-2024-0188

Hennig-Thurau, T., Aliman, D. N., Herting, A. M., Cziehso, G. P., Linder, M., & Kübler, R. V. (2022). Social interactions in the metaverse: Framework, initial evidence, and research roadmap. *Journal of the Academy of Marketing Science 2022 51:4, 51*(4), 889–913. https://doi.org/10.1007/S11747-022-00908-0

Kılıçarslan, Ö., Yozukmaz, N., Albayrak, T., & Buhalis, D. (2024). The impacts of Metaverse on tourist behaviour and marketing implications. *Current Issues in Tourism, 28*(4), 622–642. https://doi.org/10.1080/13683500.2024.2326989

Monaco, S., & Sacchi, G. (2023). Travelling the Metaverse: Potential Benefits and Main Challenges for Tourism Sectors and Research Applications. *Sustainability, 15*(4), 1–10. https://doi.org/10.3390/su15043348

Nazli, M., Bulut, C., & Ozarslan, Y. (2024). Gen Z travel intentions and museum visits in the metaverse: case of Egypt, Scotland, and Turkey. *Current Issues in Tourism*, 1–19. https://doi.org/10.1080/13683500.2024.2376885

Özdemir Uçgun, G., & Zeki Şahin, S. (2024). How does Metaverse affect the tourism industry? Current practices and future forecasts. *Current Issues in Tourism, 27*(17), 2742–2756. https://doi.org/10.1080/13683500.2023.2238111

Su, P. Y., Hsiao, P. W., & Fan, K. K. (2023). Investigating the Relationship between Users' Behavioral Intentions and Learning Effects of VR System for Sustainable Tourism Development. *Sustainability, 15*(9). https://doi.org/10.3390/su15097277

Triviño-Tarradas, P., Mohedo-Gatón, A., Carranza-Cañadas, P., & Hidalgo-Fernandez, R. E. (2024). The Application of Metaverse in the Tourism Sector as a Tool for Enhancing Sustainability–Case Study: A Medieval 'Perfume Burner' of the Local Historical Museum of Montilla (Cordoba, Spain). *Sustainability, 16*(16). https://doi.org/10.3390/su16166966

Zaman, U., Koo, I., Abbasi, S., Raza, S. H., & Qureshi, M. G. (2022). Meet Your Digital Twin in Space? Profiling International Expat's Readiness for Metaverse Space Travel, Tech-Savviness, COVID-19 Travel Anxiety, and Travel Fear of Missing Out. *Sustainability, 14*(11). https://doi.org/10.3390/su14116441

¿CÓMO INFLUYEN LOS INFLUENCERS VIRTUALES EN LA ENVIDIA BENIGNA, EL FOMO Y EL MATERIALISMO EN EL TURISMO ASPIRACIONAL?

ESTEFANIA BALLESTER
Universidad Oberta de Barcelona

ENRIQUE BIGNÉ
CARLA RUIZ
Universidad de Valencia

NATALIA RUBIO
Universidad Autónoma de Madrid

TEMÁTICA: Tecnología: Utilización de la Inteligencia artificial en la gestión de destinos turísticos

RESUMEN: El marketing de influencers continúa consolidándose como una herramienta estratégica en el ámbito turístico, especialmente a través de contenidos aspiracionales difundidos en redes sociales. Con la aparición de los influencers virtuales, surgen nuevos interrogantes sobre su eficacia emocional y persuasiva frente a los influencers humanos. El trabajo se encuentra actualmente en desarrollo y forma parte de un proyecto de investigación en curso. Este estudio, que combina medidas neurofisiológicas (atención visual, expresión emocional y activación galvánica de la piel) y un cuestionario online, presenta un análisis comparativo del impacto del tipo de influencer y del contenido turístico (lujo vs. no lujo) en Instagram sobre tres constructos clave: el miedo a perderse algo (FoMO), el materialismo y la envidia benigna. A través de un diseño experimental 2x2, se examina cómo estas respuestas emocionales y valorativas influyen en la intención de visitar el destino promocionado. Se espera que los resultados de esta investigación permitan comprender con mayor profundidad los mecanismos psicológicos que subyacen al consumo aspiracional en entornos digitales y ofrezcan implicaciones prácticas para el diseño de campañas turísticas más efectivas y emocionalmente resonantes.

Palabras clave: Influencers virtuales, envidia benigna, FoMO, Materialismo, Intención de visita

ABSTRACT: Influencer marketing continues to gain relevance as a strategic tool in the tourism sector, particularly through aspirational content shared on social media. The emergence of virtual influencers raises new questions about their emotional and persuasive effectiveness compared to human influencers. This study, which combines neurophysiological measures (visual attention, facial expression, and galvanic skin response) with an online questionnaire, presents a comparative analysis of the impact of influencer type and content type (luxury vs. non-luxury tourism) on three key constructs: Fear of Missing Out (FoMO), materialism, and benign envy. Using a 2x2 between-subjects experimental design, the research examines how these emotional and value-based responses influence consumers' intention to visit the promoted destination. The findings offer valuable insights into the psychological mechanisms underlying aspirational consumption in digital environments and provide practical implications for designing more emotionally resonant and effective tourism campaigns on social media.

Keywords: Virtual Influencers, Bening Envy, FoMO, Materialism, Visit intention

1. INTRODUCCIÓN

Las redes sociales han transformado la relación entre consumidores y marcas, especialmente mediante la figura de los influencers, quienes comparten contenidos aspiracionales que reflejan estilos de vida deseables (Dedeoglu et al., 2025). En la actualidad, en estos entornos digitales coexisten dos tipos principales de influencers: los humanos, con presencia física y vida real, y los virtuales, creados mediante inteligencia artificial con apariencias humana (Wahba et al., 2025). Los influencers humanos, reconocidos por su autenticidad y capacidad para expresar emociones reales y experiencias personales, facilitan una mayor identificación del público (Arsenyan & Mirowska, 2021; Byun et al., 2023). Por el contrario, los influencers virtuales, aunque cada vez más populares, suelen percibirse como menos auténticos y creíbles, lo que limita la conexión emocional con sus seguidores (Kim et al., 2023; Mo & Want, 2024). Esta diferencia en la percepción cobra especial relevancia en el ámbito turístico, donde el contenido aspiracional relacionado con destinos de lujo es un potente activador emocional. La combinación del tipo de influencer y la naturaleza del contenido puede, por tanto, condicionar significativamente la respuesta emocional y conductual de los usuarios, influyendo en la eficacia persuasiva del marketing de influencers.

La literatura existente ha destacado que la exposición a contenidos aspiracionales puede activar diversas emociones y motivaciones en los consumidores, entre las que destacan la envidia (Park & Lee, 2024), el miedo a perderse algo (Dinh & Lee, 2021) y el materialismo (Hussain et al., 2023). La envidia, entendida como el deseo de obtener un objeto de atención ausente en la propia vida (Tandon et al., 2021), ha sido tradicionalmente clasificada en dos formas: maliciosa y benigna (Lange & Crusius, 2015; Lim & Kim, 2018). Mientras que la envidia maliciosa se asocia con emociones negativas como la hostilidad o el resentimiento, la envidia benigna surge cuando el éxito ajeno se percibe como legítimo y alcanzable, generando admiración e impulsando el deseo de superación personal (van de Ven et al., 2011). Aunque la envidia tradicionalmente se ha estudiado en su variante maliciosa, este estudio se centra en la forma benigna debido a su potencial para motivar comportamientos positivos (Lange & Crusius, 2015; Liu et al., 2019). Por otro lado, el miedo a perderse algo (FoMO) ha sido definido como la aprensión o ansiedad experimentada ante la percepción de exclusión de experiencias placenteras que otros disfrutan (Przybylski et al., 2013). Esta sensación de carencia se ve amplificada por la naturaleza dinámica y altamente visual de las redes sociales, donde la comparación social constante con influencers u otros usuarios acentúa la percepción de estar al margen de vivencias deseables (Hussain et al., 2023). Los influencers, en particular, juegan un papel destacado en la activación del FoMO, debido a la proximidad emocional y la percepción de autenticidad que generan entre sus seguidores (Jin et al., 2020). Finalmente, el materialismo, definido como un valor que otorga a la posesión de bienes materiales un papel central en la consecución del éxito personal y la felicidad (Richins & Dawson, 1992), constituye otro factor relevante en este estudio. La exposición a contenido aspiracional compartido por influencers refuerza el materialismo al presentar estilos de vida deseables que promueven la emulación y la validación social (Lou & Kim, 2019). Esta dinámica se extiende no solo a la compra de productos tangibles, sino también a la valorización de experiencias simbólicas como los viajes, que se perciben como indicadores de estatus (Kim et al., 2021).

Desde una perspectiva teórica, este estudio se fundamenta en la Teoría de la Comparación Social (Festinger, 1954), que plantea que las personas evalúan su propia valía y situación comparándose con otros, especialmente ante estándares visibles de éxito o bienestar. En el contexto de las redes sociales, la exposición constante a contenidos cuidadosamente seleccionados que muestran estilos de vida aspiracionales intensifica las comparaciones sociales ascendentes, lo que puede generar emociones como la envidia benigna, el miedo a perderse algo (FoMO) y el materialismo (van de Ven et al., 2011; Chen et al., 2020). Por tanto, las plataformas digitales constituyen un escenario ideal para analizar cómo estas emociones sociales influyen en la conducta del consumidor y en sus decisiones relacionadas con el consumo experiencial, como la intención de visitar destinos turísticos.

Debido a su creciente relevancia en entornos digitales, las emociones de envidia benigna, miedo a perderse algo (FoMO) y materialismo han captado un notable interés académico en ámbitos como el marketing de influencers (Jin & Ryu, 2020; Lou & Kim, 2019) y el turismo aspiracional

(Liu et al., 2019; Alt & Boniel-Nissim, 2018). Aunque estudios previos han examinado el papel individual de estas emociones en variables como la actitud hacia el destino (Feng et al., 2023), la intención de visita (Dedeoglu et al., 2025) o el consumo vinculado al estatus (Gupta & Srivastav, 2016), son todavía escasas las investigaciones que analizan de forma conjunta cómo la interacción entre el tipo de contenido promocionado y el tipo de influencer afecta a la activación simultánea de estas emociones y cómo, a su vez, influyen en la intención de visitar un destino turístico. Considerando la creciente importancia de los influencers como prescriptores de experiencias aspiracionales, especialmente en sectores altamente visuales y experienciales como el turismo (Xie-Carson et al., 2023), resulta esencial abordar este fenómeno desde una perspectiva integrada que permita comprender con mayor profundidad los mecanismos emocionales y motivacionales que guían las decisiones de consumo en entornos digitales.

Aunque el trabajo empírico se encuentra actualmente en desarrollo, la presente propuesta recoge los fundamentos teóricos y el diseño metodológico que guiarán la investigación. En este marco, el presente estudio examina cómo el tipo de influencer (humano vs. virtual) y la naturaleza del contenido compartido (destinos de lujo vs. no lujo) influyen en tres constructos psicológicos centrales —la envidia benigna, el FoMO y el materialismo—, así como en su capacidad para predecir la intención de visitar los destinos promocionados. Al integrar estas variables bajo un mismo modelo, esta investigación ofrece una visión más completa sobre los mecanismos emocionales que subyacen al consumo aspiracional en entornos digitales, contribuyendo tanto al desarrollo teórico como a la toma de decisiones estratégicas en el ámbito del marketing de influencers y del turismo experiencial.

2. MARCO TEÓRICO Y PROPUESTA DE INVESTIGACIÓN

El auge de los influencers virtuales ha generado un creciente interés académico en cuanto a su efectividad en comparación con los influencers humanos (Byun et al., 2023). La literatura destaca que los influencers humanos suelen establecer conexiones más auténticas y emocionales, gracias a su capacidad para expresar emociones reales, compartir experiencias personales y mantener una presencia coherente en redes sociales (Arsenyan & Mirowska, 2021). Esta dimensión humana facilita la identificación del público, un factor clave para provocar respuestas emocionales como la envidia benigna, entendida como un impulso positivo de superación al observar los logros de alguien percibido como merecedor (Wahba et al.,

2025). Este efecto se intensifica en contextos de contenido aspiracional, como el turismo de lujo, donde la exposición a estilos de vida exclusivos tiende a provocar envidia benigna (Dedeoglu et al., 2025). En contraste, los influencers virtuales, debido a su naturaleza digital, pueden generar una menor credibilidad respecto a sus logros (Mo & Want, 2024). Por ello, se plantea que la interacción entre el tipo de influencer (humano vs. virtual) y el carácter aspiracional del contenido (destinos de lujo vs. no lujo) influye en la intensidad de la envidia benigna experimentada por los seguidores. En consecuencia, se formula la siguiente hipótesis:

- **H1.** El efecto del contenido de destinos de lujo (vs. no lujo) compartido por influencers en la envidia benigna de los consumidores es menor cuando el contenido es difundido por influencers virtuales (vs. humanos).

El miedo a perderse algo (FoMO) se define como la ansiedad ante la posibilidad de que otros estén disfrutando experiencias gratificantes de las cuales uno está ausente (Przybylski et al., 2013). Esta sensación incluye tanto la inquietud por quedar excluido de actividades sociales como la percepción de carencia de bienes o experiencias que otros poseen (Hussain et al., 2023). En redes sociales, donde la comparación social es constante, el FoMO se intensifica especialmente al exponerse a contenidos aspiracionales, como viajes a destinos de lujo (Alt & Boniel-Nissim, 2018). Los influencers juegan un papel central en la activación del FoMO, ya que su proximidad percibida y conexión emocional facilitan una vigilancia constante de sus publicaciones (Jin et al., 2019). Sin embargo, el impacto emocional varía según el tipo de influencer, pues los virtuales son percibidos como menos realistas y menos identificables, lo que atenúa la intensidad del FoMO generado (Wang et al., 2019). Por ello, se propone que la capacidad de un influencer para inducir FoMO mediante contenido de destinos de lujo es menor cuando es virtual, debido a una menor identificación y conexión emocional. De esta forma, se formula:

- **H2.** El efecto del contenido de destinos de lujo (vs. no lujo) compartido por influencers en el FoMO de los consumidores es menor cuando el contenido es difundido por influencers virtuales (vs. humanos).

El materialismo es un valor personal que refleja la creencia en la necesidad de adquirir bienes materiales para alcanzar la felicidad y el éxito (Richins & Dawson, 1992). Se articula en dimensiones como la centralidad de la adquisición, la asociación con la felicidad y la conexión con el éxito personal. En entornos digitales, la exposición a contenido aspiracional difundido por influencers intensifica estos valores al presentar estilos de vida deseables que fomentan la comparación y el deseo de emulación (Lou & Kim, 2019). Los influencers, como prescriptores de tendencias, promueven experiencias exclusivas y simbólicas, como viajes a destinos de lujo, que refuerzan la percepción de que poseer dichas experiencias contribuye a una vida satisfactoria (Freberg et al., 2011). No obstante, el impacto del contenido aspiracional en el materialismo depende del tipo de influencer: los humanos generan mayor realismo e identificación personal, mientras que los virtuales se perciben como menos alcanzables, reduciendo así la implicación emocional y la activación del materialismo (Jin et al., 2019). Por ello, se plantea:

- **H3.** El efecto del contenido de destinos de lujo (vs. no lujo) compartido por influencers en el materialismo de los consumidores es menor cuando el contenido es difundido por influencers virtuales (vs. humanos).

La experiencia de FoMO conduce a idealizar a figuras observadas como influencers y a aspirar a sus estilos de vida, generando envidia benigna. Además, el FoMO puede fomentar comportamientos de autopromoción en redes sociales como estrategia compensatoria para mitigar la ansiedad (Gómez et al., 2022; Verduyn et al., 2017). Este comportamiento motivado por la necesidad de validación social a menudo se asocia con la intención de despertar también envidia en otros, reforzando el estatus percibido (Alutaybi et al., 2019a, 2019b). En este contexto, el FoMO puede intensificar la envidia benigna, una emoción social positiva caracterizada por la admiración y el deseo de emulación sin resentimiento (van de Ven et al., 2009). Sin embargo, esta dinámica varía según el tipo de influencer, dado que los humanos generan mayor identificación e implicación emocional que los virtuales, que se perciben como menos auténticos y comparables (Jin et al., 2019). Así, se espera que el efecto del FoMO en la envidia benigna sea menor cuando el contenido proviene de influencers virtuales. Por tanto, se formula:

- **H5.** El efecto del FoMO en la envidia benigna de los consumidores es menor cuando el influencer es virtual (vs. humano).

El FoMO también se ha identificado como un motivador del comportamiento del consumidor, especialmente en entornos digitales donde la exposición a contenido aspiracional genera una sensación de urgencia y necesidad de participación (Good & Hyman, 2020). Los influencers que promueven experiencias deseables, como viajes exclusivos, aumentan la intención de visitar esos destinos mediante la activación del FoMO (Çelik et al., 2019). Sin embargo, la intensidad de este efecto depende del tipo de influencer. Los influencers humanos tienden a generar mayor realismo y cercanía, mientras que los virtuales son percibidos como menos auténticos, atenuando la respuesta emocional (Jin et al., 2019). Por ello, se plantea que la influencia del FoMO sobre la intención de visita se modera por el tipo de influencer, siendo más fuerte en presencia de humanos. Así:

- **H6.** El efecto del FoMO en la intención de visitar un destino turístico es menor cuando el influencer es virtual (vs. humano).

El materialismo, como predictor clave en el comportamiento del consumidor, está vinculado a la intención de compra y consumo experiencial (Dinh & Lee, 2021). La comparación social con influencers intensifica los deseos materialistas, fomentando tanto la adquisición de bienes como la búsqueda de experiencias que proyecten estatus y éxito (Lou & Kim, 2019). Este efecto se extiende al consumo de viajes a destinos turísticos exclusivos, percibidos como símbolos de logro. El impacto del materialismo en la intención de visitar dichos destinos está condicionado por el tipo de influencer, pues los humanos generan mayor autenticidad y credibilidad, reforzando la identificación y el impacto materialista, mientras que los virtuales atenúan esta respuesta (Jin et al., 2019). Por consiguiente:

- **H7.** El efecto del materialismo en la intención de visitar un destino turístico es menor cuando el influencer es virtual (vs. humano).

Finalmente, la envidia benigna, que puede motivar comportamientos aspiracionales y actitudes positivas hacia destinos turísticos, se activa al observar contenido aspiracional (Latif et al., 2021). Esta emoción está relacionada con la intención de visitar el destino observado, al generar inspiración y deseo de emulación (Liu et al., 2019; Feng et al., 2023). Sin embargo, su efecto también depende del tipo de influencer, siendo más fuerte cuando la fuente es humana, dada la mayor autenticidad y cercanía percibida. Por ello, se propone:

- **H8.** El efecto de la envidia benigna en la intención de visitar un destino turístico es menor cuando el influencer es virtual (vs. humano).

3. METODOLOGÍA

Para testar el modelo propuesto, se realizará un experimento entre sujetos en un Neuro Lab de una universidad europea. Se manipularán dos variables independientes: el tipo de influencer (virtual vs humano) y el tipo de destino turístico (lujo vs no lujo). Los participantes se asignarán aleatoriamente a una de las cuatro condiciones experimentales, en las que se mostrará primero el perfil de Instagram del influencer (virtual vs humano) y luego un post con una imagen y descripción del destino (lujo vs no lujo). Tras revisar la información, completarán un cuestionario online con escalas de varios ítems para la medición de las variables: FOMO (Good et al., 2021; Dinh and Lee, 2024), el materialismo (Richins, 2004; Dinh and Lee, 2024), la envidia benigna (Lange & Crusius, 2015; Ng et al., 2023) e intención de visita (Lu et al., 2016; Tian et al. 2024). Las respuestas se registrarán con una escala Likert de 7 puntos. Además, se codificarán las variables de influencer (virtual = 0; humano = 1) y tipo de contenido (no lujo = 0; lujo = 1). Los comportamientos visuales de los participantes se registrarán con un monitor de PC de 23 pulgadas y 1920 × 1080 píxeles de resolución (que también mostrará las instrucciones y los estímulos experimentales). Los datos se recogerán utilizando un rastreador ocular Tobii X2-30 Compact Eye Tracker. La duración de las emociones expresadas se medirá a través de la lectura facial y la excitación a través de las respuestas galvánicas de la piel (EDA).

4. RESULTADOS

A partir del modelo teórico propuesto, se anticipa que los resultados confirmen la influencia del tipo de influencer y del tipo de contenido turístico sobre las respuestas emocionales y comportamentales de los consumidores. En primer lugar, se espera que el contenido aspiracional de lujo genere niveles más elevados de envidia benigna, particularmente cuando es difundido por influencers humanos, percibidos como fuentes más auténticas y emocionalmente próximas. Por tanto, H1 se espera que sea apoyada.

En relación con el miedo a perderse algo (FoMO), se prevé que las publicaciones de destinos de lujo compartidas por influencers humanos produzcan un mayor grado de ansiedad por exclusión que aquellas difundidas por influencers virtuales, lo que respaldaría H2.

Respecto al materialismo, se espera que la exposición a contenido aspiracional de lujo incremente la orientación materialista de los individuos, siendo este efecto más pronunciado cuando el mensaje procede de un influencer humano. En consecuencia, H3 se espera que sea apoyada.

En cuanto al procesamiento emocional, se anticipa que el FoMO ejerza un efecto positivo sobre la envidia benigna, ya que la percepción de exclusión puede intensificar la admiración hacia quienes disfrutan de experiencias deseables. Este efecto sería más acusado en el caso de los influencers humanos, apoyando H5.

De manera similar, se prevé que el FoMO incremente la intención de visitar los destinos turísticos, especialmente cuando los contenidos provienen de influencers humanos, lo que confirmaría H6.

Asimismo, se espera que el materialismo se relacione positivamente con la intención de visita, al considerar los viajes a destinos de lujo como símbolos de estatus y logro personal. Este efecto se anticipa más fuerte en condiciones de influencia humana, por lo que H7 se espera que sea apoyada.

Finalmente, se prevé que la envidia benigna actúe como un motor aspiracional que impulse la intención de visitar los destinos promocionados. Sin embargo, debido a la menor conexión emocional que suelen generar los influencers virtuales, este efecto podría atenuarse bajo dicha condición, por lo que H8 se espera que sea apoyada.

Los resultados previstos apuntan, por tanto, a que la naturaleza humana del influencer desempeña un papel determinante en la activación de respuestas emocionales y valorativas más intensas, reforzando su eficacia en la promoción de experiencias turísticas aspiracionales.

5. CONCLUSIONES

El presente estudio pretende avanzar en la comprensión del papel que desempeñan los influencers humanos y virtuales en la formación de emociones y valores vinculados al turismo aspiracional. Basado en la Teoría de la Comparación Social (Festinger, 1954), el modelo propuesto integra constructos como la envidia benigna, el miedo a perderse algo (FoMO) y el materialismo para explicar la intención de visitar destinos turísticos. El enfoque adoptado permite analizar cómo la autenticidad percibida y la identificación emocional con los influencers pueden influir en las reacciones del consumidor frente a distintos tipos de contenido turístico.

De acuerdo con los resultados esperados, los influencers humanos tienden a generar una respuesta emocional más intensa que los influencers virtuales, debido a su capacidad para proyectar experiencias reales y conectar con el público desde la cercanía y la credibilidad. En este sentido, se anticipa que las emociones positivas como la envidia benigna o el FoMO actúen como impulsoras de la intención de visitar los destinos promocionados, mientras que el materialismo refuerce la valoración del consumo de experiencias como símbolo de logro personal.

Desde una perspectiva teórica, esta investigación busca ampliar el conocimiento sobre cómo las emociones sociales intervienen en la toma de decisiones en entornos digitales, especialmente en el contexto del marketing de influencers turísticos. El modelo propuesto permite considerar el papel motivacional de emociones tradicionalmente percibidas como negativas y explorar su contribución a comportamientos aspiracionales positivos.

En el ámbito práctico, los hallazgos previstos pueden resultar útiles para los responsables de marketing y comunicación de destinos turísticos, al ofrecer una base para seleccionar el tipo de influencer y el contenido más adecuado según los objetivos de la campaña. Los influencers humanos podrían ser más eficaces para comunicar experiencias exclusivas o de lujo, mientras que los influencers virtuales pueden aportar valor en estrategias orientadas a la innovación tecnológica o a públicos más jóvenes y digitales.

Además de las implicaciones profesionales, los resultados también pueden tener una relevante dimensión social, al contribuir a una comprensión más equilibrada del impacto de los contenidos aspiracionales en el bienestar emocional de los usuarios y en la construcción de modelos de consumo más conscientes.

Asimismo, comprender cómo las distintas figuras de influencia generan emociones y motivaciones en los consumidores puede ayudar a diseñar estrategias más equilibradas, que inspiren aspiración y deseo sin provocar frustración o comparaciones excesivas. Este equilibrio entre emoción y autenticidad resulta clave para construir relaciones más sostenibles entre las marcas turísticas y sus audiencias.

En esta etapa del proyecto, la recogida y análisis de datos todavía están en curso. No obstante, las bases teóricas y el diseño experimental desarrollados ofrecen un marco sólido para validar las relaciones planteadas y avanzar en la comprensión del papel de la influencia digital en la construcción de experiencias turísticas aspiracionales.

Agradecimientos: Los autores agradecen el apoyo de los proyectos Grant PID2023-147414OB-I00 y PID2023-153112OB-100 financiados por MCIU/AEI/10.13039/501100011033/FEDER, UE.

6. REFERENCIAS

Alutaybi, A., McAlaney, J., Arden-Close, E., Stefanidis, A., Phalp, K., & Ali, R. (2019, October). Fear of Missing Out (FoMO) as really lived: Five classifications and one ecology. In *2019 6th International Conference on Behavioral, Economic and Socio-Cultural Computing (BESC)* (pp. 1-6). IEEE.

Alutaybi, A., Arden-Close, E., McAlaney, J., Stefanidis, A., Phalp, K., & Ali, R. (2019, October). How can social networks design trigger fear of missing out?. In *2019 IEEE International Conference on Systems, Man and Cybernetics (SMC)* (pp. 3758-3765). IEEE.

Alt, D., & Boniel-Nissim, M. (2018). Links between adolescents' deep and surface learning approaches, problematic internet use, and fear of missing out (FoMO). *Internet interventions, 13*, 30-39

Arsenyan, J., & Mirowska, A. (2021). Almost human? A comparative case study on the social media presence of virtual influencers. *International Journal of Human-Computer Studies, 155*, 102694.

Byun, K. J., & Ahn, S. J. (2023). A systematic review of virtual influencers: Similarities and differences between human and virtual influencers in interactive advertising. *Journal of Interactive Advertising, 23*(4), 293-306.

Chen, F., Liu, S. Q., & Mattila, A. S. (2020). Bragging and humblebragging in online reviews. *Annals of Tourism Research, 80*, 102849.

Çelik, I. K., Eru, O., & Cop, R. (2019). The effects of consumers' FoMo tendencies on impulse buying and the effects of impulse buying on post-purchase regret: An investigation on retail stores. *BRAIN. Broad Research in Artificial Intelligence and Neuroscience, 10*(3), 124-138.

Dedeoglu, B. B., Colmekcioglu, N., & Okumus, F. (2025). Do envy and consumer-generated content boost travel motivations? *Journal of Travel Research*, 64(2), 267-283.

Dinh, T. C. T., & Lee, Y. (2021). "I want to be as trendy as influencers"–how "fear of missing out" leads to buying intention for products endorsed by social media influencers. *Journal of Research in Interactive Marketing, 16*(3), 346-364.

Dinh, T. C. T., & Lee, Y. (2024). Social media influencers and followers' conspicuous consumption: The mediation of fear of missing out and materialism. *Heliyon, 10*(16).

Feng, W., Chang, D., & Sun, H. (2023). The impact of social media influencers' bragging language styles on consumers' attitudes toward luxury brands: The dual mediation of envy and trustworthiness. *Frontiers in Psychology*, 13, 1113655.

Festinger, L. (1954). A theory of social comparison processes. *Human Relations*, 7(2), 117-140.

Freberg, K., Graham, K., McGaughey, K., & Freberg, L. A. (2011). Who are the social media influencers? A study of public perceptions of personality. *Public relations review, 37*(1), 90-92.

Good, M. C., & Hyman, M. R. (2020). 'Fear of missing out': antecedents and influence on purchase likelihood. *Journal of Marketing Theory and Practice, 28*(3), 330-341.

Gomez, M., Klare, D., Ceballos, N., Dailey, S., Kaiser, S., & Howard, K. (2022). Do you dare to compare?: The key characteristics of social media users who frequently make online upward social comparisons. *International Journal of Human–Computer Interaction, 38*(10), 938-948.

Gupta, S., & Srivastav, P. (2016). An Exploratory Investigation of Aspirational Consumption at the Bottom of the Pyramid. *Journal of International Consumer Marketing,* 28(1), 2–15.

Hussain, S., Raza, A., Haider, A., & Ishaq, M. I. (2023). Fear of missing out and compulsive buying behavior: The moderating role of mindfulness. *Journal of Retailing and Consumer Services, 75,* 103512.

Jin, S. V., & Ryu, E. (2020). "I'll buy what she's# wearing": The roles of envy toward and parasocial interaction with influencers in Instagram celebrity-based brand endorsement and social commerce. *Journal of Retailing and Consumer Services,* 55, 102–121.

Kim, D. Y., Park, M., & Kim, H. Y. (2023). An influencer like me: Examining the impact of the social status of Influencers. *Journal of Marketing Communications,* 29(7), 654-675.

Lange, J., & Crusius, J. (2015). Dispositional envy revisited: Unravelling the motivational dynamics of benign and malicious envy. *Personality and Social Psychology Bulletin,* 41(2), 284–294.

Latif, K., Weng, Q., Pitafi, A. H., Ali, A., Siddiqui, A. W., Malik, M. Y., & Latif, Z. (2021). Social comparison as a double-edged sword on social media: The role of envy type and online social identity. *Telematics and Informatics, 56,* 101470.

Lim, M. S., & Kim, J. (2018). Facebook users' loneliness based on different types of interpersonal relationships: Links to grandiosity and envy. *Information Technology and People,* 31(3), 646–665.

Liu, H., Wu, L., & Li, X. (2019). Social media envy: How experience sharing on social networking sites drives millennials' aspirational tourism consumption. *Journal of Travel Research,* 58(3), 355–369.

Lou, C., & Kim, H. K. (2019). Fancying the new rich and famous? Explicating the roles of influencer content, credibility, and parental mediation in adolescents' parasocial relationship, materialism, and purchase intentions. *Frontiers in psychology, 10,* 2567.

Mo, T., & Wang, W. (2025). The virtual new or the real old? The effect of temporal alignment between influencer virtuality and brand heritage narration on consumers' luxury consumption. *Psychology & Marketing, 42*(2), 470-492.

Park, J. Y., & Lee, H. E. (2024). How Consumer Photo Reviews and Online Platform Types Influence Luxury Hotel Booking Intentions Through Envy. *Journal of Travel Research,* 00472875241247317.

Przybylski, A. K., Murayama, K., DeHaan, C. R., & Gladwell, V. (2013). Motivational, emotional, and behavioral correlates of fear of missing out. *Computers in human behavior, 29*(4), 1841-1848.

Richins, M. L., & Dawson, S. (1992). A consumer values orientation for materialism and its measurement: Scale development and validation. *Journal of consumer research, 19*(3), 303-316.

Tandon, A., Dhir, A., Islam, N., Talwar, S., & Mäntymäki, M. (2021). Psychological and behavioral outcomes of social media-induced fear of missing out at the workplace. *Journal of Business Research, 136*, 186-197.

Tian, S., Cho, S. Y., Jia, X., Sun, R., & Tsai, W. S. (2023). Antecedents and outcomes of Generation Z consumers' contrastive and assimilative upward comparisons with social media influencers. *Journal of Product & Brand Management, 32*(7), 1046-1062.

Van de Ven, N., Zeelenberg, M., & Pieters, R. (2011). Why envy outperforms admiration. *Personality and Social Psychology Bulletin*, 37(6), 784–795.

Verduyn, P., Ybarra, O., Résibois, M., Jonides, J., & Kross, E. (2017). Do social network sites enhance or undermine subjective well-being? A critical review. *Social Issues and Policy Review, 11*(1), 274-302.

Wahba, S., El-Deeb, S., & Metry, S. (2025). The role of influencers and social comparison in shaping travel intentions. *Journal of Hospitality and Tourism Insights*, 8(3), 849-869.

Wang, P., Wang, X., Nie, J., Zeng, P., Liu, K., Wang, J., ... & Lei, L. (2019). Envy and problematic smartphone use: The mediating role of FOMO and the moderating role of student- student relationship. *Personality and Individual Differences, 146*, 136-142.

Xie-Carson, L., Magor, T., Benckendorff, P., & Hughes, K. (2023). All hype or the real deal? Investigating user engagement with virtual influencers in tourism. *Tourism Management*, 99, 104779.

TECNOLOGIAS DIGITALES PARA LA ESTIMACIÓN DE LA CAPACIDAD DE CARGA DE VISITANTES EN DIFERENTES TIPOS DE ESPACIOS PATRIMONIALES

PENÉLOPE TERUEL
MARÍA JOSÉ VIÑALS
KARIM SMAHA
Universitat Politècnica de València

RESUMEN: Este trabajo presenta un procedimiento metodológico para utilizar herramientas tecnológicas digitales con el fin de estimar y monitorear de manera eficiente la capacidad de carga de visitantes en calles y otros espacios públicos históricos, monumentos y otros lugares patrimoniales.

Los autores han basado el estudio en su experiencia en el desarrollo y aplicación de la capacidad de carga de visitantes en numerosos sitios patrimoniales de características diversas como espacios al aire libre (yacimientos arqueológicos, calles históricas y espacios públicos, áreas protegidas naturales, etc.), espacios cerrados (iglesias, museos, etc.) y espacios confinados (criptas, tumbas, capillas, sótanos históricos, etc.).

Los resultados muestran que estas herramientas digitales son eficaces y precisas para el análisis espacial de la estimación de la capacidad de carga de visitantes, pero especialmente para el recuento y monitoreo en tiempo real de los flujos de visitantes, así como para el estudio de parámetros ambientales específicos que afectan al confort y la salud de los visitantes, y a la conservación del patrimonio.

Palabras clave: Tecnologías Digitales, Capacidad de Carga de Visitantes, Gestión Turística, Espacios Patrimoniales, Monitoreo.

ABSTRACT: This paper presents a methodology for using digital technologies tools to efficiently estimate and monitor the Visitor Carrying Capacity of streets and other public historic spaces, monuments, and other heritage sites.

The methodology was tested on several heritage sites of diverse characteristics by the authors: outdoor spaces (p.e. archaeological settlements, historic streets and public spaces, natural protected areas, etc.), closed spaces (p.e. churches, museums) and confined spaces (p.e. crypts, tombs, chapels, historic basements).

The results show that these digital tools are efficient and accurate for the spatial analysis of Visitor Carrying Capacity estimation but especially for the real-time counting and monitoring of visitors, but also for surveying specific environmental parameters that affect visitors comfort and health and heritage conservation assets.

Keywords: Digital Technologies; Visitor Carrying Capacity; Tourism Management, Heritage sites, Monitoring

1. INTRODUCCIÓN Y OBJETIVOS

La Capacidad de Carga de Visitantes (CCV) es una de las herramientas más reconocidas para la gestión turística de los elementos patrimoniales (espacios naturales, culturales y urbanos, etc.) que se utilizan con el fin de garantizar la conservación del bien patrimonial y la calidad de la experiencia turística. Los estudios se centran, habitualmente, en determinar el número máximo de personas que pueden visitar un sitio patrimonial al mismo tiempo (Personas Al Mismo Tiempo —PAMT—), pero está demostrado que estimar el PAMT esto no es suficiente. La CCV resulta mucho más compleja de lo que aparenta ya que en su desarrollo intervienen muchos factores, y además analiza un fenómeno de naturaleza dinámica como son los flujos de visitantes, que están en constante evolución; por ello, debe de ser monitoreada regularmente. También hay que mencionar que, si bien estas estimaciones pueden ser pertinentes para considerar el confort y la seguridad de las personas que visitan un sitio en un momento dado, no hay apenas estudios que hablen de la afección de la rotación de las visitas en un lugar a lo largo del día, semanas o meses, ni del impacto acumulado que esos visitantes pueden causar a un lugar patrimonial a lo largo del tiempo.

Otro factor relevante para tener en cuenta en estos estudios es que no hay dos sitios patrimoniales iguales; por tanto, si bien es necesario partir de unos análisis preliminares de diagnóstico para todos los lugares, luego hay que adaptar el procedimiento a las especificidades propias de cada sitio. Es evidente que las características espaciales y vulnerabilidades de un yacimiento arqueológico o un monumento no son las mismas que las de una cueva con arte rupestre.

Por otra parte, hay que mencionar que previamente a la era digital actual, los datos se registraban, recopilaban y almacenaban en formato físico. Los cálculos matemáticos y análisis cuantitativos se realizaban en el marco de trabajos estadísticos derivados de la observación, conteos manuales, entrevistas, encuestas o test y se procesaban de forma manual o con la ayuda de dispositivos analógicos. Además, los análisis espaciales de los sitios para dimensionar los espacios patrimoniales que iban a ser objeto de un estudio de capacidad de carga, habitualmente se realizaban mediante levantamientos manuales y planimetría en 2D.

Hay que señalar también que, si bien ha habido sitios patrimoniales que siempre han tenido problemas de saturación y congestión turística, nunca como ahora se ha experimentado un crecimiento de visitantes tan alarmante en tan breve periodo de tiempo. Según datos de la OECD (2024) y de la UNTWO (2024), se esperaba la recuperación del número de turistas internacionales previos a la pandemia del COVID-19 para el 2024, como así ha ocurrido y, en 2025, en Europa está previsto que se superen las previsiones (Tourism Economics, 2024; Unión Europea, 2025). Por tanto, se puede pensar que el crecimiento en el número de visitantes en destinos turísticos no parece que vaya a disminuir en breve y que la gestión de los espacios patrimoniales, en particular la estimación y monitoreo de la capacidad de carga de visitantes, va a resultar imposible de abordar si no es con el uso de tecnologías digitales.

Por tanto, este trabajo tiene el objetivo de presentar un procedimiento metodológico para abordar el análisis y monitoreo en tiempo real de la capacidad de carga de visitantes basado en el uso tecnologías digitales. Todo ello apoyado por ejemplos que este equipo investigador ha desarrollado en diferentes tipos de espacios patrimoniales para comprobar su eficiencia. En particular se ha focalizado sobre los resultados y conclusiones del estudio de capacidad de carga de visitantes de las calles del centro histórico de Valencia circundantes a la Catedral (calle del Miguelete), y sobre los derivados del estudio de la Capilla del Santo Cáliz de la Catedral de Valencia. El primero es un espacio abierto urbano histórico, mientras que el segundo es un espacio confinado.

2. ESTADO DEL ARTE

Existen numerosas propuestas metodológicas desde finales del siglo pasado que han abordado el cálculo de la capacidad de carga de visitantes. Estas primeras aproximaciones partieron del ámbito de los espacios naturales protegidos (Cifuentes, 1992; Butler, 1996; Manning, 2002) y, poco a poco, fueron transfiriéndose a sitios patrimoniales culturales, a la vez que se refinaban los modelos de cálculo y se incorporaban otras variables como la sostenibilidad social del destino.

Desde el año 2000, los estudios sobre la capacidad de carga de visitantes van cobrando cada vez más importancia, coincidiendo con los nuevos retos relacionados con la saturación y degradación de los sitios patrimoniales, la disminución de la calidad de las experiencias turísticas y los impactos sociales negativos sobre las poblaciones residentes (gentrificación y turismofobia). Todos estos aspectos han sido abordados por autores como García Hernández (2001), Coccossis y Mexa (2007), López-Bonilla y López-Bonilla (2008), Santos y Peña Cabrera (2014), Viñals et al. (2014; 2016), Milano (2017), Muler González et al. (2018), Bin Yusoh et al. (2021), entre otros. En los últimos años, se ha podido confirmar el relevante posicionamiento de esta herramienta a la hora de abordar la gestión turística del patrimonio y la necesidad de introducir las tecnologías digitales en su estudio (Zubiaga et al., 2019; Makhadmeh et al., 2020; Salvador-García et al., 2020; de Almeida, 2021; Simou et al., 2022; Orozco et al., 2023), así como la urgencia de incorporar el estudio de sistemas de monitoreo de la capacidad de carga de visitantes para que, realmente, esta herramienta sea útil y eficiente en la gestión patrimonial y turística. De este modo, en estos momentos, comienzan a publicarse trabajos relativos a la sensorización para el conteo de personas en tiempo real y también de los parámetros ambientales relativos a la calidad del aire que limitan la utilización de determinados espacios patrimoniales, debido a las posibles afecciones a la salud de los visitantes o a la conservación del propio patrimonio (Agnew et al., 2013; Franco y Leccese, 2020; Galiano et al., 2024; Viñals et al. 2024; entre otros).

Hay que mencionar además que el análisis de los aspectos espaciales de los sitios patrimoniales propios de los estudios de capacidad de carga de visitantes se ha beneficiado enormemente de tecnologías digitales tales como el Escaneado Láser, Modelado 3D, Fotogrametría, *Heritage Building Information Modelling* —HBIM—, Sistemas de Información Geográfica —SIG—, *Simultaneous Localization and Mapping* —SLAM—, Tecnología de Drones, LIDAR, Técnicas de Procesado de Datos Geoespaciales, entre otras. Todas ellas pueden ser usadas individualmente o combinadas entre sí e integradas en plataformas de datos. De esta forma, se han aplicado para resolver aspectos como la zonificación, estimaciones métricas y volumétricas de los espacios, la determinación de los atributos espaciales y vulnerabilidades de los monumentos y espacios urbanos patrimoniales, la determinación de la Superficie Útil para la Visita (SUV), el análisis de las cuencas visuales, el patrón de la visita, la identificación de puntos de encuentro para grupos, entre otros.

Hay diversos trabajos recientes que se centran en la utilización de las tecnologías digitales para el monitoreo de la capacidad de carga de visitantes. De esta manera, empiezan a cobrar protagonismo los Sistemas de Sensorización en los espacios patrimoniales abiertos y cerrados con dispositivos de conteo de personas y de monitoreo de parámetros ambientales (Temperatura, Humedad Relativa, CO2 y otros), y se apunta a los Gemelos Digitales de los espacios patrimoniales como una oportunidad única para encontrar soluciones a desafíos diversos sin necesidad de someter al elemento patrimonial a ningún tipo de estrés (Hutson et al., 2023; Niccolucci et al., 2023; Galiano-Garrigós y López-Torres, 2024).

3. METODOLOGÍA

El reto que presentaba esta investigación ha sido cómo incorporar las tecnologías digitales en los estudios tradicionales de determinación y monitoreo de la capacidad de carga de visitantes para que realmente sean herramientas eficientes de gestión turística en tiempo real.

La investigación se ha basado tanto en la revisión bibliográfica como en la observación directa y en la experiencia de este equipo investigador en el desarrollo de estudios de capacidad de carga de visitantes. De este modo, partiendo del procedimiento habitualmente empleado y de los resultados obtenidos en casos propios de sitios patrimoniales donde se han empleado y evaluado los resultados de la aplicación de tecnologías digitales, se ha procedido a la sistematización de los procesos seguidos para generar un procedimiento metodológico de estimación y monitoreo de la capacidad de carga de visitantes basado en las tecnologías digitales. Los pasos secuenciales desarrollados se han sintetizado en diagramas de flujo.

4. RESULTADOS Y DISCUSIÓN

Se ha organizado este apartado siguiendo las siguientes fases de análisis: 1) análisis espacial del sitio patrimonial; 2) actividad turística; 3) usuarios; 4) impactos derivados; 5) monitoreo de la capacidad de carga de visitantes; 6) retroalimentación del sistema de gestión de la capacidad de carga de visitantes. A continuación, se han presentado los resultados de dos ejemplos llevados a cabo siguiendo este procedimiento.

4.1. Desarrollo del Procedimiento

El paso previo a la realización de un estudio de capacidad de carga de visitantes es el desarrollo de un diagnóstico de la situación general que presenta el sitio patrimonial en relación con la visita, para así adaptar el procedimiento metodológico a las necesidades y posibilidades del lugar. Los sitios patrimoniales, como se ha comentado, pueden ser muy diferentes y la situación de partida en lo que respecta a la visita pública, puede ser también diversa; desde sitios que tienen problemas de saturación y congestión puntual de visitantes, a sitios que abren por primera vez sus puertas al público.

En la figura 1, se presenta un diagrama de flujo que integra, de forma secuencial y jerárquica, los pasos metodológicos básicos seguidos para el cálculo o estimación de la capacidad de carga de visitantes (CCV) vinculados a tecnologías digitales. Los óvalos de este diagrama indican el inicio o resultado del proceso, los rombos representan la toma de decisiones, los rectángulos señalan tareas o procesos específicos, los paralelogramos corresponden a operaciones de entrada o salida de datos, el cilindro es la recopilación y almacenamiento de información y las flechas definen la dirección del flujo del proceso y el establecimiento de la secuencia lógica entre los elementos.

Figura 1. Diagrama de flujo para el cálculo o la estimación de la Capacidad de Carga de Visitantes mediante el uso de tecnologías digitales

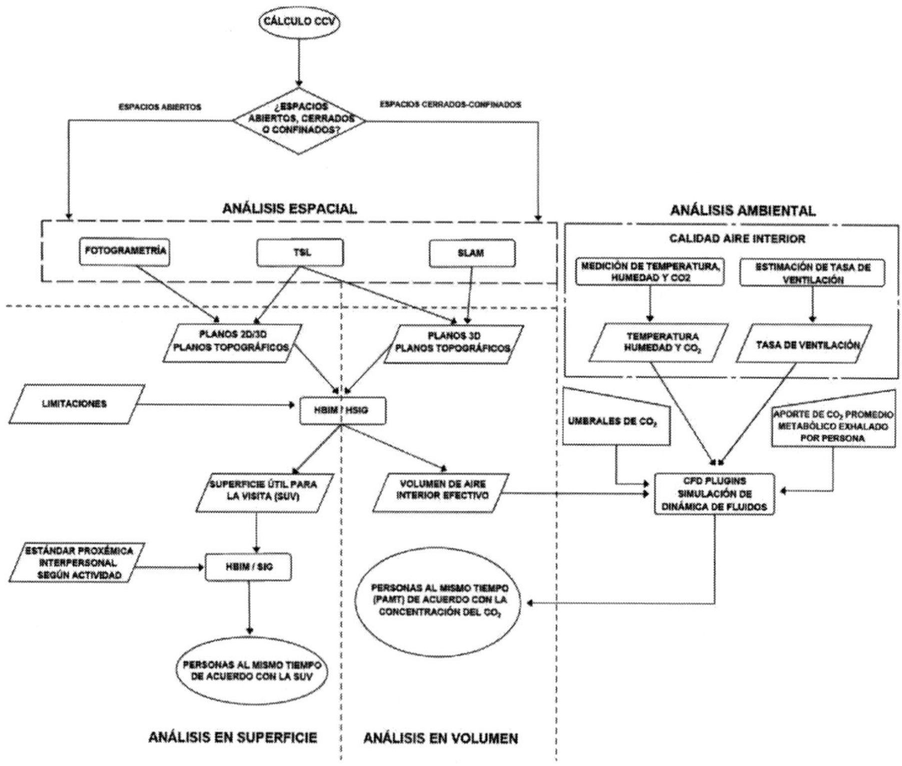

4.1.1. Análisis espacial del sitio patrimonial

El análisis espacial del sitio es fundamental en los estudios de capacidad de carga de visitantes y para ello la aplicación de tecnologías digitales da lugar a resultados muy precisos que pueden ser fácilmente actualizables.

Para este cometido herramientas digitales geoespaciales y de gestión de edificios como los Sistemas de Información Geográfica (SIG), *Simultaneous Localization and Mapping* (SLAM), Escaneado Láser, Fotogrametría, *Heritage Building Information Modeling* (HBIM), Modelado 3D entre otras.

Además de los planos topográficos en 2D o 3D, otros aspectos que se pueden abordar con estas herramientas son la determinación de las dimensiones, características físicas (rasgos morfológicos, conectividad entre unidades espaciales —pasillos, corredores, etc.—, transitabilidad —pendientes, obstáculos, etc.—, localización de accesos y ventanas, etc.), las vulnerabilidades físicas (elementos patrimoniales expuestos a riesgos diversos, etc.), y la zonificación en unidades espaciales menores si es necesario.

A continuación, se continuaría con la determinación de la Superficie Útil para la Visita (SUV)[1] que es aquella superficie (en m2) disponible para la visita después de descartar aquellos espacios que no son utilizables por razones de preservación, riesgo y seguridad, fragilidad intrínseca, falta de accesibilidad, incompatibilidad de usos, o debido a la distribución de sus componentes internos y sus propias áreas de repulsión (Viñals et al., 2017; Salvador-García et al., 2020). Esta superficie puede ser calculada y cartografiada tanto para espacios urbanos como para el interior de monumentos mediante herramientas como SIG, HBIM, u otras. También los atributos físicos de los espacios urbanos pueden ser analizados y evaluados utilizando herramientas geoespaciales, escaneados láser y Modelos Digitales del Terreno (MDT) (Orozco Carpio et al., 2024).

En el caso de los espacios confinados, además hay que calcular la volumetría del sitio para poder evaluar el volumen de aire efectivo. Para ello, se realizan los planos topográficos en 3D que luego se integrarán en HBIM.

---

1 Áreas de recepción, espacios donde están ubicados los atractivos y sus cuencas visuales, corredores de conectividad, espacios de evacuación y emergencias, espacios de equipamientos básicos, espacios museográficos, puntos de observación, puntos de reunión y encuentros, entre otros.

4.1.2. Actividad turística

Sobre la actividad a realizar, se debe destacar que una visita turística combina actividades de observación estática de los atractivos (edificios históricos, espacios urbanos, objetos en monumentos o museos —cuadros, esculturas, objetos religiosos, etc.—) desde puntos de observación o desde puntos de encuentro de grupos. Sin embargo, también es una actividad dinámica funcional puesto que los visitantes se trasladan de un punto a otro, sea en el interior de un sitio patrimonial como en los propios espacios públicos urbanos históricos; por tanto, se tiene que abordar también como un tema de gestión de flujos de visitantes.

En este paso del proceso, las herramientas digitales contribuyen de manera notable al análisis de cuencas visuales para garantizar la observación de los atractivos sin que haya obstrucciones. En el caso de espacios cerrados se puede realizar con HBIM (Salvador-García, 2020), y con herramientas geoespaciales para los espacios urbanos públicos. También la determinación de los puntos de encuentro para grupos en las calles y los patrones de visita y las opciones de tránsito se pueden llevar a cabo con herramientas geoespaciales y de optimización combinatoria de rutas (*Travelling Salesman Problem*) como se puede observar en el trabajo de Sanasaryan (2025).

4.1.3. Usuarios

En cuanto a los usuarios (visitantes u otras personas), la información relevante que se considera en estos estudios son los estándares de proxémica que se emplean para establecer la distancia interpersonal y el modo en que se realiza la visita; es decir, si se lleva a cabo de forma individual, en diadas, triadas, grupos pequeños (15 personas) o grupos más grandes. Para el establecimiento de los estándares de proxémica interpersonales en los diferentes trabajos realizados se han utilizado los propuestos por Hall (1966).

También hay que considerar si se trata de una actividad estática o de carácter dinámico. Así, la distancia interpersonal de los individuos en movimiento viene determinada en gran medida por las limitaciones físicas impuestas por otras personas y por las condiciones del entorno (Costa, 2010; Gorrini et al., 2014). En entornos de alta densidad, el distanciamiento entre individuos se basa en la necesidad de evitar colisiones con otras personas y, si se trata de un grupo, se caracteriza además por la necesidad de mantener la cohesión espacial entre sus miembros para facilitar la interacción social y la comunicación durante el desplazamiento. En el caso de visitantes individuales (que no se conocen entre sí) y debido a que se trata de una actividad dinámica, los requisitos de espacio interpersonal son mayores que en los espacios interiores; por lo tanto, resulta pertinente utilizar un estándar proxémico de «distancia pública», que podría oscilar entre 3,50 m y 7,25 m. Si la visita se realiza en grupo, se podría establecer otro estándar de «distancia social» (1,2-3,5 m) o incluso «distancia personal» (0,5-1,20 m) entre los miembros del grupo (aunque no se conozcan entre sí), ya que en ocasiones pueden identificarse como pertenecientes al mismo grupo y realizar una actividad conjunta en la que necesitan tener contacto visual y auditivo con el guía-intérprete. Sin embargo, lo importante en este caso es la distancia entre los grupos ya que está relacionada con los problemas de congestión del tráfico peatonal, sobre todo, para grupos grandes en espacios largos y estrechos. De otro lado, en espacios interiores, de forma habitual se aplica el estándar de «distancia personal» (0,5-1,20 m) y, en ocasiones, la «distancia social» (1,2-3,5 m). Estos estándares pueden ser tratados con herramientas como el ArcGIS para identificar los posibles escenarios de ocupación.

De esta forma, si se aplica un estándar de proxémica interpersonal a la Superficie Útil para la Visita (SUV), el resultado que obtendremos es el volumen de Personas Al Mismo Tiempo (PAMT) que puede acoger el espacio. Este primer resultado se refiere a una distribución aleatoria que no es realmente la que ocurre en la realidad. Las herramientas geoespaciales ayudan a identificar las áreas con capacidad para una mayor concentración de personas (puntos de encuentro de grupos, etc.) sin obstruccionar las cuencas visuales ni crear congestión de tránsito.

En el caso de espacios confinados, no son los parámetros de Superficie Útil los que comandan el análisis, sino que los factores limitantes para los usuarios tienen que ver con la calidad del aire interior (CO_2, Temperatura, Humedad etc.). Por ello, los estándares utilizados tienen que ver con el confort y la salud. Como resultado, se determina el número máximo de personas que pueden estar simultáneamente en función de la calidad del aire disponible. Este asunto está íntimamente ligado a la presencia de personas ya que son fuente de emisiones de CO_2 a través de la respiración. Hay que considerar que un número elevado de Personas Al mismo Tiempo (PAMT) en un sitio patrimonial confinado supone el disconfort físico (sobre todo termohigrométrico) y psicológico de los propios visitantes (invasión del espacio personal), pero también puede suponer un riesgo para la salud (Viñals et al., 2014; Teruel et al. 2025). Por ello, en la determinación de la capacidad de carga de visitantes debe incluirse un análisis de carácter ambiental para poder conocer las condiciones de la calidad del aire interior. En esta fase, hay que determinar los umbrales de salud de concentraciones de CO_2, determinar la tasa de ventilación del espacio en cuestión, y conocer la calidad del aire en tiempo real para estimar su disponibilidad en cada momento.

En los estudios de calidad del aire en espacios interiores, se utiliza habitualmente como valor de referencia una concentración 500 ppm (partes por millón) de CO_2, como una «calidad del aire buena» tal como sugieren el Instituto Nacional Español de Seguridad y Salud en el Trabajo (2018) y el Reglamento de Instalaciones Térmicas en los Edificios (Ministerio de la Presidencia de España, 2007; Ministerio de la Presidencia, Relaciones con las Cortes y Memoria Democrática de España, 2021) para la categoría IAQ IDA 2/Medio (oficinas, residencias, hoteles, museos y aulas). El valor de 1000 ppm se considera un umbral tolerable máximo ya que significa que es «calidad del aire aceptable, pero se recomienda ventilación», mientras que 1500 ppm supone una «calidad del aire baja, se requiere ventilación».

De cualquier manera, es necesario señalar que las concentraciones de CO2 cambian a lo largo del día según el nivel de ocupación del sitio; se trata de un elemento dinámico que necesita ser determinado en tiempo real porque está condicionando la capacidad de carga de visitantes a lo largo del horario de visita del sitio patrimonial. Si a ello se añade una tasa de ventilación baja, el CO_2 se va acumulando y la calidad del aire va empeorando mientras se produzcan visitas sucesivas, provocando un decrecimiento progresivo de la capacidad de carga de visitantes a medida que pasan las horas. Por tanto, debe ser monitoreado en tiempo real con sensores ambientales combinados con contadores de personas, o realizar ensayos puntuales del comportamiento del CO_2 del sitio frente a determinados niveles de ocupación, y considerando la tasa de ventilación. Estos ensayos pueden aportar información sobre el incremento acumulado de CO_2 a medida que van ingresando visitantes a lo largo del día y sobre la tasa de decaimiento del CO_2 una vez ha cesado la actividad de visita. Los Gemelos Digitales y la Inteligencia Artificial son de gran ayuda para establecer los escenarios relacionados con el número de visitantes en espacios confinados.

4.1.4. Impactos derivados de la actividad de visita

Respecto a los impactos derivados de las actividades de visita, se ha de mencionar que hay que tenerlos muy presentes e identificarlos tempranamente para poder abordar su mitigación o evitar que se produzcan.

Para ello, el elemento patrimonial debería dotarse de unos «estándares de conservación» y un «sistema de indicadores» en base a sus vulnerabilidades. El monitoreo de estos impactos debe enmarcarse en el contexto de la conservación preventiva de los bienes; por tanto, es necesario tenerlos en cuenta cuando se diseñan las actividades de uso público. Sin embargo, no es habitual encontrar sitios patrimoniales que dispongan de estándares e indicadores.

Los propios visitantes, como ya se ha comentado, contribuyen de forma muy significativa al propio disconfort de la actividad de visita; pero, además, son un factor de impacto sobre el patrimonio. Estos impactos pueden tipificarse en dos grandes grupos, los de carácter físico y los de tipo químico. Los primeros tienen que ver con la erosión mecánica que produce la abrasión o desgaste de los materiales debido a una acción continuada de pisoteo de los pavimentos o de rozamientos laterales. Obviamente, está relacionado con un número excesivo de visitantes (intensidad) y la persistencia (efecto permanente) de la actividad. Además, si bien los monumentos y los espacios públicos urbanos suelen ser resistentes, este tipo de impacto no es reversible. Otros riesgos, como los ataques vandálicos, son de carácter puntual, pero pueden causar graves daños al patrimonio.

Los impactos de carácter químico relacionados con los visitantes se producen también de forma continuada y presentan en ocasiones una intensidad y persistencia mayor y más extendida en superficie que los mecánicos. También son impactos de carácter irreversible. Se trata de fenómenos que afectan a la naturaleza material de los materiales constructivos (rocas y morteros) mediante el cual las rocas se desintegran o modifican debido a reacciones químicas en presencia de agentes como el agua, el oxígeno, el CO_2 y otros elementos. De esta forma, en numerosas ocasiones, se produce la disgregación y disolución de los materiales pétreos que en su composición contienen sales, infiriendo una gran fragilidad a las estructuras, además del desmantelamiento de los elementos escultóricos y los detalles arquitectónicos.

Un alto contenido de CO_2 producido por las personas en espacios confinados combinado con una humedad elevada puede disolver las rocas calcáreas, que son comunes en muchos monumentos históricos. Las temperaturas altas aceleran estas reacciones químicas. También las pinturas (cuadros, frescos, etc.) y otros elementos del patrimonio mueble se pueden ver afectados por estos impactos.

De cualquier manera, procede comentar que todavía no hay muchos estudios que analicen con detalle los impactos físicos y químicos sobre los elementos patrimoniales porque sus resultados se producen en el largo plazo. Este equipo de investigación ha puesto en marcha un programa de monitoreo en el Sitio Patrimonio de la Humanidad de Petra (Jordania) para el seguimiento de los efectos de la erosión mecánica sobre la base de la utilización de Fotogrametría y el Escaneado láser en aras de medir la denudación ocurrida por causas antrópicas.

Otra cuestión muy importante a resaltar, vinculada a la impactabilidad de los elementos patrimoniales, es que los estudios de capacidad de carga de visitantes, en su mayor parte se dedican al análisis de un «momento dado» para el cual se estima la Personas Al Mismo Tiempo (PAMT), y por tanto su objetivo se fija en el confort de las personas, pero no en los impactos sobre el elemento patrimonial. Para abordar el análisis del impacto acumulado sobre el patrimonio, se debería considerar la reiteración de visitas sobre el sitio en aras de dimensionar adecuadamente la magnitud e intensidad del impacto y considerar su persistencia, y previsibilidad a medio y largo plazo. Los Gemelos Digitales en combinación con la Inteligencia Artificial pueden contribuir decisivamente al establecimiento de potenciales escenarios de riesgo que pueden ayudar a planificar adecuadamente las actividades de uso público.

4.1.5. Monitoreo de la capacidad de carga de visitantes

El monitoreo de la capacidad de carga de visitantes es un proceso necesario para garantizar la gestión eficiente del sitio patrimonial. Se puede decir que en la fase de determinación de la capacidad de carga de visitantes se establecen los umbrales máximos de carga y en el monitoreo se realiza el seguimiento de estos parámetros y se establecen alertas para que se puedan tomar las medidas necesarias en aras de reconducir la situación a niveles de ocupación aceptables.

En esta fase del procedimiento (fig. 2), se puede decir que las tecnologías digitales son imprescindibles, sobre todo, en el caso de flujos de visitantes de grandes dimensiones que deben ser monitorizados en tiempo real. La Sensórica y los Sistemas de Transmisión de Datos son cruciales en esta fase del procedimiento.

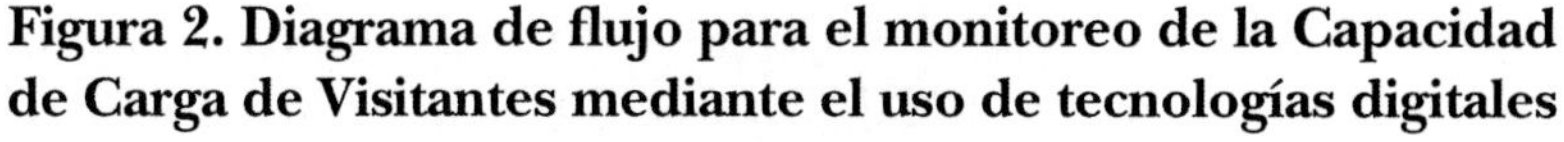

Figura 2. Diagrama de flujo para el monitoreo de la Capacidad de Carga de Visitantes mediante el uso de tecnologías digitales

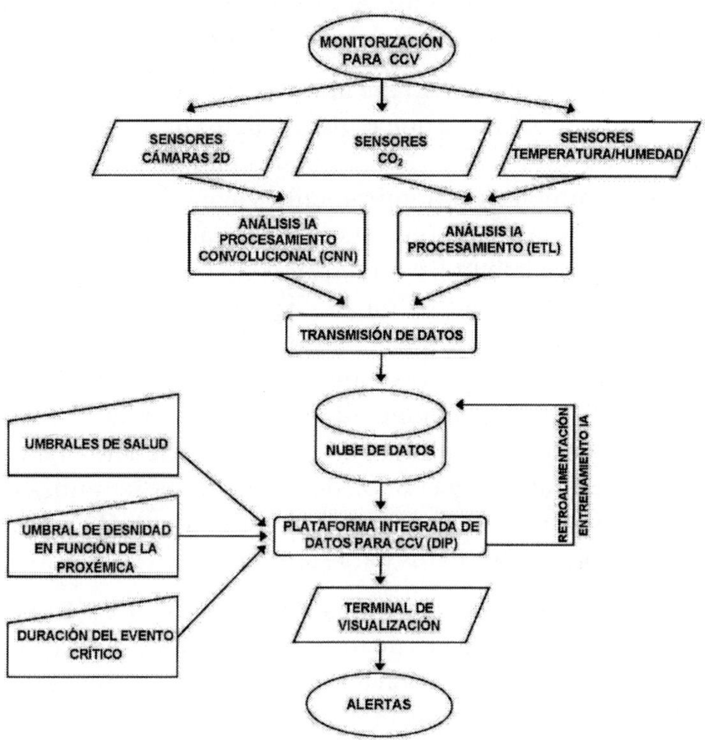

En el caso de espacios públicos urbanos históricos, el principal elemento a monitorear es el volumen y densidad del flujo de personas, para conocer cuando los umbrales de saturación y congestión se están alcanzando. Para ello, en los trabajos realizados por este equipo, se han empleado sensores de imagen 2D, ya que resultan muy viables desde el punto de vista técnico y económico para analizar el número de personas en un espacio público (Hung et al., 2012; Ashkanani et al., 2015; Liu et al., 2019; Zubiaga et al., 2019; Goto et al., 2024; Teruel et al., 2024) y tienen una alta fiabilidad de hasta el 98 % del recuento (Affluences, n.d.), con buenos resultados, especialmente a escala microurbana. En nuestro caso, por tratarse de espacios públicos, las videocámaras solamente suministraban datos numéricos (no imágenes) lo cual simplifica el procesado y el almacenamiento de la información y se salvaguardan los derechos de privacidad de las personas.

Para analizar y procesar las señales de imagen en tiempo real se utilizó tecnología de Visión Computerizada; así, el reconocimiento y conteo de personas se abordó a partir del uso de Redes Neuronales Convolucionales

(*Convolutional Neuronal Network* —CNN—), inspirándonos en los trabajos de Girshick et al. (2014) y Li (2020). La Inteligencia Artificial para desarrollar el algoritmo utiliza el Aprendizaje Automático (*Machine Learning*) en aras de crear modelos de detección de movimientos.

Para la medición de la calidad del aire en espacios patrimoniales se han utilizado sensores ambientales que registran datos de Temperatura, Humedad relativa y CO_2, entre otros. Se han usado también dispositivos comerciales que son asequibles económicamente y con gran precisión técnica. Así, en los estudios analizados por este equipo, para el registro de los parámetros ambientales se han utilizado sensores Testo 160 IAQ fijos. Los datos de los sensores son procesados con Inteligencia Artificial para organizar la información (Extract, Transform, Load —ETL—). Primero se extraen los datos de los sensores, luego se analizan y transforman a un formato comprensible y utilizable, y finalmente se cargan en bases de datos para su análisis. A continuación, la información se transmite automáticamente a través de Wi-Fi o por antena a la nube de datos, lo que garantiza el almacenamiento de la información y la obtención en tiempo real en ordenadores y dispositivos móviles de los datos para su tratamiento y análisis posterior.

Con la implementación de Plataformas Integradas de Gestión de Datos de CCV se pueden procesar los datos de forma integrada y visualizarlos en el formato conveniente. Hay que mencionar que estos datos pueden ser implementados directamente en HBIM tal como Rolin et al. (2024) han estudiado.

Los conteos de personas en el interior de los sitios patrimoniales son necesarios para poder cotejar diariamente los niveles de ocupación humana de los espacios con las concentraciones de CO2 y así conocer la evolución a lo largo del día de la calidad del aire (incremento acumulado de CO2 durante los horarios de visita y decaimiento tras el cierre) y así determinar el comportamiento de los sitios ante determinados volúmenes de afluencia de personas. Lo ideal es tener un sistema de conteo automático permanente; no obstante, se pueden hacer test ocasionales con sensores de imagen o incluso manualmente en varios días donde las condiciones de visita sean diferentes para poder extrapolar esta información a otras situaciones de visita similares. Para conteos manuales, se puede utilizar aplicaciones tipo «Count Counter» (versión 2024.12.1 para iOS) o «Contador» (Android V7.10.7), que sincronizan automáticamente los datos con sus plataformas en la nube para su visualización y gestión. También se pueden utilizar sensores de imagen con conexión Wi-Fi como por ejemplo el LoRaWAN Milesight que es un sensor con Inteligencia Artificial (IA) para detección y conteo de personas que envía los datos en tiempo real.

El objetivo de la monitorización es la identificación y activación de alertas tempranas de saturación de personas o de niveles de concentración de CO2 por encima del límite saludable (1.000 ppm). Este mecanismo permite poner en marcha mecanismos de prevención de impactos o riesgos y también mitigar posibles impactos.

Para la implementación de alertas en el sistema, hay que recurrir a la Inteligencia Artificial para que analice los datos de las series temporales obtenidas para identificar tendencias (repetitividad de los ciclos) y, además, categorizar el tipo de alerta (suave y progresiva) como sería el caso del CO2, o un crecimiento repentino como podría ser el caso de una saturación del espacio público.

4.1.6. Retroalimentación

Una vez desarrollado e implementado el sistema de Capacidad de Carga de Visitantes, procede evaluar los resultados e identificar aquellas áreas de mejora del sistema.

Tras la experiencia adquirida con el desarrollo de los casos de estudio, se pone de manifiesto la importancia que tiene el Sistema de Transmisión de Datos en Tiempo Real. Por ello, hay que estar constantemente explorando y comprobando las opciones disponibles en cada lugar. La calidad y precisión de los datos obtenidos, así como el modelo seguido, es otro objetivo que se debe contemplar en esta fase del procedimiento. Se ha de tener en cuenta como referencia que el fin último es la preservación del bien patrimonial y la calidad de la experiencia turística.

Por otra parte, con los datos obtenidos se puede desarrollar el Gemelo Digital del sitio y con la Inteligencia Artificial se pueden ensayar todos los escenarios de visita posible dotar al sistema de la máxima predictividad para adelantarse con posibles soluciones y estrategias de dispersión de carga de visitantes y conservación preventiva del bien.

4.2. Ejemplos prácticos

En este apartado se presentan los resultados obtenidos de la aplicación de tecnologías digitales en el análisis y monitoreo de la capacidad de carga de visitantes. Los casos elegidos han sido la calle del Miguelete, que es un espacio público abierto urbano en el centro histórico de Valencia, y la Capilla del Santo Cáliz que se encuentra en el interior de la Catedral de la Valencia (fig. 3).

Figura 3. Mapa de ubicación de los casos analizados: calle del Miguelete y la Capilla del Santo Cáliz en el interior de la Catedral

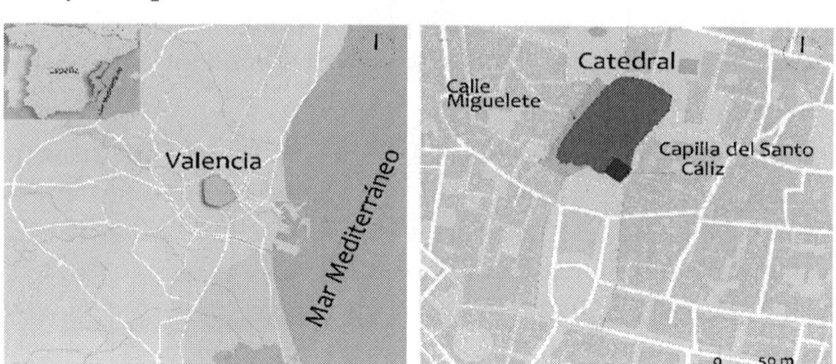

Fuente cartográfica: Ortofoto aérea 2022CVAL (Instituto Cartográfico Valenciano, 2022).

4.2.1. Capacidad de Carga de Visitantes del Entorno urbano histórico de la Catedral (calle del Miguelete)

La calle del Miguelete en Valencia es la zona experimental donde se han implementado las herramientas geoespaciales y de sensorización para el estudio de la capacidad de carga de visitantes para el caso de un espacio urbano público abierto. La elección de este sitio se debe a su ubicación estratégica y su importancia, ya que se encuentra junto a uno de los edificios patrimoniales más emblemáticos de la ciudad, la Catedral. Al mismo tiempo, la calle del Miguelete sirve de enlace vital entre dos plazas de gran importancia social y turística en Valencia, La plaza de la Virgen y la plaza de la Reina.

Se trata de una calle con una anchura que varía entre 5,00 m y 8,00 m y una longitud de 95,00 m y con mucho tráfico peatonal (especialmente visitantes), sin apenas pendiente, de características muy homogéneas, flanqueada por un lado por los muros de la Catedral y por el otro, por edificios antiguos. Presenta una escasa presencia de actividades estáticas en el espacio público (restaurantes o cafeterías con terrazas, etc.) que puedan obstruir el paso y la visibilidad, aparte de las propias personas.

En primer lugar, se realizó un escaneado láser de la calle para obtener un modelo 3D de la misma y así conocer la geometría y dimensiones de espacio urbano. Posteriormente y en base a los cálculos realizados con QGIS y otras herramientas asociadas y descritas en el trabajo de Orozco et al. (2023), se ha estimado para la calle un área de 1.246,56 m2, siendo la Superficie Útil para la Visita (SUV) aproximadamente la mitad (629,344 m^2), una vez descontadas las superficies de repulsión de las paredes (1,20 m) y otras áreas ocupadas por diferentes elementos.

Para conocer cuántas personas pueden transitar en la Superficie Útil para la Visita de esta calle, se han aplicado los estándares de proxémica interpersonal para grupos y para individuos solos y se ha establecido el número de grupos que es capaz de albergar la calle en puntos de encuentro y observación mediante la herramienta «Heatmap» de QGIS. De esta manera, se identificaron tres áreas para acoger cómodamente grupos de 15 personas (fig. 4). Para el resto del espacio urbano, se ha estimado un volumen de visitantes individuales de 40, teniendo en consideración un estándar de proxémica mayor que para las personas en grupo.

Para el monitoreo del flujo de visitantes, se implementaron sensores de imagen en tiempo real. Primero, se determinó la "escena o polígono de conteo" mediante herramientas de geoprocesamiento y considerando que el campo de visión de la cámara estuviera dentro de la Superficie Útil para la Visita. La cuenca visual se calculó con ArcGIS Pro 3.2.2.

Para dimensionar la escena (57,60 m2), se tuvo en cuenta una velocidad media fija de paso de las personas de 1,3 m/s tal como sugieren los estudios de Gianoulaki y Christoforou (2024). Los sensores de imagen en movimiento elegidos fueron cámaras de vídeo 2D con *software* de reconocimiento y conteo de personas (CPF-SENSOR, modelo WTK10070) y se instalaron a una altura de 12 m.

Figura 4. Calle del Miguelete

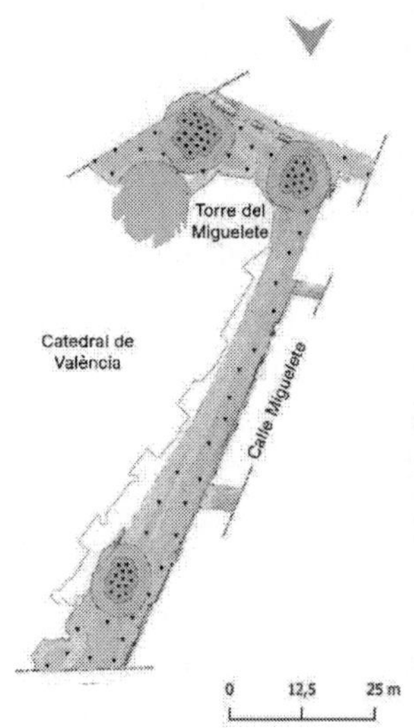

Izquierda: plano de QGIS con la localización de los tres puntos para encuentro de grupos (cerca de la fachada principal y uno cerca de la puerta gótica). Centro: imagen del punto de encuentro en la propia calle (Autora: M.J. Viñals, julio 2024). Derecha: Imagen de calle en plena celebración de la Virgen de los Desamparados (Fuente: Fotofilmax (JCF), mayo 2025)

De esta manera, fue posible recrear el campo visual en la nube de puntos de la calle, utilizando el *software* de código abierto Cloud Compare versión 2.13 Alpha para su posterior procesamiento en *software* SIG. También fue instalada una estación o unidad central con un PC y un módem USB 4G con una tarjeta SIM, con una fuente de alimentación permanente de 220V que se encargaba del almacenamiento y análisis de los datos y los enviaba de forma inalámbrica (fig. 5).

Figura 5. Escena de conteo en la calle del Miguelete

Izquierda: Localización e instalación de la cámara de vídeo 2D (Autora: M.J. Viñals, febrero 2023). Centro: cuenca visual de la cámara. Derecha: conteo de personas tras el filtrado del *software* de reconocimiento de personas.

A continuación, se presentan los resultados de tres días de conteo bajo circunstancias diferentes (Viñals et al., 2024):

- Jueves 23 de noviembre de 2023: se registraron 38.436 personas (en diez horas) y hubo dos picos críticos en los que se superaron los umbrales de capacidad de carga de visitantes de la calle: uno, a las 12:21, coincidiendo con el horario de conclusión del Tribunal de las Aguas en la puerta gótica de la Catedral recayente sobre la calle del Miguelete, y otro a las 18:04 asociado al inicio del horario gratuito de visita de la Catedral.
- Martes 5 de marzo de 2024: se registraron 54.696 personas y dos picos críticos. Uno, a las 14:13, coincidiendo con el final de los fuegos artificiales de las Fallas (Mascletà) que tenían lugar cerca de la calle Miguelete, constatándose una caída significativa en la densidad de peatones en los minutos anteriores y posteriores a las 14:00, mientras se producía el evento pirotécnico. El segundo, también se produce por la tarde y relacionado con el inicio del horario gratuito de visita de la Catedral.
- Domingo 12 de mayo de 2024: se registraron 147.058 personas, coincidiendo con la festividad religiosa del Día de la Virgen de los Desamparados. Desde las 9:00 horas, cuando se inició el conteo, se constatan cuatro picos críticos a lo largo de la mañana en que se superan los umbrales de capacidad de carga de visitantes.

En la figura 6, se presentan los resultados correspondientes a los tres días analizados, los cuales permitieron identificar cuándo, durante cuánto tiempo y con qué intensidad se superó la capacidad de visitantes establecida para la calle del Miguelete. El gráfico muestra los umbrales máximos de ocupación (en número de personas) calculados según los valores de proxémica interpersonal para la calle Miguelete. La franja azul inferior indica el rango de ocupación recomendado para la calle, correspondiente a umbrales de proxémica de distancia interpersonal entre 3.5-1.2 metros. Se observa que, el día 12 de mayo de 2024, la calle del Miguelete permaneció durante prácticamente toda la jornada fuera del rango óptimo de ocupación.

Figura 6. Curvas comparativas de flujos de visitantes en la calle del Miguelete en las fechas reseñadas

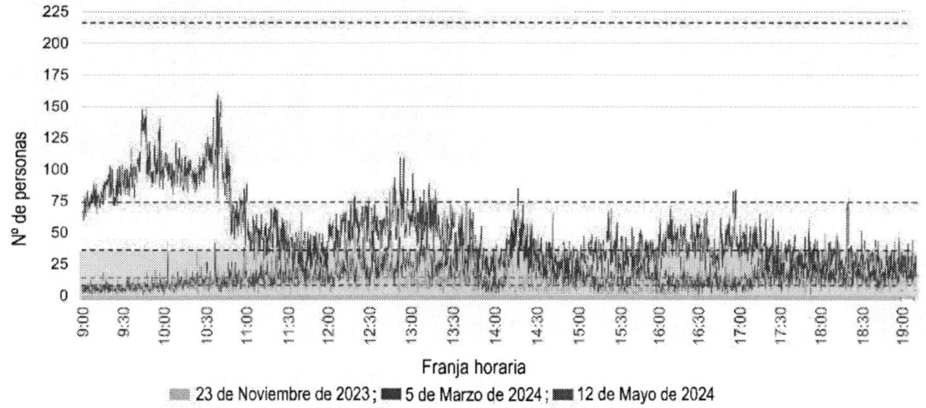

4.2.2. Capilla del Santo Cáliz (Catedral de Valencia)

La Capilla del Santo Cáliz forma parte del conjunto catedralicio y recibe a diario un número muy elevado de visitantes y feligreses. Esta capilla alberga el Santo Cáliz de la Última Cena de Jesucristo, considerado como una de las reliquias más importantes de la Cristiandad (Viñals y López González, 2022). Presenta una planta cuadrada de 13,42 m x 13,72 m, con un total de 185 m2. La altura máxima de las paredes es de 16,20 m y el punto más alto, en la clave de la cúpula, es de 18,79 m (figura 7).

Cuenta con una única entrada y una puerta interior que conecta esta Capilla con el Museo de la Catedral. No existe ventilación natural a través de ventanas, por lo que el intercambio de aire con el exterior es escaso. Se trata, por tanto, de un espacio cerrado con un marcado carácter confinado si nos atenemos a la definición del *Real Decreto 39/1997* (Ministerio de Trabajo y Asuntos Sociales de España, 1997) que describe un espacio confinado como «*un recinto con aberturas de entrada y salida restringidas y ventilación natural desfavorable, en el que pueden acumularse sustancias tóxicas o inflamables o en el que puede haber una atmósfera deficiente en oxígeno, y que no está destinado a una ocupación continua* [...]».

Figura 7. Estructura e imagen interior de la Capilla del Santo Cáliz de la Catedral de Valencia

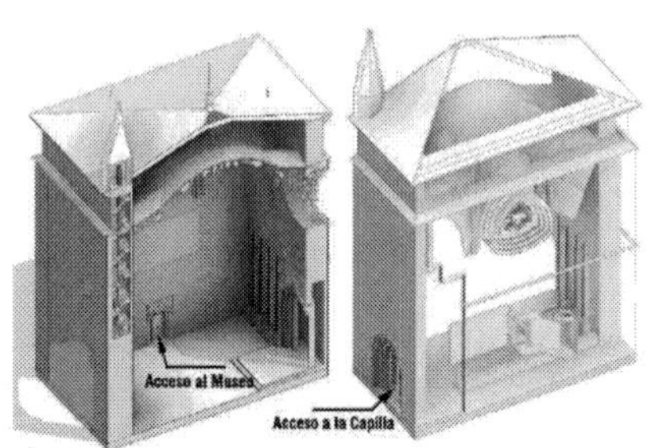

El volumen interior de la Capilla se calculó utilizando HBIM a partir de la nube de puntos 3D del modelo digital de la Catedral realizado en el marco del proyecto HBIMSIG-Turismo de la Universitat Politècnica de València, y se obtuvo un resultado de 3.100 m3.

Previamente a la estimación de la capacidad de carga de visitantes efectiva basada en la consideración de la calidad del aire interior, se estimó la capacidad de carga de feligreses (93 personas sentadas), considerando que están realizando una actividad religiosa estática, y la capacidad de carga de visitantes (33 visitantes) que aborda el análisis de una actividad más dinámica y fundamentalmente desarrollada de pie. Para ello, en ambos casos se ha llevado a cabo el establecimiento de la Superficie Útil tanto para la realización de actividades religiosas como para la visita, considerando para cada actividad estándares de proxémica diferentes.

La capacidad de carga efectiva basada en la calidad del aire interior fue estimada considerando: el volumen efectivo de espacio (una vez descontados los volúmenes ocupados por grandes objetos), y la cantidad máxima de CO2 que admite este espacio volumétrico considerando el aporte medio metabólico que exhala una persona (Tasa de generación de CO2 por persona: 22.03 L x 12 horas) y teniendo en cuenta que se no se debe superar el umbral de 1.000 ppm. Todo ello, considerando que la tasa de ventilación que en el caso de esta Capilla era nula. De esta forma, se obtuvo la cifra de 12 Personas Al Mismo Tiempo durante las 12 horas de apertura al público.

Los resultados del monitoreo realizados el 1 de noviembre de 2024 (Teruel et al., 2025) que correlacionan los valores de CO2 con la ocupación humana (feligreses y visitantes) aportan la siguiente información (fig. 5):

- Viernes 1 de noviembre de 2024: Se trata de un día festivo y la Capilla registró un total de 2.867 visitantes además de los feligreses y clero que asistieron a la misa de las 9:00 h de la mañana (30 personas). La víspera (31 de octubre) a las 12:00 de la noche, la Capilla registraba unos valores de CO2 de 958 ppm, concentración que fue bajando hasta 756 ppm a las 8:00 h del día 1 de noviembre, justo poco antes que comenzara la ocupación de la Capilla (fig. 5).

A las tres horas de la apertura al público ya habían accedido un total acumulado de 1.228 visitantes y los niveles de CO2 superaban las 1.000 ppm. El día registró tres picos máximos: dos entre las 11:00h y las 12:00h de 78 Personas Al Mismo Tiempo (PAMT) y otro entre las 14:00 y las 15:00 de 73. Estos picos de ocupación se reflejan en la concentración de CO2 de forma regular una hora más tarde. Estos niveles superiores a 1.100 ppm se mantuvieron hasta la hora del cierre (19:30). A las 21.00h comenzó el decaimiento.

Figura 5. Monitoreo del número de visitantes (histograma líneas verticales) en el interior de la Capilla del Santo Cáliz en relación con la concentración de CO2 (curva) a lo largo del 1 de noviembre de 2024

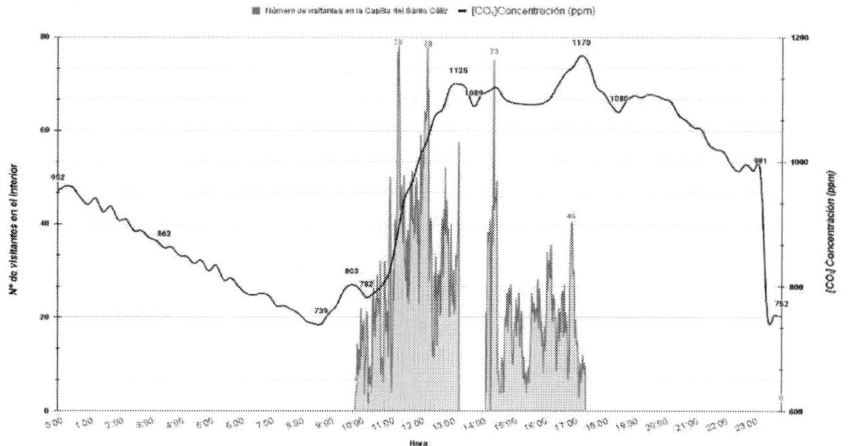

5. CONCLUSIONES

El abordaje de la estimación y monitoreo de la capacidad de carga de visitantes mediante el uso de tecnologías digitales ha supuesto un reto que solamente puede llevarse adelante con un equipo multidisciplinar, pero teniendo siempre claro el propósito que se persigue, y pensando que su posible implementación práctica debe ser sencilla y asumible por los gestores culturales y/o turísticos de los sitios.

La primera reflexión que procede comentar es que existen las suficientes herramientas tecnológicas, que son habituales en otros campos de la ciencia, pero perfectamente adaptables a este tipo de trabajos. La innovación que presenta esta investigación es la integración de todas ellas y, sobre todo, el uso combinado con los modelos urbanos en 3D y SIG. Ello ha supuesto el manejo y almacenamiento de una cantidad ingente de datos de todo tipo y el uso de sistemas efectivos de transmisión y procesado de datos en tiempo real. A cambio, los resultados han sido muy completos, precisos, fiables, y actualizados en todo momento y el método es adaptable a cualquier realidad espacial y temporal. Por tanto, se podría decir que las tecnologías digitales han aportado al estudio de capacidad de carga de visitantes una gran eficiencia y productividad. También se puede decir, que disponer de esa gran cantidad de datos dota a este procedimiento de un gran potencial para la predictividad. En primer lugar, analizar grandes volúmenes de información permite extraer patrones de comportamiento e identificar mejor las necesidades de las personas. Además, con el establecimiento de alertas tempranas de saturación de personas o de concentraciones de CO2 se pueden evitar potenciales riesgos. Por su parte, los Gemelos Digitales y la Inteligencia Artificial permiten desarrollar escenarios bajo circunstancias diversas para el sitio, lo cual beneficia a los gestores culturales y turísticos al anticiparse a los problemas y establecer estrategias y medidas que permitan la toma de decisiones para evitar situaciones que además de inconfortables para los visitantes pueden constituir una amenaza para la seguridad de las personas.

Respecto al coste de los dispositivos y herramientas digitales empleados, hay que destacar que se ha utilizado *software* de código abierto y dispositivos digitales existentes en el mercado, con lo cual se trata de un sistema totalmente asequible para las instituciones patrimoniales. Además, la información que produce el sistema es de fácil comprensión por los usuarios finales.

El uso de tecnologías digitales para el monitoreo ha permitido además tener información en tiempo real sobre un fenómeno dinámico como son los flujos de visitantes y los parámetros ambientales de los sitios. Hasta el momento, los estudios de capacidad de carga se han concebido de manera estática para situaciones, momentos y lugares concretos, pero el comportamiento de los visitantes y las circunstancias de los sitios patrimoniales varían incluso en pocas horas y los gestores culturales y turísticos necesitan llevar a cabo una gestión adaptativa que les permita abordar eficientemente cualquier situación en cualquier momento. Por ello, disponer de información en tiempo real permite tomar las decisiones más pertinentes en cada momento. Por ejemplo, en los espacios confinados, la calidad del aire varía a medida que avanzan las horas, restringiéndose así la capacidad de carga de visitantes a lo largo del día ya que se va acumulando el CO2. Otro ejemplo que se ha tratado en este trabajo son los espacios públicos urbanos, cuya congestión y saturación puede ser detectada incluso antes de que se produzca y, por tanto, actuar en consecuencia.

A lo largo de esta investigación, se han detectado algunos retos que deben ser abordados. Así, se considera que hay que trabajar más a fondo en el desarrollo de las plataformas de integración de datos ya que es el núcleo donde se concentra, almacena y procesa toda la información y todos los esfuerzos en dotarla de la mayor eficiencia es un objetivo clave. También hay que mejorar los sistemas de transmisión de datos para garantizar su funcionamiento óptimo y evitar pérdidas circunstanciales de información.

No obstante, el mayor reto que los autores de este trabajo detectan es cómo facilitar la transformación digital de las instituciones gestoras del patrimonio y del turismo. Se puede decir, que los avances científicos en la materia están ya a disposición, testados y garantizada su eficiencia pero, es verdad, que implantarlos implica cambios a nivel organizativo de la gestión en las instituciones para adaptarse a la actual situación, ya que se puede decir, sin lugar, a dudas que ya no se puede monitorear en tiempo real la capacidad de carga de visitantes de espacios patrimoniales en destinos con elevados volúmenes de turistas si no es con el soporte de las tecnologías digitales.

Esta investigación se llevó a cabo en el marco del proyecto de investigación «Análisis y desarrollo de la integración de HBIM en SIG para la creación de un protocolo para la planificación del turismo patrimonial» (ref. PID2020-119088RB-I00), financiado por el Ministerio de Ciencia e Innovación del Gobierno de España.

Con el desarrollo de este trabajo de investigación se está contribuyendo a la consecución del ODS 11, que busca hacer que las ciudades y los asentamientos humanos sean inclusivos, seguros, resilientes y sostenibles; en particular, el ODS 11.4 que se enfoca específicamente en la protección del patrimonio cultural y natural, incluyendo la identificación, protección, salvaguarda y uso sostenible de este patrimonio.

6. REFERENCIAS

Affluences (2024). *¿Por qué elegir las cámaras de conteo de personas para gestionar los flujos de visitantes?* https://www.pro.affluences.com/es/post/c%C3%A1maras-de-conteo-de-personas (consulta 2 mayo 2024).

Agnew, N., Demas, M., Jinshi, F., Xudong, W. (2013). Overview of the Methodology and Results of the Visitor Study for the Mogao Grottoes. En N. Agnew y M. Demas (eds.): *Visitor Management and Carrying Capacity at World Heritage Sites in China*, 17-19 May 2013 Mogao Grottoes, Dunhuang. The Getty Conservation Institute, LA (USA).

Ashkanani, A.M., Roza, A.S.M., Naghavipour, H. (2015). A Design Approach of Automatic Visitor Counting System Using Video Camera. IOSR *Journal of Electrical and Electronics Engineering* 10(2): 62-67. Doi:10.9790/1676-10216267.

Bin Yusoh, M.P., Mapjabil, J., Hanafi, N., bin Muhammed Idris, M.A. (2021). Tourism Carrying Capacity and Social Carrying Capacity: A Literature Review. *SHS Web of Conferences* 124(4): 02004. doi: 10.1051/shsconf/202112402004.

Butler, R.W. (1996). The concept of carrying capacity for tourism destinations: dead or merely buried? *Progress in Tourism and Hospitality Research*, 2(3-4): 283-293.

Cifuentes, M. (1992). *Determinación de Capacidad de Carga Turística en Áreas Protegidas.* Centro Agronómico Tropical de Investigación y Enseñanza (CATIE). Turrialba, Costa Rica.

Coccossis, H.; Mexa, A. (2007). *The Challenge of Tourism Carrying Capacity Assessment.* Routledge: London, UK; p. 312.

Costa, M. (2010). Interpersonal Distances in Group Walking. *Journal of Nonverbal Behaviour*, 34: 15–26.

De Almeida, D.S.B. (2021). *Urban Tourism Crowding Dynamics: Carrying Capacity and Digital Twinning.* University Institute of Lisbon: Lisbon, Portugal.

Franco, A. y Leccese, F. (2020). Measurement of CO2 concentration for occupancy estimation in educational buildings with energy efficiency purposes. *Journal of Building Engineering*, 32. doi.org/10.1016/j.jobe.2020.101714

Galiano-Garrigós, A., López González, C., García-Valldecabres, J., Pérez-Carramiñana, C., Emmitt, S. (2024). The Influence of Visitors on Heritage Conservation: The Case of the Church of San Juan del Hospital, Valencia, Spain. *Applied Scicences*, 14: 2065. doi.org/10.3390/app14052065

Galiano-Garrigós, A. y López-Torres, J. (2024). The use of Digital Twins for heritage conservation: the Church of San Juan del Hospital as a case study. En M.J. Viñals y M.C. López-González (eds.): *Heritage Digital Technologies and Tourism Management.* International Congress HEDIT 2024. June 20th-21st, 2024. Valencia, Spain. doi.org/10.4995/HEDIT2024.2024.18065

García Hernández, M. (2001). Capacidad de Acogida Turística y Gestión de Flujos de Visitantes En Conjuntos Monumentales: El Caso de La Alhambra. *PH Boletín*, 36, 124–137.

Giannoulaki, M. y Christoforou, Z. (2024). Pedestrian Walking Speed Analysis: A Systematic Review. *Sustainability*, 16: 4813.

Girshick, R., Donahue, J., Darrell, T., Malik, J. (2014). Rich Feature Hierarchies for Accurate Object Detection and Semantic Segmentation. En *Proceedings of 2014 IEEE Conference on Computer Vision and Pattern Recognition*, Columbus, OH, USA, 23–28 June 2014; pp. 580–587.

Gorrini, A., Bandini, S., Sarvi, M. (2014). Group Dynamics in Pedestrian Crowds. *Transportation Research Record Journal of the Transportation Research Board* 2421(1): 51-56. Doi: 10.3141/2421-06

Goto, I., Ueda, K., Matsuda, Y., Suwa, H., Yasumoto, K. (2024). BLESS: BLE Based Street Sensing for People Counting and Flow Direction Estimation. En *Proceedings of the 2024 IEEE International Conference on Pervasive Computing and Communications Workshops and other Affiliated Events*, Biarritz, France, 11–15 March 2024; pp. 76–81.

Hall, E.T. (1966). *The Hidden Dimension.* Anchor Books: New York, NY, USA.

Hung, D.H., Hsu, G.S., Chung, S.L., Saito, H. (2012). Real-Time Counting People in crowded areas by using local empirical templates and density ratios. *IEICE Transactions on Information and Systems*, E95.D: 1791–1803

Hutson, J., Weber, J., y Russo, A. (2023). Digital Twins and Cultural Heritage Preservation: A Case Study of Best Practices and Reproducibility in Chiesa dei SS Apostoli e Biagio. *Art and Design Review*, 11, 15-41. doi.org/10.4236/adr.2023.111003

Instituto Nacional Español de Seguridad y salud en el Trabajo (2018). NTP 742: *Ventilación general de edificios. Madrid: INSS.* Disponible en: https://www.insst.es/documentacion/colecciones-tecnicas/ntp-notas-tecnicas-de-prevencion/21-serie-ntp-numeros-716-a-750-ano-2006/ntp-742-ventilacion-general-de-edificios

Li, L. (2020). A Crowd Density Detection Algorithm for Tourist Attractions Based on Monitoring Video Dynamic Information Analysis. *Hindawi Complexity*, 2020 Article ID 6635446. doi.org/10.1155/2020/6635446

Liu, W., Salzmann, M., Fua, P. (2019). Context-Aware Crowd Counting. En *Proceedings of the 2019 IEEE/CVF Conference on Computer Vision and Pattern Recognition (CVPR).* Long Beach, CA, USA, 15–20 June 2019; pp. 5094–5103.

López-Bonilla, J.M. y López-Bonilla, L.M. (2008). La Capacidad de Carga Turística: Revisión Crítica de Un Instrumento de Medida de Sostenibilidad. *Periplo Sustentable*, 15: 123–150.

Makhadmeh, A., Al-Badarneh, M., Rawashdeh, A., Al-Shorman, A. (2020). Evaluating the Carrying Capacity at the Archaeological Site of Jerash (Gerasa) using Mathematical GIS Modeling. *Egyptian Journal of Remote Sensing and Space Sciences (EJRS)*, 23: 159–165.

Manning, R.E. (2002). How Much is Too Much? Carrying Capacity of National Parks and Protected Areas. En A. Arnberger, C. Brandenburg, A. Muhar (eds.). *Monitoring and Management of Visitor Flows in Recreational and Protected Areas. Conference Proceedings*; pp. 306-313.

Milano, C. (2017). *Overtourism y Turismofobia: Tendencias Globales y Contextos Locales.* Ostelea School of Tourism & Hospitality: Barcelona, Spain.

Ministerio de la Presidencia de España (2007). Real Decreto 1027/2007, de 20 de julio, por el que se aprueba el Reglamento de Instalaciones Térmicas en los Edificios (RITE). *BOE*, 207, de 29/08/2007. https://www.boe.es/eli/es/rd/2007/07/20/1027/con

Ministerio de la Presidencia, Relaciones con las Cortes y Memoria Democrática (2021). Real Decreto 178/2021, de 23 de marzo, por el que se modifica el Real Decreto 1027/2007, de 20 de julio, por el que se aprueba el Reglamento de Instalaciones Térmicas en los Edificios. *BOE*, 71, de 24 de marzo de 2021: 33748-33793. https://www.boe.es/eli/es/rd/2021/03/23/178

Ministerio de Trabajo y Asuntos Sociales de España. (1997). Real Decreto 39/1997, de 17 de enero, por el que se aprueba el Reglamento de los Servicios de Prevención. *BOE*, 27, de 31 de enero de 1997. https://www.boe.es

Muler González, V., Coromina, L., Galí, N. (2018). Overtourism: Residents' Perceptions of Tourism Impact as an Indicator of Resident Social Carrying Capacity—Case Study of a Spanish Heritage Town. Tour. Rev. 73: 277–296

Niccolucci, F., Markhoff, B., Theodoridou, M., Felicetti, A., Hermon, S. (2023). The Heritage Digital Twin: a bicycle made for two. The integration of digital methodologies into cultural heritage research. *arXiv:2302.07138.* doi.org/10.48550/arXiv.2302.07138

OECD. (2024). *OECD Tourism Trends and Policies 2024.* OECD Publishing, Paris, doi.org/10.1787/80885d8b-en

Orozco Carpio, P.R., Viñals, M.J., Escudero, P.A. y Rolim, R. (2023). Geospatial Tools for Determining Visitor Carrying Capacity in Tourist Streets and Public Spaces of Historic Centres. *Heritage*, 6(11): 7100–7114. doi.org/10.3390/heritage6110370

Orozco Carpio, P.R., Viñals, M.J., López-González, M.C. (2024). 3D Point Cloud and GIS Approach to Assess Street Physical Attributes. *Smart Cities*, 7: 991–1006. doi.org/10.3390/smartcities7030042

Rolim, R., López-González, C., Viñals, M.J. (2024). Analysis of the Current Status of Sensors and HBIM Integration: A Review Based on Bibliometric Analysis. *Heritage*, 7: 2071–2087. doi.org/10.3390/heritage7040098

Salvador-García, E. (2020). *Protocolo HBIM para una gestión eficiente del uso público del patrimonio arquitectónico.* Tesis doctoral, Universitat Politècnica de València. doi.org/10.4995/Thesis/10251/146811

Salvador-García, E., Viñals, M.J., García-Valldecabres, J.L. (2020). Potential of HBIM to Improve the Efficiency of Visitor Flow Management in Heritage Sites. Towards Smart Heritage Management. *International Archives of the Photogrammetry, Remote Sensing and Spatial Information Sciences*, 44: 451–456.

Santos, X.M. y Pena Cabrera, L. (2014). Management of Tourist Flows. The Cathedral of Santiago de Compostela. PASOS Revista de Turismo y Patrimonio cultural, 12: 719–735.

Simou, S., Baba, K., Nounah, A. (2022). A GIS-Based Methodology to Explore and Manage the Historical Heritage of Rabat City (Morocco). *ACM Journal on Computing and Cultural Heritage*,15(4): 1–14. doi.org/10.1145/3517142J.

Sanasaryan, A. (2025). *Geoinformation and Tourism Management of Heritage Resources: Real-World Implementation.* Tesis doctoral, Universitat Politècnica de València, 299 pp.

Teruel, P., Viñals, M.J., Gandia, J.M., Orozco Carpio, P.R. (2024). Study of visitor flows in heritage streetscapes based on counting people using motion-image sensors. The case of Valencia Cathedral (Spain). En M.J. Viñals y M.C. López-González (eds.): *Heritage Digital Technologies and Tourism Management.* International Congress proceedings HEDIT 2024. June 20th–21st, 2024. Valencia, Spain. doi.org/10.4995/HEDIT2024.2024.18435

Teruel, P., Smaha, K., Viñals, MJ. (2025). Monitoring indoor Air Quality of Heritage Buildings as a tool for Visitor's Comfort and Safety. En T. Kouider y A. Galiano: *Building FIT for Climate Change.* Conference Proceedings of the 11th International Congress on Architectural Technology (ICAT 2025), University of Alicante, Spain. 15-17 May 2025. Ed. Universidad de Alicante; pp. 413-429.

Tourism Economics (2024). *European Tourism: Trends & Prospects, European Travel Commission Quarterly Report (Q4/2024).* https://etc-corporate.org/uploads/2025/02/ETC-Quarterly-Report-Q4-2024-Public-Version.pdf

Unión Europea (2025). *Turismo de la UE en 2024: Actualizaciones clave y tendencias emergentes.* https://transition-pathways.europa.eu/articles/eu-tourism-2024-key-updates-and-emerging-trends-1?etrans=es

UNTWO. (2024). *World Tourism Barometer.* https://www.unwto.org/news/global-tourism-set-for-full-recovery-by-end-of-the-year-with-spending-growing-faster-than-arrivals

Viñals, M.J.; Morant, M.; Teruel, L. (2014). Confort Psicológico y Experiencia Turística. Casos de Estudio de Espacios Naturales Protegidos de La Comunidad Valenciana (España). *Boletín Asociación Geógrafos Españoles,* 65: 293–316.

Viñals, M.J., Planelles, M., Alonso-Monasterio, P., Morant, M. (2016). Recreational Carrying Capacity on Small Mediterranean Islands. *Cuadernos de Turismo,* 37: 437–463.

Viñals, M.J., Mayor, M., Martínez-Sanchís, I., Teruel, L., Alonso Monasterio, P., Morant, M. (2017). *Turismo Sostenible y Patrimonio. Herramientas para la Puesta en Valor y la Planificación.* Universitat Politècnica de València, 189 pp.

Viñals, M.J. y López-González, C. (2022). La interpretación el patrimonio como transmisora de los valores de los monumentos religiosos vivos. Propuesta de aplicación a la Catedral de Valencia (España), *Cuadernos de Turismo,* 9: 315-341. Ed Universidad de Murcia. doi.org/10.6018/turismo.521931

Viñals, M.J., Orozco Carpio, P.R., Teruel, P., Gandía-Romero, J.M. (2024). Real-Time Monitoring of Visitor Carrying Capacity in crowded historic streets through Digital Technologies. *Urban Science,* 8(190). doi.org/10.3390/urbansci8040190

Zubiaga, M., Izkara, J.L., Gandini, A., Alonso, I., Saralegui, U. (2019). Towards Smarter Management of overtourism in historic centres through Visitor-Flow Monitoring. *Sustainability,* 11: 7254.

HOW PASSENGERS TALK ABOUT SPANISH AIRLINES: A TOPIC MODELING APPROACH

Enrique Bigne
Universidad de Valencia

Marina Zanfardini
Universidad Nacional de Comahue, Nehuquén

Carla Ruiz
Luisa Andreu
Universidad de Valencia

TEMÁTICA: Utilización de la Inteligencia artificial en la gestión de destinos turísticos

RESUMEN: Las reseñas en línea ofrecen una valiosa perspectiva para comprender las percepciones de los pasajeros en el transporte aéreo. Este estudio emplea técnicas de modelado temático (LDA) sobre 18.597 opiniones en TripAdvisor para analizar cómo los pasajeros españoles evalúan dos tipos de aerolíneas: una de bajo coste (Vueling) y una aerolínea de bandera (Iberia). Los resultados muestran que las valoraciones se centran principalmente en atributos clave del transporte, como la puntualidad, la calidad del servicio, la comodidad de los asientos y la relación calidad-precio. De forma destacada, los pasajeros de Vueling comentan con mayor frecuencia sobre retrasos y problemas con el equipaje, mientras que Iberia recibe más evaluaciones relacionadas con el servicio a bordo. El estudio ofrece implicaciones de gestión sobre las expectativas del consumidor y los atributos críticos del servicio, con consecuencias para la comunicación y la estrategia de marca en el sector aéreo. El análisis comparativo entre una aerolínea de bajo coste y una de bandera revela diferentes patrones en la retroalimentación del cliente, lo que sugiere que las aerolíneas deben adaptar sus estrategias de comunicación según el segmento al que pertenecen.

Palabras clave: Modelado Temático, Reseñas de Aerolíneas, Contenido Generado por el Usuario, Calidad del Servicio

ABSTRACT: Online reviews offer a valuable lens to understand passenger perceptions in air travel. This study employs topic modeling (LDA) on 18,597 TripAdvisor reviews to analyze how Spanish passengers evaluate two types of airlines—low-cost (Vueling) and a flag carrier (Iberia). Results show that reviews are primarily centered on core transportation attributes—punctuality, service quality, seating, and value for money. Notably, Vueling passengers comment more on delays and baggage issues, while Iberia receives more evaluations related to onboard service. The study offers managerial insights into consumer expectations and critical service attributes, with implications for Airlines branding and customer communication. A comparative analysis between a low cost and flaf carrier airline shows different patterns in passenger feedback, suggesting airlines should adapt the communication strategies for each airline segment.

Keywords: Topic Modeling, Airline Reviews, User-Generated Content, Service Quality

1. INTRODUCTION

Airlines play a crucial role in tourism, and their scale is vast. In 2023, there were 37 million aircraft movements, indicating an evident recovery after COVID-19 and exceeding the record for movements in 2019 (IATA, 2024). A recent literature review on research in air transport (Park et al., 2025) shows that the air carrier market is a prominent research topic. Within this topic, low-cost carriers versus flagship airlines have drawn attention to their analysis of competition, service quality, and airfares. The social debate is foster by news and social media comments.

As a result, passengers use multiple criteria to choose an airline. Passenger airline choice is shaped by various factors, including convenient schedules, fare structures, perceived value for money, on-time performance (e.g., cancellations and delays), frequent flyer programs, proximity to airports, in-flight services, aircraft comfort, flight connections, ground services, and customer service (Jung & Yoo, 2014; Farzadnia et al., 2024). The array of these factors presents two main research challenges. First, the diversity of influences complicates delineating the boundaries of any given study, potentially introducing bias into variable selection. Second, objective variables, such as fare structures and schedules, interact with subjective variables, including travellers' subjective assessments and opinions, demonstrating a dynamic interplay between all these element types.

Furthermore, literature increasingly emphasizes the impact of online reviews on travellers' choices across all tourism sectors, including destinations (Bigne et al., 2024), restaurants (Wu et al., 2015), accommodations (Bigne et al., 2020), and airlines (Kim et al., 2024). The vast number of travelers indeed leads to a significant number of online reviews, which have been extensively analyzed in recent studies on airline passenger reviewers. These studies primarily rely on online reviews from platforms such as Twitter (Misopoulos et al., 2014; Lu et al., 2023), Skytrax (Xu et al., 2019; Wang et al., 2023; Lu et al., 2023; Pereira et al., 2023), and, most notably, TripAdvisor (Sezgen et al., 2019; Chang et al., 2022; Dwesar & Sahoo, 2022; Kim et al., 2024; Liu et al., 2025).

Online reviews provide a unique source of unbiased information for companies, passengers, and researchers. Indeed, passengers gather information from their peers to inform their booking decisions. Online comments on social media platforms, known as user-generated content (UGC), serve as a credible and valid information source for tourists during their booking decision process (Kitsios et al., 2022; Sparks et al., 2013). However, the commonly commented topics remain understudied (Bigne et al., 2020). Their influence on peers' choices remains fragmented (Ma et al., 2018; Bigne et al., 2021). Airlines can also gain insights from travellers' evaluations of their services. Despite the growing body of research on airline passenger online reviews, several research gaps remain. For example, in the context of restaurants, Wu et al. (2015) found that comments about restaurant quality and contextual insights based on consumer experiences hold more value than numerical ratings or objective measures of numerical online ratings. Further, the polarity of the comments needs to be addressed. Researchers alike can identify topics highlighted by users to obtain topics of interest, polarity reviews, and emotional content, referred to as sentiment analysis.

Built upon considering social media posts as a means of self-presentation, affiliation, and expression (Grewal et al., 2019) and the expectation-disconfirmation theory attributed to (Oliver, 1977), this study compares how passengers perceive low-cost carriers and flagship airlines. The expectation-disconfirmation theory addresses the differences between pre-consumption expectations and post-consumption perceptions (Wang et al., 2023; Pereira et al., 2023). Extending such theory to low-cost carriers, the expectation cannot be higher than in a premium airline and, accordingly, the passenger evaluation it should not be negative per se.

Accordingly, our research gaps involve exploring online reviews of both low-cost carriers and flagship airlines with a comparative approach. We delve into the real comments made by travellers to elucidate whether each airline type has a precise positioning. Next, we aim to analyse which elements differentiate both airline types the most.

2. CONCEPTUAL FRAMEWORK

The proliferation of online passenger reviews has increased the relevance of utilizing advanced analytical methods to gain comprehensive insights into airline service quality. This paper leverages user-generated content (UGC), specifically low-cost flight reviews on TripAdvisor, to explore passenger perceptions systematically. It employs topic modelling techniques to identify key themes from passenger online reviews.

Zaki and McColl-Kennedy (2020) provided a detailed methodological roadmap using text mining and natural language processing (NLP), demonstrating how structured analysis of large volumes of unstructured data can offer valuable insights and enhance proactive customer service management. Among the techniques, topic modelling is a widely used text mining technique capable of automatically detecting underlying topics within textual data, facilitating the identification of thematic patterns embedded in a text corpus (Çallı & Çallı, 2023; Lu et al., 2023). Topic modelling techniques significantly analyze big data's natural language processing (Farzadnia et al., 2024). Topic modelling is a technique for finding topics among several documents and clustering similar words together (Kim et al., 2024). According to Egger and Yu (2022), the most popular text modelling approach in tourism literature is Latent Dirichlet Allocation (LDA).

LDA is a Bayesian probabilistic model that identifies the underlying dimensions of words in large datasets, introduced by (Blei et al., 2003). LDA is an unsupervised machine learning technique. Compared to other topic modelling methods such as Latent Semantic Indexing and Hierarchical Dirichlet Process, LDA performs best in air flight classes (Farzadnia et al., 2024). LDA analyzes text documents composed of multiple hidden topics, each consisting of a mixture of words that adhere to a Dirichlet probability distribution. The model aims to uncover these hidden topics that most accurately represent the document's observed word patterns (Kirilenko & Stepchenkova, 2025; Bigne et al., 2025).

Since UGC (Babić Rosario et al., 2020) is acknowledged as massive and spontaneous feedback from consumers (Yan et al., 2024), its usage for topic extractions of UGC is becoming popular (Nieto García et al., 2020). Recent studies have extensively utilized topic modeling techniques to extract valuable insights from airline passenger online reviews as follows. Çallı & Çallı (2023) utilized LDA to categorize passenger complaints during COVID-19, identifying critical service issues effectively. Similarly, Lucini et al. (2020) employed LDA on over 55,000 airline reviews, uncovering key satisfaction dimensions such as onboard entertainment, comfort, and cabin service, which strongly predict passenger recommendations. Chang et al. (2022) applied deep learning and aspect-based sentiment analysis to reveal significant shifts in passenger sentiment during the pandemic, emphasizing cancellations and punctuality. Kim et al. (2024), also using topic modelling, highlighted a shift from reliability pre-pandemic to responsiveness during

COVID-19, particularly regarding refunds and booking processes, although their analysis did not differentiate between full-service and low-cost airlines. Dwesar and Sahoo (2022) expanded on these insights by exploring how service failure severity affects passenger evaluations across different cultural contexts.

Research has shown that among the factors influencing social media postings, posting behavior serves purposes such as self-presentation, affiliation, and expression (Grewal et al., 2019). Extending this research to low-cost carriers, travellers tend to comment on the basic service, which is characterized as no-frills, point-to-point service. Sezgen et al. (2019) applied Latent Semantic Analysis to analyse key drivers of customer satisfaction and dissatisfaction using TripAdvisor reviews. Research findings revealed notable differences between full-service and low-cost carriers. For low-cost passengers, monetary cost and service quality are the main attributes that make satisfaction, and for full-service airline passengers, professionalism of the staff is the key satisfaction attribute. As for customer dissatisfaction attributes, seat comfort/legroom, flight disruptions, and staff service are the main factors causing passenger dissatisfaction for full-service economy cabin passengers and low-cost airline passengers. Therefore, we aim to address whether comments differ between airlines and how they relate to core transportation elements, and less so to additional services. Accordingly, we propose the following research questions.

- *RQ1: How do low-cost and flagship airlines differ in terms of online comments?*
- *RQ2: What type of comments are related to core services by airline types?*

3. METHOD

3.1. Data collection

The dataset was collected from TripAdvisor, a widely recognized platform where travelers share their experiences with airlines, hotels, and other tourism services (Figure 1 displays an example of a TripAdvisor review). The reviews were retrieved from the website and data collection focused exclusively on user-generated content, which provides spontaneous and unfiltered opinions about airline services.

Figure 1. Example of a TripAdvisor review

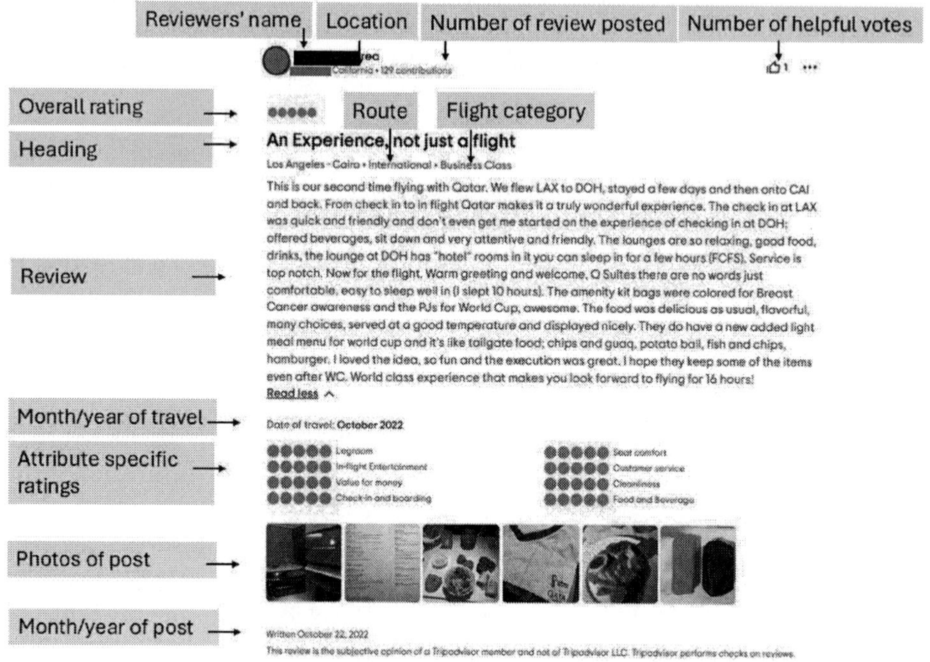

Source: TripAdvisor (2022)

To ensure the quality of the dataset, only reviews containing textual content were considered. Duplicate entries and potential spam reviews were also filtered out. To maintain consistency in the analysis, only reviews written in Spanish were included.

3.2. Dataset

The dataset comprises a total of 18,597 reviews, distributed almost equally between the two airlines under study: Iberia (52.1%) and Vueling (47.9%). Reviews were about flights from 2015 to 2023, with a peak concentration in the years 2016 to 2018 for both airlines. Specifically, Iberia's reviews volume peaked in 2018 (25.88%), while Vueling recorded its highest share that same year (28.76%). Although the volume tapers in the post-pandemic years, the presence of recent data up to 2023 maintains the relevance of insights for current managerial decisions.

Seasonal distribution by month reveals a clear peak during the high-travel season, particularly from June to September, with August being the most commented month for both Iberia (11.63%) and Vueling (14.65%). This aligns with the European summer holiday period, when demand and service stress tend to generate a higher volume of passenger feedback.

Table 1. Sample description

	Iberia (n=9,688)	Vueling (n=8,909)	Chi-square
Fligh year	2015 (5.12%); 2016 (21.15%); 2017 (20.21%); 2018 (25.88%); 2019 (17.88%); 2020 (3.12%); 2021 (2.51%); 2022 (3.28%); 2023 (0.84%)	2015 (2.14%); 2016 (19.93%); 2017 (18.06%); 2018 (28.76%); 2019 (17.85%); 2020 (3.52%); 2021 (3.70%); 2022 (4.75%); 2023 (1.30%)	187.295 (p<0.001)
Fligh month	Jan (5.14%); Feb (5.69%); Mar (6.77%); Apr (6.76%); May (10.38%); Jun (9.66%); Jul (10.89%); Aug (11.63%); Sep (11.05%); Oct (8.04%); Nov (6.69%); Dec (7.31%)	Jan (4.07%); Feb (4.72%); Mar (5.87%); Apr (6.12%); May (9.19%); Jun (10.80%); Jul (12.68%); Aug (14.65%); Sep (12.36%); Oct (7.02%); Nov (5.57%); Dec (6.96%)	104.237 (p<0.001)
Flight category	Domestic (15.99%); Europe (23.44%); International (60.57%)	Domestic (51.18%); Europe (46.66%); International (2.17%)	7298.804 (p<0.001)

Regarding flight routes, the sample shows marked differences: Iberia's corpus predominantly features international flights (60.57%), followed by European and domestic routes. In contrast, Vueling's texts are heavily weighted towards domestic operations (51.18%) and European flights (46.66%), with a minimal share for long-haul international segments (2.17%). This distribution is consistent with the airlines' business models—full-service for Iberia and low-cost short-to-medium haul for Vueling.

3.3. Components and data analysis

For each review, the following variables were downloaded: airline name, date of the review, title, text, flight route, flight category, review with photos, country of the author, number of contributions, number of useful votes, review votes, and others (overall, legroom, seat comfort, in-flight entertainment, value for money, cleanliness, check-in and boarding, and food and beverage). Text mining techniques were employed to review texts, analyze patterns, and extract relevant insights. The software KH Coder 3 Beta was utilized (Higuchi, 2017).

Tokenization was performed, yielding 820,762 words and 24,494 unique word types. After removing stop words (e.g., 'a', 'the'), the text was reduced to 622,505 words and 23,254 –word types. Next, Freeling Part-of-Speech (POS) tagging assigned grammatical categories to words based on context. Finally, lemmatization standardized word variants to their base forms; for example, *"volando"*, *"volé"*, and *"volado"* were unified under the lemma *"volar"*. We applied analysis as Word Frequency, Co-occurrence Networks and Topics Model (LDA) to the data.

4. RESULTS

Table 2 presents the top 20 most frequently occurring terms categorized by part of speech (nouns, verbs, adjectives, and adverbs) within the analyzed corpus of user-generated content related to air travel experiences. This lexical profiling provides a concise yet insightful overview of the predominant topics, actions, and evaluative language shaping passengers' discourse.

In the noun category, terms such as *"vuelo"* (flight), *"hora"* (hour/time), *"avión"* (airplane), and *"asiento"* (seat) clearly indicate that operational and logistical aspects are central to travellers' narratives. References to *"compañía"* (airline/company), *"servicio"* (service), and *"maleta"* (baggage) further confirm that passengers frequently discuss both the tangible and intangible elements that frame their overall satisfaction. Among verbs, dominant actions include *"tener"* (to have), *"hacer"* (to do), *"poder"* (to be able), and *"llegar"* (to arrive), reflecting concerns about capability, punctuality, and procedural expectations. The prevalence of verbs such as *"decir"* (to say), *"dar"* (to give), and *"viajar"* (to travel) suggests that narratives often include recommendations, complaints, or personal anecdotes. The adjective list is led by polar terms such as *"bueno"* (good), *"malo"* (bad), *"puntual"* (punctual), *"amable"* (kind), and *"correcto"* (appropriate), highlighting that customers strongly focus on service quality, staff attitude, and punctuality as key evaluative criteria. Finally, frequent adverbs like *"bien"* (well), *"siempre"* (always), *"después"* (after), and *"solo"* (only) indicate temporal framing and intensification, providing additional context to users' sentiment and sequence of events.

Overall, the distribution across parts of speech demonstrates that passengers articulate a rich blend of factual and subjective elements, confirming that text mining techniques are highly effective for uncovering the linguistic markers that signal satisfaction drivers and recurrent service challenges in the air travel sector.

Table 2. Most frequent words list (Top 20) by POS

#	nouns	TF	verbs	TF	adjectives	TF	adverbs	TF
1	vuelo	18669	tener	11348	bueno	6183	bien	3110
2	hora	7910	hacer	7701	malo	2043	siempre	2567
3	avión	6730	poder	5892	mismo	1954	después	1787
4	asiento	6361	llegar	5110	puntual	1742	solo	1713
5	compañía	5674	decir	4768	amable	1713	menos	1482
6	servicio	5121	ir	4710	correcto	1448	casi	1399
7	maleta	4072	dar	4456	cómodo	1389	así	1348
8	retraso	3996	viajar	3939	mejor	1379	bastante	1316
9	vez	3868	salir	3233	excelente	1308	nunca	1266
10	viaje	3832	volar	3146	nuevo	1235	luego	1132
11	atención	3607	pagar	2835	peor	1223	tan	997
12	día	3388	pasar	2544	normal	1080	además	983
13	personal	3313	esperar	2095	medio	1038	aun	801
14	aeropuerto	3266	deber	2042	largo	986	ahora	754
15	comida	2844	llevar	1884	único	924	dentro	727
16	problema	2774	poner	1846	pequeño	864	mal	676
17	embarque	2632	perder	1825	atento	836	tarde	670
18	vuelta	2517	dejar	1796	solo	831	incluso	560
19	pasajero	2409	volver	1732	siguiente	769	tampoco	502
20	espacio	2405	ver	1684	aéreo	750	encima	474

The co-occurrence network (Figure 2) visualizes the lexical relationships surrounding the keywords *Iberia* and *Vueling* within the corpus, revealing the most salient terms frequently mentioned in association with each airline and highlighting the linguistic proximity of shared concerns and topics, answering to RQ1 and RQ2. Both airlines share a dense cluster of high-frequency terms related to operational elements (*"vuelo"*— flight, *"hora"*— time/hour, *"compañía"*— company), passenger experience (*"asiento"*— seat, *"servicio"* — service, *"personal"* — staff), and common actions (*"tener"* — to have, *"hacer"*— to do, *"ir"*— to go). This convergence reflects that passengers discuss core aspects of air travel consistently across carriers. The relative node sizes demonstrate that *"vuelo"* and *"hora"* dominate conversations for both airlines, underscoring punctuality and flight management as pivotal topics. In addition, terms such as *"maleta"* (baggage), *"aeropuerto"* (airport), and *"problema"* (problem) emerge prominently around *Vueling*, potentially indicating a higher frequency of baggage handling or logistical issues discussed by its passengers. Peripheral nodes linked exclusively to each airline, like *"comida"* (food) or *"a bordo"* (on board) for *Iberia,* suggest distinctive aspects of the in-flight experience that customers specifically associate with this carrier.

Figure 2. Co-ocurrence network

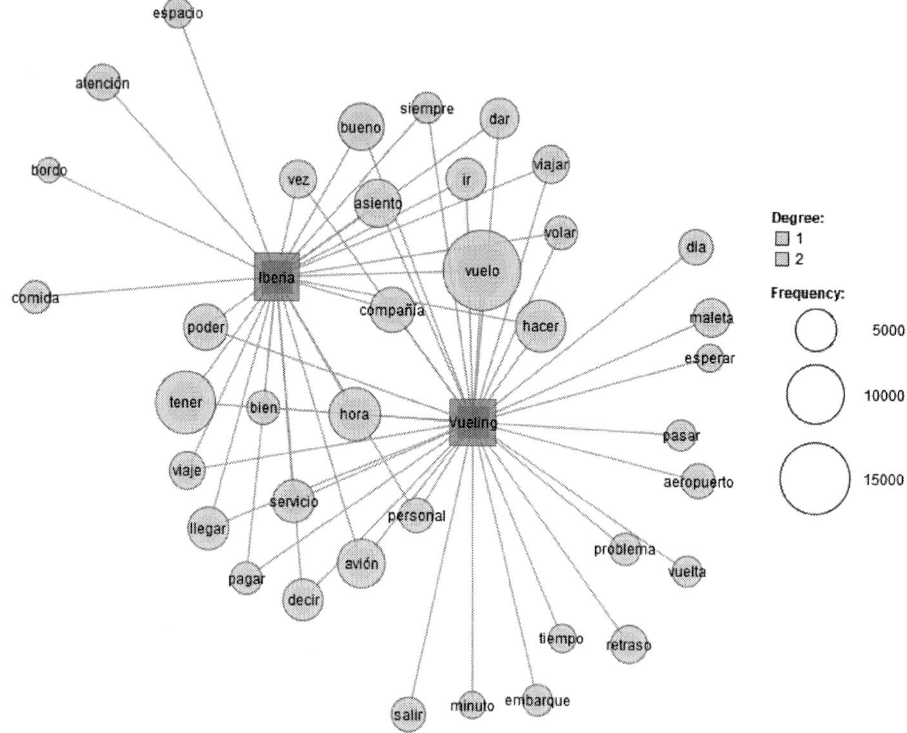

The topic modelling (LDA) results (see Table 3) highlight key aspects of passenger experiences by clustering semantically related terms into ten coherent thematic groups. Each topic encapsulates distinctive dimensions of the air travel experience, offering valuable insights into recurring priorities, concerns, and perceptions shared by passengers across the dataset.

The first topic, *In-Flight Service Quality,* centers on positive evaluations of onboard amenities, catering, entertainment, and staff attentiveness. This suggests that passengers frequently articulate satisfaction or dissatisfaction in relation to the tangible and intangible elements of cabin service. The second topic, Baggage and Boarding Issues, captures recurrent mentions of luggage handling, carry-on policies, and boarding procedures, often linked to logistical challenges or perceived inefficiencies. The third topic, Airline Reputation and Negative Experience, aggregates terms reflecting passengers' broader perceptions of the airline brand, including isolated negative experiences that impact loyalty and word-of-mouth. *Airport and Ticketing Procedures*, the fourth topic, groups reference to airport facilities, ticketing processes, and claims management, revealing operational touchpoints that influence travelers' overall satisfaction. The fifth topic, *Cabin Comfort and Seating*, underscores the importance of seat quality, available space, and cabin ergonomics, including crew interactions and seat allocation practices. The sixth topic, *Flight Duration and Timing*, highlights passengers' concerns regarding flight length, scheduling, and alignment with personal itineraries. The seventh topic, *Crew Professionalism and Courtesy*, focuses on crew behaviour, politeness, punctuality, and the perceived competence of onboard staff, reinforcing the human factor as a key determinant of perceived service quality. The eighth topic, *Delays and Boarding Timing*, zeroes in on punctuality, delays, gate procedures, and boarding efficiency—issues that frequently shape customer reviews and service complaints. The ninth topic, *Round Trip Planning and Scheduling*, reflects discussions about round-trip arrangements, return flights, and the management of itineraries, showing how customers evaluate connectivity and scheduling convenience. Finally, the tenth topic, *Value for Money and Travel Options*, encapsulates considerations about ticket prices, fare classes, perceived cost-benefit balance, and alternative travel choices, pointing to price sensitivity as a consistent evaluative factor.

Table 3. Top 10 keywords for 12 LDA topics

#1 In-Flight Service Quality		#2 Baggage and Boarding Issues		#3 Airline Reputation and Negative Experience		#4 Airport and Ticketing Procedures		#5 Cabin Comfort and Seating	
word	prob.	word	prob.	word	prob.	word	prob.	word	prob.
bueno	0,268	maleta	0,241	compañía	0,338	día	0,190	asiento	0,368
servicio	0,176	equipaje	0,136	vez	0,230	aeropuerto	0,183	avión	0,277
atención	0,149	avión	0,097	malo	0,121	mismo	0,108	espacio	0,139
Comida	0,115	problema	0,086	año	0,079	cliente	0,096	azafata	0,074
Bordo	0,094	mano	0,069	peor	0,072	billete	0,094	fila	0,067
excelente	0,076	embarque	0,065	experiencia	0,065	reclamación	0,057	pequeño	0,029
entretenimiento	0,052	persona	0,064	único	0,034	caso	0,051	pasajero	0,028
puntualidad	0,045	cabina	0,060	problema	0,024	momento	0,037	nuevo	0,007
calidad	0,019	gente	0,058	nuevo	0,020	persona	0,037	cómodo	0,002
cómodo	0,003	cosa	0,048	cosa	0,010	destino	0,034	viaje	0,001
									0,368

#6 Flight Duration and Timing		#7 Crew Professionalism and Courtesy		#8 Delays and Boarding Timing		#9 Round Trip Planning and Scheduling		#10 Value for Money and Travel Options	
word	prob.	word	prob.	word	prob.	word	prob.	word	prob.
vuelo	0,590	personal	0,206	hora	0,371	vuelo	0,526	viaje	0,225
tiempo	0,127	amable	0,105	retraso	0,226	vuelta	0,152	servicio	0,124
pasajero	0,110	puntual	0,103	minuto	0,105	ida	0,120	precio	0,115
hora	0,081	bueno	0,099	embarque	0,086	normal	0,064	aerolínea	0,097
destino	0,034	tripulación	0,096	salida	0,074	horario	0,061	mejor	0,082
parte	0,026	correcto	0,088	medio	0,059	problema	0,053	cost	0,060
salida	0,011	trato	0,083	puerta	0,056	único	0,009	largo	0,059
información	0,009	atención	0,062	información	0,011	puntual	0,005	comida	0,053
caso	0,007	cómodo	0,049	avión	0,010	puntualidad	0,005	clase	0,052
correcto	0,002	puntualidad	0,046	día	0,000	viaje	0,002	opción	0,040

To complement the analysis with the heatmap data, we can interpret how different topics vary across the two airlines in study (Figure 3). Overall, the distribution of topic proportions appears relatively balanced, indicating that passengers of both airlines discuss similar themes with comparable intensity. However, slight variations can be observed for certain topics. For instance, Topic #1 (In-Flight Service Quality) shows a higher relative weight in Iberia reviews (0.107) compared to Vueling (0.094), suggesting that passengers flying with Iberia place more emphasis on the evaluation of onboard service features such as food, entertainment, and staff attentiveness. Conversely, Topic #8 (Delays and Boarding Timing) is more prominent in Vueling (0.106) than in Iberia (0.096). This could reflect a higher frequency of comments related to punctuality, gate management, and boarding processes among Vueling passengers, aligning with its operational focus on short-haul routes where timing deviations are more noticeable. Other topics, such as Topic #10 (*Value for Money and Travel Options*), maintain a slightly higher presence in Iberia (0.103) than in Vueling (0.097), indicating that price-quality considerations may carry marginally more weight in reviews of the full-service carrier.

Figure 3. Heating map between LDA topics and airlines companies

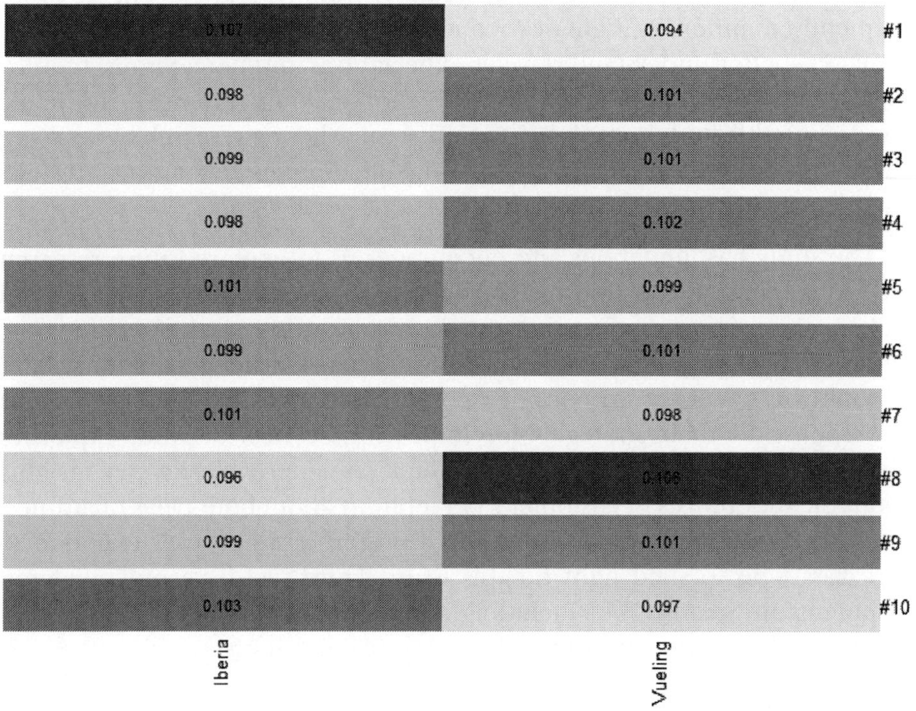

	Iberia	Vueling
#1	0.107	0.094
#2	0.098	0.101
#3	0.099	0.101
#4	0.098	0.102
#5	0.101	0.099
#6	0.099	0.101
#7	0.101	0.098
#8	0.096	0.106
#9	0.099	0.101
#10	0.103	0.097

5. DISCUSSION, CONCLUSION, AND IMPLICATIONS

Online reviews provide extensive insights into consumer opinions. This study employs a comparative analysis of different company types and airlines to elucidate whether online reviews reveal differences based on airline type. Using social media posts as a means of expressing self-expression, this research aims to explore online reviews of two types of airlines companies by revealing the most prominent topics that travellers mention in online text reviews.

The entire dataset comprises 18,597 online comments from the TripAdvisor websites of two airline companies: low-cost (Vueling) and a flag carrier (Iberia). This study demonstrates that online reviews provide valuable insights into the core elements shaping passenger experiences with different types of airlines. First, the topic modeling analysis (LDA) confirms that passengers focus their evaluations on core service attributes such as punctuality, staff treatment, seat comfort, and value for money. Second, although the main themes are common across both types of airlines, their relative weight varies: Vueling passengers tend to emphasize operational issues (e.g., delays and baggage problems), while Iberia passengers more frequently mention in-flight service aspects. These findings help tourism managers better understand traveler expectations and perceptions, thereby supporting more customer-focused decision-making. From an academic standpoint, this study contributes to tourism marketing research by applying advanced natural language processing techniques to airline reviews complementing previous research.

The study has limitations and encourages us to explore future research questions. First, we do not analyze data over time. Future studies should address these issues by focusing on the pre-, during, and post-pandemic periods to observe potential internal assessments of passengers. Additionally, it would be beneficial to consider potential changes adopted by airlines in response to their strategies for improving service. Second, exploring objectivity versus subjectivity in comments could provide deeper insights about the differences in customer's perceptions about both types of airlines. Future analyses might incorporate flight origin, distance, user experience, and class type to shed light on this issue. Third, we have only analyzed comments in Spanish, but including comments made in other languages could be valuable for capturing other types of consumers.

ACKNOWLEDGMENTS
This research (ID PID2023-153112OB) has received support from the MCIU/AEI/10.13039/501100011033/FEDER, UE).

6. REFERENCES

Babić Rosario, A., De Valck, K., & Sotgiu, F. (2020). Conceptualizing the electronic word-of-mouth process: What we know and need to know about eWOM creation, exposure, and evaluation. *Journal of the Academy of Marketing Science, 48*(3), 422–448.

Bigne, E., Fuentes-Medina, M. L., & Morini-Marrero, S. (2020). Memorable tourist experiences versus ordinary tourist experiences analysed through user-generated content. *Journal of Hospitality and Tourism Management, 45*, 309–318.

Bigne, E., Ruiz, C., Cuenca, A., Perez, C., & Garcia, A. (2021). What drives the helpfulness of online reviews? A deep learning study of sentiment analysis, pictorial content and reviewer expertise for mature destinations. *Journal of Destination Marketing & Management, 20*, 100570.

Bigne, E., Ruiz, C., & Curras-Perez, R. (2024). How consumers process online review types in familiar versus unfamiliar destinations. A self-reported and neuroscientific study. *Technological Forecasting and Social Change, 199*, 123067.

Bigne, E., Zanfardini, M., & Andreu, L. (2025). Destination online reviews: Lexicons and thematic arguments on social responsibility. *Tourism Review, 80*(4), 944–965.

Blei, D. M., Ng, A. Y., & Jordan, M. I. (2003). Latent Dirichlet Allocation. *Journal of Machine Learning Research, 3.* http://www.jmlr.org/papers/volume3/blei03a/blei03a.pdf

Çallı, L., & Çallı, F. (2023). Understanding Airline Passengers during Covid-19 Outbreak to Improve Service Quality: Topic Modeling Approach to Complaints with Latent Dirichlet Allocation Algorithm. *Transportation Research Record: Journal of the Transportation Research Board, 2677*(4), 656–673.

Chang, Y.-C., Ku, C.-H., & Le Nguyen, D.-D. (2022). Predicting aspect-based sentiment using deep learning and information visualization: The impact of COVID-19 on the airline industry. *Information & Management, 59*(2), 103587.

Dwesar, R., & Sahoo, D. (2022). Does service failure criticality affect global travellers' service evaluations? An empirical analysis of online reviews. *Management Decision, 60*(2), 426–448.

Egger, R., & Yu, J. (2022). A topic modeling comparison between lda, nmf, top2vec, and bert topic to demystify twitter posts. *Frontiers in Sociology, 7,* 886498.

Farzadnia, S., Vanani, I. R., & Hanafizadeh, P. (2024). An experimental study for identifying customer prominent viewpoints on different flight classes by topic modeling methods. *International Journal of Information Management Data Insights, 4*(1), 100223.

Grewal, L., Stephen, A. T., & Coleman, N. V. (2019). When Posting About Products on Social Media Backfires: The Negative Effects of Consumer Identity Signaling on Product Interest. *Journal of Marketing Research, 56*(2), 197–210.

Higuchi, K. (2017). A two-step approach to quantitative content analysis: KH coder tutorial using Anne of green gables (part II). *Ritsumeikan Soc Sci Rev, 53,* 137.

IATA 2024. Annual Review 2024. Available at https://www.iata.org/contentassets/c81222d96c9a4e0bb4ff6ced0126f0bb/iata-annual-review-2024.pdf Accessed on February 2025

Jung, S.-Y., & Yoo, K.-E. (2014). Passenger airline choice behavior for domestic short-haul travel in South Korea. *Journal of Air Transport Management, 38,* 43–47.

Kim, D., Lim, C., & Ha, H.-K. (2024). Comparative analysis of changes in passenger's perception for airline companies' service quality before and during COVID-19 using topic modeling. *Journal of Air Transport Management, 115,* 102542.

Kirilenko, A. P., & Stepchenkova, S. (2025). Facilitating topic modeling in tourism research: Comprehensive comparison of new AI technologies. *Tourism Management, 106,* 105007.

Kitsios, F., Mitsopoulou, E., Moustaka, E., & Kamariotou, M. (2022). User-Generated Content behavior and digital tourism services: A SEM-neural network model for information trust in social networking sites. *International Journal of Information Management Data Insights, 2*(1), 100056.

Liu, Y., Ma, L., Dou, Y., Zhu, Z., Ma, L., & Liu, Z. (2025). Injecting new insights: How do review sentiment and rating inconsistency shape the helpfulness of airline reviews? *Information Processing & Management, 62*(4), 104088.

Lu, L., Xu, P., Wang, Y.-Y., & Wang, Y. (2023). Measuring service quality with text analytics: Considering both importance and performance of consumer opinions on social and non-social online platforms. *Journal of Business Research, 169,* 114298.

Lucini, F. R., Tonetto, L. M., Fogliatto, F. S., & Anzanello, M. J. (2020). Text mining approach to explore dimensions of airline customer satisfaction using online customer reviews. *Journal of Air Transport Management, 83,* 101760.

Ma, E., Cheng, M., & Hsiao, A. (2018). Sentiment analysis–a review and agenda for future research in hospitality contexts. *International Journal of Contemporary Hospitality Management, 30*(11), 3287–3308.

Misopoulos, F., Mitic, M., Kapoulas, A., & Karapiperis, C. (2014). Uncovering customer service experiences with Twitter: The case of airline industry. *Management Decision, 52*(4), 705–723.

Nieto García, M., Muñoz-Gallego, P. A., Viglia, G., & González-Benito, Ó. (2020). Be Social! The Impact of Self-Presentation on Peer-to-Peer Accommodation Revenue. *Journal of Travel Research, 59*(7), 1268–1281.

Oliver, R. L. (1977). Effect of expectation and disconfirmation on postexposure product evaluations: An alternative interpretation. *Journal of Applied Psychology, 62*(4), 480.

Park, S.-Y., Wang, X., Oh, Y., Hong, S.-M., & Woo, S.-H. (2025). Application of structural topic modeling in a literature review of air transport. *Journal of Air Transport Management, 122,* 102708.

Pereira, F., Costa, J. M., Ramos, R., & Raimundo, A. (2023). The impact of the COVID-19 pandemic on airlines' passenger satisfaction. *Journal of Air Transport Management, 112,* 102441.

Sezgen, E., Mason, K. J., & Mayer, R. (2019). Voice of airline passenger: A text mining approach to understand customer satisfaction. *Journal of Air Transport Management, 77,* 65–74.

Sparks, B. A., Perkins, H. E., & Buckley, R. (2013). Online travel reviews as persuasive communication: The effects of content type, source, and certification logos on consumer behavior. *Tourism Management, 39,* 1–9.

Wang, X., Zheng, J., Tang, L. R., & Luo, Y. (2023). Recommend or not? The influence of emotions on passengers' intention of airline recommendation during COVID-19. *Tourism Management, 95,* 104675.

Wu, C., Che, H., Chan, T. Y., & Lu, X. (2015). The Economic Value of Online Reviews. *Marketing Science, 34*(5), 739–754.

Xu, X., Liu, W., & Gursoy, D. (2019). The Impacts of Service Failure and Recovery Efforts on Airline Customers' Emotions and Satisfaction. *Journal of Travel Research, 58*(6), 1034–1051.

Yan, Q., Jiang, T., Zhou, S., & Zhang, X. (2024). Exploring tourist interaction from user-generated content: Topic analysis and content analysis. *Journal of Vacation Marketing, 30*(2), 327–344.

Zaki, M., & McColl-Kennedy, J. R. (2020). Text mining analysis roadmap (TMAR) for service research. *Journal of Services Marketing, 34*(1), 30–47.

LA DIGITALIZACIÓN DE LOS DESTINOS RURALES: EL VEHÍCULO ELÉCTRICO COMO PROPUESTA DE VALOR PARA LAS EXPERIENCIAS TURÍSTICAS SOSTENIBLES

Elena Victoria Valero Botella
María Dolores Teruel Serrano
Juan Miguel Alberola Oltra
Universidad Politécnica de Valencia

TEMÁTICA: Innovación en la experiencia del turista

RESUMEN: La utilización del vehículo propio o de alquiler para el desplazamiento a destinos turísticos alejados del entorno urbano o alejados de importantes nodos de comunicación es una necesidad. Actualmente, el vehículo eléctrico se empieza a incorporar al parque automovilístico y se presenta como una buena alternativa para acercar a los turistas al entorno rural si bien no siempre existen infraestructuras capaces de abastecer la demanda de puntos de recarga. Es por ello por lo que la presente investigación tiene como objetivo analizar la situación actual de estos destinos para promover la digitalización de los destinos rurales a través de la incorporación de vehículos eléctricos en el diseño y comercialización de experiencias turísticas basadas en principios de sostenibilidad económica, social y ambiental.

Palabras clave: Turismo sostenible, Destinos rurales, Experiencias turísticas, Vehículos eléctricos, Inteligencia turística.

ABSTRACT: The use of private or rental vehicles for travel to tourist destinations that are far from urban areas or major communication hubs is a necessity. Currently, electric vehicles are starting to be incorporated into the automotive fleet and present a good alternative for bringing tourists closer to rural areas, although infrastructure capable of meeting the demand for charging points is not always available. Therefore, the aim of this research is to analyze the current situation of these destinations to promote the digitalization of rural destinations through the incorporation of electric vehicles in the design and marketing of tourist experiences based on principles of economic, social, and environmental sustainability.

Keywords: Sustainable tourism, Rural destinations, Tourist experiences, Electric vehicles, Tourism intelligence.

1. INTRODUCCIÓN

El turismo sostenible en zonas rurales se presenta como una alternativa respetuosa con el medio ambiente frente a los modelos turísticos tradicionales los cuales suelen implicar una explotación intensiva de los recursos naturales. En este contexto, la Organización Mundial del Turismo (OMT, 2025) define el turismo sostenible como aquel que tiene plenamente en cuenta las repercusiones actuales y futuras, económicas, sociales y medioambientales, para satisfacer las necesidades de los visitantes, de la industria, del entorno y de las comunidades anfitrionas. Este enfoque no solo promueve prácticas más responsables en el ámbito ambiental y sociocultural, sino que también se presenta como una herramienta estratégica para el desarrollo de áreas rurales. Este tipo de modelo de desarrollo es especialmente relevante en zonas afectadas por el envejecimiento demográfico o la despoblación (Johnson y Lichter, 2019). En este sentido el turismo rural, concebido desde una perspectiva sostenible puede contribuir a diversificar la economía local, generar empleo y fomentar la conservación del patrimonio natural y cultural, tal y como afirmaba Lane en 1994.

Ante esta apuesta por el desarrollo del turismo rural sostenible aparece la progresiva incorporación de tecnologías digitales y **soluciones inteligentes** las cuales están transformando la forma en que se diseñan, gestionan y disfrutan las experiencias turísticas, lo que plantea nuevas oportunidades para los destinos rurales. En este sentido, la conectividad y, en concreto, la utilización de **vehículos eléctricos**, así como el acceso a **infraestructuras sostenibles** se presentan como aspectos clave para mejorar la experiencia del visitante y avanzar hacia un modelo más eficiente y responsable. El presente artículo analiza, desde una perspectiva conceptual, los vínculos entre el **turismo sostenible, la inteligencia turística y la movilidad sostenible en entornos rurales** y se recogen algunas iniciativas representativas que ilustran cómo estos elementos pueden articularse para contribuir al desarrollo territorial sostenible.

El artículo progresa desde el desarrollo conceptual hasta la identificación de retos y propuestas de actuación, y se estructura de la siguiente manera: tras esta introducción, la **Sección 2** establece el marco conceptual del turismo rural sostenible e inteligente, donde se analizan los estándares y la normativa que articulan la gobernanza, la innovación y la sostenibilidad de los destinos turísticos (2.1). Asimismo, se abordan los principales obstáculos para la implementación del modelo de destinos turísticos inteligentes en entornos rurales, destacando la necesidad de estrategias integrales y colaborativas de desarrollo territorial (2.2). La **Sección 3** presenta un diagnóstico de las brechas infraestructurales y digitales que afectan a la movilidad eléctrica en el medio rural, evaluando su impacto sobre la sostenibilidad turística y la transición energética, con base en bibliografía especializada e informes técnicos. Finalmente, la **Sección 4** explora los retos estructurales y sociodemográficos del ámbito rural, como la despoblación o la falta de conectividad, y propone soluciones orientadas a la gobernanza colaborativa, la interoperabilidad digital y la adopción de políticas integradas que permitan transformar estos desafíos en oportunidades reales de regeneración territorial.

2. TURISMO RURAL SOSTENIBLE E INTELIGENTE: PERSPECTIVAS CONCEPTUALES SOBRE LA TRANSICIÓN DIGITAL DEL TURISMO

El paradigma del turismo con valores sostenibles en espacios rurales se ha consolidado como una estrategia clave para el desarrollo económico, la preservación del patrimonio cultural y la conservación ambiental de las zonas rurales (Rivera Mateos, 2021). Este enfoque promueve, desde una visión integral, la creación de **experiencias turísticas** que respetan y valoran tanto el **entorno natural** como las **tradiciones locales**, a la vez que favorecen el **bienestar de las comunidades anfitrionas**. De acuerdo con la Organización Mundial del Turismo (OMT, 2023), el 61 % de los turistas a nivel global considera probable que en el futuro se opte por modalidades de viaje más sostenibles, mientras que un 83 % ya reconoce la sostenibilidad como una prioridad esencial en el ámbito turístico. Las experiencias turísticas que incorporan valores sostenibles en sus dimensiones económicas, sociales y ambientales han asumido un protagonismo creciente en las agendas políticas internacionales (Organization of American States, 2018).

Este enfoque responde a la necesidad de conciliar el desarrollo y expansión del sector turístico con los principios del desarrollo sostenible. En este escenario, el turismo rural se presenta como una alternativa estratégica para dinamizar territorios tradicionalmente dependientes del sector primario (Rivera Mateos, 2018). En el caso de España, el turismo rural ha sido clave para la **diversificación económica de las zonas rurales**, así como para la conservación del patrimonio natural y cultural. Proyectos como “Enrédate en lo local”, desarrollado en el marco del programa Estrategia de Experiencias Turismo España, vinculado al Plan de Recuperación, Transformación y Resiliencia, financiado por la Unión Europea a través de los fondos NextGenerationEU, dan visibilidad al **turismo rural con valores**

sostenibles, ecológicos, socialmente responsables y/o saludables que no solo generan empleo y contrarrestan la despoblación, sino que también preservan la autenticidad cultural y fortalece la resiliencia de las comunidades locales. Estudios recientes evidencian que el turismo en entornos naturales contribuye significativamente a la desconexión del ritmo urbano y a la mejora del bienestar mental de los visitantes (Avecillas-Torres et al., 2025). En este sentido, Farkić et al. (2021) destacan prácticas como el baño de bosque que han evolucionado desde una tradición ancestral a una forma contemporánea de turismo rural en áreas naturales. En este sentido facilitar la creación y comercialización de experiencias turísticas con valores sostenibles, ecológicos, socialmente responsables y/o saludables, que promuevan la **colaboración entre los alojamientos rurales y los proveedores locales del sector primario** (agricultores, ganaderos, apicultores, etc.) se hace fundamental.

Asimismo, entre otras acciones, la **formación** dirigida a los profesionales del sector resulta crucial para garantizar un modelo turístico que promueva el consumo y la producción responsables (ODS 12), y que contribuya a la protección y restauración de los ecosistemas terrestres (ODS 15), constituyéndose como **un elemento fundamental para un desarrollo turístico verdaderamente sostenible**. El presente artículo propone un enfoque que facilita la incorporación del sector primario, como vía para dinamizar económicamente sus poblaciones, diversificando sus actividades económicas y reconociendo a través del consumo turístico el valor diferencial y de relevancia de los agricultores, ganaderos, artesanos, productores agroalimentarios, pescadores, guías de naturaleza e intérpretes de patrimonio, fortaleciendo la economía y producción local. La **diversificación económica** trae consigo una mayor estabilidad financiera y el reconocimiento social de los turistas, quienes buscan experiencias auténticas y responsables. Entre otras iniciativas de desarrollo turístico, el **agroturismo** se configura como una oportunidad para el sector primario, sirviendo de vía para dinamizar económicamente los destinos, **diversificando sus actividades económicas y contribuyendo a la repoblación rural.**

Se observa una inclinación hacia propuestas turísticas que minimicen el impacto ambiental y fomenten prácticas sostenibles, especialmente aquellas que promueven el consumo de productos locales y de proximidad (kilómetro cero). Este cambio en las prioridades del visitante ha sido respaldado por empresas que analizan la demanda como Booking, que afirmó que en el año 2022 el 58 % de los encuestados consideró esencial que sus viajes contribuyeran al **desarrollo de las comunidades locales.** En 2024, esta misma fuente, indicó que el 53 % de los viajeros manifestó interés por experiencias que integren sostenibilidad y confort, mientras que un 65 % expresó su preferencia por alojamientos que incluyan **espacios naturales**. Además, un 60 % señaló que estaría dispuesto a adoptar decisiones más responsables si estas fueran incentivadas mediante **plataformas digitales**, como las ofrecidas por **aplicaciones móviles** orientadas a la sostenibilidad turística. Tal predisposición pone de relieve el papel emergente de la tecnología como facilitadora en la reconfiguración de los comportamientos turísticos y como eje estratégico para la gestión inteligente y sostenible de los destinos rurales.

Una aportación significativa en esta línea es el estudio de Demaria et al. (2022), que analiza la viabilidad del uso de vehículos eléctricos en comunidades remotas de Australia mediante un enfoque geoespacial sustentado en el modelo *hub-and-spoke*[1]. Los resultados evidencian que la electrificación del transporte rural no solo es técnicamente viable, sino que representa una estrategia eficaz para la reducción de emisiones contaminantes, la disminución de la dependencia de combustibles fósiles y el fortalecimiento de la sostenibilidad territorial. Este marco resulta extrapolable a contextos turísticos rurales europeos, donde la **optimización de rutas y la ubicación estratégica de puntos de recarga** de vehículos eléctricos podría favorecer la conectividad de alojamientos rurales, bodegas, enclaves naturales y productores locales, reforzando así un modelo de movilidad bajo en carbono al servicio del turismo sostenible.

2.1. Hacia un modelo de destino turístico sostenible e inteligente

Dado que el turismo representa una de las principales actividades económicas y sociales en muchas regiones, su desarrollo no puede abordarse de manera aislada, sino como parte de una estrategia integral de planificación territorial. La incorporación de tecnologías avanzadas, la optimización de infraestructuras y la adopción de modelos sostenibles no solo enriquecen la experiencia turística, sino que también inciden directamente en la **calidad de vida de la población local** (Raimo et al., 2024). En este sentido, la aplicación de tecnologías emergentes en los destinos turísticos busca mejorar tanto la eficiencia operativa de los servicios públicos como el bienestar ciudadano. No obstante, estudios recientes advierten que estos beneficios solo se alcanzan cuando las iniciativas se diseñan en función del contexto

---

1 Estructura de red donde un nodo central (hub) conecta con varios nodos periféricos (spokes), optimizando la distribución de flujos y la asignación de recursos para mejorar la eficiencia operativa.

local y se promueve una **participación ciudadana efectiva** en los procesos de planificación y toma de decisiones (Albert & Klauser, 2022). La transformación de un destino turístico tradicional en uno inteligente no es un proceso automático; requiere una profunda adaptación en los modelos de gobernanza y gestión. Para ello, resulta esencial la participación activa de todas las partes interesadas, con especial atención a la cooperación entre los sectores público y privado (Khomsi y Bédard, 2024).

Para garantizar un desarrollo turístico alineado con los principios de sostenibilidad, accesibilidad e integración funcional con los servicios urbanos, resulta esencial la existencia de un marco normativo robusto que oriente la transformación de los destinos hacia modelos más inteligentes y resilientes. En este sentido, el Comité Técnico de Normalización **AEN/CTN 178**, coordinado por la Asociación Española de Normalización (AENOR) e impulsado por la Secretaría de Estado de Telecomunicaciones y la Sociedad de la Información, constituye un referente técnico clave en la transición hacia destinos inteligentes. El comité se estructura en seis subcomités que abarcan de forma holística los ámbitos críticos de un entorno inteligente: **Infraestructuras (SC1),** Indicadores y Semántica (SC2), **Gobierno y Movilidad (SC3), Energía y Medio Ambiente (SC4), Destinos Turísticos Inteligentes (SC5)** y Ámbitos Transversales (SC6). Esta arquitectura normativa permite abordar, de manera coordinada, la interoperabilidad de los sistemas territoriales, la eficiencia energética, la **movilidad sostenible** y la gobernanza participativa, garantizando siempre los criterios de sostenibilidad ambiental, económica y social.

Dentro de este marco estructural, el Subcomité 5 de destinos turísticos inteligentes cumple una función clave en la articulación del sector, al establecer directrices que favorecen la adopción de tecnologías avanzadas, el desarrollo de sistemas específicos de indicadores y la implementación de estrategias de sostenibilidad orientadas a fortalecer la competitividad de los destinos. La labor normativa desempeñada no solo incide en la mejora de la calidad y la eficiencia de la oferta turística, sino que también promueve la integración del turismo en los procesos de planificación territorial, posicionándolo como un vector estratégico que genera sinergias entre el desarrollo económico local, la cohesión social y la protección del entorno natural y cultural. Esta integración, guiada por estándares técnicos reconocidos, facilita la transición hacia un modelo territorial más eficiente, inclusivo y sostenible, en el que el turismo actúa como **catalizador del bienestar colectivo y de la innovación en la gestión de los destinos.** Es fundamental desarrollar modelos de gobernanza que permitan la integración de residentes y turistas en la planificación del destino, asegurando que las infraestructuras, servicios y políticas respondan tanto a las necesidades locales, como a sectores público y privado. En este marco, la Secretaría de Estado de Turismo, a través de SEGITTUR, lidera el proyecto de **destinos turísticos inteligentes**, una iniciativa pionera a nivel internacional cuyo objetivo es la implementación de un nuevo modelo de gestión turística basado en la gobernanza, la innovación y la sostenibilidad.

Según SEGITTUR (2025) un destino turístico inteligente es aquel que, consolidado sobre una **infraestructura tecnológica avanzada**, garantiza el desarrollo sostenible del territorio, la accesibilidad universal y la integración del visitante con el entorno. Además, este modelo de gestión incrementa la calidad de la experiencia turística y mejora la calidad de vida de los residentes, asegurando los principios de sostenibilidad. La **Norma UNE 178501:2018**, elaborada por la Asociación Española de Normalización, constituye un referente metodológico integral para la conversión de destinos turísticos convencionales en destinos turísticos inteligentes, orientados a mejorar su competitividad, sostenibilidad y eficiencia mediante una gestión accesible e innovadora (Asociación Española de Normalización, 2018).

Este marco normativo establece las bases para un modelo de gobernanza colaborativa, en el que confluyen actores públicos y privados en la articulación de una oferta turística coherente, tecnológicamente avanzada y alineada con las demandas del turista contemporáneo. En el núcleo operativo del sistema de gestión definido por la Norma UNE 178501:2018 se sitúa el **Sistema de Gestión de Destinos Turísticos Inteligentes**, estructurado en torno al ciclo de mejora continua PHVA **(Planificar-Hacer-Verificar-Actuar)**, que permite una toma de decisiones basada en evidencias objetivas a través del análisis de indicadores de desempeño específicos. Este sistema de gestión se sustenta en cinco ejes estratégicos interrelacionados **—gobernanza, innovación, tecnología, accesibilidad universal y sostenibilidad—**, cuya integración permite una respuesta coordinada y adaptativa a los desafíos del desarrollo turístico. La **gobernanza** adquiere un carácter transversal, entendida como la coordinación eficaz de todos los agentes implicados: administraciones públicas, sector privado, ciudadanía, centros de conocimiento y turistas. La norma plantea, en este sentido, la creación de un **ente gestor del destino**, responsable de liderar la planificación estratégica y operativa, garantizar la cooperación público-privada, evitar duplicidades y asegurar una visión común y participativa del desarrollo turístico. Asimismo, la **transparencia** y la **apertura de datos** se configuran como pilares fundamentales para fortalecer una gobernanza informada, inclusiva y orientada a resultados, promoviendo así un modelo de gestión que sitúe al sector turístico como motor de innovación territorial y cohesión social. La norma promueve una gestión responsable orientada a la eficiencia energética, la **reducción de emisiones**, la conservación del patrimonio natural y cultural, y la adecuada gestión de los recursos. No obstante, para que esta transformación digital sea efectiva, la norma destaca la importancia de disponer de **infraestructuras tecnológicas robustas,** como redes de conectividad 5G, plataformas de datos abiertos e instrumentos de análisis predictivo, que sustenten la inteligencia aplicada al destino.

2.2 Obstáculos para implementar el modelo de destinos turísticos inteligente en destinos rurales

A pesar de que el modelo de **destino turístico inteligente** se está consolidando progresivamente en el panorama nacional, numerosos territorios rurales siguen excluidos de este proceso de transformación. La implementación del modelo de destino turístico inteligente en estos entornos enfrenta obstáculos significativos, entre los que destaca la persistente **brecha digital**, que limita tanto el acceso a tecnologías como la conectividad básica necesaria para su desarrollo (OECD, 2018). Para que este modelo resulte viable en los contextos rurales, es imprescindible atender a sus **limitaciones estructurales**. A medida que disminuye el tamaño del municipio, aumenta la proporción de población envejecida y se reduce significativamente el acceso a **Internet**, tanto en espacios públicos como privados (Morales Romo, 2016). Esta situación no solo dificulta el **despliegue técnico de infraestructuras inteligentes**, sino que también profundiza las desigualdades entre entornos urbanos y rurales, afectando su capacidad para **competir**, **innovar** y **generar cohesión social**.

En paralelo, mientras las zonas urbanas han experimentado en las últimas décadas un notable **desarrollo tecnológico y económico**, numerosas poblaciones rurales en España y en Europa han sufrido procesos de **despoblación**. Esta tendencia ha conllevado la reducción de las inversiones y las iniciativas empresariales, debilitando aún más la posibilidad de sostener una economía local diversificada y resiliente. Además, para que el turismo rural logre consolidarse como motor de desarrollo, es fundamental que ofrezca productos diversificados, especializados y conectados con el entramado socioeconómico de los territorios, siendo la **innovación** una herramienta clave tanto para las empresas como para los destinos (Santos y Sánchez, 2021).

Un ejemplo tangible de estas **desigualdades estructurales** puede observarse en la distribución de los **puntos de recarga para vehículos eléctricos**, que en España se concentra principalmente en zonas urbanas y periurbanas (Estévez et al., 2023). En contraste, las áreas rurales presentan una red de recarga limitada, dispersa y con escasa accesibilidad, lo cual constituye una **barrera crítica** para la adopción del vehículo eléctrico, especialmente en territorios donde el **transporte privado** es esencial tanto para la movilidad cotidiana como para la actividad turística. Esta carencia compromete no solo el desarrollo de una **movilidad sostenible**, sino también la **competitividad** de estos destinos, al influir directamente en la elección del visitante. La disponibilidad de puntos de recarga para vehículos eléctricos es un factor que condiciona las decisiones del turista, cuyas preferencias actuales se orientan hacia **modalidades de viaje con menor impacto ambiental**, mayor **contacto con la naturaleza** y una relación más auténtica con las **comunidades locales**. En este contexto, la incorporación de **soluciones innovadoras** que conecten a los usuarios de vehículos eléctricos con las infraestructuras rurales de recarga de vehículos eléctricos no solo atiende una carencia técnica, sino que también representa una palanca de transformación capaz de posicionar el turismo rural como una alternativa sostenible y competitiva.

En este marco, la **cooperación multiactor** entre administraciones públicas, empresas privadas y comunidades locales resulta fundamental para garantizar una **transformación territorial equilibrada**. Esta colaboración permite articular recursos, canalizar inversiones y fortalecer esquemas de **financiación estables**, elementos esenciales para consolidar un modelo de turismo inteligente en entornos rurales. Experiencias internacionales como el **Rural EV Toolkit** desarrollado por el Departamento de Transporte de los Estados Unidos han evidenciado la eficacia de este enfoque colaborativo, subrayando la necesidad de establecer **alianzas público-privadas** y fomentar la participación ciudadana para desplegar infraestructuras de recarga de vehículos eléctricos en territorios rurales de baja densidad y alta dispersión (U.S. Department of Transportation, 2025). A este desafío se suman otros factores estructurales, como la **falta de financiación** y el **desconocimiento de ayudas** disponibles por parte de gestores locales (Hosteltur, 2022), así como la necesidad de respetar la **identidad cultural** de los territorios con el fin de evitar una pérdida de autenticidad. Por tanto, el impulso de soluciones innovadoras en materia de infraestructura sostenible, como la movilidad eléctrica, no debe abordarse de forma aislada, sino como parte de una estrategia integral de desarrollo rural inteligente.

En este escenario de desigualdad estructural, los destinos rurales enfrentan serias dificultades para adoptar el modelo de destino turístico inteligente en condiciones de equidad. Las limitaciones en conectividad, infraestructura, capacitación técnica y recursos económicos, unidas al envejecimiento poblacional y la dispersión geográfica, obstaculizan tanto la planificación estratégica como el acceso a servicios digitales de calidad. Sin embargo, esta situación también ha propiciado la aparición de enfoques adaptados a las características del medio rural, como el concepto de **pueblo inteligente**. Esta noción hace referencia a comunidades rurales que, partiendo de sus propios recursos y capacidades, integran soluciones tecnológicas y modelos de gestión innovadores con el objetivo de mejorar la calidad de vida de los residentes, combatir la despoblación y reactivar sus economías locales. Según la **Red Española de Desarrollo Rural** (REDR, 2017), estas localidades pueden configurarse como espacios de oportunidad si orientan su desarrollo hacia la prestación de servicios digitales personalizados fundamentados en la participación activa de la ciudadanía. En este sentido, la incorporación estratégica de tecnologías en los destinos turísticos rurales no solo contribuiría a mitigar los procesos de despoblación mediante la reducción de la brecha digital, sino que también permitiría avanzar de manera coordinada en la doble transición digital y ecológica, promoviendo un modelo de desarrollo territorial más equitativo, resiliente y sostenible.

3. DIAGNÓSTICO DEL PROBLEMA: BRECHAS INFRAESTRUCTURALES Y DIGITALES EN LA MOVILIDAD ELÉCTRICA ENTRE ENTORNOS RURALES Y URBANOS

Uno de los principales retos que enfrentan los destinos rurales es la conectividad, un aspecto fundamental para el desarrollo turístico. Dado que el turismo implica necesariamente el desplazamiento de personas, la conectividad se configura como un factor determinante tanto para el desarrollo de las actividades turísticas como para garantizar un acceso eficiente y planificado a los destinos. La escasez de infraestructuras de recarga para vehículos eléctricos en zonas rurales no solo limita la movilidad, sino que afecta directamente a la competitividad y sostenibilidad del turismo rural, al dificultar la atracción de visitantes comprometidos con un modelo de transporte sostenible. Su superación exige no solo la implementación de políticas públicas orientadas a fomentar la expansión de estas instalaciones, sino también el impulso de iniciativas específicas que mejoren la conectividad eléctrica y garanticen el **acceso a tecnologías de recarga rápida, eficiente y asequible**. Según datos del Instituto Nacional de Estadística (INE, 2023), a partir de la Encuesta de Turismo de Residentes y consultando la base de datos sobre viajes, pernoctaciones, duración media y gasto según el principal medio de transporte y tipo de destino, se observa que el

81,42 % de los viajes realizados en España durante 2022 se efectuaron en vehículo propio, como se recoge en la Tabla 1.

Tabla 1. Encuesta de turismo residente. (2022)

TIPOLOGÍA VEHÍCULO	4º Trimestre 2022	3º Trimestre 2022	2º Trimestre 2022	1º Trimestre 2022	TOTAL 2022
Otro medio de transporte	550446	504781	728441	345047	1,37%
Transporte aereo	2302158	2687085	2165067	1414272	5,52%
Transporte marítimo	428025	795271	349649	193239	1,14%
Transporte por autobús	1518897	2270668	1673325	1594076	4,55%
Transporte por ferrocarril	2232283	2561970	2388361	2140941	6,01%
Vehículo propio	26789235	41836986	33689775	24093028	81,42%
Total general	**33821044**	**50656761**	**40994618**	**29780603**	**100,00%**

Fuente: Instituto Nacional de Estadística.

A partir de los datos de la Encuesta de Turismo de Residentes publicada por el Instituto Nacional de Estadística (INE, 2022), relativos al volumen total de viajes turísticos a la Comunidad Valenciana y a su distribución por motivo principal, se estiman los porcentajes de utilización de los distintos medios de transporte en función de cada motivo. La estimación se realiza mediante un cálculo proporcional que combina el peso relativo de cada motivo de desplazamiento con la proporción global de uso de cada medio de transporte. Este procedimiento permite aproximar la distribución de los medios de transporte empleados según el motivo del viaje y evidencia que el vehículo particular constituye el modo de transporte predominante en los desplazamientos turísticos hacia la Comunidad Valenciana, alcanzando una incidencia destacada en la mayoría de los motivos analizados.

a) **Turismo de sol y playa**: El coche particular es el medio predominante, utilizado en el 89,5 % de los viajes, seguido por el avión (7,3 %), el tren (2,2 %) y el autobús (1,0 %).

b) **Turismo cultural**: También se caracteriza por un uso mayoritario del coche particular (77,5 %), aunque el avión (19,0 %) adquiere un peso más relevante. El tren y el autobús representan un 2,5 % y un 1,0 %, respectivamente.

c) **Turismo de naturaleza**: El coche particular es el principal medio de transporte (83,0 %), seguido del avión (13,0 %), el tren (3,0 %) y el autobús (1,0 %).

d) **Turismo de negocios**: A diferencia de los anteriores, el avión constituye el medio más utilizado (84,0 %), por delante del coche particular (12,0 %), el tren (3,0 %) y el autobús (1,0 %).

El predominio del vehículo particular como principal medio de transporte hacia destinos turísticos de naturaleza evidencia una alta dependencia del transporte privado en esta modalidad. Esta situación pone de manifiesto la necesidad de desarrollar alternativas sostenibles de movilidad, especialmente adaptadas a entornos rurales, que permitan reducir el impacto ambiental y mejorar la accesibilidad sin comprometer la conservación del territorio. Esta situación se explica, en parte, por la dispersión geográfica y la limitada conectividad mediante transporte público que caracteriza a muchos destinos rurales. Esta fuerte vinculación entre el turismo de naturaleza y el uso del automóvil plantea **tanto retos como oportunidades** en el marco de la transición hacia modelos de movilidad más sostenibles. En este contexto, el auge del vehículo eléctrico adquiere una relevancia estratégica. Según la Agencia Internacional de la Energía (IEA, 2023), el sector de la movilidad eléctrica atraviesa un crecimiento sostenido: los vehículos eléctricos representaron aproximadamente el 15 % de las ventas globales de automóviles en 2023, con proyecciones que estiman una cuota del 40 % para 2030. En 2022, las ventas superaron los 10 millones de unidades, lo que representa el 14 % del total de coches nuevos vendidos a nivel mundial, frente al 9 % en 2021 y menos del 5 % en 2020 (World Energy Outlook, 2023). La Tabla 2 muestra la tendencia creciente de ventas mundiales de coches eléctricos.

Tabla 2. Ventas mundiales de coches eléctricos (2023)

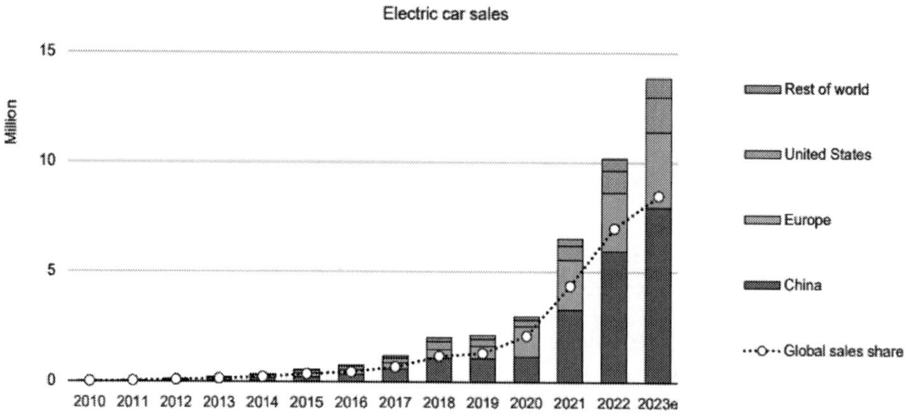

Fuente: Informe Global EV Outlook 2023 de la Agencia Internacional de la Energía extraídos del INE.

La creciente conciencia ambiental y la aspiración colectiva hacia un futuro más sostenible están impulsando una transformación en los patrones de movilidad, con una **demanda cada vez mayor de opciones de transporte de bajo impacto**. En este contexto, los vehículos eléctricos se consolidan como una alternativa energética y ambientalmente más eficiente frente a los automóviles tradicionales de combustión. Los vehículos eléctricos alimentados con la actual combinación energética vigente en Europa pueden reducir entre un 10 % y un 24 % el potencial de calentamiento global en comparación con los modelos diésel o de gasolina, considerando una vida útil de 150.000 kilómetros (Hawkins et al., 2013). La progresiva adopción de tecnologías vinculadas a la movilidad eléctrica se enmarca dentro de los compromisos internacionales adquiridos con el Acuerdo de París, que establece como objetivo mantener el aumento de la temperatura media global por debajo de los 2 °C, y preferentemente limitarlo a 1,5 °C respecto a los niveles preindustriales. Para alcanzar dicha meta, la Agencia Internacional de la Energía (IEA, 2021) advierte que es imprescindible alcanzar emisiones netas cero a nivel global para 2050. En paralelo, el Grupo Intergubernamental de Expertos sobre el Cambio Climático (IPCC, 2022) subraya que la electrificación desempeña un papel central en la descarbonización del transporte terrestre, destacando su alto potencial de mitigación cuando se alimenta con electricidad de bajo carbono. En este contexto, la movilidad eléctrica se consolida como una prioridad estratégica en la transición hacia sistemas de transporte sostenibles y climáticamente neutros.

A pesar de que más de 70 países y múltiples actores no estatales han formalizado compromisos hacia las emisiones netas cero, las proyecciones actuales advierten que las políticas vigentes resultan insuficientes para cumplir con los objetivos establecidos (Organización de las Naciones Unidas, 2022). Ante esta brecha, Naciones Unidas ha reiterado la urgencia de adoptar medidas inmediatas, coordinadas y verificables para reforzar dichos compromisos. Actualmente, la mayor parte de la demanda de recarga de vehículos eléctricos se satisface mediante sistemas de recarga domiciliaria (World Energy Outlook, 2023). No obstante, la expansión de infraestructuras de acceso público cobra cada vez más relevancia, especialmente en las zonas donde los puntos de recarga de vehículos eléctricos privados son limitados. A finales de 2022, se contabilizaban en todo el mundo cerca de **2,7 millones de puntos de recarga públicos,** lo que representa un incremento del 55 % respecto al año anterior tal y como se recoge en la Tabla 3.

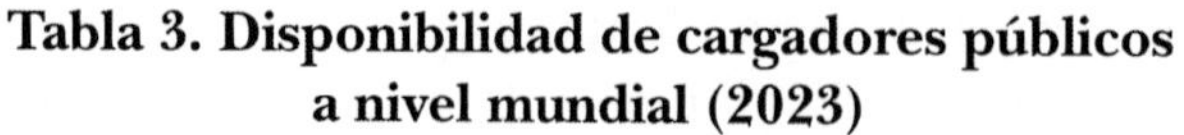

Tabla 3. Disponibilidad de cargadores públicos a nivel mundial (2023)

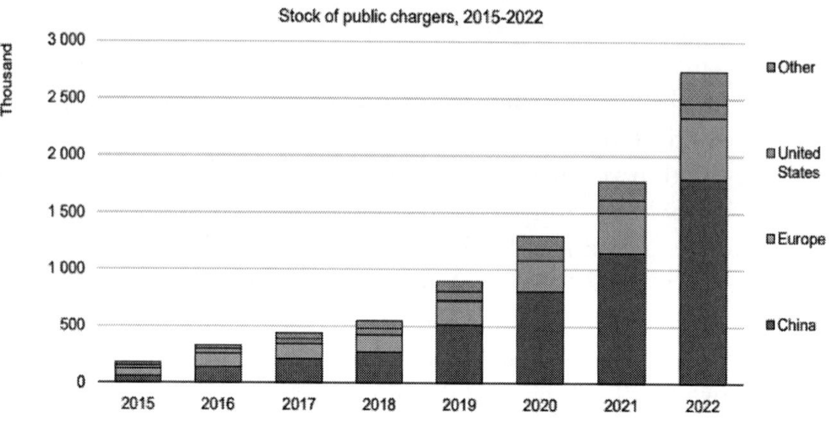

Fuente: Informe Global EV Outlook 2023 de la Agencia Internacional de la Energía.

China lidera el número de cargadores lentos y rápidos de acceso público a nivel mundial. En Europa, países como Alemania, Francia y Noruega lideran con un crecimiento substancial en el despliegue de cargadores rápidos, impulsado por iniciativas como el Reglamento sobre la infraestructura de combustibles alternativos de la Unión Europea[2]. España se posiciona por debajo de la media europea en cuanto a penetración de vehículos de turismo electrificados y eléctricos puros, así como el nivel del desarrollo de las infraestructuras de recarga (World Energy Outlook, 2023). El **despliegue adecuado de la infraestructura de recarga de vehículos eléctricos públicos** es crucial para satisfacer la creciente demanda de recarga de vehículos eléctricos y respaldar su adopción generalizada. Esto requiere una planificación estratégica y financiación adecuada, tanto a nivel nacional como internacional, para asegurar una red de recarga accesible y eficiente que promueva la transición hacia una movilidad más sostenible a nivel global.

---

2 Reglamento (UE) 2023/1804 del Parlamento Europeo y del Consejo de 13 de septiembre de 2023

4. MOVILIDAD SOSTENIBLE Y GOBERNANZA COLABORATIVA: RETOS Y CONCLUSIONES DEL MODELO DE DESTINO TURÍSTICO INTELIGENTE EN EL MEDIO RURAL

La consolidación del modelo de destino turístico inteligente en el ámbito rural exige, como punto de partida, un análisis riguroso de la compleja interdependencia entre los **desafíos estructurales** y los **retos sociodemográficos** que configuran estos territorios. La despoblación, el envejecimiento de la población, la baja densidad demográfica y la elevada dispersión territorial constituyen factores limitantes que dificultan tanto la diversificación económica como la implementación sostenida de procesos de digitalización, innovación y modernización institucional. En este marco, la digitalización no debe concebirse como un fin en sí mismo, sino como un vector de transformación sistémica orientado a fomentar la cohesión territorial, impulsar la inclusión social, **mitigar los procesos de despoblación** y consolidar la resiliencia y la identidad de los entornos rurales en el contexto del turismo del siglo XXI.

En este sentido, la superación de la **brecha digital** entre los entornos urbanos y rurales representa un prerrequisito esencial para el despliegue de estrategias eficaces encaminadas a la implementación del modelo de destinos turísticos inteligentes en zonas rurales. Esta brecha, entendida en una dimensión amplia y multidimensional, engloba tanto carencias en infraestructuras de conectividad como desigualdades en el acceso y uso de las competencias digitales por parte de la población local, constituyendo una barrera que condiciona negativamente la adopción plena de modelos de innovación territorial, gobernanza inteligente y sostenibilidad turística. La persistencia de esta brecha no solo limita el potencial transformador del modelo de destino turístico inteligente, sino que también perpetúa dinámicas de exclusión social y vulnerabilidad estructural en el medio rural. Esta problemática, analizada de manera transversal a lo largo del presente artículo, se configura como una barrera que dificulta la implementación efectiva del modelo de destino turístico inteligente en contextos rurales.

Abordar esta problemática requiere una intervención estratégica basada en una doble dimensión: por un lado, la garantía del acceso universal, asequible y de calidad a infraestructuras tecnológicas avanzadas; por otro, la promoción de procesos sostenidos de alfabetización digital y fomento de una **cultura de innovación adaptada a las especificidades del territorio.** En este contexto, la **formación y la capacitación** se consolidan como elementos transversales que permiten la implementación del modelo de destinos turísticos inteligentes. Sin una ciudadanía digitalmente alfabetizada, sin gestores públicos formados en gobernanza inteligente, sin emprendedores rurales capaces de innovar con sentido territorial, el modelo de destino turístico inteligente perdería su capacidad transformadora. Por tanto, se requieren programas formativos adaptados a la diversidad de actores del ecosistema turístico rural, desde responsables institucionales hasta colectivos vulnerables, que integren competencias digitales, habilidades en planificación estratégica, gestión sostenible, **emprendimiento social** e inteligencia turística, siempre desde una perspectiva de inclusión, equidad y continuidad.

La transición hacia un modelo de destino turístico inteligente en entornos rurales exige una **visión holística, sistémica y profundamente enraizada en las especificidades territoriales, sociales y culturales** del medio rural. Este modelo no puede ser concebido como una mera incorporación de soluciones tecnológicas, sino como una estrategia de transformación estructural orientada a reforzar las capacidades locales, dinamizar el capital endógeno y reducir las brechas históricas que afectan a estos territorios. En este contexto, la **gobernanza** adquiere un papel central, requiriendo un enfoque renovado y adaptativo, basado en la acción colaborativa, la transparencia metodológica y la rendición de cuentas. Solo así será posible activar procesos de cocreación de valor público sustentados en la evidencia empírica, la inteligencia territorial y el aprendizaje colectivo. La implementación efectiva del modelo dependerá, en gran medida, de la capacidad de los actores públicos, privados y ciudadanía para configurar marcos institucionales flexibles, inclusivos y multinivel, capaces de fomentar la innovación social, la participación activa y la gestión compartida de los recursos. Este tipo de gobernanza debe ir más allá de la mera consulta ciudadana para convertirse en un mecanismo operativo de corresponsabilidad democrática, donde la población local participe como protagonista en el diseño, ejecución y evaluación de las políticas turísticas. Solo mediante este enfoque de gobernanza integrada será posible activar dinámicas de transformación sostenibles, que permitan consolidar destinos turísticos rurales más resilientes, competitivos e inclusivos, donde el turismo actúe como motor de regeneración territorial y cohesión social.

En este sentido, la **sostenibilidad** no debe asumirse como un componente añadido al modelo, sino como un principio estructurante y transversal, presente en cada etapa del ciclo de vida del destino turístico: desde la planificación participativa hasta la evaluación de impactos. En el ámbito rural, este principio implica avanzar hacia modelos de desarrollo regenerativo que no solo mitiguen los impactos negativos del turismo, sino que contribuyan activamente a restaurar ecosistemas, revitalizar economías locales y fortalecer los lazos comunitarios. Un destino turístico inteligente basado en los principios de sostenibilidad debe optimizar el uso de recursos naturales y culturales, promover la circularidad económica y garantizar la distribución equitativa de los beneficios generados. En este marco, la transformación digital debe entenderse como un catalizador de dicha sostenibilidad, facilitando la gestión eficiente e inclusiva del destino, mediante el uso estratégico de datos abiertos, plataformas interoperables y tecnologías emergentes adaptadas al territorio.

La movilidad sostenible se configura como un componente crítico y, a la vez, un **reto de primer orden** en la implementación del modelo de destino turístico inteligente, especialmente en contextos rurales caracterizados por una fuerte dependencia del vehículo privado y por la debilidad estructural del transporte público. Estas limitaciones no solo afectan a la experiencia del visitante, sino que también condicionan la equidad en el acceso a servicios básicos por parte de la población residente. En este escenario, la electrificación progresiva de la movilidad en entornos rurales, mediante el despliegue de **infraestructuras de recarga accesibles, interoperables y territorialmente equilibradas**, constituye una **oportunidad** clave para avanzar hacia un modelo turístico bajo en carbono, más eficiente y ambientalmente responsable. No obstante, esta transición energética solo será viable si se articula a través de estrategias de planificación integradas, que combinen inversión pública y privada, participación ciudadana y adopción de tecnologías inteligentes, como sistemas de gestión en tiempo real, plataformas digitales de reserva o soluciones móviles orientadas a la optimización de flujos y recursos.

Desde una perspectiva prospectiva, se recomienda fomentar líneas de investigación e innovación orientadas al **diseño de plataformas digitales interoperables que faciliten el acceso a información en tiempo real sobre la disponibilidad, operatividad y accesibilidad de puntos de recarga,** especialmente en áreas rurales de baja densidad. La adopción de datos abiertos y estándares comunes alineados con los principios FAIR que no solo contribuirá a mejorar la transparencia y la calidad de la información, sino que también favorecerá la construcción de ecosistemas de innovación abierta, la mejora en la toma de decisiones por parte de los turistas y gestores, y el incremento de la confianza institucional y empresarial.

En definitiva, el despliegue efectivo del modelo de destino turístico inteligente en entornos rurales no puede limitarse a una mera aplicación tecnológica, sino que ha de entenderse como una estrategia integral de transformación territorial, centrada en las personas y orientada al largo plazo. Solo mediante la articulación coordinada de los ejes de sostenibilidad, digitalización, movilidad y gobernanza será posible revertir los desequilibrios estructurales del medio rural y convertir sus desafíos en palancas de innovación, cohesión social y resiliencia.

5. REFERENCIAS

Agencia Internacional de la Energía (AIE) (2023): *World Energy Outlook 2023*. París, Francia.

Albert, C., & Klauser, F. (2022). *Residents' Quality of Life in Smart Cities: A Systematic Literature Review. Land, 12*(4), 876.https://www.mdpi.com/2073-445X/12/4/876

Alonso Gallo, N., Vicent, L., & Trillo, D. (2024). *Digitalisation and rural tourism development in Europe: Assessing the impact of connectivity on service provision and demand. Tourism & Management Studies*, (Special Issue), 1–15. https://tmstudies.net/index.php/ectms/article/view/2380

Asociación Española de Normalización (UNE). (2018). UNE 178501:2018. Sistema de gestión de los destinos turísticos inteligentes: Requisitos. UNE.

Avecillas-Torres, I., Herrera-Puente, S., Galarza-Cordero, M., Coello-Nieto, F., Farfán-Pacheco, K., Alvarado-Vanegas, B., … Espinoza-Figueroa, F. (2025). *Nature tourism and mental well-being: Insights from a controlled context on reducing depression, anxiety, and stress.* Sustainability, 17(2), 654. https://www.mdpi.com/2071-1050/17/2/654

Booking.com. (2022). *Travel Predictions 2022.* https://www.booking.com/c/trends/travelpredictions2022.es.html?aid=356980&label=gog235jc1DEhV0cmF2ZWxwcmVkaWN0aW9uczIwMjIoggI46AdIClgDaEaIAQGYAQq4ARfIAQzYAQPoAQH4AQKIAgGoAgO4AryKprQGwAIB0gIkMDJmOGU0OTktNGRjNy00YWEwLWE5YWYtNDIzZjM2ODYxOWFj2AIE4AIB&sid=8bbe26d7b48b2096dda0afaa670023fa&keep_landing=1&

Booking.com. (2024). *Travel Predictions 2024.* https://www.booking.com/c/trends/travelpredictions2024.es.html

Carmona, J. (2019). *Gestión de destinos turísticos: Nuevos enfoques y paradigmas.* Editorial Universitaria.

Comisión Europea. (2021). *Una visión a largo plazo para las zonas rurales de la UE: Hacia unas zonas rurales más fuertes, conectadas, resilientes y prósperas de aquí a 2040.* eur-lex.europa.eu/legal-content/ES/TXT/HTML/?uri=CELEX:52021DC0345

Copaja-Alegre, M., & Esponda-Alva, C. (2019). Tecnología e innovación hacia la ciudad inteligente. Avances, perspectivas y desafíos. Revista Bitácora Urbano Territorial, 29(2), 1-10. https://revistas.unal.edu.co/index.php/bitacora/article/view/68333

Demaria, K., Sturmberg, B. C. P., Riley, B., & Markham, F. (2022). *Exploring the feasibility of electric vehicle travel for remote communities in Australia.* https://arxiv.org/abs/2207.05260

Estévez, R., Quílez, C., Rodríguez, M., & Prieto, F. (Junio de 2023). Infraestructura de recarga para vehículos eléctricos en España: Análisis, evaluación y recomendaciones para impulsar la movilidad eléctrica garantizando una transición justa y las particularidades territoriales. Observatorio de Sostenibilidad, ECODES. Recuperado de https://ecodes.org/hacemos/cambio-climatico/incidencia-en-politicas-publicas/estudio-infraestructura-de-recarga-para-vehiculos-electricos-en-espana

European Commission. (2021). *Sustainable and Smart Mobility Strategy – Putting European transport on track for the future.* Comunicación COM(2020) 789 final. Oficina de Publicaciones de la Unión Europea. https://op.europa.eu/en/publication-detail/-/publication/5e601657-3b06-11eb-b27b-01aa75ed71a1/language-en

Hawkins, T. R., Singh, B., Majeau-Bettez, G., & Strømman, A. H. (2013). Comparative environmental life cycle assessment of conventional and electric vehicles. *Journal of Industrial Ecology, 17*(1) https://onlinelibrary.wiley.com/doi/10.1111/j.1530-9290.2012.00532.x.

Hosteltur. (2022). *Destinos turísticos inteligentes: retos y problemáticas en municipios pequeños.* https://www.hosteltur.com/130085_retos-a-los-que-se-enfrentan-los-destinos-turisticos-inteligentes.html?utm_source=chatgpt.com

García, S. (2016, abril 28). Sistema de Inteligencia Turística. Blog SEGITTUR. Recuperado de https://www.segittur.es/transformacion-digital/proyectos-transformacion-digital/sistema-de-inteligencia-turistica-2/

Gobierno de España. (2024). Destinos Turísticos Inteligentes. https://www.destinosinteligentes.es/.

International Energy Agency. (2023). *Global EV Outlook 2023: Catching up with climate ambitions.* https://www.iea.org/reports/global-ev-outlook-2023

INE-Instituto Nacional de Estadística. (2023). Encuesta de Turismo de Residentes. https://www.ine.es/jaxiT3/Tabla.htm?cellvacia=1&t=15797

INE-Instituto Nacional de Estadística. (2023). Viajes, pernoctaciones, duración media y gasto por principal medio de transporte, según tipo de destino principal (12431). INE. https://www.ine.es/jaxiT3/Tabla.htm?t=12431&L=0

Intergovernmental Panel on Climate Change. (2022). *Chapter 10: Transport.* In P. R. Shukla et al. (Eds.), *Climate Change 2022: Mitigation of Climate Change. Contribution of Working Group III to the Sixth Assessment Report of the Intergovernmental Panel on Climate Change.* Cambridge University Press. https://www.ipcc.ch/report/ar6/wg3/chapter/chapter-10/

International Energy Agency. (2023). World Energy Outlook 2023. Recuperado de https://www.iea.org/reports/world-energy-outlook-2023

International Energy Agency. (2024). *Global EV Outlook 2024: Outlook for emissions reductions*

International Energy Agency. (2021). Net Zero by 2050: *A roadmap for the global energy sector.* IEA. *https://www.iea.org/reports/net-zero-by-2050*

Johnson, K. M., & Lichter, D. T. (2019). Rural depopulation: Growth and decline processes over the past century. *Rural Sociology*, 84(1), 3-27. https://onlinelibrary.wiley.com/doi/10.1111/ruso.12266

Khomsi, M. R., & Bédard, F. (2024). From smart city to smart destination. The case of three Canadian cities. École *des sciences de la gestion, Université du Québec à Montréal.* Recuperado de https://www.iriarteuniversidad.es/wp-content/uploads/2024/12/2024-numero-3.pdf

Lane, B. (1994). What is rural tourism? *Journal of Sustainable Tourism*, 2(1-2), 7-21. https://www.tandfonline.com/doi/abs/10.1080/09669589409510680

Melián, I. (2024). La colaboración política, empresarial y ciudadana de las organizaciones de gestión de destinos turísticos (OGD) como fórmula para el éxito. *Ibiza Melián Escuela Universitaria de Turismo IRIARTE (EUTI).* Recuperado de https://www.iriarteuniversidad.es/wp-content/uploads/2024/12/2024-numero-3.pdf

Morales Romo, N. (2016). El reto de la brecha digital y las personas mayores en el medio rural español: El caso de Castilla y León. *Fonseca, Journal of Communication: 13, 2, 2016*, 165-185.

OECD. (2018). *Bridging the rural digital divide* (OECD Digital Economy Papers, No. 265). OECD Publishing. https://www.oecd.org/en/publications/bridging-the-rural-digital-divide_852bd3b9-en.html

Organización de las Naciones Unidas. (2022). *Coalición por las emisiones netas cero.* https://www.un.org/es/climatechange/net-zero-coalition

ONU Turismo. (2025). *Informe sobre la gobernanza y la sostenibilidad en los destinos turísticos.* Organización de las Naciones Unidas para el Turismo.

Organización Mundial del Turismo (2025): Turismo sostenible. Organización Mundial del Turismo. Recuperado de https://www.unwto.org/es/desarrollo-sostenible

Organización Mundial del Turismo (2025): Turismo sostenible. Organización Mundial del Turismo. Recuperado de https://www.unwto.org/es/turismo-rural

Organización Mundial del Turismo (OMT). (2021). Encuesta mundial sobre la acción por el clima en el sector turístico. Madrid, España.

Organización Mundial del Turismo (OMT). (2023). Encuesta mundial sobre la acción por el clima en el sector turístico. Madrid, España.

Organization of American States. (2018). *Turismo sostenible en las Américas: Retos y oportunidades.* Comisión Interamericana de Turismo (CITUR), OEA. Recuperado de https://www.oas.org/en/sedi/desd/CT/Documents/OEA_LRST_s.pdf

Purnomo, E. P., Obisva, G., & Astutik, Z. A. (2019). Smart Government: The involvement of government towards public services in Yogyakarta for Smart

Raimo, N., De Marco, M., & Ricciardelli, A. (2023). *Sustainability of smart rural mobility and tourism: A key performance indicators–based approach. Technology in Society, 74,* 102287. https://www.sciencedirect.com/science/article/pii/S016079 1X23000921?via%3Dihub

Red Española de Desarrollo Rural (REDR). (2017, 17 de noviembre). *A pueblos pequeños, grandes innovaciones.* https://www.redr.es/es/noticias/smart-villages-a-pueblos-pequenos-grandes-innovaciones/

Rivera Mateos, M. (2021). Turismo sostenible en zonas rurales, oportunidad de empleo y desarrollo socioeconómico.

Santos, M., & Sánchez, J. (2021). *Retos de la innovación turística en el medio rural.* Ostelea Tourism Management School.

Secretaría de Estado de Turismo. (2025). *Smart Office DTI.* Recuperado de https://www.destinosinteligentes.es/soluciones/smart-office-dti/

SEGITTUR. (2024). Extraído de DATAESTUR y Sistema de Inteligencia Turística (SIT)

SEGITTUR. (2025). *Destinos turísticos inteligentes.* Secretaría de Estado de Turismo. Recuperado de https://www.segittur.es/destinos-turisticos-inteligentes/proyectos-destinos/destinos-turisticos-inteligentes/

Shokoohyar, M., et al. (2020). The role of tourism intelligence in strategic management: A systematic literature review. Journal of Hospitality and Tourism Management, 55, 102452.

Unión Internacional de Telecomunicaciones. (2014). *Ciudades inteligentes sostenibles: Un análisis de definiciones.* Recuperado de https://www.itu.int/en/ITU-T/focusgroups/ssc/Documents/Approved_Deliverables/TR-Definitions.docx

U.S. Department of Transportation. (s. f.). *Charging Forward: A Toolkit for Planning and Funding Rural Electric Mobility Infrastructure.* Retrieved from U.S. Department of Transportation website. https://www.transportation.gov/rural/ev/toolkit?utm_source=chatgpt.com

Vera, F., López Palomeque, F., Marchena Gómez, M., & Antón Clavé, S. (1997). *Análisis territorial del turismo.* Editorial Ariel. Barcelona.

World Tourism Organization & Organization of American States. (2018). *Tourism and the Sustainable Development Goals – Good Practices in the Americas* [Informe]. DOI: https://www.e-unwto.org/doi/book/10.18111/9789284419685

Wu, B., et al. (2021). The impact of tourism intelligence on destination competitiveness: A meta-analysis. Tourism Management, 90, 106261.

Yagüe Perales, R. (2002). Rural tourism in Spain. *Annals of Tourism Research*, 29, 1101–1110.

DATOUR LAB 360: LABORATORIO DE INTELIGENCIA TURÍSTICA PARA LA TRANSFORMACIÓN DIGITAL, LA SOSTENIBILIDAD Y LA INNOVACIÓN EN DESTINOS

CONVERTIMOS DATOS EN VALOR PARA UN TURISMO MÁS INTELIGENTE

TAMIA BELEN BOADA CHICO
DAHIANA VICENTE GONZÁLEZ
ANA MARÍA ZAMORA ORTIZ
Universitat Politècnica de València

TEMÁTICA: Tecnología-Plataformas digitales

RESUMEN: Este trabajo presenta el diseño de *DATOUR LAB 360*, una propuesta de laboratorio de inteligencia turística orientada a transformar datos multifuente en conocimiento estratégico para apoyar una toma de decisiones más sostenible, eficiente y participativa en los destinos turísticos. El laboratorio, concebido con una estructura modular, combina tecnologías de análisis avanzado, simulación de escenarios, cocreación de soluciones y gobernanza colaborativa, lo que permite anticipar impactos y validar políticas antes de su implementación. La propuesta se enmarca en los principios del modelo de Destino Turístico Inteligente (DTI) y en los Objetivos de Desarrollo Sostenible (ODS), integrando dimensiones técnicas, institucionales y sociales. Como aplicación inicial, se plantea su despliegue en el municipio de Altea. El proyecto sienta las bases para fases posteriores de validación, implementación y escalabilidad territorial.

Palabras clave: inteligencia turística, datos multifuente, gobernanza participativa, innovación territorial, sostenibilidad turística.

ABSTRACT: This paper presents the design of DATOUR LAB 360, a tourism intelligence laboratory aimed at transforming multi-source data into strategic knowledge to support more sustainable, efficient, and participatory decision-making in tourist destinations. Conceived as a modular structure, the laboratory integrates advanced analytics, scenario simulation, co-creation of solutions, and collaborative governance, enabling the anticipation of impacts and the validation of policies prior to implementation. The proposal is framed within the Smart Tourist Destination (STD) model and the Sustainable Development Goals (SDGs), combining technical, institutional, and social dimensions. As an initial application, Altea is proposed as a pilot site. The project lays the foundations for subsequent phases of validation, implementation, and territorial scalability.

Keywords: tourism intelligence, multi-source data, participatory governance, territorial innovation, tourism sustainability.

1. INTRODUCCIÓN

En los últimos años, los destinos turísticos han tenido que adaptarse a un entorno marcado por una creciente complejidad, competitividad y digitalización. En este contexto, la toma de decisiones no puede depender únicamente de la intuición o de tendencias generalizadas, sino que requiere herramientas capaces de interpretar la realidad territorial en tiempo real y anticipar escenarios futuros con mayor fiabilidad (Gretzel et al., 2015).

Si bien muchos territorios ya recogen información desde diversas fuentes como sensores urbanos, redes sociales, plataformas de movilidad o registros administrativos, en la práctica estos datos suelen estar fragmentados, no interoperan entre sí o no se analizan con enfoque estratégico. Esta realidad da lugar a una paradoja frecuente: existe abundancia de datos, pero escasa inteligencia aplicada (OECD, 2020; González-Reverté, 2019). La falta de estructuras internas y capacidades técnicas impide que dicha información se traduzca en acciones concretas y contextualizadas.

Con el objetivo de responder a esta problemática, surge *DATOUR LAB 360*, una propuesta que plantea la creación de un laboratorio especializado en inteligencia turística. Este laboratorio funcionará como un espacio de experimentación en el que los datos no solo se recopilan y analizan, sino que se utilizan para simular escenarios, validar hipótesis y testar soluciones antes de aplicarlas al territorio. Este enfoque permite reducir el margen de error, optimizar recursos y garantizar que las políticas sean pertinentes y sostenibles (UNWTO, 2022).

El laboratorio se concibe como una plataforma colaborativa e interdisciplinaria que involucra a administraciones públicas, empresas, universidades y ciudadanía, integrando principios de gobernanza participativa y alineándose con los Objetivos de Desarrollo Sostenible (ODS) y las normas ISO de turismo sostenible (SEGITTUR, 2023; UNE, 2021). Su visión impulsa un modelo de desarrollo turístico que combina tecnología, sostenibilidad e inclusión social.

La iniciativa se enmarca, además, dentro de un proceso de transformación más amplio que afecta al turismo global. El modelo de Destino Turístico Inteligente (DTI), respaldado por organismos internacionales, impulsa el uso de tecnologías como el big data, la inteligencia artificial, los sensores IoT o la realidad aumentada para mejorar la gestión, la planificación estratégica y la experiencia del visitante (Buhalis & Amaranggana, 2015; European Commission, 2023).

Sin embargo, la integración efectiva de estas herramientas sigue dependiendo de factores como la capacidad técnica local, la coordinación entre actores y la voluntad política para fundamentar las decisiones en evidencia. En muchos destinos de tamaño medio en España, América Latina y Europa persisten debilidades como la falta de estructuras de análisis, la escasa interoperabilidad de sistemas o la dependencia de consultoras externas. Estas limitaciones obstaculizan la consolidación de estrategias integradas de inteligencia territorial, tal como señalan Luque et al. (2015), quienes subrayan la necesidad de alinear la innovación tecnológica con estructuras institucionales sólidas y capacidades locales.

Ante este panorama, *DATOUR LAB 360* se propone como una solución integral que combina análisis avanzado, experimentación aplicada y transferencia de conocimiento. Su propósito es facilitar una gobernanza turística basada en datos, promoviendo decisiones más sostenibles, contextualizadas y adaptadas a los desafíos contemporáneos del sector.

2. OBJETIVOS

El presente proyecto tiene como **objetivo general** diseñar un laboratorio de inteligencia turística que funcione como una infraestructura de análisis, simulación y validación de soluciones estratégicas, orientada a transformar datos multifuente en conocimiento útil para una gestión turística más eficiente, sostenible, participativa y tecnológicamente avanzada.

Para alcanzar este propósito, se plantean los siguientes **objetivos específicos**:

a) Estructurar un modelo conceptual de laboratorio de inteligencia turística, basado en componentes tecnológicos, analíticos, experimentales y formativos, adaptable a distintos perfiles de destino.

b) Definir una arquitectura de datos interoperable, segura y ética, que articule información procedente de fuentes públicas, privadas y sensoriales, bajo criterios de calidad, anonimización y relevancia territorial.

c) Diseñar los módulos funcionales del laboratorio, incluyendo herramientas de análisis predictivo, simulación de escenarios, validación de políticas y formulación de soluciones orientadas a la sostenibilidad turística.

d) Establecer un modelo de gobernanza colaborativa, que contemple la participación activa del sector público, privado, académico y ciudadano en la toma de decisiones informadas por datos.

e) Proponer una hoja de ruta metodológica para su futura implementación, con fases escalonadas, indicadores de evaluación y condiciones de replicabilidad en distintos contextos turísticos.

3. MARCO TEÓRICO

Este apartado presenta los fundamentos teóricos que sustentan la propuesta *DATOUR LAB 360,* situándola en la intersección entre la transformación digital del turismo, la inteligencia territorial y los modelos de gobernanza colaborativa. En un escenario marcado por la creciente disponibilidad de datos, los retos de sostenibilidad y la necesidad de una toma de decisiones más eficaz, el proyecto se plantea como una infraestructura innovadora capaz de anticipar, interpretar y responder a los desafíos de los destinos turísticos contemporáneos.

3.1. Justificación de la creación del laboratorio

El concepto de turismo inteligente ha ganado relevancia como respuesta a las limitaciones de los modelos tradicionales de gestión, especialmente en un entorno caracterizado por el aumento exponencial de datos disponibles. A pesar de que muchos destinos cuentan con herramientas tecnológicas, sensores, plataformas digitales y registros administrativos, estos recursos no siempre se traducen en conocimiento estratégico para la acción (González y López, 2019; OECD, 2020).

En este contexto, *DATOUR LAB 360* se presenta como una solución para superar esta brecha estructural. Su finalidad va más allá de la observación de tendencias que busca generar hipótesis, simular escenarios, anticipar impactos y validar políticas antes de su implementación definitiva. Esta lógica de experimentación controlada permite reducir el margen de error, optimizar recursos y adaptar las decisiones a las particularidades del territorio (Valencia-Arias et al., 2020).

El enfoque del laboratorio se encuentra alineado con el modelo de Destino Turístico Inteligente (DTI), impulsado en España por SEGITTUR, que promueve la integración de cinco ejes fundamentales: tecnología, innovación, accesibilidad, sostenibilidad y gobernanza (SEGITTUR, 2025; Rucci et al., 2025). No obstante, diversos estudios advierten que, si bien este modelo ha logrado posicionar a España como referente internacional, sigue existiendo una carencia de estructuras locales estables que garanticen una gestión basada en inteligencia territorial (Flores et al., 2018).

3.2. Contribución al territorio y al ecosistema turístico

El laboratorio se concibe como un catalizador de transformación territorial, con capacidad para generar impactos positivos en cinco dimensiones clave. En el ámbito económico, contribuye a mejorar la eficiencia del gasto público, dinamiza el tejido productivo local y fomenta el empleo cualificado vinculado a la tecnología y la innovación (González y López, 2019). Desde una perspectiva ambiental, permite evaluar el impacto real del turismo sobre los recursos naturales, facilitando el diseño de políticas correctoras sostenibles. En lo social, contribuye a mitigar efectos negativos como la congestión o la sobrecarga de servicios, elevando la calidad de vida de los residentes.

A nivel competitivo, *DATOUR LAB 360* posiciona al destino como actor de referencia en turismo inteligente, con capacidad para adaptarse a nuevos contextos y exigencias del mercado. Finalmente, desde una dimensión formativa, fortalece las competencias locales mediante la capacitación técnica, la transferencia de conocimiento y la creación de redes con instituciones académicas y centros de innovación (Blasco y Cuevas, 2020; SEGITTUR, 2025).

Además, la propuesta se enmarca en una visión de inteligencia territorial que no se limita al uso de tecnología, sino que incorpora la capacidad del territorio para organizarse, interpretar su información interna y orientar el desarrollo en función de sus recursos y objetivos (Flores et al., 2018). Esta perspectiva integra el dato, la comunidad y la gobernanza en un sistema articulado de corresponsabilidad y mejora continua.

3.3. Brechas estructurales que busca resolver

El análisis del estado actual de los destinos turísticos revela cuatro brechas estructurales que obstaculizan el avance hacia modelos verdaderamente inteligentes. La primera es la brecha de análisis, derivada de la ausencia de equipos técnicos o metodologías capaces de transformar datos brutos en conocimiento útil (OECD, 2020). Le sigue la brecha de gobernanza, que se expresa en la fragmentación institucional, la duplicidad de esfuerzos y la escasa coordinación entre los diferentes actores del ecosistema turístico (Blasco y Cuevas, 2020).

En tercer lugar, se identifica una brecha de talento, vinculada a la dependencia de asesorías externas y la limitada inversión en capacidades locales. Finalmente, existe una brecha de innovación aplicada, ya que en muchos casos se adoptan soluciones tecnológicas sin realizar pruebas previas o sin verificar su compatibilidad con las dinámicas del territorio (Flores et al., 2018; Li et al., 2018).

Ante estas limitaciones, el laboratorio plantea una propuesta integral que articula tecnologías emergentes, análisis predictivo, visualización avanzada y una estructura de gobernanza colaborativa. Este modelo permite no solo generar inteligencia territorial útil, sino también transferir conocimiento, escalar soluciones y crear una base replicable para otros destinos (Rucci et al., 2025).

3.4. Comparación con plataformas y consultoras existentes

En el ecosistema actual de inteligencia turística, existen empresas privadas que ofrecen servicios de consultoría, análisis de datos y desarrollo tecnológico para destinos cuya labor ha sido clave para introducir soluciones de digitalización, visualización de indicadores turísticos, diseño de planes estratégicos y gestión basada en datos. Estas consultoras cuentan con equipos técnicos especializados, metodologías consolidadas y presencia en proyectos vinculados al modelo de Destino Turístico Inteligente promovido por SEGITTUR.

No obstante, el papel que desempeñan estas entidades suele estar enfocado en la prestación de servicios externos, sin una transferencia estructural de capacidades hacia los propios territorios. Tal como señala Ivars Baidal y Vera Rebollo (2019), la dependencia de consultorías externas puede generar soluciones desconectadas del contexto local, limitar la apropiación institucional de los datos y obstaculizar procesos de aprendizaje organizacional sostenido.

Además, aunque estas firmas integran herramientas como dashboards, análisis de sentimiento o visualización de flujos turísticos, su modelo de trabajo tiende a ser puntual o enfocado en la entrega de productos finales, sin crear espacios de experimentación continuada, ni estructuras permanentes de inteligencia territorial.

3.5. Aportación diferencial

Frente a este panorama, *DATOUR LAB 360* introduce un enfoque sustancialmente diferente. En lugar de funcionar como una consultora externa, se plantea como un laboratorio permanente de inteligencia turística, integrado dentro del propio ecosistema del destino. Su objetivo no es ofrecer diagnósticos cerrados, sino construir capacidades internas, fomentar la experimentación aplicada y generar una cultura de toma de decisiones basada en evidencia, ética y colaboración.

Las principales diferencias pueden resumirse en los siguientes ejes:

- **Carácter experimental**: espacio vivo de simulación, validación y prueba de políticas antes de su implementación real.
- **Enfoque colaborativo y de código abierto**: co-creación de soluciones con actores locales, integrando universidades, administración pública, ciudadanía y empresas tecnológicas del entorno.
- **Formación y transferencia de conocimiento**: formación continua y la generación de talento local en áreas clave como la analítica de datos, la inteligencia artificial o la sostenibilidad turística.
- **Gobernanza distribuida**: gobernanza multinivel, con mecanismos de participación, rendición de cuentas y transparencia institucional.
- **Replicabilidad y escalabilidad**: diseño modular adaptable a distintos contextos territoriales, desde municipios hasta regiones turísticas, fomentando la creación de una red descentralizada de laboratorios interconectados.

En definitiva, se propone una innovación institucional orientada a la sostenibilidad, el fortalecimiento de capacidades locales y la democratización de la inteligencia territorial.

4. METODOLOGÍA

La implementación de *DATOUR LAB 360* se basa en un enfoque metodológico progresivo, centrado en la transformación de datos en soluciones accionables para la gestión turística. Este enfoque articula infraestructuras tecnológicas, alianzas intersectoriales, formación de talento local y el desarrollo de herramientas digitales orientadas a la toma de decisiones.

La premisa fundamental es que el dato, por sí solo, no genera inteligencia: debe ser procesado, contextualizado y aplicado en escenarios reales para que contribuya a una planificación turística más eficaz, sostenible y adaptable.

4.1. Fases de implementación

El despliegue del laboratorio se realizará en tres fases sucesivas, cada una con objetivos específicos y acciones escalables que faciliten su adaptación a distintos contextos territoriales:

Fase 1 – Activación (0-12 meses):

a) Habilitación del espacio físico y digital del laboratorio.

b) Selección y contratación del equipo técnico multidisciplinar (analistas de datos, expertos en turismo, programadores, gestores territoriales).

c) Integración inicial de datos provenientes de fuentes públicas y privadas.

d) Establecimiento de convenios de colaboración con universidades, administraciones públicas y empresas tecnológicas.

Fase 2 – Consolidación (12-36 meses):

a) Desarrollo de dashboards interactivos, mapas dinámicos y sistemas de visualización.

b) Implementación de proyectos piloto mediante inteligencia artificial y modelos predictivos.

c) Análisis de impacto turístico basado en datos históricos y en tiempo real.

d) Diseño e impartición de formación especializada para técnicos y agentes locales.

Fase 3 – Innovación y Escalabilidad (36-60 meses):

a) Incorporación de gemelos digitales para simular escenarios turísticos complejos.

b) Extensión del modelo a otros municipios o regiones con características similares.

c) Desarrollo de herramientas de ayuda a la decisión en tiempo real, orientadas a la gestión pública y al sector empresarial.

4.2. Tipología y fuentes de datos

El laboratorio se regirá por una lógica multifuente e integrada, reuniendo información de naturaleza diversa bajo criterios de interoperabilidad y ética del dato. Las principales fuentes serán:

a) **Fuentes públicas:**

- Instituto Nacional de Estadística (INE), SEGITTUR, plataformas Smart Destination.
- Registros municipales de movilidad, residuos, consumo energético, tráfico.
- Información medioambiental (AEMET, SIG, sensores climáticos).

b) **Fuentes privadas:**

- Datos anonimizados de telefonía móvil (URBO, operadores telco).
- Plataformas de reservas, redes sociales, encuestas digitales.
- Transacciones comerciales y valoraciones online.

c) **Fuentes sensoriales (IoT):**

- Sensores de conteo peatonal, tráfico, calidad ambiental y aforos.
- Cámaras con análisis de comportamiento (anonimizado).
- Dispositivos instalados en puntos turísticos estratégicos (playas, senderos, cascos históricos).

4.3. Garantía de calidad del dato

Para garantizar la fiabilidad y relevancia de la información utilizada, se aplicará un protocolo técnico de validación de datos que contemplará la evaluación cruzada entre fuentes, la eliminación de duplicidades y errores, así como el análisis de la consistencia, actualidad y trazabilidad de los registros. Este proceso asegurará que los datos sean verificables, contextualizados y útiles para la toma de decisiones. Asimismo, se adoptarán criterios estrictos de anonimización y protección de la privacidad, en cumplimiento con el Reglamento General de Protección de Datos (RGPD), priorizando siempre el uso de información no personal o agregada para fines analíticos.

4.4. Tecnologías aplicadas

El funcionamiento de *DATOUR LAB 360* se apoyará en tecnologías avanzadas adaptadas a la realidad local y al tipo de datos gestionados:

a) **Big Data & Analytics:** procesamiento y análisis masivo de datos estructurados y no estructurados en tiempo real.

b) **Inteligencia Artificial:** predicción de escenarios, análisis de impacto, agrupación de perfiles turísticos y detección de patrones.

c) **Internet of Things (IoT):** captación continua de datos mediante sensores distribuidos en el territorio.

d) **GIS (Sistemas de Información Geográfica):** representación visual, análisis espacial, mapas de calor, rutas críticas.

e) **Business Intelligence (BI):** paneles de control interactivos y visualización adaptada a cada perfil usuario (gestores públicos, ciudadanía, empresas).

4.5. Actores implicados y alianzas estratégicas

DATOUR LAB 360 se configura como una iniciativa articuladora de múltiples niveles institucionales y sectores estratégicos, concebida desde una lógica de cooperación horizontal y corresponsabilidad territorial. Su implementación involucra activamente a la administración pública, incluyendo gobiernos municipales, oficinas de turismo, áreas de Smart City, diputaciones y organismos estatales como SEGITTUR, al sector privado, donde destacan empresas tecnológicas, proveedores de datos, asociaciones empresariales y clústeres turísticos, y al ámbito académico, a través de universidades, centros de innovación y programas de posgrado especializados en turismo, sostenibilidad e inteligencia territorial. A ello se suma la participación del tercer sector y de la ciudadanía organizada, mediante ONG locales, plataformas de escucha activa y consejos vecinales. Esta gobernanza multinivel no solo garantiza legitimidad social y técnica, sino que refuerza la sostenibilidad del laboratorio a largo plazo. En definitiva, el éxito del proyecto dependerá del grado de implicación, confianza y alineación entre los actores, orientándose a consolidar un modelo de gestión turística basado en inteligencia distribuida, ética y adaptativa.

5. PROPUESTA

La propuesta consiste en el desarrollo de un laboratorio modular, interdisciplinario y replicable, concebido como una infraestructura de innovación orientada a transformar datos turísticos en soluciones estratégicas mediante el análisis avanzado, la simulación prospectiva y la cocreación con actores del territorio. A diferencia de otros modelos, este laboratorio no se limita a la recolección de datos, sino que opera como un espacio real de experimentación, en el que las decisiones pueden ser modeladas y validadas antes de su implementación.

La estructura del laboratorio se organiza en seis componentes funcionales que abarcan todo el ciclo de inteligencia turística: desde la captación y procesamiento de información hasta la formulación de soluciones sostenibles, la transferencia de conocimiento y la coordinación multinivel. A continuación, se describen sus elementos esenciales.

5.1. Componentes del Laboratorio

DATOUR LAB 360 se compone de módulos interconectados, flexibles y adaptables a distintos tipos de destinos turísticos (urbanos, rurales, costeros, patrimoniales), lo que permite su implementación tanto a escala local como regional.

a) **Módulo de Captura y Recolección de Datos**: Responsable de la obtención continua de información procedente de fuentes públicas, privadas y sensoriales. Se garantiza la aplicación de protocolos de validación, anonimización y cumplimiento normativo conforme al RGPD y la LOPDGDD.

b) **Módulo de Análisis y Procesamiento Inteligente**: Núcleo analítico del laboratorio. Integra tecnologías de Big Data, inteligencia artificial, modelos predictivos y sistemas de visualización interactiva (dashboards, mapas dinámicos), permitiendo el análisis de patrones y escenarios.

c) **Módulo de Experimentación y Validación de Soluciones**: Espacio para la simulación de políticas, intervenciones o servicios. Utiliza herramientas como gemelos digitales, pruebas A/B y simuladores turísticos para evaluar impactos y ajustar propuestas de manera anticipada.

d) **Módulo de Soluciones Sostenibles y Experiencias Turísticas**: Traduce los hallazgos analíticos en acciones concretas, como rutas de movilidad sostenible, redistribución de flujos turísticos, activación de economía circular y mejora de servicios digitales, en línea con los ODS y las normas ISO.

e) **Módulo de Formación, Innovación y Transferencia de Conocimiento**: Promueve la capacitación técnica, la producción de recursos abiertos, la colaboración con universidades y la integración del laboratorio en redes de turismo inteligente a nivel nacional e internacional.

f) **Módulo de Gobernanza y Coordinación Multinivel**: Asegura el funcionamiento sistémico y participativo mediante estructuras de gobernanza compartida, estándares de interoperabilidad, evaluación por indicadores y mecanismos de transparencia y participación ciudadana.

5.2. Casos de Uso o Aplicaciones Piloto

DATOUR LAB 360 puede desplegarse en contextos concretos mediante aplicaciones piloto que respondan a problemas territoriales identificados. Algunos ejemplos incluyen:

a) Optimización de flujos turísticos en espacios sensibles.

b) Análisis de la huella de carbono generada por la actividad turística.

c) Predicción de estacionalidad y gestión anticipada de servicios.

d) Reequilibrio geográfico del gasto turístico.

e) Desarrollo de apps para senderismo con realidad aumentada.

f) Gestión inteligente del aparcamiento en zonas de alta demanda.

5.3. Ejemplo de caso de aplicación en Altea

La ciudad de Altea, reconocida por su valor patrimonial, su atractivo costero y su interés por la innovación turística, representa un entorno idóneo para la aplicación piloto de *DATOUR LAB 360*. Este municipio dispone de condiciones técnicas y voluntad institucional para avanzar hacia una gobernanza turística basada en datos. No obstante, enfrenta desafíos significativos como la estacionalidad, la saturación de zonas históricas, la desigual distribución de visitantes y la fragmentación de fuentes de información.

El laboratorio podría desplegarse en Altea como piloto temprano, centrado en: (1) la recolección y análisis de flujos turísticos mediante sensores y datos de telefonía; (2) el desarrollo de modelos predictivos para la gestión de la capacidad de carga en el casco antiguo; (3) la simulación de rutas alternativas menos saturadas; (4) la mejora de sistemas de visualización para la toma de decisiones municipales; y (5) la puesta en marcha de talleres formativos con actores locales. Este despliegue no solo aportaría soluciones concretas a los retos actuales del destino, sino que permitiría validar la replicabilidad del modelo en otros municipios de características similares.

Un aspecto clave que distingue esta propuesta es su enfoque en el fortalecimiento del capital humano local. Más allá de instalar una infraestructura tecnológica avanzada, el laboratorio busca convertirse en un centro de formación, atracción y retención de talento especializado en gestión turística basada en datos. Esta visión responde a una necesidad identificada en muchos destinos inteligentes: la dependencia estructural de consultoras externas, que si bien aportan conocimiento técnico, no garantizan la sostenibilidad ni la apropiación local del sistema. En este sentido, el laboratorio no solo funcionaría como una oficina técnica, sino como un espacio de innovación abierta que articule universidades, instituciones públicas, empresas locales y ciudadanía, generando capacidades propias en Altea. Esto permite no solo resolver problemas del presente, sino desarrollar una comunidad preparada para anticipar y liderar los desafíos del futuro.

Esta propuesta surge también gracias a la colaboración y apertura del equipo técnico municipal de Altea, quienes, en el marco de una investigación desarrollada por estudiantes del Máster en Inteligencia Turística de la Universidad Politécnica de Valencia, compartieron de forma transparente los retos que enfrentan en la gestión de los datos turísticos. Durante las entrevistas realizadas, expresaron de forma explícita: "Tenemos muchos datos, pero no sabemos qué hacer con ellos".

Esta declaración, lejos de evidenciar una carencia, reafirma la pertinencia de DATOUR LAB 360 como una respuesta estructurada y colaborativa, orientada a interpretar, integrar y dar valor a los datos existentes. Además, pone de relieve la importancia de crear capacidades locales para el análisis y la aplicación de la información, avanzando hacia una infraestructura de gobernanza inteligente diseñada desde y para el territorio.

6. DISCUSIÓN

La implementación de un laboratorio como *DATOUR LAB 360* no solo implica el desarrollo de una arquitectura técnica y organizativa sólida, sino también una reflexión crítica sobre su impacto real en el territorio. Esta sección aborda los efectos esperados del proyecto desde una perspectiva multidimensional y propone mecanismos de evaluación rigurosa que garanticen su mejora continua y sostenibilidad en el tiempo. A través de indicadores concretos y criterios de medición estructurados, se busca evidenciar cómo esta infraestructura puede contribuir a consolidar un modelo de gestión turística más eficaz, inclusivo, sostenible y basado en evidencia. En este sentido, la discusión no se limita a anticipar resultados, sino que plantea también condiciones de éxito, factores habilitantes y aprendizajes institucionales clave para su futura replicabilidad.

6.1. Evaluación de impacto

La evaluación de impacto constituye un eje fundamental para garantizar que *DATOUR LAB 360* no se limite a generar datos, sino que los traduzca en transformaciones concretas y medibles. Para ello, se han definido indicadores clave de rendimiento (KPI) que permitirán monitorear los avances del proyecto a lo largo de sus fases de desarrollo. Estos indicadores se estructuran en torno a cinco áreas estratégicas: económica, ambiental, social, tecnológica y formativa.

A continuación, se presentan los KPIs propuestos, con sus respectivas unidades de medida, frecuencias de evaluación y objetivos tentativos.

Área	Indicador Clave (KPI)	Unidad de Medida	Frecuencia	Proyección estimada (a validar en fase piloto)
Económico	% de aumento del gasto turístico en zonas no tradicionales	%	Semestral	Entre 5 % y 8 % en 3 años
	Proyectos turísticos optimizados mediante uso de datos	Nº	Anual	Entre 5 y 10 proyectos

Área	Indicador Clave (KPI)	Unidad de Medida	Frecuencia	Proyección estimada (a validar en fase piloto)
Ambiental	Reducción de huella de carbono turística	Ton CO_2 equivalente	Anual	Hasta 10 % de reducción en 5 años
	Rutas sostenibles creadas o rediseñadas	Nº	Anual	2–4 rutas nuevas/ rediseñadas
Social	Nivel de satisfacción de residentes con la gestión turística	Encuesta (1–10)	Anual	≥7.5/10
	Participación ciudadana en decisiones basadas en datos	Nº de personas / procesos	Anual	Entre 150 y 250 participantes
Tecnológico	Dashboards desarrollados y en uso activo	Nº	Semestral	3–5 paneles
	Datos integrados de fuentes públicas/ privadas	Nº de fuentes interoperables	Trimestral	6–10 fuentes
Formación / Transferencia	Personas formadas en turismo inteligente y datos	Nº	Anual	75–120 personas
	Manuales, visualizaciones y recursos generados	Nº de materiales	Anual	10–15 recursos

Nota: *Las cifras aquí presentadas constituyen una proyección estimada elaborada durante la fase de diseño. Los valores definitivos serán definidos en función de los resultados obtenidos durante el despliegue piloto del laboratorio.*

6.2. Medición de impacto multidimensional

El impacto de *DATOUR LAB 360* será evaluado desde una perspectiva integral que abarca las principales dimensiones estratégicas del desarrollo turístico. En el plano económico, se proyecta una mejora significativa en la eficiencia del gasto público, un mayor retorno económico local vinculado a decisiones basadas en datos y una reducción sustancial de los costos derivados de intervenciones poco efectivas o mal fundamentadas. Desde el enfoque ambiental, el laboratorio aspira a contribuir a la reducción de la huella ecológica de la actividad turística, mediante la promoción de modelos de movilidad sostenible, la redistribución inteligente de flujos de visitantes y la protección de entornos naturales vulnerables. En cuanto a la dimensión social, se prevé un aumento en la percepción positiva del turismo por parte de la ciudadanía, acompañado de una mayor participación de colectivos históricamente menos representados, así como una disminución de los conflictos socio-turísticos derivados de la saturación o el uso intensivo del espacio público. Finalmente, en el ámbito tecnológico e institucional, fomentará el fortalecimiento de las capacidades analíticas del territorio, mejorará la interoperabilidad entre sistemas y organismos, y consolidará una cultura organizacional orientada a la evidencia, que facilite una toma de decisiones más transparente, fundamentada y adaptativa.

6.3. Mecanismos de Monitoreo y Mejora Continua

Para garantizar una adaptación constante a los contextos cambiantes, así como la incorporación progresiva de aprendizajes institucionales, se contempla una serie de mecanismos de seguimiento que se desplegarán de manera escalonada a lo largo de las fases de implementación. Estos mecanismos permitirán evaluar la eficacia del laboratorio en tiempo real, introducir mejoras operativas y fortalecer su sostenibilidad en el largo plazo.

a) **Creación de un comité técnico de seguimiento**, con representación del sector público, privado, académico y ciudadanía, encargado de supervisar el cumplimiento de los hitos y fomentar la corresponsabilidad institucional. *(Fase 1: Planificación y Activación)*

b) **Evaluaciones trimestrales con informes ejecutivos**, para monitorear avances y detectar desviaciones en la ejecución del proyecto. *(Desde Fase 2: Implementación y Consolidación)*

c) **Sistema de alertas dinámicas basadas en KPIs**, diseñado para activar ajustes operativos en tiempo real en función del comportamiento de los indicadores clave. *(Desde Fase 2: Implementación y Consolidación)*

d) **Diseño y aplicación de encuestas periódicas** dirigidas a funcionarios, empresas, residentes y turistas, orientadas a recoger retroalimentación sobre el funcionamiento del laboratorio. La metodología será desarrollada durante la fase inicial. *(Diseño en Fase 1; aplicación desde Fase 2)*

e) **Publicación de informes abiertos y visualizaciones accesibles**, como estrategia de transparencia y rendición de cuentas hacia los distintos actores del ecosistema turístico. *(Desde Fase 2 y mantenido en Fase 3)*

f) **Ajustes metodológicos continuos**, integrando aprendizajes derivados de la práctica y la retroalimentación de los usuarios, en una lógica de mejora incremental. *(Durante Fase 2 y reforzado en Fase 3: Evaluación e Innovación)*

7. CONCLUSIONES Y LÍNEAS FUTURAS

El diseño de DATOUR LAB 360 constituye una propuesta estratégica orientada a transformar los procesos de gestión turística a través del uso inteligente de los datos. Concebido como un laboratorio modular, replicable y articulado con el territorio, su objetivo es generar conocimiento útil a partir de información fragmentada, promoviendo una toma de decisiones basada en evidencia, sostenibilidad e inclusión. A través de una estructura que integra análisis avanzado, simulación prospectiva y cocreación con actores locales, el laboratorio aborda de forma integral los desafíos que enfrentan hoy los destinos turísticos en contextos crecientemente digitales y cambiantes.

Uno de los principales aportes de esta propuesta reside en su capacidad para adaptarse a diferentes escalas y contextos, así como en su enfoque orientado al fortalecimiento de capacidades locales. Más que importar soluciones externas, DATOUR LAB 360 plantea un modelo de gobernanza participativa que fomenta la apropiación territorial del dato, el desarrollo de talento especializado y la innovación aplicada desde una lógica colaborativa. Esta perspectiva lo sitúa en consonancia con los principios del modelo de Destino Turístico Inteligente promovido por SEGITTUR y los Objetivos de Desarrollo Sostenible, aportando herramientas concretas para una planificación más resiliente, eficaz y centrada en las personas.

Aunque el laboratorio se encuentra actualmente en fase de formulación, la definición metodológica alcanzada, demuestran que se trata de una propuesta madura, técnica y conceptualmente sólida. La identificación de componentes funcionales claros, acompañados de posibles casos de uso y mecanismos de evaluación de impacto, permite visualizar su capacidad de generar resultados tangibles y medibles una vez puesto en funcionamiento.

Como línea futura, se plantea avanzar hacia la implementación de una fase piloto que permita validar en campo los módulos diseñados y su capacidad para incidir positivamente en los procesos de planificación, gestión y evaluación turística. En paralelo, será clave continuar fortaleciendo alianzas institucionales y académicas, así como generar condiciones para la consolidación de una red de laboratorios interterritoriales que compartan aprendizajes, metodologías y datos. Esta visión de inteligencia turística distribuida representa no solo una innovación metodológica, sino también un compromiso con un modelo de desarrollo más justo, colaborativo y sostenible.

8. REFERENCIAS

Blasco J y Cuevas C (2020): *Organismo inteligente para la toma de decisiones en el destino.* Instituto Valenciano de Tecnologías Turísticas (INVAT-TUR).

Buhalis D y Amaranggana A (2015): "Smart tourism destinations: Enhancing tourism experience through personalization of services". En *Information and Communication Technologies in Tourism 2015*, 377–389. Springer.

Flores Ruiz D, Perogil Burgos J y Miedes Ugarte B (2018): "¿Destinos turísticos inteligentes o territorios inteligentes? Estudios de casos en España". *Revista de Estudios Regionales*, 113, 193–219.

González J y López J (2019): "Inteligencia turística para competir: el user generated content y la reputación on-line de los establecimientos de alojamiento y hospedaje de Bogotá (Colombia)". *International Journal of Information Systems and Software Engineering for Big Companies*, 6(2), 135–144.

González-Reverté F (2019): "Building sustainable smart destinations: An approach based on the development of Spanish smart tourism plans". *Sustainability*, 11(23), 6874.

Gretzel U, Sigala M, Xiang Z y Koo C (2015): "Smart tourism: Foundations and developments". *Electronic Markets*, 25(3), 179–188.

Ivars Baidal, J. A. y Vera Rebollo, J. F. (2019): "Planificación turística en España. De los paradigmas tradicionales a los nuevos enfoques: planificación turística inteligente". *Boletín de la Asociación Española de Geografía (BAGE)*, 82, 1–27.

Li J, Xu L, Tang L y Wang S (2018): "Big data in tourism research: A literature review". *Tourism Management*, 68, 301–323.

Luque AM, Zayas B y Caro JL (2015): "Los destinos turísticos inteligentes en el marco de la inteligencia territorial: conflictos y oportunidades". *Investigaciones Turísticas*, 10, 1–25.

OECD (2020): *OECD Tourism Trends and Policies 2020.* OECD Publishing. Paris.

Rucci AC, Isoardi AE y Viletto P (2025): "Expansión del modelo español de destinos turísticos inteligentes hacia ciudades y destinos de América Latina". *ICE. Revista de Economía,* 938, 59–62.

SEGITTUR (2023): *Catálogo de Soluciones Tecnológicas para Destinos Turísticos Inteligentes 2023.* SEGITTUR. Madrid.

UNE (2021): *Norma UNE 178501: Sistema de gestión de los destinos turísticos inteligentes.* AENOR.

Valencia-Arias A, Ocampo-Osorio C, Quiroz-Fabra J, Garcés-Giraldo LF y Valencia J (2020): "Research trends in augmented reality in tourism: A bibliometric analysis". *RISTI-Revista Ibérica de Sistemas e Tecnologias de Informação,* 36, 229–242.

PÁGINAS WEB

European Commission (2023): *Towards a Common European Tourism Data Space: Boosting data sharing and innovation across the tourism ecosystem.* Disponible en: https://eur-lex.europa.eu/legal-content/EN/TXT/PDF/?uri=CELEX:52023XC0726(01)

SEGITTUR (2025): *Plataforma Inteligente de Destinos.* Disponible en: https://www.segittur.es/plataforma-inteligente/proyectos-plataforma-inteligente/plataforma-inteligente-de-destinos/

UNWTO (2022): *International tourism consolidates strong recovery amidst growing challenges.* Disponible en: https://www.unwto.org/news/international-tourism-consolidates-strong-recovery-admidst-growing-challenges

GESTIÓN SOSTENIBLE DE LA MOVILIDAD TURÍSTICA EN ESPACIOS NATURALES PROTEGIDOS: EL CASO DE L'ALBUFERA Y LA PLATAFORMA CONNECTA VALÈNCIA

Rosa Roig
Luisa Andreu
José Mª Pavía
Universitat de València

RESUMEN: La movilidad turística en espacios naturales protegidos plantea desafíos crecientes para la sostenibilidad de los destinos, especialmente durante los periodos de alta afluencia como los puentes festivos. Esta comunicación analiza los patrones espaciales y temporales de movilidad turística en el Parque Natural de L'Albufera (València), un recurso natural emblemático del destino turístico urbano, mediante el uso de datos masivos captados por sensores Wi-Fi instalados en el marco del proyecto CONNECTA, impulsado por la Diputació de València y financiado por fondos Next Generation. A través de una metodología cuantitativa basada en estadística descriptiva, se examinan 137.530 registros de conexión correspondientes a cuatro periodos clave del segundo semestre de 2024. Los resultados muestran una fuerte concentración de visitantes en determinadas zonas y franjas horarias, revelando patrones que pueden comprometer la sostenibilidad del ecosistema. Se discuten las implicaciones para una gestión turística inteligente e informada por datos, y se valora el potencial de estas herramientas para mejorar la planificación, redistribución de flujos y toma de decisiones en espacios de alta sensibilidad ecológica.

Palabras clave: movilidad turística; espacios naturales protegidos; sostenibilidad; Destino Turístico Inteligente (DTI); L'Albufera; gestión turística inteligente

ABSTRACT: Tourist mobility in protected natural areas poses growing challenges for the sustainability of destinations, especially during peak periods such as long holiday weekends. This paper analyzes the spatial and temporal patterns of tourist mobility in L'Albufera Natural Park (València), an emblematic natural asset of the urban tourism destination, using big data collected through Wi-Fi sensors installed within the framework of the CONNECTA project, promoted by the Diputació de València and funded by Next Generation funds. Through a quantitative methodology based on descriptive statistics, 137,530 connection records corresponding to four key periods in the second half of 2024 are examined. The results show a strong concentration of visitors in certain areas and time slots, revealing patterns that may compromise the sustainability of the ecosystem. The implications for smart, data-driven tourism management are discussed, and the potential of these tools to improve planning, flow redistribution, and decision-making in highly sensitive ecological areas is assessed.

Keywords: tourist mobility; protected natural areas; sustainability; Smart Tourism Destination (STD); L'Albufera; smart tourism management

1. INTRODUCCIÓN

La movilidad turística en espacios naturales protegidos plantea importantes desafíos para la sostenibilidad ambiental y la calidad de la experiencia turística (Buongiorno e Intini, 2021). En contextos de alta afluencia, como los fines de semana o los puentes festivos, estos territorios enfrentan una presión creciente sobre sus ecosistemas, infraestructuras y servicios (Rogowski, Zawilińska y Hibner, 2025). Esta situación exige nuevos enfoques de gestión que permitan equilibrar la conservación de los valores naturales con el uso público del territorio (Velmurugan, Thazhathethil y George, 2021).

En este contexto y en el ámbito provincial, la Diputació de València ha desarrollado CONNECTA, un proyecto pionero financiado mediante fondos europeos Next Generation, orientado a la gestión inteligente de los destinos turísticos de la provincia de València mediante la recopilación masiva de datos sobre movilidad, calidad ambiental, uso del espacio público y otros indicadores clave del territorio (https://connecta.dival.es/). Esta plataforma tecnológica ofrece información en tiempo real y se alinea con el modelo de Destino Turístico Inteligente (DTI) promovido por SEGITTUR, proporcionando así una base empírica sólida para la planificación estratégica basada en evidencia (SEGITTUR y Andrades, 2024).

Este estudio se inscribe en dicha iniciativa provincial y se circunscribe al caso del Parque Natural de L'Albufera, uno de los recursos naturales más emblemáticos del destino turístico ciudad de València. Este espacio natural protegido de alto valor ecológico está reconocido internacionalmente como humedal de importancia global y parte de la Red Natura 2000, lo que lo convierte en un enclave emblemático dentro del sistema de espacios naturales europeos, y en un laboratorio idóneo para estudiar los retos de la movilidad en destinos sensibles (Soria et al., 2021).

El presente estudio se enmarca en esta iniciativa y se centra en el Parque Natural de L'Albufera, uno de los principales recursos naturales del destino ciudad de València. Este espacio protegido destaca por su elevado valor ecológico, su proximidad a áreas urbanas densamente pobladas y su facilidad de acceso, factores que lo convierten en un destino turístico de alta demanda (Vizcaíno Estevan, 2024). La acumulación de visitantes en determinados momentos del año —especialmente durante puentes festivos— genera riesgos para la sostenibilidad del ecosistema y demanda nuevas herramientas de análisis y gestión.

La contribución del presente trabajo se centra en analizar los patrones espaciales y temporales de movilidad turística en el Parque Natural de L'Albufera durante los puentes festivos de 2024, a partir de datos empíricos generados por sensores Wi-Fi, con el fin de aportar evidencia útil para una gestión más sostenible e informada del uso turístico del espacio. Estos datos proceden de la plataforma CONNECTA-DIVAL. De manera específica, los objetivos de la investigación son dos: (i) observar y comparar la variación temporal y espacial de los flujos turísticos durante los principales puentes festivos del año 2024, y (ii) evaluar el potencial de los sistemas de monitorización en tiempo real como herramientas para una gobernanza más adaptativa y sostenible en espacios naturales.

2. MARCO CONCEPTUAL

2.1. Movilidad turística como reto para la sostenibilidad de los destinos

La movilidad turística representa uno de los principales retos para la sostenibilidad de los destinos, tanto urbanos como naturales. A diferencia de otras formas de movilidad cotidiana, la movilidad asociada al turismo presenta una naturaleza marcadamente estacional, irregular y concentrada, lo que genera presiones desproporcionadas sobre infraestructuras, servicios y ecosistemas en periodos muy concretos. Esta singularidad exige una aproximación específica desde las políticas de gestión del territorio y, en particular, desde una lógica de sostenibilidad y planificación estratégica.

Según la OMT y PNUD (2017), uno de los principales desafíos que enfrentan los destinos turísticos contemporáneos es precisamente la movilidad. La congestión, los impactos ambientales, la distribución desigual de visitantes y la presión sobre zonas sensibles son síntomas recurrentes de una movilidad mal gestionada. Este problema se agrava en espacios naturales protegidos, donde la afluencia masiva puede poner en riesgo los valores ecológicos que precisamente sustentan el atractivo turístico. Estudios recientes de Donici y Dumitras (2024) destacan que la planificación de la movilidad en parques naturales europeos requiere abordajes adaptativos que consideren tanto la estacionalidad como la vulnerabilidad del entorno.

La naturaleza episódica del turismo —vinculada a fines de semana, festivos o temporadas vacacionales— provoca picos de movilidad muy intensos que dificultan una respuesta adaptativa por parte de las administraciones. En este sentido, los puentes festivos constituyen un laboratorio privilegiado para analizar el comportamiento turístico bajo condiciones de alta presión. Entender estos patrones es clave para anticipar impactos y planificar medidas de mitigación que contribuyan al equilibrio entre disfrute, conservación y bienestar de las comunidades receptoras (Suárez Falcón y Álvarez García, 2016).

2.2. Gestión sostenible de destinos y el modelo DTI

En respuesta a estos retos, han emergido modelos de planificación estratégica basados en sostenibilidad y gobernanza inteligente. Entre ellos, el modelo de Destino Turístico Inteligente (DTI), promovido por la Secretaría de Estado de Turismo y desarrollado por SEGITTUR, ha identificado la movilidad como uno de sus cinco ejes estratégicos, junto con sostenibilidad, innovación, accesibilidad y tecnología (SEGITTUR, 2015).

Este enfoque se enmarca en una transformación más amplia de las políticas turísticas contemporáneas, que tienden a evolucionar desde una lógica predominantemente promocional hacia un modelo basado en datos, sostenibilidad y gobernanza pública. Según Roig (2024), esta transición responde a una necesidad creciente de gestionar los destinos de forma más integrada, considerando no solo los flujos de visitantes, sino también la capacidad de carga de los territorios, la resiliencia ecológica y el bienestar social de las comunidades receptoras.

En esta línea, El Archi et al. (2023), en una revisión sistemática, destacan cómo los modelos DTI han evolucionado hacia un enfoque multidimensional que combina eficiencia operativa, protección ambiental y gobernanza inclusiva. Según esta perspectiva, la movilidad no se trata como un fenómeno aislado, sino como una variable clave que conecta los patrones de uso del espacio, el consumo de recursos y la percepción de calidad del destino.

Por su parte, Baños-Pino et al. (2025) demuestran empíricamente, en el caso español, que los destinos que implementan el enfoque de Destino Turístico Inteligente (DTI) presentan mayores niveles de eficiencia productiva, especialmente cuando se integran tecnologías de monitorización y estrategias sostenibles en su gestión turística.

Samancioglu et al. (2024) profundizan en esta línea al mostrar que los DTI, al incorporar inteligencia de datos y planificación digital, están mejor posicionados para alcanzar objetivos de sostenibilidad ambiental y social. En particular, subrayan que los avances tecnológicos permiten no solo mejorar la eficiencia, sino también fomentar una mayor participación ciudadana y transparencia en la toma de decisiones.

2.3. Tecnología, IoT e inteligencia para la gestión de la movilidad

Dentro de este marco, la gestión inteligente de la movilidad requiere avanzar hacia sistemas de información en tiempo real, capaces de monitorizar, analizar y predecir los flujos turísticos con base en datos empíricos. La transformación digital de los destinos permite integrar herramientas de Big Data, Internet de las Cosas (IoT) e Inteligencia Artificial (IA) que abren nuevas posibilidades para una planificación más precisa, flexible y proactiva. Hardy y Aryal (2019) ya evidenciaron el potencial de estas tecnologías en parques naturales, al demostrar cómo los datos de localización pueden utilizarse para comprender los movimientos de los visitantes y mejorar la planificación y conservación de estos espacios protegidos.

El uso de sensores distribuidos en el territorio —como los desplegados en la plataforma Connecta València— posibilita la captura continua de datos sobre movilidad en puntos estratégicos. Estos datos pueden analizarse mediante técnicas de aprendizaje automático para identificar patrones, predecir escenarios de saturación y diseñar respuestas adaptativas. Como señala González-Reverté (2019), el desarrollo de destinos turísticos inteligentes no solo se basa en la eficiencia operativa a través de tecnologías digitales, sino que aspira a integrar de manera efectiva dimensiones ambientales, sociales y económicas en la toma de decisiones estratégicas del destino, favoreciendo así modelos más sostenibles de planificación y gestión.

Estudios como el de Mestre Santos et al. (2024) demuestran que la tecnología de detección inalámbrica (*wireless crowd detection*) puede emplearse eficazmente para identificar aglomeraciones en tiempo real y activar medidas de mitigación frente al overtourism. Este tipo de herramientas permite pasar de una gestión reactiva a una gestión predictiva, alineada con los principios de la smart governance.

La Plataforma Inteligente de Destino (PIT), como evolución operativa del modelo DTI, representa un paso más en esta dirección. Su capacidad para combinar datos procedentes de sensores, redes sociales, sistemas de ticketing o encuestas, permite integrar múltiples capas de información en una única infraestructura de gestión. Esta interoperabilidad facilita una visión integral del comportamiento turístico, donde la movilidad se concibe como nodo central de un sistema complejo de interacciones.

2.4. Gobernanza inteligente, redistribución de flujos y marketing basado en datos

Desde una perspectiva de gobernanza inteligente, la movilidad turística puede entenderse como un ámbito donde confluyen intereses múltiples: turistas que buscan accesibilidad y comodidad, residentes que reclaman calidad de vida, gestores que buscan equilibrio territorial, y operadores que persiguen eficiencia económica. Una gestión adecuada debe conciliar estas lógicas, lo cual requiere datos actualizados, criterios transparentes y mecanismos de participación (El Archi et al., 2023; Boes et al., 2016).

En este contexto, el marketing de destino, entendido en sentido amplio, puede desempeñar un papel clave como herramienta para informar, orientar y redistribuir la demanda. La disponibilidad de datos masivos permite diseñar campañas de promoción más segmentadas y sostenibles, que fomenten visitas en horarios valle, promuevan zonas poco conocidas o refuercen modos de transporte no motorizados. La visualización accesible de los datos (por ejemplo, mediante dashboards interactivos) puede favorecer una cultura de corresponsabilidad en la que todos los actores del destino participen en la toma de decisiones.

En definitiva, el reto de la movilidad turística en espacios naturales protegidos, como el Parque Natural de L'Albufera, debe abordarse desde una perspectiva sistémica que combine datos masivos, herramientas tecnológicas, participación de actores y principios de sostenibilidad. El presente estudio se inscribe en esta lógica, aportando evidencias y propuestas para avanzar hacia una gestión inteligente y sostenible de la movilidad en destinos turísticos naturales.

Con base en este marco conceptual, el presente estudio formula una serie de hipótesis que permitirán evaluar empíricamente los patrones de movilidad turística en el Parque Natural de L'Albufera mediante el análisis de datos generados por la plataforma Connecta València. Como se ha indicado anteriormente, la naturaleza episódica del turismo provoca picos de movilidad muy intensos que generan presión sobre los destinos turísticos naturales (Suárez Falcón y Álvarez García, 2016). En el ámbito del Parque Natural de L'Albufera, se propone la siguiente hipótesis:

H1. La movilidad turística en el Parque Natural de L'Albufera durante los puentes festivos presenta patrones espaciales y temporales concentrados que generan presión sobre zonas específicas del parque, comprometiendo su sostenibilidad.

Mediante la gestión inteligente de la movilidad, los sistemas de información en tiempo real permiten monitorizar y analizar los flujos turísticos con base en datos empíricos (Hardy y Aryal, 2019). En el presente trabajo, a partir de los sensores ubicados en las zonas de mayor accesibilidad (véase https://connecta.dival.es/appserver/public), se derivan las siguientes hipótesis:

- **H1.1.** Los sensores ubicados en las zonas de mayor accesibilidad (entradas principales, entorno del lago) registrarán un volumen de conexiones significativamente superior al resto del parque.
- **H1.2.** La mayor concentración de flujos se produce en horarios vespertinos y nocturnos, lo que complica la gestión de servicios en tiempo real.
- **H1.3.** Los flujos turísticos aumentan en los meses de octubre y diciembre en comparación con agosto, debido a la celebración de puentes festivos y condiciones climáticas más favorables.

El análisis de estas hipótesis permitirá valorar en qué medida la plataforma CONNECTA puede servir como base para una estrategia de movilidad sostenible e inteligente en espacios naturales protegidos, integrando datos empíricos, herramientas tecnológicas y principios de sostenibilidad.

3. METODOLOGÍA

Este estudio adopta un enfoque cuantitativo descriptivo, basado en el análisis empírico de datos generados por la plataforma tecnológica CONNECTA-DIVAL, desarrollada por la Diputació de València en el marco de su estrategia de Destino Turístico Inteligente (DTI). Esta plataforma integra una red de sensores que capturan datos masivos sobre movilidad mediante conexiones Wi-Fi anónimas de dispositivos móviles. Esta infraestructura tecnológica permite monitorizar los flujos turísticos en tiempo real en puntos estratégicos del territorio.

La investigación se circunscribe a nueve sensores Wi-Fi distribuidos en ubicaciones clave del Parque Natural de L'Albufera (véase Figura 1): accesos principales, áreas recreativas, zonas de tránsito y puntos de observación del entorno. Los sensores registran conexiones únicas de dispositivos móviles que transitan cerca de los emisores, lo que permite inferir patrones de afluencia, concentración y permanencia.

Figura 1. Mapa geolocalizado de los sensores en el Parque Natural de L'Albufera.

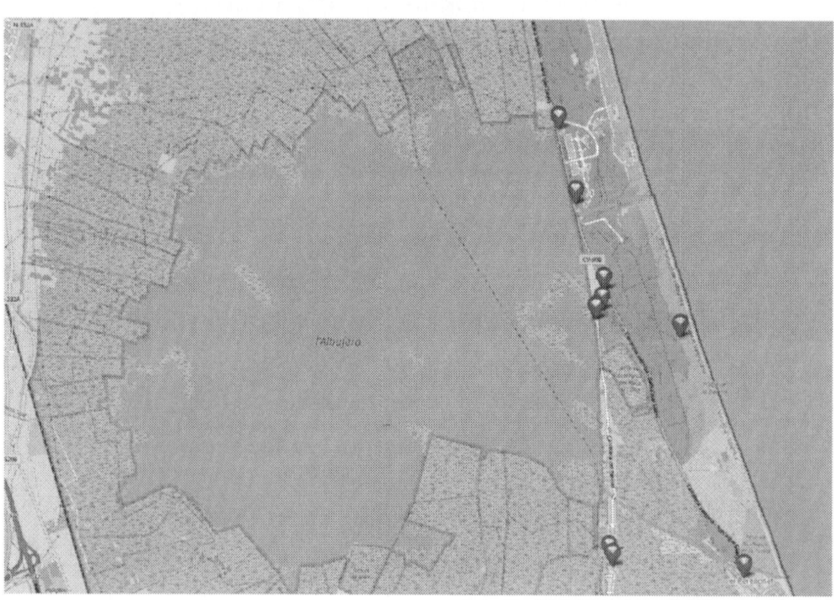

Fuente: Connecta Dival. Elaboración propia.

El análisis se centra en los puentes festivos del segundo semestre de 2024, considerados momentos de alta presión turística, que abarcan el final del verano y el inicio del invierno. En concreto, los periodos analizados son:

- Agosto (14 al 18).
- Octubre (8 al 13).
- Noviembre (30 de octubre al 3 de noviembre).
- Diciembre (5 al 8).

Estos periodos fueron seleccionados por su elevada movilidad prevista y por su valor como laboratorio natural para analizar el comportamiento turístico en espacios protegidos de alta sensibilidad ecológica.

El conjunto de datos comprende un total de 137.530 registros de conexiones Wi-Fi. El análisis se ha realizado mediante estadística descriptiva, utilizando frecuencias absolutas y relativas. El tratamiento se ha organizado en tres niveles:

Análisis espacial: distribución de conexiones por sensor, identificando zonas con mayor o menor afluencia relativa.

Análisis temporal: distribución de registros por franjas horarias (07:00–10:00, 10:00–14:00, etc.), con el objetivo de detectar picos de intensidad y horarios críticos para la gestión.

Análisis estacional: comparación entre los puentes festivos seleccionados, con el fin de identificar variaciones significativas en el comportamiento de los visitantes.

La ubicación de los sensores ha sido verificada mediante herramientas de georreferenciación (Google Maps), lo que permite relacionar los datos obtenidos con características físicas del territorio como accesibilidad, tipología del uso público o cercanía al lago.

Si bien este análisis no plantea indicadores nuevos en sentido estricto, las variables empleadas —volumen de conexiones por espacio, franja horaria y momento del año— permiten inferir niveles de presión turística y constituyen una base empírica útil para orientar decisiones de gestión.

Una consideración metodológica relevante se refiere al puente de noviembre, cuyo comportamiento turístico estuvo condicionado por la DANA del 29 de octubre de 2024. Este episodio de lluvias torrenciales provocó graves daños humanos y materiales en varios municipios al sur de València, particularmente en la comarca de L'Horta Sud. El Parque Natural de L'Albufera, como principal cuenca de desagüe natural de estas localidades, se convirtió en zona operativa prioritaria para cuerpos de seguridad, bomberos y servicios de emergencia. Durante varios días, la movilidad turística quedó suspendida, permitiéndose únicamente el acceso institucional. No obstante, los sensores registraron un volumen significativo de conexiones, atribuible a los desplazamientos intensivos de los servicios de emergencia dentro del parque. Esta circunstancia debe ser tenida en cuenta al interpretar los datos correspondientes a ese periodo.

Además, como parte de un proyecto piloto en desarrollo, pueden haberse producido fallos puntuales de cobertura o conectividad en algunos sensores, lo que podría afectar de forma leve la representatividad de los datos. Aun así, se aplicaron procedimientos de depuración técnica para garantizar la validez del conjunto.

En su conjunto, esta metodología permite establecer correlaciones entre comportamiento turístico, localización geográfica y temporalidad, sentando así las bases para el diseño de estrategias de gestión inteligente de la movilidad, especialmente relevantes en espacios naturales protegidos con alta presión ecológica y social.

4. RESULTADOS

Este estudio analiza los patrones de movilidad turística en el Parque Natural de L'Albufera durante los puentes festivos de agosto, octubre, noviembre y diciembre de 2024, a partir de los datos empíricos obtenidos por los sensores Wi-Fi del sistema CONNECTA València. El análisis revela diferencias significativas tanto en la distribución espacial como en los ritmos temporales de uso, con implicaciones directas para la sostenibilidad del espacio natural.

4.1. Distribución por zonas

La mayor concentración de actividad se registró en los sensores C0102S01 (20,3%), C0067S01 (18,9%) y C0101S01 (16,0%), ubicados en las zonas más accesibles y de mayor atractivo turístico del parque. Estos puntos se corresponden con áreas cercanas a los accesos principales, al lago y a las rutas más transitadas. En cambio, sensores como C0147S01 (2,9%) y C0068S01 (4,0%) muestran una menor afluencia, lo que evidencia la existencia de zonas con menor uso turístico. Esta información permite identificar "zonas calientes" de uso turístico y abre la posibilidad de promover alternativas u orientar políticas de redistribución de flujos y descongestión de áreas saturadas.

Tabla 1. Distribución de conexiones por sensor, coordenadas y zona estimada.

Sensor	Latitud	Longitud	Zona estimada	% conexiones
C0002S01	39,309568	-0,31774	Entrada sur (El Saler)	4,8
C0023S01	39,33497	-0,307823	Centro-norte (El Palmar)	15,6

Sensor	Latitud	Longitud	Zona estimada	% conexiones
C0026S01	39,349727	-0,323365	Mirador norte / zona de paseos	9,2
C0067S01	39,357918	-0,325868	Acceso interior norte	18,9
C0068S01	39,336875	-0,320283	Zona este, área recreativa	4
C0101S01	39,310453	-0,318284	Entrada sur principal	16
C0102S01	39,30841	-0,29833	Paseos/lago	20,3
C0119S01	39,337934	-0,319347	Zona recreativa este-central	8,4
C0147S01	39,340153	-0,319126	Senderos este menos concurridos	2,9

Fuente: Connecta Dival. Elaboración propia.

4.2. Distribución por franja horaria

El análisis por franja horaria revela que, en términos temporales, la franja con mayor volumen de conexiones corresponde al intervalo nocturno de 21:00 a 07:00 horas, que concentra el 40,3% del total. Aunque este dato puede reflejar conexiones pasivas o residuales, como pernoctaciones, autos estacionados, residentes.

También destaca la presencia de visitantes en horarios que coinciden con el momento más atractivo para visitas, que es al atardecer y al amanecer. La franja de tarde (17:00 a 21:00) representa el 17,5%, mientras que las franjas de mañana (07:00 a 14:00) suman el 28,9%. Este patrón horario señala picos de presión vespertinos, lo que plantea retos para la planificación de transporte público, control de accesos y gestión de residuos.

Tabla 2. Conexiones por franja horaria con frecuencia y porcentaje

Franja horaria	Frecuencia	Porcentaje (%)
07:00–10:00	17638	12,8
10:00–14:00	22164	16,1
14:00–17:00	18254	13,3
17:00–21:00	24070	17,5
21:00–07:00	55404	40,3

Fuente: Connecta Dival. Elaboración propia.

Figura 2. Gráfico de barras apiladas con la distribución horaria.

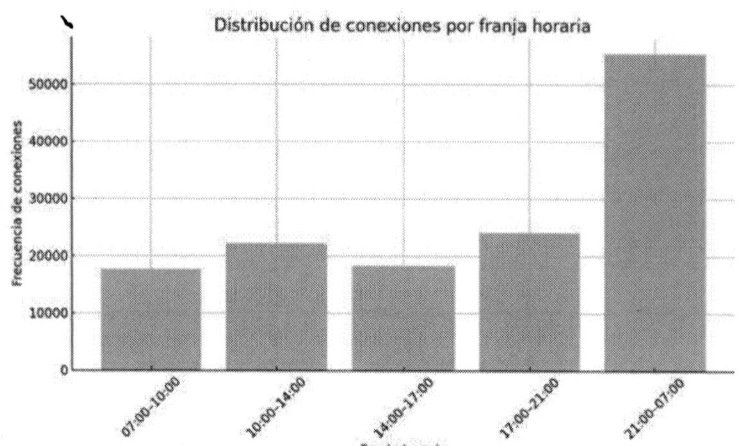

Fuente: Connecta Dival. Elaboración propia.

4.3. Distribución por meses

Desde una perspectiva estacional mensual, se observó un mayor número de registros en octubre (33,8%) y diciembre (28,3%), seguidos por noviembre (20,5%) y agosto (17,5%). Esta evolución muestra la importancia creciente del turismo vinculado a puentes festivos de otoño/invierno, así como un menor uso en agosto, posiblemente debido al calor o preferencias de otros entornos costeros más cercanos. Esta alta afluencia en los meses otoñales e invernales puede estar vinculada con los puentes festivos, pero también con un clima más propicio para la visita con temperaturas más moderadas.

Cabe señalar que el periodo de noviembre estuvo afectado por la DANA del 29 de octubre, que distorsionó la movilidad habitual. Esta variabilidad climática apunta a la necesidad de integrar indicadores de resiliencia en la planificación turística.

Tabla 3. Conexiones por mes.

Mes	Frecuencia	Porcentaje (%)
Agosto	24099	17,5
Octubre	46419	33,8
Noviembre	28158	20,5
Diciembre	38854	28,3

Fuente: Connecta Dival. Elaboración propia.

Figura 3. Gráfico de sectores o barras comparando la estacionalidad.

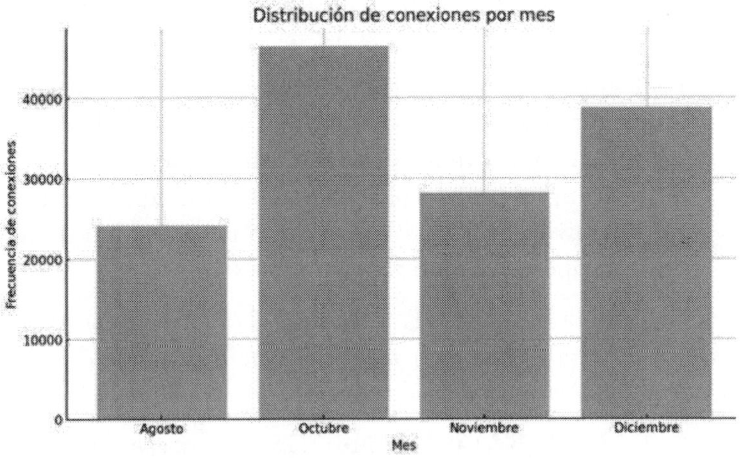

Fuente: Connecta Dival. Elaboración propia.

4.4. Evaluación de hipótesis

Los resultados obtenidos permiten contrastar las hipótesis formuladas al inicio del estudio con base en la evidencia empírica recopilada por los sensores de la plataforma Connecta València.

- Se confirma la hipótesis H1. *La movilidad turística en el Parque Natural de L'Albufera durante los puentes festivos presenta patrones espaciales y temporales concentrados que generan presión sobre zonas específicas del parque, comprometiendo su sostenibilidad.*
    - o Los datos evidencian una fuerte concentración de visitantes en determinadas zonas (especialmente accesos y entorno del lago) y en franjas horarias específicas (tarde y noche), lo que plantea retos de capacidad de carga y conservación ambiental.
- Se confirma la hipótesis H1.1. *Los sensores ubicados en las zonas de mayor accesibilidad registrarán un volumen de conexiones significativamente superior al resto del parque.*
    - o Los sensores C0102S01, C0067S01 y C0101S01, situados en zonas accesibles y de gran atractivo, acumulan más del 55% de las conexiones totales. En cambio, los sensores en zonas periféricas muestran una actividad muy reducida.

- Se confirma parcialmente la hipótesis H1.2. *La mayor concentración de flujos se produce en horarios vespertinos y nocturnos, lo que complica la gestión de servicios en tiempo real.*
    - La franja nocturna (21:00–07:00) es la más intensa (40,3%), aunque parte de estas conexiones podrían deberse a factores no turísticos (vehículos estacionados, residencias). No obstante, la franja de tarde (17:00–21:00) también muestra un pico significativo (17,5%), confirmando la necesidad de mejorar la gestión operativa en este tramo horario.
- Se confirma la hipótesis H1.3. *Los flujos turísticos aumentan en los meses de octubre y diciembre en comparación con agosto, debido a la celebración de puentes festivos y condiciones climáticas más favorables.*
    - Octubre (33,8%) y diciembre (28,3%) presentan mayor intensidad de visitas que agosto (17,5%), a pesar de que noviembre estuvo afectado por una DANA. Este patrón confirma la estacionalidad asociada a los puentes festivos y a factores climáticos.

Esta evaluación empírica demuestra la utilidad de los sistemas de monitorización inteligente como base para una gobernanza más eficaz, sostenible y basada en datos en entornos naturales de alta sensibilidad.

5. CONCLUSIONES

Este estudio ha permitido identificar patrones espaciales y temporales significativos en la movilidad turística del Parque Natural de L'Albufera durante los principales puentes festivos del año 2024. A partir de los datos recogidos por los sensores Wi-Fi del sistema CONNECTA-DIVAL, se confirma que la movilidad en este entorno natural protegido presenta una alta concentración en determinados puntos de acceso (especialmente en la zona del lago y los accesos norte y sur), así como una elevada intensidad en franjas vespertinas y nocturnas.

Estos hallazgos refuerzan la hipótesis de que el parque experimenta una presión turística focalizada, tanto en términos territoriales como temporales, lo que genera tensiones en la conservación del entorno y en la gestión de infraestructuras y servicios. Asimismo, la estacionalidad identificada —con mayores flujos en octubre y diciembre— sugiere que la planificación turística en espacios naturales no debe limitarse a la temporada estival, sino abordar también los impactos de eventos festivos fuera del verano.

En este contexto, se demuestra el valor estratégico de los sistemas de inteligencia turística para la gobernanza sostenible de los destinos. La plataforma CONNECTA València se presenta como una herramienta eficaz para recopilar y analizar datos masivos de movilidad en tiempo real, facilitando una toma de decisiones más adaptativa, basada en evidencia y alineada con los principios del modelo de Destino Turístico Inteligente (DTI).

Estos resultados son especialmente relevantes para espacios frágiles como L'Albufera, donde los impactos de la actividad turística deben ser equilibrados con la protección de sus valores ecológicos. El análisis empírico pone en valor la necesidad de disponer de información en tiempo real sobre los flujos de visitantes clave para diseñar estrategias de redistribución de flujos, establecer límites operativos de carga y mejorar la coordinación interadministrativa en situaciones de alta presión turística o emergencia ambiental en aras de la sostenibilidad del destino.

6. LIMITACIONES

El presente estudio se enmarca en un proyecto piloto en curso, por lo que existen algunas limitaciones relevantes a considerar:

- Funcionamiento parcial de sensores: En determinados periodos o ubicaciones, algunos sensores Wi-Fi podrían haber registrado datos incompletos o inconsistentes, bien por desconexiones técnicas o por interferencias en la detección de dispositivos móviles. Esta limitación afecta principalmente a la precisión del análisis espacial detallado.
- DANA del 29 de octubre de 2024: La Depresión Aislada en Niveles Altos (DANA) que tuvo lugar a finales de octubre provocó lluvias torrenciales en la Comunidad Valenciana, con graves consecuencias humanas y materiales. L'Albufera, como espacio húmedo y cuenca receptora natural, actuó como vía de evacuación del agua acumulada, lo que implicó la alteración total de los usos turísticos habituales durante el puente de Todos los Santos. Además, la presencia de cuerpos de seguridad, trabajos de limpieza y zonas inaccesibles influyó en los registros recogidos en ese periodo.
- Carencia de datos cualitativos: Aunque el análisis cuantitativo de conexiones permite inferencias significativas sobre flujos y densidad, no es posible obtener información sobre la motivación del visitante, el tipo de actividad realizada o su percepción de la experiencia. Se-

ría útil combinar estos datos con encuestas o fuentes cualitativas en futuras fases del proyecto.

- Cobertura espacial limitada: El estudio se basa en nueve sensores ubicados en zonas clave del parque, lo que implica una representación parcial del conjunto del espacio natural. Aunque suficiente para detectar patrones relevantes, una cobertura más amplia podría ofrecer una visión más precisa del comportamiento global de los visitantes.

A pesar de estas limitaciones, el estudio ofrece una base empírica sólida para avanzar en el diseño de estrategias de movilidad sostenible en espacios naturales protegidos. Los resultados deben interpretarse como una aproximación inicial dentro de un sistema de gestión basado en datos que sigue en desarrollo y perfeccionamiento.

7. REFERENCIAS

Baños-Pino, J. F., Sustacha, I., Boto-García, D., & Del Valle, E. (2025). Are Smart Tourism Destinations more productive efficient? The Spanish case. *Tourism Economics, 0*(0). https://doi.org/10.1177/13548166241313413

Boes, K., Buhalis, D., & Inversini, A. (2016). Smart tourism destinations: Ecosystems for tourism destination competitiveness. *International Journal of Tourism Cities, 2*(2), 108–124. https://doi.org/10.1108/IJTC-12-2015-0032

Buongiorno, A., & Intini, M. (2021). Sustainable tourism and mobility development in natural protected areas: Evidence from Apulia. *Land Use Policy*, 101, 105220. https://doi.org/10.1016/j.landusepol.2020.105220

Donici, D. S., & Dumitras, D. E. (2024). Nature-Based Tourism in National and Natural Parks in Europe: A Systematic Review. *Forests, 15*(4), 588. https://doi.org/10.3390/f15040588

El Archi, Y., Benbba, B., Nizamatdinova, Z., Issakov, Y., Vargáné, G. I., & Dávid, L. D. (2023). Systematic literature review analysing smart tourism destinations in context of sustainable development: Current applications and future directions. *Sustainability, 15*(6), 5086. https://doi.org/10.3390/su15065086

Vizcaíno Estevan, A. V. (2024). Agentes e imaginarios en la construcción de la marca patrimonial "Albufera" (València, España). El caso de la gastronomía y la restauración en el parque natural de L'Albufera. *Revista Andaluza de Antropología,* (27), 41-66. https://doi.org/10.12795/RAA.2024.i27.03

González-Reverté, F. (2019). Building Sustainable Smart Destinations: An Approach Based on the Development of Spanish Smart Tourism Plans. *Sustainability, 11*(23), 6874. https://doi.org/10.3390/su11236874

Hardy, A., & Aryal, J. (2019). Using innovations to understand tourist mobility in national parks. *Journal of Sustainable Tourism, 28*(2), 263–283. https://doi.org/10.1080/09669582.2019.1670186

Mestre Santos, T., Pérez Álvarez, R., & Molina, R. (2024). *Wireless crowd detection for smart overtourism mitigation. arXiv.* https://doi.org/10.48550/arXiv.2402.09158. [Preprint].

OMT & PNUD (2017). *Tourism and the Sustainable Development Goals – Journey to 2030.* OMT, Madrid. https://www.undp.org/sites/g/files/zskgke326/files/publications/UNWTO_UNDP_Tourism%20and%20the%20SDGs.pdf?utm_source=chatgpt.com

Rogowski, M., Zawilińska, B., & Hibner, J. (2025). Managing tourism pressure: Exploring tourist traffic patterns and seasonality in mountain national parks to alleviate overtourism effects. *Journal of Environmental Management,* 373, 123430. https://doi.org/10.1016/j.jenvman.2024.123430

Roig, R. (2024). La política turística más allá de la promoción, la coordinación y la innovación. En Roig, R., Bigné, E. y Pavía, J.M. (eds.): *Digitalización turística para la sociedad 5.0*; pp 25-52. València: Publicacions Universitat de València (PUV).

Samancioglu, E., Kumlu, S. T., & Ozkul, E. (2024). Smart tourism destinations and sustainability: Evidence from the tourism industry. *Worldwide Hospitality and Tourism Themes,* Vol. 16 No. 6, pp. 680-693. https://doi.org/10.1108/WHATT-07-2024-0167

SEGITTUR. (2015). *Guía metodológica para la conversión de destinos turísticos en destinos turísticos inteligentes.* Sociedad Mercantil Estatal para la Gestión de la Innovación y las Tecnologías Turísticas (SEGITTUR). https://www.segittur.es/destinos-turisticos-inteligentes/proyectos-destinos/libro-blanco-destinos-turisticos-inteligentes/

SEGITTUR. y Andrades, L. (2024). The Technology Pillar of the Spanish Smart Tourism Destination (DTI) Model. En: Andrades, L., Romero-Dexeus, C., Martínez-Marín, E. (eds) *The Spanish Model for Smart Tourism Destination Management. Tourism, Hospitality & Event Management.* Springer, Cham. https://doi.org/10.1007/978-3-031-60709-7_6

Soria, J., Vera-Herrera, L., Calvo, S., Romo, S., Vicente, E., Sahuquillo, M., & Sòria-Perpinyà, X. (2021). Residence time analysis in the albufera of Valencia, a Mediterranean Coastal Lagoon, Spain. *Hydrology,* 8(1), 37.

Suárez Falcón, J. C., & Álvarez García, J. (2016). Movilidad y sostenibilidad en destinos turísticos urbanos: una aproximación desde la planificación estratégica.

PASOS: Revista de Turismo y Patrimonio Cultural, 14(2), 319–333. https://doi.org/10.25145/j.pasos.2016.14.022

Velmurugan, S., Thazhathethil, B. V., & George, B. (2021). A study of visitor impact management practices and visitor satisfaction at Eravikulam National Park, India. *International Journal of Geoheritage and Parks*, 9(4), 463-479. https://doi.org/10.1016/j.ijgeop.2021.11.006

BLOQUE 3

GESTIÓN Y GOBERNANZA INTELIGENTE

MARCO JURÍDICO DE LA GESTIÓN DE RIESGOS Y CRISIS EN DESTINOS TURÍSTICOS INTELIGENTES: LA RESILIENCIA Y LA SOSTENIBILIDAD EN EL PAÍS VASCO. EL EJEMPLO DE SAN SEBASTIÁN DTI

EVA MARÍA LÓPEZ TUBÍA

RESUMEN: Gestionar riesgos y crisis en destinos turísticos es una tarea imprescindible para garantizar su sostenibilidad y resiliencia. La preparación, la comunicación efectiva y la adaptación continua son las mejores herramientas para afrontar los desafíos del presente y del futuro. En España contamos con un marco legal bien estructurado que regula la gestión de riesgos y crisis en destinos turísticos, promoviendo la coordinación entre diferentes niveles de administración y garantizando la protección tanto de turistas como de residentes. España cuenta con un corpus jurídico sólido en materia ambiental (Ley 42/2007, Ley 26/2007) y de seguridad turística (Ley Orgánica 4/2015, planes de protección civil). Las comunidades autónomas complementan esta normativa con marcos propios, destacando las normativas autonómicas en Cataluña (Decreto 75/2020), que exige planes de emergencia en alojamientos, Andalucía (Decreto 28/2016), con protocolos de seguridad en viviendas turísticas, y Canarias (Ley 7/1995) con Planes Municipales de prevención de riesgos naturales en zonas turísticas. En el País Vasco, la Ley 13/2016 de Turismo y sus decretos de desarrollo refuerzan la seguridad, accesibilidad y gestión sostenible como ejes clave en la ordenación turística. El LABI (Consejo Asesor del Lehendakari) fue un referente en la gobernanza de la crisis sanitaria, articulando decisiones basadas en datos y priorizando la seguridad turística. Su impacto se evidenció en la regulación de aforos, eventos y protocolos de movilidad durante la Semana Grande Donostiarra. Esta experiencia ha sido modelo de buenas prácticas en gestión de eventos en contextos de crisis. San Sebastián cuenta con proyectos como SmartKalea, ha liderado la implantación del modelo DTI, renovando su distintivo en 2023 y consolidando una visión de turismo urbano inteligente, seguro y participativo.

Palabras clave: gobernanza, destino turístico inteligente, gestión de riesgos y crisis, sostenibilidad y resiliencia

ABSTRACT: Managing risks and crises in tourist destinations is essential to ensure their sustainability and resilience. Preparation, effective communication, and continuous adaptation are the most valuable tools for facing today's and tomorrow's challenges.In Spain, a well-structured legal framework regulates risk and crisis management in tourist destinations, promoting coordination among different levels of government and safeguarding both tourists and residents. The country has a solid legal corpus regarding environmental protection (Law 42/2007, Law 26/2007) and tourist safety (Organic Law 4/2015, civil protection plans).

Autonomous communities complement this with their own regulations. Notable examples include: Catalonia (Decree 75/2020), which requires emergency plans in tourist accommodations;Andalusia (Decree 28/2016), which implements safety protocols in tourist housing; Canary Islands (Law 7/1995), which introduces Municipal Plans for the prevention of natural hazards in tourist zones.

In the Basque Country, Law 13/2016 on Tourism and its implementing decrees reinforce security, accessibility, and sustainable management as key pillars of tourism planning. The LABI (Lehendakari's Advisory Council) became a reference for crisis governance during the health emergency, basing decisions on data and prioritizing tourist safety. Its impact was evident in the regulation of capacities, events, and mobility protocols during Donostia's Semana Grande. This experience has become a model of good practice in event management under crisis conditions.

San Sebastián, through initiatives like SmartKalea, has led the implementation of the DTI (Smart Tourist Destination) model, renewing its official recognition in 2023 and strengthening a vision of smart, safe, and inclusive urban tourism.

Keywords: sustentable tourism, Smart Tourist Destination, risk and crisis management, sustainability and resilience

1. CONSIDERACIONES SOBRE EL CONCEPTO DE GOBERNANZA Y GESTIÓN DE RIESGOS Y CRISIS EN DESTINOS TURÍSTICOS

1.1. El concepto amplio de gobernanza: herramienta analítica y práctica

El concepto de gobernanza ha cobrado protagonismo desde los años noventa como una herramienta analítica y práctica para comprender las nuevas formas de gestión pública y toma de decisiones colectivas. Su carácter amplio y su aplicabilidad en distintos niveles institucionales lo convierten en un enfoque clave, especialmente en el contexto europeo y en sectores como el turismo, dónde se aprecia sus principales dimensiones, su vínculo con el territorio y su potencial como marco para la acción pública.

Y es que, desde la década de 1990, el concepto de gobernanza ha ganado relevancia, tanto en el discurso académico como en el diseño de políticas públicas. Esta noción ha surgido como respuesta a la creciente complejidad de la gestión estatal, el papel de múltiples actores en la toma de decisiones y la necesidad de adaptar las estructuras institucionales a contextos cada vez más dinámicos y descentralizados (Rhodes, 1996; Kooiman, 2003). Lejos de ser un concepto unívoco, la gobernanza es una idea compleja, de contornos flexibles y significados diversos. En esencia, hace referencia al proceso mediante el cual diferentes actores –públicos, privados y sociales– participan, influyen y cooperan en la toma de decisiones que afectan al conjunto de la sociedad. No se limita al accionar del Estado, sino que reconoce la multiplicidad de voces y escalas implicadas en la gestión de los asuntos públicos.

1.1.1. La definición de gobernanza y su relación con la sociedad, el territorio e instituciones

La gobernanza no posee una definición única. Autores como Pierre y Peters (2000) destacan que se trata de un concepto de difícil concreción, que abarca una pluralidad de procesos y actores. En términos generales, puede entenderse como un sistema de interacciones entre el gobierno, el sector privado y la sociedad civil, orientado a la toma de decisiones y la implementación de políticas públicas (Aguilar, 2006). Mediante este enfoque, se aleja de la idea tradicional de gobierno jerárquico y vertical, promoviendo en su lugar redes horizontales de cooperación, corresponsabilidad y participación (Jessop, 1998). De esta forma, la gobernanza no reemplaza al Estado, sino que redefine su papel en un contexto de mayor interdependencia entre los distintos niveles y sectores sociales (Benz & Papadopoulos, 2006).

Uno de los aspectos clave de la gobernanza es su capacidad para vincular la gestión institucional con las características y necesidades de los territorios. La gobernanza implica una articulación entre los actores locales, regionales y nacionales, permitiendo una mayor adecuación de las políticas a la realidad social y espacial (Kooiman, 2003). Este vínculo es especialmente importante en contextos donde los problemas son multidimensionales y exigen respuestas integradas. La gobernanza territorial, por ejemplo, permite la planificación conjunta de actores públicos y privados para el desarrollo sostenible, la gestión ambiental o la planificación urbana (Vallejo & Hausner, 2004).

Así pues, la gobernanza se posiciona como un concepto clave para entender la relación entre sociedad, territorio e instituciones. Se ha de reconocer que los desafíos contemporáneos —como el desarrollo sostenible, la urbanización acelerada o el cambio climático— requieren de una mirada integrada y colaborativa. Así, más que una estructura de gobierno vertical, propone redes horizontales donde se promueve la participación, la transparencia y la corresponsabilidad.

1.1.2. La gobernanza multinivel en Europa: el Libro Blanco sobre la Gobernanza Europea

En Europa, el concepto de gobernanza ha adquirido particular relevancia debido a la necesidad de coordinar políticas entre diferentes niveles de gobierno y organismos supranacionales. La gobernanza multinivel, promovida por la Unión Europea, reconoce la importancia de la cooperación entre instituciones europeas, nacionales, regionales y locales (Benz & Papadopoulos, 2006).

Esta estructura busca responder a la creciente fragmentación de competencias y a la necesidad de una gestión eficaz en contextos complejos, promoviendo procesos de deliberación inclusivos y mecanismos de coordinación transversales. La gran complejidad de la gestión pública contemporánea, caracterizada por múltiples niveles de decisión (local, regional, nacional e internacional), ha hecho de la gobernanza un concepto particularmente útil en el contexto europeo.

Allí donde las políticas suelen surgir del diálogo entre instituciones supranacionales, gobiernos nacionales y administraciones locales, la gobernanza se convierte en una herramienta de articulación y eficacia. Sus principios, según el Libro Blanco de la Gobernanza de la Unión Europea (2001) son la Transparencia en la gestión, la Participación pública en el diseño y la aplicación de políticas de Responsabilidad de todos los agentes que intervienen en dichas políticas. De esta forma, se evalúa la eficacia (mediante medidas objetivas) y la coherencia en las acciones. Y es que el Libro Blanco sobre la Gobernanza Europea (Comisión Europea, 2001) nació en un momento clave para la integración europea. Frente a una ciudadanía cada vez más distante de las instituciones, el documento propuso cinco principios fundamentales para renovar la acción pública, fortalecer la legitimidad institucional y mejorar la relación entre la Unión y sus ciudadanos.

La gobernanza es, en esencia, una invitación a repensar cómo se ejerce el poder. Los principios propuestos por la Unión Europea en 2001 siguen siendo plenamente vigentes: abrir las instituciones, promover la participación, exigir responsabilidad, actuar con eficacia y asegurar la coherencia de las decisiones. En tiempos de desafíos globales y crisis, gobernar bien no es una opción, sino una necesidad. Aunque el Libro Blanco fue pensado para la Unión Europea, sus principios han inspirado reformas institucionales en otros ámbitos, desde gobiernos nacionales hasta la gestión del turismo o el desarrollo territorial. El sector turístico es uno de los ámbitos donde el concepto de gobernanza presta una gran utilidad, puesto que la planificación y gestión del turismo requiere de una visión integral, que contemple la sostenibilidad, la participación de la comunidad local y la articulación entre actores públicos y privados (UNWTO, 2013).

1.1.3. Gobernanza y turismo. El papel de las Administraciones Publicas en la Organización de Gestión de Destino (OGD). Modelos de gobernanza de destinos turísticos, en especial, la gobernanza de los Destinos turísticos inteligentes (DTI)

La gobernanza se concibe como un punto de vista para abordar los desafíos contemporáneos de la gestión pública. Su énfasis en la cooperación, la participación y la adecuación territorial la convierte en una herramienta eficaz para la formulación de políticas más democráticas y efectivas. En sectores como el turismo, su aplicación resulta especialmente valiosa para fomentar un desarrollo inclusivo, sostenible y coordinado. Sin duda, el ámbito donde la gobernanza adquiere un valor especial es el del turismo. Este sector, altamente dependiente del territorio y con múltiples impactos sociales, económicos y ambientales, requiere de una gestión integral. Las Administraciones Públicas desempeñan un protagonismo especial, no solo como ente regulador, sino como facilitador de procesos colaborativos, dada cuenta de que la gobernanza turística permite identificar intereses diversos, coordinar acciones y promover el desarrollo equilibrado del territorio (Aguilar, 2006).

Por ello, el papel de las Administraciones Públicas no solo es el de regular o planificar, sino también el de articular intereses, fomentar alianzas y promover un desarrollo turístico que sea sostenible e inclusivo. La gobernanza turística implica, por tanto, trabajar con una lógica de red, en la que participan empresarios, comunidades locales, ONGs, y otros actores clave del territorio.

La gobernanza presenta dos caracteres, en primer lugar, la capacidad directiva de la Administración, determinada por la coordinación y la colaboración, así como por la participación de las redes de agentes interesados. En segundo lugar, la eficacia directiva, determinada por las capacidades y los recursos institucionales que ayudan a llevar a cabo los procesos de definición de objetivos y búsqueda de soluciones y oportunidades para los agentes interesados, así como por las herramientas y medios que se ofrecen para su ejecución conjunta.

La gobernanza de destinos turísticos se refiere a la gestión coordinada de todos los elementos que componen un destino turístico, involucrando la participación de diferentes actores públicos y privados. Este proceso busca una planificación y gestión turística efectiva y sostenible, involucrando a la sociedad civil, los organismos públicos y los actores privados.

En este contexto se distinguen los varios modelos de gobernanza de destinos turisticos, como los Modelos de Gestión Turística, que incluyen modelos generales o sistemas, modelos de proceso, modelos de funciones, modelos organizacionales, modelos estructurales-funcionales, modelos de demanda, modelos de desarrollo de destino y modelos de impacto. Por otra parte, surge el Modelo de Competitividad del Destino, modelo que evalúa la capacidad de un destino para atraer y retener turistas, considerando factores como la calidad de la oferta, la infraestructura y la imagen del destino. También se encuentra el Modelo del Sistema Turístico de Leiper, modelo que conceptualiza el turismo como un sistema complejo, considerando la interacción entre diferentes componentes como la demanda, la oferta, la infraestructura y el ambiente. Y el Modelo Irridex de Doxey, modelo que describe el impacto del turismo en la comunidad local, destacando diferentes fases como euforia, aversión, apatía y conflicto. Y el Ciclo de Vida del Área Turística de Butler (TALC), modelo que analiza el desarrollo turístico a lo largo del tiempo, identificando diferentes etapas como exploración, crecimiento, madurez y estancamiento.

Finalmente, el modelo de Destinos Turísticos Inteligentes (DTI). Este modelo enfatiza la gestión del destino desde la perspectiva local, considerando la participación de los diferentes grupos de interés y la implementación de tecnologías para mejorar la gestión turística. Se basa en cinco ejes principales: gobernanza, innovación, tecnología, sostenibilidad y accesibilidad. En el enfoque de los destinos turísticos inteligentes (DTI) se ha ganado relevancia al integrar tecnología, sostenibilidad, gobernanza participativa y planificación basada en datos (Segittur, 2022). Los DTI se caracterizan por el uso de tecnologías digitales para mejorar la experiencia del visitante, optimizar la gestión de recursos y fomentar la sostenibilidad. Según Buhalis y Amaranggana (2015), un DTI utiliza tecnologías de la información y la comunicación (TIC) para mejorar la experiencia del turista, la gestión del destino y la sostenibilidad

Los Componentes de la gobernanza de destinos turísticos son la visión estratégica, la definicion de objetivos y metas claras para el desarrollo turístico, alineando los intereses de los diferentes actores, y sobre todo, la Participación de los grupos de interés, involucrando a la sociedad civil, los organismos públicos y los actores privados en la toma de decisiones.

Respecto a la transparencia, se pretende asegurar que la información sobre la gestión turística sea accesible y clara para todos los actores involucrados. Con relación a la Evaluación del desempeño, se monitorean los resultados de las acciones de gestión turística y evaluar su impacto en el destino. En cuanto a la Co-gestión, esta se refiere a la gestión compartida del destino entre los diferentes actores, fomentando la colaboración y el trabajo en equipo. Y con relación a las Redes de colaboración público-privada, se fomenta la participación de la sociedad civil, los organismos públicos y los actores privados en la gestión del destino.

Así pues, se obtiene una resolución participada de conflictos, estableciendo mecanismos para la resolución de conflictos de manera participativa, involucrando a todos los actores involucrados, teniendo en cuenta la Transversalidad, es decir, la importancia de la gestión turística en todos los sectores económicos y sociales.

En este sentido, ONU Turismo trabaja para ayudar a sus Miembros en sus esfuerzos por desarrollar modelos/estructuras y políticas de gobernanza eficientes, centrándose en la política turística y la planificación estratégica, la gobernanza y la cooperación vertical, (es decir, a nivel nacional-regional-local), y las alianzas público-privadas.

ONU Turismo ha detectado tres áreas clave para el rendimiento de la gestión de destinos de las Organizaciones de gestión de destino (OGD): liderazgo estratégico, ejecución eficaz y gobernanza eficiente.En las últimas décadas, el turismo se ha consolidado como un motor de desarrollo económico global, pero también como un sector altamente vulnerable a las crisis. La pandemia de COVID-19 evidenció la necesidad de fortalecer la resiliencia sistémica de los destinos frente a perturbaciones imprevistas (Gössling, Scott & Hall, 2020).

1.2. Gestión de riesgos y crisis en Destinos Turísticos Inteligentes (DTI): claves para la resiliencia y la sostenibilidad.

Los Destinos Turísticos deben prepararse para afrontar escenarios de riesgo de forma proactiva, integrada y tecnológica. Los DTI precisamente ofrecen un marco útil para fortalecer la capacidad de adaptación ante crisis, garantizando la sostenibilidad del sector a largo plazo. Y es queel desarrollo y la gestión de los destinos turísticos requiere un enfoque holístico para abordar las políticas y la gobernanza. Un DTI es definido por SEGITTUR (2022) como "un destino innovador, consolidado sobre una infraestructura tecnológica que garantiza el desarrollo sostenible del territorio turístico, accesible para todos, que facilita la interacción e integración del visitante con el entorno y mejora la calidad de vida del residente". Esta concepción permite abordar riesgos de forma anticipativa, coordinada y sostenible.

La gestión de riesgos y crisis en destinos turísticos inteligentes (DTI) es un tema actual, donde los destinos enfrentan una serie de desafíos, desde desastres naturales hasta crisis sanitarias. La resiliencia y la sostenibilidad se han convertido en pilares fundamentales para garantizar la continuidad y el éxito del turismo en un entorno cada vez más incierto.

1.2.1. Gestión de Riesgos en DTI: Identificación y Evaluación de Riesgos

La primera etapa en la gestión de riesgos consiste en identificar y evaluar los riesgos potenciales, que incluye desastres naturales, crisis económicas, problemas de seguridad, y pandemias. Las herramientas de análisis de datos y la inteligencia artificial pueden ser fundamentales para anticipar y mitigar estos riesgos.

1.2.2. Planificación y Preparación desde la sostenibilidad: involucrar a la población

La planificación es esencial para enfrentar crisis. Los destinos deben desarrollar planes de contingencia que incluyan protocolos claros para diferentes tipos de crisis. La formación y capacitación del personal son igualmente importantes para asegurar una respuesta efectiva.

Con respecto a la Sostenibilidad en DTI, se pretende que sean prácticas Sostenibles, y la sostenibilidad debe ser un enfoque central en la gestión de DTI. Es decir, la implementación de prácticas que reduzcan la huella ecológica, promueve el uso responsable de recursos y fomenten el bienestar de las comunidades locales. Según el Informe de la OMT sobre Turismo Sostenible (2021), los destinos que integran la sostenibilidad en su planificación son más resilientes ante crisis. Además, se intenta Involucrar a la Comunidad. El involucrar a las comunidades locales resulta fundamental para la sostenibilidad de los DTI. Las comunidades deben ser parte activa en la toma de decisiones y en la planificación de estrategias turísticas, asegurando que sus necesidades y perspectivas sean consideradas (Bramwell y Lane, 2011).

1.2.3. Resiliencia en DTI: Adaptabilidad e Innovación

La resiliencia se refiere a la capacidad de un destino para adaptarse a situaciones adversas. Esto implica no solo recuperarse de una crisis, sino también aprender de ella y mejorar los procesos existentes. La colaboración entre los sectores público y privado es clave para fomentar esta adaptabilidad (Ritchie, 2004).

La innovación es otro componente esencial de la resiliencia. Los DTI deben estar dispuestos a adoptar nuevas tecnologías y estrategias que les permitan enfrentar los desafíos de manera más efectiva. Por ejemplo, el uso de plataformas digitales para la promoción y gestión del turismo puede ayudar a diversificar la oferta y atraer a nuevos visitantes (Sigala, 2020).

1.3. El sistema de certificación de OGD UNTourism.QUEST

La certificación UNTourism.QUEST evalúa las tres áreas clave del rendimiento en la gestión de destinos a nivel de OGD: liderazgo estratégico, ejecución eficaz y gobernanza eficiente. Mediante la UNTourism.QUEST se promueve la calidad y la excelencia en la planificación, la gestión y la gobernanza del turismo de las OGD, dotándolas de nuevas capacidades. Con un componente de formación y capacitación, UNTourism.QUEST es una herramienta estratégica que permite a las OGD llevar a cabo un plan de mejora que les permite alcanzar los criterios y estándares de la certificación, a fin de mejorar sus procesos de gestión y contribuir así a la competitividad y sostenibilidad de los destinos que representan.

2. BREVE REFERENCIA AL MARCO LEGISLATIVO VIGENTE EN ESPAÑA EN MATERIA DE GESTIÓN DE RIESGOS, CON ESPECIAL ATENCIÓN A LOS ÁMBITOS DE LA PROTECCIÓN DEL MEDIO AMBIENTE Y LA SEGURIDAD TURÍSTICA

La legislación española articula un sistema normativo para la prevención y gestión de riesgos tanto en el ámbito ambiental como en el turístico, combinando leyes estatales, reales decretos y normativa autonómica. Su cumplimiento es esencial para salvaguardar la sostenibilidad, la seguridad y la calidad de vida, especialmente en contextos de alta exposición al riesgo. Tanto las entidades públicas cómo las privadas han de revisar periódicamente esta legislación y actualizar sus protocolos de actuación en base a los marcos normativos vigentes.

El marco legislativo vigente en España en materia de gestión de riesgos presta una especial atención a los ámbitos de la protección del medio ambiente y la seguridad turística. Estos sectores son fundamentales para garantizar el desarrollo sostenible, la prevención de daños y la preservación de la integridad de personas, bienes y ecosistemas.

2.1. La legislación estatal general sobre Protección del Medio Ambiente

España dispone de una normativa extensa que regula la gestión de riesgos ambientales. Las principales disposiciones son la Ley 26/2007, de 23 de octubre, de Responsabilidad Medioambiental, dónde se recoge el Principio de "quien contamina paga" y regula la prevención, evitación y reparación de daños al medio ambiente. En esta ley se obliga a las empresas a evaluar riesgos y aplicar medidas preventivas. Y en Ley 21/2013, de 9 de diciembre, de Evaluación Ambiental, se regula la Evaluación Ambiental de Planes, Programas y Proyectos susceptibles de generar impactos significativos sobre el medio ambiente, integrando medidas de mitigación de riesgos.

También se ha de tener en cuenta la aplicación del Real Decreto 815/2013, por el que se aprueba el Reglamento de emisiones industriales y de desarrollo de la Ley de prevención y control integrados de la contaminación, dónde se regulan los riesgos asociados a actividades industriales contaminantes. Y la Ley 42/2007, de 13 de diciembre, del Patrimonio Natural y de la Biodiversidad, más enfocada en la conservación de los ecosistemas, especies y espacios naturales frente a riesgos ambientales.

2.2. La legislación sobre Seguridad Turística

En cuanto a la seguridad turística, España cuenta, —como normativa específica para garantizar la protección de los visitantes y la adecuada gestión de emergencias en zonas de alta afluencia turística—, con la Ley Orgánica 4/2015, de Protección de la Seguridad Ciudadana, dónde se incluyen medidas para la protección de personas en espacios públicos, aplicables a zonas turísticas. A su vez, y a través de la coordinación establecida en la Ley 17/2015, del Sistema Nacional de Protección Civil, son de aplicación los

Planes Territoriales de Emergencias de Protección Civil (PLATER), desarrollados por las Comunidades Autónomas para gestionar riesgos naturales y antrópicos, incluyendo zonas turísticas.

Además, en algunas Comunidades Autónomas se ha regulado una Normativa autonómica específica, como, por ejemplo, el Decreto 135/2021 de la Generalitat Valenciana sobre seguridad en playas y zonas de baño o el Decreto 151/2014 de la Junta de Andalucía para la gestión de emergencias en establecimientos turísticos.

Por otro lado, también hay que tener en cuenta la aplicación de la Ley 34/2002, de Servicios de la Sociedad de la Información y Comercio Electrónico (LSSI), aunque enfocada en el entorno digital, incluye disposiciones que afectan a plataformas turísticas y sistemas de información para viajeros.

2.3. La regulación autonómica de la seguridad y la gestión de riesgos en destinos turísticos

La regulación autonómica de la seguridad y la gestión de riesgos en destinos turísticos es fundamental para proteger a los visitantes y asegurar la sostenibilidad del sector. Aunque se han realizado avances significativos, es crucial seguir trabajando en la armonización de normativas, la capacitación del personal y la mejora de los recursos disponibles. Solo así se podrá garantizar que los destinos turísticos sean seguros y atractivos para todos. En la regulación Autonómica de la Seguridad y Gestión de Riesgos en Destinos turísticos, la seguridad y la gestión de riesgos en destinos turísticos son aspectos esenciales para garantizar la protección de los visitantes y la sostenibilidad del sector turístico. En España, la regulación de estos aspectos no solo se realiza a nivel nacional, sino que también depende de las competencias autonómicas, que varían según la comunidad.

2.3.1. El marco normativo autonómico general

Cada Comunidad Autónoma tiene la capacidad de establecer su propia normativa en materia de turismo, lo que incluye regulaciones sobre seguridad y gestión de riesgos. La Ley de Turismo de cada Comunidad Autónoma proporciona un marco general, pero es en los reglamentos específicos donde se abordan los temas de seguridad. Las normativas autonómicas son esenciales para la identificación y prevención de riesgos en destinos turísticos. Por ejemplo, la regulación de actividades de aventura establece estándares de seguridad que deben cumplir las empresas, lo que reduce la probabilidad de accidentes y mejora la confianza del visitante (González, 2022).

A pesar de los esfuerzos realizados, existen desafíos en la regulación de la seguridad y la gestión de riesgos en destinos turísticos, como es la propia diversidad normativa. La variabilidad en las regulaciones entre Comunidades Autónomas puede generar confusión tanto para los turistas como para los operadores turísticos.

Por ende, se cuenta con recursos limitados, dado que algunas Comunidades Autónomas se enfrentan a limitaciones en recursos para implementar y supervisar las normas de seguridad. Además, la creciente incidencia de fenómenos naturales extremos requiere de una adaptación constante de los planes de emergencia. En situaciones de crisis, como desastres naturales o emergencias sanitarias, las regulaciones han de permitir una respuesta rápida y coordinada, así pues, las Comunidades Autónomas pueden activar planes de emergencia que incluyan medidas de evacuación, atención médica y comunicación con los turistas, asegurando su protección y bienestar (Martínez, 2021).

Con relación a la normativa de Seguridad, las normas autonómicas suelen incluir disposiciones sobre Seguridad en las Instalaciones Turísticas, y regulaciones sobre la seguridad en hoteles, restaurantes y otras instalaciones turísticas, incluyendo requisitos de accesibilidad y medidas de emergencia. En cuanto a la Salud Pública, se legislan normas relacionadas con la higiene y salubridad en servicios turísticos, especialmente tras la pandemia de COVID-19, motivo por el que se han ido intensificado los controles sanitarios.

Por otro lado, con respecto a la Protección Civil, —materia de competencia autonómica—, cada Comunidad Autónoma tiene su propio sistema de protección civil y establece protocolos para la gestión de emergencias, incluyendo evacuaciones y asistencia a turistas en situaciones de riesgo.

La gestión de riesgos en destinos turísticos implica identificar, evaluar y mitigar riesgos potenciales que puedan afectar a los visitantes. Las Comunidades Autónomas implementan diversas estrategias, como los Planes de Emergencia, mediante el desarrollo de planes específicos para hacer frente a situaciones de emergencia, como desastres naturales, atentados o crisis sanitarias. También se pretende mejorar la formación y capacitación mediante Programas de formación para el personal del sector turístico en gestión de riesgos y atención al cliente en situaciones de emergencia.

Y se fomente la colaboración interinstitucional, mediante la coordinación entre diferentes administraciones (local, autonómica y nacional) para garantizar una respuesta efectiva ante situaciones de riesgo.

2.3.2. Regulación Autonómica turística con referencias a normas de seguridad

En la normativa autonómica se puede constatar la existencia de una variada regulación autonómica turística con referencia expresa a las normas de seguridad: en Cataluña, el Decreto 75/2020, de ordenación de los alojamientos turísticos, realiza una mención a los planes de emergencia, en Andalucía, el Decreto 28/2016, que incluye protocolos de seguridad en viviendas turísticas, y Canarias, la Ley 7/1995, de 6 de abril, de ordenación del turismo, establece los requisitos de prevención de riesgos en zonas de uso turístico intensivo.

En Cataluña, la Ley 13/2002, de 21 de junio, de turismo de Cataluña contiene un amplio conjunto de disposiciones que buscan garantizar la calidad y sostenibilidad del turismo en Cataluña, así como proteger los derechos de los turistas, si bien no hace referencia especial a las normas sobre seguridad en el sector. Empero si cuenta con la Agencia de Salud Pública de Cataluña, que regula aspectos relacionados con la salud y la higiene en los establecimientos turísticos. Y además, mediante el Decreto 75/2020, de 4 de agosto se regula la ordenación de los alojamientos turísticos (hoteles, campings, apartamentos, etc.), y este Decreto catalán contempla aspectos de seguridad como la obligación de los establecimientos de disponer de planes de emergencia y autoprotección, especialmente en función de su capacidad y localización. Además, el Decreto catalán 75/2020 fomenta la integración de los alojamientos en las redes de protección civil y en la planificación municipal de riesgos, regulando las condiciones de accesibilidad, seguridad estructural, sistemas de detección y extinción de incendios.

En Aragón, destaca el Decreto Legislativo 1/2016 y el Decreto 204/2018 introducen requisitos de seguridad y planes de autoprotección para alojamientos rurales y turismo activo. Se valora especialmente la capacidad de respuesta en zonas de montaña o de difícil acceso.

En el caso del Principado de Asturias, la Ley 7/2001, de 22 de junio, de turismo, establece criterios de higiene, salubridad y seguridad en alojamientos rurales y servicios turísticos, con énfasis en el cumplimiento de los estándares técnicos y medioambientales. En el mismo sentido, en Cantabria, la Ley 5/1999, de 24 de marzo, de ordenación del turismo exige condiciones de seguridad reforzada en alojamientos y actividades turísticas, con especial atención al turismo activo en zonas rurales y costeras.

En la Comunidad Autónoma de Castilla-La Mancha, la Ley 8/1999, de 26 de mayo, de ordenación del turismo, establece el marco para la seguridad estructural y la accesibilidad universal en alojamientos turísticos, reforzando el papel de la planificación local. Y en la Comunidad Autónoma de Castilla y León, la Ley 14/2010, de 9 de diciembre contempla aspectos específicos de seguridad en el medio rural, desde alojamientos hasta rutas de senderismo, fomentando la coordinación con protección civil.

Por su parte, en la Comunidad Valenciana, la Ley 15/2018, de 7 de junio, de turismo, ocio y hospitalidad, integra seguridad, accesibilidad y gestión de riesgos en destinos turísticos. De esta forma se incorpora la figura del "municipio turístico" con requisitos específicos en cuanto a capacidad de respuesta ante emergencias y sostenibilidad.

En la Comunidad Autónoma de Extremadura, la Ley 2/2011, de 31 de enero, de desarrollo y modernización del turismo, impone a los establecimientos turísticos el deber de garantizar condiciones básicas de seguridad y salubridad. Se fomenta la coordinación entre ayuntamientos y empresas turísticas para la preparación ante crisis. En la Comunidad Autónoma de Galicia, la Ley 7/2011, de 27 de octubre, contempla medidas específicas para el turismo rural y costero, y promueve la implantación de sistemas de gestión ambiental y de alerta temprana ante riesgos hidrometeorológicos.

En la Comunidad de Madrid, cuenta con la Ley 1/1999, de 12 de marzo, de ordenación del turismo, y la normativa madrileña de desarrollo, presta especial interés en la calidad y seguridad de los alojamientos, sin olvidar la preparación ante eventos masivos o situaciones excepcionales en entornos urbanos. Por su parte, en la Región de Murcia, la Ley 12/2013, de 20 de diciembre, introduce medidas para la seguridad en actividades turísticas marítimas, enoturismo y senderismo, incluyendo registros y autorizaciones específicas con fines preventivos.

En Navarra, la Ley Foral 7/2003, de 14 de febrero, de turismo de Navarra, exige condiciones de seguridad en establecimientos turísticos y promueve la formación obligatoria del personal en primeros auxilios y evacuación. En la Rioja, la Ley 2/2001, de 31 de mayo, prevé medidas de seguridad en alojamientos rurales e impulsa la prevención de incendios en entornos naturales. Se exige señalización, botiquines y formación básica en seguridad.

La Ley de Turismo de Andalucía, Ley 13/2011, de 23 de diciembre, del Turismo de Andalucía establece el marco regulatorio para la planificación, ordenación y promoción del sector turístico en la Comunidad Autónoma. Incluye expresamente medidas de seguridad y salud pública. Y por su parte, la Junta de Andalucía ha implementado protocolos específicos para la gestión de crisis, especialmente en el contexto de la pandemia. Además, se encuentran regulados en el Decreto andaluz 28/2016, protocolos de seguridad en viviendas turísticas. Este Decreto 28/2016, de 2 de febrero regula las viviendas con fines turísticos. Dentro de los aspectos de seguridad, se regula la obligatoriedad de que las viviendas dispongan de hojas informativas con teléfonos de emergencia, normas básicas de uso y evacuación, con extintores y detectores de humo o monóxido de carbono, en función del tipo de vivienda, y se vincula con las ordenanzas municipales y la normativa autonómica de seguridad contra incendios.

También se debe mencionar la regulación de Canarias, la Ley 7/1995, de 6 de abril, de ordenación del turismo en Canarias, que incluye referencias explícitas a la prevención de riesgos naturales y medioambientales, por tratarse de un territorio con volcanes, barrancos y zonas costeras. En su Ley 7/1995, se incorporan referencias específicas a la prevención de riesgos naturales como erupciones volcánicas, fenómenos costeros adversos y afecciones climáticas. Exige a los municipios turísticos elaborar Planes Municipales de Seguridad frente a emergencias, en prevención de riesgos naturales. Promueve campañas de concienciación a turistas sobre riesgos costeros, senderismo y fenómenos volcánicos.

Finalmente, se ha de destacar cómo las Islas Baleares, mediante la Ley 8/2012, de 19 de julio, del Turismo de las Illes Balears, han desarrollado un Plan de Seguridad Turística que incluye medidas específicas para la protección de los turistas, así como protocolos de actuación en caso de emergencias y de Seguridad en Zonas saturadas y medidas ambientales. La Ley 8/2012, muy centrada en la modernización del sector, establece planes de intervención en ámbitos turísticos (PIAT), que permiten la actuación coordinada ante riesgos naturales y emergencias urbanísticas en zonas turísticas maduras.

2.3.3. Turismo en Euskadi: la Ley 13/2016, de 28 de julio de turismo y Decretos de desarrollo

En el País Vasco, la Ley 13/2016 y Decretos como el 101/2018 establecen criterios de seguridad en viviendas turísticas y actividades guiadas.

Se destaca el papel del LABI (Lehendakariaren Aholku Batzordea) como órgano de coordinación en tiempos de crisis, especialmente durante la pandemia.

El turismo en Euskadi se regula principalmente por la Ley 13/2016, de 28 de julio, de Turismo, que establece los principios de sostenibilidad, calidad y accesibilidad. En un contexto global marcado por pandemias, fenómenos meteorológicos extremos y la creciente sensibilidad hacia la sostenibilidad, la Ley 13/2016, de 28 de julio, de Turismo del País Vasco se presenta como una herramienta legal avanzada que no solo regula la actividad turística, sino que también incorpora principios de prevención, seguridad y gestión de riesgos. Desde su preámbulo, la Ley 13/2016 reconoce el turismo como una actividad estratégica para Euskadi, pero también como un fenómeno que debe ser gestionado con criterios de sostenibilidad, accesibilidad y seguridad. En este sentido, la norma establece que la política turística debe estar alineada con otros ámbitos como la protección civil, el medio ambiente y la salud pública. Durante la pandemia de la COVID-19, esta ley sirvió de base para adaptar normativas específicas, como decretos y órdenes del LABI, que regularon aforos, movilidad y protocolos sanitarios en alojamientos, agencias de viajes y actividades turísticas. Asimismo, en zonas rurales o costeras, se activaron planes de contingencia ante incendios forestales o temporales, en coordinación con Protección Civil. La Ley 13/2016 anticipa un modelo de turismo que no solo busca atraer visitantes, sino también proteger a las personas, los recursos y el entorno. En un escenario de cambio climático y riesgos globales, esta visión resulta más vigente que nunca.

Aunque la ley no dedica un capítulo específico a la gestión de crisis, sí incorpora disposiciones que son de aplicación, como el Artículo 5 (Competencias), que establece que las administraciones públicas deben coordinarse con otros departamentos en materia de seguridad, sanidad y medio ambiente, especialmente en situaciones que afecten al normal desarrollo de la actividad turística. En el Artículo 9 (Deber de preservación y respeto medioambiental) se obliga a los agentes turísticos a adoptar medidas que minimicen el impacto ambiental y promuevan la resiliencia ante riesgos naturales.

En el Artículo 13 (Planes Directores de Destino Turístico) se permite incluir en los planes directores medidas de prevención y respuesta ante emergencias, como parte de la planificación estratégica del destino. Y en el Artículo 31 (Deberes de las empresas turísticas) se incluye la obligación de garantizar la seguridad de las personas usuarias, lo que puede implicar la elaboración de planes de evacuación, protocolos ante fenómenos meteorológicos adversos o medidas sanitarias.

Esta ley ha sido complementada por diversos decretos, entre ellos:

- Decreto 112/2019, sobre el Registro de Empresas y Actividades Turísticas.
- Decreto 101/2018, sobre viviendas de uso turístico.
- Decreto 26/2024, sobre la actividad de guía de turismo.
- Decreto 52/2025, que modifica la regulación de viviendas turísticas.

En un mundo donde el turismo ya no puede desligarse de la sostenibilidad, la Ley 13/2016, de Turismo del País Vasco, se posiciona como una norma pionera, porque no solo regula la actividad turística, sino que incorpora Principios que dialogan directamente con los Objetivos de Desarrollo Sostenible (ODS) impulsados por Naciones Unidas, conectando los siguientes Principios y Objetivos:

1. **Turismo como motor de desarrollo sostenible.** Desde su artículo 3, la ley vasca establece como fines la promoción de un turismo sostenible, accesible, inclusivo y de calidad, en línea con el ODS 8 (Trabajo decente y crecimiento económico) y el ODS 12 (Producción y consumo responsables). Se reconoce así el turismo como herramienta de cohesión territorial y dinamización del medio rural.

2. **Protección del entorno y resiliencia climática.** El artículo 9 impone el deber de preservación y respeto medioambiental a todos los agentes turísticos, lo que conecta directamente con el ODS 13 (Acción por el clima) y el ODS 15 (Vida de ecosistemas terrestres). Además, la ley permite incorporar medidas de adaptación al cambio climático en los planes directores de destino (art. 13).

3. **Gestión de crisis y riesgos naturales.** Aunque no se dedica un capítulo específico a emergencias, la Ley vasca si establece mecanismos de coordinación interdepartamental (art. 5) y exige a las empresas turísticas garantizar la seguridad de las personas usuarias (art. 31), lo que se alinea con el ODS 11 (Ciudades y comunidades sostenibles) y el ODS 3 (Salud y bienestar). Durante la pandemia, estas disposiciones sirvieron de base para aplicar medidas del LABI.

4. **Igualdad, accesibilidad y participación.** La ley promueve la igualdad de género en el acceso a servicios turísticos y la accesibilidad universal (art. 3 y 4), en consonancia con el ODS 5 (Igualdad de género) y el ODS 10 (Reducción de las desigualdades). También fomenta la participación ciudadana en la planificación turística, reforzando el ODS 16 (Instituciones sólidas).

3. INNOVACIÓN CON SEGURIDAD: PROYECTOS Y EXPERIENCIAS DE GESTIÓN DE RIESGOS EN DESTINOS TURÍSTICOS INTELIGENTES

3.1. LABI y Turismo en Euskadi: Gobernanza en Tiempos de Crisis. Ejemplos de Turismo seguro e inteligente en la gestión de riesgos en destinos turísticos inteligentes del País Vasco

3.1.1. LABI y Turismo en Euskadi: Gobernanza en Tiempos de Crisis

El LABI (*Lehendakariaren Aholku Batzordea*), como órgano asesor del Gobierno Vasco, desempeñó un papel clave en la gestión de la movilidad, la seguridad sanitaria y la comunicación institucional durante la pandemia de la COVID-19, lo que obligó también a repensar el modelo turístico en Euskadi.

El LABI fue creado en virtud del Decreto 153/1997, por el que se aprueba el Plan de Protección Civil de Euskadi. Este plan se apoya en la Ley 1/1996, de Gestión de Emergencias, y establece un sistema de coordinación interinstitucional para responder a situaciones de grave riesgo, catástrofe o calamidad.

El LABI fue creado para dar respuesta a las emergencias sanitarias, con funciones de asesoramiento al Lehendakari en la toma de decisiones estratégicas. Su composición multidisciplinar permite integrar criterios sanitarios, económicos y sociales. Aunque no legisla directamente, sus recomendaciones se han traducido en decretos y órdenes que han afectado directamente al turismo. Durante la pandemia, la normativa se adaptó mediante resoluciones específicas que limitaban aforos, horarios y movilidad, siguiendo las directrices del LABI.

El LABI cuenta con un consejo asesor político y técnico, presidido por el Lehendakari, e integrado por consejeros clave (Salud, Seguridad, Gobernanza, Turismo, etc.), así como representantes de las tres Diputaciones Forales y alcaldías de las capitales vascas. Esta estructura garantiza una respuesta transversal y consensuada. En situaciones críticas, como en 2021, el LABI activó la Fase 2 de Emergencia, lo que permitió al Gobierno Vasco asumir la coordinación de todas las instituciones implicadas. Esta Fase2 refuerza la capacidad de respuesta y centraliza la toma de decisiones estratégicas.

Entre las actuaciones más relevantes del LABI, destacan:

- **Emergencia Sanitaria por COVID-19 (2020–2022):** El LABI fue activado formalmente el 13 de marzo de 2020. Coordinó medidas como el cierre de centros escolares, restricciones de movilidad, limitación de aforos y protocolos para eventos culturales y deportivos.
- **Eventos Meteorológicos y Naturales:** Antes de la pandemia, el LABI ya había sido activado en múltiples ocasiones por temporales, inundaciones o nevadas intensas. Aunque pasaban desapercibidas para el público general, estas activaciones permitieron coordinar recursos de emergencia y protección civil.
- **Gestión de Eventos Masivos:** Aunque no es su función principal, el LABI ha influido indirectamente en la planificación de eventos multitudinarios durante la pandemia, estableciendo criterios de seguridad sanitaria, control de aforos y planes de evacuación. Esto afectó a festivales, partidos de fútbol, ferias y celebraciones populares.

3.1.2. Impacto del LABI en el Turismo

El LABI no solo gestionó una crisis sanitaria, sino que dejó un legado en la gobernanza turística. Su enfoque basado en datos, su coordinación interinstitucional y comunicación clara, son ya modelo para futuras crisis, como las climáticas o energéticas, en cuestiones como:

a. **Restricciones y resiliencia:** Las decisiones del LABI supusieron cierres temporales, restricciones de movilidad y limitaciones de aforo. Esto afectó gravemente al sector, pero también impulsó la digitalización, la diversificación de la oferta y el turismo de proximidad. Con la irrupción del virus, el LABI impulsó medidas drásticas que paralizaron temporalmente la movilidad, afectando a uno de los motores económicos del País Vasco: el turismo. Las restricciones de entrada, los toques de queda, y la limitación de aforos supusieron un duro golpe para hoteles, casas rurales, agencias de viajes, restaurantes y guías turísticos. Sin embargo, también propiciaron una reflexión sobre el modelo turístico vasco, encaminada hacia el Turismo Responsable, generando una promoción de un turismo más sostenible y responsable. Y es que, al limitar las aglomeraciones, se redescubrieron destinos menos masificados, y los pequeños pueblos, las rutas de montaña y los enclaves naturales ganaron protagonismo frente a los tradicionales puntos turísticos urbanos. Todo ello favoreció una mayor diversificación de la oferta, y propició la puesta en valor de la riqueza del medio rural.

b. **Turismo activo y rural:** Según un informe de Aktiba, el turismo activo en Euskadi creció en relevancia durante la pandemia, con más de 220 empresas registradas en 2019. El LABI, al fomentar actividades al aire libre y en espacios menos concurridos, contribuyó indirectamente a este auge.

c. **Comunicación institucional:** Las ruedas de prensa del LABI y sus comunicados oficiales generaron confianza en residentes y visitantes. Euskadi fue percibida como un destino seguro, lo que facilitó la recuperación del sector. A través de sus comparecencias y comunicados, el LABI mantuvo informada a la población y a los sectores afectados, entre ellos el turístico. La claridad en la normativa fue esencial para generar seguridad, tanto en los residentes como en los viajeros. Con el tiempo, Euskadi se posicionó como un destino preparado y responsable, lo que ayudó a recuperar la confianza tras la crisis. Aunque el LABI ya no opera como consejo activo, muchas de sus actuaciones siguen vigentes, como la colaboración entre Administraciones, sector turístico y ciudadanía, lo que marcó un antes y un después en la forma de gestionar situaciones de crisis.

3.1.3. La relación del LABI con los Destinos Turísticos Inteligentes

La relación entre el LABI (*Lehendakariaren Aholku Batzordea*) y los Destinos Turísticos Inteligentes (DTI) no es directa en términos estructurales, pero sí existe una conexión funcional y estratégica en la forma en que ambos conceptos abordan la gestión de crisis, la gobernanza colaborativa y la toma de decisiones basada en datos.

a. Gobernanza y coordinación interinstitucional

El LABI, como órgano de coordinación en situaciones de emergencia, demostró durante la pandemia la importancia de una gobernanza ágil, transversal y basada en evidencia, principios que también son pilares del modelo DTI promovido por SEGITTUR. En este sentido, el LABI actuó como un precursor práctico de modelos de gobernanza que hoy se aplican en destinos turísticos inteligentes para gestionar eventos, flujos de visitantes y situaciones de riesgo.

b. Gestión de eventos y seguridad turística

Uno de los ejes de los DTI es la gestión inteligente de eventos masivos, como festivales, ferias o celebraciones populares. Durante la pandemia, el

LABI estableció protocolos específicos para este tipo de eventos, incluyendo control de aforos, trazabilidad y medidas de seguridad sanitaria. Estas prácticas han sido recogidas por muchos destinos que hoy integran plataformas de gestión de eventos inteligentes, como el caso de Pamplona con los Sanfermines.

c. Uso de datos y digitalización

El LABI basó sus decisiones en datos epidemiológicos y modelos predictivos, lo que guarda paralelismo con el enfoque de los DTI, que utilizan inteligencia turística para analizar flujos, medir impactos y anticipar necesidades. Esta cultura de la toma de decisiones basada en datos ha sido uno de los legados más valiosos del LABI para el ecosistema turístico vasco.

d. Confianza y comunicación institucional

Tanto el LABI como los DTI comparten la necesidad de generar confianza ciudadana y transparencia. Las comparecencias del LABI durante la pandemia sirvieron como modelo de comunicación clara y eficaz, algo que los destinos inteligentes han adoptado para mejorar la experiencia del visitante y la percepción del destino.

3.2. Proyectos y Experiencias de gestión de riesgos en destinos turísticos inteligentes en el País Vasco ejemplos concretos de la coordinación del LABI con la gestión de eventos: la Semana Grande donostiarra

Durante la pandemia de la COVID-19, el LABI (*Lehendakariaren Aholku Batzordea*) desempeñó un papel clave en la coordinación de eventos multitudinarios en Euskadi, y la Semana Grande Donostiarra (*Aste Nagusia*) fue uno de los casos más representativos de esa gestión adaptativa.

3.2.1. Cancelación y rediseño del evento con eventos alternativos y controlados (2020–2021).

En 2020 y 2021, el LABI recomendó la suspensión de las celebraciones tradicionales de la Semana Grande, incluyendo los fuegos artificiales, conciertos masivos y actos populares. Esta difícil decisión, se tomó en base a criterios epidemiológicos y fue respaldada por el Ayuntamiento de Donostia, priorizando la salud pública. En lugar de cancelar por completo todas las actividades de la Semana Grande donostiarra, se promovieron actividades culturales descentralizadas y con aforo limitado, como conciertos en recintos cerrados, exposiciones y espectáculos infantiles. Estas actividades se diseñaron en coordinación con las recomendaciones del LABI, aplicando protocolos de acceso, distancia interpersonal y uso obligatorio de mascarilla. El LABI, junto con Donostia Kultura y Donostia Festak, facilitó una comunicación clara y anticipada sobre las medidas adoptadas. Esto permitió a residentes y visitantes planificar su participación de forma segura, y reforzó la imagen de Donostia como un destino responsable.

3.2.2. Reanudación progresiva del programa de festejos tradicional de Semana Grande (2022-2023)

Con la mejora de la situación sanitaria, el LABI autorizó la reanudación gradual de los eventos masivos, incluyendo los conciertos en Sagüés y los fuegos artificiales. Sin embargo, se mantuvieron medidas de vigilancia y planes de contingencia, como refuerzos sanitarios y dispositivos de seguridad coordinados con Protección Civil y Ertzaintza. Este modelo de gestión colaborativa entre el LABI y las entidades locales ha sido citado como ejemplo de gobernanza resiliente en contextos turísticos.

3.2.3. Lecciones del LABI: propuesta de Buenas Prácticas para la Gestión de Eventos en Destinos Turísticos

De la experiencia de coordinación del LABI en la gestión de eventos durante la pandemia, tomando como referencia la experiencia de la Semana Grande Donostiarra, se puede obtener una Propuesta de Buenas Prácticas, que proporcione un modelo replicable para la gestión de eventos multitudinarios en Destinos Turísticos, basado en la experiencia de coordinación interinstitucional, comunicación efectiva y toma de decisiones según la experiencia del LABI.

1. Planificación Multiescalar y Coordinación Institucional	2. Protocolos de Adaptabilidad Sanitaria y Seguridad Preventiva	3.Comunicación Clara, Multicanal y Anticipada	4. Digitalización y Monitorización del Evento	5. Evaluación Post-evento y Mejora Continua
Buena práctica: Establecer mesas de coordinación entre gobiernos locales, autonómicos y cuerpos de seguridad.	**Buena práctica:** Elaborar planes de contingencia para adaptar o modular el evento ante distintos escenarios epidemiológicos.	**Buena práctica:** Diseñar campañas de información para residentes y visitantes que generen confianza y reduzcan incertidumbre	**Buena práctica:** Utilizar herramientas digitales para control de aforo, análisis de flujos y seguimiento en tiempo real.	**Buena práctica:** Realizar evaluaciones cualitativas y cuantitativas tras cada edición del evento

1. Planificación Multiescalar y Coordinación Institucional	2. Protocolos de Adaptabilidad Sanitaria y Seguridad Preventiva	3.Comunicación Clara, Multicanal y Anticipada	4. Digitalización y Monitorización del Evento	5. Evaluación Post-evento y Mejora Continua
Ejemplo: Donostia y el LABI articularon decisiones mediante reuniones con Donostia Kultura, Ertzaintza, Osakidetza y Protección Civil	**Ejemplo:** En 2021, se sustituyeron los conciertos masivos de la Semana Grande por actividades culturales con aforo controlado.	**Ejemplo:** El LABI comunicó con antelación la suspensión de actos clave mediante ruedas de prensa y soportes digitales multilingües.	**Ejemplo:** Aunque no se aplicaron plenamente durante la Semana Grande, varios municipios desarrollaron apps de localización y control de acceso a recintos culturales inspiradas en protocolos LABI.	**Ejemplo:** Donostia Festak recogió informes sobre impacto económico, percepción ciudadana y cumplimiento de medidas.
Recomendación: Formalizar protocolos de gobernanza compartida y comisiones técnicas con competencias específicas (salud, logística, movilidad).	**Recomendación:** Incluir matrices de decisión que permitan activar fases restrictivas o de recuperación en función de indicadores sanitarios.	**Recomendación:** Centralizar la información en plataformas oficiales y establecer portavoces institucionales coordinados	**Recomendación:** Integrar soluciones DTI (Destinos Turísticos Inteligentes) como sensores, Big Data y dashboards operativos.	**Recomendación:** Sistematizar informes postevento y convertirlos en insumos para rediseñar ediciones futuras.

3.3. El distintivo de Destino Turístico Inteligente de la ciudad de San Sebastián/Donostia

El Ayuntamiento de Donostia/San Sebastián forma parte de la Red de Destinos Turísticos Inteligentes desde 2019, lo que prueba el interés del Consistorio donostiarra por la transformación de la ciudad como destino turístico, lo que finalmente se materializó a través de la implantación de la metodología de Destino Turístico Inteligente.

Este reconocimiento distintivo DTI tiene una validez de dos años y está sujeto a un proceso de renovación, por lo que somete al destino a un proceso de mejora continua, comprometiéndose a una renovación de los Objetivos y Estrategias y una adaptación a las necesidades del entorno futuro, lo que se traduce en una revalorización del destino a través de la gobernanza, la sostenibilidad, la tecnología, la innovación y la accesibilidad que sustentan el modelo DTI.

La entrega del diagnóstico DTI da comienzo la Fase de Estrategia y Planificación, en la que se establece el proceso de ejecución de las Acciones integradas en dicho Plan de Acción, desde su priorización o calendarización, hasta la identificación de inversiones, en aquellas que sea necesaria.

3.3.1. El Programa Destino Turístico Inteligente

El programa Destino Turístico inteligente es un proyecto promovido por la Secretaría de Estado de Turismo (SETUR) y gestionado por la Sociedad Mercantil Estatal para la Gestión de la Innovación y las Tecnologías Turísticas (SEGITTUR), que persigue contribuir a mejorar la competitividad de los destinos turísticos y la calidad de vida de sus residentes. Este Programa de Destino Turístico Inteligente incide en cinco ámbitos de actuación: gobernanza, innovación, tecnología, sostenibilidad y accesibilidad. Esta iniciativa, surgida del Plan Nacional e Integral de Turismo 2012-2015, genera los mecanismos adecuados para facilitar la rápida incorporación de innovaciones en los destinos turísticos. Y es que el Destino Turístico Inteligente, por definición, es un destino turístico innovador, consolidado sobre una infraestructura tecnológica de vanguardia, por lo que se garantiza el desarrollo sostenible del territorio turístico, siendo accesible para todos, y facilita la interacción e integración del visitante con el entorno, con la consiguiente mejora en la calidad de su experiencia en el destino y en la calidad de vida del residente, que es otro factor importante que tradicionalmente no se suele tener en consideración.

Para alcanzar estos objetivos, el programa DTI promueve la implantación de un Modelo de Gestión que valora la transversalidad de la actividad turística y las características diferenciadoras de cada destino. Se articula sobre una Metodología de Diagnóstico, basada en 97 requisitos y 261 indicadores, lo que a su vez deriva en un Sistema de Recomendaciones, un Plan de Acción y un Sistema de Monitorización, y todo ello conforma el conjunto de los elementos fundamentales del modelo, permitiendo un proceso de mejora continuo de la gestión del Destino Turístico, adaptada siempre a los retos presentes y futuros del turismo en el País Vasco.

Donostia/San Sebastián ha realizado un importante esfuerzo, siendo destacable la participación del personal técnico de las distintas áreas municipales del Ayuntamiento y de Turismo de San Sebastián, que ha contribuido a proporcionar la información necesaria para evaluar a este Destino Turístico en base a los requisitos e indicadores que la componen, para el conjunto de ejes clave de un DTI.

3.3.2. La renovación del Distintivo de Destino turístico Inteligente en la ciudad de San Sebastián

En diciembre de 2024 se ha procedido a la renovación del distintivo de Destino Turístico Inteligente obtenido en 2022 por la ciudad de Donostia/ San Sebastián, al constatar que sigue cumpliendo los requisitos exigidos por la metodología DTI, ciudad Destino Turístico Inteligente.

Por ello, Donostia/San Sebastián permanece en el grupo de destinos que lideran la excelencia en materia de implantación del modelo DTI, situándose a la vanguardia del desarrollo turístico y con una estrategia de futuro basada en la gobernanza, la sostenibilidad, la accesibilidad, la innovación y la tecnología como ejes vertebradores. Así pues, además de Donostia/San Sebastián, a nivel nacional han logrado este objetivo/distintivo los siguientes destinos: Barcelona, Bilbao, Benidorm, Gijón/Xixón, Málaga, Lloret de Mar y Santander, y todos estos destinos así considerados conforman el grupo de Destinos Turísticos Inteligentes plenos, a los que sigue perteneciendo.

El distintivo Destino Turístico Inteligente se adjudica sólo si el destino obtiene una puntuación en el grado de cumplimiento de los requisitos que integran la metodología DTI, igual o superior al 80%. En 2022, Donostia/ San Sebastián cumplía en un 83,1% con los requisitos de la metodología DTI. Y en la actualidad, en diciembre de 2024, tras la revisión de los requisitos, el grado de cumplimiento alcanza el 84,5%. El proceso metodológico se inició con la solicitud de revisión del diagnóstico DTI por parte de Donostia/San Sebastián y, por ende, con el compromiso de ejecución del plan de acción y el diagnóstico DTI. De esta forma, con la aceptación de esta solicitud se inició la fase de diagnóstico a través de 97 requisitos y 261 indicadores en los que se ha valorado el grado de madurez del destino en relación con la metodología, obteniéndose además un 'feedback' de recomendaciones que derivan en un plan de acción para el destino.

En la presentación de la revisión del Informe diagnóstico y Plan de acción Destino Turístico Inteligente de Donostia/San Sebastián, se ha utilizado la misma metodología que en el informe anterior, y ha sido realizado mediante el Sistema de gestión o Plataforma DTI. El proceso de revisión DTI en Donostia/San Sebastián ha contado con el apoyo de la Consejería de Turismo, Comercio y Consumo del Gobierno Vasco a través de Basquetour, Agencia Vasca de Turismo, y con la implicación de todas las áreas municipales y de los agentes privados del destino, que han contribuido a proporcionar la información necesaria para esta revisión DTI.

3.3.3. El proyecto SmartKalea de San Sebastián: la Calle Inteligente que impulsa el Turismo del Futuro en Donostia

En una ciudad donde la innovación se pasea entre edificios históricos y playas urbanas, SmartKalea se ha convertido en el emblema de cómo la tecnología puede transformar no solo la vida cotidiana, sino también la experiencia turística. Este proyecto pionero, impulsado por Fomento de San Sebastián, ha sido clave para que la ciudad obtuviera el distintivo de Destino Turístico Inteligente (DTI), otorgado por SEGITTUR en 2023.

El proyecto SmartKalea comenzó en 2014 en la emblemática calle Mayor de la Parte Vieja de San Sebastian, fue creado a fin de testear un modelo integral de ciudad inteligente que pudiera aplicarse en otros barrios y ciudades. Pero su impacto fue más allá de lo técnico: mejoró la experiencia del visitante, redujo la huella ambiental del turismo y fortaleció la colaboración entre ciudadanía, comercios y administración. Su enfoque combina tecnología, sostenibilidad y colaboración público-privada, integrando a ciudadanía, comercios, empresas tecnológicas y administraciones locales en un mismo ecosistema. Entre las acciones implementadas destacan:

- **Sistemas de iluminación LED inteligente**, que ajustan su intensidad según la presencia de personas.
- **Sensores de consumo energético y ambiental**, instalados en viviendas, comercios e infraestructuras públicas.
- **Compra agrupada de energía renovable**, que ha permitido a los negocios locales reducir su factura eléctrica y su huella de carbono.
- **Monitorización de afluencia peatonal**, útil para la planificación urbana y la gestión de eventos.

Todos estos datos se integran en una plataforma digital abierta, accesible a la ciudadanía, fomentando la transparencia y la participación. Gracias a la infraestructura de SmartKalea, San Sebastián ha podido ofrecer a sus visitantes información en tiempo real sobre afluencia y movilidad, comercios más eficientes y sostenibles y espacios urbanos más seguros y adaptados a las necesidades del turista digital.

Estas acciones se alinean con los cinco ejes del modelo DTI: gobernanza, sostenibilidad, accesibilidad, innovación y tecnología. En 2023, Donostia fue la única ciudad española en obtener el distintivo DTI con la nueva metodología de SEGITTUR, situándose junto a destinos como Medellín, Benidorm o Málaga. El papel de SmartKalea fue decisivo: demostró que es posible aplicar soluciones inteligentes a escala local y luego escalar su impacto a nivel de ciudad.

Por otra parte, el Proyecto SmartKalea también ha servido como banco de pruebas para startups y empresas tecnológicas locales, que han podido testar sus productos en condiciones reales. Esta sinergia ha generado nuevas oportunidades de negocio y ha fortalecido el tejido innovador de la ciudad.

Gracias a sus resultados, el proyecto ha sido galardonado con premios como el Premio Progreso a Ciudades Inteligentes (2020) y el Premio CNIS a la mejor colaboración público-privada (2017). Actualmente, SmartKalea se ha expandido a otros barrios como Altza, Sancho el Sabio y Txomin Enea, consolidando a Donostia como referente en el ámbito de las smart cities. SmartKalea no es solo una calle inteligente: es una visión de ciudad donde la tecnología mejora la vida cotidiana, impulsa la economía local y fortalece el vínculo entre instituciones y ciudadanía.

4. CONCLUSIONES

1. **Importancia de la Gestión de Riesgos:** La gestión de riesgos y crisis es fundamental para garantizar la sostenibilidad y resiliencia de los destinos turísticos. La preparación, la comunicación efectiva y la adaptación son claves para enfrentar desafíos actuales y futuros.

2. **Marco Legal en España:** se regula la gestión de riesgos y crisis en la legislación autonómica del turismo, incluyendo leyes ambientales y de seguridad turística. Se promueve la coordinación entre los diferentes niveles de las Administraciones, asegurando la protección de turistas y residentes.

3. **Normativa Autonómica**: Las comunidades autónomas han complementado la legislación estatal con normativas específicas, como las de Cataluña, Andalucía y Canarias, que establecen protocolos de seguridad y planes de emergencia adaptados a sus contextos particulares.

4. **Gobernanza Multinivel:** La gobernanza multinivel es esencial para la gestión eficaz de los destinos turísticos, facilitando la cooperación entre instituciones a nivel europeo, nacional y local. El LABI (Lehendakariaren Aholku Batzordea) en el País Vasco ha sido un ejemplo de cómo una estructura de gobernanza puede responder a crisis sanitarias.

5. **Experiencias Prácticas en San Sebastián:** San Sebastián ha implementado el modelo de Destino Turístico Inteligente (DTI), desta-

cando iniciativas como SmartKalea, que integran tecnología y sostenibilidad en la gestión turística. Estas experiencias son ejemplos de buenas prácticas en la gestión de eventos durante crisis.

6. **Resiliencia y Sostenibilidad:** La resiliencia se define como la capacidad de adaptarse y recuperarse de situaciones adversas. Los DTI deben adoptar enfoques innovadores y sostenibles que involucren a las comunidades locales en la toma de decisiones, asegurando que sus necesidades sean consideradas.

5. REFERENCIAS

Aguilar Villanueva, L. F. (2006). Gobernanza: el nuevo proceso de gobernar. Instituto Nacional de Administración Pública (INAP), 35-55.

Aktiba. (2022). Informe sobre Turismo Activo en Euskadi. https://www.aktiba.eus/wp-content/uploads/2023/07/202211-INFORME-COMPETENCIA-TURISMO-ACTIVO_rev.pdf.

Benz, A., & Papadopoulos, Y. (Eds.). (2006). Governance and democracy: Comparing national, European and international experiences. Routledge, London, 273-295.

Bianci, R. (2020). "Tourism, crisis and the COVID-19 pandemic: Discursive shifts and implications for policy". Journal of Sustainable Tourism, 29(11-12), 1931-1950.

Bramwell, B., & Lane, B. (2011). Tourism Collaboration and Partnerships: Politics, Practice and Sustainability. Channel View Publications.

Buhalis, D., & Amaranggana, A. (2015). "Smart Tourism Destinations". Information and Communication, Technologies in Tourism 2015, 553-564.

Gössling, S., Scott, D., & Hall, C. M. (2020). "Pandemics, tourism and global change: a rapid assessment of COVID-19". Journal of Sustainable Tourism, 29(1), 1-20.

Hall, C. M., Scott, D., & Gössling, S. (2020). Tourism and climate change: Impacts, adaptation and mitigation. Channel View Publications

Kooiman, J. (2003). Governing as governance. Sage Publications.

Ritchie, B. W. (2004). "Chaos, Crisis and Disaster Management in Tourism". Tourism Management, 25(6), 669-683.

SEGITTUR. (2022). Destinos Turísticos Inteligentes: Informe de evolución y tendencias. Secretaría de Estado de Turismo, Gobierno de España.

UNWTO. (2020). Tourism and COVID-19: Understanding the impact. Organización Mundial del Turismo. https://www.unwto.org
https://www.fomentosansebastian.eus

LA PERCEPCIÓN DE LOS ACTORES PÚBLICOS SOBRE LA CORRESPONSABILIDAD EN LAS DECISIONES ESTRATÉGICAS EN TURISMO. LOS LÍMITES A LA PARTICIPACIÓN EN TIERRA BOBAL (VALÈNCIA, SPAIN)

RUBEN ARNANDIS I AGRAMUNT
Universitat de València

ALEJANDRO COLOMINA MARTÍNEZ
Soluciones Turísticas

TEMÁTICA: Gobernanza: Transparencia y toma de decisiones participativas

RESUMEN: La Mancomunidad del Interior Tierra del Vino implementó en el periodo 2019–2021 el Plan de Dinamización y Gobernanza Turística. De entre las diferentes actuaciones propuestas, se identificó la creación de un equipo de gobernanza integrado por agentes públicos, privados y civiles para propiciar una toma de decisiones más participada y acorde con el desarrollo turístico sostenible. Tras la identificación inicial de los integrantes de este equipo, surge el presente trabajo. Mediante entrevistas personales estructuradas analizadas con el software MACTOR, el estudio identifica los puntos convergentes y divergentes entre los agentes públicos sobre cuál debe ser el alcance de este equipo (potestad y funciones). Los primeros resultados muestran que todos los municipios están a favor de la participación de otros actores en la gestión del turismo, pero es en el debate sobre las funciones a desarrollar y su potestad donde aparecen las divergencias más acusadas.

Palabras clave: gobernanza turística, participación, actores públicos, MACTOR

ABSTRACT: The Mancomunidad del Interior Tierra del Vino implemented the **Tourism Revitalization and Governance Plan** during the 2019–2021 period. Among the various actions proposed, the establishment of a governance body composed of public, private, and civil society actors was identified as a key measure to foster more participatory decision-making aligned with the principles of sustainable tourism development. Following the initial identification of the members comprising this body, the present study was undertaken. Through structured personal interviews, subsequently analysed using the MACTOR methodology, the research identifies points of convergence and divergence among public-sector actors concerning the scope—specifically the powers and functions—that this governance team should possess. Preliminary findings indicate broad consensus among municipalities in favor of incorporating diverse stakeholders into tourism management. However, significant discrepancies emerge regarding the precise functions to be performed and the extent of authority to be granted to the governance body.

Keywords: tourism governance, participation, public stakeholders, MACTOR

1. INTRODUCCIÓN

Uno de los rasgos distintivos del turismo contemporáneo —y cuya comprensión ha ganado profundidad en años recientes— es el reconocimiento de que su planificación y gestión no pueden abordarse exclusivamente desde el ámbito público ni desde el privado, como si se tratara de esferas inconexas, antagónicas o irreconciliables. La complejidad sociocultural y territorial inherente al desarrollo turístico justifica esta necesidad, la cual, cabe señalar, varía en función de las características específicas de cada destino. En este contexto, se hace imperativa la adopción de modelos de gestión turística sustentados en los principios de la gobernanza (López y López, 2004).

Uno de los objetivos fundamentales de la gobernanza es conducir a los territorios hacia modelos de gestión colaborativa, a través de esfuerzos sinérgicos que permitan identificar de forma conjunta las barreras y fortalezas existentes con miras a alcanzar metas comunes (Comisión Europea, 2001). Esta necesidad se explica, en parte, por la multiplicidad de agentes que intervienen en la actividad turística —tanto en el plano horizontal como en el vertical, tanto públicos como privados, tanto internos como externos al destino— así como por la diversidad de intereses que con frecuencia convergen, y en ocasiones se contraponen. Tal complejidad exige un modelo de gestión que facilite y potencie la comunicación entre los distintos grupos de interés (Pulido-Fernández y Pulido-Fernández, 2014).

Un análisis de los fundamentos que sustentan los actuales modelos de Destino Turístico Inteligente —como los desarrollados por Segittur, Invat·tur o la norma ISO 178501— permite observar el papel central que se le asigna a la gobernanza. Esta transita desde una concepción centrada en la legitimidad de la gestión de los bienes públicos (gobernabilidad), hacia una formulación basada en la participación activa de los actores estratégicos. El objetivo es generar confianza y coherencia institucional, capaces de articular voces, movilizar recursos y planificar de manera consensuada con una visión de largo plazo (Segittur, 2016).

Entre los principios que configuran el renovado concepto de gobernanza europea, la participación se erige como un pilar fundamental, en tanto que la calidad democrática se vincula estrechamente con la capacidad de la ciudadanía para involucrarse en el debate público (Comisión Europea, 2001). No obstante, para que esta participación sea efectiva, debe articularse con otros principios igualmente esenciales: la transparencia en la información, la rendición de cuentas, la oportunidad en la toma de decisiones y el compromiso asumido por los diversos actores implicados.

Cabe destacar que corresponde a la administración pública, en sus distintos niveles, garantizar las condiciones necesarias para una participación efectiva (coordinación público–pública). Si bien el ordenamiento democrático otorga legitimidad al poder institucional, el creciente interés de la ciudadanía por los asuntos públicos —especialmente cuando estos inciden directamente en su realidad cotidiana— y la creciente complejidad de la formulación de políticas públicas, representan una oportunidad para compartir responsabilidades en ámbitos que generan especial sensibilidad social.

Cuando los asuntos públicos en cuestión tienen un impacto significativo sobre determinados colectivos —como los actores turísticos— en el mediano o largo plazo, la voluntad política de avanzar hacia procesos de toma de decisiones consensuadas y coherentes se vuelve crucial. Sin embargo, dicha voluntad puede verse condicionada por intereses de difícil identificación —como los relacionados con afinidades políticas— que explican, en parte, las distintas posturas que adoptan los gobiernos locales.

Esta dificultad se acentúa en contextos de gobernanza compartida, como es el caso del ámbito mancomunado, donde las posibilidades de alcanzar acuerdos tienden a reducirse (Generalitat Valenciana, 2022). A diferencia de los municipios, las mancomunidades no siempre cuentan con la delegación de la competencia en materia de turismo, ya sea por una falta de visión estratégica, por desequilibrios en el potencial turístico entre los municipios que las integran, o simplemente porque se considera que una gestión individual resulta más operativa. En este sentido, el éxito de cualquier medida que incida en la gestión turística a este nivel dependerá en gran medida del compromiso, la visión compartida y la capacidad de articulación entre los actores implicados (Generalitat Valenciana, 2022).

En consecuencia, los mecanismos de colaboración público–privada, la coordinación interinstitucional, así como la participación ciudadana y del visitante —a través de órganos de cooperación, consulta o asesoramiento— constituyen las herramientas más idóneas para la construcción de espacios de participación real. En este marco se inscribe la presente investigación, cuyo objetivo es analizar el grado de consenso existente entre los distintos actores públicos locales de la Mancomunidad del Interior Tierra del Vino (MITV) en relación con el recientemente constituido órgano asesor participativo (equipo de gobernanza), conformado por representantes del sector público, privado y de la sociedad civil, y en particular, en torno a las funciones que se le han atribuido.

2. DE LA GOBERNANZA, EL TURISMO Y LA PARTICIPACIÓN

El modelo de gobernanza comienza a adquirir relevancia a partir de la segunda mitad de la década de 1990, impulsado por una serie de transformaciones estructurales que afectan la capacidad tradicional del Estado para ejercer el gobierno de manera unilateral. Entre estas nuevas realidades se incluyen la creciente incapacidad de los gobiernos para sostener los niveles previos de provisión de servicios públicos, las demandas sociales por una participación más activa en los procesos de toma de decisiones, y la progresiva complejidad de los asuntos públicos y políticos (Ledesma, 2023). En este contexto, emergen distintas corrientes dentro de la literatura académica que abordan diversas formas de materializar el modelo de gobernanza, tales como la gobernanza colaborativa, la gobernanza participativa, la buena gobernanza, la gobernanza multinivel o las redes de gobernanza. Si bien estas aproximaciones presentan matices conceptuales y metodológicos específicos, en su esencia comparten una orientación común: la reducción de estructuras jerárquicas tradicionales y la promoción de una mayor interacción, cooperación y deliberación entre los actores implicados en los territorios, con el fin de mejorar la formulación de políticas públicas y los procesos de toma de decisiones.

No será, sin embargo, hasta el 2001 que la Comisión Europea decidió establecer las bases para el desarrollo de un nuevo modelo de gobernanza, visto el descenso progresivo en los niveles de participación ciudadana en los asuntos de política europea (Comisión Europea, 2001). En dicho informe se sostenía que una mayor transparencia, acompañada del incremento en la rendición de cuentas por parte de los actores no gubernamentales, permitiría formular e implementar políticas públicas más eficaces y ajustadas a los problemas reales de la sociedad. Y es que es el ámbito local el espacio estratégico donde han de promoverse las soluciones a los problemas de la sociedad para la cogestión de bienes y servicios públicos, y es a través de la articulación de la gobernanza democrática como pueden establecerse mecanismos para intervenir colectivamente en la política pública (Talón et al., 2024)

El objetivo último era, por tanto, promover una participación más activa y significativa de los actores sociales en el diseño, ejecución y evaluación de las políticas públicas. Para ello, la Comisión propuso cinco principios fundamentales que debían constituir los pilares sobre los cuales asentar un sistema de gobernanza sólido, legítimo y eficaz: apertura, participación, responsabilidad, eficacia y coherencia (tabla 1). Estos principios, concebidos como los fundamentos de la "buena gobernanza", buscaban guiar tanto las instituciones europeas como a los Estados miembros en la consolidación de una gobernanza más inclusiva, transparente y democrática.

Tabla 1. Principios para establecer los pilares de la gobernanza. Comisión Europea (2001)

Principio	Descripción
Apertura	Instituciones y estados deben trabajar de forma más abierta. Se deberá utilizar un lenguaje accesible y fomentar la comunicación sobre el papel y las acciones que se llevan a cabo.
Participación	Mayor participación de la ciudadanía de todos los países de la Unión en la toma de decisiones políticas. Desde la concepción hasta la aplicación y evaluación.
Responsabilidad	Establecer quiénes son los agentes que participan en cada proceso para determinar el nivel de implicación y la rendición de cuentas.
Eficacia	Las medidas que se lleven a cabo deben ser válidas y oportunas, basadas en objetivos claros. Estas medidas deben ser ejecutadas por los niveles administrativos más pertinentes y adecuados.
Coherencia	Las políticas que se diseñen deben estar relacionadas con el fin que persiguen y ser fáciles de entender para la ciudadanía. Esa coherencia debe de tener un liderazgo político y un firme compromiso por parte de las instituciones.

Pero ¿qué es la gobernanza? Definir con precisión el concepto de gobernanza no resulta una tarea sencilla. Como señalan Olaya et al. (2021), pueden identificarse al menos seis modalidades distintas, lo que da cuenta de su complejidad conceptual y de su carácter polisémico. Ante esta diversidad de enfoques, es a través de las definiciones ofrecidas por la academia y las instituciones donde pueden extraerse los elementos estructurales que configuran el concepto.

Una de las definiciones más tempranas es la propuesta por Calame y Talmant (1997), quienes entienden la gobernanza como la "capacidad de las sociedades para dotarse de sistemas de representación, de instituciones, de procesos y órganos sociales, para administrarse a sí mismas mediante una acción voluntaria" (en Rosas et al., 2012). Esta noción introduce un componente esencial: el carácter voluntario de la acción por parte de los agentes involucrados, es decir, la autogestión como base del proceso.

Desde un enfoque institucional, el Instituto Nacional de Administración Pública (INAP, 2005) define la gobernanza como el conjunto de "normas y reglas que pautan la interacción en el marco de las redes de actores públicos, privados y sociales interdependientes en la definición del interés general en entornos complejos y dinámicos" (2005:9), lo que implica, además, una mayor implicación de los actores no gubernamentales tanto en el diseño como en la implementación de las políticas públicas. Esta definición pone el acento en la regulación de las relaciones entre actores en contextos de creciente complejidad.

Por su parte, Jiménez (2008) aporta una visión centrada en la toma de decisiones y la concertación, definiendo la gobernanza como las "formas y procesos de interacción y cooperación horizontal entre sector público, sector privado y actores sociales dentro de un marco institucional en mayor o menor grado proclive al logro de decisiones y acuerdos societales" (2008:61). Esta perspectiva comparte con la anterior la idea de interacción multisectorial, pero se enfoca en el resultado colectivo y consensuado de dicha cooperación.

Finalmente, Velasco (2008) define la gobernanza como el conjunto de "instituciones y reglas que fijan los límites y los incentivos para la constitución y funcionamiento de redes independientes de actores que actúan en ámbitos sociales determinados" (2008:1). Esta definición introduce el concepto de incentivos y límites como condiciones estructurantes del sistema de gobernanza, destacando su dimensión normativa.

A partir del análisis de estas definiciones, pueden identificarse una serie de elementos comunes que permiten comprender la importancia de la gobernanza en la formulación y gestión de políticas públicas. En primer lugar, la gobernanza es un proceso de naturaleza voluntaria, en el que intervienen actores públicos, privados y sociales. En segundo lugar, se configura en torno a un conjunto de normas, principios y reglas consensuadas, orientadas a guiar las relaciones entre actores y fomentar dinámicas de cooperación horizontal. En tercer lugar, su finalidad última es la construcción colectiva de decisiones públicas que generen beneficios compartidos y sostenibles para el territorio.

Así, la implantación de la gobernanza supone el diseño de políticas públicas que respondan a intereses diversos, mediante la inclusión activa de los distintos agentes en los procesos de deliberación y decisión. En este marco, la administración pública —como única instancia con legitimidad para legislar— debe asumir un papel proactivo, facilitando espacios de interlocución e integrando las propuestas del resto de actores sociales y económicos.

A la luz de las definiciones revisadas y de los planteamientos recogidos en el informe de la Comisión Europea (2001), se desprende que los actores públicos deben velar por garantizar ciertos principios fundamentales: proporcionar información clara, veraz y actualizada (transparencia); asegurar que dicha información responda a demandas reales de todos los actores implicados (participación); asumir un compromiso con la ejecución de las políticas acordadas (responsabilidad); y plantear objetivos realistas y alcanzables, capaces de generar transformaciones tangibles (coherencia y eficacia).

Los diferentes organismos, tanto a nivel nacional como internacional, han adaptado este concepto integrador a las especificidades de sus respectivos campos de actuación. Un ejemplo ilustrativo es la definición propuesta por la Organización Mundial del Turismo (OMT), en el marco de la Declaración de Madrid (2014), donde se concibe la gobernanza turística como un "proceso de conducción de los destinos turísticos a través de los esfuerzos sinérgicos y coordinados de los gobiernos en sus diferentes niveles y atribuciones, de la sociedad civil que habita en las comunidades receptoras y del tejido empresarial relacionado con la operación del sistema turístico" (2014:165).

Esta definición enfatiza la necesidad de articular a los actores operativos del destino —instituciones, comunidad local y sector empresarial— y la importancia de establecer mecanismos de comunicación efectivos entre ellos. De esta idea se deriva una de las consignas más repetidas en la gestión contemporánea de destinos: la necesidad de construir alianzas que trasciendan los límites organizativos tradicionales, incluyendo a la comunidad local y a los actores no gubernamentales en la toma de decisiones (OMT, 2019).

No obstante, como advierte Bichler (2021), en la mayoría de los destinos analizados, si bien existe representación de los actores económicos, la participación de la comunidad local sigue siendo insuficiente o marginal.

Esto resulta particularmente relevante si se considera que el valor de la participación en la gestión pública local constituye la base sobre la cual se construyen los esfuerzos por incorporar a los distintos actores —directos e indirectos— en el diseño, implementación y evaluación de las políticas públicas. Sin embargo, como señalan Hernández et al. (2018), activar mecanismos estables de participación requiere no solo voluntad política, sino también un aumento en la disponibilidad de recursos, mayor carga organizativa y un esfuerzo sostenido de coordinación interinstitucional.

En consecuencia, este esfuerzo debe ir acompañado, en una primera etapa, de estrategias de sensibilización y difusión sobre los beneficios de la participación en los asuntos públicos, con el fin de legitimar socialmente el esfuerzo que implica y de consolidar una cultura democrática que valore la inclusión activa de la ciudadanía y los agentes no estatales en la toma de decisiones (véase Tabla 2).

Tabla 2. Beneficios de la participación. Hernández et al. (2018)

Refuerza la cercanía entre responsables públicos y sociedad
Mejora el conocimiento disponible de la organización
Introduce nuevos asuntos y alternativas en la agenda política local
Mejora la información disponible por parte de la sociedad
Aumenta la eficacia de las políticas públicas
Facilita la detección temprana de errores y la rendición de cuentas

Queda así evidenciado que ciertas prácticas comúnmente asociadas con la participación no pueden ser consideradas como tales si se atiende a los criterios teóricos establecidos por Arnstein (1969) en su célebre escala de participación ciudadana. Consultas unidireccionales —a menudo carentes de mecanismos reales para modificar decisiones—, la delegación irresponsable de competencias bajo una retórica de consenso, procesos carentes de reglas claras y límites institucionales, o incluso mecanismos utilizados como meros ejercicios de validación social (cuando las decisiones ya han sido adoptadas), no constituyen formas genuinas de participación. Como advierten Cerradas et al. (2017), estas prácticas, más que empoderar a la ciudadanía o a los actores sociales, funcionan como estrategias de legitimación o maquillaje institucional, reproduciendo dinámicas verticales que contradicen el espíritu deliberativo y transformador de la participación auténtica.

Tabla 3. Niveles de la participación. Hernández et al. (2018)

Autoría	**Arnstein (1969)**	**IAPP (2018)**	**OCDE (2001)**
Ámbito de aplicación	**Escalera de participación ciudadana**	**Espectro de la participación pública**	**Relaciones entre instituciones públicas y ciudadanía**
Poder ciudadanía	Control ciudadano	–	–
	Delegación poder	Dar poder de decisión	–
	Colaboración	Colaborar	–
Participación “de fachada”	Asesoría	Involucrar	Participación activa
	Consulta	Consultar	Consulta
	Información	Informar	Información
No participación	Terapia	–	–
	Manipulación	–	–

La participación, en el marco de la gobernanza, debería situarse en el nivel del “poder de la ciudadanía”, entendido como el estadio en el que se transfiere capacidad de decisión real a la sociedad civil. Es precisamente en este nivel donde las instituciones públicas dejan de ser meros canales de consulta para convertirse en agentes que promueven la corresponsabilidad, reconociendo a los actores sociales como interlocutores legítimos y co-constructores de las políticas públicas.

3. LA MANCOMUNIDAD DEL INTERIOR TIERRA DEL VINO COMO ESPACIO DE ESTUDIO

La MITV es una mancomunidad situada en la comarca de Utiel-Requena (Valencia) compuesta por nueve municipios: Camporrobles, Caudete de las Fuentes, Fuenterrobles, Requena, Sincarcas, Utiel, Venta del Moro, Villargordo del Cabriel y Chera. Requena y Utiel concentran más del 95% del total de la población, lo que deja de manifiesto el poder que ambos municipios ejercen sobre el resto de los integrantes de la mancomunidad. La MITV no posee en su estructura organizativa ninguna área, departamento o servicio de turismo, de modo que la gestión queda supeditada al personal técnico de otras áreas (desarrollo económico, fundamentalmente) y las decisiones son tomadas en el seno del Pleno de la mancomunidad. Este hecho es también trasladable al nivel municipal de los entes integrantes de la mancomunidad.

El desarrollo turístico de la MITV está principalmente gestionado por la Ruta del Vino Utiel-Requena, enfocada únicamente a la promoción del turismo enológico, sin desplegar grandes ofertas turísticas complementarias (Marcos & Arnandis, 2014). Esta delegación de funciones queda plasmada en los estatutos de la mancomunidad, pues, estos ya parten de la adaptación a la Ley 27/2013 de Racionalización y Sostenibilidad de la Administración Local, que establece en el art. 25 *la información y promoción de la actividad turística de interés y ámbito local* como competencia específica de las entidades locales.

A pesar de contar en la actualidad con diferentes entidades de gestión vinculadas al desarrollo territorial, en la MITV existe una "ausencia de planificación y estrategia conjunta, agregada y participativa, que aúne esfuerzos y recursos en beneficio de un desarrollo sostenible a largo plazo." (Cuevas, 2021: 6)

Este individualismo presente en la gestión local del turismo desde hace tiempo pretende ser solucionado mediante la inclusión de espacios de encuentro participativo y colaborativo para la creación de sinergias. Y ese proceso comienza con la aprobación del Plan de Dinamización y Gobernanza Turística en 2019. El plan recoge la necesidad de crear un órgano de asesoramiento y evaluación permanente, que mejore la gestión turística del destino (Cuevas, 2019). Se plantea para tal fin un equipo de alto desempeño, multidisciplinar, especializado y con experiencia en el desarrollo turístico. Se busca la horizontalidad, la fluidez y el equilibrio en las redes de colaboración, involucración y compromiso y, sobre todo, personas de diferentes ámbitos vinculadas al territorio.

Se identificaron para tal fin unos 150 registros de potenciales integrantes del equipo. De todos ellos se filtró una muestra de 45 perfiles relevantes. Fueron 28 los finalmente entrevistados. De los resultados de las entrevistas, y a través del análisis de sus redes de contactos (Análisis de Redes Sociales), se identificaron un total de 11 actores, correspondientes tanto al sector público (36%), privado (45%) como civil (19%) y que fueron el punto de partida para la creación del equipo de gobernanza de la MITV (Arnandis y Cuevas, 2022)

4. METODOLOGÍA

El objetivo principal de esta investigación consiste en analizar las distintas posiciones que sostienen los actores públicos integrantes de la Mancomunidad del Interior Tierra del Vino (MITV) en relación con las funciones que debería desempeñar el equipo de gobernanza recientemente constituido, en el marco de la estrategia turística Tierra Bobal.

Para ello, se ha considerado pertinente la aplicación del método MACTOR, por ser una herramienta de análisis estratégico utilizada por Godet (2000) para estudiar las relaciones entre actores en un sistema determinado.

A través de la aplicación de esta herramienta se posibilita la identificación de los niveles de convergencia y divergencia existentes entre dichos actores en torno a una serie de dimensiones clave: la gobernanza, la participación, la transparencia, la situación actual de la gestión turística en Tierra Bobal, la posible cesión de competencias, la composición del equipo de gobernanza, sus funciones específicas y su articulación institucional con la mancomunidad.

La recolección de información se llevó a cabo mediante entrevistas personales estructuradas dirigidas a los representantes públicos de los nueve municipios que integran el Pleno de la MITV. El instrumento de recogida de datos se organizó en siete bloques temáticos distribuidos en once secciones, e incluyó un total de sesenta y siete preguntas, de las cuales dieciocho fueron de carácter abierto y cuarenta y nueve cerradas, estas últimas valoradas mediante una escala tipo Likert de 1 a 5. El análisis se desarrolló siguiendo un protocolo metodológico de seis fases, adaptado de la propuesta de Monge y Arnandis (2016), estructurado de la siguiente manera:

- Fase 1: Identificación de todos los actores públicos con competencias decisorias sobre la constitución del equipo de gobernanza.
- Fase 2: Elaboración de un cuestionario estructurado por bloques temáticos, con el fin de recabar evaluaciones individuales de cada actor sobre las dimensiones consideradas.
- Fase 3: Traslación de las respuestas obtenidas a los formatos y escalas propias de las matrices MACTOR.
- Fase 4: Construcción de la matriz de influencia-dependencia, con el objetivo de determinar la posición de poder relativa de cada actor en el sistema analizado.
- Fase 5: Análisis cualitativo de las respuestas obtenidas en las preguntas abiertas del cuestionario.
- Fase 6: Integración de los resultados cuantitativos con las valoraciones cualitativas manifestadas por los entrevistados durante el desarrollo de las entrevistas.

5. RESULTADOS

El primer paso para determinar las relaciones de poder y la posición relativa de cada actor en el sistema analizado consistió en la elaboración de la matriz de influencias directas e indirectas (véase Figura I). Dado que los actores implicados pertenecen al ámbito público, las valoraciones asignadas se han establecido, en primer término, atendiendo a la capacidad de voto que ostenta cada representante en el Pleno de la Mancomunidad, ya que esta no es homogénea entre los distintos municipios. En consecuencia, la ponderación de la influencia de cada actor responde a un criterio institucional objetivo, vinculado al peso específico que cada municipio posee dentro del órgano de representación.

Figura 1. Plano de influencias y dependencias entre actores

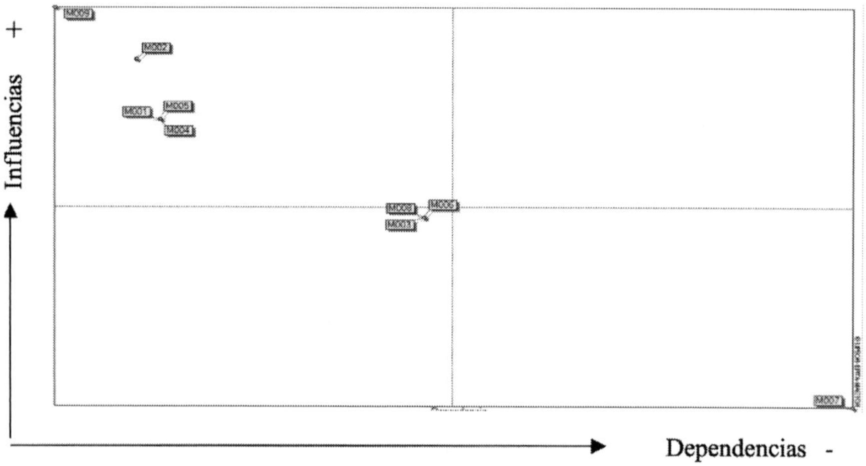

Fuente: Elaboración propia.

Se identifican cuatro grupos claramente diferenciados en la matriz de influencias. En primer lugar, el actor M009 se posiciona como el más influyente de manera independiente, configurándose como el actor dominante debido a su alta influencia y baja dependencia respecto al resto. Le sigue el actor M002, que ocupa la segunda posición en términos de dominancia. Estos dos municipios, actuando conjuntamente, cuentan con la capacidad suficiente para vetar cualquier propuesta presentada por los demás actores públicos.

En el mismo cuadrante superior izquierdo, pero un poco más hacia abajo se observa un grupo compuesto por tres agentes (M001, M004 y M005) que, si bien individualmente no poseen poder de decisión significativo, en conjunto superan la influencia de M009. De manera análoga, en el cuadrante inferior izquierdo se sitúa otro grupo similar (M003, M006 y M008), caracterizado por una menor influencia y una mayor dependencia, pero que, unidos, ostentan el mismo número de votos que M009. Es importante destacar que estos dos bloques podrían incrementar su poder efectivo mediante el establecimiento de consensos y votaciones conjuntas.

Finalmente, el actor M007, que carece de capacidad de voto en el Pleno, ocupa una posición relegada en términos decisorios. No obstante, debido a su posición estratégica dentro del territorio de Tierra Bobal, puede aportar información relevante, evaluaciones y conocimientos que enriquecen el proceso de planificación turística de la Mancomunidad del Interior Tierra del Vino, sin llegar a incidir directamente en la toma de decisiones.

Figura 2. Gráfico de convergencias sobre el poder de decisión de la administración pública en los procesos de gobernanza

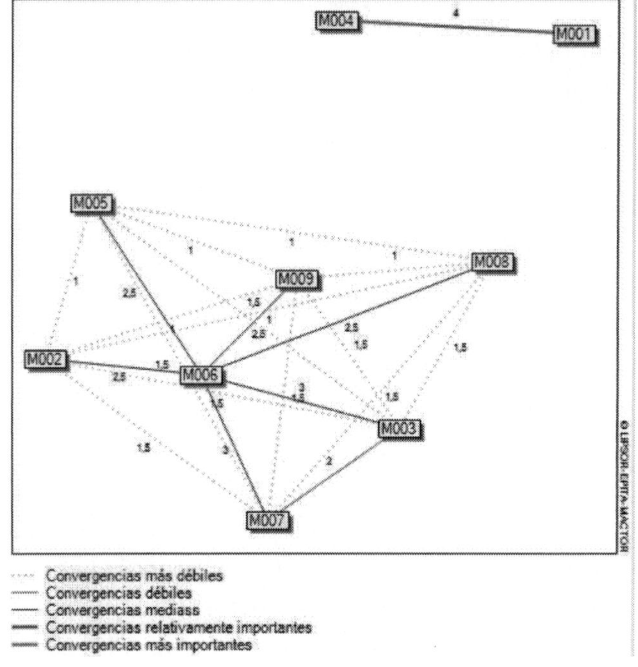

En primer lugar, se planteó la cuestión de si la administración pública debe ostentar, en última instancia, el poder decisorio dentro de los procesos de gobernanza. Como se observa en la parte izquierda de la Figura 2, se identifican dos grupos claramente diferenciados. Por un lado, los municipios M004 y M001 (línea roja, convergencia más importante), que consideran que la administración pública no debería tener la última palabra en estos procesos. Por otro lado, el resto de los municipios expresan una convergencia hacia el actor M006, que defiende que la administración sí debe poseer la autoridad final en la toma de decisiones relacionadas con la gobernanza. Asimismo, es este actor M006 el que destaca como el de mayor divergencia respecto a las posturas de M001 y M004.

Figura 3. Gráfico de convergencias (izquierda) y divergencias (derecha) sobre el papel del equipo como decisor

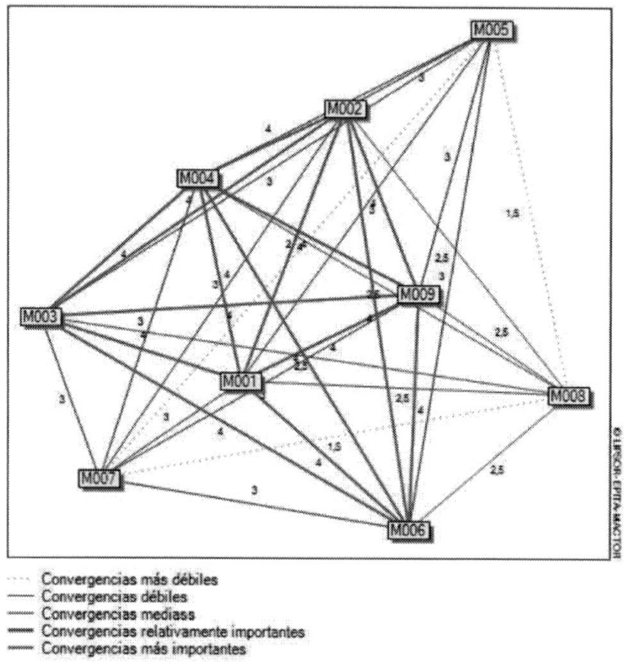

De acuerdo con los resultados reflejados en la Figura 3, los agentes entrevistados coinciden en que la responsabilidad de tomar decisiones en materia de gestión turística debe recaer en el Pleno de la Mancomunidad. Todos los municipios, con la única excepción de M008, manifiestan, en distintos grados, su conformidad con que el equipo de gobernanza actúe como un órgano asesor en asuntos turísticos.

Este resultado pone de manifiesto una limitada visión, por parte de los representantes públicos de la Mancomunidad, respecto al principio de corresponsabilidad en la gestión del turismo. Cabe señalar que no se plantea, en ningún caso, una cesión de competencias —cuestión que, desde un punto de vista jurídico, no sería viable—, sino más bien la posibilidad de que el equipo de gobernanza asuma un papel más activo, implicado y corresponsable en el desarrollo e implementación de políticas turísticas.

Figura 4. Gráfico de convergencias sobre el valor de las propuestas del equipo para el Pleno de la mancomunidad.

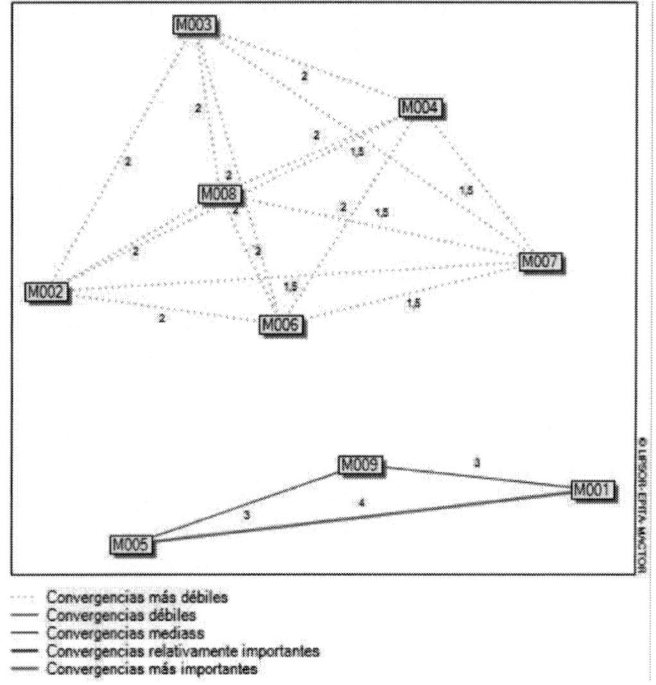

Una vez identificado el carácter asesor del equipo de gobernanza, resulta pertinente analizar el grado de valor o vinculación que sus propuestas pueden tener para el Pleno. El objetivo de esta cuestión es establecer en qué medida las decisiones formuladas por dicho equipo —que requieren aprobación por parte del Pleno— deben ser tenidas en cuenta (véase Figura 4). Los resultados obtenidos en relación con las convergencias revelan nuevamente la existencia de dos grupos claramente diferenciados. El primero, compuesto por seis municipios —entre los que se incluyen tanto actores dominantes como dependientes—, muestra una convergencia débil en torno al reconocimiento del carácter vinculante de las decisiones del equipo de gobernanza. Es decir, en este grupo predomina la postura de que las propuestas del equipo no deben ser obligatoriamente consideradas por el Pleno. Frente a este grupo, se identifica un segundo conjunto de tres municipios que presentan una mayor convergencia en cuanto al reconocimiento del valor de las propuestas del equipo de gobernanza y su consideración dentro de los procesos deliberativos del Pleno.

Se planteó a los agentes públicos la cuestión relativa a la posibilidad de que el equipo de gobernanza dispusiera de capacidad de voto en el Pleno en lo referido a asuntos turísticos. Dado que son los representantes públicos —a través del Pleno— quienes ostentan las competencias formales para aprobar o rechazar propuestas, esta pregunta busca indagar hasta qué punto, pese al carácter asesor atribuido al equipo, existiría disposición a otorgarle cierto margen de actuación cuando se trate de propuestas relacionadas con cuestiones turísticas de especial relevancia. Los resultados obtenidos (véase Figura 5) indican que, en coherencia con su naturaleza consultiva, siete de los nueve municipios se manifiestan a favor de que el equipo de gobernanza tenga únicamente voz, pero no voto, en el Pleno. Sin embargo, la ausencia de capacidad de voto permanente no implica necesariamente que las recomendaciones del equipo puedan ser ignoradas. En este sentido, si el equipo considera que determinadas acciones son prioritarias o estratégicas, sus propuestas deberían ser tenidas en cuenta con el debido respeto institucional y valoradas en función de su contribución al desarrollo turístico del territorio.

Figura 5. Gráfico de convergencias sobre la capacidad de voto del equipo de gobernanza

Convergencias más débiles
Convergencias débiles
Convergencias mediass
Convergencias relativamente importantes
Convergencias más importantes

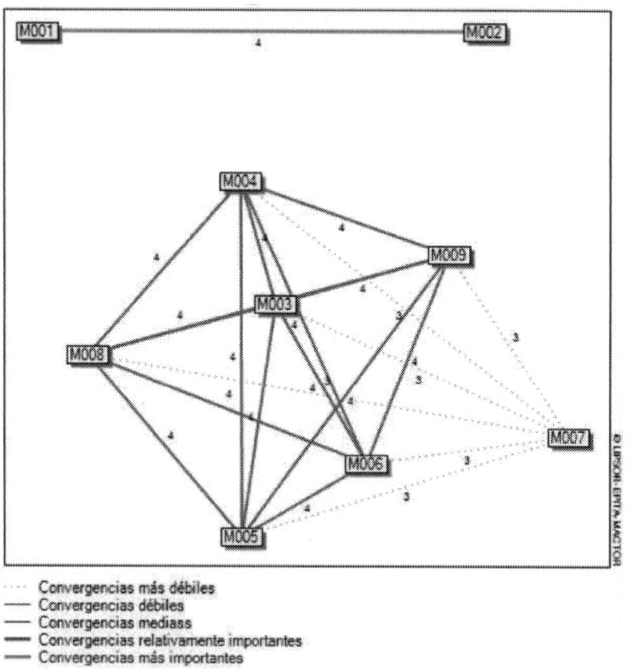

La Figura 6 permite analizar el grado de dependencia institucional que los agentes públicos desean atribuir al equipo de gobernanza. Si bien hasta el momento se le reconoce un carácter estrictamente asesor, se espera también que sus aportaciones sean consideradas en materia turística. Ante la pregunta sobre si dicho equipo debería estar directamente vinculado al Pleno —es decir, no integrarse en ningún departamento o área técnica de la MITV, sino funcionar como un órgano adjunto al máximo órgano de decisión—, se observa una clara tendencia a centralizar las competencias y a limitar la autonomía operativa del equipo. Esta orientación resulta paradójica si se considera que, en su concepción original, el equipo de gobernanza debía constituirse como un ente técnico, apolítico e integrador, capaz de representar de manera equitativa los intereses turísticos de todo el territorio. Sin embargo, los resultados muestran una amplia convergencia entre los actores (véase Figura 6) en favor de mantenerlo exclusivamente vinculado al Pleno, sin conferirle independencia estructural. De hecho, solo dos de los nueve representantes entrevistados expresaron su apoyo a un modelo en el que el equipo de gobernanza pudiera actuar de forma autónoma respecto de la estructura política de la MITV. Este posicionamiento refleja una voluntad predominante de control institucional sobre un órgano que, por su naturaleza, requeriría de cierto grado de flexibilidad y autonomía para cumplir adecuadamente su función estratégica.

Figura 6. Gráfico de convergencias sobre la vinculación del equipo con el Pleno

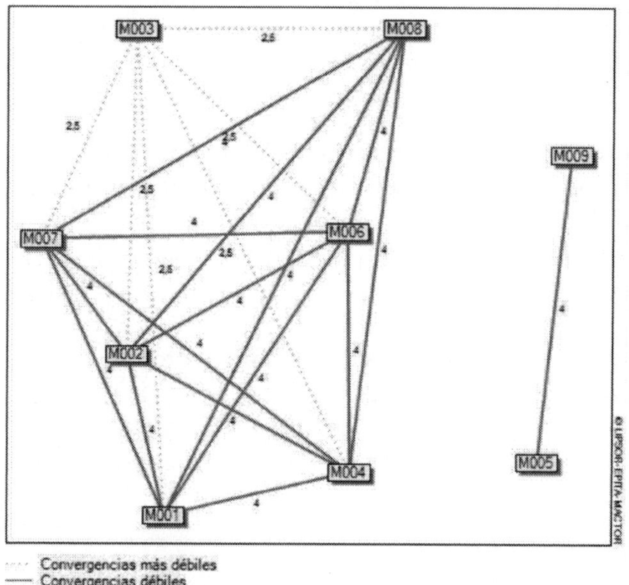

En el último apartado, relativo a las competencias que debe asumir el equipo de gobernanza, es esencial partir de la premisa de que la potestad sobre cualquier materia o asunto público recae exclusivamente en la administración pública. No obstante, como señala Rodríguez-Arana (2008), los entes locales pueden ejercer competencias que les hayan sido delegadas, refiriéndose así a posibles cesiones por parte de entidades municipales.

Los resultados obtenidos a partir de las entrevistas revelan que únicamente dos municipios consideran que el equipo de gobernanza debería asumir la totalidad de las funciones propuestas (véase Tabla 3). De las dieciséis funciones planteadas, en diez se identificaron divergencias de distinta intensidad entre los actores públicos entrevistados. Las discrepancias se acentúan particularmente cuando se trata de atribuciones que no requieren la aprobación directa del Pleno. Existe, en cambio, un consenso generalizado en torno a aquellas funciones de carácter estrictamente asesor.

Se observan posiciones mayoritariamente restrictivas en relación con la posibilidad de que el equipo de gobernanza suscriba convenios, gestione ayudas públicas o represente al Pleno en asuntos turísticos. Estas funciones son percibidas como intrínsecamente vinculadas al ejercicio de autoridad institucional, lo que refuerza la necesidad de supervisión y validación por parte del órgano plenario. Las valoraciones recogidas confirman esta orientación: aunque los representantes municipales manifiestan su interés en que el equipo contribuya a la mejora del turismo en el territorio de la MITV, insisten en que cualquier acción o iniciativa deberá estar previamente revisada y autorizada por el Pleno.

Se concluye, por tanto, que tanto los municipios con mayor capacidad de influencia como aquellos con menor poder optan por un modelo de gobernanza en el que se prioriza el control institucional sobre la autonomía operativa, restringiendo así la capacidad del equipo de gobernanza para incidir de manera directa en el diseño y ejecución de políticas turísticas.

Tabla 4. Funciones del equipo de gobernanza

Órgano	Funciones	Votos
Equipo de gobernanza	Revisar informes de la MITV u otros organismos sobre la actividad turística en el territorio (a iniciativa propia o petición del Pleno) y emitir una valoración argumentada	9
	Valorar y proponer la creación de productos turísticos	9
	Asesorar sobre la gestión de los recursos turísticos actuales y potenciales	9

Órgano	Funciones	Votos
Equipo de gobernanza	Trasladar al Pleno cuantos asuntos en materia turística recojan de la ciudadanía	9
	Velar por la consecución de los objetivos establecidos en materia turística	9
	Orientar la estrategia de promoción de la actividad turística propuesta por la MITV	8
	Aconsejar en la resolución de conflictos entre agentes durante el desarrollo de la actividad turística	8
	Fomentar el intercambio de conocimiento con organismo públicos y privados turísticos	8
	Reflexionar sobre las estrategias turísticas de órganos superiores y su adecuación a Tierra Bobal	8
	Promover el desarrollo de instalaciones públicas y privadas que fomente la recuperación del patrimonio cultural y natural	8
Área/Departamento de turismo	Proponer la estrategia turística y su planificación	9
	Definir la estrategia turística de la mancomunidad	8
	Redactar planes que dinamicen la actividad turística en el territorio	7
	Gestionar ayudas públicas que mejoren el desarrollo turístico de la mancomunidad	5
	Actuar como representante en materia turística de la MITV ante otros organismos	5
MITV	Suscribir convenios de colaboración con entidades públicas y/o privadas que persigan mejorar la imagen de Tierra Bobal	4

Fuente: Elaboración propia.

6. CONCLUSIONES

El turismo es una actividad compleja que se desarrolla en espacios públicos, donde confluyen visitantes, población residente, empresas privadas y organismos públicos. Por ello, su análisis no puede limitarse únicamente a una dimensión económica. Se trata de un fenómeno multidimensional en el que intervienen actores de naturaleza diversa, lo que exige considerar sus respectivas necesidades e intereses con el fin de desarrollar políticas que, en la medida de lo posible, beneficien al conjunto del sistema o, al menos, al interés general, objetivo último de toda administración pública.

Esta investigación ha examinado cómo los actores públicos comprenden y valoran la participación del resto de agentes implicados en los procesos de toma de decisiones en el ámbito turístico. En la medida en que la administración pública detenta la potestad exclusiva de regular y ordenar esta actividad, es necesario que sean estos mismos actores quienes, de forma proactiva, impulsen mecanismos y espacios de colaboración que favorezcan el consenso, la corresponsabilidad y el compromiso entre los distintos actores del territorio.

Uno de los hallazgos más significativos derivados del análisis MACTOR es que las posiciones de convergencia o divergencia entre los agentes públicos no se explican tanto por su nivel de influencia o dependencia, sino por las visiones y valores que defienden. Así, pueden observarse coincidencias entre municipios con distinto peso decisional cuando comparten una postura común respecto a mantener el control institucional sobre la toma de decisiones.

Existe una clara conciencia, compartida por todos los actores entrevistados, sobre el potencial que ofrece el turismo para el desarrollo del territorio, así como sobre la necesidad urgente de gestionar esta actividad de forma coherente y profesionalizada. Todos ellos reconocen la oportunidad que representa la creación de un equipo de gobernanza turística y apoyan su participación en múltiples funciones. Sin embargo, esta aparente apertura se ve limitada por una resistencia persistente a ceder espacios de poder o permitir su autonomía operativa. Esta contradicción revela una tensión estructural entre el reconocimiento del valor de la gobernanza colaborativa y la preferencia por estructuras jerárquicas de control.

En este contexto, la utilidad del equipo de gobernanza se pone de manifiesto especialmente en su capacidad para operar con flexibilidad, ya sea en tareas de planificación, coordinación o evaluación de las políticas turísticas. No obstante, su actual dependencia del Pleno de la mancomunidad compromete seriamente la implementación efectiva de un modelo de gobernanza participativa. Como consecuencia, las políticas públicas que se formulen en este marco difícilmente reflejarán las necesidades y valores reales del territorio.

Según los niveles de participación ciudadana establecidos por Arnstein (1969), los resultados de esta investigación sitúan el grado de participación impulsado por los actores públicos en un nivel de tipo "decorativo" o de "fachada". Esto corresponde, según los marcos conceptuales del IAPP y la OCDE, a un estadio de involucración o participación activa, pero sin llegar a la delegación real de poder. Para avanzar hacia formas más genuinas de gobernanza, sería necesario que las administraciones públicas comprendan en profundidad los beneficios estructurales de la participación, no solo como un principio democrático, sino como una herramienta eficaz de formulación de políticas más inclusivas, legitimadas y sostenibles.

7. REFERENCIAS

Arnandis-i-Agramunt, R.; Cuevas Paredes, E. (2022) *La participación organizada en la toma de decisiones sobre turismo: el equipo de gobernanza en la Mancomunidad de Interior Tierra del Vino.* XI Congreso Internacional en gobierno, administración y políticas públicas (GIGAPP). Madrid, España, 21–23 de septiembre de 2022.

Arnstein, S. (1969) A ladder of citizen participation. JAIP *Journal of the American Institute of Planners,* 35 (4), pp. 216–224.

Bichler, Bernhard F. (2021) Designing tourism governance: The role of local residents. *Journal of Destination Marketing & Management.* Vol. 19, pp. DOI: https://doi.org/10.1016/j.jdmm.2019.100389

Cerradas, A., Chao, L., y Pineda, C. (2017) Participación ciudadana: de la participación en la gestión a la gestión de la participación, *Política y Sociedad,* 54 (1), pp. 163-189.

Comisión Europea (2001) L*a Gobernanza Europea. Un libro blanco.* Fecha de acceso: 21/06/2024 https://eur-lex.europa.eu/legal-content/ES/TXT/?uri=celex%3A52001DC0428

Cuevas, E. (2021) Estructura de gobernanza turística, Tierra Bobal, Plan de Dinamización y Gobernanza Turística 2019–2021. Mancomunidad del Interior Tierra del Vino.

Generalitat Valenciana (2022) *Estudio sobre la adaptación de la metodología e indicadores del modelo DTI-CV al ámbito supramunicipal.* Fecha de acceso: 05/05/2024 https://invattur.es/news/el-modelo-de-destino-turistico-inteligente-de-la-comunitat-valenciana-llega-a-los-espacios-supramunicipales

Godet. M. (2000) La caja de herramientas de la prospectiva estratégica. Laboratoire d'Investigation Prospective et Stratégique. Paris. Cuarta Edición actualizada.

Hernández, E.; Camacho, R.; Silván, A.; Rojas-Martín, F.; Stan, L. (2018) Gobernanza Participativa Local. Construyendo un nuevo marco de relación con la ciudadanía. Madrid. Federación Española de Municipios y Provincias.

Instituto Nacional de Administración Pública (2005) La gobernanza hoy: 10 textos de referencia, 1ª ed, 262 p., Madrid, ISBN 84-7351-239-1

International Association for Public Participation-IAPP (2018): IAPP's Public Participation Spectrum. Recuperado de: https://iap2.org.au/wp-content/uploads/2020/01/2018_IAP2_Spectrum.pdf

Jiménez, B. (2008) El enfoque de políticas públicas y los estudios sobre gobierno. Propuestas de encuentro, Revista del CLAD Reformas y Democracia, 41, pp. 57–80

Ledesma González, O. (2023) Analysis of governance networks in tourist destinations: a practical application. Boletín de la Asociación de Geógrafos Españoles, 97, DOI: https://doi.org/10.21138/bage.3367

López, J. M., y López, L. M. (2004) Evolución y perspectivas del enfoque interdisciplinario en el estudio del turismo. *Estudios Turísticos* (160), 31–44.

Madrid, F. (2014) *Gobernanza turística. El caso de los pueblos mágicos de México,* México: Universidad Anáhua México Norte, Facultad de Turismo, 348 pp., ISBN 978-607-7652-45-B

Marcos, R., y Arnandis-i-Agramunt, R. (2014) El turismo enológico como articulador del territorio: La ruta del vino Utiel-Requena. *Cuadernos de Geografía,* 94, pp. 79-94.

Monge, J., y Arnandis-i-Agramunt, R. (2016) Participación, intereses y relaciones de fuerza: análisis de divergencias y convergencias de los actores sobre la política pública turística del cantón Ambato (Tungurahua, Ecuador) para el periodo 2009–2019, *VII Congreso Internacional en Gobierno, Administración y Políticas Públicas GIGAPP,* Madrid.

OCDE (2001). Participación ciudadana: manual de la OCDE sobre información, consulta y participación en la elaboración de políticas públicas. París: OCDE.

Olaya, S. I., Cruz, G., Castillo, M. (2021) La gobernanza en los estudios sobre turismo: estado del arte (2013–2019) *Gran Tour: Revista de Investigaciones Turísticas,* 23, pp. 50–75

Organización Mundial del Turismo (2019) Directrices de la OMT para el fortalecimiento de las organizaciones de gestión de destinos (OGD) – Preparando las OGD de cara a nuevos retos. OMT, Madrid, DOI: https://doi.org/10.18111/9789284420933

Pulido-Fernández, M., y Pulido-Fernández, J. I. (2014) ¿Existe gobernanza en la actual gestión de los destinos turísticos? Estudio de caso. *Pasos: Revista de turismo y patrimonio Cultural, 12*(4), 685–705.

Rosas, F., Calderón, J., y Alanís, H. (2012) Elementos conceptuales para el análisis de la gobernanza territorial. *Quivera Revista de Estudios Territoriales, 14*(2), pp. 113–136.

Segittur, 2016, *Gobernanza en un destino turístico inteligente: juntos, más inteligentes.* Fecha de acceso: 01/06/2024 https://www.segittur.es/blog/destinos-turisticos-inteligentes/gobernanza-destino-turistico-inteligente-juntos-mas-inteligentes/

Talón Villacañas, A., Belda-Miquel, S., Cuesta Fernández, I., Palau Salvador, G. (2024) Social innovation from the citizenship to advance in urban democratic governance. Study of Valencia City Council. Boletín de la Asociación de Geógrafos Españoles, 100, DOI: https://doi.org/10.21138/bage.3377

Velasco, M. (2008) Gestión de destinos ¿gobernabilidad del turismo o gobernanza del destino? Actas del XVII Simposio Internacional de Turismo y Ocio. ESADE.

Rodríguez-Arana, J. (2008) Sobre la distribución de competencias en materia de turismo. Revista Aragonesa de Administración Pública, 32, pp. 389-406.

TRANSPARENCIA EN LAS EMPRESAS TURÍSTICAS: UN ANÁLISIS SOBRE SUS EFECTOS EN EL COMPROMISO Y LOS COMPORTAMIENTOS DE AYUDA

JACOB GUINOT REINDERS
RICARDO CHIVA GÓMEZ
ZINA BARGHOUTI ABRINI
Universidad Jaume I

TEMÁTICA: Gobernanza (transparencia y toma de decisiones participativas)

RESUMEN: Este estudio explora el impacto de la transparencia organizacional en la confianza interpersonal, el compromiso organizacional afectivo y los comportamientos ciudadanos organizacionales dirigidos hacia individuos (OCBI, por sus siglas en inglés) en el sector turístico. Con base en una muestra de 249 empleados de 50 empresas turísticas en España, los datos se recolectaron mediante encuestas estructuradas y se analizaron utilizando modelos de ecuaciones estructurales (SEM) con el software EQS 6.4. Los resultados revelan que la transparencia organizacional influye positivamente en la confianza interpersonal y en el compromiso afectivo, siendo este último un mediador parcial en la relación entre transparencia y confianza. Además, se encontró que la confianza interpersonal fomenta el OCBI, lo que indica que los ambientes transparentes no solo fortalecen el compromiso emocional, sino también comportamientos voluntarios y prosociales entre los empleados. Esta investigación contribuye a la literatura existente al integrar en un solo modelo causal constructos que tradicionalmente han sido estudiados de forma separada, y destaca la importancia de la confianza entre pares, más allá de las perspectivas tradicionales basadas en la confianza vertical o institucional. Los resultados ofrecen valiosas orientaciones para estrategias de recursos humanos y liderazgo orientadas a cultivar confianza y cooperación a través de la transparencia, sin depender únicamente de incentivos formales.

Palabras clave: Transparencia, Confianza Interpersonal, Compromiso, OCBI

ABSTRACT: This study explores the impact of organizational transparency on interpersonal trust, affective organizational commitment, and organizational citizenship behaviors toward individuals (OCBI) in the tourism sector. Based on a sample of 249 employees from 50 tourism companies in Spain, data were collected through structured surveys and analyzed using structural equation modeling (SEM) with EQS 6.4 software. The results show that organizational transparency has a positive influence on interpersonal trust and affective commitment, with the latter partially mediating the relationship between transparency and trust. Furthermore, interpersonal trust was found to promote OCBI, suggesting that transparent environments not only strengthen emotional attachment but also encourage voluntary and prosocial behaviors among employees. This research contributes to existing literature by integrating previously studied constructs into a single causal model and highlighting the importance of peer-based trust, beyond traditional vertical or institutional perspectives. The findings provide valuable guidance for human resource and leadership strategies aimed at fostering trust and cooperation through transparency, without relying solely on formal incentives.

Keywords: Transparency, Interpersonal Trust, Commitment, OCBI

1. INTRODUCCIÓN

En el contexto del sector turístico, altamente competitivo y cada vez más sensible a las exigencias de sostenibilidad, responsabilidad social y gobernanza corporativa, la transparencia organizacional se configura como un factor estratégico clave para generar confianza entre los distintos agentes involucrados, mejorar la reputación institucional y fomentar relaciones laborales y comerciales más sólidas (Albu & Flyverbom, 2019). La comunicación clara, la toma de decisiones basada en criterios éticos y el acceso facilitado a la información son prácticas que inciden directamente en la percepción que empleados, clientes y otros stakeholders tienen de la organización (Sifry, 2011). Este cambio de paradigma refleja cómo la transparencia ha dejado de ser solo un valor normativo para convertirse en una herramienta operativa que contribuye al fortalecimiento de la cultura organizacional y a la construcción de ventajas competitivas sostenibles dentro del ecosistema turístico.

Según Schnackenberg y Tomlinson (2016), la transparencia organizativa es una cualidad que las personas perciben en una empresa cuando esta actúa con claridad y apertura. Se basa en tres dimensiones fundamentales: compartir información relevante, comunicar con precisión y explicar de manera comprensible las decisiones y acciones que se toman. La literatura ha reconocido ampliamente que la transparencia organizativa contribuye al desarrollo de la confianza institucional, facilitando percepciones de responsabilidad y buena gestión (Auger, 2014; Rawlins, 2008; Schnackenberg & Tomlinson, 2016). Cuando los empleados perciben que la información es accesible, las decisiones son razonables y los canales de comunicación están abiertos, tienden a sentirse más seguros y depositar mayor confianza en la organización y sus líderes (Dirks & Ferrin, 2001; Rousseau et al., 1998; Barghouti et al., 2022). Esta relación suele explicarse desde la teoría de la justicia, donde la equidad en los procedimientos e interacciones mejora las percepciones de fiabilidad (Colquitt et al., 2007). Por ello, en el contexto del turismo, la transparencia se considera un factor crítico para construir y mantener la confianza dentro de las organizaciones, especialmente en entornos altamente competitivos y dependientes de la reputación.

Sin embargo, aunque la transparencia organizativa se ha vinculado ampliamente con las percepciones generales de confianza en las organizaciones, la mayoría de las investigaciones se han centrado en la confianza en el liderazgo o en la confianza institucional, prestando relativamente poca atención a la confianza interpersonal entre colegas del mismo nivel jerárquico. En este sentido, en este estudio vamos más allá de evaluaciones globales de confianza y examinamos formas más específicas de confianza interpersonal que surgen en las relaciones laborales cotidianas. Nuestro análisis considera la confianza interpersonal en sus múltiples dimensiones, incluyendo la confianza entre pares y entre supervisores y subordinados. Además, exploramos cómo la transparencia configura un clima organizativo de confianza más amplio — uno que refleje tanto relaciones horizontales como verticales en el lugar de trabajo. Dado que gran parte de la colaboración diaria en empresas turísticas depende no solo de las interacciones entre pares sino también del grado en que los líderes se sienten seguros delegando tareas y empoderando a los empleados, comprender cómo la transparencia refuerza tanto la confianza horizontal como vertical ofrece valiosas perspectivas sobre cómo las empresas turísticas pueden fomentar ambientes de mutua confianza, cooperación voluntaria y trabajo en equipo efectivo.

Aunque la asociación entre transparencia y confianza a menudo se trata como directa, la investigación también indica que esta conexión puede entenderse mejor a través de mecanismos psicológicos y relacionales. Por ejemplo, el compromiso organizativo ha sido propuesto como una variable que moldea cómo los individuos perciben la transparencia y la confianza institucional (Sofyani et al., 2022). De manera similar, Klimchak et al. (2020) encontraron que la transparencia se percibe como una señal de fiabilidad organizativa, lo cual a su vez afecta el compromiso afectivo de los empleados. Por tanto, una vía prometedora para comprender este proceso radica en el compromiso afectivo organizativo. El compromiso afectivo hace referencia a una identificación emocional con la organización y el deseo de formar parte de ella (Meyer, Allen & Smith, 1993). Este vínculo emocional puede actuar como un mecanismo psicológico a través del cual la transparencia mejora la confianza interpersonal al moldear cómo los empleados interpretan las intenciones y comportamientos de sus compañeros (De Jong & Elfring, 2010). En el sector turístico, donde la rotación laboral es alta y la motivación del personal influye directamente en la experiencia del cliente, el compromiso afectivo se convierte en un factor clave para mantener equipos estables y cohesionados.

Aunque algunos estudios han explorado la relación entre transparencia organizativa y variables como la confianza y el compromiso organizativo (Klimchak et al., 2020; Pepper et al., 2010), estas investigaciones suelen centrarse en la confianza institucional o generalizada en la organización, más que en la confianza interpersonal entre empleados. La mayor parte de esta investigación se ha desarrollado desde una perspectiva de la teoría de señales, destacando cómo las prácticas transparentes influyen en las percepciones de fiabilidad organizativa (Klimchak et al., 2020) o analizando la transparencia en contextos específicos como la educación superior (Pepper et al., 2010). De forma similar, otros estudios han analizado su papel en entornos post-crisis, donde sirve como mecanismo clave para reconstruir la confianza pública (Jahansoozi, 2006), aunque con frecuencia centrándose más en las relaciones externas que en las internas.

A pesar de este cuerpo de investigación, aún hay evidencia limitada sobre cómo la transparencia afecta a formas más específicas de confianza — especialmente la confianza interpersonal — y cómo estas podrían influir finalmente en el comportamiento de los empleados dentro de las empresas turísticas. Mientras que el impacto de la transparencia en resultados actitudinales generales como la confianza en la organización o el compromiso afectivo ha sido examinado en cierta medida, se ha prestado menos atención a si y cómo fomenta la confianza entre individuos, y cómo esto podría llevar a acciones discrecionales que beneficien a compañeros y a la organización en su conjunto.

Entre estos comportamientos discrecionales, particular relevancia tienen aquellos dirigidos hacia personas, tales como ayudar a compañeros, mostrar cortesía o resolver proactivamente conflictos. Estas acciones suelen denominarse en la literatura como Comportamientos Ciudadanos Organizacionales dirigidos hacia Individuos (OCBI) (Williams & Anderson, 1991). Una importante cantidad de investigación ha establecido la importancia de la confianza interpersonal en fomentar apoyo mutuo, compartir recursos y coordinación espontánea (Altuntas & Baykal, 2010; Podsakoff et al., 1990; Singh & Srivastava, 2009), todos ellos elementos esenciales para una efectiva colaboración y funcionamiento organizativo en sectores como el turismo, donde la calidad del servicio depende en gran medida de la interacción entre empleados y la resolución ágil de situaciones imprevistas.

Este estudio busca abordar esta brecha investigadora proponiendo un modelo integrador que examine cómo la transparencia organizativa percibida influye en la confianza interpersonal, considerando el rol mediador del compromiso afectivo organizativo, y cómo esta confianza, a su vez, se traduce en OCBI. Aunque la transparencia, la confianza, el compromiso afectivo y los comportamientos extra-rol han sido extensamente estudiados de forma aislada o en combinaciones parciales, existe una carencia de investigación que explore una cadena causal completa que integre todos estos constructos en el contexto específico del sector turístico. Este estudio busca cubrir esa laguna proponiendo un modelo integral que explique cómo las prácticas transparentes moldean la confianza interpersonal entre empleados — tanto entre pares como entre supervisores y subordinados — y cómo esta confianza impulsa comportamientos prosociales que mejoran la calidad del servicio y la cohesión del equipo. Al hacerlo, ofrece una contribución novedosa a la literatura aplicada al turismo al destacar los procesos psicológicos internos a través de los cuales la transparencia fomenta no solo actitudes positivas de los empleados, sino también comportamientos prosociales concretos que potencian la efectividad organizativa.

2. MARCO TEÓRICO

2.1. Transparencia Organizativa

En los últimos años, la transparencia organizativa ha emergido como un valor central en el discurso público, en las prácticas de gobierno corporativo y en las relaciones entre organizaciones y sus grupos de interés (Albu & Flyverbom, 2019; Heimstädt, 2017). Más allá de ser percibida únicamente como una herramienta de comunicación o una estrategia para legitimidad institucional, la transparencia se ha consolidado como un fenómeno complejo e integrador que abarca múltiples niveles de análisis — desde lo individual hasta lo institucional — y se manifiesta a través de prácticas como la divulgación sistemática de información, la comunicación clara y el acceso facilitado a datos relevantes para los grupos de interés.

Uno de los contextos donde la transparencia organizativa adquiere particular relevancia es dentro de la estructura interna de la empresa, especialmente en la relación entre la dirección y sus empleados. Este tipo específico de transparencia, referido como transparencia organizativa hacia los empleados, implica una comunicación constante, honesta y accesible sobre cuestiones como estrategias corporativas, cambios organizativos, políticas internas, resultados financieros, evaluaciones de desempeño y criterios de promoción y compensación. La transparencia organizativa hacia los empleados es un aspecto crucial en la dinámica laboral moderna, destacando la importancia de la apertura y la honestidad en el intercambio de información dentro de la organización (Albu & Flyverbom, 2019). Esta forma específica de transparencia conlleva una comunicación clara, coherente y comprensible respecto a las decisiones, políticas y acciones de la organización, permitiendo a los empleados entender no solo qué está ocurriendo, sino también por qué ocurre y cómo pueden influir en ello.

Los fundamentos teóricos de la transparencia organizativa hacia los empleados se basan en varios marcos. La Teoría del Agente sugiere que la transparencia ayuda a mitigar el problema principal-agente asegurando que los gerentes actúen en el mejor interés de los empleados y de la organización (Jensen & Meckling, 1976). Al proporcionar información clara y precisa, las organizaciones pueden alinear los intereses de los gerentes y los empleados, reduciendo el riesgo de comportamiento oportunista. Además, la Teoría de los Grupos de Interés sostiene que las organizaciones tienen la responsabilidad de considerar los intereses de todos sus grupos de interés, incluidos los empleados (Freeman, 1984). La transparencia es un componente clave en la gestión de los grupos de interés, ya que permite a los empleados comprender las acciones y decisiones de la organización, fomentando un sentido de inclusión y confianza. Asimismo, la Teoría Institucional sugiere que las organizaciones están influenciadas por las normas y expectativas del entorno institucional en el que operan (DiMaggio & Powell, 1983). La transparencia puede verse como una respuesta a estas presiones externas, ya que las organizaciones buscan cumplir con las expectativas sociales de apertura y rendición de cuentas.

La transparencia organizativa hacia los empleados es fundamental para mejorar la toma de decisiones, fomentar un ambiente de trabajo positivo y potenciar el desempeño organizativo. Al implementar prácticas transparentes, las organizaciones pueden crear un entorno más eficiente, productivo y armonioso. Según Schnackenberg y Tomlinson (2016), la transparencia organizativa proporciona a los empleados información clara y precisa, clave para una toma de decisiones efectiva. Además, Albu y Flyverbom (2019) destacan que la transparencia permite a los empleados tomar decisiones más informadas y eficaces. A su vez, la transparencia organizativa es clave para mejorar el desempeño empresarial, ya que posibilita una ejecución más efectiva de la estrategia, alinea los objetivos individuales con los de la organización, motiva a los empleados mediante un sistema justo de reconocimiento y facilita la retención del talento al crear un entorno de confianza y claridad en el que cada persona comprende su rol en el éxito colectivo (Berggren y Bernshteyn, 2007).

2.2. Confianza Interpersonal

La confianza interpersonal se define como el grado en que una persona tiene seguridad y está dispuesta a actuar basándose en las palabras, acciones y decisiones de otra (Mayer, Davis y Schoorman, 1995). Implica la creencia de que la otra parte es confiable y competente, y que genuinamente se preocupa por su bienestar (McAllister, 1995). Los fundamentos teóricos de la confianza interpersonal en las organizaciones se enraizan en varios marcos clave que ayudan a explicar cómo se desarrolla y mantiene entre los empleados. La Teoría del Intercambio Social plantea que la confianza se construye a través de intercambios recíprocos de beneficios y favores. Básicamente, cuando los empleados reciben apoyo, recursos o ayuda de sus compañeros, sienten un sentido de obligación de devolver el favor. Este intercambio continuo crea un sentido de obligación mutua y fiabilidad. Con el tiempo, a medida que continúan estas interacciones recíprocas, los individuos llegan a depender unos de otros para recibir apoyo, construyendo así confianza. Por ejemplo, si un empleado ayuda a un compañero en un proyecto difícil, el compañero probablemente se sienta agradecido y dispuesto a ofrecer ayuda cuando sea necesario. Este ciclo de dar y recibir fomenta una relación de confianza (Blau, 1964).

Además, la teoría de la Justicia Organizacional destaca la importancia de la equidad en los procesos e interacciones organizativas. Cuando los empleados perciben que son tratados con justicia en términos de distribución de recursos, equidad procedural y trato respetuoso, es más probable que confíen en sus colegas y líderes. El trato justo crea un sentido de seguridad y predictibilidad, componentes esenciales de la confianza. Por ejemplo, si una organización aplica consistentemente sus políticas y procedimientos de manera justa, los empleados se sentirán más seguros de que serán tratados con justicia, lo que incrementará los niveles de confianza. Por el contrario, las percepciones de injusticia pueden erosionar la confianza y generar escepticismo y desconfianza entre los empleados (Colquitt et al., 2007).

También, la Teoría del Apego sugiere que las experiencias tempranas con cuidadores moldean la capacidad de una persona para confiar en otros, y estos patrones pueden extenderse a las relaciones laborales. Según esta teoría, las personas que han desarrollado estilos de apego seguros —caracterizados por un sentido de seguridad y confianza en sus cuidadores

— son más propensas a confiar y formar relaciones positivas en el entorno laboral. Estas personas suelen ser más abiertas, cooperativas y confiadas en sus interacciones con colegas. Por otro lado, personas con estilos de apego inseguros, que pueden haber experimentado cuidados inconsistentes o poco confiables, podrían tener dificultades para confiar y mostrarse más cautelosas o vigilantes en sus relaciones laborales. Esto puede generar dificultades para formar vínculos de confianza con colegas y líderes (Mikulincer y Shaver, 2007).

En resumen, estos marcos teóricos proporcionan colectivamente una comprensión integral de cómo se desarrolla y mantiene la confianza interpersonal en entornos organizativos. La confianza interpersonal en las organizaciones conduce a varios resultados positivos. Facilita el trabajo en equipo eficaz y la colaboración, ya que los empleados están más dispuestos a compartir información y cooperar (Dirks y Ferrin, 2001). Los empleados que confían en sus colegas y líderes tienden a tener mayores niveles de satisfacción laboral y compromiso organizativo (Dirks y Ferrin, 2002). Además, la confianza puede mejorar el desempeño organizativo al fomentar un ambiente laboral positivo y reducir conflictos (Kramer, 1999).

2.3. Compromiso Organizativo

El compromiso organizativo es un estado psicológico que caracteriza la relación de un empleado con su organización y tiene implicaciones sobre su decisión de continuar siendo miembro de ella (Meyer y Allen, 1991). Uno de los componentes más significativos del compromiso organizativo es el compromiso afectivo, que se refiere al vínculo emocional, identificación y participación que un empleado tiene con su organización (Mercurio, 2015).

El compromiso afectivo se define como el vínculo emocional positivo que un empleado siente hacia su organización (Meyer y Allen, 1991). Los empleados con alto compromiso afectivo se identifican fuertemente con los objetivos y valores de la organización y genuinamente desean seguir formando parte de ella porque "quieren hacerlo" (Meyer, Allen y Smith, 1993). Este tipo de compromiso se caracteriza por sentimientos de lealtad, pertenencia y orgullo por estar asociado con la organización. Los fundamentos teóricos del compromiso afectivo se basan en la idea de que los empleados que experimentan emociones positivas y satisfacción en sus roles son más propensos a desarrollar un fuerte vínculo emocional con su organización. Factores como liderazgo de apoyo, relaciones positivas en el lugar de trabajo y alineación con los valores organizativos pueden mejorar significativamente el compromiso afectivo (Meyer y Allen, 1991).

El compromiso afectivo tiene varias implicaciones importantes para los resultados organizativos. Los empleados afectivamente comprometidos son más propensos a mostrar altos niveles de desempeño laboral, participar en Comportamientos Ciudadanos Organizacionales dirigidos hacia Individuos (OCBI) y demostrar menores intenciones de rotación (Mercurio, 2015). Este vínculo emocional motiva a los empleados a ir más allá de sus responsabilidades formales, contribuyendo al éxito general y efectividad de la organización. Además, el compromiso afectivo puede verse influenciado por diversas características demográficas, como edad, antigüedad, género y educación, aunque estas influencias no siempre son fuertes o consistentes (Meyer y Allen, 1991). El desarrollo del compromiso afectivo suele ser resultado de experiencias positivas dentro de la organización, incluyendo reconocimiento, oportunidades de desarrollo profesional y un entorno laboral de apoyo.

2.4. Comportamiento Ciudadano Organizacional dirigido hacia Individuos (OCBI)

El Comportamiento Ciudadano Organizacional dirigido hacia Individuos (OCBI) hace referencia a acciones voluntarias y discrecionales realizadas por empleados para ayudar y beneficiar a otras personas dentro de la organización, más allá de sus responsabilidades formales. Este concepto es una subdimensión del Comportamiento Ciudadano Organizacional (OCB), que engloba comportamientos que no son directamente recompensados ni exigidos por la organización pero que contribuyen al funcionamiento efectivo y armonioso del lugar de trabajo (Organ, 1988; Organ, 1997). El OCBI incluye comportamientos como ofrecer ayuda a colegas, compartir conocimientos y recursos, brindar apoyo emocional y colaborar en tareas que no están estrictamente relacionadas con el rol formal del empleado. Estas acciones fomentan un entorno laboral positivo y pueden mejorar tanto el bienestar individual como colectivo (Organ, 1988; Organ, 1997). El OCBI se basa en la teoría de la reciprocidad y el intercambio social, donde los empleados que participan en estos comportamientos suelen hacerlo con la expectativa implícita de recibir apoyo similar en el futuro. Además, el OCBI puede estar motivado por valores prosociales y altruistas, así como por el deseo de mejorar la cohesión y el desempeño del equipo (Organ, 1988; Organ, 1997). Participar en OCBI puede llevar a varios resultados positivos tanto para los individuos como para las organizaciones.

Al ayudar a colegas, los empleados contribuyen a la efectividad y eficiencia general de sus equipos (Podsakoff et al., 2009). Los empleados que participan en OCBI suelen experimentar niveles más altos de satisfacción laboral y un mayor sentido de realización personal (Bateman y Organ, 1983).

El OCBI representa un aspecto crítico del comportamiento organizativo que enfatiza la importancia de acciones voluntarias y de apoyo entre empleados. Al fomentar estos comportamientos, las organizaciones pueden crear un entorno de trabajo más colaborativo y solidario, contribuyendo finalmente a la efectividad organizativa global (Organ, 1988; Organ, 1997).

3. HIPÓTESIS

Con base en el marco teórico y la literatura existente, este estudio propone tres hipótesis para explorar las relaciones entre transparencia organizacional, confianza interpersonal, compromiso organizacional y comportamientos ciudadanos organizacionales dirigidos hacia individuos (OCBI, por sus siglas en inglés).

Como se ha discutido previamente, la transparencia organizacional implica una comunicación clara y abierta de decisiones y acciones, así como la provisión de información precisa y relevante a los empleados (Schnackenberg & Tomlinson, 2016). Schnackenberg y Tomlinson (2016) argumentan que cuando las organizaciones son transparentes, los empleados tienden a percibirlas como justas y confiables, dimensiones clave que fomentan la confianza institucional. La transparencia también reduce la asimetría informativa y promueve un acceso igualitario al conocimiento, lo cual contribuye a una percepción de justicia procedimental y predictibilidad en las relaciones organizacionales.

La confianza interpersonal, a su vez, se fundamenta en intercambios recíprocos y en expectativas mutuas de integridad y benevolencia (Blau, 1964). Investigaciones sugieren que dicha confianza se fortalece cuando los individuos perciben justicia en los procesos de toma de decisiones (Colquitt et al., 2007), y cuando desarrollan estilos relacionales seguros que facilitan la cooperación (Mikulincer & Shaver, 2007). Además, Rawlins (2008) encontró una asociación positiva entre la transparencia organizacional y la confianza de los empleados en la organización, reforzando la idea de que la apertura fomenta percepciones de fiabilidad y conducta ética.

Es importante destacar que la transparencia no solo construye confianza en la organización, sino que también puede incentivar la confianza entre los empleados mismos (Barghouti et al., 2022). Al señalar la disposición de la dirección a compartir información e involucrar a los empleados en los procesos organizacionales, la transparencia puede iniciar un ciclo de confianza recíproca (Blau, 1964), en el cual los empleados se sienten confiados y responden extendiendo confianza hacia otros. Esta dinámica respalda la visión de que la transparencia no solo moldea la confianza institucional, sino también la confianza interpersonal dentro de la organización.

Por lo tanto, proponemos la siguiente hipótesis:

- *H1: Existe una relación positiva y significativa entre la transparencia organizacional percibida y la confianza interpersonal entre empleados.*

Estudios han demostrado que la transparencia organizacional mejora el compromiso afectivo al fomentar un sentido de inclusión y una identificación emocional con la organización. Por ejemplo, Klimchak et al. (2020) encontraron que la transparencia permite a los empleados tomar decisiones más informadas y efectivas, lo cual fortalece su vínculo emocional con la organización. De manera similar, Rawlins (2008) argumentan que la transparencia promueve una cultura de apertura y responsabilidad, incrementando así el sentido de pertenencia y lealtad de los empleados. Jahansoozi (2006) enfatiza además que una comunicación honesta y transparente, basada en apertura e integridad, sirve como base fundamental para fortalecer el vínculo emocional y la identificación de los empleados con su organización. Estos hallazgos coinciden con la definición clásica del compromiso afectivo como un vínculo emocional que lleva a las personas a permanecer en la organización debido a la identificación y el involucramiento (Meyer & Allen, 1991). En conjunto, estas investigaciones sugieren que cuando los empleados perciben altos niveles de transparencia organizacional, es más probable que desarrollen fuertes vínculos emocionales caracterizados por lealtad, orgullo y sentido de pertenencia.

Además, hay evidencia que respalda una conexión entre el compromiso afectivo y la confianza interpersonal. Nyhan (1999), por ejemplo, encontró que la confianza en los directivos está fuertemente asociada con el compromiso organizacional, lo que sugiere que los empleados emocionalmente comprometidos tienden a extender mayor confianza hacia otros. Dirks y Ferrin (2002) destacan también que el liderazgo transformacional —estrechamente vinculado con la transparencia y la justicia— fortalece tanto el compromiso afectivo como la confianza en los líderes. Además, Ouedraogo y Laid Ouakouak (2018) mostraron que la confianza interpersonal está positivamente relacionada con el compromiso afectivo, indicando que este último desempeña un papel mediador clave en el éxito del cambio organizacional.

Este conjunto de evidencia sugiere que el compromiso afectivo puede actuar como un mecanismo psicológico a través del cual la transparencia fomenta la confianza interpersonal. Los empleados que se sienten emocionalmente conectados con su organización son más propensos a interpretar las acciones de los demás de manera positiva, lo que lleva a una mayor confianza mutua y comportamiento cooperativo.

Con base en esta fundamentación teórica, proponemos la siguiente hipótesis:

- *H2: La relación entre la transparencia organizacional y la confianza interpersonal está mediada por el compromiso organizacional afectivo.*

La confianza interpersonal en el lugar de trabajo puede desempeñar un papel crucial en la promoción de los OCBI. Un creciente cuerpo de investigación ha demostrado consistentemente que la confianza interpersonal influye significativamente en la medida en que los empleados participan en acciones discrecionales que van más allá de los requisitos formales del trabajo, como ayudar a compañeros, compartir conocimientos y brindar apoyo emocional (por ejemplo, Dirks & Ferrin, 2001; Kim & Park, 2019; Singh & Srivastava, 2009).

Por ejemplo, Ghasemy y Frömbling (2024) encontraron que el afecto positivo media la relación entre la confianza interpersonal en compañeros y los OCBI. Su estudio reveló que los empleados que confían en sus colegas tienden a mostrar más OCBI, impulsados por las emociones positivas generadas a través de estas relaciones de confianza. De manera similar, Dirks y Ferrin (2001) exploraron las implicaciones más amplias de la confianza en entornos organizacionales y concluyeron que la confianza facilita un trabajo en equipo y colaboración efectivos, ya que los empleados están más dispuestos a compartir información y cooperar cuando confían en sus colegas. La confianza en los demás permite a los empleados interpretar las acciones de sus compañeros de manera más favorable, reduciendo conflictos y malentendidos, y facilitando así el desempeño de comportamientos de ayuda discrecional (Colquitt et al., 2007; Rousseau, 1998). Estos hallazgos coinciden con la Teoría del Intercambio Social (Blau, 1964), que plantea que la confianza surge de intercambios recíprocos de beneficios y favores. Este intercambio continuo fomenta un sentido de obligación mutua y fiabilidad, reforzando la disposición de los empleados a involucrarse en comportamientos de apoyo (Mayer, Davis, & Schoorman, 1995). Como resultado, se espera que niveles más altos de confianza interpersonal estén asociados con un mayor involucramiento en OCBI.

Con base en esta fundamentación teórica y empírica, proponemos la siguiente hipótesis:

- *H3: Existe una relación positiva y significativa entre la confianza interpersonal y los Comportamientos Ciudadanos Organizacionales dirigidos hacia individuos (OCBI).*

4. METODOLOGÍA

4.1. Diseño de investigación

Este estudio emplea un diseño de investigación cuantitativo y transversal para examinar las relaciones entre la transparencia organizacional, la confianza interpersonal, el compromiso organizacional y los comportamientos ciudadanos organizacionales dirigidos hacia individuos (OCBI). Los diseños transversales son especialmente útiles para capturar una instantánea de las relaciones entre variables en un único momento en el tiempo. Los datos se recopilaron mediante encuestas aplicadas a empleados del sector turístico, lo que proporcionó una visión integral de sus percepciones y comportamientos. Las encuestas se administraron en dos periodos: la primera entre noviembre y diciembre de 2022, y la segunda en enero de 2023. Este enfoque aseguró que la recolección de datos cubriera diferentes momentos del año, posiblemente captando variaciones en las percepciones y comportamientos de los empleados. Las encuestas se distribuyeron por teléfono y las respuestas se recopilaron de forma anónima para fomentar respuestas honestas y precisas.

4.2. Muestra

El estudio se basa en una encuesta realizada en el sector turístico en 2023, abarcando diversas empresas y empleados de las provincias de Alicante, Castellón de la Plana y Valencia. La muestra consta de un total de 249 encuestados, con una distribución casi igual entre hombres (124) y mujeres (125). La muestra incluye empleados de 50 empresas turísticas diferentes, cada una contribuyendo con cinco empleados al estudio, asegurando así una representación diversa de roles y departamentos dentro del sector. La selección de los empleados fue aleatoria para minimizar sesgos y garantizar representatividad. La mayoría de las empresas son hoteles y resorts que ofrecen servicios de alojamiento y turismo.

En cuanto al nivel educativo, los participantes presentan una variedad de calificaciones, desde educación obligatoria (12) hasta doctorado (2), siendo la mayoría graduados universitarios (105). La antigüedad en la empresa actual varía considerablemente, con un grupo importante de empleados que lleva entre 2 y 5 años (110) en su puesto, seguido por aquellos con experiencia de entre 5 y 10 años (70).

Los cargos desempeñados por los encuestados también son diversos e incluyen directores, gerentes, jefes de departamento, técnicos de mantenimiento, camareros, recepcionistas y gerentes de recursos humanos, entre otros. Esta diversidad en cargos y niveles educativos ofrece una visión amplia y representativa del sector turístico, permitiendo comprender mejor las dinámicas y características de los empleados en esta industria.

4.3. Instrumentos de medición

Para medir los constructos de interés, utilizamos escalas validadas que han sido ampliamente adoptadas en numerosos estudios para analizar estas variables. Específicamente, empleamos una escala Likert que va del 1 al 7, donde 1 significa "totalmente en desacuerdo" y 7 significa "totalmente de acuerdo". Las propiedades psicométricas de estas escalas han sido previamente analizadas y la validez de los instrumentos de medición ha sido confirmada por otros estudios.

- Transparencia organizacional: Se midió utilizando la escala desarrollada por Rawlins (2008), que incluye ítems como "La organización quiere entender cómo sus decisiones afectan a personas como yo" y "La organización proporciona información útil para personas como yo, para tomar decisiones informadas".
- Compromiso organizacional: Se midió utilizando la escala desarrollada por Meyer y Allen (1991), adaptada por Bulut y Culha (2010). Esta escala incluye ítems como "Estaría muy feliz pasando el resto de mi carrera en esta organización" y "Realmente siento que los problemas de esta organización son mis propios problemas".
- Confianza interpersonal: Se midió utilizando la escala desarrollada por Huff y Kelley (2003), que incluye ítems como "Existe un alto nivel de confianza a través de toda esta organización" y "Los gerentes en esta empresa confían en que sus subordinados tomen buenas decisiones".

Esta escala evalúa el grado de confianza dentro de la organización, centrándose en la confianza que los empleados tienen en sus directivos, la fiabilidad de las promesas realizadas dentro de la organización y la cultura general de confianza que impregna a la organización.

- Comportamiento ciudadano organizacional dirigido hacia individuos (OCBI): Se midió utilizando la escala desarrollada por Lee y Allen (2002), que incluye ítems como "Ayudar a otros que han estado ausentes" y "Dar voluntariamente tu tiempo para ayudar a otros que tengan problemas relacionados con el trabajo".

4.4. Estadística descriptiva y fiabilidad de las escalas de medida

Las estadísticas descriptivas de los indicadores considerados en el estudio (medias y desviaciones estándar) y los factores de correlación se presentan en la Tabla I. Para verificar la fiabilidad de la escala, además del coeficiente alfa de Cronbach (Cronbach, 1951), se utilizaron dos indicadores más: la fiabilidad compuesta (Fornell y Larcker, 1981) y la varianza media extraída (Alegre y Chiva, 2008) (ver Tabla II). Tanto los valores del coeficiente alfa de Cronbach como la fiabilidad compuesta están por encima del valor mínimo aceptable de 0,7 (Nunnally, 1978). Además, la varianza media extraída muestra valores superiores al mínimo recomendado de 0,5 (Hair et al., 1998; Nunnally, 1978).

Dado que estos son medidas de evaluación subjetiva, se realizó una prueba de un solo factor de Harman (Podsakoff et al., 2003). Esta prueba permite determinar si un único factor explica la mayor parte de la varianza en nuestros datos, lo cual indicaría una varianza común de método (CMV). Los resultados de la prueba indican que el primer factor explica el 46,274% de la varianza total. Este valor es menor al 50%, lo que indica que no hay un único factor dominante que explique la mayor parte de la varianza en los datos. Por lo tanto, se puede concluir que la varianza común de método no es un problema significativo en este estudio. Además de la prueba de un solo factor de Harman, se realizó la técnica CFA Marker usando EQS. Se incluyó una variable marcadora teóricamente no relacionada en el modelo de análisis factorial confirmatorio. Los índices de ajuste del modelo, incluyendo el CFI (0,934), NNFI (0,926), IFI (0,935) y RMSEA (0,072), indicaron un buen ajuste del modelo tanto con, como sin la variable marcadora. Los resultados mostraron que la inclusión de la variable marcadora no mejoró significativamente el ajuste del modelo, reforzando la conclusión de que la CMV no representa un problema significativo en este estudio.

Tabla 1. Medias, desviaciones estándar y factores de correlación (N=249)

	Mean	S.D.	OCBI1	OCBI2	OCBI3	OCBI4	OCBI5	OCBI6	OCBI7	OCBI8	COMIT1	COMIT2	COMIT3	COMIT4	COMIT5	COMIT6	TRUST1	TRUST2	TRUST3	TRUST4	TRANSP1	TRANSP2	TRANSP3	TRANSP4
OCBI1	5,655	1,212	1	,529**	,414**	,441**	,405**	,431**	,475**	,244**	,321**	,299**	,298**	,297**	,189**	,278**	,286**	,166**	,238**	,204**	0,116	,166**	0,111	,172**
OCBI2	5,968	1,153	,529**	1	,336**	,640**	,609**	,498**	,630**	,283**	,412**	,393**	,462**	,390**	,356**	,354**	,355**	,165**	,272**	,270**	,195**	,277**	,263**	,312**
OCBI3	5,193	1,662	,414**	,336**	1	,295**	,375**	,270**	,416**	,389**	,234**	,304**	,265**	,363**	,281**	,344**	,355**	,224**	,319**	,258**	,175**	,135*	,176**	,188**
OCBI4	6,149	1,062	,441**	,640**	,295**	1	,805**	,704**	,701**	,425**	,389**	,384**	,424**	,382**	,379**	,365**	,377**	,272**	,402**	,380**	,294**	,277**	,304**	,338**
OCBI5	5,900	1,235	,405**	,609**	,375**	,805**	1	,723**	,682**	,518**	,368**	,340**	,393**	,370**	,328**	,326**	,308**	,216**	,318**	,341**	,249**	,216**	,276**	,314**
OCBI6	5,687	1,260	,431**	,498**	,270**	,704**	,723**	1	,681**	,527**	,314**	,327**	,284**	,302**	,271**	,319**	,242**	,286**	,360**	,361**	,293**	,228**	,299**	,348**
OCBI7	5,767	1,255	,475**	,630**	,416**	,701**	,682**	,681**	1	,502**	,410**	,450**	,398**	,366**	,314**	,389**	,340**	,279**	,403**	,372**	,323**	,258**	,323**	,347**
OCBI8	5,305	1,597	,244**	,283**	,389**	,425**	,518**	,527**	,502**	1	,195**	0,123	,172**	,187**	0,100	,151*	,177**	,134*	,241**	,229**	,158*	0,109	,165**	,207**
COMIT1	4,153	1,886	,321**	,412**	,234**	,389**	,368**	,314**	,410**	,195**	1	,640**	,555**	,528**	,586**	,575**	,480**	,384**	,368**	,454**	,398**	,425**	,325**	,356**
COMIT2	4,121	1,805	,299**	,393**	,304**	,384**	,340**	,327**	,450**	0,123	,640**	1	,617**	,649**	,636**	,664**	,485**	,505**	,506**	,502**	,487**	,466**	,435**	,418**
COMIT3	4,345	1,783	,298**	,462**	,265**	,424**	,393**	,284**	,398**	,172**	,555**	,617**	1	,810**	,769**	,769**	,661**	,537**	,523**	,481**	,512**	,591**	,586**	,546**
COMIT4	4,241	1,800	,297**	,390**	,363**	,382**	,370**	,302**	,366**	,187**	,528**	,649**	,810**	1	,811**	,821**	,721**	,617**	,571**	,569**	,550**	,626**	,588**	,598**
COMIT5	4,032	1,811	,189**	,356**	,281**	,379**	,328**	,271**	,314**	0,100	,586**	,636**	,769**	,811**	1	,823**	,667**	,656**	,599**	,556**	,588**	,589**	,583**	,555**
COMIT6	4,032	1,842	,278**	,354**	,344**	,365**	,326**	,319**	,389**	,151*	,575**	,664**	,769**	,821**	,823**	1	,693**	,609**	,602**	,607**	,549**	,614**	,600**	,606**
TRUST1	4,382	1,742	,286**	,355**	,355**	,377**	,308**	,242**	,340**	,177**	,480**	,485**	,661**	,721**	,667**	,693**	1	,724**	,717**	,532**	,654**	,702**	,689**	,683**
TRUST2	3,964	1,817	,166**	,165**	,224**	,272**	,216**	,286**	,279**	,134*	,384**	,505**	,537**	,617**	,656**	,609**	,724**	1	,744**	,735**	,863**	,781**	,757**	,696**
TRUST3	4,289	1,791	,238**	,272**	,319**	,402**	,318**	,360**	,403**	,241**	,368**	,506**	,523**	,571**	,599**	,602**	,717**	,744**	1	,637**	,712**	,678**	,653**	,621**
TRUST4	4,438	1,809	,204**	,270**	,258**	,380**	,341**	,361**	,372**	,229**	,454**	,502**	,481**	,569**	,556**	,607**	,532**	,735**	,637**	1	,746**	,711**	,624**	,612**
TRANSP1	4,121	1,753	0,116	,195**	,175**	,294**	,249**	,293**	,323**	,158*	,398**	,487**	,512**	,550**	,588**	,549**	,654**	,863**	,712**	,746**	1	,832**	,802**	,749**
TRANSP2	4,277	1,780	,166**	,277**	,135*	,277**	,216**	,228**	,258**	0,109	,425**	,466**	,591**	,626**	,589**	,614**	,702**	,781**	,678**	,711**	,832**	1	,812**	,746**
TRANSP3	4,040	1,866	0,111	,263**	,176**	,304**	,276**	,299**	,323**	,165**	,325**	,435**	,586**	,588**	,583**	,600**	,689**	,757**	,653**	,624**	,802**	,812**	1	,829**
TRANSP4	4,366	1,881	,172**	,312**	,188**	,338**	,314**	,348**	,347**	,207**	,356**	,418**	,546**	,598**	,555**	,606**	,683**	,696**	,621**	,612**	,749**	,746**	,829**	1

**. The correlation is significant at the 0.01 level (two-tailed).

*. The correlation is significant at the 0.05 level (two-tailed).

Tabla 2. Fiabilidad de los instrumentos de medida.

Constructo	Cronbach's α	Fiabilidad compuesta	Varianza media extraída
Transparencia organizativa	0.939	0.938	0.793
Confianza interpersonal	0.895	0.898	0.688
Compromiso organizativo	0.928	0.929	0.689
OCBI	0.876	0.891	0.519

5. RESULTADOS

Los datos recopilados se analizaron utilizando EQS 6.4 para Windows, una herramienta diseñada específicamente para el modelado de ecuaciones estructurales (SEM). El SEM es especialmente adecuado para este estudio ya que permite examinar relaciones complejas entre múltiples variables simultáneamente. Los resultados obtenidos muestran que la transparencia organizacional tiene un impacto significativo tanto en la confianza interpersonal como en el compromiso organizacional (Figura 1). Específicamente, la transparencia organizacional influye positivamente en la confianza interpersonal con un coeficiente de 0,676 y un estadístico de prueba de 13,221, lo que indica una relación positiva fuerte. Además, la transparencia organizacional también tiene un impacto positivo en el compromiso organizacional, con un coeficiente de 0,541 y un estadístico de prueba de 9,451, lo que sugiere que los empleados que perciben transparencia en su organización tienden a sentirse más comprometidos con ella.

A su vez, el compromiso organizacional tiene un impacto significativo en la confianza interpersonal. Los resultados muestran que el compromiso organizacional influye positivamente en la confianza interpersonal con un coeficiente de 0,313 y un estadístico de prueba de 5,308. Esto sugiere que el compromiso organizacional media parcialmente la relación entre transparencia y confianza, confirmando la hipótesis de que la relación entre la transparencia organizacional y la confianza interpersonal está mediada por el compromiso organizacional. Finalmente, la confianza interpersonal tiene un impacto significativo en el OCBI. Los resultados indican que la confianza interpersonal influye positivamente en el OCBI con un coeficiente de 0,202 y un estadístico de prueba de 5,616, confirmando la hipótesis de que la confianza interpersonal está positivamente relacionada con el OCBI.

Los índices de ajuste del modelo sugieren que el modelo tiene un buen ajuste general. El índice de ajuste normado de Bentler-Bonett (NFI) es de 0,887, el índice de ajuste no normado de Bentler-Bonett (NNFI) es de 0,923, el índice comparativo de ajuste (CFI) es de 0,931, el índice incremental de ajuste de Bollen (IFI) es de 0,932 y el error cuadrático medio aproximado (RMSEA) es de 0,074, con un intervalo de confianza del 90% para el RMSEA entre 0,065 y 0,082.

En resumen, los resultados del análisis de modelado de ecuaciones estructurales confirman las hipótesis planteadas en el estudio. La transparencia organizacional tiene un impacto significativo en la confianza interpersonal y el compromiso organizacional. El compromiso organizacional media parcialmente la relación entre transparencia y confianza, y la confianza interpersonal influye significativamente en el OCBI. Estos hallazgos destacan la importancia de la transparencia organizacional para fomentar la confianza y el compromiso entre los empleados, así como para promover comportamientos positivos en el lugar de trabajo.

Figura 1. Resultados del modelo de investigación.

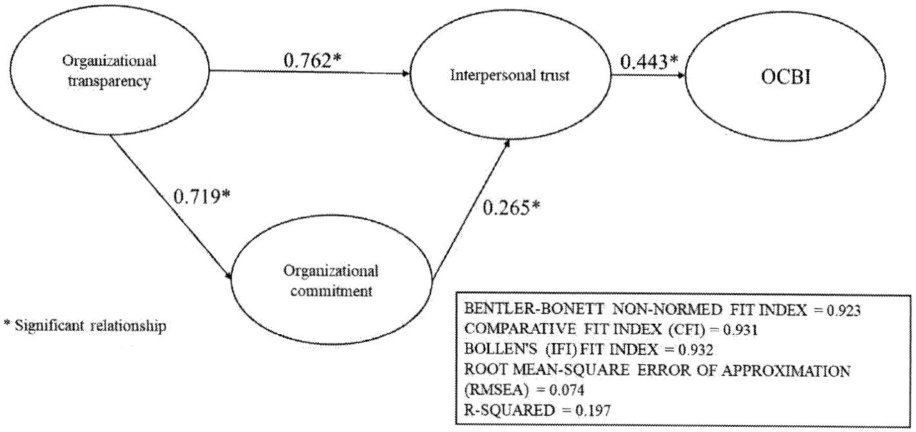

Organizational transparency
0.762*
Interpersonal trust
0.443*
OCBI
0.719*
0.265*
Organizational commitment
* Significant relationship

BENTLER-BONETT NON-NORMED FIT INDEX = 0.923
COMPARATIVE FIT INDEX (CFI) = 0.931
BOLLEN'S (IFI) FIT INDEX = 0.932
ROOT MEAN-SQUARE ERROR OF APPROXIMATION (RMSEA) = 0.074
R-SQUARED = 0.197

6. DISCUSIÓN

Los resultados de este estudio ofrecen valiosas perspectivas sobre cómo la transparencia organizativa influye en la confianza interpersonal, el compromiso afectivo y los comportamientos prosociales entre empleados del sector turístico. Al examinar estas relaciones dentro de un marco integrado, no solo confirmamos hallazgos previos, sino que también ampliamos su aplicación a contextos específicos del turismo, donde la colaboración humana, la experiencia del cliente y la coordinación interna son esenciales.

Una de las contribuciones más destacadas del estudio radica en demostrar que la transparencia organizativa desempeña un papel fundamental en la construcción de la confianza interpersonal entre empleados del sector turístico. En industrias como la hotelería o el transporte vacacional, donde la calidad del servicio depende en gran medida de la cooperación entre equipos, la percepción de una comunicación clara y coherente por parte de la dirección fortalece la confianza mutua entre trabajadores. Cuando los empleados perciben que la organización actúa con integridad y justicia, se sienten más seguros y dispuestos a colaborar, compartir información y apoyarse mutuamente — factores clave para ofrecer una experiencia positiva al cliente. Estos resultados coinciden con literatura previa que destaca la transparencia como un pilar fundamental de la confianza en entornos organizacionales (Dirks & Ferrin, 2001), pero lo extienden al contexto turístico, subrayando su relevancia en sectores altamente interpersonales.

De forma aún más significativa, el estudio realiza una novedosa contribución teórica al mostrar que el compromiso afectivo organizativo media la relación entre transparencia y confianza interpersonal en empresas turísticas. Aunque estudios anteriores han explorado por separado los efectos de la transparencia sobre la confianza y sobre el compromiso, pocos han analizado cómo estos constructos interactúan dentro de un único modelo aplicado al turismo. Nuestros hallazgos sugieren que la transparencia no solo fortalece directamente la confianza, sino que también refuerza la identificación emocional de los empleados con la organización, lo cual a su vez incrementa su disposición a confiar en sus compañeros y líderes. Este descubrimiento tiene implicaciones prácticas importantes en un sector caracterizado por alta rotación laboral y trabajo en equipo intensivo, ya que una cultura transparente puede ayudar a retener talento y mejorar la cohesión del equipo.

A su vez, el análisis respalda la idea de que la confianza interpersonal es un fuerte predictor de los Comportamientos Ciudadanos Organizacionales dirigidos hacia Individuos (OCBI) en el ámbito turístico. Reforzando evidencia existente (Podsakoff et al., 1990; Dirks & Ferrin, 2001), nuestros datos muestran que los empleados que confían en sus colegas están más dispuestos a ayudar, compartir recursos y resolver conflictos proactivamente, todo ello esencial para garantizar un servicio eficiente y personalizado. Esta relación cobra especial relevancia en el sector turístico, donde la atención al cliente muchas veces depende de la resolución rápida de imprevistos y la coordinación espontánea entre empleados. Por tanto, fomentar la transparencia desde la dirección puede traducirse en un ambiente laboral más colaborativo, lo cual impacta directamente en la experiencia del viajero.

Desde una perspectiva académica, esta investigación aborda una laguna en la literatura al proponer y validar empíricamente un modelo mediado que integra cuatro constructos centrales —transparencia, compromiso afectivo, confianza interpersonal y OCBI — que suelen estudiarse de manera aislada. Al hacerlo, proporciona una comprensión más holística de los mecanismos psicológicos y sociales que conectan las prácticas organizativas con los comportamientos de los empleados en el ámbito turístico. Este enfoque permite ir más allá de simples asociaciones estadísticas y explorar cómo la transparencia estructural influye en las dinámicas informales del lugar de trabajo, especialmente en hoteles, agencias de viajes y servicios turísticos donde la calidad humana del servicio es un factor diferenciador clave.

Además, al centrarse en la confianza horizontal entre empleados, el estudio amplía el alcance habitual de la investigación en comportamiento organizacional, que suele priorizar la confianza vertical (hacia líderes) u organizacional (hacia la institución). Sin embargo, en el sector turístico, donde los equipos deben trabajar de forma ágil y coordinada para responder a necesidades cambiantes de los clientes, la confianza entre pares es igualmente crítica para la toma de decisiones rápidas, el intercambio de conocimientos y la resolución de problemas en tiempo real.

Desde un punto de vista práctico, los resultados sugieren que la transparencia debe considerarse una herramienta estratégica para moldear una cultura organizativa positiva en empresas turísticas. Directivos y responsables de RR.HH. interesados en construir equipos cohesionados pueden beneficiarse de implementar estrategias de comunicación transparente, procesos participativos de toma de decisiones y un trato consistente y justo hacia todos los empleados. Estos esfuerzos no solo mejoran la claridad y reducen la incertidumbre, sino que también fomentan vínculos emocionales más fuertes con la organización y animan a la cooperación voluntaria, incluso en ausencia de incentivos extrínsecos. En un sector donde la rotación laboral es elevada y la motivación del empleado impacta directamente en la satisfacción del cliente, estas prácticas pueden convertirse en una ventaja competitiva sostenible.

Esta investigación también responde a un desafío real: cómo promover comportamientos prosociales y colaboración espontánea sin recurrir exclusivamente a recompensas financieras. Los resultados indican que cultivar un ambiente transparente puede lograr este objetivo, convirtiéndose en un elemento clave en estrategias de gestión del talento y desarrollo organizativo en el sector turístico.

A pesar de sus contribuciones, el estudio presenta ciertas limitaciones. El tamaño de la muestra, compuesto por 249 empleados de 50 empresas turísticas en Alicante, Castellón y Valencia, podría limitar la generalización de los hallazgos a otros tipos de organizaciones o regiones. Además, la recolección de datos se realizó en dos periodos distintos (noviembre-diciembre de 2022 y enero de 2023), lo cual podría haber introducido variabilidad debido a fluctuaciones estacionales propias del sector turístico.

Futuras investigaciones podrían explorar cómo estas relaciones se manifiestan en otros contextos culturales o subsectores del turismo (como cruceros, plataformas digitales de viaje o turismo rural), y si variables como el estilo de liderazgo, la cultura organizacional o las políticas de formación afectan o modulan dichos efectos. Estudios longitudinales permitirían además observar cómo la transparencia influye en la evolución del compromiso y la conducta prosocial a largo plazo, especialmente en temporadas de alta y baja demanda.

En resumen, este estudio contribuye al creciente cuerpo de literatura sobre la transparencia organizativa al demostrar su influencia en el compromiso afectivo, la confianza interpersonal y los comportamientos prosociales, todo ello contextualizado en el ecosistema del turismo. Subraya el valor de la transparencia no solo como una práctica gerencial, sino como un elemento fundamental para construir una cultura organizativa saludable, colaborativa y éticamente sólida, capaz de mejorar tanto la experiencia del empleado como la del cliente final.

7. REFERENCIAS

Albu, O.B. & Flyverbom, M. 2019. Organizational transparency: Conceptualizations, conditions, and consequences. *Business & Society,* 58(2), pp. 268–297.

Alegre, J. & Chiva, R. 2008. Assessing the impact of organizational learning capability on product innovation performance: An empirical test. *Technovation,* 28(6), pp. 315–326.

Altuntas, S. & Baykal, U. 2010. Relationship between nurses' organizational trust levels and their organizational citizenship behaviors. *Journal of Nursing Scholarship,* 42(2), pp. 186–194.

Auger, G.A. 2014. Trust me, trust me not: An experimental analysis of the effect of transparency on organizations. *Journal of Public Relations Research,* 26(4), pp. 325–343.

Bateman, T.S. & Organ, D.W. 1983. Job satisfaction and the good soldier: The relationship between affect and employee "citizenship". *Academy of Management Journal,* 26(4), pp. 587–595.

Barghouti, Z., Guinot, J. & Chiva, R. 2022. Humanizing organizations: The role of organizational trust and transparency. In: *Towards humanizing workplaces and organizations: enriching theory and practice through multiple approaches.* Tirant lo Blanch, pp. 121–131.

Berggren, E. & Bernshteyn, R. 2007. Organizational transparency drives company performance. *Journal of Management Development,* 26(5), pp. 411–417.

Blau, P.M. 1964. *Exchange and power in social life.* New York: Wiley.

Bratley, K.J. & Aloysius, S.M. 2019. Transparency in managerial practices and affective commitment. *Journal of Business Studies,* 6(2), pp. 61–81.

Bulut, C. & Culha, O. 2010. The effects of organizational training on organizational commitment. *International Journal of Training and Development,* 14(4), pp. 309–322.

Colquitt, J.A., Scott, B.A. & LePine, J.A. 2007. Trust, trustworthiness, and trust propensity: A meta-analytic test of their unique relationships with risk taking and job performance. *Journal of Applied Psychology,* 92(4), pp. 909–927.

DiMaggio, P.J. & Powell, W.W. 1983. The iron cage revisited: Institutional isomorphism and collective rationality in organizational fields. *American Sociological Review,* 48(2), pp. 147–160.

Dirks, K.T. & Ferrin, D.L. 2001. The role of trust in organizational settings. *Organization Science,* 12(4), pp.450–467.

Freeman, R.E. 1984. *Strategic management: A stakeholder approach.* Boston: Pitman.

Ghasemy, M. & Frömbling, L. 2024. Lecturers' interpersonal trust in peers, job performance, and OCBI: examining the mediating role of positive affect during the Covid-19 pandemic utilizing the PLSe2 estimator. *International Journal of Productivity and Performance Management,* 73(6), pp. 1996–2015.

Hair, J.F., Black, W.C., Babin, B.J., Anderson, R.E. & Tatham, R.L. 1998. *Multivariate data analysis* (5th ed.). Upper Saddle River, NJ: Prentice Hall.

Heimstädt, M. 2017. Openwashing: A decoupling perspective on organizational transparency. *Technological Forecasting and Social Change,* 125, pp. 77–86.

Huff, L. & Kelley, L. 2003. Levels of organizational trust in individualist versus collectivist societies: A seven-nation study. *Organization Science,* 14(1), pp. 81–90.

Jahansoozi, J. 2006. Organization-stakeholder relationships: exploring trust and transparency. *Journal of Management Development,* 25(10), pp. 942–955.

Jensen, M.C. & Meckling, W.H. 1976. Theory of the firm: Managerial behavior, agency costs and ownership structure. *Journal of Financial Economics,* 3(4), pp .305–360.

Kim, E.J. & Park, S. 2019. The role of transformational leadership in citizenship behavior: Organizational learning and interpersonal trust as mediators. *International Journal of Manpower,* 40(7), pp. 1347–1360.

Klimchak, M., Ward Bartlett, A.K. & MacKenzie, W. 2020. Building trust and commitment through transparency and HR competence: A signaling perspective. *Personnel Review,* 49(9), pp. 1897–1917.

Kramer, R.M. 1999. Trust and distrust in organizations: Emerging perspectives, enduring questions. *Annual Review of Psychology,* 50, pp. 569–598.

Lee, K. & Allen, N.J. 2002. Organizational citizenship behavior and workplace deviance: The role of affect and cognitions. *Journal of Applied Psychology,* 87(1), pp. 131–142.

Mayer, R.C., Davis, J.H. & Schoorman, F.D. 1995. An integrative model of organizational trust. *Academy of Management Review,* 20(3), pp. 709–734.

McAllister, D.J. 1995. Affect– and cognition-based trust as foundations for interpersonal cooperation in organizations. *Academy of Management Journal,* 38(1), pp. 24–59.

Mercurio, Z.A. 2015. Affective commitment as a core essence of organizational commitment: An integrative literature review. *Human Resource Development Review,* 14(4), pp. 389–414.

Meyer, J.P. & Allen, N.J. 1991. A three-component conceptualization of organizational commitment. *Human Resource Management Review,* 1(1), pp. 61–89.

Meyer, J.P., Allen, N.J. & Smith, C.A. 1993. Commitment to organizations and occupations: Extension and test of a three-component conceptualization. *Journal of Applied Psychology,* 78(4), pp. 538.

Mikulincer, M. & Shaver, P.R. 2007. *Attachment in adulthood: Structure, dynamics, and change.* New York: Guilford Press.

Nunnally, J.C. 1978. *Psychometric theory* (2nd ed.). New York: McGraw-Hill.

Nyhan, R.C. 1999. Increasing affective organizational commitment in public organizations: The key role of interpersonal trust. *Review of Public Personnel Administration,* 19(3), pp. 58–70.

Organ, D.W. 1988. *Organizational citizenship behavior: The good soldier syndrome.* Lexington, MA: Lexington Books.

Organ, D.W. 1997. Organizational citizenship behavior: It's construct clean-up time. *Human Performance,* 10(2), pp. 85–97.

Ouedraogo, N. & Ouakouak, M.L. 2018. Impacts of personal trust, communication, and affective commitment on change success. *Journal of Organizational Change Management,* 31(3), pp. 676–696.

Pepper, M.B., Tredennick, L. & Reyes, R.F. 2010. Transparency and trust as antecedents to perceptions of commitment to stated diversity goals. *Journal of Diversity in Higher Education,* 3(3), pp. 153.

Podsakoff, P.M., MacKenzie, S.B., Moorman, R.H. & Fetter, R. 1990. Transformational leader behaviors and their effects on followers' trust in leader, satisfaction, and organizational citizenship behaviors. *The Leadership Quarterly,* 1(2), pp. 107–142.

Podsakoff, P.M., MacKenzie, S.B., Paine, J.B. & Bachrach, D.G. 2000. Organizational citizenship behaviors: A critical review of the theoretical and empirical literature and suggestions for future research. *Journal of Management,* 26(3), pp. 513–563.

Rawlins, B.L. 2008. Measuring the relationship between organizational transparency and employee trust. *Public Relations Journal,* 2(2), pp. 1–21.

Schnackenberg, A.K. & Tomlinson, E.C. 2016. Organizational transparency: A new perspective on managing trust in organization-stakeholder relationships. *Journal of Management,* 42(7), pp. 1784–1810.

Sifry, M.L. 2011. *WikiLeaks and the age of transparency.* Berkeley, CA: Counterpoint.

Singh, U. & Srivastava, K.B. 2009. Interpersonal trust and organizational citizenship behavior. *Psychological Studies,* 54, pp. 65–76.

Sofyani, H., Pratolo, S. & Saleh, Z. 2022. Do accountability and transparency promote community trust? Evidence from village government in Indonesia. *Journal of Accounting & Organizational Change,* 18(3), pp. 397–418.

FROM TECHNOLOGY TO GOVERNANCE: THEMATIC EVOLUTION OF SMART TOURISM DESTINATION RESEARCH

Beatriz Forés
José María Fernández-Yáñez
Alba Puig-Denia
Montserrat Boronat-Navarro
Universitat Jaume I

Alexandra García-Joerger
Universitat de València

TEMÁTICA: Innovación

ABSTRACT: Smart Tourism Destinations (STDs) have emerged as a key paradigm in tourism studies, building on smart city principles to integrate digital technologies, sustainability, governance, and accessibility. This paper provides a comprehensive bibliometric and thematic analysis of STD research published between 2013 and 2025 in the Web of Science (WoS) database. Using keyword co-occurrence techniques with VOSviewer software, the study identifies major research fields, leading authors, and influential journals, as well as three thematic clusters: (1) tourist experience, co-creation, and destination image; (2) competitiveness, governance, sustainability, and accessibility; and (3) innovation and advanced technologies. The results reveal the multidisciplinary nature of the field, highlighting the interplay between technological innovation, participatory governance, and sustainability in shaping competitive and resilient destinations. This study contributes to the consolidation of STD research by mapping its intellectual structure, identifying knowledge gaps, and suggesting future directions for academics, practitioners, and policymakers.

Keywords: Smart Tourism Destinations; bibliometric analysis; thematic clusters; innovation and governance; sustainability; tourism competitiveness

1. INTRODUCTION

The concept of Smart Tourism Destinations (STDs) has rapidly evolved and progressed into one of the most influential concept in tourism studies, drawing inspiration from the smart city paradigm that combines digitalization, sustainability, and open governance model to improve territorial competitiveness and urban life (Ivars et al., 2016; Buhalis & Amaranganna, 2015). Specifically in the tourism, this framework has been expanded to encompass not only the technological upgradings of destinations, but also the integration of the tenets of governance, sustainability development, and universal accessibility as a core pillars that would benefit both tourist and residents (Forés et al., 2022; López de Ávila & García-Sánchez, 2015).

Spain has played a pioneering role in promoting this new tourism destination management, with SEGITTUR defining and institutionalizing the STD model through a comprehensive certification system and UNE standards that have projected the concept internationally (SEGITTUR, 2025). Therefore, both practitioners and academic research propose that STD must be viewed as tourism ecosystems capable of aligning innovation, with economic, social, and environmental goals, orchestrating territorial resources through participatory dialogue among all the stakeholders involved, and data-driven decision making (Xu et al., 2025).

The growing attention in academia mirrors the rising importance of innovation and sustainability for tourism destinations competitiveness. Beyond technology as a backbone for promoting operational efficiency and personalization of services (Gursoy et al., 2023), recent publications underline the relevance of aspects like sustainability (Ndou et al., 2023), governance (Giaccone & Bonacini, 2019); accessibility (Buhalis et al., 2023), and innovation (Tian & Tang, 2021), as equally drivers and promoter of this new tourism paradigm. This strategic multidimensionality positions STDs as a central research domain to understand how destinations can enhance tourists experiences, achieve resources resilience, and respond to structural challenges such as overtourism, climate change, resource depletion, or phenomenon such as gentrification (del Vals et al., 2024; Shafiee et al., 2022). Despite this rapid expansion, the field remains relatively young, with fragmented approaches and evolving conceptual boundaries. This makes bibliometric analysis a valuable tool for mapping the structure, key contributors, and emerging themes in STD research.

The purpose of this paper is therefore to provide a comprehensive bibliometric and thematic analysis of the academic literature on Smart Tourism Destinations. Using 138 publications indexed in the Web of Science (WoS) database over the period 2013-2025 and applying keyword co-occurrence techniques with VOSviewer software, the study identifies major research streams, influential authors, and leading journals. Specifically, the analysis highlights three thematic clusters: tourism experience and co-creation, governance and sustainability, and innovation and advanced technologies that together illustrate how the STD paradigm has evolved into a multidimensional framework. By synthesizing these contributions, this paper aims to clarify the intellectual structure of the field, underline its main theoretical and practical implications, and suggest avenues for future research.

The remainder of this paper is structured as follows: Section 2 introduces the conceptual framework of the STD model and its main dimensions. Section 3 outlines the methodology employed in this exploratory bibliometric study, including data collection, filtering, and analysis procedures. Section 4 presents the results. Section 5 discusses the implications of the findings, offering insights into how STD research is consolidating as a field, as well as recommendations to navigate the transition toward smart, sustainable, and inclusive tourism ecosystems.

2. SMART TOURISM DESTINATIONS: AN OVERVIEW

2.1. Definition and Evolution of the STD Concept

The concept of Smart Tourism Destination (STD) originates in the paradigm of smart cities (Ivars et al., 2016; Buhalis & Amaranggana, 2015), an urban development model that integrates the intensive use of digital technologies with environmental sustainability and policies aimed at enhancing citizens' quality of life. While smart cities primarily address urban challenges through digital and sustainable solutions, STDs transfer this logic to the tourism domain, explicitly incorporating governance and universal accessibility to create shared value for businesses, public institutions, tourists, and residents (Forés et al., 2022; Ivars et al., 2016). In doing so, the smart city vision is expanded into a tourism-oriented approach that reinforces competitiveness, fosters collaborative governance, and extends its impact beyond metropolitan boundaries (López de Ávila & García Sánchez, 2015).

In Spain, the State Secretariat for Tourism, through SEGITTUR, has spearheaded the definition and implementation of the concept, defining STDs as "an innovative space built upon the territory and state-of-the-art technological infrastructure. A territory committed to the environmental, cultural, and socio-economic factors of its habitat, equipped with an intelligence system that procedurally captures information, analyzes and interprets events in real time, in order to facilitate visitor interaction with the environment and decision-making by destination managers, thereby enhancing efficiency and substantially improving the quality of the tourism experience" (SEGITTUR, 2025). This conception has been projected internationally and has inspired certification methodologies such as the UNE standards promoted by the Spanish Network of STDs (Forés & Fernández-Yáñez, 2020).

Beyond being understood as conventional destinations enhanced by new technologies, STDs must be conceived as tourism ecosystems that integrate knowledge, innovation, and sustainability in pursuit of more inclusive, efficient, and environmentally respectful experiences (Bastidas-Manzano et al., 2021). True "intelligence" lies in orchestrating territorial resources through participatory and collaborative governance models supported by reliable data, aligning innovation not only with economic goals but also with social and environmental objectives (Xu et al., 2025). In this vein, recent studies show that STDs contribute to productivity and efficiency, as well as to the quality of destination management, when they integrate data analysis, policy design, and inter-actor coordination (Zhou et al., 2024).

2.2. Core dimensions of the STD model

The literature advances a systemic model based on five key dimensions: governance, innovation, sustainability, accessibility, and technology articulated across three levels of action: (i) the strategic-relational level, which sets the conditions for competitiveness through governance, innovation, and sustainability; (ii) the instrumental level, which incorporates accessibility (physical and digital) and data intelligence; and (iii) the applied level, where technological solutions are deployed in domains such as transport, safety, heritage, or marketing (Forés & Fernández-Yáñez, 2020; Ivars et al., 2017, 2019). This framework coexists with ongoing efforts to measure and standardize the STD construct, advancing the development of scales and impact indicators (Wei et al., 2024).

2.2.1. Sustainability

Sustainability in an STD seeks balanced development that respects the natural environment, fosters the local economy, and preserves cultural identity. It involves reducing environmental impacts, promoting responsible practices, supporting local communities, and deploying technologies that allow for the monitoring and optimization of natural and cultural resources (Ndou et al., 2023; Garcia et al., 2021). Recent research highlights the adoption of tools for carrying capacity management and tourist pressure, particularly in coastal areas, as well as the need to legitimize interventions through social acceptance (del Vas et al., 2024). At the policy level, there is increasing interconnection between tourism and urban sustainability strategies (Samancioglu et al., 2024).

2.2.2. Technology

Technology functions as a backbone that, when strategically implemented, enhances competitiveness and resilience (Boes et al., 2016). The deployment of 5G, the Internet of Things, Artificial Intelligence, Big Data, or blockchain is transforming tourism resources into smart assets, enabling personalization, automation, and new service models (Suanpang & Pothipassa, 2024; Gursoy et al., 2023). This dimension also connects with risk management in digital tourism ecosystems (Popova et al., 2023), with open data platforms for planning and decision-making (Alcaraz et al., 2024), and with vertical domains such as smart stadiums (Panagopoulos et al., 2025).

2.2.3. Accessibility

Universal accessibility ensures that all individuals, regardless of physical, sensory, or cognitive conditions, can enjoy the destination equally. It entails the removal of architectural, communicative, and digital barriers, and the adaptation of both physical infrastructures and virtual services (Buhalis et al., 2023). Recent evidence identifies drivers of inclusivity in destinations through stakeholder analysis (Rubio-Escuderos et al., 2025) and emphasizes the role of geospatial data governance in guiding interventions (Radojevic et al., 2023).

2.2.4. Governance

Governance in an STD is understood as a dynamic process of inclusive, collaborative, and data-driven decision-making involving the active participation of multiple stakeholders (SEGITTUR, 2023; Giaccone & Bonacini, 2019). In practice, this translates into open innovation and co-creation in living labs and urban labs, where solutions are tested prior to large-scale deployment, thereby reducing uncertainty and fostering social acceptance (Zhou et al., 2024; Gretzel et al., 2018). It encompasses initiatives ranging from policies to attract digital nomads to open data schemes that institutionalize transparency (Alcaraz et al., 2024).

2.2.5. Innovation

Innovation in STDs encompasses both technological and non-technological outcomes (organizational, institutional, marketing) aimed at transforming tourism management into more efficient, sustainable, and differentiated practices. It encourages co-creation of products, the development of servitized services, and personalization, anticipating emerging demands (Xu et al., 2025; Tian & Tang, 2021). Bibliometric evidence indicates increasing field consolidation and the evolution of research lines (Palomo Santiago & Parra López, 2024). In this vein, it is worth highlighting the approval of UNE Standard 178501:2018, which establishes the requirements for an STD management system. This standard provides the basis for official certification in Spain, setting verifiable criteria that destinations must meet to implement, maintain, and improve an STD management system. Its scope spans the five key dimensions: governance, innovation, technology, universal accessibility, and sustainability, and it applies to any type of destination, whether vacation, urban, or rural, regardless of its size or managing entity (Forés & Fernández-Yáñez, 2020).

Figure 1. STD model

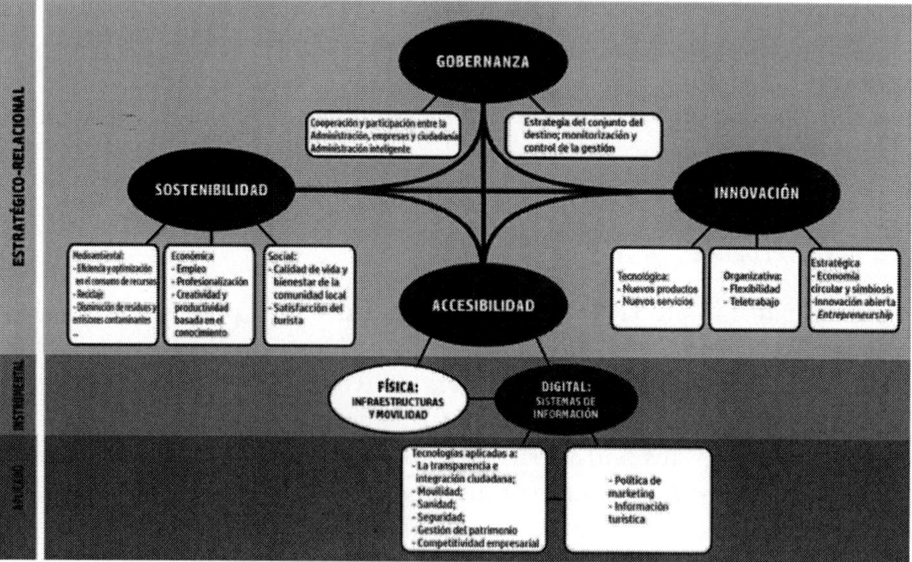

Source: Forés & Fernández-Yáñez (2020)

3. METHODOLOGY

To explore existing STD research, we carried out a bibliometric study based on an analysis of the co-occurrences of the keywords used in publications on the subject, with the aid of VOSviewer software (Sainaghi et al., 2019). Keyword co-occurrence analysis involves looking at the keywords that occur together in articles. This type of quantitative analysis can reveal the structure underpinning a certain topic in a discipline and its evolution, as well as the most relevant related concepts. Furthermore, the analysis of the thematic clusters identified may show networks among papers, based on their keywords and topics, helping to reveal trends (Forés et al. 2021).

To identify and retrieve the articles, we used the Clarivate WoS database, considered one of the main academic databases for the assessment of scientific output worldwide, filtering by articles published in English. The data retrieval was performed on 11 April 2025.

To gain a general overview of the publications, we searched for the terms that we consider capture STD research ("smart touris* destination*") in titles, abstracts, or indexing terms of a dataset limited to articles. This search yielded 156 results. After filtering out articles not related to the topic, we were left with a sample composed of 138 publications on STD.

We treated the input text file with the keywords before obtaining the results of the bibliometric analysis with VosViewer. Specifically, we integrated words with the most co-occurrences that have a similar meaning, acronyms and plural forms of the keywords.

4. RESULTS

4.1. Evolution of Published Papers and Main STD Research Streams

Figure 2 shows the evolution in the number of papers related to STD published during the 13-year period 2013–2025 (April). According to the Clarivate WoS database, the first article on STD, Wang et al. (2013) appears in 2013 and was cited on this basis 21 times; since then, articles on the subject have regularly been published. A clear upward trend over time, especially after 2018, can be observed, indicating the increased importance of the subject in scientific research.

Figure 2. Annual publications in Web of Science (WoS) on STD research

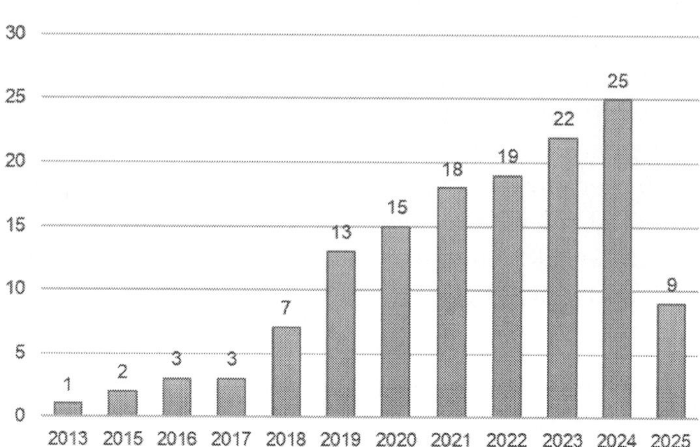

Source: own elaboration based on data from WoS

4.2. Main research fields on STD

The bibliometric analysis also highlights the main research fields contributing to the study of STD. The most prominent area is Hospitality, Leisure, Sport, and Tourism (108 publications), reflecting the central role of tourism-specific research in addressing innovation, technology adoption, and visitor experience within smart destinations. Other significant domains include Environmental Studies (25) and Environmental Sciences (23), which indicate a strong focus on sustainability, resource management, and the integration of ecological considerations into smart destination strategies. Closely linked, the field of Green and Sustainable Science and Technology (21) underlines the importance of technological solutions that support sustainable development goals in tourism.

From a managerial and business perspective, Management (25), Business (10), and Economics (10) demonstrate how STD are also examined through organizational efficiency, governance models, competitiveness, and economic impacts. These areas provide insights into how businesses and policymakers can integrate smart technologies to create value. Overall, the results suggest that while the core research remains tourism-oriented, there is a clear multidisciplinary engagement involving environmental sciences, sustainability, and management disciplines, which enrich the understanding of smart tourism destinations from both ecological and socio-economic perspectives.

Figure 3. Main research areas on STD

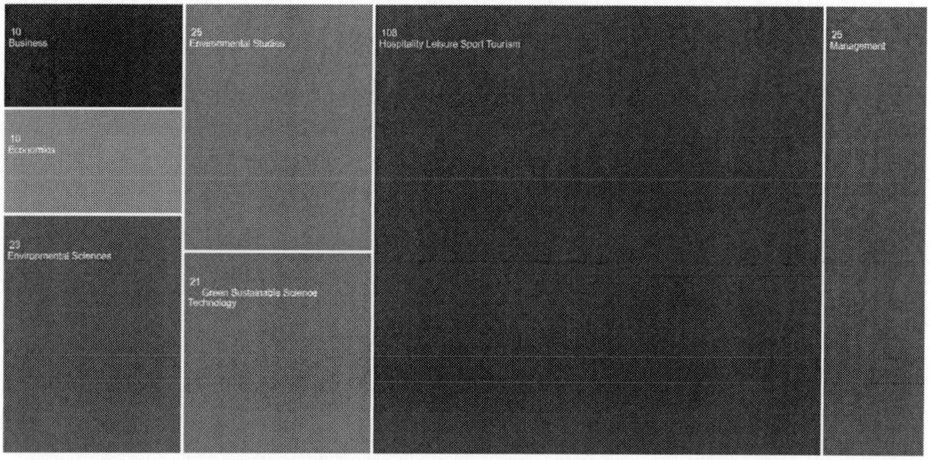

Source: own elaboration based on data from WoS

4.3. Top articles, authors and journals on STD

In Figure 3 we can find the top authors by number of publications in order to gain an understanding of the most influential participants. The top 4 authors displayed in Figure 4 represent 14.5% of all the publications in this recent field, with a total of 20 published articles.

Figure 4. Main authors on STD

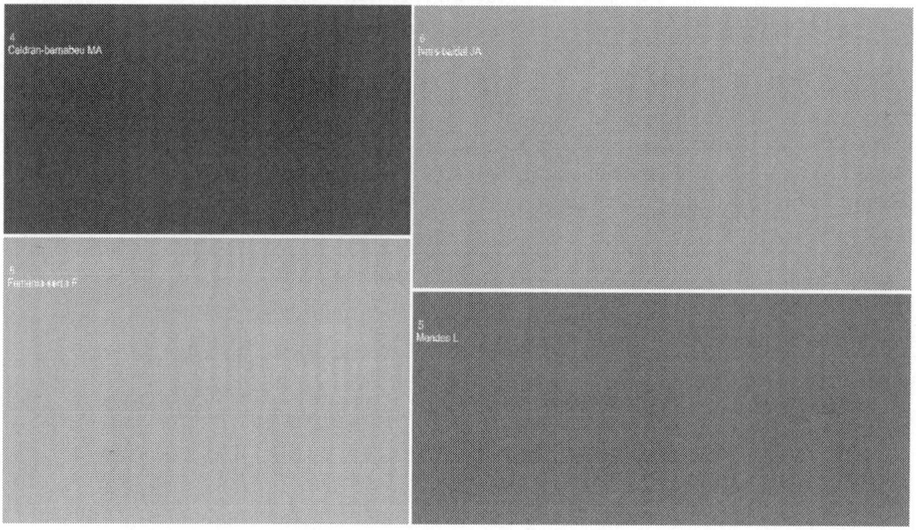

Source: own elaboration based on data from WoS

In terms of authorship, the scholar who has contributed most extensively to this topic is Ivars-Baidal, J.A., with six articles. He is followed closely by Femenia-Serra, F., Mendes, L., and Celdrán-Bernabeu, M.A., who also stand out as leading researchers in this field. Table 1 of the analysis presents the top 10 most-cited articles, which is an indicator of both the quality and the influence of specific contributions (Garrigos-Simon et al., 2018). Among these highly cited works is the influential paper by Ivars-Baidal et al. (2016), Smart destinations and the evolution of ICTs: a new scenario for destination management, which has become a key reference in understanding how the evolution of information and communication technologies (ICTs) has reshaped destination management and provided the foundations for the smart destination paradigm.

Table 1. Top 10 articles on STD with highest number of citations

Authors and publication	**Number of citations**
Boes, K; Buhalis, D; Inversini, A Smart tourism destinations: ecosystems for tourism destination competitiveness	360
Buonincontri, P; Micera, R The experience co-creation in smart tourism destinations: a multiple case analysis of European destinations	161
Del Chiappa, G; Baggio, R Knowledge transfer in smart tourism destinations: Analyzing the effects of a network structure	229
Del Vecchio, P; Mele, G; Ndou, V; Secundo, G Creating value from Social Big Data: Implications for Smart Tourism Destinations	231
Ivars-Baidal, JA; Celdrán-Bernabeu, MA; Mazón, JN; Perles-Ivars, AF Smart destinations and the evolution of ICTs: a new scenario for destination management?	202
Jeong, M; Shin, HH Tourists' Experiences with Smart Tourism Technology at Smart Destinations and Their Behavior Intentions	221
Jovicic, DZ From the traditional understanding of tourism destination to the smart tourism destination	165
Marine-Roig, E; Clavé, SA Tourism analytics with massive user-generated content: A case study of Barcelona	255

Authors and publication	Number of citations
Pencarelli, T The digital revolution in the travel and tourism industry	282
Wang, D; Li, X; Li, YP China's smart tourism destination initiative: A taste of the service-dominant logic	218

Source: own elaboration based on data from WoS

Figure 4 shows the journals that publish the highest number of papers, with four journals standing out from thc others. The first one is *Sustainability* (19 publications), followed by *Current Issues in Tourism* (9 publications), *Journal of Destination Marketing and Management* (8 publications) and *International Journal of Tourism Cities* (7 publications). These four journals represent 31.16% of the total publications.

Figure 5. Publications on STD by journal

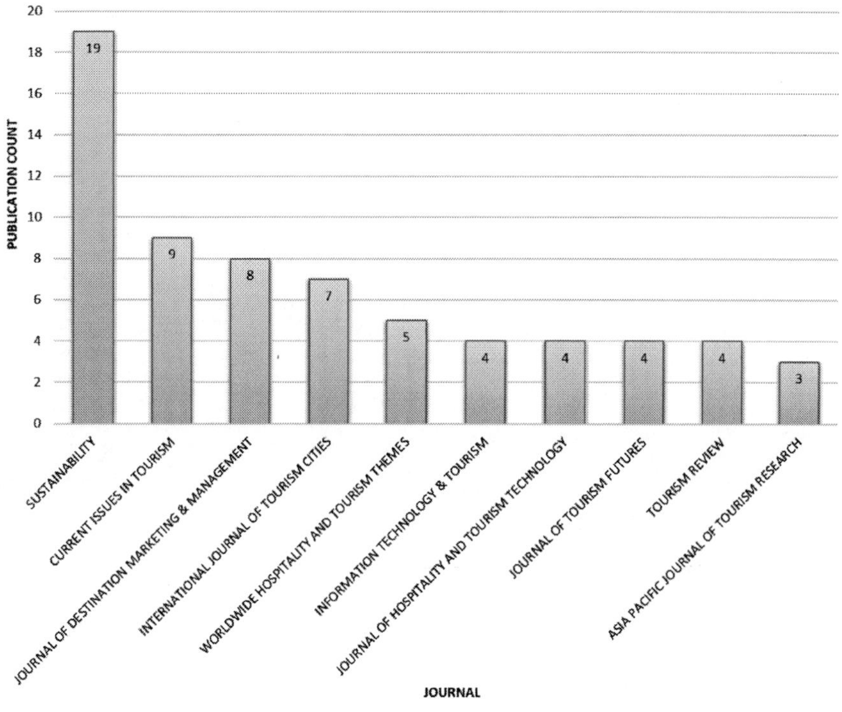

Source: own elaboration based on data from WoS

4.4. Keyword co-occurrence analysis

We analyzed articles using the VOSviewer program to identify the most frequent keywords, shown below. The analysis of the networks can be used to create a graphic map of the relationships between the data. Figure 6 displays the networks created by taking the 461 keywords (introduced by the authors), filtered to obtain a minimum of four occurrences; this process resulted in 19 keywords related to STD in the articles. Nodes represent keywords and links between nodes show co-occurrence. Using VOSviewer software, a node can be made to represent the number of papers in which a keyword is used, such that the larger the node, the greater the frequency of the keyword. The same color indicates a group of connected keywords or cluster. The lines depict the number of articles in which a specific keyword appears in conjunction with another. The distance between nodes represents how many articles the two keywords are in together compared to co-occurrences with other keywords.

Figure 6. Network of key concepts linked to STD with the highest frequency of occurrences

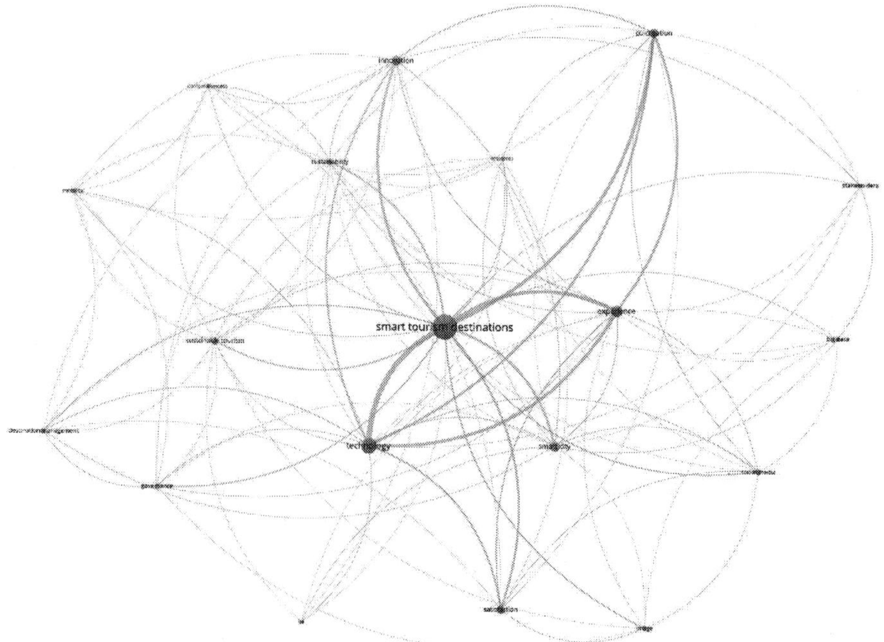

Source: own elaboration based on data from WoS and VOSviewer

Based on this information, the next step was to conduct a cluster analysis of these 19 concepts. The program identified three clear groups of theoretical analysis, based on keywords that appear together or keyword occurrence. The resulting clusters are shown in Table 2. We describe these three clusters below, together with their main focuses of analysis and publications in the literature.

Table 2. Keyword co-occurrence in clusters

CLUSTER 1:
Co-creation Experience Image Satisfaction Smart tourism destinations Social media Technology
CLUSTER 2:
Competitiveness Destination management Governance Mobility Residents Sustainability Sustainable tourism
CLUSTER 3:
Big data Innovation IoT Smart city Stakeholders

Source: own elaboration based on data from WoS and VOSviewer

4.5. Identified Cluster Analysis

4.5.1. Cluster 1: STD image and management: tourism experience and involvement (co-creation)

An analysis of the articles comprising this first cluster reveals a clear conceptual convergence that positions the tourist at the core of the investigation. These studies examine not only the traveler's objective experience but also their subjective perceptions, levels of satisfaction, and the range of emotions that accompany their engagement with the destination.

Within this framework, technology emerges as a mediating factor as an instrument intended to enhance the tourist experience, rather than an end in itself.

A consistent emphasis across the literature in this cluster is placed on analyzing the degree to which travelers feel connected, inspired, safe, or pleasantly surprised when engaging with smart technologies. This emotional dimension is essential, as several authors demonstrate that the interactivity and accessibility of such tools exert a direct effect on tourist satisfaction and on their intention to revisit or recommend the destination (Anjum & Ali, 2025; Jeong & Shin, 2020). Moreover, privacy concerns and perceived risk are shown to mediate the relationship between technological interaction and behavioral outcomes, as trust becomes a critical variable influencing tourists' willingness to adopt services and share personal data (Afolabi et al., 2021). It is therefore insufficient for a digital solution to merely operate efficiently; what ultimately matters is how it shapes the traveler's emotional response, generating pleasure, arousal, and hedonic value that enrich the experience (Jeong & Shin, 2020).

Complementarily, technology is consistently presented as a means rather than an end in itself. The literature discusses the use of mobile applications, augmented and virtual reality, and phygital environments that merge physical and digital layers to create richer experiences (Stankov et al., 2025; Femenia-Serra et al., 2018). The emphasis is placed on the ability of these solutions to provide relevant information, smooth the travel process, facilitate communication, and enable more immersive and personalized journeys. Several studies also highlight that real-time data analytics allows destinations to deliver dynamic, context-aware recommendations—such as suggesting restaurants, cultural events, or alternative routes—reinforcing the traveler's perception of a tailored, responsive experience (Shafiee et al., 2023; Femenia-Serra et al., 2018).

Value co-creation emerges as another cornerstone of this cluster. Tourists are not merely passive recipients of information; rather, they actively participate in shaping their own journeys by selecting when and how to interact with technologies, contributing feedback, and leaving digital footprints that destinations use to improve services (Stankov et al., 2025). Research on phygital tourism experiences shows that visitors combine physical and digital touchpoints in unique ways, effectively constructing personalized narratives of their trips (Stankov et al., 2025).

The literature also pays special attention to post-experience behaviors, extending the analysis beyond immediate satisfaction. Variables such as revisit intention, willingness to pay a premium, and electronic word-of-mouth (eWOM) are frequently examined (Tian & Tang, 2021; Jeong & Shin, 2019). Empirical studies suggest that technologically enhanced experiences create stronger emotional bonds with destinations, which, in turn, increase loyalty and the likelihood of recommending the destination to others. Moreover, scholars have noted that tourists' sharing of their experiences through social media produces a multiplier effect, shaping the overall image of the destination and inspiring potential future visitors—thus positioning eWOM as both an outcome and a mechanism of value co-creation (Ghaderi et al., 2024; Femenia-Serra et al., 2018).

Another relevant dimension is the focus on aesthetics and emotional resonance of digital services. Perceived value depends not only on functionality but also on the design, usability, and seamless integration of digital tools into the flow of the visit (Nadee et al., 2024). Technological mediation can even reshape visitors' perceptions of space and time, transforming routine moments into memorable, immersive episodes (Stankov et al., 2025). Recent contributions also raise the concept of "digital well-being," arguing that excessive notifications or information overload may lead to cognitive fatigue and detract from the overall experience, underscoring the need for mindful, balanced design (Stankov et al., 2025). Gamification is another mechanism gaining scholarly attention, with evidence showing that incorporating challenges, rewards, and playful elements extends engagement and enhances memorability (Anjum & Ali, 2025). Similarly, inclusivity has been identified as a crucial design principle: accessible interfaces for travelers with disabilities improve not only individual experiences but also the global image of the destination as equitable and socially responsible (Ghaderi et al., 2024).

At the same time, the literature recognizes the tensions inherent in digital tourism. Concerns regarding privacy, data misuse, or poorly designed interfaces can erode trust and compromise the overall experience. Consequently, perceived security and user control over personal data are repeatedly identified as preconditions for technology adoption and for consolidating the tourist–destination relationship (Afolabi et al., 2021; Stankov et al., 2025).

Finally, there is consensus that the integration of physical and digital dimensions is no longer optional. Tourists increasingly expect digital layers to enrich physical spaces, offering contextualized information, guidance, and real-time personalization that situate them at the center of the service ecosystem (Nadee et al., 2024; Femenia-Serra et al., 2018).

4.5.2. Cluster 2: STD competitiveness: governance, sustainability and accessibility

Unlike the experiential immediacy of Cluster 1, Cluster 2 adopts a systemic and strategic perspective, observing the destination as a complex socio-technical organism in constant evolution. The literature invites us to picture the destination as a network of interdependent actors — public administrations, businesses, residents, and visitors — whose coordinated action is necessary to ensure long-term sustainability and competitiveness (Gretzel et al., 2018; Boes et al., 2016). Rather than focusing on the design of a single app or visitor-facing interface, these studies emphasize the institutional, strategic, and regulatory frameworks that enable destinations to function as coherent and adaptive systems.

A key dimension repeatedly highlighted by scholars is management and governance. Authors argue that technological deployment alone is insufficient; a robust decision-making architecture is required to define long-term objectives, allocate responsibilities, and coordinate stakeholders across multiple levels (Gretzel et al., 2018; Femenia-Serra et al., 2018). Destination Management Organizations (DMOs) are often described as "coordination hubs," bringing together public authorities, private sector actors, civil society, and residents to align interests and foster collective action (Boes et al., 2016). More recent contributions underscore the need for governance agility — the ability to respond rapidly to crises such as pandemics or climate shocks — highlighting examples where destinations used real-time data to reorient flows during COVID-19 or to adapt to sudden demand fluctuations (Shafiee et al., 2022). This literature consistently advocates collaborative governance models based on public–private partnerships, participatory forums, and co-design processes rather than purely top-down planning (Del Chiappa & Baggio, 2015).

Sustainability emerges as a central guiding principle, going beyond a rhetorical commitment to become a normative anchor for destination planning. Studies consistently stress that tourism development must be compatible with ecosystem preservation, cultural heritage protection, and social well-being (Boes et al., 2016). Core concepts such as carrying capacity, destination resilience, inclusiveness, and universal accessibility are frequently employed to frame the challenge of balancing economic growth with community welfare (Moreno-Izquierdo et al., 2018). Moreover, some authors emphasize the importance of operationalizing sustainability through digital tools — for instance, deploying IoT sensors to monitor visitor density or environmental impact in real time, enabling more informed decisions and proactive interventions (Shafiee et al., 2023).

The concept of destination resilience is another prominent theme. Recent works analyze how destinations can absorb and adapt to systemic shocks — health crises, extreme weather events, or economic downturns — without compromising their viability (Shafiee et al., 2022; Moreno-Izquierdo et al., 2018). Proposed strategies include diversifying tourism products, distributing visitor flows across underutilized areas, and creating contingency plans supported by data-driven early warning systems. Open data governance is also highlighted as a mechanism to foster transparency and empower citizens and firms to co-create innovative solutions (Femenia-Serra et al., 2018).

Strategic planning frameworks are a defining feature of this cluster. Many studies propose detailed roadmaps for the transition toward smart destinations, identifying phases, investment priorities, and resource needs (Gretzel et al., 2018). Others employ efficiency metrics — such as DEA-Tobit models — or develop indicator systems to continuously monitor progress and benchmark destinations against peers (Wu et al., 2024). Several contributions additionally emphasize the role of real-time dashboards and data visualization tools as decision-support systems that allow destination managers to act proactively rather than reactively (Shafiee et al., 2022; 2023). This approach embodies evidence-based governance, where data becomes a compass guiding investments, service improvements, and regulatory adjustments, always with the ultimate aim of enhancing residents' and visitors' quality of life.

Resident participation is a cornerstone consistently emphasized across the literature. Surveys, focus groups, and sentiment analyses are widely employed to gauge local perceptions of tourism impacts (Femenia-Serra et al., 2018; Moreno-Izquierdo et al., 2018). Social acceptance is framed as a precondition for a destination to be considered truly "smart" (Boes et al., 2016). If residents perceive declining quality of life — whether due to congestion, rising housing costs, or loss of cultural authenticity — the model loses legitimacy. Several articles propose mechanisms for civic participation, including digital suggestion platforms, deliberative workshops, and living labs where residents collaborate directly with planners (Del Chiappa & Baggio, 2015). Recent research even explores gamification of participation, suggesting reward systems to encourage resident engagement and strengthen a sense of shared responsibility for tourism development (Shafiee et al., 2023).

Mobility and accessibility are also recurrently addressed as pillars of destination management. The literature explores integrated solutions that combine public transport, micromobility, and pedestrian networks, often supported by real-time data to redistribute flows and mitigate congestion (Moreno-Izquierdo et al., 2018). Some contributions recommend nudging strategies embedded in mobility apps, encouraging tourists to explore less crowded routes or visit during off-peak hours, thus reducing pressure on sensitive areas and improving overall visitor experience.

In this line, Cluster 2 adopts a long-term, policy-oriented vision of destination management. Many contributions resemble practical handbooks for planners, proposing tourism observatories, regulatory frameworks for balancing short-term rental markets, and circular economy initiatives to minimize waste in heavily visited areas (Gretzel et al., 2018). This cluster ultimately calls on destinations to engage in anticipatory governance: to define not only how to attract visitors tomorrow, but what kind of community they aspire to be in ten or twenty years, and to make the strategic decisions today that will lead them there.

4.5.3. Cluster 3: STD innovation and advanced technologies

Cluster 3 represents the bridge between the original concept of smart cities and its application to tourism through Smart Tourism Destinations (STDs) (Ivars et al., 2017). Its aspirational goal is to enable smarter destination management, enhancing both competitiveness and the well-being and satisfaction of tourists and residents (Buhalis, 2020; Gretzel et al., 2018).

Studies in this cluster describe STDs as tourism ecosystems that, while relying heavily on digital technologies, strengthen governance, sustainability, and especially innovation processes. In this context, tourism organizations not only adapt but also develop capacities for learning, anticipation, and strategic coevolution with their environment (Stankov et al., 2019).

According to the canonical STD model, innovation stands alongside sustainability, governance, and accessibility as a strategic pillar. Its relevance extends beyond technological products and processes to include organizational, institutional, and marketing innovations that are critical to sustainable competitiveness (Tian & Tang, 2021). Increasingly, innovation is conceived as a mechanism for creating shared value among stakeholders, reinforcing social and environmental goals that broaden the scope of competitiveness as was suggested previously in the Cluster 2 (Anjum & Ali, 2025; Porter & Kramer, 2011).

In this sense, STDs inherit from industrial clusters (Porter, 1998) and innovation districts (Barceló, 2023) the ability to leverage territorial co-location and tacit knowledge to stimulate open innovation (Chesbrough,

2003; Markusen, 1996). Accordingly, studies in this cluster emphasize public–private collaboration and experimental settings such as living labs or urban innovation labs, where firms, administrations, universities, and tourists co-design and test servitization solutions, reducing uncertainty before large-scale deployment and fostering social acceptance (Forés et al., 2021; Gretzel et al., 2018).

Digital technologies also represent the instrumental backbone whose application, as shown in Figure 1, enhances transparency and citizen participation, mobility programs, health and safety systems, heritage management, and firm competitiveness. A defining feature of this cluster is the emphasis on Big Data and the Internet of Things (IoT), conceived not merely as analytical tools but as strategic instruments for generating innovations that address latent needs of consumers and residents. In this regard, research highlights that Big Data enables demand forecasting, consumption pattern detection, identification of unmet needs, and service personalization, while IoT and machine learning enable the interconnection of systems through sensor–actuator mechanisms, dynamically optimizing transport, energy, and tourism operations (Panagopoulos et al., 2025).

The predictive capacities of these technologies further support the development of intelligent open information systems (open data) that allow stakeholders to adapt their offerings and operations in real time when facing events such as health crises or adverse weather conditions, thereby reinforcing the resilience of destinations (Akbar et al., 2024; Buhalis & Sinarta, 2019).

Equally relevant is the integration of information flows into a comprehensive territorial management system, covering not only the optimization of natural resource use and the protection of cultural heritage (Garcia et al., 2021), but also the prevention of undesirable effects linked to tourism growth, such as gentrification and overtourism (Barceló, 2023). Moreover, these technologies can serve as platforms for institutional governance innovation, promoting transparency, democratization of data use, and stakeholder collaboration, thereby reinforcing the open innovation model previously highlighted (Chesbrough, 2003).

This technological shift, however, is not without risks as already mentioned in Cluster 1. Articles highlight concerns regarding cybersecurity, data privacy, and excessive reliance on automation, with potential negative effects on lower-skilled employment (Ghaderi et al., 2024; Suanpang & Pothipassa, 2024). Some scholars also warn that prioritizing more profitable segments may exacerbate inequities and risks of social exclusion.

Overall, the studies comprising this cluster converge on the idea that innovation is a fundamental strategy for ensuring the coevolution of STDs with the changing tourism environment. These innovations, grounded in data and predictive systems, in turn reinforce the governance, accessibility, and sustainability pillars of the model, ensuring adaptive capacity and balanced development in the long term.

5. DISCUSSION, IMPLICATIONS, LIMITATIONS AND FUTURE RESEARCH

This study provides a comprehensive overview of the academic landscape surrounding STDs by carrying on a bibliometric study and a thematic analysis of the clusters identified. The results suggest that while the core research remains tourism-oriented, there is a clear multidisciplinary engagement involving environmental sciences, sustainability, and management disciplines. At the same time, the contributions of leading authors and highly cited works demonstrate the growing consolidation of STDs as a distinct and influential line of academic inquiry.

Through a co-occurrence analysis of keywords using VOSviewer software (Sainaghi et al., 2019), we identified three main thematic clusters: 1) STD image and management: tourism experience and co-creation; (2) STD competitiveness: governance, sustainability and accessibility, which emphasize participatory planning, long-term resilience, and inclusive destination management; and (3) STD innovation and advanced technologies This methodological approach allowed us to not only map the most influential concepts and their interconnections but also to detect emerging patterns and trends that define the STD discourse.

The three clusters identified collectively reflect the multidimensional evolution of STDs, where technological innovation, emotional engagement, and strategic governance intersect to shape more sustainable and competitive tourism ecosystems. Cluster 1 emphasizes the centrality of the tourist experience, highlighting the emotional, interactive, and co-creative dimensions of travel enhanced through digital and phygital tools. Meanwhile, Cluster 2 shifts the focus toward long-term governance, stressing the importance of institutional coordination, sustainability, inclusivity, and anticipatory planning to ensure the resilience and social legitimacy of tourism development. Finally, Cluster 3 underlines the importance of the strategic role of innovation, driven by Big Data, IoT, and open systems, in enabling adaptive, efficient, and participatory tourism ecosystems aligned with smart city principles.

The results have several implications for both academics and practitioners. For researchers, the clusters highlight the consolidation of a multidisciplinary field and provide a roadmap for organizing future theoretical and empirical contributions. For practitioners and policymakers, the findings emphasize the need to move beyond a narrow focus on digital infrastructure and adopt holistic strategies that integrate innovation, sustainability, and stakeholder participation. The prominence of authors such as Ivars-Baidal and highly cited works also underlines the importance of building on established conceptual foundations while adapting to emerging challenges such as overtourism, climate change, and digital ethics.

This study presents certain limitations that should be acknowledged. First, the analysis is based exclusively on publications indexed in the Web of Science database, which may have excluded relevant works found in other databases or grey literature. Second, the bibliometric method, while useful for identifying thematic patterns and conceptual structures, does not capture the full depth of qualitative insights or theoretical nuances present in the field. Additionally, the keyword co-occurrence analysis depends heavily on author-selected terms, which may vary in consistency and specificity. Finally, as the field of smart tourism is rapidly evolving, the findings represent a snapshot in time and may need to be updated as new technologies, policies, and research trends emerge.

Future research could address these limitations by expanding the scope of analysis to include other databases such as Scopus or Google Scholar, and by incorporating qualitative content analysis to deepen the understanding of emerging themes. Moreover, longitudinal analyses could help track the evolution of key concepts within STD, for example, regarding how they adapt to global challenges such as climate change or overtourism. Additionally, more qualitative and mixed-method approaches could enrich the analysis of co-creation, inclusivity, and residents' perspectives, areas often underrepresented in large-scale bibliometric studies. Finally, future work should explore the ethical and social dimensions of smart destinations, particularly regarding data privacy, digital well-being, and the distributional effects of technological innovation on local communities.

ACKNOWLEDGEMENTS

This research was funded by "Plan Estatal de Investigación Científica y Técnica y de Innovación 2024-2027" of the Ministerio de Ciencia, Innovación y Universidades, with reference PID2024-162887NB-100 and by "subvencions a grups d'investigació emergents GE 2024" of the Generalitat Valenciana CIGE 2024/84.

6. REFERENCES

Afolabi, O., Ozturen, A., & Ilkan, M. (2021). Effects of privacy concern, risk, and information control in a smart tourism destination. *Economic research-Ekonomska istraživanja, 34*(1), 3119-3138.

Akbar, P. N. G., Auliya, A., Pranita, D., & Oktadiana, H. (2024). The readiness assessment of Jakarta as a smart tourism city. *Cogent Social Sciences, 10*(1), 2364386.

Alcaraz, O., Berenguer, A., Tomás, D., Celdrán-Bernabeu, M. A., & Mazón, J. N. (2024). Augmenting retail data with open data for smarter tourism destinations. *IEEE Access.*

Anjum, F., & Ali, Y. (2025). Smart tourism technologies and destination perception: implications for revisit intentions in mountainous destinations. *Tourism and hospitality management, 31*(1), 107-123.

Barceló, M. (2023). *Distritos innovadores.* Ediciones Piramide.

Bastidas-Manzano, A. B., Sánchez-Fernández, J., & Casado-Aranda, L. A. (2021). The past, present, and future of smart tourism destinations: a bibliometric analysis. *Journal of Hospitality & Tourism Research, 45*(3), 529-552.

Boes, K., Buhalis, D., & Inversini, A. (2016). Smart tourism destinations: ecosystems for tourism destination competitiveness. *International Journal of Tourism Cities, 2*(2), 108-124.

Buhalis, D., & Amaranganna, A. (2015). Smart tourism destinations: Enhancing tourism experience through personalisation of services. In I. Tussyadiah & A. Inversini (Eds.), Information and Communication Technologies in Tourism 2015—Proceedings of the International Conference in Lugano, Switzerland (pp. 377–389). Springer.

Buhalis, D., & Sinarta, Y. (2019). Real-time co-creation and nowness service: lessons from tourism and hospitality. *Journal of Travel & Tourism Marketing, 36*(5), 563-582.

Buhalis, D., Lin, M. S., & Leung, D. (2023). Metaverse as a driver for customer experience and value co-creation: implications for hospitality and tourism management and marketing. *International Journal of Contemporary Hospitality Management, 35*(2), 701-716.

Buhalis, D. (2020). Technology in tourism-from information communication technologies to eTourism and smart tourism towards ambient intelligence tourism: a perspective article. *Tourism review, 75*(1), 267-272.

Buonincontri, P., & Micera, R. (2016). The experience co-creation in smart tourism destinations: a multiple case analysis of European destinations. *Information Technology & Tourism, 16*(3), 285-315.

Chesbrough, H. W. (2003). *Open innovation: The new imperative for creating and profiting from technology.* Harvard Business Press.

Del Chiappa, G., & Baggio, R. (2015). Knowledge transfer in smart tourism destinations: Analyzing the effects of a network structure. *Journal of Destination Marketing & Management, 4*(3), 145-150.

del Vas, G. M., Puig-Cabrera, M., Cádiz-Gómez, M., & de Diego, A. A. (2024). Smart management of tourist coastal areas in a reborn tourism era: Transitioning from safe to sustainable beaches within the Spanish sun and sand model. *Journal of Tourism, Sustainability and Well-being, 12*(1), 21-34.

Del Vecchio, P., Mele, G., Ndou, V., & Secundo, G. (2018). Creating value from social big data: Implications for smart tourism destinations. *Information processing & management, 54*(5), 847-860.

Femenia-Serra, F., Neuhofer, B., & Ivars-Baidal, J. A. (2018). Towards a conceptualisation of smart tourists and their role within the smart destination scenario. *The Service Industries Journal, 39*(2), 109-133.

Forés, B. & Fernández-Yáñez, J. M. (2020). Los destinos turísticos inteligentes en un contexto de crisis: principales retos a nivel empresarial y de destino. *Economía industrial,* (418), 73-88.

Forés, B., Fernández-Yáñez, J. M. & Puig-Denia, A. (2021). Servitización del sector turístico: el modelo de Destinos Turísticos Inteligentes (DTI) como impulsor del proceso de digitalización de los servicios turístico. *Economía industrial,* (422), 81-90.

Forés, B., Breithaupt Janssen, Z., & Takashi Kato, H. (2021). A bibliometric overview of tourism family business. *Sustainability, 13*(22), 12822.

García-Milon, A., Juaneda-Ayensa, E., Olarte-Pascual, C., & Pelegrín-Borondo, J. (2020). Towards the smart tourism destination: Key factors in information source use on the tourist shopping journey. *Tourism management perspectives, 36,* 100730.

Ghaderi, Z., Beal, L., Hall, C. M., Zaman, M., Ahmad Rather, R., & Mat Som, A. P. (2024). Cybersecurity and smart tourist destinations resilience. *Tourism Recreation Research,* 1-17.

Giaccone, S. C., & Bonacini, E. (2019). New technologies in smart tourism development: The# iziTRAVELSicilia experience. *Tourism Analysis, 24*(3), 341-354.

Gretzel, U., & Scarpino-Johns, M. (2018). Destination resilience and smart tourism destinations. *Tourism Review International, 22*(3-4), 263-276.

Gursoy, D., Luongo, S., Della Corte, V., & Sepe, F. (2024). Smart tourism destinations: an overview of current research trends and a future research agenda. *Journal of Hospitality and Tourism Technology, 15*(3), 479-495.

Ivars-Baidal, J. A., Celdrán, M. A., Mazón, J., y Perles, Á. (2017). Towards an ICT roadmap for smart tourism destinations based on prospective analysis. *E-Review Tourism Res, 8*: 1-5.

Ivars-Baidal, J. A., Celdrán-Bernabeu, M. A., Mazón, J. N., & Perles-Ivars, Á. F. (2019). Smart destinations and the evolution of ICTs: a new scenario for destination management?. *Current Issues in Tourism, 22*(13), 1581-1600.

Jeong, M., & Shin, H. H. (2020). Tourists' experiences with smart tourism technology at smart destinations and their behavior intentions. *Journal of Travel Research, 59*(8), 1464-1477.

López de Ávila, A., y García, S. (2015). Destinos turísticos inteligentes. *Economía Industrial, 395*: 261-69.

Jovicic, D. Z. (2019). From the traditional understanding of tourism destination to the smart tourism destination. *Current Issues in Tourism, 22*(3), 276-282.

Marine-Roig, E., & Clavé, S. A. (2015). Tourism analytics with massive user-generated content: A case study of Barcelona. *Journal of Destination Marketing & Management, 4*(3), 162-172.

Markusen, A. (1996), Sticky places in slippery space: a typology of industrial districts, Economic Geography 72, 293–313.

Moreno-Izquierdo, L., Ramón-Rodríguez, A. B., & Such Devesa, M. J. (2018). The challenge of long-term tourism competitiveness in the age of innovation: Spain as a case study.

Nadee, W., Kaewkitipong, L., Ractham, P., & Sayruamyat, S. (2024). An Investigation of the Intention to Visit Smart Tourism Destinations: Domestic Travelers vs. International Travelers. *Sustainability, 16*(23), 10484.

Ndou, V., Hysa, E., & Maruccia, Y. (2023). A methodological framework for developing a smart-tourism destination in the southeastern Adriatic–Ionian area. *Sustainability, 15*(3), 2057.

Palomo Santiago, M., & Parra LARRA López, E. (2024). Preparation of papers–intellectual influence of smart tourism destinations 2000-2023. *Tourism and hospitality management, 30*(3), 301-316.

Panagopoulos, A., Matika, V., Nikas, I. A., & Paraschi, E. P. (2025). A comprehensive structural framework for smart stadiums as essential components of smart tourism destinations. *Worldwide Hospitality and Tourism Themes, 17*(1), 106-119.

Pencarelli, T. (2020). The digital revolution in the travel and tourism industry. *Information technology & tourism, 22*(3), 455-476.

Porter, M. E., & Kramer, M. R. (2011). Creating shared value. *Harvard Business Review, 89*(1–2), 62–77.

Porter, M. E. (1998, November–December). Clusters and the new economics of competition. *Harvard Business Review, 76*(6), 77–90.

Radojević, B., Stankov, U., & Vujičić, M. D. (2023). Governing geospatial aspects of smart destination development-The case of Novi Sad, Serbia. *Geographica Pannonica, 27*(3).

Rubio-Escuderos, L., García-Andreu, H., & Ullán de la Rosa, J. (2025). What is leading destinations towards inclusivity? Analysis of accessible tourism drivers from a stakeholders' perspective. *Tourism Planning & Development, 22*(1), 19-40.

Sainaghi, R., Köseoglu, M. A., d'Angella, F., & Tetteh, I. L. (2019). Foundations of hospitality performance measurement research: A co-citation approach. *International Journal of Hospitality Management, 79*, 21-40.

Samancioglu, E., Kumlu, S., & Ozkul, E. (2024). Smart tourism destinations and sustainability: evidence from the tourism industry. *Worldwide Hospitality and Tourism Themes, 16*(6), 680-693.

SEGITTUR (2025). Destinos turísticos inteligentes. Available from: https://www.segittur.es/destinos-turisticos-inteligentes/ [1/9/2025].

Shafiee, S., Ghatari, A. R., Hasanzadeh, A., & Jahanyan, S. (2022). Developing a model for smart tourism destinations: an interpretive structural modelling approach. *Information Technology & Tourism, 24*(4), 511-546.

Shafiee, S., Jahanyan, S., Ghatari, A. R., & Hasanzadeh, A. (2023). Developing sustainable tourism destinations through smart technologies: A system dynamics approach. *Journal of Simulation, 17*(4), 477-498.

Stankov, U., Gretzel, U., & Vujičić, M. D. (2025). AI-powered smartphones and phygital tourism experiences: implications and future research directions. *Information Technology & Tourism*, 1-10.

Suanpang, P., & Pothipassa, P. (2024). Integrating generative AI and IoT for sustainable smart tourism destinations. *Sustainability, 16*(17), 7435.

Tian, Y., & Tang, X. (2025). The use of artificial neural network algorithms to enhance tourism economic efficiency under information and communication technology. *Scientific Reports, 15*(1), 8988.

Wang, D., Li, X. R., & Li, Y. (2013). China's "smart tourism destination" initiative: A taste of the service-dominant logic. *Journal of Destination Marketing & Management, 2*(2), 59-61.

Wei, W., Önder, I., & Uysal, M. (2024). Smart tourism destination (STD): developing and validating an impact scale using residents' overall life satisfaction. *Current Issues in Tourism, 27*(17), 2849-2872.

Wu, D., Li, H., Huang, Q., Li, C., & Liang, S. (2024). Measurement and determinants of smart destinations' sustainable performance: a two-stage analysis using DEA-Tobit model. *Current Issues in Tourism, 27*(4), 529-545.

Xu, J., Shi, P. H., & Chen, X. (2025). Exploring digital innovation in smart tourism destinations: i

Zhou, L., Buhalis, D., Fan, D. X., Ladkin, A., & Lian, X. (2024). Attracting digital nomads: Smart destination strategies, innovation and competitiveness. *Journal of Destination Marketing & Management, 31*, 100850.